# Handbook of Nonverbal Assessment

R. Steve McCallum

Editor

# Handbook of Nonverbal Assessment

Second Edition

 Springer

*Editor*
R. Steve McCallum
Department of Educational Psychology and
  Counseling
University of Tennessee
Knoxville, TN
USA

ISBN 978-3-319-84439-8          ISBN 978-3-319-50604-3    (eBook)
DOI 10.1007/978-3-319-50604-3

Printed on acid-free paper

This Springer imprint is published by Springer Nature
The registered company is Springer International Publishing AG
The registered company address is: Gewerbestrasse 11, 6330 Cham, Switzerland

*This book is dedicated to those who have been most influential in my life: my wife Sherry and the memory of my mother, Nevada—both experts in nonverbal communication! the children (Ross, Ryan, Daniel, Lauren); and my students. I continue to learn from each of them!*

# Acknowledgements

Any project of this magnitude requires help from many others. I would like to acknowledge the strong contribution of each of the authors of the various chapters. The thoughtful content they provided ensures that it will be useful to practitioners and researchers alike. In addition, I would like to thank Judy Jones and Michelle Tam of Springer, Judy as Senior Editor and Michelle as Editorial Assistant. Their capable guidance was invaluable and they created an appealing and user-friendly format. Finally, I would like to thank Baileigh Kirkpatrick. Without her thoughtful contributions, tireless efforts, and editorial assistance this book would not have been possible.

# Contents

# Editor and Contributors

## About the Editor

**R. Steve McCallum Ph.D.** is Professor of School Psychology in the Department of Educational Psychology and Counseling at the University of Tennessee (UT). Before coming to UT in 1986, Dr. McCallum worked for 4 years as a practicing school psychologist, then for six years as a faculty member in the Department of Psychology at the University of Southern Mississippi. During his tenure at UT, Dr. McCallum served both as Program Coordinator for the School Psychology Program (6 years) and Department Head (22 years). He contributes to the assessment field as an author or co-author of numerous scholarly works, including books, book chapters, journal articles, tests, and national and international conference presentations (e.g., *Universal Nonverbal Intelligence Test 2* (UNIT2), published by PRO-ED Publishing Company; a software interpretive program for the UNIT2 called *UNIT Compuscore; Essentials of Nonverbal Assessment*, published by John Wiley & Sons; the *Handbook of Nonverbal Assessment*, (2nd ed.), published by Springer Publishing Company; the *Handbook of Reading Assessment*, (2nd ed.) published by Rougledge, Taylor & Frances Group; and the *Universal Multidimensional Abilities Scales (UMAS)*, published by PRO ED). Finally, he is co-founder and contributing editor of the *Journal of Psychoeducational Assessment.* For his contributions to the profession, Dr. McCallum was elected a Fellow of the American Psychological Association in 1992 and has been the recipient of many honors (e.g., Chancellors Research and Creative Achievement Award and the UT/Quest Scholar Award, University of Tennessee; Alumnus of Distinction Award, University of Georgia; Distinguished Alumus Award, Georgia Southern University).

## Contributors

**Achilles Bardos** Division of School Psychology, University of Northern Colorado, Greeley, CO, USA

**Sherry Mee Bell** Department of Theory and Practice in Teacher Education, University of Tennessee, Knoxville, TN, USA

**Bruce A. Bracken** College of William and Mary, Williamsburg, VA, USA

**Jeffrey P. Braden** College of Humanities and Social Sciences, North Carolina State University, Raleigh, NC, USA

**Maris Doropoulou** Athens, Greece

**Ruth A. Ervin** University of British Columbia, Vancouver, BC, Canada

**Trish Franklin** University of Tennessee, Knoxville, USA

**Alex Friedlander Moore**  College of William and Mary, Williamsburg, VA, USA

**Craig L. Frisby**  University of Missouri, Columbia, MO, USA

**Donald D. Hammill**  Austin, TX, USA

**Caroline M. Jaquett**  University of Tennessee, Knoxville, USA

**Susan K. Johnsen**  Department of Educational Psychology, School of Education, Baylor University, Waco, TX, USA

**Baileigh A. Kirkpatrick**  University of Tennessee, Knoxville, USA

**Christopher Koch**  George Fox University, Newberg, OR, USA

**Susan J. Maller**  Department of Educational Studies, Purdue University, West Lafayette, IN, USA

**R. Steve McCallum**  Department of Educational Psychology and Counseling, University of Tennessee, Knoxville, TN, USA

**Ryan E. McCallum**  School of Osteopathic Medicine, A. T. Still University, Pinetop, AZ, USA

**Merilee McCurdy**  Department of Educational Psychology and Counseling, University of Tennessee, Knoxville, TN, USA

**Nils Pearson**  Austin, TX, USA

**Lai-Kwan Pei**  Houston Independent School District, Houston, TX, USA

**Gale H. Roid**  Testing Research, Keizer, OR, USA

**Christopher H. Skinner**  Department of Educational Psychology and Counseling, University of Tennessee, Knoxville, TN, USA

**Amber Stieg Green**  University of Northern Colorado, Greeley, CO, USA

**John D. Wasserman**  Burke, VA, USA

**Brian Wilhoit**  Department of Educational Psychology and Counseling, University of Tennessee, Knoxville, TN, USA

R. Steve McCallum

Although verbal responses are assumed to provide a window on the intellect, personality, and related functioning of individuals, in some cases verbal interactions during assessment may be inappropriate because of the characteristics of the examinee. For example, some individuals cannot be assessed via verbal interactions (e.g., those with speech and language impairments and/or hearing deficits, culturally different backgrounds, neurological trauma, emotional problems such as selective mutism). For those individuals language is a confound, and nonverbal tests may provide a fair(er) and less biased assessment.

## Context for Nonverbal Assessment

Currently, the terms used to characterize nonverbal assessment are somewhat confusing (e.g., nonverbal assessment, nonverbal intellectual assessment, nonverbal scales, and nonverbal testing). For example, the term nonverbal assessment may be used to describe a test administration process in which *no receptive or expressive language demands are placed on either* the examinee or the examiner (Bracken and McCallum 1998, 2016). Alternatively, some test manuals for nonverbal tests claim that tests are

nonverbal if the examinees are not required to speak even though the tests are administered using verbal directions. In fact, traditionally most so-called nonverbal tests could be best described as language-reduced instruments with verbal directions—sometimes with lengthy and complex verbal directions. For example, some nonverbal subtests/scales from cognitive measures such as the Nonverbal Scales of the *Kaufman Assessment Battery for Children* (K-ABC II; Kaufman and Kaufman 1983), the *Differential Ability Scales* (DAS 2; Elliot 2007), and the Stanford-Binet V (Roid 2003)—all may be presented with verbal directions. There are a few intelligence tests that are truly nonverbal. The *Test of Nonverbal Intelligence* (TONI-4; Brown et al. 1980, 1990, 1997, 2010), the *Comprehensive Test of Nonverbal Intelligence* (CTONI 2; Hammill et al. 1997, 2009), and the *Universal Nonverbal Intelligence Test* (UNIT-2; Bracken and McCallum 1998, 2016) can be administered in a 100% nonverbal fashion. The *Leiter International Performance Scale—III* (Roid et al. 2013) and the *Wechsler Nonverbal Scale of Ability* (WNV, Wechsler and Naglieri 2006) are administered in a nonverbal manner, but the examiner may use some verbalizations.

To add to the confusion, although nonverbal intellectual assessment may characterize the *process* of assessing the construct of intelligence in a nonverbal fashion, some test authors use this term to describe the assessment of a construct called nonverbal intelligence, nonverbal reasoning, or nonverbal abilities (Brown et al. 1980, 1990, 1997; Hammill et al. 2009; Wechsler and

R.S. McCallum (✉)
Department of Educational Psychology &
Counseling, University of Tennessee,
523 BEC, 1126 Volunteer Blvd,
Knoxville, TN 37996-3452, USA
e-mail: mccallum@utk.edu

© Springer International Publishing AG 2017
R.S. McCallum (ed.), *Handbook of Nonverbal Assessment*,
DOI 10.1007/978-3-319-50604-3_1

Naglieri 2006). In spite of these different labels, Bracken and McCallum (1998, 2016) suggest that the central construct assessed by most nonverbal intelligence tests is in fact general intelligence. This distinction in terminology is important because it has implications for how instruments are used with diverse populations. For example, if those intelligence tests that purportedly assess nonverbal intelligence (e.g., *TONI-IV*, *C-TONI 2*) do in fact assess a construct that is theoretically different from the construct assessed on traditional intelligence tests (i.e., general intelligence), then the inferences drawn from these tests may be different from the inferences drawn from tests purporting to assess general intelligence (e.g., inferences about eligibility for special educational services).

The use of the term nonverbal assessment is equally confusing as it relates to assessment of related constructs (e.g., personality, academic achievement). Not all examiners use the term in the same way. Practitioners should read the manuals of tests they use to clearly understand the nature of the construct assessed and the techniques and strategies employed to do so.

## Brief Historical Context

Jean Itard was among the first to assess nonverbal cognitive (and related) abilities. He attempted to determine the capabilities of the so-called Wild Boy of Aveyron, a feral youth discovered wondering the countryside in the 1800s. He tried to determine whether the youth could acquire functional language skills and attempted to elicit both verbal and nonverbal responses (Carrey 1995). Eventually, Itard concluded that the boy could not produce meaningful speech; consequently, he was relegated to exploring the nonverbal domain. Similarly, other eighteenth century clinicians pursued the problem of assessing the intellectual abilities of children who did not speak, such as Seguin (1907), who is known for the development of unique instrumentation to aid in nonverbal assessment of childrens' abilities. He developed a form board test, which required placement of common geometric shapes into inserts of the same shape; the *Sequin Form Board* has since been modified and has been adapted for use in many instruments and across multiple cultures.

Practical use of nonverbal assessment on a large scale occurred in response to a very real problem in the United States during the early part of the twentieth century. During the First World War, the armed forces needed to assess the cognitive abilities of foreign born and illiterate military recruits. The Committee on the Psychological Examination of Recruits was formed to collect/design assessment strategies (Thorndike and Lohman 1990). According to the Examiners Guide for the Army Psychological Examination (Government Printing Office 1918), military testing was used to classify soldiers according to mental ability, identify potential problem soldiers, identify potential officers, and discover soldiers with special talents. The Army Mental Tests included both the Alpha and Beta forms. The Group Examination Alpha (Army Alpha) was administered to recruits who could read and respond to the written English version of the scale; the Group Examination Beta portion of the Mental Tests (Army Beta) was developed as a nonverbal supplement to Army Alpha. In addition, the army also developed the Army Performance Scale Examination, an individually administered test to use for those who could not be tested effectively in group form using the Alpha and Beta tests. Together, the Army Performance Scale Examination and the Army Beta served an important need in a country with a diverse population. These instruments included a variety of performance tasks, many of which were to appear later on various scales developed by David Wechsler and others (e.g., puzzles, cube constructions, digit symbols, mazes, picture completions, picture arrangements).

The need for nonverbal assessment did not end with the war. For example, in 1924 Arthur developed the *Arthur Point Scale of Performance Tests* (Arthur 1943, 1947). The *Point Scale* combined and modified a variety of existing performance tests, including a revision of the *Knox Cube Test* (Knox 1914), *Sequin Form Board*, *Arthur Stencil Design Test*, *Porteus Maze*

Deaf / Hard of Hearing

*Test* (Porteus 1915), and an adaptation of the *Healy Picture Completion Test* (Healy 1914, 1918, 1921) into a battery. This scale was made for examinees who were deaf or otherwise hard of hearing and was designed by Arthur to provide a multidimensional assessment of cognition.

Refinement of nonverbal or language-reduced tests continued and several were widely used by psychologists and other professionals for examinees who could not respond to traditional verbally laden measures (e.g., *Leiter International Performance Scale*; Leiter 1938, 1948; *Columbia Mental Maturity Scale*, Burgmeister et al. 1972; *Draw a Person*; Goodenough 1926). However, during the 60s and 70s these tests eventually fell into disfavor because their norms, stimulus materials, or procedures became outdated. Consequently, many psychologists began to rely on tests with language-reduced performance tasks from standard verbal batteries in an effort to provide fairer assessments (e.g., the Wechsler Performance Scale of the *Wechsler Intelligence Scale for Children* (Wechsler 1949), and its later editions. These became popular as nonverbal tests, and typically were used whenever hearing or language skills were considered a confound, even though each of the Wechsler Performance subtests had test directions that contain verbal instructions and basic language concepts (Bracken 1986; Kaufman 1990, 1994). Other "nonverbal measures" were being developed by those studying cognitive development during the 50s, 60s, and 70s, but these measures did not become part of the mainstream intelligence testing movement [e.g., see the tests of conservation by Jean Piaget (1963) and the processing tasks of Guilford (1967)]. These measures are highly dependent on understanding naturally occurring phenomenon depicted via (nonverbal) abstractions. But, they are difficult to administer and score in a standardized format and most required at least some language.

By the early 1990s psychologists began to provide updated alternatives to language-based tests to assess the intellectual ability of those with language difficulties. Consequently, several nonverbal intelligence tests were developed during the decade of the 90s, and the development

continues. Currently, practitioners have more and better nonverbal intelligence tests available than ever before, as is apparent from the information presented in later chapters of this *Handbook*.

Even though there are several psychometrically sound nonverbal intelligence tests currently available, nonverbal assessment of related areas such as academics, personality, neuropsychological functioning is still shrouded in confusion and uncertainty. Some behavioral strategies seem particularly well suited for nonverbal assessment. As McCurdy, Skinner, and Ervin note in Chap. 16 of this text, core functional assessment procedures do not require clients to produce verbal or written reports of their behavior, making functional behavioral assessment (FBA) readily adaptable for assessment of many nonverbal behaviors. FBA relies on direct application of basic principles from the behavioral learning literature (i.e., operant conditioning primarily), and has as a goal to identify the current environmental contingencies that serves to maintain or reinforce behaviors of interest (e.g., hand flapping, fighting). Once antecedent conditions, target behaviors, and consequent events that are contingent upon target behaviors have been specified, assessment, and intervention follows naturally. Nonverbal behaviors are no more difficult to assess and track than verbal behaviors; both rely on tight operationalizations.

When more traditional assessment of nonverbal academic skills are needed, the task is more difficult, primarily because academic content in nearly all areas is delivered orally or in writing, and students are expected to communicate in kind. Typically, individual or group administered tests are used, and in many cases these tests are standardized. As Frisby notes in Chap. 15 of this text, nonverbal assessment of academic achievement appears to be an oxymoron, given these realities. However, he notes that nonverbal assessment of behaviors is possible using limited means of responding (e.g., pointing, gestures) or adaptive education practices first used for certain disabled populations (e.g., use of American Sign Language, augmentative and alternative communication devices, adapted computer access).

Traditionally assessment of personality has relied on use of pencil and paper, just like assessment of academics. And nonverbal assessment of personality is just as difficult as nonverbal assessment of academic functioning, perhaps more so. Nonverbal assessment of academics has been perceived by certain educational personnel as very important (e.g., special educators); consequently, adaptive techniques have been developed for those with severe impairments and those techniques can be adapted for nonverbal assessment in some cases. No similar technology exists for personality assessment. As Wasserman notes in Chap. 14 of this text, modification and adaptations are possible however, and some assessment techniques already available can be implemented with little or no change. For example, drawings of human figures and other common objects (e.g., house, tree) may be completed without use of verbal directions, and they are sometimes used as measures of personality.

Unlike nonverbal assessment of personality, nonverbal assessment of neuropsychological functioning has a long history. That is, neuropsychological assessment has long relied on certain nonverbal strategies as part of an overall general assessment of verbal and nonverbal functioning. This tradition arises in part because of the need to assess functions assumed to be controlled by different central nervous system localization sites, some of which are presumed to be primarily nonverbal (e.g., right hemisphere for most left handed people, and Wernicke's area of the left hemisphere, cite of receptive language skills). And research from the neuropsychological literature have identified a subset of learning difficulties sometimes referred to as nonverbal learning disabilities (see Rourke 1995). In addition, certain "neurological" measures can be (and have been) adapted already for nonverbal assessment (e.g., mazes tasks, presumed to assess prefrontal lobe planning abilities). However, there is no single source that describes the state of the art/science of nonverbal neuropsychological assessment until. In Chap. 17 of this text Wasserman summarizes the current status of nonverbal assessment of neuropsychological functioning.

## Sociopolitical Context of Nonverbal Assessment

Assessment does not exist in isolation; it is embedded in a social context. In fact, assessment operates in the service of social goals, in the broad sense. As George Orwell (1946) humorously conveys in his classic book *Animal Farm*, societies seem to select some traits to value over others, even in those cultures that espouse equality. Societies develop informal and formal methods to measure prized abilities, then to sort and reward them. For example, in most societies intelligence, by whatever name, is highly valued; and in many societies formal tests have been developed to quantify intelligence and to use these measures to predict and/or improve performance.

One of the early documented uses of formal ability tests occurred over 2000 years ago in China, where test results were used to select civil service workers. The use of exams to select government employees communicates considerable information about that culture. For example, the practice suggests that jobs were given based on merit, rather than family connections, money or favors, birthright, etc. Apparently, the principles underlying a meritocracy prevailed, at least to some degree, and served to guide the social and cultural zeitgeist. See Herrnstein and Murray (1994) for a more recent attempt to describe intelligence and its operationalizations as primary influences in a meritocracy and Serwer (2011) for one of several critical articles in response to Herrnstein and Murray's perspective.

Of course, the qualities of intelligence, achievement, and personality valued by a particular society are not necessarily the same as those prized in other cultures (Dasen 1984). For example, even though all cultures use a term like "intelligence," the operationalization varies considerably. In the Baoulé culture of Africa, Dasen found a term with roughly the same meaning as intelligence, *n'glouélê*, meaning the ability and motivation to complete activities which enhance family and community life. Some of the descriptive terms and phrases used by Baoulé community members to illustrate the concept of n'glouélê include: responsibility, politeness, story-telling ability, writing and drawing ability, academic ability, memory, obedience, and maturity. Dasen notes that the social skills are prized above the academic; in fact, academic skills are considered practically useless unless they are applied directly to improving the quality of community life. The correlations among Piagetian concrete operational tasks for the n'glouélê typically were very small or even negative. In this culture intelligence is related to the ability to further social/cultural needs, and cannot be considered in the abstract. So, the effects of culture on the way intelligence, achievement, and personality are conceptualized are significant.

The effects of culture may be subtle, but may still impact the way members of society think about intelligence and the way experts measure the construct. For example, McCallum et al. (2001) and others (e.g., Valencia and Rankin 1985) have discussed the difficulties inherent in developing equivalent forms of a test of intelligence in two relatively *similar* cultures. Valancia and Rankin administered the standard English version of the *McCarthy Scales of Children's Abilities* (McCarty 1972) and a Spanish translation of that test to over 300 children; 142 were judged to be primarily English language dominant and the standard English version was administered to them; 162 were judged to be Spanish language dominant and they were administered the Spanish version. Using an item X group partial correlational analyses, six of 16 subtests showed some evidence of bias, as indicated by a significant partial correlation between language and subtest score. Twenty-three of 157 McCarthy items were biased; six were biased against the English dominant children and 17 against the Spanish dominant group. The six items showing bias against the English dominant group came from a variety of subtests and did not appear to reflect a systematic bias. However, most of the items biased against the Spanish dominant group came from subtests measuring verbal and numerical memory. The authors claim that the biasing effect can be attributed to language differences.

Valencia and Rankin (1985) identified two effects they referred to as "word length effect" and "acoustic similarity effect." That is, because Spanish words of the same meaning are often longer (word length effect) and because Spanish contains fewer vowel sounds (Spanish, 5 and English, 11), similar sounding words are subject to greater misunderstanding (by the Spanish dominant children), placing the Spanish-speaking children at a disadvantage. Obviously, language differences can be powerful across cultures, even though the cultures may be similar in many ways, and assessment of individuals in one culture with a language loaded test developed in another culture and in another language, even when the test has been translated by experts, is a questionable practice. Experts suggest that tests developed in one culture are not typically useful in another unless massive changes are made, including adding items designed specifically for the target culture and restandardization in the target culture.

Of interest, McCallum et al. (2001) described a relatively efficient procedure to adapt/adopt a nonverbal test designed in one culture for use in another. This procedure requires collection of data in the target population from a small representative sample (e.g., 200 cases), then using those cases in a statistical weighting process to link with the original standardization sample. Such a procedure is more defensible for adaptation of a nonverbal test, but even then, is not without its problems.

Assessment, educational, rehabilitation, and psychotherapeutic goals are determined in part by broad societal goals and by cultural consensus regarding the importance of education and mental health treatment. In some societies, the educationally disadvantaged are not prioritized; in the U.S. the bulk of special education money is spent on children who have educational and cognitive limitations, rather than on improving the opportunities of the brightest portion of the population. Additionally, during the past 50 years or so, considerable attention has been focused on providing optimal instructional opportunities for culturally or racially different children with learning problems and mental retardation. Of course, many of these children are identified primarily by using intelligence tests; the use of tests for this purpose has been the subject of considerable litigation.

## Social (Re)Action to Assessment

In the United States the influence of increasingly larger minority populations is growing; consequently, there is heightened sensitivity about the use of ability tests (e.g., intelligence and achievement tests) designed primarily for the majority culture to evaluate ethnic minority children. Back in 1988 Sattler identified ethnic minority children as those who belong to a recognized ethnic group and whose values, customs, patterns of thought, and/or language are significantly different from those of the majority of the society in which they live. In this country such ethnic groups include African–Americans, Mexican–Americans, American Indians, Puerto Ricans, Asian Americans, and many others. Using this definition, the U.S. is very diverse indeed. According to a report from the U.S. Department of Education (2016) 19 prominent languages are spoken by students in English-Language Learner (ELL) programs, with Spanish was the most prominent (71% of ELL students nationally). Other prominent languages included Chinese, Arabic, Vietnamese, Haitian, Russian, Navajo. Significant diversity was apparent many of the largest school systems in the nations around the turn of the past century. More than 200 languages were spoken by the children who attended the Chicago City Schools (Pasko 1994), over 140 in the California schools (Unz 1997), and 61 in Knoxville, Tennessee (Forrester, personal communication, March 13, 2000). Projections for the future show an ever increasing pattern of diversity. Sattler (2008) reports percentages from the U.S. Census Bureau showing that the proportion of Euro Americans will shrink to a bare majority (50.1%) by mid-century.

Sattler (2008) suggests that health service providers adopt a multifactor, pluralistic approach, to appreciate cultural values and coping patterns, and to guard against inappropriate generalizations when working with minority group children. He notes that the issues involved in the assessment of ethnic minority children are complex, partly because they are part and parcel of the greater woes and injustices of society. Experts have criticized the use of tests for minority children; others have argued that such tests are necessary to prevent injustices which may occur when other less objective methods are used to make educational decisions, particularly placement decisions. In some cases identification of minority children for special education increases when only teacher recommendations are used, as opposed to traditional assessment measures. The use (and misuse) of intelligence tests and other standardized assessments for ethnic minority children has become an intensely debated topic in recent years.

For years, proponents of discontinuing the use of intelligence tests claim that the tests have a cultural bias against ethnic minority group children—that the national norms are inappropriate for minority children, that minority children are handicapped in test-taking skills because they fail to appreciate the achievement aspects of the test situation, lack motivation, and have limited exposure to the culture of the test builders; that most examiners are white, which tends to depress the scores of minority children; and that test results lead to inferior educational opportunities. These and related complaints have been addressed in the courts, in the professional literature, and in the popular press. In particular, concern about the role of intelligence tests in identifying children in need of special education came under strong scrutiny when that practice resulted in overrepresentation of minority group children in special education classes in the early 1970s, primarily because minority group children tended to earn lower overall IQs.

One of the first cases was brought in California–*Diana v. State Board of Education*, in

1970. Others followed (e.g., in 1979 *Larry P. v. Riles*; in 1984, *PACE v. Hannon*; in 1980, *Marshall v. Georgia*, 2004, etc.). The outcomes have varied from case to case, but the overall result has been to encourage test authors to develop better means to assess culturally difference children. In addition, these cases have positively influenced statutory innovations, as included in the Individuals with Disabilities Education Act (2004).

In summarizing the findings from case and statutory law, Gopaul-McNicol and Thomas-Presswood (1998) and Padilla (2001) describe some of the guidelines and safeguards now provided to protect the rights of linguistically and culturally diverse students. In essence, these guidelines require that a student be assessed in his/her native language, whenever possible; tests evaluate what they were intended to evaluate; examiners be appropriately trained; tests results not be confounded by sensory, manual, or speaking impairments; special educational placement decisions be made by a team of professional educators and not on the basis of any single test; students be evaluated in all areas of suspected disability; special education students be reevaluated every three years; and initial evaluations (for special education eligibility) focus on instructionally relevant information in addition to information necessary to make an eligibility decision.

Further, Gopaul-McNicol and Thomas-Presswood and others describe some of the competencies assessment psychologists should possess, including the ability to recognize the limits of their skills, training, and expertise in working with culturally/linguistically diverse students and willingness to ask for appropriate guidance and training when needed. In addition, psychologists must understand the technical and practical limits of the assessment instruments they use, particularly as those limitations relate to particular diverse groups. For example, if a student is bilingual or Limited English Proficient (LEP) the psychologist should be able to appreciate the culturally determined nonverbal messages of the student *and* interact in the dominant language of the student if possible (or find

someone who can). The psychologist is expected to document the cultural, sociological, and sociopolitical factors, which may impact the assessment process. In fact, Prifitera et al. (1998) note that the minority versus majority group differences typically cited (e.g., 7–15 IQ points) would be reduced drastically or disappear with a more refined match on SES and related variables (e.g., use of household income, accounting for home environment, time parents spend with children, medical history), and there some empirical evidence to justify this recommendation (see Upson 2004). Finally, as discussed in the next section, the assessment of many culturally and linguistically diverse students may be enhanced by using nonverbal assessment instruments. Psychologists should be appropriately trained to use those instruments and should use instruments that have been developed to promote fair(er) assessment using (see McCallum 1999).

**Some Promising Remedies**. Overall, the result of litigation and social consciousness raising have been positive, i.e., the assessment of diverse students is better informed and "fairer" than before the cases were brought. Also, clarifications in the assessment process have resulted as well. For example, it has become apparent that many of the problems associated with using major individualized intelligence tests have resulted from abuse of the tests, rather than psychometric flaws in the instruments themselves. Data have shown that most of the major individual intelligence tests are not systematically biased in a psychometric sense (see Reynolds and Lowe 2009). But the tests are not without problems and they often have been misapplied, over interpreted, and misused. Because of the heightened sensitivity to the bias issue, most test authors now are careful to address this issue in the test development phase, which is an important change in the way publishers and authors do business. Also as a result of court action and changes in the law (and the related consciousness raising), the number of students in classes serving children with Intellectuall Disabilities (ID) has declined dramatically from the late 60s. Many children who would have been labeled ID in the late 60s and before are now helped in regular classrooms or in classes for learning disabled children. Of course, the numbers of children diagnosed with a learning disability are decreasing now also as a result of implementation of the response to intervention (RtI) model, which requires evidence-based interventions before a full-blown assessment is conducted.

Of historical note, one of the first assessment strategies designed to promote fairer testing was the System of Multicultural Pluralistic Assessment (SOMPA, Mercer 1976). This system took into account socioeconomic status and related cultural variables and made adjustments accordingly. The SOMPA produced an overall score, the Estimated Learning Potential or ELP. A somewhat similar system produces a PROIQ, or projected IQ, and takes into account low SES levels and other environmental factors, as described by Thorndike and Hagen (1986); these factors are presumed to reduce IQ scores and may include a home language other than standard English, home values which do not appreciate academic success, and/or undereducated parents. The PROIQ was actually developed by Van den Berg (1986), who believed that the PROIQ could be used as a reasonable estimate of the IQ for a deprived child, given intensive long-term remediation, including upgrading the environment. The efficacy of using the SOMPA or of the Van den Berg's technique has not been demonstrated in practice and they are studied today primarily for historical purposes.

Another promising procedure designed to address the limitations associated with assessing deprived, low SES, limited English proficient children with conventional individual intelligence tests include the assessment paradigm favored by Feuerstein and colleagues, which has produced the Learning Potential Assessment Device (LPAD) and related instruments. The rationale for the development of the LPAD is based on the work of Vygotsky (1978a, b), who believed strongly in the social influences of intellectual development. According to Vygotsky children learn from interacting with competent models, particularly adults. As they mature and

become more sophisticated from previous interaction, the more intellectually sophisticated they become. The process is summarized by his notion of the zone of proximal development (ZPD). The ZPD is conceptualized by the difference between the child's current level of development, as determined by history and maturation, and the level of development possible when the child is aided by a competent model.

The ZPD has implications for teaching and seems conceptually similar to the notion of "readiness." Feuerstein et al. (1979) and others (e.g., Budoff 1987; Lidz 2001) have developed strategies to assess the ZPD, and have conceptualized these strategies as a way of determining the malleability of intelligence via a test-teach-test model. The teaching phase relies on "mediated learning," implementation of effective strategies and prompts conveyed to the child by a competent model. Budoff's (1975) version of the paradigm requires the use of nonverbal intelligence test items. Presumably these items are less influenced by cultural diversity (e.g., Kohs Block Design Test, Raven's Progressive Matrices). During the mediated learning (teaching) phase the model provides problem-solving strategies (e.g., avoidance of impulsive responding, active planning, checking progress). Finally, the pretest items are re-administered and the gain scores are determined. This gain score becomes an operationalization of the ZPD.

According to Braden (1984) results from this kind of dynamic assessment are often different from the results of traditional assessment strategies and the interactions between examiner and examinee are more fluid. Proponents also report that children who perform competently following dynamic assessment do better in other learning and social situations. In addition, dynamic assessment yields results which are more directly relevant for educational interventions, are more growth oriented (as opposed to being categorical), and are more descriptive of the student's behavior. But these authors cite some of the problems associated with dynamic assessment also. For example, the test-teach-test paradigm is complicated and characterized by nonstandard-ized administration, and the assessment and mediation is multifaceted. Due to the complexity of the technique Braden (1984) concludes that the LPAD requires extensive training and much social interaction. Consequently, the procedure may be difficult to implement for individual with disabilities or for the culturally different (e.g., new immigrants). Glutting and McDermott (1990) criticize the methodology of the LPAD and Budoff's techniques and concluded that Budoff's technique identifies gainers, those making strong pre- to post-test gains, twice as often as do diagnostic techniques that control statistical artifacts better. Further, they conclude that gainer diagnoses are incorrect over 50% of the time. In summary, in spite of the promise of dynamic assessment techniques much more research is needed to verify its long-term utility.

Of course, one very positive outcome of the consciousness raising produced by the litigation is the emphasis of development of psychometri-cally sound nonverbal tests of intelligence. Results of court cases made educators and psy-chologists more aware of the need to assess minority and culturally different children care-fully, without bias, and made them more aware that good nonverbal tests of intelligence are rare.

According to Coleman et al. (1993), tests that measure intelligence nonverbally should possess three essential characteristics. First, the test must not require the examinee to demonstrate another knowledge base (e.g., a particular language); secondly, the test must require complex reason-ing; finally, the test must require flexibility in the application of reasoning strategies. According to Coleman et al., many traditional measures of intelligence have relied too heavily on language for limited English proficient children; they note that such students are best assessed using tests which are untimed, require no listening, speak-ing, reading or writing skills, and use a test-teach-test model of assessment. Many of the innovations designed to aid in the assessment of culturally different children also benefit assess-ment of deaf or hearing-impaired children (see

Braden 1984 and Chap. 4 in this volume; Braden et al. 1994; Kamphaus 1993; Sattler 2008). Jen-sen (1998) recommends the use of highly "g" loaded nonverbal tests to assess those who are deaf or hard of hearing. Good nonverbal tests are only recently becoming available, and seven of the best are described in this book in (Chaps. 7 through 13).

In lieu of using nonverbal tests solely to assess culturally different individuals, Gopaul-McNicol and Thomas-Presswood (1998) describe a comprehensive approach, one that takes into account some of the techniques men-tioned above and could include nonverbal assessment as one component. They refer to their approach as "bio-ecological," and describe it in a four-tier system to include Psychometric Assessment, Psychometric Potential Assessment, Ecological Assessment, and Other Intelligences. Each tier is assumed to contribute 25% to an individual's overall intellectual functioning, and taken together the four tiers address three inter-related and dynamic dimensions of intelligence: biological cognitive processes, culturally coded experiences, and cultural contexts.

Each of the four tiers is multifaceted. The Psychometric Assessment strategy allows the use of traditional standardized measures of intelli-gence. The Psychometric Potential Assessment measure consists of procedures to be used in conjunction with the psychometric measure; these procedures provide supplementary information, and include Suspending Time (tabulation of scores without penalties associated with speeded performance), Contextualizing Vocabulary (al-lowing the examinee to define words by using them in sentences), Paper and Pencil (e.g., allowing examinees to use pencil and paper for arithmetic problems), and Test-Teach-Retest (al-lowing the examinee who is unfamiliar with certain tasks such as puzzles to be taught those tasks and then assessed). This procedure is similar to the dynamic assessment strategies described in the previous section. Finally, the examiner is instructed to answer relevant questions designed to determine how much the student gained.

Examinees in a tropical climate might be asked "In what way are a mango and a banana alike.").

Some experts complain that many important *intelligences* are not typically assessed well by traditional cognitive measures including skills/knowledge/functioning within the following areas: music, bodily kinesthetic, interpersonal, intrapersonal, nature. Presumably, these intelligences can be assessed in this model using interviews and observation. Some of these abilities are also considered important by experts who study emotional intelligence (Goleman 1995, 2010). Assessment of some of these skills are consistent with the suggestions provided by the American Psychological Association (2016) for examiners who work with culturally and linguistically diverse populations.

Like APA, the American Association of Colleges for Teacher Education (AACTE; 2016) endorses cultural pluralism in testing. For example, AACTE encourages teachers to consider the learning styles of their students (e.g., extent to which immigrants are familiar with multiple-choice tests, computers, assessment of basic curriculum content, and independent versus cooperative work format). Such creative assessments may be particularly helpful for students from diverse backgrounds who are new to U.S. classrooms. Curriculum-based assessment may be helpful because it is tied to the student's curriculum, which should be made relevant by teachers. In turn, teachers can then make even more relevant instructional materials based on their assessment. Additionally, consistent with the need to make assessment more relevant for all children, authentic or "real world" assessment techniques should be particularly helpful for diverse students. For example, teachers should include culturally relevant problems in their testing and the instructional goals. Finally, assessment of achievement should include personalized content for diverse students, who may feel marginalized already. Portfolios are particularly useful for this purpose and may include a picture of the student and examples of work over time (Payne 2003).

## Impetus for Nonverbal Assessment

Several factors have contributed to the recent interest in developing and/or adapting technologies for nonverbal assessment. In addition to litigation and related governmental action, there is an increasing need for accountability in education, making assessment data necessary for documenting student progress. In addition, the advent of computers and computer technology makes testing adaptations more user friendly; that is, the adaptations are increasingly easier for clients to use and for educators and health professionals to adapt. For many students assessment with heavily verbally laden tests is not optimal, and may even be unethical. In some cases language is not a window on the intellect, but a barrier, as is true for many minority students. The rapidly shifting world population and rapid influx of immigrants into communities of all sizes and all regions of the U.S. has produced multicultural, multilingual, multiethnic, and multiracial environments. Although quality test translations are both possible and available (e.g., Bracken 1998; Muñoz-Sandoval et al. 1998, 2005), test translations and subsequent norming and validation efforts are costly and time consuming for a single dominant language (e.g., Spanish), let alone 200 or more low-incidence languages. In addition, subtle dialect differences even within the same language presents translation problems. And, given the relative lack of bilingual school psychologists, the primary alternative to testing children in their native languages is to remove language as a variable and employ nonverbal tests (Frisby 1999). Many of the issues described above are related to the notions of *test bias* and *fairness in testing*, and in the next section I explore those terms in some detail.

## Bias in Testing and Fairness

Traditionally experts considered a test to be fair if it was free from *test bias*. Test bias generally refers to elements of a test that produce construct irrelevant variance, which leads to error in measurement. Thus, a test can be characterized as biased if it leads to systematic error in the measurement of some construct as a function of membership in a particular cultural or racial subgroup (Reynolds and Lowe 2009). Bias may lead to systematically different levels or patterns of performance by members of various groups as a result of construct irrelevant variance. Importantly, cultural bias must be distinguished from cultural loading. A test can be culture loaded without being culturally biased; similarly, in may be biased but not culturally loaded. That is, a test may be free of bias in a technical sense but still may be influenced by cultural or linguistic characteristics that can impact performance negatively and lead to erroneous conclusions regarding ability.

As implied from the definition of bias above and from a strictly psychometric perspective, bias is a technical term, operationalized by results from particular statistical tests (e.g., correlational and related factor analytic and model-testing comparisons across groups, use of the chi square-based Mantel-Haenszel procedure). These techniques have been applied to cognitive tests in particular, in part because of the history of test abuse described above. For example, an IQ test item can be considered biased against a particular group if it yields lower mean scores for those group members relative to members of another group when overall ability is held constant across the two groups. In addition, bias may be present if a test predicts less well for the marginalized group members relative to members from other groups, if the test yields a factor structure for the marginalized group that is different from the mainstream group, leads to poorer treatment outcomes among marginalized group members relative to members of other groups, and in general produces more error in the obtained or predicted scores for the marginalized group relative to the mainstream group (Reynolds and Lowe 2009). As noted above technical bias can be operationalized by specific statistical techniques.

Even though a test may be free of technical bias, and most of the nonverbal cognitive tests currently available are, examiners may want to minimize the effects of culture or language

influences, because they consider use of culturally and linguistically loaded tests to be *unfair* for some examinees, i.e., those who are unfamiliar with the particular culture and/or language embedded in the tests. Consequently, examinees will need to know the extent to which particular tests/subtest are culturally or linguistically loaded before they use them for certain examinees. Fortunately, the field has advanced sufficiently that test authors can evaluate a test to determine the influence of technical bias *and/or* cultural/linguistic characteristics. As noted above there is little or no bias present in commonly used (verbal) and nonverbal cognitive tests currently available. Does that mean they are not culturally or linguistically loaded, and hence appropriate for culturally different or language challenged examinees?

## Are Nonverbal Tests Free of Cultural and Linguistic Content?

The short answer to this question is "no." According to Flanagan et al. (2007, 2013), even "nonverbal" tests like UNIT-2 and Leiter-3 contain elements of the culture within the stimulus materials (e.g., pictured objects that may be more prevalent in the U.S. than in other cultures, or more prevalent in some subcultures than others) and the administration format (e.g., choice of gestures). And, some would argue that measures of intelligence cannot and should not be completely devoid of cultural influences if the intent is to predict performance within that particular culture (Reynolds and Lowe 2009). Nonetheless, experts in the field have contributed significantly to the creation of guidelines that can inform practitioners about culture and language loadings, and hence help examiners assess and/or reduce the influence of these variables to a considerable extent. For example, according to a model of nondiscriminatory testing Ortiz (2002) created, examiners should: (a) develop culturally and linguistically based hypotheses; (b) assess language history, development, and proficiency; (c) assess effects of cultural and linguistic differences; (d) assess environmental and community factors; (e) evaluate, revise, and retest hypotheses; (f) determine appropriate languages of assessment; (g) reduce bias in traditional practices; (h) use authentic and alternative assessment practices; (i) apply cultural-linguistic context to all data; and (j) link assessment to intervention. Although testing is only a small part of this overall model, use of nonverbal tests is consistent with his perspective, subsumed under the admonition to reduce bias in traditional (testing) practices.

According to Salvia and Ysseldyke (2004) examiners often erroneously begin the assessment process by accepting the *assumption of comparability*, the belief that the acculturation of examinees is similar to those on whom the test was standardized—an assumption that is not always justified. Similarly, Flanagan et al. (2013) note that a test may produce lower scores for individuals whose cultural background and experiences are dissimilar from those in the standardization sample, primarily because the tests samples cultural or language content related to the mainstream milieu, and not the full range of experiences of the examinee (also see Valdés and Figueroa 1994). To aid in this process of determining acculturation examiners may explore some general guidelines provided by Cummins (1979), who recommends that practitioners consider the time required by immigrant children to acquire conversational fluency in their second language (about 2 years), versus the time required to catch up to native speakers in the academic aspects of the second language (about 5 years). The skill level acquired within the initial 2-year period is referred to as *basic interpersonal communicative skills* (BICS), and the skill level referenced by the initial 5-year period is called *cognitive academic language proficiency* (CALP).

Language differences among examinees can impact test performance just as different cultural histories can. That is, an examinee's language proficiency may be limited by lack of exposure to the language, and less well developed than the proficiency level of the typical examinee in the standardization sample. For example, language exposure certainly is limited for examinees with

hearing deficits, as well as those who speak English as a second language; these examinees may be penalized by highly loaded language tests, and the *assumption of comparability* regarding language may be invalid. Consequently, Figueroa (1990) cautions examiners to take into account the language history of the examinee within his/her cultural context, not just the obvious language proficiency level.

In the best of all world, test authors and publishers would develop tests using standardization samples that are "leveled" by culture and language (i.e., large and targeted samples, representative of all examinees in the population, selected based on knowledge of various levels of cultural and language proficiency). Because the U.S. population is much too diverse to make leveling feasible test authors have typically adopted one of two other solutions. They have either developed tests in the native language of examinees (e.g., the *Bateria Woodcock-Munoz III*) or language reduced or nonverbal tests. The second option is more practical because it is not possible to create tests and find examiners proficient in all the languages spoken by examinees in the U.S. As mentioned previously, even nonverbal tests have some cultural and linguistic loadings, and in the next section we discuss the value of using a model for determining language and cultural loading of tests/subtests developed by Flanagan et al. (2013). This model provides a strategy to match an examinee's level of proficiency and the language and/or cultural demands of particular tests. Use of their model allows examiners to characterize the cultural and language loading within their Culture-Language Test Classification (C-LTC) and the Culture-Language Interpretative Matrices (C-LIM).

**Use of C-LTC and C-LIM**. Flanagan et al. (2007) caution examiners to keep four essential assumptions in mind: (a) all tests are culturally loaded and reflect the value, beliefs, and knowledge deemed important within the culture; (b) all tests, even nonverbal ones, require some form of language/communication from the examiner and the examinee which will influence performance; (c) the language and culture loadings of test vary significantly; and (d) interpretation of standardized tests results (using existing normative data) may be invalid for diverse individuals. The use of C-LTC and C-LIM ensures that these assumptions are addressed in a systematic and logical fashion.

To determine the influence of language and culture on tests results, Flanagan et al. (2007, 2013) relied on systematic strategies for determining cultural and linguistic loading, including for example, a review of existing test data in order to determine the nature and extent of cultural and linguistic impact (of these tests); consideration of distributions of scores on various tests for relevant samples to determine the attenuating effects of culture and language (e.g., bilinguals score about one standard deviation below the mean of monolinguals on many available tests, based on a number of studies (see Cummins 1984; Mercer 1976); and, consensus of experts to determine potential effects of either based on the test characteristics. From this information these authors created a two by two matrix for commonly used tests/subtests, reflecting on one dimension the degree of (mainstream U.S.) cultural loading and on the other, degree of (English) language demand, with three levels of impact, low, moderate, and high.

Flanagan et al. (2007, 2013) characterize the culture and language loadings of many tests using their model, including *UNIT, Leiter,* and the verbal and nonverbal subtests of the most

widely used tests of intelligence and neuropsychological functions (e.g., *Wechsler scales, Stanford-Binet intelligence scales, fifth edition [SB5], Woodcock Johnson, Fourth Edition* (WJ-IV; Schrank et al. 2014). To illustrate use of the C-LTC and C-LIM matrices cultural and language influences for the *UNIT-2* subtests are shown in this chapter in Fig. 1.1. The cell assignment from Flanagan et al. for the four *UNIT* original subtests are retained and are shown in the matrix as they were characterized in the Flanagan et al. 2007 book. Two new *UNIT 2* subtests, Nonsymbolic Quantity and Symbolic Quantity are placed in the matrix cells based on the perspective of the *UNIT-2* authors from the *UNIT-2* Manual, *not* Flanagan et al. (*UNIT-2* subtests were not included by Flanagan et al. in their 2013 book as the test was in development at the time the book was written.) Subtests in the top, leftmost cell are the least influenced, and those in the bottom, rightmost cell are the most affected. Impact is operationalized by the extent to which subtests within particular cells increase (or not) as a function of their distance from the top, left cell to the bottom right cell. Subtests that are least impacted by culture and language include Spatial Memory, Cube Design, and Nonsymbolic Quantity and Symbolic Quantity, which is slightly impacted by linguistic demand in the opinion of the *UNIT2* authors and has a low degree of cultural loading as all developed countries use Arabic numbers to quantify and

**Fig. 1.1** Matrix of cultural loading and linguistic demand classifications of the UNIT 2 subtests

**DEGREE OF LINGUISTIC DEMAND**

| | | Low | Moderate | High |
|---|---|---|---|---|
| **DEGREE OF CULTURAL LOADING** | Low | Spatial Memory<br>Cube Design<br>Nonsymbolic Quantity<br>Symbolic Memory | Symbolic Quantity | |
| | Moderate | Analogic Reasoning | | |
| | High | | | |

operationalize numerical concepts. *UNIT2* authors placed Nonsymbolic Quantity in the least impacted cell of the grid as it assesses quantitative reasoning *without* Arabic numbers.

Examiners can use the matrix to choose subtests and subtests from commonly used test batteries as shown in Flanagan, et al. (2007, 2013) for specific purposes (e.g., cross-battery assessment, screening). Examinees who want to minimize language and culture before administration will select subtests that are depicted in cells that reflect less (language and cultural) impact, i.e., they are placed near the top left of the matrix. If examinees want to determine the relative influence of language and culture *after* a battery of subtests have been administered they might examine the scores of the subtests within the matrix; if the scores are systematically lower from left to right and from top to bottom the scores may have been negatively impacted by linguistic or cultural influences, assuming other hypotheses for the pattern of scores can be ruled out. There is a computer software package included on a disc that accompanies Flanagan et al. (2007, 2013) to aid examiners in this process.

**Distinction between Nonverbal Unidimensional and Multidimensional Nonverbal Tests**. As is apparent from using the C-LTC and C-LIM matrices nonverbal cognitive tests possess various degrees of cultural and language loadings. Within the category of nonverbal tests, there are two basic types. There are nonverbal cognitive tests that assess cognition narrowly through the use of one operationalization (e.g., use of progressive matrices for intelligence). On the other hand, there are comprehensive tests of intelligence that assess multiple facets of intelligence (e.g., memory, reasoning, attention). Similarly, there are both narrow operationalizations of achievement available (e.g., those that assess oral reading for reading achievement) and comprehensive measures (e.g., tests that assess oral reading, vocabulary, fluency, and comprehension). The distinction between more narrow unidimensional and comprehensive multidimensional testing is clear in the area of nonverbal assessment of intelligence. For example, there is

a plethora of unidimensional progressive matrix tests available (*TONI-4; C-TONI-2*); however, there are fewer comprehensive nonverbal tests of intelligence (e.g., the *UNIT-2* and the *Leiter-3*). Given the narrow focus of the matrix analogy type tests and the fact that many of these tests employ verbal directions, these instruments may be best suited for 'low stakes' screening applications or in some cases large-scale group assessments. When psychoeducational assessments are conducted for 'high stakes' placement, eligibility, or diagnostic decision-making reasons, broader, more comprehensive (multidimensional) measures of intelligence might be more appropriate.

In any areas of noncognitive assessment (e.g., achievement, personality) the distinction between unidimensional and multidimensional testing is less salient. For example, most tests of achievement, even screening tests, assess more than one facet of performance. Similarly, personality tests are typically multifaceted also, assessing various aspects (e.g., paranoia, inattentiveness, depression). Importantly, nonverbal assessment of achievement, personality, and neurological functioning is not nearly as well defined and developed as nonverbal assessment of intelligence. The content devoted to nonverbal assessment of achievement, personality, and neuropsychological functioning in first edition of the *Handbook of Nonverbal Assessment* represented seminal treatments of these topics. This second edition reflects an update.

## Summary

This chapter provides context for nonverbal assessment of intelligence and related abilities. The goal is to present the rationale and history of nonverbal assessment along with the sociopolitical context, focusing particularly on the developments since the early 1900s. One of the strongest early initiatives for the development of nonverbal measures emerged because of the practical needs associated with illiterate personnel selection in wartime. Similar needs were being expressed in the private sector during the first half of the twentieth century. In addition, psychologists and related healthcare specialists began to demand more sophisticated measures of language-impaired individuals, such as those with central nervous system trauma, psychiatric diagnoses, and so on. Nonverbal tests were developed to meet these needs. Most recently, two major types of nonverbal tests have been developed, unidimensional or low stakes tests and more comprehensive high stakes multidimensional ones. Importantly, the nonverbal assessment of intelligence is relatively sophisticated; the nonverbal assessment of related constructs is ill-defined and/or in its infancy, depending on the particular ability in question. In fact, the content devoted to the nonverbal assessment of achievement, personality, and neurological functioning in the *Handbook of Nonverbal Assessment* represents the first systematic treatment of that topic.

In general, the assessment strategies mentioned in this chapter and discussed in detail in later chapters are very relevant for assessing individuals who have language-related limitations when expected to perform in mainstream English-speaking environments, i.e., those who are often described as culturally and linguistically diverse. Even so, the most defensible assessment should be multifaceted, and should consist of a nonverbal *and* a verbal component when possible. Of course, not all children are verbal, and in those cases a nonverbal assessment is the only option.

# References

American Association of Colleges of Teacher Education. (2016). *Preparing teachers for diverse students and settings.* Research-to-Practice Spotlight. Series 2: Building Partnerships. Retrieved from https://secure.aacte.org/apps/rl/resource.php?resid=552&ref=rl

American Psychological Association. (2016). *Guidelines for providers of psychological services to ethnic, linguistic, and culturally diverse populations.* Retrieved from http://www.apa.org/pi/oema/resources/policy/provider-guidelines.aspx

Arthur, G. (1943). *A point scale of performance tests: Clinical manual.* New York: The Commonwealth Fund.

Arthur, G. (1947). *A point scale of performance tests: clinical manual.* New York: The Commonwealth Fund.

Bracken, B. A. (1986). Incidence of basic concepts in the directions of five commonly used American tests of intelligence. *School Psychology International, 7,* 1–10.

Bracken, B. A. (1998). *Bracken basic concept scale: Spanish form.* San Antonio, TX: The Psychological Corporation.

Bracken, B. A., & McCallum, R. S. (1998). *Universal nonverbal intelligence test.* Itasca, IL: Riverside.

Bracken, B. A., & McCallum, R. S. (2016). *Universal nonverbal intelligence test.* Austin, TX: PRO-ED.

Braden, J. P. (1984). The factorial similarity of the WISC-R performance scale in deaf and hearing samples. *Personality and Individual Differences, 5* (4), 403–409.

Braden, J. P., Kostrubala, C. E., & Reed, J. (1994). Why do deaf children score differently on performance vs. motor-reduced nonverbal intelligence tests? *Journal of Psychoeducational Assessment, 12*(4), 357–363.

Brown, L., Sherbenou, R. J., & Johnsen, S. K. (1980). *Test of nonverbal intelligence.* Austin: PRO-ED.

Brown, L., Sherbenou, R. J., & Johnsen, S. K. (1990). *Test of nonverbal intelligence* (2nd ed.). Austin: PRO-ED.

Brown, L., Sherbenou, R. J., & Johnsen, S. K. (1997). *Test of nonverbal intelligence* (3rd ed.). Austin: PRO-ED.

Brown, L., Sherbenou, R. J., & Johnsen, S. K. (2010). *Test of nonverbal intelligence* (4th ed.). Austin, TX: PRO-ED, Publishing Company.

Burgmeister, B. M., Blum, L. H., & Lorge, I. (1972). *Columbia mental maturity scale* (3rd ed.). San Antonio. The Psychological Corporation.

Budoff, M. (1975). Measuring learning potential: An alternative to the traditional intelligence test. In *Ethical and legal factors in the practice of school psychology: Proceedings of the first annual conference in school psychology* (pp. 75–89).

Budoff, M. (1987). The validity of learning potential assessment. In L. C. Schneider (Ed.), *Dynamic assessment: An interactional approach to evaluating learning potential* (pp. 53–81). New York, NY: Guilford Press.

Carrey, N. J. (1995). Itard's 1828 memoire on "Mutism caused by a lesion of the intellectual functions": A historical analysis. *Journal of the American Academy of Child and Adolescent Psychiatry, 341,* 655–1661.

Coleman, M., Scribner, A. P., Johnsen, S., & Evans, M. K. (1993). A Comparison between the Wechsler Adult Intelligence Scale-Revised and the Test of Nonverbal Intelligence-2 with Mexican-American Secondary Students. *Journal of Psychoeducational Assessment, 11*(3), 250–258.

Cummins, J. (1979). Linguistic interdependence and the educational development of bilingual children. *Review of Educational Research, 49*(2), 222–251.

Cummins, J. (1984). *Bilingualism and special education: Issues in assessment and pedagogy* (Vol. 6). Clevedon: Multilingual Matters.

Dasen, O. R. (1984). The cross-cultural study of intelligence—Piaget and the Baoule. *International Journal of Psychology, 19*(4–5), 407–434.

Diana v State Board of Education. (1970).

Elliot, C. D. (2007). *Differential Ability Scales-II*. San Antonio, TX: Pearson Education, Inc.

Feuerstein, R., Rand, Y. A., & Hoffman, M. B. (1979). *The dynamic assessment of retarded performers: The learning potential assessment device, theory, instruments, and techniques*. Scott Foresman & Co.

Figueroa, R. A. (1990). Best practices in the assessment of bilingual children. *Best Practices in School Psychology, II*, 93–106.

Frisby, C. L. (1999). Straight talk about cognitive assessment and diversity. *School Psychology Quarterly, 14*, 195–207.

Flanagan, D. P., Ortiz, S. O., & Alfonso, S. O. (2007). *Essentials of Cross-Battery Assessment* (2nd ed.). Hoboken, NJ: John Wiley & Sons Inc.

Flanagan, D. P., Ortiz, S. O., & Alfonso, S. O. (2013). *Essentials of Cross-Battery Assessment* (3rd ed.). Hoboken, NJ: John Wiley & Sons Inc.

Goleman, D. (1995). *Emotional intelligence*. New York: Bantam Books.

Goleman, D. (2010). *Emotional intelligence* (10th Anniversary ed.). New York: Bantam Books.

Goodenough, F. L. (1926). *Measurement of intelligence by drawings*. New York: World Book.

Gopaul-McNicol, S. A., & Thomas-Presswood, T. (1998). *Working with linguistically and culturally different children: Innovative clinical and educational approaches*. Allyn & Bacon.

Glutting, J. J., & McDermott, P. A. (1990). Principles and problems in learning potentials. In C. R. Reynolds & R. W. Kamphaus (Eds.), *Handbook of psychological and educational assessment of children's intelligence and achievement* (pp. 296–347). New York: Guilford.

Government Printing Office. (1918). *Examiners Guide for Psychological Examining in the Army*. Washington, DC: Author.

Guilford, J. P. (1967). *The nature of human intelligence*. New York: McGraw-Hill.

Hammill, D. D., Pearson, N. A., & Wiederholt, J. L. (1997). *Comprehensive Test of Nonverbal Intelligence*. Austin, TX: PRO-ED.

Hammill, D. D., Pearson, N. A., & Wiederholt, J. L. (2009). *C-TONI: Comprehensive Test of Nonverbal Intelligence-2*. Austin, TX: PRO-ED Publishing Company.

Healy, W. L. (1914). A pictorial completion test. *The Psychological Review, 21*(3), 189–203.

Healy, W. L. (1918). *Pictorial completion test II*. Chicago: C.H. Stoelting.

Healy, W. L. (1921). Pictorial completion test II. *Journal of Applied Psychology, 5*, 232–233.

Herrnstein, R. J., & Murray, C. (1994). *The bell curve: Intelligence and class structure in American life*. New York: Simon & Schuster.

Individuals with Disabilities Education Improvement Act Amendments (IDEIA) of 2004, 20, U.S.C. (2004).

Jensen, A. R. (1998). *The g factor: The science of mental ability*. Westport, CT: Praeger.

Kamphaus, R. W. (1993). *Clinical assessment of children's intelligence: A handbook for professional practice*. Needham Heights, MA: Allyn & Bacon.

Kaufman, A. S. (1990). *Assessing adolescent and adult intelligence*. Boston: Allyn & Bacon.

Kaufman, A. S. (1994). *Intelligent testing with the WISC-II*. New York: Wiley.

Kaufman, A. S., & Kaufman, N. L. (1983). *K-ABC: Kaufman assessment battery for children: Interpretive manual*. American Guidance Service.

Knox, H. A. (1914). A scale based on the work at Ellis Island for estimating mental defect. *Journal of the American Medical Association, 62*, 741–747.

Larry P. By Lucille P. v. Riles, 793 F.2d 969 (9th Cir. 1984).

Leiter, R. G. (1938). *A comparative study of the general intelligence of Caucasian and Asian children as measured by the Leiter International Performance Scale* (Unpublished doctoral dissertation). University of Southern California, Los Angeles, CA.

Leiter, R. G. (1948). *Leiter international performance scale*. Chicago: Stoeling.

Marshall v. Georgia, 543 U.S. 962 (Supreme Court 2004).

Mercer, J. R. (1976). Cultural diversity, mental retardation, and assessment: The case for nonlabeling.

Lidz, C. S. (2001). Multicultural issues and dynamic assessment. In L. A. Suzuki, J. G. Ponterotto, & P. J. Meller (Eds.), *Handbook of multicultural assessment: Clinical psychological, and educational applications* (2nd ed., pp. 4–28). San Francisco: Jossey-Bass.

McCallum, R.S. (1999). A bakers dozen criteria for evaluation fairness in nonverbal testing. *The School Psychologist*, 40–43.

McCallum, R. S., Bracken, B. A., & Wasserman, J. (2001). *Essentials of nonverbal assessment*. New York: Wiley.

McCarthy, D. (1972). *McCarthy scales of children's abilties*. New York: The Psychological Corporation.

Muñoz-Sandoval, A. F., Cummins, J., Alvarado, C. G., & Ruef, M. L. (1998). *Comprehensive manual for the bilingual verbal ability tests*. Itasca, IL: Riverside Publishing Company.

Muñoz-Sandoval, A. F., Woodcock, R. W., McGrew, K. S., & Mather, N. (2005). *Bateria III-Woodcock-Muñoz*. Itasca, IL: Riverside Publishing.

Ortiz, S. O. (2002). Best practices in nondiscriminatory assessment. *Best Practices in School Psychology IV, 2*, 1321–1336.

Orwell, G. (1946). *Animal farm*. New York: Harcourt, Brace, and Company.

Padilla, A. M. (2001). Issues in culturally appropriate assessment. In L. A. Suzuki, J. G., Ponterotto, J. G., & Meller, P. L. (Eds.), *Handbook of multicultural assessment* (pp. 5–27). San Francisco: John Wiley & Sons.

Parents in Action on Special Ed. (Pase) v. Hannon, 506 F. Supp. 831 (N.D. Ill. 1980).

Pasko, J. R. (1994). Chicago-don't miss it. *Communique, 23*(4), 2.

Payne, D. A. (2003). *Applied educational assessment* (2nd ed.). Belmont, CA: Wadsworth/Thomson Learning.

Piaget, J. (1963). *The origins of intelligence in children.* New York: Norton.

Porteus, S. D. (1915). Mental tests for the feebleminded: A new series. *Journal of Psycho-Asthenics, 19,* 200–213. Minneapolis, MN: NCS Assessments.

Prifitera, A., Weiss, L. G., & Saklofske, D. H. (1998). The WISC-111 in context. In D. Rapaport & M. Gill (Eds.), *SchaferWISC-11 clinical use and interpretation.* New York: Academic Press.

Reynolds, C. R., & Lowe, P. A. (2009). The problem of bias in psychological testing. In T. G. Gutkin & C. R. Reynolds (Eds.), *School psychology handbook* (4th ed., pp. 332–374). Hoboken, NJ: John Wiley & Sons Inc.

Roid, G. (2003). Stanford-Binet intelligence scales-fifth Ed. San Antonio, TX: PRO-ED.

Roid, G.H., Miller, L.J., Pomplun, M. & Koch, C. (2013). *Leiter international performance scale-3.* Torrance, CA: Western Psychological Services. Examiner's manual. In G. H. Roid & L. J. Miller (Eds.), *Leiter international performance scale revised.* Wood Dale: Stoelting.

Rourke, B. P. (1995). *Syndrome of nonverbal learning disabilities: Neurodevelopmental manifestations.* New York: Guilford Press.

Salvia, J., & Ysseldyke, J. E. (2004). *Assessment in special and inclusive education.* Boston: Houghton Mifflin Company.

Sattler, J. (1988). *Assessment of children.* San Diego: Sattler.

Sattler, J. (2008). *Assessment of children. Cognitive foundations.* San Diego: Sattler.

Schrank, F. A., Mather, N., & McGrew, K. S. (2014). *Woodcock-Johnson IV tests of achievement.* Riverside: Rolling Meadows, IL, USA.

Serwer, A. (2011, May). The Bell swerve: Charles Murray surveys the crisis in white America and isn't sure whom to blame. *The American Prospect, 22*(5). Retrieved from http://prospect.org/artcile/bell-serve

Seguin, E. (1907). *Idiocy and its treatment by the physiological method.* New York: Teachers College, Columbia University.

Thorndike, R. L., & Hagen, E. P. (1986). *Measurement in evaluation in psychology and education* (4th ed.). Ney York: Wiley.

Thorndike, R. M., & Lohman, D. F. (1990). *A century of ability testing.* Chicago: Riverside Publishing.

Upson, L. M. (2004). Effects of an increasingly precise socioeconomic match on mean score differences in nonverbal intelligence test scores. (Doctoral dissertation). University of Tennessee-Knoxville. Retrieved from http://trace.tennessee.edu/utk_graddiss/2250/

Unz. (1997, October 19). Perspective on education; bilingual is a damaging myth; a system that ensures failure is kept alive by the flow of federal dollars. A 1998 initiative would bring change. *Los Angeles Times,* Opinion section, part M, p. 5

U.S. Department of Education. (2016). National Center for Education Statistics, ED*Facts* file 141, Data Group 678, extracted May 13, 2016, from the ED*Facts* Data Warehouse (internal U.S. Department of Education source); Common Core of Data (CCD), "State Non-fiscal Survey of Public Elementary and Secondary Education," 2008–09 through 2013–14. http://nces.ed.gov/programs/digest/d15/tables/dt15_204.27.asp.

R. R. Valencia & R. J. Rankin (1985). Evidence of content bias on the McCarthy Scale with Mexican-American children—Implications for test translation and nonbiased assessment. *Journal of Educational Psychology, 77* (2), 197-207.

Valencia, R. R., & Rankin, R. J. (1985). Evidence of content bias on the McCarthy scale with Mexican-American children—Implications for test translation and nonbiased assessment. *Journal of Educational Psychology, 77*(2), 197–207.

Valdés, G., & Figueroa, R. A. (1994). *Bilingualism and testing: A special case of bias.* Westport, CT: Ablex Publishing.

Van den Berg, A. R. (1986). *The problems of measuring intelligence in a heterogeneous society and possible solutions to some of the problems.* Pretoria: Institute for Psychological and Edumetric Research, Human Sciences Research Council.

Wechsler, D. (1949). *Wechsler intelligence scale for children.* San Antonio, TX: The Psychological Corporation.

Wechsler, D., & Naglieri, J. A. (2006). *Wechsler nonverbal scale of ability.* San Antoniok TX: The Psychological Corporation.

Vygotsky, L. (1978a). Interaction between learning and development. *Readings on the Development of Children, 23*(3), 34–41.

Vygotsky, L. S. (1978b). Mind in society: The development of higher mental process.

# Best Practices in Detecting Bias in Cognitive Tests

Susan J. Maller and Lai-Kwan Pei

In the 1970s, concerns regarding potential bias of intelligence tests led to several court cases (e.g., Diana v. the California State Board of Education 1970; Larry P. v. Wilson Riles 1979), and studies of item bias, with conflicting findings (cf., Cotter and Berk 1981; Ilai and Willerman 1989; Jastak and Jastak 1964; Koh et al. 1984; Ross-Reynolds and Reschly 1983; Sandoval 1979; Sandoval et al. 1977; Turner and Willerman 1977). Bryk (1980) found methodological flaws in the above-mentioned mean score difference score definition and related item bias studies, noting that the current psychometric methodologies (e.g., latent trait theory) had not even been mentioned by Jensen (1980). However, studies using such methods continue to be promoted as evidence of bias (e.g., Braden 1999; Frisby 1998).

*Bias* refers to systematic error in the estimations of a construct across subgroups (e.g., males vs. females, minority vs. majority). All forms of bias eventually lead to a question of construct validity due to the potential influence of unintended constructs. The presence of bias ultimately suggests that scores have different meanings for different subgroups. Bias can be investigated empirically at the item or test score levels. The various methods to investigate bias relate to the source of bias or differential validity (content, construct, and criterion-related).

*Fairness* is a more inclusive term and refers specifically to the (a) absence of bias, (b) equitable treatment of examinees during the testing process, (c) equitable test score interpretations for the intended uses, and (d) equitable opportunities to learn the content of the test (American Educational Research Association [AERA], American Psychological Association [APA], & National Council on Measurement in Education [NCME] 2014). Clearly, there is no such thing as a "nonbiased test" or a test that "is fair" or "is valid" for all subgroups under all conditions. Furthermore, test developers can go to extensive lengths to create instruments that lack evidence of bias against subgroups; however, test consumers ultimately are responsible for selecting, administering, and interpreting the results of tests with evidence of validity for the purpose in which tests are used.

Various professional entities have developed guidelines related to fairness in testing. For example, the Standards for Educational and Psychological Testing (AERA, APA, & NCME 2014) devotes an entire chapter to "Fairness in Testing". The section "fairness as lack of measurement bias" states that mean score differences are insufficient evidence of bias. When mean score differences are found for subgroups, construct irrelevant variance, or construct underrepresentation should be investigated as an explanation. Construct irrelevant

S.J. Maller (✉)
Department of Educational Studies, Purdue University, West Lafayette, IN 47907, USA
e-mail: maller@purdue.edu

L.-K. Pei
Houston Independent School District, 4400 West 18th Street, Houston, TX 77092-8501, USA
e-mail: lpei@houstonisd.org

© Springer International Publishing AG 2017
R.S. McCallum (ed.), *Handbook of Nonverbal Assessment*,
DOI 10.1007/978-3-319-50604-3_2

variance may occur as a function of test development, administration, and scoring procedures. Four guidelines are provided to help test developers and users to minimize construct irrelevant variance and ensure the validity of the test and test score interpretation.

Code of Professional Responsibilities in Educational Measurement (National Council on Measurement in Education [NCME] 1995) states that those who develop assessments are responsible for making their products "as free as possible from bias due to characteristics irrelevant to the construct being measured, such as gender, ethnicity, race, socioeconomic status, disability, religion, age, or national origin" (Sect. 1.2a).

Code of Fair Testing in Education (Joint Committee on Testing Practices [JCTP] 2004) Section A states that test developers should obtain and provide evidence on the performance of test takers of diverse subgroups, and evaluate the evidence to ensure that differences in performance are related to the skills being assessed, while test users should evaluate the available evidence on the performance of test takers of diverse subgroups, and determine to the extent feasible which performance differences may have been caused by factors unrelated to the skills being assessed.

Test publishers routinely enlist the assistance of experts in the test content domain to conduct sensitivity reviews or evaluate the items for content unfairness, including offensive language, insensitivity, or other content that may have unintended influences on the performances of members of various subgroups. Panel reviews of the item contents in several achievement and scholastic aptitude tests have tied differential item performance to differences in opportunities to learn or differences in socialization. For example, items favoring females have been linked to specific topics involving humanities, esthetics, human relationships, whereas items that favoring males have been linked to contents about science, sports, mechanics (Lawrence and Curley 1989; Lawrence et al. 1988; Scheuneman and Gerritz 1990; Wild and McPeek 1986). Unfortunately, panel reviews of the item content

bias have neither yielded consistent nor accurate results (Engelhard et al. 1990; Plake 1980; Sandoval and Miille 1980).

To study whether a test is biased toward specific groups, the psychometric properties of the test can be investigated for invariance (equality) across groups. The type of the invariance investigation depends on the suspected nature of bias and can include a variety of methods to (a) detect differential item functioning (DIF), and (b) examine measurement invariance. Item bias/DIF detection examines the characteristics of the test and item itself to check whether the test/items are measuring irrelevant construct. Measurement invariance refers to whether the scale is measuring the same construct at different occasions or across different groups.

## Item Bias and Differential Item Functioning (DIF)

Although the terms item bias and differential item functioning (DIF) are often used interchangeably, the term DIF was suggested (Holland and Thayer 1988) as a somewhat neutral term to refer to differences in the statistical properties of an item between groups of examinees of equal ability. These groups are often referred to as the reference (e.g., majority) and focal (e.g., minority) groups. DIF detection methods "condition on" or control for ability, meaning that examinees are necessarily matched on ability; thus, only examinees of equal ability (e.g., overall test score) in the reference and focal groups are compared. The item that is being tested for DIF is referred to as the study item. There are two types of DIF: uniform DIF and non-uniform DIF. Uniform DIF, also called unidirectional DIF, occurs when an item favors one group over another across all ability levels. Alternatively, non-uniform DIF, also called crossing DIF, occurs when an item discriminates across the ability levels differently for the groups. Items that exhibit DIF threaten the validity of a test and may have serious consequences for groups as well as individuals, because the probabilities of correct responses are determined not only by the trait that the test claims to measure, but also by factors specific to group membership, such as ethnicity or gender. Thus, it is critical to identify DIF items in a test.

Numerous methods have been proposed for detecting DIF. The methods can be classified into two groups, depending on whether the method is based on item response theory (IRT). In non-IRT DIF detection methods, the observed total score is usually used to indicate the examinee's ability level. Non-IRT methods are better than IRT methods when the sample size is small, because they do not require item parameter estimation. However, without item parameter estimation, it is more difficult to figure out the source of DIF when an item is flagged as a DIF item. Non-IRT detection methods include: the (a) Mantel–Haenszel procedure (Holland and Thayer 1988; Mantel and Haenszel 1959); and (b) logistic regression modeling (Zumbo 1999); and (c) SIBTEST (Shealy and Stout 1993).

In IRT DIF detection methods, the probability of a correct response to an item is assumed to follow an IRT model. The examinee ability levels and item parameters are estimated based on item responses. DIF detection is then performed by comparing the estimated models for the reference and focal groups. IRT methods require larger sample size and more computational load for parameter estimation. However, with the known item parameters, the test developers can learn more about the source of the DIF and revise the item/test. IRT DIF detection methods include: (a) Lord's chi-square test (Kim et al. 1995; Lord 1980); (b) area method (Raju 1988, 1990); and (c) IRT likelihood ratio test (Thissen et al. 1988, 1993).

In the following sections, the more popular DIF detection methods, including Mantel–Haenszel procedure, logistic regression modeling, SIBTEST, and IRT likelihood ratio test, are described. Details of the other methods, as well as some older methods not mentioned above, can be found in the overviews given by Camilli and Shepard (1994), Clauser and Mazor (1998), Holland and Wainer (1993), Millsap and Everson

(1993), Osterlind and Everson (2009), and Penfield and Camilli (2007).

## Ability Matching

When detecting DIF, only examinees of equal ability in the reference and focal groups are compared. Thus, ability matching is very important in DIF detection. For example, if examinees with different ability levels are matched by mistake, then a non-DIF item could be flagged incorrectly as a DIF item. If external criterion is not available to match the reference and focal groups, then the matching has to be performed with the item responses of the study items. Because the inclusion of DIF items in the matching step would likely result in incorrect matches, a purification step is usually used to remove DIF items that might contaminate the matching criterion. The remaining DIF-free items, also known as *anchor items*, can then be used in ability matching. The purification is usually performed with an initial Mantel–Haenszel procedure, in which the observed total score from all items is used to match ability levels.

## Mantel–Haenszel Procedure (MH)

Mantel and Haenszel (1959) introduced a procedure to study matched groups. Holland (1985) and later Holland and Thayer (1988) adapted the procedure for detection of DIF. The MH procedure compares the odds of a correct response of the reference and focal groups on a dichotomous item. For each ability level, a contingency table is constructed for the study item, resulting in $J$ $2 \times 2$ tables, where $J$ is the number of ability levels. Each cell of the table indicates the frequency of correct/incorrect responses to the item for reference/focal group. An example of contingency table is shown in Table 2.1.

Under the null hypothesis of no DIF, the two groups have the same odds of getting a correct response in all ability levels, i.e., $A_j/B_j = C_j/D_j$ for all ability levels $j$. The chi-square statistic for the null hypothesis is

**Table 2.1** Example of a 2 × 2 contingency table for an item at ability level $j$

|  | 1 (correct response) | 0 (incorrect response) | Total |
|---|---|---|---|
| Reference group | $A_j$ | $B_j$ | $N_{Rj}$ |
| Focal group | $C_j$ | $D_j$ | $N_{Fj}$ |
| Total | $N_{1j}$ | $N_{0j}$ | $N_{.j}$ |

$$\text{MH} - \chi^2 = \frac{\left[\left|\sum_j \left(A_j - E(A_j)\right)\right| - 0.5\right]^2}{\sum_j \text{var}(A_j)}, \quad (2.1)$$

where

$$E(A_j) = \frac{N_{Rj}N_{1j}}{N_{.j}} \quad \text{and}$$

$$\text{var}(A_j) = \frac{N_{Rj}N_{Fj}N_{1j}N_{0j}}{\left(N_{.j}\right)^2 \left(N_{.j} - 1\right)}.$$

The statistic follows chi-square distribution with one degree of freedom. The $-0.5$ term in the statistic is a continuity correction, which is supposed to improve accuracy of Type I error (Holland and Thayer 1988). Note that when detecting DIF on a study item, examinees are matched on the purified subtest and the study item. Although it may be counter-intuitive to include the study item in the matching, exclusion of the studied item would change the calculation of the test statistic (Holland and Thayer 1988) (Table 2.2).

An additional statistic can be used with the MH procedure to facilitate interpretation of DIF by taking the natural logarithm of the chi-square statistic. Zieky (1993) suggested multiplying $\ln(\text{MH} - \chi^2)$ by $-2.35$, denoted as $\delta$, resulting in a statistic that centers at zero and ranges from $-4$ to $+4$. Educational testing service (ETS) developed a scheme for classifying a dichotomous item into one of three categories of DIF: A (negligible), B (slight to moderate), and C (moderate to severe). The classification guidelines are as follows (Dorans and Holland 1993; Zieky 1993):

| Level | $\delta$ |
|---|---|
| A | $|\delta| < 1.0$ |
| B | $1.0 < |\delta| < 1.5$ |
| C | $|\delta| > 1.5$ |

Samples of 100 examinees are adequate for the MH procedure (Hills 1989), and as small as 50 examinees in the reference group and 10 examinees in the focal group have been suggested for MH DIF screening (Kromrey and Parshall 1991). The MH procedure is not designed to detect non-uniform DIF. If non-uniform DIF is present, the term $A_j - E(A_j)$ in Eq. (2.1) is positive for some ability levels and negative for the others. The statistic will then be small because of cancelation, giving a false conclusion of no DIF. To detect non-uniform DIF, the modified version proposed by Mazor et al. (1994) can be used. The MH procedure has been extended to detect DIF for polytomous items, and to detect DIF for multiple groups simultaneously (Penfield 2001; Zwick et al. 1993). The MH procedure can easily and quickly be run in statistical analysis packages such as SAS, SPSS, Stata, R, and Systat.

## Logistic Regression DIF Detection Method (LR DIF)

Unlike the MH procedure, LR DIF can be used to test non-uniform DIF directly (Rogers and Swaminathan 1993; Swaminathan and Rogers 1990). In LR DIF, the probability of a correct response to an item follows a logistic regression model:

$$P(x = 1|\theta, g)$$
$$= \frac{\exp(\beta_0 + \beta_1\theta + \beta_2 g + \beta_3(\theta g))}{1 + \exp(\beta_0 + \beta_1\theta + \beta_2 g + \beta_3(\theta g))},$$
$$(2.2)$$

where $x$ is the item response, $\theta$ is the ability level, and $g$ is the group membership, which is usually coded as 1 for reference group and 0 for focal

**Table 2.2** Summary of bias studies for several nonverbal intelligence tests

| Test | Item bias/DIF | Factor invariance | Differential prediction | Other |
|---|---|---|---|---|
| CTONI-2 | Logistic regression was used to detect DIF across gender, race, and ethnicity. No DIF item was found | No examination was conducted | Sensitivity and specificity indices between CTONI-2 and TONI-4, PTONI were larger than 0.70, which meet acceptability Level I when predicting TONI-4 and PTONI<br><br>Correlation coefficients were used to be the predictive validity for achievement test<br><br>Differential prediction across subgroups was not investigated | The reliability coefficients are consistently large for a general population and subgroups: gender, racial, and exceptionality categories |
| Leiter-3 | Correlations between separately calibrated difficulty parameters of 1-PL IRT model were used to detect DIF across race and ethnicity. Two DIF items were found | No examination was conducted | Correlation between Leiter-3 and the California Achievement Test was used as the predictive validity coefficient. It was not significant for samples of 50 Caucasians/nor-Hispanic and 20 African Americans<br><br>Differential prediction across subgroups was not investigated | The lack of mean score differences was used as evidence of fairness, although a few differences were found between the following: Caucasians/Hispanics, Normative sample members/Navajos, and males/females |
| UNIT2 | Logistic regression was used to detect DIF across gender, race, and ethnicity. No DIF item was found according to Jodoin and Gierl's (2001) criteria | CFA for various subgroups, including males, females, African Americans, Hispanics, all showed good fit to the data, although hypotheses regarding invariance were not tested using simultaneous, multisample CFA | The correlations between the UNIT2 and seven criterion measures was used as the predictive validity<br><br>The correlations between the UNIT2 composites and the criterion tests range from moderate to nearly perfect<br><br>However, the predictive validity across subgroups were not examined | Mean score comparisons of several subgroups indicated some differences between groups<br><br>Internal consistency reliability coefficients were consistently high across subgroups (males, females, African Americans, Hispanics) |

(continued)

**Table 2.2** (continued)

| Test | Item bias/DIF | Factor invariance | Differential prediction | Other |
|---|---|---|---|---|
| TONI-4 | Logistic regression was used to detect DIF across gender, race, and ethnicity. One DIF item was found | No examination was conducted | Predictive validity was measured by the correlations between TONI-4 and two selected criterion measures, TONI-3 and CTONI-2 | Internal consistency reliability coefficients were uniformly high across subgroups (gender, race/ethnicity, intellectual ability, English language proficiency) |
| | | | Differential prediction across subgroups was not investigated | |
| Wechsler Nonverbal Scale of Ability (WNV) | No DIF detection was conducted | No examination was conducted | Correlations between corresponding subtests on the WNV and other selected cognitive tests were moderate | The authors indicated that the majority of the subtests reliability coefficients across special groups were similar to, or higher than, those of the U.S. normative sample, and claimed that the WNV was an equally reliable tool for this population |
| | | | Differential prediction across subgroups was not investigated | |

group. Equation (2.2) can be written as an additive function by taking the log odd ratio:

$$\log\left(\frac{P}{1-P}\right) = \beta_0 + \beta_1\theta + \beta_2 g + \beta_3(\theta g), \quad (2.3)$$

where the parameters $\beta_0$, $\beta_1$, $\beta_2$ and $\beta_3$ represent the intercept, slopes for ability, membership and the interaction term (ability $\times$ group), respectively. The item exhibit non-uniform DIF if $\beta_3 \neq 0$, and exhibit uniform DIF if $\beta_2 \neq 0$ and $\beta_3 = 0$. If $\beta_2 = \beta_3 = 0$, then the item does not exhibit DIF.

To test whether the item exhibits non-uniform DIF, two different models are fitted to the data, yielding two likelihood ratio chi-squares. The *compact* model only has the first three terms of Eq. (2.3), while the *augmented* model has all the terms. Because chi-squares are additive, the explanatory power of the interaction term can be tested by subtracting the likelihood ratio of the less restrictive (augmented) model from the more restrictive (compact) model, yielding a difference chi-square with one degree of freedom. If the difference is significant, the interaction term is necessary, and the item is concluded to exhibit non-uniform DIF. Otherwise, the item is tested for uniform DIF, in which a compact model including only the first two terms ($\beta_0$, $\beta_1$), and an augmented model including the first three terms ($\beta_0$, $\beta_1$, $\beta_2$), are fitted to the data. If the difference chi-square between the compact and augmented models is significant, the item is concluded to exhibit uniform DIF, and the direction of uniform DIF is indicated by the sign of $\beta_2$. Uniform DIF favors the reference group when $\beta_2 > 0$, and favors the focal group when $\beta_2 < 0$. Zumbo and Thomas (1997) proposed to use the difference between Nagelkerke's $R^2$ (1991) of two logistic models, denoted $\Delta R^2$, to be the effect size of DIF. They provided the following interpretation of DIF: (a) negligible DIF if $\Delta R^2 \leq 0.13$; (b) moderate DIF if $0.13 < \Delta R^2 \leq 0.26$; and (c) large DIF if $\Delta R^2 > 0.26$. LR DIF is widely available in statistical software like SAS, SPSS, Stata, R, and Systat. The method has been extended to polytomous items and to multiple groups (Agresti 1996; Magis et al. 2011).

## SIBTEST Procedure

Simultaneous item bias test (SIBTEST) was developed by Shealy and Stout (1993) to detect and estimate DIF. The procedure was later extended to polytomous items (Chang et al. 2005). SIBTEST tests the following hypothesis:

$$H_0 : \beta_{uni} = 0 \text{ versus } H_1 : \beta_{uni} \neq 0,$$

where $\beta_{uni}$ is the parameter specifying the magnitude of unidirectional DIF. $\beta_{uni}$ is defined as:

$$\beta_{uni} = \int_\theta d(\theta) f_F(\theta) d\theta, \quad (2.4)$$

where $d(\theta) = P(x = 1|\theta, F) - P(x = 1|\theta, R)$ is the difference in probability of correct response at ability $\theta$, and $f_F(\theta)$ is the density function of ability in the focal group. When the reference and focal groups have the same ability distribution, the observed total score is an unbiased estimator of ability, and $\beta_{uni}$ can be estimated by

$$\hat{\beta}_{uni} = \sum_{j=0}^{J} p_j (\bar{Y}_{Fj} - \bar{Y}_{Rj}), \quad (2.5)$$

where $\bar{Y}_{gj}$ is the average score on the study item for the group $g$ examinees with observed score $j$, $p_j$ is the proportion of examinees with observed score $j$, and $J$ is the total number of items (Bolt and Stout 1996). In practice, the two groups usually have different ability distributions, and the observed total score is a biased estimator of ability. To adjust the estimation bias, Shealy and Stout (1993) introduced regression correction step into SIBTEST procedure to correct for mean difference in the ability distribution of the reference and focal groups. The regression correction step was later improved by Jiang and Stout (1998) for better control of Type I error inflation. Replacing the observed item score $\bar{Y}_{gj}$ in

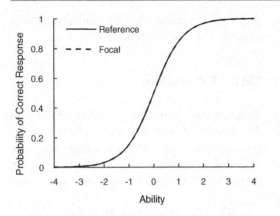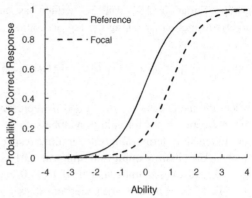

**Fig. 2.1** Item characteristic curves for non-DIF (*left*) and DIF (*right*) items

Eq. (2.5) with the adjusted item score $\bar{Y}_{gj}^*$ yields an unbiased estimator for the DIF size regardless of the difference in the ability distribution of two groups. Positive values of $\hat{\beta}_{\text{uni}}$ indicate DIF favoring the reference group and negative values indicate DIF favoring the focal group. The test statistic for the null hypothesis of no DIF is then given by

$$B_{\text{uni}} = \frac{\hat{\beta}_{\text{uni}}}{\hat{\sigma}\left(\hat{\beta}_{\text{uni}}\right)},$$

where $\hat{\sigma}(\hat{\beta}_{\text{uni}})$ is the standard error of the estimator $\hat{\beta}_{\text{uni}}$. $B_{\text{uni}}$ follows a normal distribution with mean 0 and standard deviation 1 under the null hypothesis (Shealy and Stout 1993).

SIBTEST was designed to detect uniform DIF. If non-uniform DIF is present, the term $d(\theta)$ in Eq. (2.4) changes sign at a certain ability. The magnitude of $\beta_{\text{uni}}$ will then be small because of cancelation, giving a false conclusion of no DIF. To address this problem, crossing simultaneous item bias test (CSIBTEST) was developed by Li and Stout (1996) to detect crossing DIF. Unfortunately, the distribution of the test statistic in CSIBTEST cannot be derived easily, and a randomization test has to be used to determine statistical significance. SIBTEST is the computer program for this DIF detection method (Li and Stout 1994).

## IRT-Based DIF Detection

One problem of non-IRT DIF detection methods is the use of the observed score as an indicator of ability level, which may not be reliable. For example, both theoretical studies and simulation studies showed that when the item responses are generated by complex IRT models, the MH procedure can falsely indicate DIF when no bias is present (Meredith and Millsap 1992; Millsap and Meredith 1992; Uttaro 1992; Zwick 1990). In IRT models, ability is conceptualized as a latent trait. The probability of a correct response to an item for a given ability is given by the *item characteristic curve* (ICC). Figure 2.1 shows the ICCs for non-DIF and DIF items. The first set of ICCs, which are the same for the reference and focal groups, shows that the item does not exhibit DIF. The second set of ICCs is for an item that exhibit uniform DIF, because the reference group always has a higher probability of correct response than the focal group. If an item exhibits non-uniform DIF, then the ICCs will cross each other.

IRT models commonly used to investigate DIF in intelligence tests include the one-, two-, and three-parameter models, as well as Samejima's (1969) graded response model. In the two-parameter logistic (2-PL) model, the probability of correct response is for an examinee with ability $\theta$ is:

$$P(x = 1|\theta) = \frac{1}{1 + e^{-a(\theta-b)}},$$

where $x$ is the item response, $a$ is the item discrimination parameter (proportional to the slope of the ICC), and $b$ is the item difficulty parameter (at which the examinee has a 50% probability of correct response). The one-parameter logistic (1-PL; also known as Rasch) model differs from the 2-PL model in that the discrimination parameter is held constant across items. This is a very stringent assumption that rarely can be met in practice. However, examination of fit statistics can indicate whether the assumption is met. Regardless, if sufficient sample sizes are available, the 2-PL model is generally preferable to test the invariance of item discriminations across groups. A three-parameter logistic (3-PL) model is recommended for multiple choice items, because the model includes a guessing parameter $c$. The parameter ranges from 0 to 1, but is typically <0.3. The 3-PL model is defined as:

$$P(x = 1|\theta) = c + \frac{1 - c}{1 + e^{-a(\theta-b)}}.$$

When items are scored using necessarily ordered categories, they can be fitted with Samejima's graded response model (Samejima 1969). For example, for an item scored 0, 1, or 2, the graded response model provides two item difficulty estimates (based on the probability of scoring 1 or the probability of scoring 2). The graded response model is as follows:

$$P_k^*(\theta) = P(x \geq k|\theta) = \frac{1}{1 + e^{-a(\theta-b_k)}},$$

where $P_k^*(\theta)$ is the probability of an examinee with ability $\theta$ reaching category $k$ or higher, and $b_k$ is the difficulty parameter in reaching category $k$. For an examinee with ability $\theta$, $P_0(\theta) = 1 - P_1^*(\theta)$ is the probability of scoring 0, $P_1(\theta) = P_2^*(\theta) - P_1^*(\theta)$ is the probability of scoring 1, and $P_2(\theta) = P_2^*(\theta)$ is the probability of scoring 2.

## IRT Likelihood Ratio Test (IRT-LR)

IRT-based likelihood ratio test for DIF is designed to determine whether the ICC of the study item differs for the reference and focal groups. The method used the likelihood ratio test statistic to test the null hypothesis that the item parameters of the study item do not differ between groups. In this method, two models are fitted for the anchor items and the study item. In the *free* model, all parameters for the anchor items are constrained to be equal across groups, whereas the parameters for the study item are not. The *constrained* model poses an additional equality constraint on one of the parameters for the study item, such as lower asymptote parameter, discrimination parameter, or difficulty parameter. The likelihood goodness-of-fit statistic, $G^2$, is then used to test the hypothesis that the parameter estimate is invariant across groups:

$$G^2 = 2 \sum_{g \in \{R,F\}} \sum_{\mathbf{x}} n_g(\mathbf{x}) \cdot \ln\left(\frac{P_{\text{free}}(\mathbf{x}|g)}{P_{\text{constrained}}(\mathbf{x}|g)}\right),$$

where $g$ is the group (reference or focal); $\mathbf{x}$ is a response pattern; $n_g(\mathbf{x})$ is the count for pattern $\mathbf{x}$ in group $g$; $P_{\text{free}}(\mathbf{x}|g)$ and $P_{\text{constrained}}(\mathbf{x}|g)$ are the probabilities of pattern $\mathbf{x}$ under the free and constrained models, respectively. The statistic follows the chi-square distribution approximately with degree of freedom equal to the difference in the number of free parameters in the two models. IRT-LR test can be carried out with IRTLRDIF (Thissen 2001).

## Test Bias

Evidence of *Test bias* is reflected in test/subtest scores if there is differential validity as a function of group membership. Investigations of test bias usually include studies of (a) unequal psychometric properties, (b) unequal factor structures, or (c) differential prediction of performance between groups. Traditionally, test developers and consumers believed that special subgroup norms may be useful for comparing individuals to a more representative peer group. For example, special norms were developed for Wechsler Intelligence Scale for Children—Revised Performance Scale for deaf children (Anderson and Sisco 1977). However, subgroup norms may be a superficial solution to a larger problem concerning content and construct validity. If test items have different meanings for examinees belonging to different subgroups, then subgroup norms result in comparing members to other members on some trait not claimed to be measured by the test (Maller 1996).

Differences in reliability coefficients also may indicate bias. Reliability coefficients provide an indication of how consistently a construct, such as intelligence, is measured across groups. Statistical tests are used to assess differences in the reliability coefficients (Feldt and Brennan 1989). Differences found in the internal consistency coefficients between groups may indicate bias. However, differences in the test–retest and alternate forms coefficients may also be a result of the time between testings (test–retest) or nonequivalent forms (alternate forms) and not a result of bias.

## Factor Invariance

*Construct equivalence* suggests that test constructs are conceptualized and measured similarly across groups (Shelley-Sireci and Sireci 1998; Sireci et al. 1998). Factor analytic methods are used to examine the internal structure of a test and to investigate whether a construct is equally indicated for groups. Exploratory (EFA) and confirmatory (CFA) factor analyses are used to examine the similarity of the factor structures. In EFA, the *coefficient of congruence*, a type of correlation, is used to determine the similarity of the factor loadings for groups. Values above 0.90 indicate factor invariance, meaning factors are equivalently indicated across groups and provides evidence against test bias (Cattell 1978).

Reynolds (1982) stated "bias exists in regard to construct validity when a test is shown to measure different hypothetical traits (psychological constructs) for one group than another or to measure the same trait but with different degrees of accuracy" (p. 194). Furthermore, Reynolds added that multisample CFA based on the techniques of Jöreskog (1971) is a more promising and sophisticated method in detecting such construct bias than the method of exploratory factor analysis, which examines factorial similarity using the coefficient of congruence.

Multisample CFA has been used to test the invariance of factor structures (Alwin and Jackson 1981; Bollen 1989; Jöreskog and Sörbom 1989; Jöreskog 1971; McGaw and Jöreskog 1971). Following the procedures recommended by Bollen (1989) and Jöreskog and Sörbom (1989), the general form (hereafter referred to as the Model$_{baseline}$) of the theoretical model is tested for invariance across samples which equal the sum of the chi-squares for the individual group analyses, and to obtain fit statistics of the model across groups. To assess the fit of the model, the following fit indices can be used: GFI, TLI, CFI, and RMSEA. The GFI is interpreted as the proportion of the observed variances and covariances that can be accounted for by the model. The TLI is recommended by Tucker and Lewis (1973), with values greater than or equal to 0.90 indicating reasonable fix. The CFI is recommended by Bentler (1990, 1992) and Rigdon (1996) to indicate the difference in fit of the null and target models relative to the fit of the null model, with values greater than or equal to 0.90 indicating reasonable fit. The RMSEA is recommended by Browne and Cudeck (1993) and Rigdon (1996) to indicate the fit of the empirical and modeled variance-covariance matrices, with values less than 0.05 indicating excellent fit and values less than 0.08 indicating reasonable fit (Rigdon 1996). In addition, the Satorra–Bentler scaled chi-square (Satorra and Bentler 1988) also might be examined, because it has been reported to be reliable for various distributional conditions and sample sizes (Hu et al. 1992).

If the general form does not fit across groups, test constructs are measured differently across the groups and a more exploratory approach might be taken to reveal a model that fits the data. These approaches may include exploratory factor analytic studies or model fitting approaches in CFA. If, however, the general form of the model adequately fits across groups, progressively more restrictive models are then tested for invariance. Three progressively more restricted models may be tested by adding one additional constrained matrix of: (a) factor loadings or path coefficients, describing the relationships between the latent and observed variables and are interpreted like regression coefficients, (b) error variances, and (c) factor variances and covariances. The chi-squares for each of the restricted models, Model$_{nested}$, are compared to the chi-square for the Model$_{baseline}$, using a difference chi-square test, which involves subtracting the Model$_{baseline}$ chi-square from the chi-square obtained for the restricted model, with degrees of freedom equal to the degrees of freedom for the Model$_{nested}$ minus the degrees of freedom for the Model$_{baseline}$.

Factor loading invariance is the most critical concern regarding construct validity, because factor loadings indicate the relationship between the observable item response and factor (construct). If the matrix of factor loadings is not invariant, at least one element of the matrix lacks invariance, individual elements of the matrix subsequently should be individually tested for invariance to isolate the source(s) of invariance (Maller and Ferron 1997; Maller et al. 1998). The restricted model is the Model$_{nested}$ with one equality constraint of the studied parameter. The chi-square difference is obtained by comparing the restricted and Model$_{baseline}$ chi-squares with one degree of freedom. A lack of factor loading invariance suggests that factor loadings should not be constrained to be invariant when testing the invariance of error variances and factor variances and covariances. In fact, a lack of factor loading invariance is sufficient to lead to the conclusion of differential validity.

If the factor loadings are invariant, the matrix of error variances should be tested for invariance. If the matrix is not invariant, individual elements subsequently can be tested for invariance, as described above. A lack of error variance invariance suggests that the measurement of the

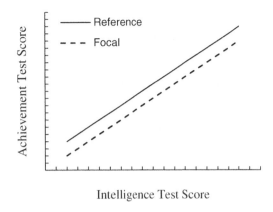

**Fig. 2.2** Regression lines for reference and focal groups where intelligence scores under-predict achievement test scores for the focal group

variables (subtests) is differentially affected by extraneous sources of variance.

If factor covariances are found to lack invariance, differential variability in the factors may be the source of invariance, resulting in smaller or greater redundancy in the constructs claimed to be measured by the factors. In other words, the "separate" factors may be measuring overlapping abilities for one of the groups.

If factor variances and covariances are invariant, it makes sense to do a follow-up test of the invariance of means structures to investigate whether the latent means differ across groups. A lack of invariance suggests that, although the measurement of test constructs do not differ, the groups differ in terms of ability.

## Prediction Bias

The examination of differential predictive validity is especially important when tests are used for placement and selection decisions. Differential prediction has been used as an indication of test bias (Cleary 1968). Predictive validity coefficients that significantly differ between groups indicate that the test has different relationships with the criterion across the groups. Another type of differential prediction refers to a systematic under or overestimation of a criterion for a given group (Cleary 1968; Scheuneman and Oakland

1998). Specifically, differential prediction occurs when examinees belonging to different subgroups, but with comparable ability based on some predictor test score, tend to obtain different scores on some criterion test. To investigate differential prediction, regression lines for criterion (e.g., intelligence) and predictor (e.g., achievement) test scores are compared for reference and focal groups.

Figure 2.2 depicts an example of regression lines with different intercepts. The criterion is underpredicted for the focal group through achievement test. Suppose the achievement test in Fig. 2.2 is required for admission to a gifted education program. Members of the focal group actually will obtain lower scores on the achievement test than would be expected based on their intelligence scores, when using the regression line for the reference group. Focal group members who would be successful on the criterion may be denied acceptance into the gifted program based on their achievement test scores. A test that does not exhibit differential predictive validity still may be biased based on other definitions of bias. Furthermore, predictor and criterion tests may be spuriously correlated due to systematic factors, including construct bias. That is, factors specific to group membership that similarly affect scores on both tests may actually inflate predictive validity coefficients. Consistent with Messick's (1989) concerns, this method is not recommended in the absence of other bias investigations related to construct validity.

## Current Status and Recommendations

The best practices in detecting bias in nonverbal tests are really no different from the best practices for detecting bias in other psychoeducational tests. Until recently, there were few published studies of invariance at the item or test levels in intelligence tests using state-of-the-art methods, though these methods have been used for quite some time to study bias in various scholastic aptitude tests (e.g., Dorans and Kulick 1983;

Green et al. 1989; Holland and Thayer 1988; Linn et al. 1981; Scheuneman 1987). Recently, nonverbal and verbal intelligence test manuals and independent researchers have begun to report investigations of DIF and factor invariance. However, some popular test manuals do not include DIF investigation, such as Wechsler Nonverbal Scale of Ability technical manual (WNV; Wechsler and Naglieri 2006).

The comprehensive test of nonverbal intelligence–second editionmanual includes a report of DIF analysis for three dichotomous groups (male vs. female, African American vs. non-African American, Hispanic vs. non-Hispanic) (CTONI-2; Hammill et al. 2009). Using the entire normative sample as subjects, the LR DIF approach was applied to all items contained in each of the CTONI-2 subtests. Of the 150 items, at least 24 were found to be statistically significant at the 0.001 level, but had negligible effect sizes according to Jodoin and Gierl's (2001) criteria ($\Delta R^2 < 0.035$).

The Leiter International Performance Scale-3 manual includes a report of DIF analysis for two dichotomous groups (Caucasian vs. African American, Anglo vs. Hispanic) (Leiter-3; Roid and Miller 2013). For each item, the difficulty parameters for the 1-PL IRT model were derived separately for each ethnic/racial sample. The correlations between difficulty parameters were then used to indicate the uniformity of indices across groups. Out of the 152 items tested, 2 items were found to departed slightly from the linear trend in the scatter plots. However, this method suffers from at least two flaws. First, no mention was made regarding whether item difficulty estimates were placed on a similar scale. Second, like traditional methods, this method used a summary statistic, ignoring the functioning of specific items.

The Universal Nonverbal Intelligence Test–Second Edition manual includes a report of DIF analysis for three dichotomous groups (male vs. female, African American vs. non-African American, Hispanic vs. non-Hispanic) (UNIT2; Bracken and McCallum 2016). The LR DIF approach was applied to all items contained in each of the UNIT2 subtests. Of the 241 items, 25 were found to be statistically significant at the 0.001 level, but had negligible effect sizes according to Jodoin and Gierl's (2001) criteria. The manual also reports a multigroup invariance study across gender, race, and ethnic groups. The TLI, CFI, and RMSEA fit indices were reported for four different models, with TLI and CFI values greater than 0.90, and RMSEAs of less than 0.12.

The Test of Nonverbal Intelligence–Fourth Edition manual includes a report of DIF analysis for three dichotomous groups (male vs. female, African American vs. non-African American, Hispanic vs. non-Hispanic) (TONI-4; Brown et al. 2010). The LR DIF approach was applied to all items contained in TONI-4. Of the 120 items, at least 5 were found to be statistically significant at the 0.001 level, with 1 item found to have moderate effect size according to Jodoin and Gierl's (2001) criteria.

The Wechsler Intelligence Scare for Children-Fifth Edition technical manual states that MH DIF analysis and IRT-LR approach were used to examine DIF across race (WISC-V; Wechsler 2014). However, no details were provided on specific items in terms of results. A study of invariance across age groups with a five-factor higher order models was reported in the technical manual. However, Canivez and Watkins (in press) was not able to replicate the five-factor baseline structural model in WISC-V, which was used for invariance study in the technical model. Therefore, the conclusion of the invariance study in the technical manual may be questionable. Besides, to capture the bias of the test, the invariance study should be conducted across gender, race groups instead of age group to ensure the test is free of bias against any one minority group.

A test may contain considerable DIF, yet focal and reference groups may have similar score distributions due to cancelation DIF, which occurs when some items favor the reference group and other favor the focal group. Scores may be based in part on different items systematically scored as correct. Although some might believe that DIF cancelation results

in a fairer test, the presence of even a one point systematic raw score difference on individual subtests due to DIF may result in systematic age-based standard score differences at the subtest level and may have cumulative effects at the scale score level for individuals. Furthermore, when ceiling rules are used and numerous adjacent items exhibit DIF against one group, individual examinees may reach a ceiling for reasons related to both group membership and intelligence. It is very likely that different items systematically scored as correct comprise the scores of examinees from different groups with the same test scores.

The scores from tests that lack item or test invariance cannot be assumed to have the same meaning across groups. Differential prediction studies are not recommended in the absence of DIF and factor invariance investigations, because tests may be correlated due to construct irrelevant factors. Thus, bias studies should begin with DIF studies, move to factor invariance studies, and conclude with differential prediction studies. The results of bias studies are crucial to the interpretation of test scores. A lack of item and test score invariance can be a function of possible differential opportunities to learn or other differences in socialization. Unfortunately, results of state-of-the-art item and test structure invariance investigations traditionally have not been reported for individually administered intelligence tests. Thus, conclusions regarding intellectual similarities or differences may be unfounded, and the interpretation of test scores influenced by unintended constructs may have serious consequences for individuals and groups. Although such investigations are labor intensive and expensive, and it is impossible to compare psychometric properties for all possible groups, test developers are encouraged to conduct more invariance investigations for nonverbal and other psychoeducational tests used for high-stakes educational decisions.

Even if a test developer makes a thorough attempt to create a test that lacks evidence of bias against a variety of subgroups, the test cannot be assumed to fair for all subgroups under all conditions. Ultimately, practitioners must take responsibility for understanding the psychometric properties and potential unintended consequences, as discussed by Messick (1989), of using tests without the necessary validity evidence. Specifically, practitioners should question whether (a) the test should be used for a given purpose, based on the empirical validity evidence, and (b) score interpretation reflects intended test constructs. That is, adverse outcomes for examinees should not be a result of construct irrelevant variance. Messick (1989) points out that, given the social consequences of test use and value implications of test score interpretation, testing practices should be based on both scientific evidence and ethical consideration.

# References

Agresti, A. (1996). Logit models with random effects and quasi-symmetric loglinear models. In Proceedings of the 11th International Workshop on Statistical Modelling (pp. 3–12).

Alwin, D. F., & Jackson, D. J. (1981). Applications of simultaneous factor analysis to issues of factorial invariance. In D. Jackson & E. Borgatta (Eds.), *Factor analysis and measurement in sociological research: A multi-dimensional perspective* (pp. 249–279). Beverly Hills: Sage.

Anderson, R. J., & Sisco, F. H. (1977). *Standardization of the WISC-R performance scale for deaf children* (Office of Demographic Studies Publication Series T, No. 1). Washington, DC: Gallaudet College.

American Educational Research Association, American Psychological Association, & National Council on Measurement in Education. (2014). *Standards for educational and psychological testing*. Washington, DC: American Psychological Association.

Bentler, P. M. (1990). Comparative fit indexes in structural models. *Psychological Bulletin, 107*, 238–246.

Bentler, P. M. (1992). On the fit of models to covariances and methodology in the Bulletin. *Psychological Bulletin, 112*, 400–404.

Bollen, K. A. (1989). *Structural equations with latent variables*. New York: Wiley.

Bolt, D., & Stout, W. (1996). Differential item functioning. Its multidimensional model and resulting SIBTEST detection procedure. *Behaviormetrika, 23*, 67–95.

Bracken, B. A., & McCallum, R. S. (2016). *Examiner's manual: Universal nonverbal intelligence test-second edition (UNIT2)*. Austin, TX: PRO-ED.

Braden, J. P. (1999). Straight talk about assessment and diversity: What do we know? *School Psychology Review, 14*, 343–355.

Brown, L., Sherbenou, R. J., & Johnsen, S. K. (2010). *Test of nonverbal intelligence (TONI–4)*. Austin, TX: PRO-ED.

Browne, M. W., & Cudeck, R. (1993). Alternative ways of assessing model fit. In K. A. Bollen & J. S. Long (Eds.), *Testing structural equation models* (pp. 136–162). Beverly Hills, CA: Sage.

Bryk, A. (1980). Review of Bias in mental testing. *Journal of Educational Measurement, 17*, 369–374.

Camilli, G., & Shepard, L. A. (1994). *Methods for identifying biased test items*. Thousand Oaks, CA: Sage.

Canivez, G. L., & Watkins, M. W. (in press). Review of the Wechsler intelligence scale for children-fifth edition: Critique, commentary, and independent analyses. In A. S. Kaufman, S. E. Raiford, & D. L. Coalson (Authors), *Intelligent testing with the WISC-V* (pp. xx–xx). Hoboken, NJ: Wiley.

Cattell, R. B. (1978). *The scientific use of factor analysis in behavioral and life sciences*. New York: Plenum.

Chang, H. H., Mazzeo, J., & Roussos, L. (2005). Detecting DIF for polytomously scored items: An adaption of the SIBTEST procedure. *Journal of Educational Measurement, 33*, 333–353.

Clauser, B. E., & Mazor, K. M. (1998). Using statistical procedures to identify differentially functioning test items. *Educational Measurement: Issues and Practice, 17*, 31–44.

Cleary, T. A. (1968). Test bias: Prediction of grades of Negro and White students in integrated colleges. *Journal of Educational Measurement, 5*, 115–124.

Cotter, D. E., & Berk, R. A. (1981, April). *Item bias in the WISC-R using Black, White, and Hispanic learning disabled children*. Paper presented at the Annual Meeting of the American Educational Research Association, Los Angeles, CA.

Diana v. the California State Board of Education. Case No. C-70-37 RFP. (N.D. Cal., 1970).

Dorans, N. J., & Holland, P. W. (1993). DIF detection and description: Mantel-Haenszel and Standardization. In P. W. Holland & H. Wainer (Eds.), *Differential item functioning* (pp. 35–66). Hillsdale, NJ: Erlbaum.

Dorans, N. J., & Kulick, E. (1983). Assessing unexpected differential item performance of female candidates on SAT and TSWE forms administered in December 1977: An application of the standardization approach. *ETS Research Report Series, 1983* (pp. i–14).

Engelhard, G., Hansche, L., & Rutledge, K. E. (1990). Accuracy of bias review judges in identifying differential item functioning on teacher certification tests. *Applied Psychological Measurement, 3*, 347–360.

Feldt, L. S., & Brennan, R. L. (1989). Reliability. In R. L. Linn (Ed.), *Educational measurement* (3rd ed., pp. 105–146). New York: American Council on Education & Macmillan.

Frisby, C. L. (1998). Poverty and socioeconomic status. In J. L. Sandoval, C. L. Frisby, K. F. Geisinger, J. D. Scheuneman, & J. R. Grenier (Eds.), *Test interpretation and diversity: Achieving equity in assessment* (pp. 241–270). Washington, DC: American Psychological Association.

Green, B. F., Crone, C. R., & Folk, V. G. (1989). A method for studying differential distractor functioning. *Journal of Educational Measurement, 26,* 147–160.

Hammill, D. D., Pearson, N. A., & Wiederholt, J. L. (2009). *Comprehensive test of nonverbal intelligence–2 (CTONI–2).* Austin, TX: PRO-ED.

Hills, J. R. (1989). Screening for potentially biased items in testing programs. *Educational Measurement: Issues and Practice, 8,* 5–11.

Holland, P. W. (1985). On the study of differential item performance without IRT. In Proceedings of the 27th Annual Conference of the Military Testing Association (Vol. 1, pp. 282–287). San Diego, CA.

Holland, P. W., & Thayer, D. T. (1988). Differential item functioning and the Mantel-Haenszel procedure. In H. Wainer & H. I. Braun (Eds.), *Test validity* (pp. 129–145). Hillsdale, NJ: Erlbaum.

Holland, P. W., & Wainer, H. (Eds.). (1993). *Differential item functioning.* Hillsdale, NJ: Erlbaum.

Hu, L., Bentler, P. M., & Kano, Y. (1992). Can test statistics in covariance structure analysis be trusted? *Psychological Bulletin, 112,* 351–362.

Ilai, D., & Willerman, L. (1989). Sex differences in WAIS-R item performance. *Intelligence, 13,* 225–234.

Jastak, J. E., & Jastak, S. R. (1964). Short forms of the WAIS and WISC vocabulary subtests. *Journal of Clinical Psychology, 20,* 167–199.

Jensen, A. R. (1980). *Bias in mental testing.* New York: Free Press.

Jiang, H., & Stout, W. (1998). Improved Type I error control and reduced estimation bias for DIF detection using SIBTEST. *Journal of Educational Statistics, 23,* 291–322.

Jodoin, M. G., & Gierl, M. J. (2001). Evaluating Type I error and power rates using an effect size measure with the logistic regression procedure for DIF detection. *Applied Measurement in Education, 14,* 329–349.

Joint Committee on Testing Practices. (2004). *Code of fair testing practices in education.* Washington, DC.

Jöreskog, K. G. (1971). Simultaneous factor analysis in several populations. *Psychometrika, 57,* 409–426.

Jöreskog, K. G., & Sörbom, D. (1989). *LISREL7: A guide to the program and applications* (2nd ed.). Chicago: SPSS.

Kim, S.-H., Cohen, A. S., & Park, T.-H. (1995). Detection of differential item functioning in multiple groups. *Journal of Educational Measurement, 32,* 261–276.

Koh, T., Abbatiello, A., & McLoughlin, C. S. (1984). Cultural bias in WISC subtest items: A response to Judge Grady's suggestions in relation to the PASE case. *School Psychology Review, 13,* 89–94.

Kromrey, J. D., & Parshall, C. G. (1991, November). *Screening items for bias: An empirical comparison of the performance of three indices in small samples of examinees.* Paper presented at the annual meeting of the Florida Educational Research Association, Clearwater, FL.

Larry P. v. Wilson Riles, Superintendent of Public Instruction for the State of California. Case No. C-71-2270 (N.D. Cal., 1979).

Lawrence, I. M., & Curley, W. E. (1989, March). *Differential item functioning of SAT-Verbal reading subscore items for males and females: Follow-up study.* Paper presented at the annual meeting of the American Educational Research Association, San Francisco, CA.

Lawrence, I. M., Curley, W. E., & McHale, F. J. (1988, April). *Differential item functioning of SAT-Verbal reading subscore items for male and female examinees.* Paper presented at the annual meeting of the American Educational Research Association, New Orleans, LA.

Li, H.-H., & Stout, W. (1994). *SIBTEST: A FORTRAN-V program for computing the simultaneous item bias DIF statistics [Computer software].* Urbana-Champaign, IL: University of Illinois, Department of Statistics.

Li, H.-H., & Stout, W. (1996). A new procedure for detection of crossing DIF. *Psychometrika, 61,* 647–677.

Linn, R. L., Levine, M. V., Hastings, C. N., & Wardrop, J. L. (1981). Item bias in a test of reading comprehension. *Applied Psychological Measurement, 5,* 159–173.

Lord, F. M. (1980). *Applications of item response theory to practical testing problems.* Hillsdale, NJ: Lawrence Erlbaum.

Magis, D., Raîche, G., Béland, S., & Gérard, P. (2011). A generalized logistic regression procedure to detect differential item functioning among multiple groups. *International Journal of Testing, 11,* 365–386.

Maller, S. J. (1996). WISC-III Verbal item invariance across samples of deaf and hearing children of similar measured ability. *Journal of Psychoeducational Assessment, 14,* 152–165.

Maller, S. J., & Ferron, J. (1997). WISC-III factor invariance across deaf and standardization samples. *Educational and Psychological Measurement, 7,* 987–994.

Maller, S. J., Konold, T. R., & Glutting, J. J. (1998). WISC-III Factor invariance across samples of children displaying appropriate and inappropriate test-taking behavior. *Educational and Psychological Measurement, 58,* 467–475.

Mantel, N., & Haenszel, W. (1959). Statistical aspects of the analysis of data from the retrospective studies of disease. *Journal of the National Cancer Institute, 22,* 719–748.

Mazor, K. M., Clauser, B. E., & Hambleton, R. K. (1994). Identification of nonuniform differential item functioning using a variation of the Mantel-Haenszel procedure. *Educational and Psychological Measurement, 54,* 284–291.

Meredith, W., & Millsap, R. E. (1992). On the misuse of manifest variables in the detection of measurement bias. *Psychometrika, 57,* 289–311.

Messick, S. (1989). Validity. In R. L. Linn (Ed.), *Educational measurement* (3rd ed., pp. 13–103). New York: American Council on Education & Macmillan.

McGaw, B., & Jöreskog, K. G. (1971). Factorial invariance of ability measures in groups differing in intelligence and socio-economic status. *British Journal of Mathematical and Statistical Psychology, 24*, 154–168.

Millsap, R. E., & Everson, H. T. (1993). Methodology review: Statistical approaches for assessing measurement bias. *Applied Psychological Measurement, 17*, 297–334.

Millsap, R. E., & Meredith, W. (1992). Inferential conditions in the statistical detection of measurement bias. *Applied Psychological Measurement, 16*, 389–402.

Nagelkerke, N. D. (1991). A note on a general definition of the coefficient of determination. *Biometrika, 78*, 691–692.

National Council on Measurement in Education. (1995). Code of professional responsibilities in educational measurement. *Educational Measurement: Issues and Practice, 14*, 17–24.

Osterlind, S. J., & Everson, H. T. (2009). *Differential item functioning* (2nd ed.). Thousand Oaks, CA: Sage.

Penfield, R. D. (2001). Assessing differential item functioning across multiple groups: A comparison of three Mantel-Haenszel procedures. *Applied Measurement in Education, 14*, 235–259.

Penfield, R. D., & Camilli, G. (2007). Differential item functioning and item bias. In C. R. Rao & S. Sinharay (Eds.), *Handbook of statistics: Vol. 26. Psychometrics* (pp. 125–167). Amsterdam: Elsevier.

Plake, B. S. (1980). A comparison of a statistical and subjective procedure to ascertain item validity: One step in the test validation process. *Educational and Psychological Measurement, 40*, 397–404.

Raju, N. S. (1988). The area between two item characteristic curves. *Psychometrika, 53*, 495–502.

Raju, N. S. (1990). Determining the significance of estimated signed and unsigned areas between two item response functions. *Applied Psychological Measurement, 14*, 197–207.

Reynolds, C. R. (1982). The problem of bias in psychological assessment. In C. R. Reynolds & T. B. Gutkin (Eds.), *The handbook of school psychology* (pp. 178–208). New York: Wiley.

Rigdon, E. E. (1996). CFI versus RMSEA: A comparison of two fit indexes for structural equation modeling. *Structural Equation Modeling, 3*, 369–379.

Roid, G. H., & Miller, L. J. (2013). *Leiter international performance scale-3rd edition (Leiter-3) manual*. Wood Dale, IL: Stoelting.

Rogers, H. J., & Swaminathan, H. (1993). A comparison of logistic regression and the Mantel-Haenszel procedures for detecting differential item functioning. *Applied Measurement in Education, 17*, 105–116.

Ross-Reynolds, J., & Reschly, D. J. (1983). An investigation of item bias on the WISC-R with four sociocultural groups. *Journal of Consulting and Clinical Psychology, 51*, 144–146.

Samejima, F. (1969). *Estimation of latent ability using a response pattern of graded scores* (Psychometrika Monograph Series No. 17). Richmond, VA: Psychometric Society.

Sandoval, J. (1979). The WISC-R and internal evidence of test bias with minority groups. *Journal of Consulting and Clinical Psychology, 47*, 919–927.

Sandoval, J., & Miille, M. P. W. (1980). Accuracy of judgments of WISC-R item difficulty for minority groups. *Journal of Consulting and Clinical Psychology, 48*, 249–253.

Sandoval, J., Zimmerman, I. L., & Woo-Sam, J. M. (1977). Cultural differences on the WISC-R verbal items. *Journal of School Psychology, 21*, 49–55.

Satorra, A., & Bentler, P. M. (1988). Scaling corrections for chi-square statistics in covariance structure analysis. *Proceedings of the Business and Economic Statistics Section of the American Statistical Association* (pp. 303–313).

Scheuneman, J. D. (1987). An experimental, exploratory study of causes of bias in test items. *Journal of Educational Measurement, 24*, 97–118.

Scheuneman, J. D., & Gerritz, K. (1990). Using differential item functioning procedures to explore sources of item difficulty and group performance characteristics. *Journal of Educational Measurement, 27*, 109–131.

Scheuneman, J. D., & Oakland, T. (1998). High stakes testing in education. In J. Sandoval, C. L. Frisby, K. F. Geisinger, J. D. Scheuneman, & J. R. Greiner (Eds.), *Test interpretation and diversity: Achieving equity in assessment* (pp. 77–103). Washington, DC: American Psychological Association.

Shealy, R. T., & Stout, W. F. (1993). A model based standardization approach that separates true bias/DIF from group ability differences and detects test bias/DIF as well as item bias/DIF. *Psychometrika, 58*, 159–194.

Shelley-Sireci, & Sireci, S. G. (1998, August). *Controlling for uncontrolled variables in cross-cultural research*. Paper presented at the annual meeting of the American Psychological Association, San Francisco, CA.

Sireci, S. G., Bastari, B., & Allalouf, A. (1998, August). *Evaluating construct equivalence across adapted tests*. Paper presented at the annual meeting of the American Psychological Association, San Francisco, CA.

Swaminathan, H., & Rogers, H. J. (1990). Detecting differential item functioning using logistic regression procedures. *Journal of Educational Measurement, 27*, 361–370.

Thissen, D. (2001). Psychometric engineering as art. *Psychometrika, 66*, 473–486.

Thissen, D., Steinberg, L., & Wainer, H. (1988). Use of item response theory in the study of group differences in trace lines. In H. Wainer & H. I. Braun (Eds.), *Test validity* (pp. 149–169). Hillsdale, NJ: Erlbaum.

Thissen, D., Steinberg, L., & Wainer, H. (1993). Detection of differential item functioning using the parameters of item response theory. In P. W. Holland & H. Wainer (Eds.), *Differential item functioning* (pp. 67–114). Hillsdale, NJ: Erlbaum.

Tucker, L. R., & Lewis, C. (1973). A reliability coefficient for maximum likelihood factor analysis. *Psychometrika, 38*, 1–8.

Turner, R. G., & Willerman, L. (1977). Sex differences in WAIS item performance. *Journal of Clinical Psychology, 33*, 795–798.

Uttaro, T. (1992). *Factors influencing the Mantel–Haenszel procedure in the detection of differential item functioning.* Unpublished doctoral dissertation, Graduate Center, City University of New York.

Wechsler, D. (2014). *Wechsler intelligence scale for children-fifth edition technical and interpretive manual.* San Antonio, TX: NCS Person.

Wechsler, D., & Naglieri, J. A. (2006). *Wechsler nonverbal scale of ability technical and interpretive manual.* San Antonio, TX: Pearson.

Wild, C. L., & McPeek, W. M. (1986, August). *Performance of the Mantel–Haenszel statistic in identifying differentially functioning items.* Paper presented at the annual meeting of the American Psychological Association, Washington, DC.

Zieky, M. (1993). Practical questions in the use of DIF statistics in item development. In P. W. Holland & H. Wainer (Eds.), *Differential item functioning* (pp. 337–364). Hillsdale, NJ: Erlbaum.

Zumbo, B. D. (1999). *A handbook on the theory and methods of differential item functioning (DIF): Logistic regression modeling as a unitary framework for binary and Likert-type (ordinal) item scores.* Ottawa ON: Directorate of Human Resources Research and Evaluation, Department of National Defense.

Zumbo, B. D., & Thomas, D. R. (1997). *A measure of effect size for a model-based approach for studying DIF.* Working Paper of the Edgeworth Laboratory for Quantitative Behavioral Science, University of Northern British Columbia, Prince George, B.C.

Zwick, R. (1990). When do item response function and Mantel-Haenszel definitions of differential item functioning coincide? *Journal of Educational Statistics, 15*, 185–197.

Zwick, R., Donoghue, J. R., & Grima, A. (1993). Assessing differential item functioning in performance tasks. *Journal of Educational Measurement, 30*, 233–251.

# Best Practices in Multicultural Assessment of Cognition

## Trish Franklin

The demographic makeup of students in the United States is shifting radically. According to the National Center for Education Statistics (2015), between fall 2002 and fall 2012 enrollment in public schools increased from 48.2 million to 49.8 million. With the increase in enrollment, there has also been a change in the distribution of students of particular racial/ethnic groups. In 2002, the percentage of white public school students was 56%; in 2012, that percentage decreased to 51%. It is projected that public schools will enroll 52.9 million students by fall 2024, and only 46% of those students will be white. Of the other major racial groups that make up the US student population, Hispanic students constitute the second largest and fastest-growing subset. In 2002, 18% of public school students were of Hispanic origin; that number stood at 24% in 2012 and is expected to increase to 29% by 2024.

Similarly, the percentage of students who are English language learners is increasing. In the 2012–2013 school year, 9.2% of public school students were reported to be English language learners, up from 8.1% in 2002. These students are present to different degrees throughout the United States, with a higher concentration of English language learners in the western part of the country.

This increase in the population of diverse individuals in the United States has led to heightened awareness of the issues facing psychologists who seek to provide a fair assessment of their abilities (Bracken and Naglieri 2003). A survey of school psychologists conducted by Ochoa et al. (1997) revealed that 83% of school psychologists who reported conducting evaluations of students with limited English proficiency felt less than adequately trained to conduct the assessments, and 56% reported that they were not well prepared to interpret the results. While this study focused on examiners who had evaluated Hispanic children for specific learning disabilities or intellectual disability, similar results were reported when examiners were surveyed regarding their perceived competency in evaluating students for serious emotional disabilities (Ochoa et al. 1999). The dramatic increase in the Spanish-speaking population in the United States (and, by extension, in schools) has led to a demand for psychologists who speak fluent Spanish. However, Spanish is only one of the many languages that are spoken in our school system. Because psychologists are charged with assessing all public school students, it is impossible to employ enough individuals to address each student's native language.

The most important and ubiquitous purpose of assessment is to gain information for use in making decisions about an individual; often, these are high-stakes decisions, such as recommendations for treatment, diagnosis, or educational placement and services (Oakland 2009). The use of assessment data to guide these

T. Franklin (✉)
University of Tennessee, 535 BEC,
1122 Volunteer Blvd, Knoxville 37996, USA
e-mail: tfrankl5@vols.utk.edu

© Springer International Publishing AG 2017
R.S. McCallum (ed.), *Handbook of Nonverbal Assessment*,
DOI 10.1007/978-3-319-50604-3_3

decisions relies on the assumption that the test itself was administered and interpreted fairly and equitably with respect to individual cultural differences (Mpofu and Ortiz 2009). According to the *Standards for Educational and Psychological Testing*, equitable assessment allows individuals to achieve at a similar level to those with equivalent ability on a measured construct without having their performance impacted by confounding factors (AERA, APA, and NCME 1999).

## Multicultural Assessment, Test Bias, and Fairness

"Test bias" refers to a global sense of systematic error in the estimation of some "true" value for a group of individuals. This is in contrast to random error, which all tests possess and exists equally for any individual taking the test (Reynolds and Kaiser 2003). The issue of test bias has been an ongoing source of controversy in the area of mental measurement (Reynolds and Kaiser 2003). In the past, it was assumed that cultural and linguistic differences would cause bias to be evident in the reliability of a test. Apparently this is not the case when bias is defined strictly as a statistical phenomenon; tests inherently follow a developmental pattern of difficulty, which allows within-examinee results to remain reliable and valid over time and across multicultural groups. Reynolds and Lowe (2009) summarize the research on technical test bias in the assessment of intelligence (i.e., bias in content, construct, and predictive validity) and conclude, "There is no strong evidence to support contentions of differential or single-group validity" and when bias occurs, "it is most often in the direction of favoring low-SES, disadvantaged, ethnic minority children or other low-scoring groups." (p. 363). However, this conclusion does not satisfy all experts and some still question the extent to which construct validity can be demonstrated/determined by conventional statistical analyses for multicultural individuals (Ortiz et al. 2012). And related to this point, other experts distinguish between test bias and test

fairness. For example, in the first chapter of this volume McCallum notes, "Even though a test may be free of technical bias…examiners may want to minimize the effects of culture or language influences, because they consider use of culturally and linguistically-loaded tests to be *unfair* for some examinees, i.e., those who are unfamiliar with the particular culture and/or language embedded in the tests." (p. ?).

In order to address the impact of culture and language on test performance it may be helpful to consider a developmental perspective. A developmental model of assessment acknowledges the interrelationship between biology and culture as individuals master developmental tasks. The developmental perspective examines the impact of race, ethnicity, language, and SES on the psychosocial task of growing up in a complex physical and social environment. While some aspects of maturation are universal, there is great variation in the behavior associated with and emphasis placed on certain developmental outcomes (Berk 1996). Most of our current knowledge of development is based on studies with non-Latino, White, middle-class children and families (McLoyd 1998).

## Addressing Issues of Reliability, Validity, Fairness

Examiners charged with evaluating students who are not members of the dominant cultural group and/or have limited proficiency in English must select a testing battery that presents the best opportunity for each student to achieve at a level that is reflective of their ability. This requires that instruments measure the intended construct (e.g., intelligence) while minimizing irrelevant or confounding factor to negatively impact scores (e.g., the ability to speak fluent English). Such confounding factors increase the level of measurement error for a test. One common source of measurement error occurs when an examinee's racial or ethnic membership is either not represented in the norm group of the test or is underrepresented. Standard 4.5 of the *Standards for Educational and Psychological Testing* states that "norms, if used, should refer to clearly described populations" with whom a practitioner intends to compare an examinee (AERA, APA, and NCME 1999). While normative samples are stratified with the intention of being representative of the general population, an important oversight almost always occurs when considering students who are not members of the dominant culture. Generally, cultural groups are represented in the sample by including members of varying races and ethnicities. This practice assumes that all students of a particular race or ethnicity come from a similar cultural background and are equally acculturated into the dominant culture (Oakland 2009). However, socially constructed categories such as race and ethnicity may not adequately address factors that actually affect test performance. An examinee's developmental background with respect to acculturation and language acquisition, rather than skin color or ethnic heritage, significantly impacts performance on tests. Constructs included on each test may manifest differently in an examinee's native culture, and the examinee may have had less exposure to the construct than his peers represented in the normative group. This leads to uneven performance on test items, placing inadequately represented students at a disadvantage (Ortiz et al. 2012). In fact, some adopt a hard line regarding this point and conclude that any time a test relies on culture-specific knowledge to test an individual's ability or achievement, the test may be invalid, as it is instead testing the student's knowledge of U.S. culture (Salvia et al. 2012).

Oakland (2009) suggested a remedy, i.e., that construct equivalence must be established when considering the validity of constructs measured by an instrument. Construct equivalence relies on consideration of three factors: whether the construct in question exists in a particular culture, and if so, whether it has equivalent meaning and is present in the same manner and to a similar magnitude. Test developers and users can gain information about construct equivalence by involving individuals from the culture in question, and collecting information from sources such as interviews, published literature, and observation.

## Language Acquisition

It can be taken as a given that language proficiency impacts test results. The debate lies in how much, in what ways, and in how examiner can best compensate for the effects of language when assessing nonnative English speakers. First, they must acknowledge that any degree of language demand is significant. Even a minimal level of language demand will affect performance; this is consistent with the view of language as a developmental process. Language is not a threshold performance, and there is no predetermined level of proficiency beyond which performance is no longer impacted. Test performance is affected on a linear basis by language proficiency, rather than either being "affected" or "not affected" (Ortiz et al. 2012).

One cannot make assumptions based on one or two factors about a bilingual individual's experiences. Even information about factors such as what language is spoken in the home, at what age the individual arrived in the United States, and what language is spoken most frequently or was learned first does not predict a bilingual individual's relative strengths in each language. Even if all these factors are the same many for bilingual individuals, his or her abilities may still present very differently (Valdes and Figueroa 1994).

Even the term "bilingual" offers some inherent ambiguity. Individuals are not simply mono-, bi-, or multilingual; language proficiency is not an either/or prospect (i.e., the issue is more complex than simply designating individuals as are "proficient" or "not proficient", "bilingual" or "not bilingual"). Instead, an individual's language proficiency may be best viewed as a continuum that reflects a number of factors related to their acquisition of each language. Valdes and Figueroa (1994) describe bilingual individuals as being sequential or simultaneous, and circumstantial or elective. These categories refer to the sequence in which languages are learned and the individual's reasons for learning the language. Sequential bilingualism occurs when an individual becomes fluent in a single language, and then begins to learn another (for example, an individual who relocates to another country where a language other than their own is spoken). Simultaneous bilingualism takes place when an individual learns two languages concurrently at an early age. An example of an individual with simultaneous bilingualism may be a child who speaks Spanish at home, but has been enrolled since early childhood in an English-speaking school program. Circumstantial bilingualism is most often sequential, as it occurs when an individual finds himself in a situation that requires the use of his nonnative language in order to participate in society, while elective bilingualism happens when an individual learns a second language because they want to do so. Hayman and Damico (1991, as cited in Ochoa et al. 1997) also categorize bilingual individuals as having nonbalanced, balanced, or mixed-dominant bilingualism. This is based on their assertion that there are four domains in which language manifests: reading, writing, speaking, and listening, along which individual skill levels vary. Nonbalanced bilingual individuals will show better development among the four domains in one particular language, while balanced bilingual individuals show even development in each domain in both languages. Mixed-dominant bilingual individuals show preference for one language in some domain(s), and a second language in the other domain(s). Mixed-dominant bilingualism may occur when an individual has spoken a language fluently in the home since early childhood, but have been taught academic skills in the other language. Thus, they may perform better when asked to read or write English, but may understand and speak Spanish more competently. School psychologists are most likely to be charged with assessing students who have sequential, circumstantial, non- or mixed-dominant bilingualism, presenting several challenges to administering and interpreting assessment measures (Ochoa 2003; Rhodes et al. 2005).

Ideally, verbal communication should be very limited or nonexistent, and information should be communicated clearly. Test format is also a factor; measures that allow the examinee to select from an array of responses are preferable to those who require an open-ended verbal or written response. Scoring for a multiple-choice measure also allows for objectivity, while open-ended responses often require an examiner to subjectively interpret scoring criteria in order to evaluate their accuracy (Oakland 2009).

Many tests incorporate time as a factor in scoring, whether by adding extra points for speed (for example, the Block Design subtests of the Wechsler measures) or by placing a time limit on responses (for example, the Pattern Completion subtest of the Kaufman Assessment Battery for Children, Second Edition; Kaufman and Kaufman 2004). Cultures value speed differently; while American children are accustomed to an emphasis on fluency, children from other cultures may not be accustomed to being asked to work quickly and less able to demonstrate their ability within time constraints. What may be considered a skill deficit (a lack of the requisite knowledge or ability to complete a task) may actually be a performance deficit (when this ability or knowledge is present, but not demonstrated). A child who has been taught to value accuracy over speed may work slowly and carefully, and may appear deficient in the area of fluency (Oakland 2009).

Other cultural differences may manifest in an examinee's level of comfort in speaking to an adult. Some cultures consider it disrespectful when children speak directly to adults at length, and some may find answering questions or displaying one's knowledge immodest (Salvia et al. 2012). Evidence also shows that examinees perform better on tests when the examiner is from the same cultural background (Fuchs and Fuchs 1989).

## Culture-Specific Response Patterns

In addition to considerations regarding normative group representation, a number of factors must be taken into account during test administration.

## Approaches to Multicultural Testing

Ortiz et al. (2012) have identified four approaches to dealing with validity issues related to testing individuals with cultural and linguistic differences. The first approach involves modified or adapted testing. This may include eliminating certain items from administration, repeating or simplifying verbal instructions, removing time constraints, or administering only subtests that require the examinee to respond nonverbally. Unfortunately, while this approach does reduce aspects of the testing process that attenuate the scores, this practice almost always constitutes a nonstandardized administration of the test. This leads to unknown levels of test error, and likely invalidates the results of the test.

Another adaptation involves the use of a translator or interpreter, with the assumption that testing results will be valid as long as the examinee understands what is being said. However, this approach neglects to address the fact that the items themselves may contain information that is culturally bound. Additionally, aside from issues with content and accurate translation aside, the use of a translator also violates standardization procedures. Altering the standardization procedures of a test in any way leads to a lack of validity of the results. Thus, these procedures do little more than allow for an examiner to gain qualitative data about the examinee from the testing session.

Another approach to dealing with validity issues related to testing for culturally and linguistically diverse individuals is native language testing. Recently, instruments have been developed in languages other than English, and their use among bilingual psychologists has increased. This process is sometimes referred to as "bilingual testing"—a misnomer, as "bilingual" implies that the testing is conducted concurrently in two languages, when in fact the instruments are standardized using only the language in which they were developed. Most importantly when considering native language testing is that the examiner must be fluent in the language of the test. While this approach is promising, it is relatively new, and there is little information regarding the performance of bilingual individuals when tested using a monolingual instrument in their native language. Additionally, native language tests are often normed on individuals who are monolingual speakers of that language

residing in other countries. This fails to account for performance differences that may come as a result of factors related to bilingualism and concurrent exposure to different cultures and instructional practices. Monolingual individuals that speak an individual's native language are just as different from them as individuals who are monolingual in the individual's second language. Even when bilingual individuals are included, they are not sampled based on factors most likely to influence their test performance (level of acculturation and linguistic proficiency).

Another adaptation involves the use of a translator or interpreter, with the assumption that testing results will be valid as long as the examinee understands what is being said. However, this approach neglects to address the fact that the items themselves may contain information that is culturally bound. Additionally, aside from issues with content and accurate translation, the use of a translator also violates standardization procedures. Altering the standardization procedures of a test in any way leads to a lack of validity of the results. Thus, these procedures do little more than allow for an examiner to gain qualitative data about the examinee from the testing session.

## Nonverbal Testing

The fourth, and arguably the best, method for assessing individuals from culturally and linguistically diverse individuals is to use a nonverbal intelligence test. Bracken and McCallum (2016) define "nonverbal assessment" as a test administration procedure in which no receptive or expressive language demands are placed on either the examinee or the examiner. While nonverbal tests may have different formats, they all measure general cognitive ability (Bracken and Naglieri 2003). It should be noted that there is a distinction between "tests of nonverbal intelligence" and "nonverbal intelligence testing." Nonverbal intelligence, which is usually assessed by performance tasks such as matrices, has historically been used to assess individuals with limited verbal abilities. The thought process behind this practice is that no knowledge of the English language is necessary to complete these tasks. However, there are two major limitations of this approach. The first is that most of these tasks, while they do include verbal information as a component of the task itself, are presented with verbal instructions that are often lengthy and relatively complex (e.g., the Performance tasks on the Wechsler scales). The second, and arguably most important limitation, is that ability to complete nonverbal tasks is only one component of general intelligence. General intelligence is a composite measure that is made up of abilities in several different domains, and assessment of multiple constructs allows an examiner to gain an understanding of an examinee's strengths and weaknesses. Nonverbal intelligence testing is a process that seeks to obtain a composite score that is representative of an examinee's general intelligence, while placing minimal or no verbal demands on either the examiner or the examinee. For the purpose of this chapter, "nonverbal intelligence testing" refers to the practice of a comprehensive assessment of a culturally and linguistically diverse individual with the intention of attaining a measure of their general intelligence, among other factors.

As noted earlier, students in our school system come from a wide variety of cultural backgrounds, and we are home to students who speak hundreds of languages. It is infeasible to be able to find psychologists who are fluently multilingual, and beyond that, to find tests that are appropriate for each student, given the considerations outlined above. This is where the utility of nonverbal testing becomes apparent. As early as 1922, Pintner and Keller collected data from a variety of groups and concluded that students from non-English-speaking homes were at a disadvantage when compared to those from homes where English was the primary language. They concluded that nonverbal intellectual testing increased the scores of the former group (Reynolds and Kaiser 2003).

Ideally, verbal communication during a test administration should be very limited or nonexistent (Oakland 2009). Many tests calculate nonverbal indices using subtests that do not require a verbal response from the examinee; however, administration of these subtests still requires the examinee to attend to directions given in spoken English, regardless of the medium for their response. Nonverbal tests such as the Universal Nonverbal Intelligence Test 2 (UNIT-2) and Comprehensive Test of Nonverbal Intelligence, Second Edition (Hammill et al. 2009) remove language from the equation entirely, instead employing the use of pantomime for instructions (Athanasiou 2000). It is also suggested that examinees have the opportunity to respond in various ways. Some examples may include pointing to an answer, arranging cards, or building with blocks.

Obviously, the issue of multicultural assessment is complex, and some would argue that measures should not be completely devoid of cultural influences if the intent is to predict performance within that particular culture (Reynolds and Lowe 2009). Even so, experts in the field have contributed significantly to the creation of guidelines that can inform practitioners about the effects of culture and language loadings, and hence help examiners assess and/or reduce the influence of these variables to a considerable extent. For example, according to a model of nondiscriminatory testing Ortiz's (2002) created examiners should: (a) develop culturally and linguistically based hypotheses; (b) assess language history, development, and proficiency; (c) assess effects of cultural and linguistic differences; (d) assess environmental and community factors; (e) evaluate, revise, and retest hypotheses; (f) determine appropriate languages of assessment; (g) reduce bias in traditional practices; (h) use authentic and alternative assessment practices; (i) apply cultural-linguistic context to all data; and (j) link assessment to intervention. Although testing is only a small part of this overall model, use of nonverbal tests is consistent with the model.

In the interest of helping examiners improve fairness in testing Flanagan et al. (2007, 2013) provide a specific strategy which allows potentially allows examiners to determine the impact of culture and language on cognitive test scores. In Chap. 1 of this volume McCallum provides a somewhat detailed description of this strategy and an example of how to use it. Briefly, the strategy allows an examiner to match an examinee's level of proficiency and the language and/or cultural demands of particular tests. This model allows examiners to characterize the cultural and language loading within Culture-Language Test Classification (C-LTC) and the Culture-Language Interpretative Matrices (C-LIM). Depending on the magnitude of scores of particular subtest and the cultural or linguistic loading of those subtests, examiners can estimate the extent to which cognitive performance impacts performance negatively, and by inference the extent to which assessment is "fair."

Importantly, Flanagan et al. (2007) caution examiners to keep four essential assumptions in mind: (a) all tests are culturally loaded and reflect the value, beliefs, and knowledge deemed important within the culture; (b) all tests, even nonverbal ones, require some form of language/communication from the examiner and the examinee which will influence performance; (c) the language and culture loadings of test vary significantly; and (d) interpretation of standardized tests results (using existing normative data) may be invalid for diverse individuals. The use of C-LTC and C-LIM ensures that these assumptions are addressed in a systematic and logical fashion.

## Summary

The continuing demographic shift in the United States has created an increasing need for assessment procedures that accurately reflect the abilities and skills of individuals who are culturally and linguistically diverse. Assessment of these individuals presents a variety of challenges, including but not limited to availability of tests that include nonnative English speakers and bilingual individuals in the standardization sample, knowledge about the cultural and language loading of assessment items, examiners with proficiency in understanding the issues related to culture and language acquisition, and with the ability to determine the potentially negative

impact of cultural and linguistic loading of particular tests on examinee performance. By considering the factors presented above, as well as careful selection of instruments, examiners can work toward more accurate evaluation of an individual's abilities and skills.

## References

American Educational Research Association (AERA), American Psychological Association (APA), National Council on Measurement in Education (NCME), Joint Committee on Standards for Educational, & Psychological Testing (US). (1999). *Standards for educational and psychological testing.* American Educational Research Association.

Athanasiou, M. S. (2000). Current nonverbal assessment instruments: A comparison of psychometric integrity and test fairness. *Journal of Psychoeducational Assessment, 18*(3), 211–229.

Berk, L. (1996). *Infants, children, and adolescents* (2nd ed.). Boston, MA: Allyn & Bacon.

Bracken, B. A., & McCallum, R. S. (2016). *Universal nonverbal intelligence test* (2nd ed.). Chicago, IL: Riverside.

Bracken, B. A., & Naglieri, J. A. (2003). Assessing diverse populations with nonverbal tests of general intelligence. In C. R. Reynolds & R. W. Kamphaus (Eds.), *Handbook of psychological and educational assessment of children: Personality, behavior, and context* (2nd ed., pp. 243–274). New York, NY: Guilford Press.

Flanagan, D. P., Ortiz, S. O., & Alfonso, S. O. (2007). *Essentials of cross-battery assessment* (2nd ed.). Hoboken, NJ: Wiley.

Flanagan, D. P., Ortiz, S. O., & Alfonso, S. O. (2013). *Essentials of cross-battery assessment* (3rd ed.). Hoboken, NJ: Wiley.

Fuchs, D., & Fuchs, L. S. (1989). Effects of examiner familiarity on Black, Caucasian, and Hispanic children: A meta-analysis. *Exceptional Children, 55*(4), 303–308.

Hammill, D. D., Pearson, N. A., & Weiderholt, J. L. (2009). *Comprehensive test of nonverbal intelligence* (2nd ed.). Austin, TX: PRO-ED.

Kaufman, A. S., & Kaufman, N. L. (2004). *Kaufman assessment battery for children* (2nd ed.). Circle Pines, MN: American Guidance Service.

McLoyd, V. C. (1998). Changing demographics in the American population: Implications for research on minority children and adolescents. In V. C. McLoyd & L. Steinberg (Eds.), *Studying minority adolescents: Conceptual, methodological, and theoretical issues* (pp. 3–28). Mahwah, NJ: Lawrence Erlbaum Associates.

Mpofu, E., & Ortiz, S. O. (2009). Equitable assessment practices in diverse contexts. In E. L. Grigorenko

(Ed.), *Multicultural psychoeducational assessment* (pp. 41–76). New York, NY: Springer.

National Center for Education Statistics. (2015). *The condition of education 2015.* Retrieved from http://nces.ed.gov/pubs2015/2015144.pdf

Oakland, T. (2009). How universal are test development and use? In E. L. Grigorenko (Ed.), *Multicultural psychoeducational assessment* (pp. 1–40). New York, NY: Springer.

Ochoa, S. H. (2003). Assessment of culturally and linguistically diverse children. In C. R. Reynolds & R. W. Kamphaus (Eds.), *Handbook of psychological and educational assessment of children: Personality, behavior, and context* (2nd ed., pp. 563–583). New York, NY: Guilford Press.

Ochoa, S. H., Garza, S., & Amado, A. (1999). School psychology training pertaining to psychological assessment of African Americans. In *Poster session presented at the annual meeting of the American Psychological Association*, Boston, MA.

Ochoa, S. H., Rivera, B. D., & Ford, L. (1997). An investigation of school psychology training pertaining to bilingual psychoeducational assessment of primarily Hispanic students: Twenty-five years after Diana v California. *Journal of School Psychology, 35*(4), 329–349.

Ortiz, S. O. (2002). Best practices in nondiscriminatory assessment. *Best Practices in School Psychology IV, 2,* 1321–1336.

Ortiz, S. O., Ochoa, S. H., & Dynda, A. M. (2012). Testing with culturally and linguistically diverse populations: Moving beyond the verbal-performance dichotomy into evidence-based practice. In D. P. Flanagan & P. L. Harrison (Eds.), *Contemporary intellectual assessment: Theories, tests and issues* (3rd ed., pp. 526–552). New York, NY: Guilford Press.

Pintner, R., & Keller, R. (1922). Intelligence tests of foreign children. *Journal of Educational Psychology, 13*(4), 214.

Reynolds, C. R., & Kaiser, S. M. (2003). Bias in assessment of aptitude. In C. R. Reynolds & R. W. Kamphaus (Eds.), *Handbook of psychological and educational assessment of children: Personality, behavior, and context* (2nd ed., pp. 519–562). New York, NY: Guilford Press.

Reynolds, C. R., & Lowe, P. A. (2009). The problem of bias in psychological testing. In T. G. Gutkin & C. R. Reynolds (Eds.), *School psychology handbook* (4th ed., pp. 332–374). Hoboken, N.J.: Wiley.

Rhodes, R. L., Ochoa, S. H., & Ortiz, S. O. (2005). *Assessing culturally and linguistically diverse students: A practical guide.* New York: Guilford Press.

Salvia, J., Ysseldyke, J., & Witmer, S. (2012). *Assessment: In special and inclusive education* (11th ed.). Boston, Massachusetts: Cengage Learning.

Valdes, G., & Figueroa, R. A. (1994). *Bilingualism and testing: A special case of bias.* Westport, CT: Ablex Publishing.

# Best Practices in Assessing Those Who Are Deaf or Hard-of-Hearing

**4**

Jeffrey P. Braden

## Introduction

Experts in the psychological and educational assessment of deaf and hard-of-hearing (D/HoH) clients have long recommended the use of non verbal assessment approaches (e.g., Pintner and Paterson 1915; Vernon 1967; Sligar et al. 2013). Although there have been many cases in which otherwise well-meaning examiners were ignorant of the specialized needs (and concurrent recommendations) related to D/HoH clients, and some cases in which commitment to ideological approaches to educating D/HoH students (e.g., oralism, or speech-only methods) may have led examiners to rely on oral, language-based assessment approaches, the literature regarding professional practices within the D/HoH community has long held that nonverbal assessment approaches must be included in any valid assessment of D/HoH clients. In fact, some have even argued for the exclusive use of nonverbal tools; cf).

In this chapter, I will attempt to summarize and add to the rich history of this literature. I will begin by defining challenges in the assessment of D/HoH clients, considering the arguments for (and against) the use of nonverbal assessment approaches with D/HoH clients, and conclude with a set of recommendations drawn from research, professional guidelines, and legal perspectives to suggest recommended practices in the use of nonverbal assessment with D/HoH clients.

## Challenges in Assessing D/HoH Clients

Perhaps the greatest challenge to those who wish to examine D/HoH clients is understanding the impact of hearing loss on linguistic, psychological, and educational development, and how those factors then influence assessment. Table 4.1 lists some critical terms and concepts that appear in the literature on people who are D/HoH; however, that list is not intended to imply that other principles relevant to audiology, otolaryngology, disability studies, and other areas of scholarship are irrelevant. One point should be made at the outset of this discussion: When using the acronym D/HoH, I am referring to clients who are deaf (i.e., a hearing loss of sufficient magnitude to substantially impair spoken communication) and not Deaf (i.e., those who identify with Deaf culture and use ASL as their primary language). There are two reasons why I use D/HoH to refer to clients who are deaf rather than Deaf. The first is that there are far more individuals who are deaf than who are Deaf; current estimates suggest about 25,000–500,000 people (i.e., less than 0.24%) in the US are Deaf (Mitchell et al. 2006). Second, the literature on psychological assessment tends to

J.P. Braden (✉)
College of Humanities and Social Sciences,
North Carolina State University, 106 Caldwell Hall,
Raleigh, NC 27695-8101, USA
e-mail: jpbraden@ncsu.edu

© Springer International Publishing AG 2017
R.S. McCallum (ed.), *Handbook of Nonverbal Assessment*,
DOI 10.1007/978-3-319-50604-3_4

focus on individuals who are deaf rather than Deaf (although I will identify and discuss some exceptions).

The broad challenge confronting examiners is that D/HoH clients are exceptionally heterogeneous; in addition to varying as other clients do on the basis of gender, age, ethnicity, language, culture, and so on, they also vary with respect to the type, severity, onset, and impact of hearing loss, as well as their response to assistive technologies and educational/linguistic interventions (e.g., use of signs, speech). Given that D/HoH clients are a small fraction of the general population (about 4–10 in 1000, or 0.4–1%, under the age of 18 have a hearing loss that significantly impairs spoken language use) (Reilly and Qi

**Table 4.1** Terms and concepts essential to understanding D/HoH Clients

| Term | Definition |
|---|---|
| Deaf | A hearing loss that is of sufficient severity to inhibit effective spoken communication |
| Hard-of-hearing | A hearing loss that is moderate to mild, but that interferes with spoken communication |
| Deaf | Designates people who use American Sign Language (ASL) as their primary form of communication and identify with Deaf culture. These people are usually also deaf, but may be hard-of-hearing or have no hearing loss at all (e.g., hearing children of deaf parents) |
| Onset of hearing loss | Hearing loss is typically defined by audiologists as being congenital (present at birth) or adventitious (acquired after birth); however, most psychologists consider the critical onset factor to be whether the hearing loss occurs prior to the acquisition of spoken language (prelingual) or after the acquisition of spoken language (postlingual) |
| Response to assistance or amplification | Most children are given some form of technology to assist or amplify hearing (e.g., hearing aid, cochlear implant); however, children vary widely in their responsiveness to these technologies (i.e., some function as if they have normal-hearing, whereas others may find the technology intrusive or disruptive to social and linguistic interactions) |
| Sign language | A means of expressing ideas through gestures formed on the hands, body, and face. Most sign language used in North America is a mix of American Sign Language (ASL) and English. Members of the Deaf community more likely signing ASL with little English, in contrast to educators, who tend to use English and little ASL |
| Cued speech | Using hand shapes and/or technology (e.g., special glasses) to help improve understanding of speech |
| Severity of hearing loss | The mean psychophysical threshold for sound sensation measured in decibels (dB) across the speech range. Means are categorized into normal, mild, moderate, severe, and profound ranges |
| Type of hearing loss | Conductive (i.e., problems in the outer or middle ear), sensorineural (i.e., a problem within the cochlea, nerve, or brain), or mixed (i.e., both conductive and sensorineural) |
| Etiology of hearing loss | Generally classified as adventitious (i.e., due to trauma or illness) or genetic, with genetic causes being further identified as dominant or recessive. Certain etiologies are associated with additional disabilities |
| Bi/Bi movement | The Bilingual (i.e., intentional alternation between ASL and sign English) Bicultural (Deaf vs. normal-hearing) educational philosophy |
| Total communication | Philosophy of using all available means (e.g., speech, signs, assistive devices) to communicate with D/HoH individuals. This approach is the most widely used in education of D/HoH students, although its implementation varies greatly within and among sites |
| Oralism | Philosophy of using only speech for receptive and expressive communication with D/HoH individuals (generally no longer used without cochlear implants) |

2011), and nearly 40% have at least one disability in addition to deafness (Gallaudet Research Institute 2011), D/HoH clients are a low-incidence, highly complex population to serve. The myriad ways in which etiology, onset, and other factors influence linguistic, educational, and psychological development of D/HoH clients' challenges even those professionals who have dedicated their careers to understanding these issues to provide reliable and valid assessment findings.

## Reasons to Use Nonverbal Assessment Approaches

It is precisely the fact that D/HoH clients are low-incidence yet highly complex cases that leads to most professionals recommending the use of nonverbal assessment approaches. That is, by using approaches that minimize the use of language in understanding, mediating, and responding to assessment tasks (i.e., nonverbal methods), examiners hope to circumvent the complex interactions among variations in hearing loss and other client characteristics. Whereas language-intensive assessment approaches (e.g., those relying on language to convey directions, mediate processes, and produce responses) confound hearing loss, language, and cognitive abilities, nonverbal approaches attempt to eliminate that confound by placing D/HoH clients on a "level playing field" so that their results may be fairly compared to those of the normative sample.

Although the justification in the preceding paragraph has great intuitive appeal, a better justification from an assessment perspective draws on Messick's (1989) work on the sources of invalidity. Essentially, Messick argues that there are two sources that undermine the validity of assessment results: (1) construct-irrelevant variance, and (2) construct under-representation. Construct-irrelevant variance is created when assessment items or approaches unintentionally require the use of knowledge or processes that are not intended to be included in the assessment. For example, word problems intended to assess

mathematical reasoning may use sports-related examples in an effort to provide a more familiar or meaningful context to test-takers. However, sports knowledge is not equally distributed among genders (e.g., males are more likely to know more about baseball, whereas females are more likely to know about figure skating) or economic class (e.g., golf-related knowledge is more available to middle- and upper-class examinees than to lower SES test examinees). Therefore, the use of sports-related word problems may introduce construct-irrelevant variance into assessments of mathematical reasoning. This principle—that language-loaded assessments are likely to introduce construct-irrelevant variance into assessments of D/HoH clients—is the primary justification that experts consistently recommend nonverbal assessments for D/HoH examinees.

A related argument that might be put forward in arguing for the use of nonverbal assessment tools with D/HoH clients relates to "opportunity to learn." The *Standards for Educational and Psychological Testing* (American Educational Research Association, American Psychological Association, National Council on Measurement in Education 2014) (hereinafter referred to as "the *Standards*") identifies opportunity to learn as a major influence on test fairness. The *Standards* defines opportunity to learn as "the extent to which individuals have had exposure to instruction or knowledge that affords them the opportunity to learn the content and skills targeted by the test...." (p. 56). Given that D/HoH individuals have dramatically limited opportunities to acquire knowledge that is mediated through spoken communication (e.g., the definition of words, rules for social interaction, verbal analogies), it is logical to argue that tests of knowledge acquired intentionally (i.e., through instruction) or incidentally (i.e., through interactions and experiences outside of the classroom) would violate the principle that test-takers should have equal opportunity to learn the content being assessed. These related ideas—that is, that tests may inappropriately demand knowledge or skills not intended to be a focus of the assessment, or that examinees may not have equal opportunity to acquire the knowledge or skills in the assessment—have driven the recommendations to use nonverbal assessment approaches with D/HoH clients.

However, experts have given far less attention to Messick's second source of invalidity (i.e., construct under-representation). Construct under-representation occurs when, in an effort to accommodate unique needs of test-takers, examiners alter assessments or select assessments that may inadvertently reduce the representation of the construct they seek to assess. For example, reading a passage aloud to examinees with reading disabilities might help reduce the impact of their reading disability on the assessment outcome, but it also results in construct under-representation by changing the test from a reading comprehension test to a spoken comprehension test. Understanding text and speech are not the same thing, and therefore one cannot be reasonably substituted for the other without reducing the representation of the construct (i.e., reading comprehension) and therefore undermining the validity of the assessment result. In contrast, providing glasses to a test-taker with visual acuity limitations reduces construct-irrelevant variance (i.e., poor performance due to being unable to discern letters) while maintaining construct representation (see Braden and Joyce 2008; Elliott et al. 2001). I will return to this issue when considering limitations to nonverbal assessment approaches later in this chapter.

Some experts cite additional reasons to use nonverbal tests with D/HoH examinees. These include the observation that D/HoH examinees score higher on nonverbal assessments than on language-loaded assessments; that there are nonverbal assessments that provide normative samples composed entirely of D/HoH examinees; that nonverbal assessment must be included to avoid damaging consequences of assessment for D/HoH clients; and that D/HoH clients be examined only by those with significant expertise in understanding and serving those with hearing impairment, and that experts exercise their clinical judgment in interpreting assessment results and making recommendations. I shall address each of these arguments in turn.

## Using Tests that Produce Higher Scores

The oft-stated observation that D/HoH examinees often score below normal-hearing examinees, even on tests that ostensibly minimize the use of language in administration, content, and response, is usually accurate. Some in the field (e.g., Vonderhaar and Chambers 1975) go on to argue that higher scores provide prima facie evidence of greater fairness of tests for D/HoH examinees. However, "group differences in [test] outcomes do not in themselves indicate that a testing application is biased or unfair" (*Standards* 2014, p. 54). Given that educators serving D/HoH students believe that nearly 40% of all D/HoH students have disabilities in addition to hearing impairment (Gallaudet Research Institute 2011), it would be surprising if the mean score on tests of intelligence, achievement, or other forms of cognitive, social, or physical performance were *not* lower for D/HoH populations. Furthermore, selecting only tests where prior research shows D/HoH individuals to perform higher would bias the outcomes of an assessment towards higher scores. The decision regarding whether a test may be used with D/HoH examinees rests not on average outcomes, but rather on evidence of differential reliability/accuracy or validity (see the *Standards* Chapter 2).

## Norms Based Entirely on D/Hoh Test-Takers Are Inherently Superior to Other Norms

Some experts (e.g., Anderson and Sisco 1977; Vernon 1976; Vernon and Andrews 1990) have argued that norms based on D/HoH test-takers (aka "deaf norms") are inherently preferable for assessing D/HoH clients than norms based on representative groups of normal-hearing test-takers. Reesman et al. (2014) advance a more nuanced argument, stating that deaf norms should be preferred when assessing language-based reasoning skills, but not for other situations. For example, examiners may find deaf norms useful when characterizing the academic achievement of D/HoH students, as measured by the tenth edition of the Stanford Achievement Test; given the gap between D/HoH and normal-hearing peers, and the fact those gaps increase with age, it can be helpful to know how the D/HoH student compares to others (Metz et al. 2010). Gallaudet University (2016) provides age-based percentiles drawn from its annual survey of D/HoH students in the US; however, because the focus of this chapter is on nonverbal assessment, the argument advanced by Reesman et al. (2014) regarding the use of deaf norms for nonverbal tests deserves further attention.

Ironically, Reesman et al. claim that "the argument for use of a deaf normative sample increases when one considers… the heterogeneous group of neurological conditions often associated with hearing loss" (p. 102). In contrast, the *Standards* argues "when some groups are much more heterogeneous than others, the construction and interpretation of group norms is problematic" (p. 104). In most cases, examiners use nonverbal tests with D/HoH clients to identify abnormalities in general or specific intellectual deficits. Use of tests normed on a population where such deficits are more prevalent is likely to mask the presence of such deficits (i.e., unusual scores or score patterns are likely to appear more common when compared to atypical samples than to typical samples) (Braden 1990). Given that D/HoH examinees are likely to have similar opportunities to learn those skills and processes assessed by nonverbal tests relative to normal-hearing peers, it makes more sense to compare their performance to non-clinical (i.e., normal-hearing) samples—provided there is no evidence that the test demonstrates differential reliability, accuracy, and validity for D/HoH examinees.

## Nonverbal Tests Are Needed to Avoid Unintended Consequences of Assessment

Experts in the field argue that there is danger inherent in reporting the results of language-loaded tests, and that therefore nonverbal tests must be used when assessing D/HoH clients. The argument is as follows: (1) D/HoH examinees lack opportunities to acquire language and related knowledge; (2) language-loaded tests assess language and related knowledge; (3) therefore, D/HoH examinees will score poorly on language-loaded tests; (4) those low scores may be interpreted as evidence of low cognitive abilities rather than lack of opportunity to learn; and (5) the inappropriate interpretation of scores will drive inappropriate decisions about clients. Some experts (e.g., Vernon 1976) are so concerned about the potential for inappropriate score interpretation that they argue *only* nonverbal tests should be used in assessing D/HoH clients, whereas others (e.g., Kelly and Braden 1990; Braden 2006; Reesman et al. 2014) argue that there is some value in assessing the degree to which D/HoH clients have acquired incidental knowledge despite their hearing impairments.

As is true for normal-hearing examinees (see Braden and Shaw 2009), there is no systematic research on the consequential validity of tests (language-loaded or nonverbal) for D/HoH examinees. However, there is a single case study reported by Vernon and Andrews (1990) that illustrates the dramatic potential that invalid score interpretations might have for a D/HoH client. They cite the case of a D/HoH female (who also had mild cerebral palsy) who, on the basis of a low IQ produced by a language-loaded intelligence test, was placed in an institution serving children with severe to profound intellectual impairments. Although she acquired many of the mannerisms and dress of her fellow students, she was eventually retested with a nonverbal test that yielded an IQ in the normal range; based on that IQ, she was transferred from the institution to an educational program serving D/HoH students. The young lady eventually graduated from high school and went on to obtain an advanced professional degree after earning an undergraduate degree.

Although this is the only specific case I have found of unintended test consequences for D/HoH clients in the professional literature, it illustrates the profound impact inappropriate interpretation of test scores may have. Therefore, although experts disagree regarding whether results from language-loaded tests should ever be used (given their potential for misinterpretation), there is clear consensus among experts that nonverbal tests are strongly recommended whenever examiners seek to estimate the intellectual ability of a D/HoH examinee.

## Use of Experts (and Expert Judgment) in Assessing D/HoH Clients

There is consensus among those writing about the assessment of D/HoH examinees that assessments are best conducted by experts who have deep understanding of the ways in which hearing and hearing loss influences human development and performance (e.g., Metz et al. 2010; Reesman et al. 2014; Sligar et al. 2013). Furthermore, experts encourage examiners to either have fluency in the examinee's primary mode of communication (often American Sign Language, or ASL, but which might be pidgin Sign English, or PSE, cued speech, or other specially developed communication approaches), or to have experience and expertise in working with interpreters who have such fluency (e.g., Sligar et al. 2013). Examiner expertise is considered especially important in the interpretation of assessment results, as the integration of test scores, observational data, background information, and data from other sources requires both expertise and nuance. It is difficult to argue that less knowledge and expertise would better inform the interpretation of assessment outcomes and yet, there is a body of work within the psychological literature that does just that. The body of work examines clinical versus statistical interpretation of scores; Mcchl (1954/1996) proposed over half a century ago that the evidence showed the inclusion of clinical judgment *decreased* the accuracy of interpretation and prediction of psychological test data. The years since the publication of that work have consistently supported Meehl's original contention (Grove and Lloyd 2006), at the very least inviting those who argue that clinicians should

actively nuance their interpretation of scores for D/HoH clients (e.g., Metz et al. 2010) provide evidence that to support clinical (as opposed to statistical) interpretation. To the best of my knowledge, no such evidence is available, nor has the argument been identified as one worthy of empirical study. I will return to this issue when discussing the limitations of recommended practices; for now, suffice it to say that there is no disagreement among experts that clinical interpretation of D/HoH assessment results is superior to statistical interpretation, but it is equally true that there is no evidence to inform the practice one way or the other.

## Limitations of Nonverbal Tests with D/HoH Clients

The most significant limitation to the use of nonverbal tests is the threat to construct under-representation. That is, because there are essentially no reasonable nonverbal alternatives to assessing domains mediated by, or based upon, language (e.g., crystallized abilities, verbal reasoning, vocabulary knowledge, general information, short-term memory for digits or words), examiners greatly increase the risk of under-representing the constructs they wish to assess.

Fortunately for the domain of intellectual abilities, appropriately designed and administered nonverbal assessments can do a good job of capturing fluid reasoning abilities. Because fluid reasoning is the cognitive ability most closely associated with general intelligence (indeed, some scholars argue that fluid reasoning is synonymous with general intelligence) (Braden 2008), there is good reason to believe that a well-conducted assessment using nonverbal tests would capture the cognitive characteristic most highly associated with meaningful educational, vocational, and social outcomes—general intelligence.

However, the same is not true for many other attributes that are important to educational, vocational, and social success (and failure). Because performance in these domains is profoundly influenced by prior knowledge, comprehension and expression of written and spoken forms of language, social interaction, and other attributes that are significantly or profoundly limited by the immediate and cumulative impact of hearing loss, an exclusive focus on the use of nonverbal assessment strategies with D/HoH clients would dramatically underrepresent constructs that are essential to understanding the client's ability to learn, perform, and function in educational, vocational, and community settings. It therefore is incumbent upon examiners to clearly define the constructs they intend to measure, and to identify those constructs that they have reason to believe influence important examinee outcomes, yet which they have not assessed.

A second concern is whether expert clinical judgment is superior to statistical interpretation of nonverbal assessment results. As noted earlier in this chapter, there is unanimity among experts that expert clinical judgment is needed to understand and interpret assessment results—but there is also an impressive body of work spanning multiple decades suggesting clinical interpretations are inferior to statistical interpretation of assessment results (Grove and Lloyd 2006; Meehl 1954/1996). Because there are no studies comparing clinical versus statistical interpretation approaches using D/HoH clients, the debate must for the present be argued from the basis of theory.

Research studies suggest that clinical judgment is far more likely to introduce bias and attenuate, rather than improve, prediction. For example, I have read hundreds of psychological reports by professionals and graduate students that report outcomes for D/HoH clients, and cannot recall one that suggested the assessment results probably over-estimated the client's intellectual abilities. In contrast, a majority of those reports suggested that the client's abilities were likely to be higher than the score or range reported—despite the fact that, statistically speaking, over-estimation occurs just as often as under-estimation. Based on these data (which admittedly lack rigorous control, but enjoy the virtue of being collected in authentic contexts

over multiple decades), I believe the potential for clinical judgment to *reduce* accuracy of interpretation to be a real threat to the accuracy of interpretation.

The one exception to the superiority of statistical interpretation versus clinical judgment is known as the "broken leg case" (see Grove and Lloyd 2006, p. 193). In this hypothetical example, the statistically derived probability that Professor A will go see a movie on Tuesday night (0.90) is less accurate only when the examiner has information that would clearly contradict it (i.e., knowing that Professor A broke her leg and was put in a hip cast Tuesday morning). This knowledge is referred to as a "special power of the clinician," and comes about because researchers cannot gather actuarial data on all of the distinct, unanticipated factors that have a meaningful influence on the probability of one or more outcomes. The question becomes: Is hearing loss a "broken leg case" in the interpretation of assessment results—that is, does knowing the client is D/HoH create a situation in which the clinician has special power or knowledge that substantially changes the relationship between test results and outcomes based on general research?

Any answer to that question is speculative in the absence of research—but given the ways in which hearing loss profoundly influences outcomes linked to language (and there are few that are not), it seems likely. For example, research on normal-hearing examinees shows modest to moderate correlations between nonverbal test scores and scores from academic achievement tests—but no difference in means or variance between groups. In contrast, whereas D/HoH clients also show modest correlations between nonverbal tests and achievement tests, and have average or near-average scores on nonverbal tests of cognitive abilities, they typically score one or more standard deviations lower on tests of academic achievement (Braden 1994; Reesman et al. 2014). Failure to account for this phenomenon might, indeed, constitute a "broken leg case"—and given the heterogeneity and complexity of the D/HoH population, it seems possible that there may be other instances in which examiners have knowledge available to them that outweigh the actuarial predictions derived from research on normal-hearing populations. However, whether these "broken leg cases" outweigh the biases that cause the vast majority of studies to show clinical judgment is inferior to statistical interpretation is not yet known (and could make for a fruitful area for future research).

## Research on Nonverbal Tests with D/HoH Clients

There are a number of published sources that review the use of nonverbal cognitive tests with D/HoH clients (e.g., Braden 1994, 2005; Maller and Braden 2011; Reesman et al. 2014). Original studies and reviews are remarkably consistent in reporting the following findings regarding nonverbal cognitive tests used with D/HoH clinical samples:

- Reliability coefficients are either similar to data reported for normative (normal-hearing) samples, or are higher (e.g., Krouse and Braden 2011).
- Correlations with other nonverbal tests are similar to values reported for normative samples.
- Correlations with verbal tests of cognitive ability and achievement are similar to or somewhat lower than those for normative samples, although substantial (1–2 standard deviation) differences are found on verbal test means.
- Mean scores for nonverbal tests are generally similar to or slightly lower than means for normative samples, with performance test means (i.e., those emphasizing speed and manipulation of objects) being closer to the normative means than nonverbal tests that do not use manipulatives (which tend to be 0.33 to 0.50 standard deviations below the normative sample mean) (see Braden 1994; Braden et al. 1994).
- Factor structures extracted from nonverbal test batteries tend to be quite similar to those extracted using the same methods from normative samples (Braden 1985; Perez and Braden 2013).

Taken collectively, the bulk of the research suggests nonverbal tests maintain their accuracy/consistency, and exhibit similar evidence of validity, when used with D/HoH clients. However, two caveats to this conclusion must be noted. First, although the correlations between nonverbal tests and achievement tests are similar or only somewhat lower in D/HoH clinical samples relative to normative, normal-hearing samples, verbal test score means are substantially (1–2 standard deviations) lower. This finding provides direct evidence in support of the oft-repeated admonition among experts in the field that language-loaded (i.e., verbal) tests are likely to produce substantially lower results for clients than nonverbal tests. Given that hearing loss, and not intellectual abilities, is likely to be the cause of the lower score, language-loaded tests should be used with caution (if at all) with D/HoH clients.

Second, the available evidence supporting validity is positive—but is substantially limited. There are no systematic studies of item content, test processes, or test consequences for D/HoH clients—meaning most of the claims made by nonverbal test publishers (i.e., that test scores have value for selecting educational interventions, deciding program placement, predicting vocational success, or other uses) are not supported. The same characterizations have been offered for normal-hearing populations, especially with respect to test consequences (Braden and Niebling 2012; Braden and Shaw 2009). Although equity is something generally to be sought, the dearth of evidence showing test results actually support better selection of interventions, influence response to placements, or otherwise have value in predicting educational, vocational, or social outcomes may show equity but it should not encourage confidence.

## Recommendations for Nonverbal Assessment

Given that the evidence of validity for nonverbal (and, for that matter, verbal) tests with D/HoH clients is almost exclusively limited to intra-test (i.e., internal consistency, intercorrelations, factor structure) and inter-test (i.e., correlation coefficients) metrics, how should clinicians best assess D/HoH clients? Table 4.2 provides a list of specific recommendations that are drawn from the literature to guide examiners in making decisions about whether/how to assess a D/HoH client, and the appropriate role of nonverbal tools and tests in an assessment.

In addition to those specific recommendations, it is imperative for the clinician to keep in mind that, in most cases, objective data are better than subjective impressions regarding a client's abilities. The same is true for D/HoH clients. So,

**Table 4.2** Recommended practices for assessing D/HoH clients

| Practice | Justification/explanation |
| --- | --- |
| Refer to or consult with a specialist | Because D/HoH clients are low-incidence and often highly complex, most experts recommend examiners refer to (or consult with) specialists. Specialists may be identified via the research directory maintained by Gallaudet University (http://research.gallaudet.edu/resources/mhd/), the American Deafness and Rehabilitation Association (http://www.adara.org/), the Deafness special interest group of Division 22 of the American Psychological Association (https://division-rehabpsych.squarespace.com/deafness/), or the School Psychologists Working with Students Who Are Deaf or Hard of Hearing special interest group of the National Association of School Psychologists (http://bit.ly/2bxD8CF) |
| Determine child's primary mode of communication | For children, primary caregivers or educators may identify the primary mode of communication; for adults, most clients can write or tell the examiner. Note that clients may not be proficient even in their primary mode of communication |
| Obtain interpreting services | If the examiner is not proficient in the client's primary mode of communication, interpreting services may be needed. In educational settings, one or more interpreters familiar with the client may be available (however, ensure the interpreters are appropriately credentialed). Alternatively, interpreters may be identified through the Registry of Interpreters for the Deaf (http://rid.org/), state or regional health and human services units, or through educational programs serving D/HoH clients (see list at Gallaudet University http://bit.ly/2bKzi9L). Examiners must budget time to train interpreters in the issues surrounding standardized test administration, and can learn from interpreters issues of communication and culture that may help them understand their client |
| Determine assessment objectives | Although assessments may occur for many reasons, the most common are: Intervention selection, program eligibility, and program placement. Rules and regulations may govern program eligibility, requiring certain tests to be administered or procedures to be followed |
| Determine client's assessment setting needs | Many D/HoH clients will have amplification assistance (e.g., hearing aids; cochlear implants), visual acuity assistance (e.g., glasses or contact lenses), and may have medical issues that benefit from pharmacological or other (e.g., diet) management. Consulting with the client, caregivers, educators, and prior records can help examiners identify relevant issues and take steps to minimize their effect on the assessment process |
| Select tests and other assessment approaches | As is true with all assessment, the use of multiple methods, settings, and opportunities is important to reducing error and enhancing generalization. Particular attention should be given to minimizing construct-irrelevant variance *and* construct under-representation. Generally, examiners should consider administering one or more nonverbal cognitive test to rule out generalized intellectual deficits |

(continued)

**Table 4.2** (continued)

| Practice | Justification/explanation |
| --- | --- |
| Implement the assessment | Examiners should position the interpreter slightly behind the examiner so the examinee can see both the examiner and the interpreter, and so the interpreter can voice (if needed) the examinee's responses |
| Interpret the results | As is true for all clients, examiners should be careful to separate likely from speculative interpretations, and to make inferences supported by theory and research. Ruling out general intellectual deficits is often useful for D/HoH clients. It is also useful to note that eligibility for a program or intervention is not the same as evidence the program or intervention will help the client (see comments on low-inference assessments and RTI) |
| Ensure assessment contributes to client well-being | Viewing assessment as a process rather than an event can help examiners attend to outcomes beyond writing a report and making recommendations. Using trial placements and other approaches to making assessment an in vivo rather than an in vitro process is likely to enhance outcomes and reduce the unintended (negative) consequences of assessment |

although there are substantial limitations to the clinical research base to support the use of non-verbal (and other) tests with D/HoH clients, some data are likely to be better than no data. There are exceptions to even this generalization, as shown by the tragic case presented by Vernon and Andrews (1990). When combined with concerns raised about the potential for clinical judgment to degrade predictive accuracy, what should examiners do?

First, there is strong consensus among experts in the field that the administration of one or more nonverbal tests of cognitive ability are useful as a means to make informed differential diagnoses regarding intellectual deficits. Essentially, an IQ from a nonverbal test in or above the normal range rules out general intellectual deficit or delay. The converse is not necessarily true (i.e., an IQ below the normal range does not prove a general deficit exists); rather, IQs from nonverbal tests in the normal range rule out mental retardation or generalized developmental deficits. This is an important contribution to any assessment, as many of the presenting behaviors (e.g., delayed, distorted, limited or absent speech; lack of sustained attention; deficits in incidentally acquired knowledge) for generalized intellectual deficits are similar to behaviors seen in typical D/HoH individuals.

Second, although there is an implicit sense that the complexity and heterogeneity of D/HoH clients is best handled by experts, I would suggest that lower, not higher, inference assessment approaches may be of greater use. The special education field as a whole has moved away from high-inference differential diagnosis towards low-inference response to intervention (RTI) approaches early in assessing students with difficulties. Examiners who are asked to answer questions such as "What intervention might work with this client?" or "Is Program X or Program Y more likely to foster vocational, social, and educational growth?" or "Are social services provided in this context/program better than social services provided in that context/program?" might be better off seeking answers from nontraditional assessment approaches that use low-inference, high-context means. These include, but are not limited to, intervention trials (i.e., RTI) and trial placements in which the D/HoH client is given an intervention or placed in a setting, and then the examiner (or other professionals) carefully assess the outcomes in response to the intervention, placement, or program. These approaches are nonverbal only by technicality (i.e., the examiner observes silently without verbal intrusion), but in fact would be assessing the client's response to rich social, educational, vocational, and linguistic stimuli.

I would like to note that the primary reasons such low-inference approaches are generally avoided is for organizational concerns, not client welfare. That is, educational and social organizations serving D/HoH clients have been built around the assumption that an examiner, working in isolation with a D/HoH client for a matter of hours, can accurately identify client needs and predict outcomes in response to educational, social, and vocational programs and interventions. As I have argued in this chapter, that assumption is not supported by research. There are institutional tools available that would allow low-inference, high-context assessments (e.g., students with disabilities can be placed into any program an IEP team recommends for up to 30 days, and that placement is renewable for an unlimited number of 30 day intervals), but they are rarely used as a means of answering "Will this intervention/program help this client?" Of course, there are good reasons to avoid some trial observations (e.g., some medical interventions are risky or irreversible), but there are mechanisms in place (e.g., multi-disciplinary assessment teams) that likely mitigate against unintended consequences. These approaches have the added value of rendering the clinical versus statistical interpretation argument moot, as in vivo assessment removes the uncertainty of in vitro prediction.

## Summary

In summary, nonverbal assessment tools are an important—and most experts would argue essential—tool in the psychological and educational assessment of any D/HoH client. Although nonverbal tools are necessary, they are not sufficient, and emerging low-inference, high-context approaches may provide stronger evidence of positive outcomes for individual (and eventually, groups of) D/HoH clients.

## References

American Educational Research Association, American Psychological Association, & National Council on Measurement in Education. (2014). *Standards for educational and psychological testing.* Washington, DC: American Educational Research Association.

Anderson, R. J., & Sisco, F. H. (1977). *Standardization of the WISC-R Performance Scale for deaf children* (Office of demographic studies publication series T, No. 1). Washington, DC: Gallaudet College.

Braden, J. P. (1985). The structure of nonverbal intelligence in deaf and hearing subjects. *American Annals of the Deaf, 131,* 496–501.

Braden, J. P. (1990). Do deaf persons have a characteristic psychometric profile on the Wechsler performance scales? *Journal of Psychoeducational Assessment, 8,* 518–526.

Braden, J. P. (1994). *Deafness, deprivation, and IQ.* New York: Plenum.

Braden, J. P. (2005). Using the WISC-IV with clients who are hard-of-hearing or deaf. In D. Saklofske, A. Prifitera, L. Weiss, & E. Rolfhus (Eds.), *WISC IV clinical use and interpretation* (pp. 351–380). New York: Academic Press.

Braden, J. P. (2006, March). *(When) Do we need "deaf norms?"* Invited symposium address, annual meeting of the National Association of School psychologists special interest group for deaf/hard of hearing children and families, Anaheim, CA.

Braden, J. P. (2008). Fluid intelligence. In N. Salkind (Ed.), *Encyclopedia of educational psychology.* Thousand Oaks, CA: Sage.

Braden, J. P. & Joyce, L. B. (2008). Best practices in making assessment accommodations. In A. Thomas & J. Grimes. (Eds.), *Best practices in school psychology* (5th ed., pp. 589–608). Silver Spring, MD: National Association of School Psychologists.

Braden, J. P., Kostrubala, C., & Reed, J. (1994). Why do deaf children score differently on performance v. motor-reduced nonverbal intelligence tests? *Journal of Psychoeducational Assessment, 12,* 357–363.

Braden, J. P., & Niebling, B. C. (2012). Using the joint test standards to evaluate the validity evidence for intelligence tests. In D. P. Flanagan & P. L. Harrison (Eds.), *Contemporary intellectual assessment: theories, tests and issues* (3rd ed., pp. 739–757). New York: Guilford.

Braden, J. P., & Shaw, S. R. (2009). Intervention validity of cognitive assessment: Knowns, unknowables, and unknowns. *Assessment for Effective Intervention, 34* (2), 106–115.

Elliott, S. N., Braden, J. P., & White, J. L. (2001). *Assessing one and all: Educational accountability for students with disabilities.* Reston, VA: Council for Exceptional Children.

Gallaudet Research Institute (April, 2011). Regional and National summary report of data from the 2009-10 annual survey of deaf and hard of hearing children and youth. Washington, DC: GRI, Gallaudet University. Retrieved July 4, 2016 from http://research.gallaudet.edu/Demographics/2010_National_Summary.pdf

Grove, M. W., & Lloyd, M. (2006). Meehl's contribution to clinical versus statistical prediction. *Journal of Abnormal Psychology, 115*(2), 192–194.

Kelly, M., & Braden, J. P. (1990). Criterion-related validity of the WISC-R performance scale with the Stanford achievement test-hearing impaired edition. *Journal of School Psychology, 28,* 147–151.

Krouse, H. E., & Braden, J. P. (2011). The reliability and validity of WISC-IV scores with deaf and hard-of-hearing children. *Journal of Psychoeducational Assessment, 29*(3), 238–248.

Maller, S. J. & Braden, J. P. (2011). Intellectual assessment of deaf people: A critical review of core concepts and issues. In M. Marschark & P. E. Spencer (Eds.), *The Oxford handbook of deaf studies, language, and education,* (Vol. 1, 2nd ed., pp. 473–485). New York: Oxford University Press.

Meehl, P. E. (1996). *Clinical versus statistical prediction: A theoretical analysis and a review of the evidence.* Northvale, NJ: Jason Aronson (Original work published 1954).

Messick, S. (1989). Validity. In R. L. Linn (Ed.), *Educational measurement* (3rd ed., pp. 13–103). New York: American Council on Education/Macmillan.

Metz, K., Miller, M., & Thomas-Presswood, T. N. (2010). Assessing children who are deaf and hard of hearing. In D. C. Miller (Ed.), *Best practices in school neuropsychology: Guidelines for effective practice, assessment, and evidence-based intervention* (pp. 419–463). New York: Wiley.

Mitchell, R. E., Young, T. A., Bachleda, B., & Karchmer, M. A. (2006). How many people use ASL in the United States? Why estimates need updating. *Sign Language Studies, 6*(3), 306–335.

Perez, H. E., & Braden, J. P. (2013). *The structure of intelligence of deaf and hard of hearing children: A factor analysis of the WISC-IV* (Manuscript under review).

Pintner, R., & Paterson, D. G. (1915). The Binet scale and the deaf child. *Journal of Educational Psychology, 6,* 201–210.

Reesman, J. H., Day, L. A., Szymanski, C. A., Hughes-Wheatland, R., Witkin, G. A., Kalback, S. R., et al. (2014). Review of intellectual assessment measures for children who are deaf and hard-of-hearing. *Rehabilitation Psychology, 59*(1), 99–106.

Reilly, C., & Qi, S. (2011). Snapshot of deaf and hard of hearing people, postsecondary attendance and unemployment. [Document compiled for US Senate HELP Committee]. Available: http://research.gallaudet.edu/Demographics/deaf-employment-2011.pdf Retrieved July 13, 2016.

Sligar, S. R., Morere, D., Cawthon, S., & Moxley, A. (2013). Equity in assessment for individuals who are deaf or hard-of-hearing. *Journal of the American Deafness and Rehabilitation Association, 47*(1), 110–127.

Vernon, M. (1967). Relationship of language to the thinking process. *Archives of Genetic Psychiatry, 16,* 325–333.

Vernon, M. (1976). Psychological evaluation of hearing impaired children. In L. Lloyd (Ed.), *Communication assessment and intervention strategies.* Baltimore, MD: University Park Press.

Vernon, M., & Andrews, J. F. (1990). *The psychology of deafness: Understanding deaf and hard-of-hearing people.* New York: Longman.

Vonderhaar, W. F., & Chambers, J. F. (1975). An examination of deaf students' Wechsler performance subtest scores. *American Annals of the Deaf, 120,* 540–543.

# Best Practices in Cross-Battery Assessment of Nonverbal Cognitive Ability

**5**

## Brian Wilhoit

The Cattell–Horn–Carroll (CHC) Cross-Battery approach, originally known as the Gf-Gc Cross-Battery model of assessment, has been defined as "a time efficient method of intellectual assessment that allows practitioners to validly measure a wider range (or a more in-depth but selective range) of cognitive abilities than that represented by any one intelligence battery in a way consistent with contemporary psychometric theory and research on the structure of intelligence" (McGrew and Flanagan 1998, p. 357). The CHC Cross-Battery approach provides two unique advantages: (a) data gathered both within and across test batteries can be interpreted theoretically and empirically within meaningful patterns; and (b) cognitive test data leads to examination of empirically validated links between specific cognitive abilities and specific academic areas (Flanagan et al. 2013). The approach provides practitioners with a classification system of cognitive abilities; existing cognitive tests can be evaluated according to the model, i.e., subcomponents/subtests can be described based on their ability to assess cognitive abilities within the CHC model.

According to Flanagan and McGrew (1997) the CHC Cross-Battery Assessment system is

based on three pillars. The three pillars provide the theoretical underpinnings of the Cross-Battery approach, and depict a relatively complete taxonomic framework for describing the structure and nature of intelligence. Pillar one classifies cognitive abilities at three levels, or "strata", that differ on degree of generality, as described in the next section. Pillar two illustrates the placement of subtests of major published cognitive batteries along the ten broad (Stratum II) abilities. Pillar three illustrates the placement of subtests of the major published cognitive batteries according to their ability to assess multiple narrow (Stratum I) abilities described in the CHC theory. The second and third pillars are described in later sections for the major nonverbal cognitive batteries and tests. For a complete description of all traditional intelligence batteries' ability to assess Stratum II and Stratum I abilities, readers are referred to McGrew and Flanagan (1998), Flanagan and Ortiz (2001), and Flanagan et al. (2013).

## The Theoretical Foundation of CHC Cross-Battery Assessment

The theoretical underpinnings of the Cross-Battery approach lie within an enormous body of literature beginning with only the two basic abilities—fluid (Gf) and crystallized (Gc; Cattell 1941, 1957, 1963), and later expanding to several abilities (Horn 1965, 1968, 1985, 1988, 1991; Woodcock 1994). Further empirical research conducted by Carroll (1993) clarified a

B. Wilhoit (✉)
Department of Educational Psychology &
Counseling, University of Tennessee,
407 Claxton Education Complex,
1122 Volunteer Blvd, Knoxville,
TN 37996-3452, USA
e-mail: bwilhoit@utk.edu

© Springer International Publishing AG 2017
R.S. McCallum (ed.), *Handbook of Nonverbal Assessment*,
DOI 10.1007/978-3-319-50604-3_5

multiple-component intelligence theory, elaborated upon by Flanagan and McGrew (1997). McGrew (1997) proposed a model designed to synthesize Horn, Cattell, and Carroll's work, with refinements following factor analyses by Flanagan and McGrew (1997). Finally, McGrew and Flanagan (1998) outlined a taxonomy of intellectual abilities that came to be known as the Cattell–Horn–Carroll (CHC) Theory of Cognitive Abilities (Flanagan and Ortiz 2001).

The CHC Theory of Cognitive Abilities as outlined by McGrew and Flanagan (1998) included ten broad cognitive abilities and approximately 70 narrow cognitive abilities (Flanagan and Ortiz 2001; Flanagan et al. 2013). The ten broad cognitive abilities located at the Stratum II level include: Crystallized Intelligence (Gc), Fluid Intelligence (Gf), Quantitative Knowledge (Gq), Reading and Writing Ability (Grw), Short-Term Memory (Gsm), Visual Processing (Gv), Auditory Processing (Ga), Long-Term Storage and Retrieval (Glr), Processing Speed (Gs), and Decision/Reaction Time or Speed (Gt). These abilities form the cornerstone of interpretation within the CHC model. The broadest, or most general level, is represented by Stratum III and is located at the apex of the hierarchy. Stratum III subsumes both the broad Stratum II and narrow Stratum I abilities and represents a general factor "g" that is presumed to represent complex higher order cognitive processes (Gustafsson and Undheim 1996); however, McGrew (1997) and McGrew and Flanagan (1998) judge it to have very little practical relevance for assessment and interpretation of cognitive abilities. Below we describe the 10 Stratum II and the multiple Stratum I abilities (notation as outlined by Flanagan et al. 2013, is followed).

## Gc—Crystallized Intelligence

Crystallized Intelligence is the breadth and depth of cultural information that is acquired and applied. There are 12 Stratum I narrow abilities within Gc. These include: Language Development (LD), Lexical Knowledge (VL), Listening Ability (LS), General Information (KO),

Information about Culture (K2), General Science Information (K1), Communication Ability (CM), Oral Production and Fluency (OP), Grammatical Sensitivity (MY), Foreign Language Proficiency (KL), and Foreign Language Aptitude (LA).

## Gf—Fluid Intelligence

Fluid Intelligence can be characterized as the ability to solve novel tasks. Five component narrow abilities comprise Gf. These narrow abilities include: General Sequential Reasoning (RG), Induction (I), Quantitative Reasoning (RQ), Piagetian Reasoning (RP), and Speed of Reasoning (RE).

## Gq—Quantitative Knowledge

Quantitative Knowledge is the acquired factual and conceptual knowledge possessed by an individual. Gq is comprised of two component narrow abilities: Mathematical Knowledge (KM) and Mathematical Achievement (A3).

## Grw—Reading and Writing Ability

Reading and Writing Ability is the acquired basic reading and writing skills necessary to comprehend and express ideas in written language. There are eight component narrow abilities comprising Grw: Reading Decoding (RD), Reading Comprehension (RC), Verbal Language Comprehension (V), Cloze Ability (CZ), Spelling Ability (SG), Writing Ability (WA), English Usage Knowledge (EU), and Reading Speed (RS). Grw is not typically assessed via intelligence tests.

## Gsm—Short-Term Memory

Short-Term Memory can be characterized as the ability to apprehend, hold, and use information within a few seconds. Gsm is comprised of two narrow abilities: Memory Span (MS) and Learning Abilities (L1).

## Gv—Visual Processing

Visual Processing "is the ability to generate, perceive, analyze, synthesize, manipulate, transform, and think with visual patterns and stimuli" (p. 23). Eleven component narrow abilities comprise Gv. These narrow abilities include: Visualization (VZ), Spatial Relations (SR), Visual Memory (MV), Closure Speed (CS), Flexibility of Closure (CF), Spatial Scanning (SS), Serial Perceptual Integration (PI), Length Estimation (LE), Perceptual Illusions (IL), Perceptual Alternations (PN), and Imagery (IM).

## Ga—Auditory Processing

Auditory Processing is the ability to "perceive, analyze, and synthesize patterns among auditory stimuli, especially the ability to perceive and discriminate subtle nuances of patterns of sound…and speech that may be presented under distorted conditions" (p. 23). Ga is comprised of 13 component narrow abilities: Phonetic Coding (PC), Speech Sound Discrimination (US), Resistance to Auditory Stimulus Distortion (UR), Memory for Sound Patterns (UM), General Sound Discrimination (U3), Temporal Tracking (UK), Musical Discrimination and Judgment (U1, U9), Maintaining and Judging Rhythm (U8), Sound-Intensity/Duration Discrimination (U6), Sound-Frequency Discrimination (U5), Hearing and Speech Threshold Factors (UA, UT, UU), Absolute Pitch (UP), and Sound Localization (UL). Ga is not currently assessed via nonverbal intelligence tests.

## Glr—Long-Term Storage and Retrieval

Long-Term Storage and Retrieval is the ability to store and retrieve information for more than a few minutes. Thirteen component narrow abilities comprise Glr: Associative Memory (MA), Meaningful Memory (MM), Free Recall Memory (M6), Ideational Fluency (FI), Associational Fluency (FA), Expressional Fluency (FE), Naming Facility (NA), Word Fluency (FW),

Figural Fluency (FF), Figural Flexibility (FX), Sensitivity to Problems (SP), Originality/Creativity (FO), and Learning Abilities (L1).

## Gs—Processing Speed

Processing Speed is the ability to "fluently perform cognitive tasks…when under pressure to maintain focused attention and concentration" (p. 24) and may last for minutes. Three narrow abilities comprise Gs: Perceptual Speed (P), Rate-of-Test Taking (R9), and Number Facility (N).

## Gt—Decision/Reaction Time or Speed

Decision/Reaction Time or Speed can be characterized as quickness in reacting and/or making decisions and is described as latency to respond. Gt is comprised of four component narrow abilities: Simple Reaction Comparison Speed (R7). Gt is not typically assessed by currently available intelligence tests.

## Application of CHC Cross-Battery Assessment to Nonverbal Assessment

The use of CHC Cross-Battery Assessment procedures, while comprehensive in scope, carries an implied assumption that the examinee presents with language faculties intact. There are many cases; however, when the examinee presents with language deficits so severe that traditional language laden instruments cannot be utilized to obtain a measure of cognitive abilities. In these cases, nonverbal measures of cognitive abilities may be more appropriate. Use of the CHC Cross-Battery Assessment procedures is possible even for those with limited English proficiency; the procedures simply require nonverbal assessment techniques and instruments. Unfortunately, there are fewer measures that are appropriate for nonverbal assessment, and of those measures there are salient differences that practitioners must consider when making assessment choices.

Some nonverbal instruments such as the Universal Nonverbal Intelligence Test, Second Edition (UNIT-2; Bracken and McCallum 2016), require the use of pantomime and gestures and can be administered completely nonverbally; on the other hand, the majority of "nonverbal" instruments include some verbal communication either of expression or reception. Additional training may be necessary before practitioners can administer some instruments requiring non-verbal presentations. Most of the nonverbal instruments are individually administered, but a few may allow group administration. Adminis-tration characteristics may limit a practitioner's choices of instruments depending on the indi-vidual needs of the clients (e.g., motor require-ments). So, practitioners need to acquaint themselves with the unique characteristics of each instrument and be aware of the task demands during interpretation of the results.

Another consideration that practitioners must consider when selecting an instrument is whether the standardization sample included verbally limited individuals in proportion to the general population, or whether there were less than pro-portional numbers of verbally limited individuals included. Obviously, when available, an instru-ment that most closely and inclusively resembles the general population would be more appropri-ate for normative comparisons; even so, instru-ments with less proportionate standardization samples may provide adequate measures of nar-row abilities in some cases.

Several nonverbal instruments are considered unidimensional; that is, they measure only one aspect or narrow sliver of intelligence. For a comprehensive assessment of intelligence, a unidimensional instrument will not be appropri-ate, unless combined with other measures. Mul-tidimensional nonverbal instruments provide better coverage of broad abilities than unidi-mensional tests and are generally appropriate for high stakes assessment (e.g., placement deci-sions); however these tests may not be inclusive enough to measure the total range of broad cognitive abilities that have been identified. Use

of the CHC Cross-Battery Assessment approach addresses this limitation.

The primary principle of CHC Cross-Battery Assessment and Nonverbal Assessment is the same: to obtain the most accurate measure of cognitive abilities available. It is through the combination of these procedures that a more comprehensive evaluation can be completed for verbally limited individuals.

## Nonverbal CHC Cross-Battery Assessment

### Seven Steps of the Nonverbal Cross-Battery Assessment Approach

The steps in a Cross-Battery assessment are adapted from McGrew and Flanagan (1998) and Flanagan et al. (2013), and rely heavily on the processes they describe and on their categoriza-tions of existing nonverbal instruments according to their ability to assess Stratum II and Stratum I cognitive components. These steps are appro-priate for verbal and nonverbal assessment, and are presented below, along with elaboration and specific directions.

1. Choose the most appropriate core intelligence battery
   The evaluator should select a core intelli-gence battery that is multidimensional. A multidimensional battery provides more coverage of Gf-Gc abilities. Thus, the exam-iner reduces the need to supplement the bat-tery with a large number of subtests selected from other batteries. Generally, a battery is also selected to meet respective States' requirements for a Full-Scale IQ score. For nonverbal assessment, examiners have a choice of three multidimensional batteries currently—the Wechsler Nonverbal Scale of Ability (Wechsler and Naglieri 2006), the Leiter International Performance Scale, Third Edition (Leiter-3; Roid and Miller 2013) and the Universal Nonverbal Intelligence Test, Second Edition (UNIT-2; Bracken and McCallum 2016).

2. Decide which Gf-Gc abilities are adequately represented in core intelligence battery.

Once a comprehensive intelligence battery has been selected, the examiner needs to attend to the scope of Gf-Gc broad and narrow ability coverage. The examiner can accomplish this by simply reviewing the worksheets found in Appendix 1 or in tables found in McGrew and Flanagan (1998), Flanagan and Ortiz (2001), and Flanagan et al. (2013) to determine those abilities assessment by particular subtests. In order for a broad Stratum II ability to be adequately represented, it must consist of at least two qualitatively different narrow Stratum I abilities that measure the broad ability of interest. For example, if fluid reasoning is the broad ability of interest, two qualitatively different narrow abilities, such as induction and general sequential reasoning, would suffice to adequately measure the broad ability characterized as fluid reasoning. However, two measures of the same narrow ability would be insufficient coverage of a broad ability. It is important to use the fewest number of batteries necessary to provide adequate coverage (Flanagan et al. 2013) to avoid confounds associated with the use of multiple standardization samples.

3. Decide which Gf-Gc abilities are un- or underrepresented.

Deciding which Gf-Gc abilities are un- or underrepresented is accomplished by examining the worksheets in Appendix 1 or those worksheets and tables provided by McGrew and Flanagan (1998), Flanagan and Ortiz (2001), and Flanagan et al. (2013). There are no currently published intelligence batteries that provide adequate coverage of all broad and narrow abilities (Flanagan and Ortiz 2001). Some batteries provide two or more narrow abilities within a broad ability; however, in many cases, these narrow abilities do not differ qualitatively within the respective broad abilities (McGrew and Flanagan 1998).

4. Determine which supplemental subtests are needed to assess those un- or underrepresented abilities.

Nonverbal cognitive batteries provide a good source for Gf-Gc ability measures for visual processing, fluid reasoning, processing speed, and long-term retrieval. In addition, selective subtests of another nonverbal battery, or other nonverbal tests (e.g., Test of Nonverbal Intelligence—Fourth Edition; TONI-4; Brown et al. 2010) provide further narrow abilities of interest that may be used in conjunction with subtests already present on the core cognitive battery. Importantly, nonverbal assessment is necessarily limited due to constraints associated with the examinee. For example, nonverbal assessment is usually indicated when examinees are deaf, culturally different, have language impairments, etc.; consequently, the choice of measures will be limited due, in part, to the level of reliance upon language-related skills. In some cases, receptive language can be assessed using instruments such as the Peabody Picture Vocabulary Test—Fourth Edition (PPVT-4; Dunn and Dunn 2007).

5. Administer core battery and supplemental subtests.

The core battery is administered to obtain the needed Full-Scale IQ using the standardized procedures specified by the respective test publishers. The supplemental subtests that are necessary to complete the cross-battery assessment are also administered as specified by the test publishers. Standardized procedures should be followed unless there are extenuating circumstances, and documentation of breaking standardization would be necessary in those circumstances.

6. Complete Cross-Battery worksheets.

Cross-Battery worksheets are located in Appendix 2 for the nonverbal intelligence tests discussed in this chapter. Broad Stratum II Abilities can be calculated for visual processing, fluid reasoning, processing speed, short-term memory, and crystallized intelligence. A Narrow Stratum I Ability score can be calculated for associative memory; a measure of long-term retrieval. As necessary, all standard scores must be converted to the most common metric, which uses a mean of 100 and standard deviation of 15. Once the scores obtained are entered into the worksheets, all the necessary computations are entered within the worksheets to compute Broad or Narrow abilities. (Importantly, some Broad Stratum II abilities are operationalized by only one Narrow Stratum I measure.) If considered helpful, examiners may transfer the Gf-Gc narrow ability standard scores and broad ability averages from the worksheets to a Gf-Gc profile. The profile provides a visual graphic depicting strengths and weaknesses at a glance. An example of a typical Gf-Gc profile worksheet can be found in either McGrew and Flanagan (1998), Flanagan and Ortiz (2001), or Flanagan et al. (2013).

7. Interpret the results.

Interpreting test results is itself a multistep process. Results can be interpreted using the guidelines provided by McGrew and Flanagan (1998), Flanagan and Ortiz (2001), or Flanagan, Ortiz, and Alfonso (2013). In general, the goal of interpretation is to determine cognitive strengths and weaknesses, which are assumed to underlie real-world performance in school and in the workplace. Interpretation of abilities at the Stratum II level requires at least one measure of two different Stratum I abilities; these measures operationalize the broader Stratum II ability. The two scores are averaged to provide a particular Stratum II score. (If the two narrow Stratum I abilities are significantly different one from the other, each of the two Stratum I abilities should be assessed with an additional measure, and the four subtests averaged—significance is defined for our purposes as a difference greater than 15 points.). In order to interpret cognitive strengths and weaknesses at the Stratum II level Stratum II ability scores are averaged and each measure is compared to the overall Stratum II average (to determine whether there are outliers). If so, these outliers are assumed to be strengths and weaknesses. Again, outliers are defined as those (Stratum II) abilities that deviate more than 15 points from the overall mean. As Flanagan and McGrew note,

Stratum II abilities have been empirically linked to and are assumed to underlie certain real-world skills. For example, processing speed is assumed to relate to reading because it influences the ability to rapidly call words (Bowers and Wolf 1993). See McGrew and Flanagan (1998) and Mather (1991) for other important relationships between CHC Stratum II abilities and academic areas (e.g., visual processing and math). The astute examiner will be able to relate these abilities to referral problems. Parents and teachers can use this information to plan curricular changes. Following our example above, a child who exhibits slow processing may be given more time to call words and may be instructed using a particular strategy designed to enhance word calling speed, such as "reading previewing;" reading previewing requires that a model gradually increase oral reading speed as a student reads along silently.

## Summary

The purpose of cross-battery assessment is to provide psychological assessment specialists/examiners with an overall cognitive assessment strategy. More specifically, it is designed to make examiners aware of the subconstructs of intelligence, as defined by the Cattell–Horn–Carroll Model of Intelligence, and to make them aware of how these constructs can be assessed, using the best available operationalizations (of the constructs). Cross-battery assessment principles can be used by examiners to determine cognitive strengths and weaknesses, and is generally considered to provide the steps necessary to complete a very comprehensive evaluation of cognitive abilities. I have adapted the guidelines and principles from McGrew and Flanagan (1998) and Flanagan et al. (2013) for those examiners who engage in nonverbal assessment of cognitive abilities and intelligence. In addition, I provide a listing of the best nonverbal assessment instruments (Appendix 1) and a set of worksheets to guide interpretation of scores obtained from nonverbal cross-battery assessment (Appendix 2). Finally, I provide a case for illustrative purposes in Appendix 3. As is apparent from reading the case, the basic principles and strategies are the same for both verbal and nonverbal assessment, but the number and quality of instruments available for nonverbal assessment are less than for verbal assessment.

## Appendix 1 Broad and Narrow Abilities Measured by Nonverbal Intelligence Batteries and Tests

| Battery/Test | Test/Subtest | Broad ability | Narrow ability |
|---|---|---|---|
| UNIT-2 | Spatial memory<br>Symbolic memory | Visual processing | Visual memory |
| | Cube design | Fluid intelligence | General sequential reasoning |
| | | Visual processing | Spatial relations |
| | Nonsymbolic quantity<br>Numerical series | Fluid intelligence | Quantitative reasoning |
| | Analogic reasoning | Fluid intelligence | Induction |
| Raven's | Raven's progressive matrices | Fluid intelligence | Induction |
| Leiter-3 | Classification<br>Design analogies<br>Repeated patterns<br>Sequential order | Fluid intelligence | Induction |
| | Picture context<br>Visual coding | Fluid intelligence | General sequential reasoning |
| | Figure rotation | Visual processing | Spatial relations |
| | Matching<br>Form completion<br>Paper folding | Visual processing | Visualization |
| | Immediate recognition<br>Forward memory | Visual processing | Visual memory |
| | Figure ground | Visual processing | Flex of closure |
| | Delayed recognition<br>Associated pairs<br>Delayed pairs | Long-term retrieval | Associative memory |
| | Attention sustained | Processing speed | Perceptual speed |
| Matrix analogies | Matrix analogies | Fluid intelligence | Induction |
| Beta IV | Coding | Processing speed | Rate-of-test-taking |
| | Picture completion | Visual processing | Closure speed |
| | Clerical checking | Processing speed | Perceptual speed |
| | Picture absurdities | Crystallized intelligence | Language development |
| | Matrix reasoning | Fluid intelligence | Induction |
| CTONI-2 | Pictorial analogies | Fluid intelligence | Induction |
| | Geometric analogies | | |
| | Pictorial categories | Fluid intelligence | Induction |
| | Geometric categories | | |
| | Pictorial sequences | | |
| | Geometric sequence | | |

(continued)

**Appendix 1** (continued)

| Battery/Test | Test/Subtest | Broad ability | Narrow ability |
|---|---|---|---|
| GAMA | Matching | Visual processing | Visualization |
| | Sequences | Fluid intelligence | General sequential reasoning |
| | Analogies | Fluid intelligence | Induction |
| | Construction | Visual processing | Spatial relations |
| NNAT-2 | Pattern completion | Visual processing | Visualization |
| | Reasoning by analogy | Fluid intelligence | Induction |
| | Serial reasoning | Fluid intelligence | General sequential reasoning |
| | Spatial visualization | Visual processing | Spatial relations |
| TONI-4 | TONI-4 | Fluid intelligence | Induction |
| PPVT-4 | PPVT-4 | Crystallized intelligence | Lexical knowledge |
| WNV | Matrices | Fluid intelligence | Induction |
| | Coding | Processing speed | Rate-of-test taking |
| | Object assembly | Visual processing | Closure speed |
| | Recognition | Visual processing | Visual memory |
| | Spatial span | Short-term memory | Memory span |
| | Picture arrangement | Visual processing | Visualization |

*UNIT-2* Universal Nonverbal Intelligence Test—Second Edition
*Raven's* Raven's Progressive Matrices
*Leiter-3* Leiter International Performance Scale—Third Edition
*MAT* Matrix Analogies Test
*Beta IV* Beta IV
*CTONI-2* Comprehensive Test of Nonverbal Intelligence—Second Edition
*GAMA* General Ability Measure for Adults
*NNAT-2* Naglieri Nonverbal Ability Test—Second Edition
*TONI-4* Test of Nonverbal Intelligence—Fourth Edition
*PPVT-4* Peabody Picture Vocabulary Test—Fourth Edition
*WNV* Wechsler Nonverbal Scale of Ability

# Appendix 2 Cross-Battery Worksheets for Use with Nonverbal Intelligence Tests

Visual processing (Gv)

| Spatial relations | | |
|---|---|---|
| Battery/Test | Test/Subtest | Standard Score (M = 100, SD = 15) |
| UNIT-2 | Cube design | |
| Leiter-3 | Figure rotation | |
| NNAT-2 | Spatial visualization | |
| Sum of subtests | | |
| Number of subtests | | |
| Sum of subtests/Number of subtests | | |
| Spatial relations standard score | | |

(continued)

**Appendix 2** (continued)

| Visualization | | |
|---|---|---|
| Battery/Test | Test/Subtest | Standard Score (M = 100, SD = 15) |

| Visualization | | |
|---|---|---|
| Battery/Test | Test/Subtest | Standard Score (M = 100, SD = 15) |
| Leiter-3 | Matching | |
| | Form completion | |
| | Paper folding | |
| GAMA | Matching | |
| NNAT-2 | Pattern completion | |
| WNV | Picture arrangement | |
| Sum of subtests | | |
| Number of subtests | | |
| Sum of subtests/Number of subtests | | |
| Visualization standard score | | |

| Flexibility of closure | | |
|---|---|---|
| Battery/Test | Test/Subtest | Standard Score (M = 100, SD = 15) |
| Leiter-3 | Figure ground | |
| Flexibility of closure standard score | | |

| Closure speed | | |
|---|---|---|
| Battery/Test | Test/Subtest | Standard score (M = 100, SD = 15) |
| Beta-4 | Picture completion | |
| WNV | Object assembly | |
| Sum of subtests | | |
| Number of subtests | | |
| Sum of subtests/Number of subtests | | |
| Closure speed standard score | | |

| Visual memory | | |
|---|---|---|
| Battery/Test | Test/Subtest | Standard Score (M = 100, SD = 15) |
| UNIT-2 | Spatial memory | |
| | Symbolic memory | |
| Leiter-3 | Immediate recognition | |
| | Forward memory | |
| WNV | Recognition | |
| Sum of subtests | | |
| Number of subtests | | |
| Sum of subtests/Number of subtests | | |
| Visual memory standard score | | |
| Sual processing broad ability score conversion | | |
| Spatial relations narrow ability score | | |
| Spatial scanning narrow ability score | | |

(continued)

**Appendix 2** (continued)

| Sual processing broad ability score conversion |
| Visualization narrow ability score |
| Flexibility of closure narrow ability score |
| Closure speed narrow ability score |
| Visual memory narrow ability score |
| Sum of narrow ability scores |
| Number of narrow ability scores |
| Sum of narrow ability scores/Number of narrow ability scores |
| Visual processing broad ability score (Gv) |

Fluid reasoning (Gf)

Induction

| Battery/Test | Test/Subtest | Standard Score (M = 100, SD = 15) |
|---|---|---|
| UNIT-2 | Analogic reasoning | |
| Raven's | Raven's progressive matrices | |
| Leiter-3 | Classification | |
| | Design analogies | |
| | Repeated patterns | |
| | Sequential order | |
| Matrix analogies | Matrix analogies | |
| Beta-4 | Matrix reasoning | |
| CTONI-2 | Pictorial analogies | |
| | Geometric analogies | |
| | Pictorial categories | |
| | Geometric categories | |
| | Pictorial sequences | |
| | Geometric sequences | |
| GAMA | Analogies | |
| NNAT-2 | Reasoning by analogy | |
| TONI-4 | TONI-4 | |
| WNV | Matrices | |
| Sum of subtests | | |
| Number of subtests | | |
| Sum of subtests/Number of subtests | | |
| Induction standard score | | |

Quantitative reasoning

| Battery/Test | Test/Subtest | Standard Score (M = 100, SD = 15) |
|---|---|---|
| UNIT-2 | Nonsymbolic quantity | |
| | Number series | |
| Sum of subtests | | |
| Number of subtests | | |

(continued)

**Appendix 2** (continued)

| Quantitative reasoning | | |
| --- | --- | --- |
| Battery/Test | Test/Subtest | Standard Score (M = 100, SD = 15) |
| Sum of subtests/Number of subtests | | |
| Quantitative reasoning standard score | | |

| General sequential reasoning | | |
| --- | --- | --- |
| Battery/Test | Test/Subtest | Standard Score (M = 100, SD = 15) |
| UNIT-2 | Cube Design | |
| GAMA | Sequences | |
| NNAT-2 | Serial Reasoning | |
| Leiter-3 | Picture Context | |
| | Visual Coding | |
| Sum of subtests | | |
| Number of subtests | | |
| Sum of subtests/Number of subtests | | |
| General sequential reasoning standard score | | |
| Fluid reasoning broad ability score conversion | | |
| Induction narrow ability score | | |
| Quantitative reasoning narrow ability score | | |
| General sequential reasoning narrow ability score | | |
| Sum of narrow ability scores | | |
| Number of narrow ability scores | | |
| Sum of narrow ability scores/Number of narrow ability scores | | |
| Fluid reasoning broad ability score (Gf) | | |

Long-term retrieval (Glr)

| Associative memory | | |
| --- | --- | --- |
| Battery/Test | Test/Subtest | Standard Score (M = 100, SD = 15) |
| Leiter-3 | Delayed recognition | |
| | Associated pairs | |
| | Delayed pairs | |
| Sum of subtests | | |
| Number of subtests | | |
| Sum of subtests/Number of subtests | | |
| Associative memory standard score | | |

Processing speed (Gs)

| Perceptual speed | | |
| --- | --- | --- |
| Battery/Test | Test/Subtest | Standard Score (M = 100, SD = 15) |
| Leiter-3 | Attention sustained | |
| Beta-4 | Clerical checking | |
| Sum of subtests | | |
| Number of subtests | | |

(continued)

**Appendix 2** (continued)

| Perceptual speed | | |
|---|---|---|
| Battery/Test | Test/Subtest | Standard Score (M = 100, SD = 15) |
| Sum of subtests/Number of subtests | | |
| Perceptual speed standard score | | |

| Rate of test taking | | |
|---|---|---|
| Battery/Test | Test/Subtest | Standard Score (M = 100, SD = 15) |
| Beta-4 | Coding | |
| WNV | Coding | |
| Sum of Subtests | | |
| Number of Subtests | | |
| Sum of subtests/Number of subtests | | |
| Rate of test taking standard score | | |

| Processing speed broad ability score conversion |
|---|
| Induction narrow ability score |
| General sequential reasoning narrow ability score |
| Sum of narrow ability scores |
| Number of narrow ability scores |
| Sum of narrow ability scores/Number of narrow ability scores |
| Processing speed broad ability score (Gs) |

**Crystallized intelligence (Gc)**

| Language development | | |
|---|---|---|
| Battery/Test | Test/Subtest | Standard Score (M = 100, SD = 15) |
| Beta-4 | Picture absurdities | |
| Language development standard score | | |

| Lexical knowledge | | |
|---|---|---|
| Battery/Test | Test/Subtest | Standard Score (M = 100, SD = 15) |
| PPVT-4 | PPVT-4 | |
| Lexical knowledge standard score | | |

| Crystallized intelligence broad ability score conversion |
|---|
| Induction narrow ability score |
| General sequential reasoning narrow ability score |
| Sum of narrow ability scores |
| Number of narrow ability scores |
| Sum of narrow ability scores/Number of narrow ability scores |
| Crystallized intelligence broad ability score (Gc) |

(continued)

Short-term memory (Gsm)

| Visual memory | | |
|---|---|---|
| Battery/Test | Test/Subtest | Standard Score (M = 100, SD = 15) |
| UNIT-2 | Spatial memory | |
| | Symbolic memory | |
| Leiter-3 | Immediate recognition | |
| | Forward memory | |
| Sum of subtests | | |
| Number of subtests | | |
| Sum of Subtests–Number of Subtests | | |
| Visual memory standard score | | |
| Memory span | | |
| Battery/Test | Test/Subtest | Standard Score (M = 100, SD = 15) |
| WNV | Spatial span | |
| Memory span standard score | | |
| Short-term memory broad ability score conversion | | |
| Visual memory narrow ability score | | |
| Memory span narrow ability score | | |
| Sum of narrow ability scores | | |
| Number of narrow ability scores | | |
| Sum of narrow ability scores/Number of narrow ability scores | | |
| Short-term broad ability score (Gf) | | |

# Appendix 3

## Confidential Psychoeducational Report

**Name**: Miguel D.
**Birth Date**: 01/21/2008
**Age**: 8 years 1 month 20 days
**School**: Green Valley Elementary School
**Grade Placement**: 2nd grade
**Sex**: Male
**Examiner**: Jamie L. Smith
**Test Dates**: 3/16/2016, 3/27/2016

**Referral Question**: Miguel was referred for testing by his teacher because of reading difficulty, particularly reading comprehension. According to his teacher, Miguel can decode words, but this skill is not automatic and his reading lacks fluency. His general academic progress has been much slower than the other students in his classroom, and is marked by poor grades. She requested a psycho-educational evaluation to determine whether this problem is a function of intellectual disability, a specific learning disability, or a language-related limitation.

**Background Information**: Miguel is an eight-year-old boy who is in the second grade at Green Valley Elementary School. He is of Hispanic origin and moved with his family from Venezuela one year ago. Miguel's parents are migrant workers and work on a local farm. He has two older brothers and a younger sister. Spanish is the dominant language within Miguel's household. His current academic functioning has been described as low by both his teacher and parents, though they say that his

English is average when compared to other children his age of Hispanic origin. Miguel's mother states that he works diligently on his homework every day but struggles to find the right answers. An interview with Miguel's mother revealed that he has had no significant health, medical, or emotional problems. He is not currently taking any medications. Miguel interacts well with his peers and is well liked by the other children in his classroom. Miguel is right-handed and does not wear glasses. A recent vision/hearing exam revealed no visual or auditory acuity problems.

**Tests Administered**:

Beta-4 (select subtests; 3/16/16)

Leiter International Performance Scale—Third Edition (Leiter-3) (select subtests; 3/16/16)

Woodcock- Johnson IV Tests of Achievement (WJ-ACH-IV) (select subtests; 3/16/16)

Universal Nonverbal Intelligence Test—Second Edition (UNIT-2) (3/27/16)

Peabody Picture Vocabulary Test—Fourth Edition, Spanish Version (PPVT-4) (3/27/16)

Wechsler Nonverbal Scale of Ability (select subtests; 3/27/16)

**Clinical and Behavioral Observations**: Miguel was tested on a couple of occasions in the school psychology clinic. He was dressed casually and appeared somewhat reserved. Rapport was easily established and maintained. During the testing sessions, he was quiet yet cooperative. He maintained eye contact easily, but took several minutes to respond to many questions. Miguel's language skills seemed below average for his age, and his activity level was generally low during testing. He took longer than usual to answer questions, and seemed to have trouble selecting the word that he wanted to use. At times, Miguel had difficultly articulating his thoughts and needed to be queried to facilitate a response. He became frustrated when the items became more difficult (e.g., he bit his nails, frowned). He would not voluntarily admit that he did not know the answer to the more difficult items, but rather, would wait until prompted by the examiner to say that he did not know. Miguel's concentration level was extremely high

during all of the tests. He did not display any unusual habits or mannerisms, and conveyed a sense of respect towards the examiner. Overall, the testing conditions were deemed adequate to obtain valid responses from this child.

**Referral Question Determination**:
Universal nonverbal intelligence test—second edition

| Global scale | Standard score | Percentile rank |
|---|---|---|
| Full-scale IQ | 82 | 12th |
| Memory | 91 | 27th |
| Reasoning | 77 | 6th |
| Nonsymbolic | 91 | 27th |

State regulations and guidelines require the use of standard scores to diagnose intellectual disability and a discrepancy score to diagnose specific learning disabilities. The UNIT-2 was administered to obtain a Full Scale IQ, from which a discrepancy score could be calculated. Miguel obtained a Full-Scale IQ of 82, which falls at the 12th percentile nationally and is classified as Low Average. We can be 90% certain that Miguel's true score falls somewhere between 77 and 89. This score rules out intellectual disability, because it falls in the low average range and is considerably above the cutoff score necessary to help establish a diagnosis of intellectual disability (two standard deviations below the mean). In addition, the similarity between Miguel's IQ score and achievement scores (discussed later) rules out the possibility of a specific learning disability, as defined by a discrepancy score. Strengths and weaknesses from the UNIT-2 are discussed as part of the cross-battery assessment.

**Assessment of Cognitive Strengths and Weaknesses**: Certain subtests from the Leiter-3 (3/16/16), Beta-4 (3/16/16), UNIT-2 (3/27/16), and PPVT-4 (3/27/16) were combined by CHC Cross- Battery principles and procedures. These scores yielded six broad cognitive ability clusters, which include Fluid Intelligence (G$f$), Crystallized Intelligence (G$c$), Visual Processing (G$v$), Short- Term Memory (G$sm$), Long-Term Retrieval (G$lr$), and Processing Speed (G$s$). A summary of Miguel's performance across these domains is provided below.

**Cross-Battery Assessment of G*f***: Fluid intelligence applies to mental operations that are used when one is faced with a novel task that cannot be performed automatically. It includes forming concepts, identifying relationships, problem solving, drawing inferences, and reorganizing information. Miguel's G*f* ability was assessed through tasks that required him complete conceptual or geometrical analogies presented in matrix format (Analogic Reasoning, SS = 75 ± 7, *Low*). In addition, G*f* was assessed by tasks requiring him to construct abstract, geometrical designs with cubes while viewing a picture of the design (Cube Design, 75 ± 7, *Low*). Miguel's Fluid Intelligence cluster score of 75 ± 5 is ranked at the 5th percentile and is classified as *Low*. The variation of scores Miguel earned in this area was not statistically significant, suggesting uniform ability within this domain. Overall, Miguel's ability to reason and form concepts is low, compared to peers.

**Cross-Battery Assessment of G*c***: Crystallized intelligence is defined as the breadth and depth of a person's acquired knowledge. Included in this category is verbal communication, cultural knowledge, and reasoning with abilities that have already been developed. Miguel's G*c* ability was assessed through tasks that required him to place an X on one picture out of four that illustrates an object that is wrong or foolish (Picture Absurdities, 74 ± 7, *Low*) and to identify pictures which corresponded to words that are presented orally (PPVT-4, 76 ± 7, *Low*). The variation in scores Miguel earned in this area was not statistically significant, suggesting uniform ability within this domain. Miguel's Crystallized Intelligence cluster score of 75 ± 5 is ranked at the 5th percentile nationally and is classified as *Low*. Overall, Miguel's ability to use his acquired knowledge and accumulated experiences to solve everyday problems is low.

**Cross-Battery Assessment of G*v***: Visual processing refers to the ability to perceive, generate, synthesize, analyze, and think with visual patterns and stimuli. Miguel's G*v* ability was assessed by constructing abstract, geometrical designs while viewing a picture of the design (Cube Design, 75 ± 7, *Low*). In addition, Miguel was asked to reorder a prearranged set of picture cards to tell a logical story within a specified time limit (Picture Arrangement, 80 ± 7, *Low*). Because there is little variance, Miguel's obtained scores on these G*v* subtests combined to yield a cluster score of 78 ± 5, which is ranked at the 8th percentile nationally. This score suggests Miguel's Visual Processing is low.

**Cross-Battery Assessment of G*sm***: Short-term memory describes the ability to apprehend and hold information in immediate awareness and then use it within a few seconds. Miguel's G*sm* was assessed through tasks that required him to recreate a random pattern of dots after viewing the stimulus for five seconds (Spatial Memory, 105 ± 7, *Average*) and by asking him to reproduce sequences of symbols after being exposed to the stimulus for five seconds (Symbolic Memory, 95 ± 7, *Average*). Because there was no variation in Miguel's scores, a Short-Term Memory cluster score of 100 ± 5 was obtained. This score is ranked at the 50th percentile nationally and falls in the Average Classification.

**Cross-Battery Assessment of G*lr***: Long-term retrieval refers to the ability to store information and concepts in long-term memory and retrieve it later through association. Miguel's G*lr* was assessed through tasks that required him to recall objects depicted on the Associated Pairs subtest after approximately 30 min (Delayed Pairs, 93 ± 7, *Average*). More specifically, this subtest measured Miguel's Associative Memory, which is a narrow cluster included in the G*lr* factor. Because this was the only subtest that Miguel was administered in this factor, the narrow cluster of Associative Memory is the only representation of long-term retrieval.

**Cross-Battery Assessment of G*s***: Processing speed is defined as the ability to perform cognitive tasks automatically, particularly when under pressure to concentrate. Miguel's G*s* ability was assessed through tasks that required him to identify and cross out target stimuli embedded within rows of stimuli on a page that includes both target stimuli and several foils (Attention Sustained, 70 ± 7, *Low*), and to write numbers that correspond to symbols, based upon a number-symbol key provided at the top of the page (Coding, 75 ± 7, *Low*). Miguel's cluster score was 73 ± 5, which is ranked at the 3rd percentile and is classified as *Low*. Because there was no variation of scores in this area, Miguel's processing speed can be considered uniform.

**Assessment of Academic Achievement**: Miguel's achievement scores are consistent with his scores on the various tests of cognitive functioning. On the Woodcock Johnson IV Tests of Achievement (3/16/16), Miguel earned scores that ranged from *Very Low* to *Low Average*.

**Reading**: The Letter-Word Identification subtest measures the child's word identification and basic reading skills, including sight vocabulary, phonics, and structural analysis. Miguel's score of 68 (66–71, *Very Low*) on this test is equivalent to the average score of a child aged 6 years, 6 months. This score is low for Miguel's age and is ranked at the 2nd percentile nationally.

The Reading Fluency subtest provides a measure of the child's ability to quickly read and comprehend simple sentences. This test is part of the Broad Reading Cluster, which measures reading decoding, reading speed, and the ability to comprehend connected discourse while reading. Miguel's score of 73 (69–77, *Very Low*) on this subtest is equivalent to the average score of a child aged 6 years, 6 months. This score is ranked at the 4th percentile.

**Math**: The Calculation subtest falls in the Broad Math and Math Calculation Clusters, which provide a measure of math achievement including problem solving, number facility, automaticity, and reasoning. The Calculation subtest requires the child to perform mathematical computations. Miguel's score of 83 (78–89, *Low Average*) on this subtest is equivalent to the average score of a child aged 7 years, 0 months. This score falls at the 13th percentile nationally.

Lastly, the Applied Problems subtest is included in the Broad Math and Math Reasoning subtests and provides a measure of problem solving, analysis, reasoning, and vocabulary. Miguel's score of 88 (84–91, *Low Average*) on this subtest is equivalent to the score of a child aged 6 years, 11 months. This score is ranked at the 20th percentile.

**Data Integration and Interpretation**: Data derived from the administration of selected cognitive and achievement tests suggest that Miguel demonstrates low to average functioning across the various cognitive and academic domains. According to the cross-battery analyses, Miguel exhibits an intrapersonal strength in short and long-term memory. However, in general Miguel's pattern of cognitive weaknesses helps to explain the referral concerns and appear to underlie his reported difficulties in reading. For example, his low processing speed, fluid reasoning, crystallized intelligence, and visual processing all fall within the borderline to low average range. A pattern of scores such as Miguel's often predict limited academic functioning, particularly as the content becomes more complex and relies less on rote memorization. The shift in task demands from a high dependence on memory to stronger emphasis on understanding patterns and relationships is particularly salient at the third grade level.

Because Miguel's specific cognitive weaknesses appear to underlie his academic difficulties, his poor academic skills do not appear to be solely nor even primarily the result of factors such as limited English proficiency, nonsupportive educational environment, or cultural differences, although these variables may reduce academic skill acquisition to some degree.

**Summary and Recommendations**: Miguel is an eight-year-old boy who was administered selected cognitive and achievement tests. Data from these tests indicate that his cognitive functioning is low average and his academic achievement is considerably below average in Reading. Other academic areas are slightly below average also. He has several cognitive weaknesses. Miguel's memory scores were average when compared to other children his age, suggesting that his abilities in this area are not impaired. However, as the academic content becomes more sophisticated and less memory-dependent he will experience increasing difficulty unless instructional strategies are developed to take advantage of his relatively good memory. The integration of data from the various tests and teacher reports has provided the basis for the following recommendations:

1. Reading skills will be enhanced via exposure to a strong code-emphasis approach (e.g., Language! by Sopris West, and Slingerland's multisensory approach).
2. In order to address Miguel's reading comprehension difficulties, he should be provided with organizational strategies and worksheets to use when reading a passage or story. And, in general he will be aided by the use of advance organizers and other structural devices to facilitate awareness of relationships and structure inherent into-be-learned content.
3. Miguel will profit from the use of mnemonics and other strategies designed to take advantage of his relatively strong memory. He will benefit from exposure to concrete, factual information, using memory aids, rather than through discovery learning instructional techniques. Instruction requiring higher order comprehension should rely on well-learned rules, principles and laws (e.g., "a pint is a pound the world round.")

Jamie L. Smith, M.S.
Examiner in School Psychology

# References

Bracken, B. A., & McCallum, R. S. (2016). *Universal nonverbal intelligence test* (2nd ed.). Itasca, IL: Riverside.

Brown, L., Sherbenou, R. J., & Johnson, S. K. (2010). *Test of nonverbal intelligence* (4th ed.). Austin, TX: Pro-Ed.

Bowers, P., & Wolf, M. (1993). Theoretical links among naming speed, precise timing mechanisms, and orthographic skill in dyslexia. *Reading and Writing, 5,* 69–86.

Carroll, J. B. (1993). *Human cognitive abilities: A survey of factor-analytic studies.* Cambridge, England: Cambridge University Press.

Cattell, R. B. (1941). Some theoretical issues in adult intelligence testing. *Psychological Bulletin, 38,* 592.

Cattell, R. B. (1957). *Personality and motivation structure and measurement.* New York: World Book.

Cattell, R. B. (1963). Theory of crystallized and fluid intelligence. *Journal of Educational Psychology, 54,* 1–22.

Dunn, L. M., & Dunn, D. M. (2007). *Peabody picture vocabulary test—Fourth Edition.* Circle Pines, MN: American Guidance Services.

Flanagan, D. P., & McGrew, K. S. (1997). A cross-battery approach to assessing and interpreting cognitive abilities: Narrowing the gap between practice and cognitive science. In D. P. Flanagan, J. L. Genshaft, & P. L. Harrison (Eds.), *Contemporary intellectual assessment: Theories, tests, and issues* (pp. 314–325). New York: Guilford.

Flanagan, D. P., & Ortiz, S. (2001). *Essentials of cross-battery assessment.* New York: John Wiley & Sons.

Flanagan, D. P., Ortiz, S., & Alfonso, V. (2013). *Essentials of cross-battery assessment* (3rd ed.). New York: John Wiley & Sons.

Gustafsson, J. E., & Undheim, J. O. (1996). Individual differences in cognitive functions. In D. C. Berliner & R. C. Calfee (Eds.), *Handbook of educational psychology* (pp. 186–242). NY: Prentice Hall International.

Horn, J. L. (1965). *Fluid and crystallized intelligence: A factor analytic and developmental study of the structure among primary mental abilities.* Unpublished doctoral dissertation, University of Illinois, Champaign.

Horn, J. L. (1968). Organization of abilities and the development of intelligence. *Psychological Review, 75,* 242–259.

Horn, J. L. (1985). Remodeling old theories of intelligence: Gf-Gc theory. In B. B. Wolman (Ed.), *Handook of intelligence* (pp. 267–300). New York: Wiley.

Horn, J. L. (1988). Thinking about human abilities. In J. R. Nesselroade & R. B. Cattell (Eds.), *Handbook of multivariate psychology* (rev ed., pp. 645–685). New York: Wiley.

Horn, J. L. (1991). Measurement of intellectual capabilities: A review of theory. In K. S. McGrew, J. K. Werder, & R. W. Woodcock (Eds.), *Woodcock-Johnson technical manual* (pp. 197–232). Chicago: Riverside.

Mather, N. (1991). *An instructional guide to the Woodcock Johnson Psychoeducational Battery-Revised.* Brandon, VT: Clinical Psychology Publishing Company.

McGrew, K. S. (1997). Analysis of the major intelligence batteries according to a proposed comprehensive Gf-Gc framework. In D. P. Flanagan, J. L. Genshaft, & P. L. Harrison (Eds.), *Contemporary intellectual assessment: Theories, tests, and issues* (pp. 151–179). New York: Guilford.

McGrew, K. S., & Flanagan, D. P. (1998). *The intelli-gence test desk reference (ITDR): Gf-Gc cross-battery assessment*. Boston: Allyn & Bacon.

Roid, G. H., & Miller, L. J. (2013). *The leiter interna-tional performance scale—Fourth Edition* (3rd ed.). Torrance, CA: Western Psychological Services.

Wechsler, D., & Naglieri, J. A. (2006). *Wechsler nonverbal scale of ability*. San Antonio, TX: Pearson Clinical Assessment.

Woodcock, R. W. (1994). Measures of fluid and crystallized intelligence. In R. J. Sternberg (Ed.), *The encyclopedia of intelligence* (pp. 452–456). New York: Macmillan.

# Psychological and Physiological Influences on Multicultural and Nonverbal Assessment

Ryan E. McCallum and R. Steve McCallum

Performance on individualized, standardized test may be either enhanced or inhibited by the examinee's internal or external environment, a fact acknowledged by Terman and Merrill back in 1937 (as cited in McLoughlin and Lewis 2008). They noted the importance of following standardized procedures, ensuring accurate scoring of results, and obtaining the examinee's best effort as a result of establishing and maintaining adequate rapport. The *Standards for Educational and Psychological Testing* (Joint Committee of AERA, APA, and NCME 2014) acknowledge the importance of these recommendation and go on to provide several more admonitions (e.g., ensure that the examiner has adequate training, mention any deviation from standardized administration, ensure test item security). In general, the examiner is charged with eliminating test error, which leads to construct-irrelevant variance in the scores. Construct-irrelevant variance may occur as a result of within-the child or external influences that contribute to an examinee's score beyond the focus of the test, i.e., the

target abilities. Any test score is a function of systematic variance (construct relevant and construct irrelevance), as well as nonsystematic variance. Below we discuss some of the variables that contribute to both.

Acknowledging in a humorous way the biological reality that animals, including humans, really are not created equally one of the animals in George Orwell's *Animal Farm* (1946) says, "All animals are equal, but some animals are more equal than others." For example, some of us inherit genes that contribute to better (or worse) memory than most of our peers; similarly, some are more capable in other ways than their peers (e.g., faster processing speed, better reasoning skills, longer attention spans, better visual, or auditory processing). Some are born into more affluent family environments, with all the advantages inherent in that situation; others are born into poverty, and face the associated problems. Many of these differences will influence assessment results directly and in fact, some are the target of the assessment process, i.e., the examiner is interested in measuring these differences (e.g., working memory, processing speed). Other differences tend to be temporary, situational, and subject to change; they are created by the examinee, examiner, parents, or teachers and may be sources of construct-irrelevant variance and assessment error. It is these latter differences that are the primary focus of this chapter, and the goal for the examiner is to minimize them. Such sources of error may include negative assessment environments such as excessive room temperature, poor lighting, and inappropriate fit of

R.E. McCallum (✉)
School of Osteopathic Medicine, A. T. Still
University, 726 West Sequoia Lane,
Pinetop, AZ 85935, USA
e-mail: mccallum@astu.edu

R.S. McCallum
Department of Educational Psychology &
Counseling, University of Tennessee,
523 BEC, 1126 Volunteer Blvd,
Knoxville, TN 37996-3452, USA
e-mail: mccallum@utk.edu

© Springer International Publishing AG 2017
R.S. McCallum (ed.), *Handbook of Nonverbal Assessment*,
DOI 10.1007/978-3-319-50604-3_6

furniture to the examinee; other sources of within-the-examinee error may include hunger, exhaustion, too much or too little anxiety, poor motivation, negative influence of medication, and so on. Also, examinees bring both positive and/or negative perceptions of the testing enterprise forged in their particular subcultural milieus and examiners may need to spend more time gaining rapport with examinees who do not trust the intentions of the examiner.

Bracken (2007) notes four potential sources of construct-irrelevant influences on test results: (a) the examinee, (b) the examiner, (c) the environment, and (d) the instruments used. It is not our intent to address every possible influence, even if we could, but rather to address those most amenable to short-term control of the examiner and other caregivers. For example, the assessment environment should be created to increase the motivation of the examinee, to establish the optimal testing situation, and thereby obtain the most valid score. In this chapter, we discuss some of the more salient psychological and physiological characteristics of the assessment process, and focus most on the impact of these variables on nonverbal assessment.

## Psychological Influences

Psychological influences on the assessment process could be considered from a variety of perspectives. But one truism exists. All influences can be dichotomized into global categories as either within-the-child, such as personality or cognitive strengths/weaknesses, and outside-the-child, such as the environment, reinforcement history for effort, etc. For the purposes of this chapter, discussion will focus on psychological influences produced by certain unique characteristics of the examiner, by the environment of the test session, and by the examinee.

## Examiner Characteristics

Examiners who conduct complicated individualized assessments should possess the necessary training, and those who provide specialized individualized assessment beyond the traditional strategies should receive even more extensive training (e.g., examiners who work primarily with examinees who are not proficient in English, who are not from the mainstream culture, who live in poverty). Those who use individualized standardized tests of intelligence, personality, or achievement will have typically been trained to administer those tests in university training programs under close supervision. For example, standardized tests must be administered using the same procedures created when the test was developed (and normed). If administration procedures are not followed, the obtained scores contain error, more or less, depending on the amount of deviation (Cronbach 1960). Because nonverbal tests may require use of pantomime, gestures, etc. administration of nonverbal measures require even more extensive training, building on the basic skills. Bracken (2007) describes several psychometric considerations that should guide examiners choice of test selection for a particular examinee, including: reliability, validity, age, and appropriateness of norms, test floor, ceiling, and item gradients. It is the responsibility of the examiner to ensure the test chosen has adequate psychometric properties. Experts have provided some general rules for examiners to follow to ensure test quality. For example, for high-stakes educational decisions tests should possess an internal consistency reliability of 0.90, for screening purposes 0.80, and test floors and ceilings that adequately reflect extremes of performance (i.e., at least two standard deviations below and above the population mean, respective). Fortunately, several experts have provided guidelines for optimal test selection (e.g., Bracken and McCallum 1998; Joint Committee of AERA, APA, and NCME 2014; Sattler 2008).

After a test is selected but before the assessment actually starts, examiners need to know how to establish rapport, deal with unusual or oppositional examinees and obtain extra-test data to provide a context for the obtained scores— skills typically taught in university training programs. In addition to these basic skills, it is the responsibility of each examiner to know particular test instruments extremely well so that the routine test administration procedures are automatized. As mentioned above, particular tests may use unique administration procedures. For example, the UNIT and UNIT2 (Bracken and McCallum 1998, 2016) use eight specific administration gestures—the examiner should know how to use the gestures well before administering this test. In short, the examiner should not have to devote energy and attention to the mechanics of test administration, but should be relatively free to observe the examinee's behavior in the test situation and to establish a good pace, with little or no dead time between activities and subtests. Automatizing the test administration process allows the examiner time to observe carefully examinee and test environment characteristics, such as obvious health status of the examinee, size compared to peers, dress, grooming, effort, problem-solving strategies, external distractions, and so on. The examiner should be pleasant, sincere, encouraging, even cheerful, but should maintain a structured and somewhat business-like attitude. Encouragement for effort (but not contingent on correct responses) is essential, particularly early on in the session, and the examiner should be attuned to the tempo of the examinee and follow suit, allowing those who are more comfortable with a rapid pace to proceed accordingly. Examiners should be sensitive to the other needs of the examinees. For example, younger examinees may need restroom breaks more often; examinees who are easily frustrated or give up easily should be given more encouragement; and examinees who become bored easily should be moved along quickly to allow them to engage in the more difficult items.

Examiners should communicate important information to examinees before the exam begins, or before particular subtests. Some examples of information that could be critical to include: examinees need to know that they are not expected to answer all questions accurately, about how long they will be expected to work, task requirements and the nature of the responses expected (e.g., pointing, verbal responses),

whether a subtest is timed (e.g., by prominently displaying a stopwatch), whether questions can be repeated, and any unique test demands (e.g., use of gesture, constructing puzzles).

Although the examiner characterizations described in this section generally apply to most examinees, Santos de Barona and Barona (2007) note that examiners may need to make accommodations for culturally different examinees, and the same generalization hold for examinees who are different in other respects (e.g., hard of hearing, have emotional problems, limited cognitive abilities). Stantos de Barona and Barona urge examinees to consider the optimal style and tempo for a particular examinee and modify their behavior accordingly, noting that examiners may have to adopt a facilitative style for some culturally different examinees. They note that in the U.S. failure to make eye contact is considered a sign of disrespect, but just the opposite is the case in some other cultures. Similarly, examiners may need to modify the administration and/or interpretation process due to language difficulties. For example, examiners may need to choose a language reduced or nonverbal test, or conduct an analysis to determine whether the culture and language loading of subtests administered negatively impacted performance according to the guidelines offered by Flanagan et al. (2013). In some cases, examiners may choose to test-the-limits by modifying administration directions, as described below, but only after the test was administered using standardized directions initially.

As with examinees who are culturally different, examiners must be particularly vigilant when evaluating special needs examinees. McLoughlin and Lewis (2008) do a fine job of discussing the importance of making modifications in test administration and the conditions under which modifications are allowed. For example, they note that modifications can be made after a test has been administered according to the standardization directions initially. In this test-the-limits procedure examinees may engage in a variety of modifications, including paraphrasing, allowing additional modeling of the task demands, reducing the difficulty of the language used to convey task demands, allowing a different response mode ,such as pointing rather than verbalizations, providing additional feedback, and so on. Any deviations from the standard administration procedures should be acknowledged.

## Testing Environment Characteristics

The testing environment should provide the optimal space and atmosphere in order to maximize test results, i.e., it should convey an upbeat atmosphere, safety, and comfort. It should be pleasant, but not distracting. Materials should be accessible to the examinee, which requires furniture of the appropriate height and size. For example, the furniture should be small enough for the examinee's feet to touch the floor to increase comfort and decrease the likelihood of circulation problems and the distracting tingling sensation that accompanies it. Lighting, temperature, and noise levels should be appropriate. The testing room should be pleasing but not filled with too many distracting bulletin boards, decorations, or windows. If there is a window the examinee should be oriented away from it to prevent outside distractions. The examiner should be positioned closer to the door than the examinee to discourage the examinee from suddenly leaving the room. Test materials should be presented in a manner consistent with standardization, but close enough to the examinee to facilitate easy use. Most test administration manuals describe the juxtaposition of materials, examiner, and examinee. For standardized testing, it is typical for the examinee and the examiner to sit at an angle across the corner of the testing table; the examiner usually sits closest to the examinee's dominant hand to facilitate manipulating the materials more easily and seeing the examinee's responses. The table should be flat and smooth, and cleared of all material except the test stimuli. Typically, the testing room contains only the examiner and examinee, but occasionally a third person may be necessary, at least initially (e.g., an interpreter, a parent for a very young or frightened child). If a third party is present, the testing guidelines should be explained to prevent spoiling the examinee's responses. For example, parents need to know that the examinee should provide answers to the particular test questions without help.

To allow examiners to address the extent to which the testing environment is optimal McLoughlin and Lewis (2008) provide a testing environment checklist. The checklist allows examinees to assess room, seating, and equipment characteristics as optimal, adequate, or poor. Room characteristics include variables, such as size, lighting, temperature, ventilation, noise level, distractions, interruptions. Seating characteristics include appropriateness of chairs, table, arrangement of furniture. Equipment characteristics include quality of testing materials, writing implements, timing devices. Of course, to update this list of important characteristics, we might add the quality and fit of computer equipment, if relevant.

## Examinee Characteristics

Many of the general guidelines presented in this chapter are appropriate for verbal and nonverbal assessment. However, the primary focus of the chapter and book is on nonverbal assessment, which is appropriate in a number of situations (e.g., for deaf children, those with language deficits, and those from other cultures). Examinees from cultures other than the mainstream culture may possess shared characteristics, i.e., behaviors associated with membership in their particular culture. These shared characteristics allow for some generalizations about the problem-solving strategies and general test-taking strategies, attitudes, etc. of examinees from that culture (e.g., the reflective styles of some Asian cultures), though examiners must guard against making stereotypical judgments that would negatively impact performance (see Santos de Barona and Barona 2007; Sattler 2008). Seasoned examiners will want to explore the subculture of examinees before the testing session. For example, speeded performance, wearing high-status clothes, and glibness are prized in the U.S., but are not emphasized in some cultures. As Bracken and Barona (1991) note, "The specific individual experiences of non majority culture individuals will greatly influence their educational, emotional, and language development" (p. 129). Examinees from non-mainstream cultures (as well as those who are deaf and/or from other language-deficit populations) may have unique styles of problem solving. For example, they may not prize an independent problem-solving milieu, but may be much more comfortable working in a cooperative arrangement. They may not value speeded performance, or appreciate the "logic" inherent in western-style categorization and classification (Sternberg and Grigorenko 2001). And, for those examinees whose first language is not English, an interpreter or bilingual psychologist or teacher may be needed to interact successfully with the examinee and/or family members. Importantly, examiners must not assume that the primary instrument used for *bilingual* examinees should be an English language instrument; often, bilingual students are not sufficiently proficient for a valid assessment in English, and would be better served by administration of a nonverbal measure. The successful examiner will be alert to these types of population differences and know in advance how best to address them. As noted in the Examiner section above, test results of examinees who may be disenfranchised by administration of highly language or culturally loaded tests/subtests should be subjected to analyses within the framework created by Flanagan et al. (2007, 2013) and described in some detail in Chap. 1 of this volume. This analysis allows the cultural/language influences of subtests to be determined using the Culture-Language Test Classification scheme (C-LTC). Using, this procedure examiners can get some sense of test performance as a function of the language and cultural loading of the subtests administered.

Examiners should be aware that parents' perceptions of their child's social skills, cognitive sophistication, academic motivation, and integration into the U.S. culture may be helpful in interpreting test behavior and results. Parent interviews are often extremely helpful to establish a more meaningful context (e.g., the extent to which education is valued, the extent to which the examinee's nonverbal behavior is encouraged/discouraged). Takushi and Uomoto (2001) describe the components of a successful multicultural clinical interview, and many of their suggestions are relevant for interviewing parents of referred children as well as the children themselves.

As previously noted, examinees who have special needs (e.g., speech and language problems, difficulty hearing, very limited cognitive ability, as is typical for examinees with Down's Syndrome, serious emotional, or psychiatric disorders) require unique expertise. But, unlike culturally different examinees who have a history of adequate communication in a language other than English, these examinees sometimes have a long history of frustration associated with their inability to hear and/or express themselves effectively in any language. In some cases, there is an emotional overlay associated with this frustration that negatively impacts assessment. For example, these individuals may exhibit less persistence when they are not understood. Examiners should bring to bear all their behavior management skills to establish rapport, gently but firmly maintain control of the session, and implement assessment in a timely and efficient manner. Usually, the best strategy for the examiner is to spend a short amount of time establishing a productive relationship, then relatively quickly engage the examinee in the test process. Remember, the goal of the examiner is not to provide treatment, but to obtain optimal test performance in a timely manner.

Examinees who have physical disabilities, such as Cerebral Palsy, present particular challenges. The examiner must observe the examinee beforehand to determine the level of proficiency available relative to the test demands. Some modifications may be necessary, such as altering the height of the testing table, providing smaller or larger chairs than the room initially provides, obtaining unusually bright lighting for those with limited vision, etc. Recent innovations in technology make certain aspects of existing tests available to physically limited individuals via menu-driven computer programs and laser-guided "pointers," guided only by head movement. Examiners must report the extent to which a particular test administration differs from standardized administration, and estimate the effects on the obtained scores.

Finally, examinees with limited verbal skills due to emotional problems are particularly challenging. For example, selective/elective mutes will not talk to the examiner in all likelihood; in addition, they may be very shy and noncompliant in other ways as well. And examinees with certain emotional problems and poor reality testing, such as autism, or Asperger's Disorder may be particularly difficult to motivate, as are those who are socially maladjusted or oppositional. Establishing rapport may be very difficult. These examinees are socially disconnected and will seem distant and uninvolved. Similarly, establishing rapport with examinees who are oppositional or defiant may be difficult if not impossible. Examiners should know the characteristics of these diagnostic categories and not be surprised or discouraged by examinee behavior. Examinees who have poor reality testing (e.g., those with diagnoses of psychotic conditions, including schizophrenia) may be completely uncooperative. Time spent in reviewing records to determine hobbies and interests of the examinees may be useful. Seasoned examiners will be aware of the characteristics associated with typical "diagnostic categories" in general and will take the time to become familiar with the particular characteristics of specific examinees before the evaluation begins. Certainly, it is important to know how diagnostic characteristics may vary as a function of particular examinee characteristics.

## Some Physiological Influences

Although detailed treatment of physiological influences on test performance is beyond the scope of this chapter, some of those influences were mentioned in the sections above. For example, examiners need to accommodate to biologically determined conditions, such as deafness, Cerebral Palsy, Down's Syndrome, etc. These impairments result from physiological anomalies and trauma and they impact in a mutually reciprocal fashion both the external and the internal environments of examinees. In addition, there are other subtle physiological influences that result primarily from the contribution of multiple-gene pairs (interacting with the environment). In their important article entitled "The Genetic Basis of Complex Human Behaviors" Plomin et al. (1994) discuss the case genetic research has built for the importance of genetic factors in the acquisition of many complex personality and cognitive abilities (and disabilities), including reading disability, autism, affective disorders, schizophrenia, Alzheimer's disease, memory, processing speed, extraversion, verbal and spatial reasoning, and general intelligence. Using twin studies and other sources of data these researchers discuss the "heritability factor" for these characteristics, noting that heritability can be estimated roughly by doubling the differences between the intraclass correlations obtained from monozygotic and dizygotic twins. This statistic is considered to represent the proportion of phenotypic variance in a population that can be attributed to genetic influence. According to the calculations reported by Plomin, Owen and McGuffin, heritabilities for personality, scholastic achievement, verbal and spatial reasoning, and general intelligence range from 40 to 50%. Others discuss how genes contribute to very specific individual personality differences, such as optimism, risk taking, gregariousness, even homosexuality (e.g., Pool 1997). It is increasingly apparent that many behavioral scientists have shifted dramatically from "nurture," to "nature" as an explanation of the origin of behavior. In fact, environmentalism peaked in 1950s and 1960s and has been on the decline since, due in part to the increasing sophisticated knowledge base now available via innovative medical technologies. These medical advances are capable of showing the power of biology to explain behaviors once thought to be totally environmentally determined (e.g., autism).

Many of the physiological influences are so powerful that they restrict assessment totally to nonverbal means (e.g., Cerebral Palsy, deafness). In fact, most of this book is devoted to describing nonverbal strategies to assess intelligence and related constructs. However, as mentioned above, many physiological influences on the assessment process are subtle, and those less obvious influences are the primary focus of this chapter.

Examiners are becoming increasingly aware that even the subtle physiological contributions to the testing session can have significant impact. How does this information help in the evaluation of nonverbal behavior? This awareness can sensitize examiners to be alert to these sources of behavioral variation. One important line of research that is helping to define the link between the influence of physiology and test behavior focuses on behavior constellations or traits referred to as temperaments; temperaments are assumed to be the building blocks of personality and produce individual differences in problem-solving abilities in general and influence the manner in which intelligence is displayed in testing situations in particular.

Although a number of child development experts have discussed the origin and typology of temperaments (e.g., Kagan 1994a, b), perhaps the most comprehensive description has been offered by Thomas et al. (1968) and colleagues. Chess and Thomas (1984) describe temperament as akin to a "behavioral style," and note that it may be best viewed as referring to the how of behavior. They note that two children may dress themselves alike and may have similar interests and even similar success in meeting life's challenges. However, they may differ significantly with regard to the quickness with which they move, the ease with which they approach a new task or physical environment, the intensity of their mood, the effort they display, the activity level, and so on. Thomas et al. (1968) note that temperaments are forged by biology via interactions with the environment; however, biology seems to be a strong determinant because variation in temperaments can be distinguished very early in an infant's life.

Thomas et al. (1968) identified temperaments by observing (and following over time) the behavior of very young infants. They identified nine basic temperaments along continua, as follows: activity level, rhythmicity (regularity of habits), distractibility, tendency to approach or avoid new situations, adaptability, attention span and task persistence, quality of mood, intensity of reaction, and threshold of responsiveness. In a longitudinal study children were followed for years, from infancy through the toddler stage, and even into adolescence. Using these nine categories, Thomas et al. (1968) found that most children could be identified as either "easy," "difficult" or "slow to warm up." Easy children where those positive in mood, adaptable, regular in feeding, eating, sleeping habits, able to attend, and persevere. The difficult children exhibited very irregular habits, responded impulsively, were labile in mood, unable to maintain task persistence, etc. The "slow to warm up" group exhibited behaviors somewhere in between, e.g., showing a reluctance to engage the environment until they were sure it held no surprises, somewhat irregular in habits and mood, somewhat persistent, etc. A few of the children were not easy to categorize and did not fit nicely into the three groups.

Obviously, it is possible to see how temperaments can impact the testing situation. For example, examinees who are highly distractible, show little task persistence, highly active, impulsive, or extremely shy will present significant challenges to the examiner. Of course, these characteristics may interact with other influences, such as medications, lack of sleep, hunger, etc. Examiners should be aware of and report whether the examinee was on or off medications. Of course, examiners may request that parents refrain from administering behavior-altering medications on the day of the evaluation if the intent is to assess the child's natural state.

Examiners should become aware of the power of certain commonly administered medications to affect testing behavior. There are several resources available to examiners that describe behavioral effects of medications (e.g., Wilens 1999). And many children take either over the counter or prescribed medicines currently. Some of the more commonly used medications includes methylphenidate, pemoline, or dextroamphetamine for attention deficits or hyperactivity, diazepam, or clorazepate for anxiety, haloperidol, thioridazine, or clorzapine for psychoses, imipramine, amitriptyline, desipramine, bupropion, or trazodone for affective disorders and/or obsessive-compulsive disorders and/or enuresis, albuterol for asthma, diphenhydramine, hydroxyzine, promethazine, or cyproheptadine for congestion, and phenobarbitol for seizures. All of these medications can cause side effects, including impulsivity, excitability, drowsiness, agitations, etc. (See the next section and related tables for a more detailed description of medication effects on the assessment process).

Examiners who are knowledgeable regarding physiological influences will be alert to how these influences can affect the examinee in the testing session, realizing that many of these behaviors will be present also in the classroom and home settings, and will impact the success of the child in social and academic situations. Examiners who possess this knowledge can help parents and teachers modify the environment to facilitate behavior change, but they can also help parents and teachers understand the relative influences of physiology and environment. Thus, they can help target environmentally based behavior change efforts toward those behaviors more amenable to environmental impact.

Obviously, the physiological environment of the examinee significantly contributes to the quality of the testing session, and by inference to the quality of the child's life in general. The experienced examiner will be alert to these influences and note those that are salient, in either a positive or negative manner. Because these influences will also contribute to the examinee's success outside the testing session the experienced examiner will help teachers and parents identify and link appropriate treatments to problem behaviors, treatments that take into account the extent to which particular problem behaviors are amenable to environmental influences (vs. those which might be more resistant to environmentally focused treatments but more amenable to biological treatments, such as medication).

## Effects of Medications, Supplements, and Drugs of Abuse

Medications, supplements, and drugs of abuse can affect the examinee's physiology, thereby potentially altering mental capacity (e.g., working and long-term memory, attentional control, processing speed), as well as mood, affect, motor skills, and other organ system functioning. Overall, the effects of substances can indeed impact assessment results, either positively or negatively; for example, some medication affects are intended and therapeutic. On the other hand, substances may cause unintended adverse effects and potentially lower assessment results.

In this section, commonly used medications, supplements, and drugs of abuse are outlined, as is the extent to which these substances can affect the examinee and skew assessment results. The goals of this section of the chapter for the examiner are threefold. First, it is critical for the examiner to recognize and anticipate physiological, behavioral, and cognitive effects of commonly used medications and supplements, particularly, as they relate to assessment, and relevant information is provided below. Second, it may be advantageous to recommend discontinuing medication for assessment purposes, and strategies for doing so safely are shared. Third, it is important for examiners to recognize the effects of illicit drugs on complex test behavior; examiners may terminate the testing session if it obvious that the examinee is in an altered state precipitated or exacerbated by drug abuse. Below we describe the basic function of common medications by class, and generic descriptors are provided. In addition, detailed information about commonly prescribed medications by trade name, illicit drugs, and the effects of common supplements is provided in tables at the end of the chapter.

## Prescription and Over the Counter Medications

Initially, we consider commonly used prescription and nonprescription, or over the counter, medicines that can alter examinee behaviors. In this section, the following classes of medication will be described: central nervous system (CNS) stimulants and atomoxetine, antidepressants, sedative-hypnotics, antipsychotics (typical and atypical), lithium, antiseizure medications, and both prescription and over the counter nonpsychiatric medications with psychotropic effects. This is significant because examiners are likely to encounter examinees who are taking at least some of the following medications and should have a working knowledge of how they could impact testing results.

## CNS Stimulants and the Nonstimulant, Atomoxetine

For the purposes of this section, CNS stimulants, or stimulants for short, will be subdivided into three smaller subcategories: methylphenidate products, amphetamine products, and other stimulants. Also Atomoxetine, a nonstimulant used as a second-line agent to treat ADHD will be described in this section.

**Methylphenidate products and amphetamine products.** These two subclasses of stimulants have been the mainstay of attention deficit/hyperactivity disorder (ADHD) treatment for decades and remain first-line pharmacotherapy agents used to treat it. Additionally, many of the stimulants that are used to treat ADHD are also used to treat the daytime sleepiness component of narcolepsy (e.g., dextroamphetamine and methylphenidate).

When examiners encounter examinees taking stimulants, a few principals should be considered. First, they are often prescribed to improve academic, behavioral, emotional, and social functioning associated with ADHD by addressing hyperactivity, impulsivity, and/or inattention, and as a result, can assist in improving assessment results (American Academy of Pediatrics (AAP) 2011; American Psychiatric Association (APA) 2013). Also, the active ingredients in the methylphenidate and amphetamine subclasses have different durations of activity, and, therefore different dosing recommendations (see Table 6.1 for duration of medication action). The unintended and unwanted adverse effects should also be weighed. These include anxiety, insomnia and irritability that could potentially affect the examinee and his or her test results (see Table 6.1 for a more exhaustive list). Finally, if the decision to discontinue stimulate medications is made, physical affects from abrupt discontinuation are not life-threatening; however, depression and excessive sleeping are common, and proper supervision and monitoring of the examinee should be arranged (Breggin 2013).

**Other stimulants.** Another subclass of stimulants we call "other stimulants" has a wide range of uses. For instance, some of these medicines (armodafinil and modafinil) can be used to treat ADHD (although not approved by the United States Food and Drug Administration, or FDA, for this purpose). However, these medications are less often prescribed for ADHD and instead used primarily to treat narcolepsy and obstructive sleep apnea (see Table 6.1 for specific information on the names of agents in this subclass and their respective indications). As expected, daytime sleepiness does return after discontinuation of these medications; however, stopping modafinil abruptly typically does not cause dangerous withdrawal symptoms (Provigil prescribing information, 2015).

Two other stimulants, phentermine and phendimetrazine, exploit the "adverse effect" of appetite suppression that commonly occurs with many CNS stimulants to treat patients struggling with obesity. These medications can also cause anxiety and irritability, potentially altering assessment scores. Phentermine, the most commonly used medication in this subclass, causes only minor discontinuation symptoms if discontinued abruptly. For example, in one study, some subjects that stopped phentermine abruptly reported excessive hunger as the only adverse effect (Hendricks and Greenway 2011).

**Table 6.1** Stimulants and Other Medications for Attention Deficit Hyperactive Disorder (ADHD)

| Subclass and indication, generic name (brand name) | Clinical application | Physiological/adverse effects |
|---|---|---|
| **Amphetamine Stimulants** | | |
| Amphetamine and Dextroamphetamine (Adderall); Dextroamphetamine (Dexedrine, Dextrostat); long-acting Amphetamine and Dextroamphetamine (Adderall XR); Lisdexamfetamine (Vyvanse) | ADHD, narcolepsy | Appetite suppression, weight loss, insomnia, irritability, tics, restlessness, dependence. Duration of action: amphetamine and dextroamphetamine combination, dextroamphetamine, long-acting amphetamine and dextroamphetamine combination: 3-8 h; dextroampheamine and lidexamfetamine: 8–12 h |
| **Methylphenidate Stimulants** | | |
| Methylphenidate (Ritalin, Methylin); Dexmethylphenidate (Focalin); long-acting Methylphenidate (Metadate ER, Methylin ER, Ritalin LA, Concerta, Quillivant XR, Daytrana patch); long-acting Dexmethylphenidate (Focalin XR) | ADHD, narcolepsy | Appetite suppression, weight loss, insomnia, irritability, tics, restlessness, dependence. Duration of action: methylphenidate, dexmethyphenidate: 3–4 h; long-acting methylphenidate, long-acting dexmethylphenidate: 6–12 h |
| **Other Stimulants** | | |
| Armodafinil (Nuvigil); Modafinil (Provigil) | Narcolepsy, obstructive sleep apnea, shift-work disorder | Headache, palpitations, insomnia, anxiety, dizziness, depression, agitation, gastrointestinal upset, dependence. Duration of action: armodafinil, modafinil: 6–12 h |
| Phendimetrazine (Bontril PDM); Phentermine (Adinex-P, Suprenza); Benzphetamine (Regimex); Diethylpropion (Tenuate) | Obesity | Flushing, high blood pressure, increased heart rate, agitation, dizziness, headache, insomnia, psychosis, restlessness, gastrointestinal upset, tremor, blurred vision, dependence. Duration of action: phendimetrazone: 8–12 h (capsule) or 4–6 h (tablet); phentermine: 6–12 h; benzphetamine: 3–4 h; diethylproprion: 4–12 h |
| **Nonstimulant (Norepinephrine Reuptake Inhibitor) for ADHD** | | |
| Atomoxetine[a] (Strattera) | ADHD | Insomnia, anxiety, fatigue, gastrointestinal upset, dizziness, dry mouth. Duration of action: 24 h |

Note: Information in table adapted from WebMD http://www.webmd.com/add-adhd/guide/adhd-medication-chart and Lexicomp Online http://www.wolterskluwercdi.com/lexicomp-online/
[a]Medications that include United States Food and Drug Administration (FDA) Boxed Warning for suicide ideation in children and adolescents. *Source* FDA Website

**Nonstimulant—atomoxetine**. Atomoxetine is a nonstimulant used to treat ADHD. This medication avoids some of the side effects and abuse potential of stimulants; consequently, it is an option for stimulant therapy failure or in cases where narcotics are not appropriate. Although not a stimulant, atomoxetine can, nevertheless, cause side effects like irritability and anxiety. Notably, some evidence suggests that atomoxetine may increase suicide ideation and action, particularly soon after starting the medication. This prompted the FDA to issue a Boxed Warning regarding the increased risk of suicide in children and adolescents taking atemoxetine (Labbate et al. 2010). Atomoxetine can be stopped abruptly without ill effect, although many practitioners still opt to discontinue this medication slowly over 2–4 weeks (Wernicke et al. 2004).

## Antidepressants

Many medications comprise the antidepressant class, and many of the agents within this class are prescribed to treat multiple psychological, behavioral, and cognitive diagnoses (see Table 6.2). Therefore, the examiner is bound to encounter these medicines frequently. Below, we discuss the following medication subclasses: monoamine oxidase inhibitors (MAOIs), tricyclic antidepressants (TCAs), selective serotonin reuptake inhibitors (SSRIs), serotonin-norepinephrine reuptake inhibitors (SNRIs), benzodiazepines, and finally, we examine a small group containing medicines that do not fit neatly in the above antidepssant categories. Although it may seem counterintuitive, some evidence suggests that all antidepressants may increase suicide ideation and/or action, although many of these findings are somewhat controversial. In any case, the FDA directed the manufacturers of antidepressants to include a Boxed Warning regarding the increased risk of suicidality.

**Monoamine oxidase inhibitors**. MAOIs are indicated for depression and related mood disorders. Although prescribed infrequently because of dangerous interactions with certain foods and many medications, examiners may still see these medications used to treat adults with difficult-to-treat depression, panic disorder and anxiety (Gelenberg et al. 2010; Kalikow 2011). Mixing MAOIs with larger quantities of tyramine-rich foods, such as aged cheese, soy sauce, tofu, sourdough bread, and draft beer can cause dangerous spikes in blood pressure called hypertensive crises. Additionally, combining MAOIs with other medications that increase serotonin levels in the brain (e.g., SSRIs and SNRIs, discussed below) can be dangerous and is strongly discouraged. Too much serotonin can cause serotonin syndrome, which manifests as constellation of signs and symptoms, such as anxiety, delirium, restlessness, tachycardia, hyperthermia, hypertension, vomiting, and diarrhea (Katzung 2015). MAOI discontinuation should occur over a slow taper (over two to four weeks), which helps avoid delirium, agitation, and insomnia that can accompany an abrupt cessation (Labbate et al. 2010; Lejoyeux and Adès 1997).

**Tricyclic antidepressants**. Before the advent of SSRIs and newer SNRIs, TCAs were the mainstay in psychopharmacologic depression therapy. Along with depression disorders, TCAs are prescribed to treat a wide range of diagnoses, including chronic pain disorders, incontinence, obsessive-compulsive disorder, ADHD, migraine headaches, chronic pain syndrome, and others but these medications are associated with several and potentially dangerous side effects (Katzung 2015). Notably, TCAs have marked anticholinergic and antihistaminic actions that cause adverse effects, such as dry mouth, constipation, confusion, and delirium, which may influence assessment results. TCA discontinuation should occur over a slow taper (over two to four weeks) in order to avoid withdrawal-associated gastrointestinal distress, malaise, chills, and muscle aches that can accompany an abrupt cessation (Labbate et al. 2010; Breggin 2013).

**Selective serotonin reuptake inhibitors**. SSRIs are used frequently to treat many psychological, behavioral, and cognitive disorders, such as depression, anxiety, disruptive disorders,

**Table 6.2** Antidepressants

| Subclass, generic name (brand name) | Clinical applications | Physiological/adverse effects |
|---|---|---|
| **Monoamine Oxidase Inhibitors (MAOIs)** | | |
| Phenelzine[a] (Nardil)<br>Tranylcypromine[a] (Parnate)<br>Selegiline[a] (Eldepryl, Emsam, Zelapar) | Major depression unresponsive to other drugs, Parkinson's disease (selegiline) | Low blood pressure, insomnia. Drug-food interactions: hypertensive crisis with tyramine-containing food/drink. Adds to risk of serotonin syndrome (signs and symptoms include agitation, confusion, dilated pupils, sweating, high blood pressure, vomiting) |
| **Tricyclic Antidepressants (TCAs)** | | |
| Amitriptyline[a] (Elavil)<br>Clomipramine[a] (Anafranil)<br>Desipramine[a] (Norapramin)<br>Doxepin[a] (Silenor)<br>Imipramine[a] (Tofranil)<br>Nortriptyline[a] (Pamelor) | Major depression not responsive to other drugs, chronic pain disorders, incontinence, attention deficit/hyperactivity disorder, obsessive-compulsive disorder (clomipramine) | Anticholinergic effects (dry mouth, constipation, blurred vision, delirium), headache, dizziness, low blood pressure, sedation, weight gain, seizures in overdose |
| **Selective Serotonin Reuptake Inhibitors (SSRIs)** | | |
| Fluoxetine[a] (Prozac, Sarafem)<br>Citalopram[a] (Celexa)<br>Escitalopram[a] (Lexapro)<br>Paroxetine[a] (Paxil, Pexeva)<br>Sertraline[a] (Zoloft)<br>Fluvoxamine[a] (Luvox) | Major depression, anxiety disorders, panic disorders, obsessive-compulsive disorder, posttraumatic stress disorder, bulimia | Sexual dysfunction, drowsiness, weight gain, insomnia, anxiety, dizziness, headache, dry mouth, tremor, gastrointestinal upset, adds to risk of serotonin syndrome (signs and symptoms include agitation, confusion, dilated pupils, sweating, high blood pressure, vomiting) |
| **Serotonin-Norepinephrine Reuptake Inhibitors (SNRIs)** | | |
| Duloxetine[a] (Cymbalta, Irenka)<br>Venlafaxine[a] (Effexor XR)<br>Levomilnacipran[a] (Fetzima)<br>Desvenlafaxine[a] (Khedezla, Pristiq)<br>Milnacipran[a] (Savella) | Major depression, chronic pain disorders, fibromyalgia | Anticholinergic effects (dry mouth, constipation, blurred vision, delirium), albeit less than TCAs, sedation, nausea, dizziness, high blood pressure |
| **Tetracyclics, Unicyclics** | | |
| Bupropion[a] (Aplenzin,<br>Budeprion, Buproban, Wellbutrin, Zyban)<br>Mirtazapine[a] (Remeron) | Major depression, smoking cessation (bupropion) | Lowers seizure threshold, anxiety (bupropion); sedation and weight gain (mirtazepine) |
| **Serotonin Receptor Modulators** | | |
| Nefazodone[a] (Serzone)<br>Trazodone[a] (Oleptro) | Major depression, insomnia (off label trazodone indication) | Headache, dizziness, fatigue, drowsiness, blurred vision, low blood pressure, dry mouth, delirium: trazodone |
| Vortioxetine[a] (Brintellix) | Major depression | Gastrointestinal upset, sexual dysfunction |

Note: Information in table adapted from Summary Antidepressants table: Basic and Clinical Pharmacology, 13e and Handbook of Psychiatric Drug Therapy and Lexicomp Online http://www.wolterskluwercdi.com/lexicomp-online/

[a]Medications that include a United States Food and Drug Administration (FDA) Boxed Warning for suicide ideation in children and adolescents

posttraumatic stress disorder, and others. Compared to MAOIs and TCAs, the adverse affects of these medications and drug–drug interactions are fewer and less severe (see Table 6.2). Importantly, there are a couple of adverse effects that could skew testing results. For example, agitation and anxiety have been reported in over 10% of the individuals using SSRIs and usually occurs early in therapy (usually within the first few days). Additionally, 10–30% of patients experience cognitive and memory symptoms, such as difficulties with focusing and recall, as well as trouble finding words (Labbate et al. 2010). Examiners should be aware of the effects of abrupt cessation of SSRIs, which may lead to dizziness, nausea, fatigue, muscle aches, chills, anxiety, and irritability within days of stopping medication. Instead it is recommended to taper these medications over days to weeks, the exact time frame depending on the elimination half-life of the particular agent (van Geffen et al. 2005).

**Serotonin-norepinephrine reuptake inhibitors.** SNRIs treat depression and anxiety as well as chronic pain disorders. Broadly speaking, SSRIs and SNRIs share many adverse effects, see Table 6.2, including potential suicidal thoughts. It is also worth mentioning SNRIs can cause deliurm, albeit this side effect occurs infrequently in this class. As with SSRIs, a slow taper is preferred over abrupt termination of SNRIs (Labbate et al. 2010; Kalikow 2011).

**Tetracyclics, unicyclics.** Bupropion has been shown to be helpful in major depressive disorder as well as ADHD (Labbate et al. 2010). Bupropion also has the unique indication of assisting individuals with smoking cessation (Katzung 2015). Pertinent adverse effects include anxiety as well as lowering seizure threshold in susceptible individuals. No rapid discontinuation symptoms have been recognized for bupropion.

Mirtazapine is an example of a medication in this subclass of antidepressants that affects several receptors and neurotransmitters, which makes it an effective option for depression, but can also add side effects that other, more precisely targeted antidepressants do not produce. For example, examiners may note that examinees

exhibit sedation, dry mouth, delirium, and dizziness. Abrupt cessation reports are varied and inconsistent and guidelines advise slowly discontinuing mirtazapine over a few weeks (Shelton 2001).

**Serotonin Receptor modulators.** There are two medications in this subclass, trazodone and nefazodone. Trazodone is used more often and primarily treats insomnia as well as depression. These medications are not prescribed often because they have been replaced by more effective, better tolerated antidepressants discussed earlier. Examiners should be aware that side effects can include headache, dizziness, fatigue, and blurred vision (Katzung 2015).

## Sedative-Hypnotics

The aim of prescribing a sedative medication is to reduce anxiety and exert a calming effect, although many sedatives are also prescribed to treat insomnia (see Table 6.2). Hypnotics, on the other hand, are used almost exclusively to promote onset and maintenance of sleep (Katzung 2015). Included under the sedative-hypnotic classification are benzodiazepines, barbiturates, newer hypnotics used for insomnia, melatonin receptor agonists and serotonin receptor antagonists, namely buspirone.

**Benzodiazepines.** Benzodiazepines (often recognizable by their characteristic–epam ending, alprazolam, lorazepam, etc.) are prescribed often to treat insomnia and anxiety disorders. As expected, these medicines cause drowsiness and sedation, which assist in treating insomnia and anxiety disorders, but, paradoxically, benzodiazepines are noted to cause disinhibition as well. Disinhibition is a rare, unintended effect of benzodiazepine therapy that examinees may see manifested as aggressive (or other socially inappropriate) behavior, insomnia, irritability, sleep disturbances, and even psychoses (Katzung 2015). If these symptoms occur, the examiner may choose to consult with school personnel and parents. Of note, sudden discontinuation of benzodiazepines is dangerous and should be avoided because it can precipitate seizures. Instead, a slow taper discontinuation over weeks or months is indicated (Labbate et al. 2010).

**Barbiturates**. Barbiturates, such as phenobarbital and secobarbitol, interact at multiple areas of the synapse in several areas in the CNS, and, therefore, cause several pronounced CNS affects (i.e., sedation) as well as other adverse effects that examiners may notice, like difficulty concentrating, drowsiness, behavioral changes, hyperactivity, impaired coordination of muscle movements, all which can potentially impair various testing outcomes (Katzung 2015). See Tables 6.3 and 6.5 (phenobarbital) for more complete list of barbiturate adverse effects. This undesirable adverse effect profile, in addition to potentially fatal respiratory depression in overdose (unlike with other medications in this section), many medication–medication interactions, and the potential for dependence make barbiturates an unpopular class of medications for outpatient use for anxiety and insomnia. Instead, for outpatient use, this class (mainly phenobarbital) is used most often in seizure prevention (discussed in the Antiseizure section below). If this medication is discontinued abruptly examinees may exhibit tremors, sweating, anxiety, agitation, hypertension, delirium, and seizures.

**Novel hypnotics**. This newer class of medications (sometimes referred to as "Z drugs" because the generic names all contain the letter "Z"), commonly prescribed to treat insomnia, is chemically unrelated to the benzodiazepines, zolpidem, zaleplon, and eszopiclone often prescribed for this purpose. Understandably, daytime drowsiness may occur and, interestingly, these medications may cause sleep-related behavior changes along with associated amnesia. For example, while in a state of apparent sleep patients may prepare and cook food or even drive their vehicle but will not remember the episode after awakening. Extreme cases like these two are rare. If this adverse effect occurs or if there are other reasons to stop these medications it is important to know that abrupt discontinuation is associated with withdrawal symptoms like difficulty sleeping, restlessness, and irritability (Ambien prescribing information,

2014). As a result, these should be slowly tapered.

**Melatonin receptor agonists**. Ramelteon and tasimelteon treat insomnia by maintaining circadian rhythms, which controls the sleep-wake cycle (Katzung 2015). These medications have minimal adverse effects and are not likely to negatively effect assessment by contributing to fatigue; nor are these medications are associated with withdrawal symptoms (Katzung 2015).

**Serotonin receptor agonist—buspirone**. Buspirone is prescribed for anxiety and may be considered as a first choice in treating isolated anxiety disorders because it does not cause marked sedation or euphoric effects. Rarely, buspirone can cause numbness, tingling, or increased heart rate that could affect examinees; stopping buspirone abruptly does not elicit rebound or withdrawal effects (Katzung 2015).

## Antipsychotic Medications

Typically antipsychotic medications are prescribed for treatment of schizophrenia and related disorders, and reduce frequency or intensity of hallucinations, delusions, and erratic behavior. These medications can also improve symptoms of bipolar disorder, psychotic depression, acute psychoses and are adjunctives for mood disorder treatment. There are two types, or generations, of antipsychotics: typical antipsychotics (e.g., haloperidol and chlorpromazine), and atypical antipsychotics (e.g., aripiprazole and olanzapine). Generally speaking, medications within both generations treat the above disorders and share similar potency profiles. However, typical antipsychotics are older than the atypicals, and these medications have been linked to a myriad of adverse effects. In contrast, atypical antipsychotics are newer and associated with fewer and less severe side effects that can interfere with assessment results. For example, atypical antipsychotics as a rule, cause less sedation/anticholinergic effects, restlessness, and involuntary muscle movements/tremor than typical antipsychotics (see Table 6.4 for more details of antipsychotic medication applications

**Table 6.3**  Sedative-hypotics

| Subclass, generic name (brand name) | Clinical applications | Physioloical/adverse effects |
|---|---|---|
| **Benzodiazepines** | | |
| Alprazolam (Nirvam, Xanax); Chlordiazepoxide (Librium); Clonazepam (Klonopin); Clorazepate (Tranxene-T); Diazepam (Valium, Diastat); Flurazepam (Dalmane); Lorazepam (Ativan); Midazolam (Versed); Oxazepam (Serax); Temazepam (Restoril); Triazolam (Halcion) | Acute anxiety states, panic attacks, generalized anxiety disorder, insomnia and other sleep disorders, relaxation of skeletal muscle, anesthesia , seizure disorders | Dizziness, fatigue, disorientation, irritability, hostility, blurred vision, dependence |
| **Barbituates** | | |
| Amobarbital (Amytal); Butabarbital (Butisol); Pentobarbital (Nembutol); Phenobarbital (Luminal); Secobarbital (Seconal) | Daytime sedation, insomnia (butabarbitol), insomnia (secobarbital), seizure disorders (pentobarbital, phenobarbital) | Dizziness, fatigue, disorientation, irritability, hostility, blurred vision, dependence, sleep-related activities (e.g., sleep-cooking, driving, eating) behavior changes |
| **Novel Hypnotics** | | |
| Eszopiclone (Lunesta); Zaleplon (Sonata); Zolpiden (Ambien, Edular, Intermezzo, Zolpimist) | Sleep disorders | Dizziness, fatigue, disorientation, irritability, hostility, blurred vision, dependence, sleep-related activities (e.g., sleep-cooking, driving, eating) behavior changes |
| **Melatonin Receptor Agonists** | | |
| Ramelton (Rozerem) | Sleep disorders | Dizziness, fatigue, minimal rebound insomnia or withdrawal symptoms |
| Tasimelteon (Hetlioz) | Sleep disorders | Headache, abnormal dreams |
| **Serotonin Receptor Agonists** | | |
| Buspirone (Buspar) | Generalized anxiety states | Increased heart rate, tingling/numbness/burning sensation, gastrointestinal upset, minimal psychomotor impairment |

Note: Information in table adapted from Summary Sedative-Hypnotics table, Basic and Clinical Pharmacology, 13e and Lexicomp Online

and adverse effects; Katzung 2015; Labbate et al. 2010). Also noteworthy for assessment purposes, both typical and atypical antipsychotics may cause patients to become listless, uninvolved, and unmotivated (Kalikow 2011). Finally, stopping either generation of antipsychotic medications suddenly is not advised, and may elicit withdrawal symptoms, which could consist of psychotic episodes, emotional instability, abnormal movements, cognitive dysfunction, and gastrointestinal problems (Breggin 2013).

**Lithium**. Lithium is prescribed frequently, primarily to treat manic episodes of bipolar disorder, but has clinical applications as well. Considering it is commonly prescribed, it is important to consider the following adverse affects and their potentially detrimental implications for the performance of the examinee: confusion, fatigue, memory impairment, psychomotor impairment, and restlessness (Lithobid or lithium carbonate 2014). Because of the substantial risk of mania or depression following abrupt cessation of lithium,

**Table 6.4** Antipsychotics and Lithium

| Subclass, generic name (brand name) | Clinical applications | Physiological/adverse effects |
|---|---|---|
| **Typical (First Generation) Antipsychotics** | | |
| Chlorpromazine (Thorazine); Fluphenzine (Permitil, Prolixin); Thioridazine (Mellaril); Thiothixene (Nevane); Haloperidol (Haldol) | Psychiatric: schizophrenia, bipolar disorder (manic phase). Nonpsychiatric uses include antiemesis, preoperative sedation, itching | Low blood pressure, sedation, anticholinergic effects (dry mouth, constipation, blurred vision, delirium), involuntary motor movements like akathisia, dystonia, parkinsonism tardive dyskinesia |
| **Atypical (Second Generation) Antipsychotics** | | |
| Aripiprazole (Abilify); Clozapine (Clozaril, FazaClo); Olanzapine (Zyprexa); Quetiapine (Seroquel); Risperidone (Risperdal); Ziprasidone (Geodon) | Schizophrenia, bipolar disorder (olanzapine or risperidone adjunctive with lithium), agitation in Alzheimer's and Parkinson's patients, major depression (aripiprazole) | Involuntary motor movements, weight gain (clozapine, olanzapine) |
| **Mood Stabilizer** | | |
| Lithium (Lithobid, Lithane) | Bipolar affective disorder | Low blood pressure, confusion, fatigue, memory impairment, psychomotor impairment, restlessness, blue-gray skin pigmentation, tremor |

Note: Information in table    adapted from Antipsychotic Drugs: Relation of Chemical Structure to Potency and Toxicities table, and Antipsychotic Drugs and Lithium table, Basic and Clinical Pharmacology, 13e and Lexicomp Online

it is best to slowly discontinue it over a minimum of two- to four-week period (Breggin 2013; Kalikow 2011).

## Antiseizure Medications

In addition to treating all types of seizure disorders, antiseizure medicines are indicated for sedation, mood disorders, neuralgias, and migraine headaches (see Table 6.5 for a more complete list of clinical applications). Most antiseizure medications can be split into the following subclasses: cyclic ureides, benzodiazepines (discussed in the sedative-hypnotic section), tricyclics (different from TCAs discussed in the antidepressant section), GABA (short for gamma-aminobutyric acid, a major inhibitory CNS neurotransmitter) derivatives, and a group of medications that do not fit neatly in any of these categories, i.e., "other antiseizure medications" (Katzung 2015). These medications

have wide-ranging mechanisms of actions and adverse effects. For example, phenytoin, a commonly prescribed antiseizure medication can cause several adverse effects that could impact test performance, such as confusion, slurred speech, double vision, and impaired coordination of muscle movement. Another example of a commonly used antiseizure medicine is levetiracetam, which is typically well tolerated by patients but can cause nervousness, dizziness, fatigue, anxiety, and depression. Topiramate is also prescribed for multiple seizure disorders as well as migraine headache prophylaxis. It produces a myriad of adverse affects pertinent to examinee performance, such as cognitive slowing, tingling/numbness/burning sensation, fatigue, nervousness, difficulty concentrating, confusion, depression, anorexia, language problems, anxiety, mood problems, and tremor. Also, phenobarbital, briefly mentioned in the barbiturate section above can cause pertinent side effects like confusion, hyperactivity, alteration of sleep cycles, sedation, lethargy, behavioral changes, hyperactivity, and impaired coordination of muscle movements. Again, the list of antiseizure medications is lengthy and covers many subclasses and mechanisms of action; for a more comprehensive list of these medications, details on how they work, and adverse effects see Table 6.5. Abrupt discontinuation of these medicines can cause seizures, particularly if patient has a seizure disorder or is prone to seizures (Labbate et al. 2010).

## Nonpsychiatric Prescription and Nonprescription Medicines with Psychotropic Effects

There are many nonpsychiatric medications that can affect behavior, mood, cognition, and level of consciousness—and thus can potentially alter assessment performance; in this section, we review a few of the more commonly used prescription medications: isotretinoin, corticosteroids, specific blood pressure medicines, inhaled beta-2 agonists, and blood pressure medications used in ADHD therapy. Additionally, we review the following notable nonprescription medications with psychotropic effects: pseudoephedrine, antihistamines and caffeine.

**Nonpsychiatric prescription medicines.** Isotretinoin is synthetic relative of vitamin A that is used to treat severe, nodulocystic acne. Isotretinoin is associated with adverse psychiatric effects, including depression, aggressive behavior, psychosis, and suicidal ideation. Consequently, this medicine is usually used only once for a 15–20 week period (Kalikow 2011; Absorica prescribing information 2014).

Glucocorticoid steroids like prednisone, hydrocortisone, triamcinolone, and dexamethasone treat and prevent inflammation and are prescribed and purchased over the counter often and used treat a multitude of ailments, including autoimmune disorders, asthma, cancer and other disorders. Indeed these medicines have significant medical utility; but, they also have many side effects. For example, systemically delivered glucocorticoids (injected into the body or taken orally) can cause neuropsychiatric effects (e.g., euphoria, depression, insomnia, mania, psychosis, and restlessness) that can obviously affect assessment results. In addition, these medications can produce skin and soft tissue effects (e.g., acne, hair loss), eye effects (e.g., cataracts and eyeball protrusion from the eye socket), cardiovascular effects (e.g., heart arrhythmias and hypertension), gastrointestinal distress (e.g., peptic ulcer disease, gastritis, and pancreatitis), fluid volume shifts, infertility, osteoporosis, diabetes mellitus, and increased risk of infection (Kalikow 2011; Rayos prescribing information 2013).

The beta-blocker class of hypertension medications is typically used for hypertension and heart failure, but these medications have other uses as well. This class of medicines includes acebutolol, atenolol, betaxolol, bisoprolol, careolol, carvedilol, esmolol, labetalol, metoprolol, nadolol, nebivolol, oxprenolol, penbutolol, pindolol, propranolol, sotalol, and timolol. These medicines have been shown to cause fatigue and possibly depression; but whether or not they cause depression is debatable (Gheorghiade and Eichhorn 2001; Ko et al. 2002). We mention it here because it is listed in the prescribing information/package inserts of many beta-blockers (e.g., Inderal prescribing information 2015; Tenormin prescribing information 2012; Toprol XL prescribing information 2014; Zebeta prescribing information 2010).

The inhaled beta-2 agonists are frequently used for breathing problems, especially asthma. In fact, they are considered first-line therapy for asthma, making them commonplace among all age groups. This class includes albuterol, salmertol, and formoterol. Dizziness, anxiety, jitters, are common adverse effects associated with these mediations that may limit test performance (Foradil Aerolizer prescribing information 2010; Proventil HFA inhalation aerosol prescribing information 2012; Serevent Diskus prescribing information 2014).

Two alpha-2-adrenergic agonists that were initially marketed to treat hypertension are now used to treat ADHD as well. Guanfacine and clonidine are considered less effective than

**Table 6.5** Antiseizure Medications

| Subclass, generic name (brand name) | Clinical applications | Physiological/adverse effects |
|---|---|---|
| **Cyclic Ureides** | | |
| Phenytoin (Phenytek, Dilantin); Fosphenytoin (Cerebyx) | Generalized tonic-clonic seizures, partial seizures | Confusion, slurred speech, double vision, impaired coordination, swollen gums, abnormal hair growth, tingling/numbness/burning sensation |
| Primidone (Mysoline) | Generalized tonic-clonic seizures, partial seizures | Sedation, cognitive issues, hyperactivity, nausea, rash, alteration of sleep cycles, sedation, lethargy, behavioral changes, hyperactivity, impaired coordination, dependence |
| Phenobarbital (Luminal) | Generalized tonic-clonic seizures, partial seizures, myoclonic seizures, neonatal seizures, status epilepticus | Same as primidone |
| Ethosuximide (Zarontin) | Absence seizures | Nausea, headache, dizziness, lethargy, sleep disturbance, drowsiness, hyperactivity |
| **Tricyclics** | | |
| Carbamazepine (Tegretol, Carbatrol, Equetro, Epitol) | Generalized tonic-clonic seizures, partial seizures, acute mania | Nausea, impaired coordination, headache, drowsiness, dizziness, blurred or double vision, lethargy |
| **Gamma-aminobutyric Acid (GABA) Derivatives** | | |
| Gabapentin (Gralise, Neurontin, Horizant, Fanatrex) | Generalized tonic-clonic seizures, partial seizures | Somnolence, dizziness, impaired coordination |
| Pregabalin (Lyrica) | Partial seizures | Somnolence, dizziness, impaired coordination, weight gain |
| Vigabatrin (Sabril) | Partial seizures, infantile spasms | Drowsiness, dizziness, psychosis, visual field loss |
| **Other** | | |
| Valproic acid (Depakene, Depacon, Depakote, Stavzor, Valproic) | Generalized tonic-clonic seizures, partial seizures, absence seizures, myoclonic seizures, acute mania | Nausea, tremor, weight gain, hair loss |
| Lamotrigine (Lamitctal) | Generalized tonic-clonic seizures, partial seizures, absence seizures, acute mania | Dizziness, headache, double vision, rash |
| Levetiracetam (Keppra) | Generalized tonic-clonic seizures, partial seizures | Nervousness, dizziness, fatigue, anxiety, depression, seizures |
| Ezogabine (Potiga) | Partial seizures | Dizziness, somnolence, confusion, blurred vision |
| Rufinamide (Banzel) | Lennox-Gastaut syndrome | Somnolence, vomiting, fever, diarrhea |
| Tiagabine (Gabitril) | Partial seizures | Nervousness, dizziness, depression, tremor, seizures, difficulty concentrating |

(continued)

**Table 6.5**  (continued)

| Topiramate (Qudexy XR, Topamax, Trokendi XR) | Generalized tonic-clonic seizures, partial seizures, absence seizures, migraine | Somnolence, cognitive slowing, tingling/numbness/burning sensation, fatigue, nervousness, difficulty concentrating, confusion, depression, anorexia, language problems, anxiety, mood problems, tremor |
|---|---|---|
| Zonisamide (Zonegran) | Generalized tonic-clonic seizures, partial seizures, myoclonic seizures | Drowsiness, depression, cognitive impairment, confusion, rash |
| Lacosamide (Vimpat) | Generalized tonic-clonic seizures, partial seizures | Dizziness, headache, nausea |
| Permpanel (Fycompa) | Partial seizures | Dizziness, somnolence, headache, aggression, mood alteration |

*Note:* Information in table adapted from Antiseizure Drugs table, Basic and Clinical Pharmacology, 13e, and Common Side Effects of Anti-Epileptics Drugs table, Up to Date: https://www-uptodate-com.p.atsu.edu/contents/search?search= Anti-Epileptics+Drug&sp=0&searchType=PLAIN_TEXT&source=USER_INPUT&searchControl=TOP_ PULLDOWN&searchOffset= and Bipolar Disorder in Adults: Pharmacotherapy for Acute Mania and hypomania, Up to Date: https://www-uptodate-com.p.atsu.edu/contents/bipolar-disorder-in-adults-pharmacotherapy-for-acute-mania-and-hypomania?source=search_result&search=mood+stabilizers&selectedTitle=1%7E32

stimulants and atomoxetine and are therefore second-line agents to improve inattention and hyperactivity/impulsivity associated with ADHD, or they can be used when side effects preclude the use of stimulants (AAP 2011). More common side effects of these two medications include dizziness and drowsiness, fatigue. Discontinuing clonidine and guanfacine abruptly can cause dangerous rebound hypertension. Discontinuation must be slowly tapered over days or weeks (Kapvay prescribing information 2015; Intuniv prescribing information 2015).

**Nonpsychiatric over the counter medicines.** Pseudoephedrine is commonly prescribed for nasal decongestion. This medication that was once easy to obtain over the counter but has become regulated in most states because it is an ingredient used to make methamphetamine illegally. Pseudoephedrine produces side effects that can affect examinee (e.g., heart palpitations, confusion, impaired coordination, dizziness, drowsiness, excitability, hallucination, insomnia, anxiety, and blurred vision). Stopping pseudoephedrine suddenly can cause rebound nasal congestion (Pseudoephedrine: Drug information 2015).

Oral antihistamines treat ailments such as seasonal allergies, allergic reactions, and insomnia. These medications can be split into two groups. The first group is called first generation antihistamines and includes diphenhydramine, chlorpheniramine, hydroxyzine, brompheniramine, and others. These medications pass through the blood–brain barrier, which accounts for their adverse CNS effects including drowsiness and intellectual and motor function impairment (Church 2001; Simons and Simons 1999). They have been shown to cause fatigue, memory impairment, irritability, and insomnia/excitement, particularly in children (Carson et al. 2010). The other antihistimines fall under the second or third generation antihistamines and includes loratidine, cetirizine, fexodinadine, desloratadine, levocetirizine, and others. These medications do not cross the blood–brain barrier and, therefore, cause less CNS-related side effects (Verster and Volkerts 2004). This group of medications is used for allergic rhinitis primarily. The side effect profile of these medications is more favorable when compared to the first generation medications and includes drowsiness, anxiety, fatigue, insomnia, particularly in children) (Carson et al. 2010; Ousler et al. 2004). Typically, antihistamines can be discontinued without negative consequences.

A commonly used but perhaps overlooked over the counter medicine is caffeine, which is easily accessible and present in coffee, tea, many soft drinks, energy drinks, and in pill form as well—both by itself and mixed with other ingredients/medicines. Most commonly, caffeine is used to combat fatigue and can also treat headaches. Notably, it can cause anxiety, agitation, restlessness, insomnia, and in extreme cases, psychotic-like behavior (Caffeine: Drug information 2015), and may be the most commonly abused drug by examinees.

## Drugs of Abuse

Ingesting ethyl alcohol and/or taking illicit drugs can cause drastic changes in the examinee's behavior, mood, cognition, and health, escalating to a medical emergency if the doses are high enough (see Table 6.6). There are acute effects and chronic sequelae of substance use disorders. In this section, we concentrate on the effects of acute intoxication with ethanol and a several other commonly abused drugs.

Importantly, there are various screening tools available to assess ethanol abuse and drug use, but these are not commonly available to examiners. Nonetheless, awareness of the clinical features of intoxication can help alert the examiner to the use of these substances. For example, signs of acute alcohol intoxication include slurred speech, lowered inhibitions, loss of coordination, and emotional volatility. Signs of acute marijuana intoxication, a cannabinoid, include euphoria relaxation, slowed reaction time, impaired learning and memory, anxiety, and red (or blood-shot) eyes.

Another commonly abused drug is the CNS stimulant cocaine, which can cause several affects that can acutely alter the examinee's test performance, including increased energy, mental alertness, tremors, irritability, anxiety, paranoia, violent behavior, psychosis, insomnia, and seizures. Lysergic acid diethylamide, or LSD for short, is a hallucinogen that can cause the following constellation of notable effects: altered states of perception and feeling, hallucinations, flashbacks, weakness, tremors, impulsive behavior, and rapid shifts in emotion. Of course,

there are numerous drugs of abuse, many with their own list of unique effects (American Psychiatric Association (APA) 2011). For more information about these drugs of abuse and others, refer to Table 6.6.

As should be obvious by now, it is important for examiners to recognize the effects of commonly used medications. Before a test is administered examiners should determine whether or not examinees are currently taking medications and the dosage level. This information should be included in the psychological report. If the medications are assumed to affect test results these observations should also be included in the report. In some cases, examiners may delay testing until the examinee is drug free. This decision should be made in concert with parental knowledge and approval and upon the advice of a physician.

## Complementary and Alternative Therapies

The alternative therapies market as a whole is burgeoning, and the mental health niche of alternative therapy is no different. Although robust data supporting their use is lacking, there are many alternative options available, which could impact various behavior in general and test results in particular. We review a couple of the more commonly used agents in this section.

St. Johns Wort is derived from an herb and has been used for centuries to treat a variety of ailments, most notably, psychiatric-related diagnoses such as depression (Kalikow 2011). However, because the data supporting its use compared to placebo or standard of care for depression and ADHD is weak, it is not recommended as first-line for either diagnosis (AAP 2011; APA 2010; Fava et al. 2005; Shelton et al. 2001; Weber et al. 2008). Side effects of this herb when taken alone are mild, but combining St. John's Wort with other medications can cause dangerous interactions. For example, co-administration with SSRIs can cause dangerous increases in serotonin level (dubbed

**Table 6.6** Commonly Abused Drugs

| Category, name | Commercial and street names | How administered | Acute effects/health ricks |
|---|---|---|---|
| **Alcohol** | | | |
| Alcohol (ethyl alcohol) | Found in liquor, beer, and wine | Swallowed | In low doses, euphoria, mild stimulation, relaxation, lowered inhibitions; in higher doses, drowsiness, slurred speech, nausea, emotional volatility, impaired coordination, visual distortions, impaired memory, loss of consciousness/ increased risk of injuries, violence, depression; neurologic deficits, hypertension, dependence. Overdose/withdrawal potentially fatal |
| **Cannabinoids** | | | |
| Marijuana | Blunt, dope, ganja, grass, herb, joint, bud, Mary Jane, pot, reefer, green, trees, smoke, sinsemilla, skunk, weed | Smoked, swallowed | Euphoria, relaxation, slowed reaction time, distorted sensory perception, impaired balance and coordination, increased heart rate and appetite, impaired learning/memory, anxiety, panic attacks, psychosis, cough, frequent respiratory infections, possible mental health decline, dependence |
| Hashish | Boom, gangster, hash, hash oil, hemp | Smoked, swallowed | Same as marijuana |
| **Opioids** | | | |
| Heroin | Diacetylmorphine: smack, horse, brown sugar, dope, H, junk, skag, skunk, white horse, China white; cheese (with OTC cold medicine and antihistamine) | Injected, smoked, snorted | Euphoria, drowsiness, impaired coordination, dizziness, confusion, nausea, sedation, feeling of heaviness in the body, slowed or arrested breathing/constipation, dependence, fatal overdose |
| Opium | Laudanum, paregoric: big O, black stuff, block, gum, hop | Swallowed, smoked | Same as heroin |
| **Stimulants** | | | |
| Cocaine | Cocaine hydrochloride: blow, bump, C, candy, Charlie, coke, crack, flake, rock, snow, toot | Snorted, smoked, injected | Increased heart rate/blood pressure, feelings of exhilaration, increased energy, mental alertness, tremors, reduced appetite, irritability, anxiety, panic, paranoia, violent behavior, psychosis, weight loss, insomnia, seizures, dependence |
| Amphetamine | Biphetamine, dexedrine: bennies, black beauties, crosses, hearts, LA turnaround, speed, truck drivers, uppers | Swallowed, snorted, smoked, injected | Same as cocaine |

(continued)

**Table 6.6** (continued)

| | | | |
|---|---|---|---|
| Methamphetamine | Meth, ice, crank, chalk, crystal, fire, glass, go fast, speed | Swallowed, snorted, smoked, injected | Same as cocaine |
| **Club Drugs** | | | |
| MDMA (methylenedioxy-methamphetamine) | Ecstasy, Adam, clarity, Eve, lover's speed, peace, uppers | Swallowed, snorted, injected | Mild hallucinogenic effects, increased tactile sensitivity, empathetic feelings, lowered inhibition, anxiety, chills, sweating, teeth clenching, muscle cramping/sleep disturbance, depression, impaired memory, hyperthermia, dependence |
| Flunitrazepam | Rohypnol: forget-me pill, Mexican Valium, R2, roach, Roche, roofies, roofinol | Swallowed, snorted | Sedation, muscle relaxation, confusion, memory loss, dizziness, impaired coordination, dependence |
| GHB (Gamma-hydroxybutyrate) | G, Georgia home boy, grievous bodily harm, liquid ecstasy, soap, scoop, goop, liquid X | Swallowed | Drowsiness, nausea, headache, disorientation, impaired coordination, memory loss, seizures, coma |
| **Dissociative Drugs** | | | |
| Ketamine | Ketalar SV: cat, Valium, K, Special K, vitamin K | Injected, snorted, smoked | Feelings of being separated from one's body and environment, impaired motor function, anxiety, tremors, numbness, memory loss, nausea. Also, for ketamine only: analgesia, impaired memory, delirium |
| Phenyl cyclohexyl piperidine (PCP) and analogs | Phencyclidine: angel dust, boat, hog, love boat, peace pill | Swallowed, smoked, injected | Same as ketamine. Also, for PCP and analogs: analgesia, psychosis, aggression, violence, slurred speech, impaired coordination, hallucinations |
| Salvia divinorum | Salvia, Shepherdess's Herb, Maria Pastora, magic mint, Sally-D | Chewed, swallowed, smoked | Same as ketamine |
| Dextromethorphan (DXM) | Found in some cough and cold medications: Robotripping, Robo, Triple C | Swallowed | Same as ketamine. Also, for DXM: euphoria, slurred speech, confusion, dizziness, distorted visual perceptions |

(continued)

**Table 6.6** (continued)

**Hallucinogens**

| | | |
|---|---|---|
| Lysergic acid diethylamide (LSD) | Lysergic acid diethylamide: acid, blotter, cubes, microdot, yellow sunshine, blue heaven | Swallowed, absorbed through mouth tissues | Altered states of perception and feeling, hallucinations, nausea. Also, for LSD: :flashbacks, hallucinogen persisting perception disorder. Also, for LSD and mescaline: increased heart rate/blood pressure, loss of appetite, sweating, sleeplessness, numbness, dizziness, weakness, tremors, impulsive behavior, rapid shifts in emotion |
| Mescaline | Buttons, cactus, mesc, peyote | Swallowed, smoked | Same as LSD |
| Psilocybin | Magic mushrooms, purple passion, shrooms, little smoke | Swallowed | Same as LSD. Also, for psilocybin only: nervousness, paranoia, panic attacks |

**Other compounds**

| | | |
|---|---|---|
| Anabolic steroids | Anadrol, Oxandrin, Durabolin, Depo-Testosterone, Equipoise: roids, juice, gym candy, pumpers | Injected, swallowed, applied to skin | Hostility and aggression, acne, premature stoppage of growth (in adolescents) In males: breast enlargement In females: development of beard and other masculine characteristics |
| Inhalants | Solvents (paint thinners, gasoline, glues), gases (butane, propane, aerosol propellants, nitrous oxide), nitrites (isoamyl, isobutyl, cyclohexyl): laughing gas, poppers, snappers, whippets | Inhaled through nose or mouth | Loss of inhibition, headache, nausea or vomiting, slurred speech, impaired coordination, wheezing, cramps, muscle weakness, depression, memory impairment, unconsciousness, sudden death |

Note: Information in table adapted from American Psychiatric Association website: http://www.psychiatry.org/addiction via National Institute of Health—National Institute of Drug Abuse. 2011 serotonin syndrome, discussed in the MAOI section) and is discouraged (Kalikow 2011).

The leaf extract of the *Gingko biloba* tree has been used for years to treat dementia, especially in the elderly (Kalikow 2011). Although the data supporting its use is somewhat mixed, a 2009 *Cochrane Review* found that the evidence for cognitive improvement in demented patients is inconsistent and unconvincing (Birks and Grimley 2009). Adverse effects reported with *Gingko biloba* supplements, such as headaches, rashes, and gastrointestinal upset, are generally mild and probably would not affect assessment results.

## Summary

This chapter describes some salient physiological and psychological influences on multicultural and nonverbal assessment. Obviously, examinees who require nonverbal assessment, those from culturally diverse settings and those with emotional problems and/or language deficits, may behave in ways that are different from mainstream examinees and those who present no language-related problems. Examiners who are sensitive to these differences, to the psychological impact of the testing environment, and the impact of biology on test behavior will be more successful in reducing construct-irrelevant variance in test scores and in obtaining more accurate estimates of intellectual, educational, and emotional functioning. In particular, examiners should determine whether medications have been administered to examinees before testing, and the dosage level; this information should be included in the psychoeducational report. If an examiner suspects that an examinee is under the influence of illicit drugs the session should be terminated until the examinee is drug free. Examiners who are aware of the conditions under which tests are administered, who can relate the impact of these influences to the success or failure of the child in the testing session, and who can extrapolate the impact of these influences to the school and home will be more successful in helping teachers and parents help children.

## References

Absorica (isotretinoin) prescribing information. (2014). Ranbaxy Laboratories Inc. Jacksonville, FL: Retrieved from http://www.absorica.com/absorica_pi.pdf

Ambien (zolpidem tartrate tablet) prescribing information. (2014). *Bridgewater*. NJ: Sanofi-Aventis.

American Academy of Pediatrics. (2011). ADHD: Clinical practice guideline for the diagnosis, evaluation, and treatment of attention-deficit/hyperactivity disorder in children and adolescents. *Pediatrics, 128*(5), 1007–1022. doi:10.1542/peds.2011-2654F

American Educational Research Association, American Psychological Association, & National Council on Measurement in Education. (2014). *Standards for educational and psychological testing.* Washington, DC: American Educational Research Association.

American Psychiatric Association. (2010). *Practice guideline for the treatment of patients with major depressive disorder* (3rd ed.). Washington, DC: A. J. Gelenberg, M. P. Freeman, J. C. Markowitz, J. F. Rosenbaum, M. E. Thase, M. H. Trivedi, & R. S. van Rhoads.

American Psychiatric Association. (2011). *Help with addiction and substance use disorders.* Retrieved from http://www.psychiatry.org/addiction

American Psychiatric Association. (2013). Attention-deficit/hyperactivity disorder. In *Diagnostic and statistical manual of mental disorders* (5th ed.). Washington, DC: Author.

Birks, J., & Grimley Evans, J. (2009). Ginkgo biloba for cognitive impairment and dementia. *The Cochrane Database of Systematic Reviews*, (1), CD003120. doi:10.1002/14651858.CD003120.pub3

Bracken, B. A. (2007). Clinical observation of preschool assessment behavior. In B. A. Bracken & R. J. Nagle (Eds.), *Psychoeducational assessment of preschool children* (4th ed., pp. 95–110). Mahwah, NJ: Lawrence Erlbaum Associates Inc.

Bracken, B. A., & Barona, A. (1991). State of the art procedures for translating, validating, and using psychoeducational tests in cross-cultural education. *School Psychology International, 12*(1–2), 119–132.

Bracken, B. A., & McCallum, R. S. (1998). *Universal nonverbal intelligence test.* Itasca, IL: Riverside.

Bracken, B. A., McCallum, R. S. (2016). *Universal nonverbal intelligence test* (2nd ed.). Itasca, IL: Riverside.

Breggin, P. R. (2013). *Psychiatric drug withdrawal: A guide for prescribers, therapists, patients, and their families.* New York: Springer Publishing Company.

Caffeine: Drug information. (2015). *Lexicomp Online.* Retrieved from https://www-uptodate-com.p.atsu.edu/contents/caffeinedruginformation?source=search_result&search=caffeine&selectedTitle=1%7E150

Carson, S., Lee, N., & Thakurta, S. (2010). *Drug class review: Newer antihistamines: Final report update 2.* Portland (OR): Oregon Health & Science University.

Chess, S., & Thomas, A. (1984). *Origins and evolution of behavior disorders from infancy to early adult life.* New York: Brunner/Mazel.

Church, M. K. (2001). H(1)-antihistamines and inflammation. *Clinical and Experimental Allergy: Journal of the British Society for Allergy and Clinical Immunology, 31*(9), 1341–1343.

Cronbach, L. J. (1960). *Essentials of psychological testing* (2nd ed.). New York: Harper.

Fava, M., Alpert, J., Nierenberg, A. A., Mischoulon, D., Otto, M. W., Zajecka, J., et al. (2005). A double-blind, randomized trial of St John's wort, fluoxetine, and placebo in major depressive disorder. *Journal of Clinical Psychopharmacology, 25*(5), 441–447. doi:10.1097/01.jcp.0000178416.60426.29.

Flanagan, D. P., Ortiz, S. O., & Alfonso, V. C. (2007). *Essentials of cross-battery assessment* (2nd ed.). Hoboken, NJ: Wiley.

Flanagan, D. P., Ortiz, S. O., & Alfonso, V. C. (2013). *Essentials of cross-battery assessment* (3rd ed.). Hoboken, NJ: Wiley.

Foradil Aerolizer (formoterol) prescribing information. (2010). Merck & Co, Inc. Whitehouse Station, NJ. Retrieved from https://www.merck.com/product/usa/pi_circulars/f/foradil/foradil_pi.pdf

Gelenberg, A. J., Freeman, M. P., Markowitz, J. C., Rosenbaum, J. F., Thase, M. E., Trivedi, M. H., van Rhoads, R. S. (2010). *Practice guideline for the treatment of patients with major depressive disorder* (3rd ed.). Washington, DC: Retrieved from the American Psychiatric Association website http://psychiatryonline.org/pb/assets/raw/sitewide/practice_guidelines/guidelines/mdd.pdf

Gheorghiade, M., & Eichhorn, E. J. (2001). Practical aspects of using beta-adrenergic blockade in systolic heart failure (Supplemental material). *The American Journal of Medicine, 110*, 68–73. doi:10.1016/S0002-9343(00)00575-1.

Hendricks, E. J., & Greenway, F. L. (2011). A study of abrupt phentermine cessation in patients in a weight management program. *American Journal of Therapeutics, 18*(4), 292–299. doi:10.1097/MJT.0b013e3181d070d7.

Inderal XL (propranolol) prescribing information. (2015). *Mist Pharmaceuticals.* Cranford, NJ. Retrieved from http://inderalxl.com/wpcontent/uploads/2014/06/InderalXL_prescribing_information_highlights.pdf

Intuniv (guanfacine) prescribing information. (2015). Wayne, PA: Shire Inc.

Kagan, J. (1994a). *Galen's prophecy: temperament in human nature.* New York, NY: Basic Books.

Kagan, J. (1994b). *The nature of the child.* New York, NY: Basic Books (Original work published 1984).

Kalikow, K. T. (2011). *Kids on meds: Up-to-date information about the most commonly prescribed psychiatric medications.* New York, NY: W W Norton & Co.

Kapvay (clonidine) prescribing information. (2015). St. Michael, Barbados: Concordia.

Katzung, B. G. (2015). *Basic and clinical pharmacology.* New York: McGraw-Hill Education.

Ko, D. T., Hebert, P. R., Coffey, C. S., Sedrakyan, A., Curtis, J. P., & Krumholz, H. M. (2002). Beta-blocker therapy and symptoms of depression, fatigue, and sexual dysfunction. *Journal of the American Medical Association, 288*(3), 351–357.

Labbate, L. A., Rosenbaum, J. F., Fava, M., & Arana, G. W. (2010). *Handbook of psychiatric drug therapy* (6th ed.). Philadelphia: Lippincott Williams & Wilkins.

Lejoyeux, M., & Adès, J. (1997). Antidepressant discontinuation: A review of the literature (Supplemental material). *Journal of Clinical Psychiatry, 58*, 11–16.

Lithobid (lithium carbonate) prescribing information. (2014). Baudette, MN: Ani Pharmaceuticals.

McLoughlin, J. A., & Lewis, R. B. (2008). *Assessing students with special needs* (7th ed.). Upper Saddle River, NJ: Pearson.

Orwell, G. (1946). *Animal Farm.* New York: Harcourt Broace Jovanovich.

Ousler, G. W., Wilcox, K. A., Gupta, G., Abelson, M. B., & Fink, K. (2004). An evaluation of the ocular drying effects of 2 systemic antihistamines: loratadine and cetirizine hydrochloride. *Annals of Allergy, Asthma & Immunology, 93*(5), 460–464. doi:10.1016/S1081-1206(10)61413-5.

Plomin, R., Owen, M. J., & McGuffin, P. (1994). The genetic basis of complex human behaviors. *Science, 264*, 1733–1739.

Pool, R. (1997). Portrait of a gene guy. *Discover*, 51–57.

Proventil HFA (Albuterol sulfate) inhalation aerosol prescribing information. (2012) Merck & Co., Inc. Whitehouse Station, NJ. Retrieved from https://www.merck.com/product/usa/pi_circulars/p/proventil_hfa/proventil_hfa_pi.pdf

Provigil (modafinil) prescribing information. (2015). *Teva Pharmaceuticals.* North Wales, PA. Retrieved from http://www.provigil.com/media/pdfs/prescribing_info.pdf

Pseudoephedrine: drug information. (2015). *Lexicomp Online.* Retrieved from https://www-uptodate-com.p.atsu.edu/contents/pseudoephedrine-drug-information?source=search_result&search=pseudoephedrine&selectedTitle=1%7E140

Rayos (prednisone) prescribing information. (2013). *Horizon Pharma,* Deerfield, IL. Retrieved from http://www.rayosrx.com/PI/RAYOS-Prescribing-Information.pdf

Santos de Barona, M., & Barona, A. (2007). Assessing multicultural preschool children. In B. A. Bracken & R. J. Nagle (Eds.), *Psychoeducational assessment of preschool children* (4th ed., pp. 69–92). Mahwah, NJ: Lawrence Erlbaum Associates Inc.

Sattler, J. M. (2008). *Assessment of children: Cognitive foundations* (5th ed.). San Diego, CA: Jerome M. Sattler, Publisher Inc.

Serevent Diskus (salmeterol xinafoate inhalation powder) prescribing information. (2014). GlaxoSmithKline. Research Triangle Park, NC. Retrieved from https://www.gsksource.com/pharma/content/dam/GlaxoSmithKline/US/en/Prescribing_Information/Serevent_Diskus/pdf/SEREVENT-DISKUS-PI-MG.PDF

Shelton, R. C. (2001). Steps following attainment of remission: Discontinuation of antidepressant therapy. *Primary Care Companion to the Journal of Clinical Psychiatry, 3*(4), 168–174.

Shelton, R. C., Keller, M. B., Gelenberg, A., Dunner, D. L., Hirschfeld, R., Thase, M. E., … Halbreich, U. (2001). Effectiveness of St John's wort in major depression: a randomized controlled trial. *Journal of the American Medical Association, 285*(15), 1978–1986.

Simons, F. E., & Simons, K. J. (1999). Clinical pharmacology of new histamine H1 receptor antagonists. *Clinical Pharmacokinetics, 36*(5), 329–352.

Sternberg, R. J., & Grigorenko, E. L. (2001). Ability testing across cultures. In L. A. Suzuki, J. G. Ponterotto, & P. J. Meller (Eds.), *Handbook of multicultural assessment: Clinical, psychological, and educational applications* (2nd ed., pp. 335–358). San Francisco: Jossey-Bass.

Takushi, R., & Uomoto, J. M. (2001). The clinical interview from a multicultural perspective. In L. A. Suzuki, J. G. Ponterotto, & P. J. Meller (Eds.), *Handbook of multicultural assessment: Clinical, psychological, and educational applications* (2nd ed., pp. 47–66). San Francisco: Jossey-Bass.

Tenormin (atenolol) prescribing information. (2012). *AstraZeneca Pharmaceuticals*. Wilmington, DE. Retrieved from http://www1.astrazeneca-us.com/pi/tenormin.pdf

Thomas, A., Chess, S., & Birch, H. G. (1968). *Temperament and behavior disorders in children*. New York, NY: New York University Press.

Toprol XL (metoprolol) prescribing information. (2014). *AstraZeneca Pharmaceuticals*. Wilmington, DE. Retrieved from http://www1.astrazeneca-us.com/pi/toprol-xl.pdf

van Geffen, E. G., Hugtenburg, J. G., Heerdink, E. R., van Hulten, R. P., & Egberts, A. G. (2005). Discontinuation symptoms in users of selective serotonin reuptake inhibitors in clinical practice: tapering versus abrupt discontinuation. *European Journal of Clinical Pharmacology, 61*(4), 303–307.

Verster, J. C., & Volkerts, E. R. (2004). Antihistamines and driving ability: Evidence from on-the-road driving studies during normal traffic. *Annals of Allergy, Asthma & Immunology, 92*(3), 294–304. doi:10.1016/S1081-1206(10)61566-9

Weber, W., Stoep, A. V., McCarty, R. L., Weiss, N. S., Biederman, J., & McClellan, J. (2008). Hypericum perforatum (St John's wort) for attention-deficit/hyperactivity disorder in children and adolescents: A randomized controlled trial. *JAMA Journal of The American Medical Association, 299* (22), 2633–2641. doi:10.1001/jama.299.22.2633

Wernicke, J. F., Adler, L., Spencer, T., West, S. A., Allen, A. J., Heiligenstein, J., … Michelson, D. (2004). Changes in symptoms and adverse events after discontinuation of atomoxetine in children and adults with attention deficit/hyperactivity disorder: A prospective, placebo-controlled assessment. *Journal of Clinical Psychopharmacology, 24*(1), 30–35. doi:10.1097/01.jcp.0000104907.75206.c2

Wilens, T. E. (1999). *Straight talk about psychiatric medications for kids*. New York: The Guilford Press.

Zebeta (bisoprolol) prescribing information. (2010). *Duramed Pharmaceuticals*. Pomona, NY. Retrieved from http://dailymed.nlm.nih.gov/dailymed/drugInfo.cfm?setid=a11548a0-9c0f-4729-907c-75d8f99a6c85

# Part II

# Selected Nonverbal Cognitive Tests

# The Universal Nonverbal Intelligence Test: Second Edition

7

## Alex Friedlander Moore, R. Steve McCallum and Bruce A. Bracken

The *Universal Nonverbal Intelligence Test-Second Edition* (UNIT2; Bracken and McCallum 2016), the latest edition of the *Universal Nonverbal Intelligence Test* (UNIT; Bracken and McCallum 1998), was conceptualized as a comprehensive measure of intelligence, assessed through a nonverbal administration format. The revised and renormed UNIT2 preserved the many benefits of the original test, while also adding a number of advancements that made the current instrument even more useful.

Many of the original UNIT's strengths were derived from its aforementioned nonverbal assessment approach. As with the UNIT, the UNIT2 is administered in a completely nonverbal format. This feature renders the UNIT2 especially useful for assessing students who have speech, language, or hearing impairments; students who come from diverse cultural or language backgrounds, or students who are verbally uncommunicative. As a nonverbal test the UNIT2 provides a fair, equitable, and comprehensive assessment of general intelligence for students who otherwise would be disadvantaged by the administration of a language-loaded ability test.

In addition to retaining its most salient features, the UNIT2 authors addressed limitations of the original test with the following improvements:

1. To address the issue of dated norms, all new normative data were collected.
2. To ensure the test was appropriate for all high school and many college-age students the upper age range was extended to 21 years, 11 months.
3. To address floor effects for young, low functioning examinees, items were added to the lower end of all subtests.
4. To address ceiling effects for the older, high-functioning examinees, items were added to the upper end of all subtests.
5. To facilitate ease of administration, a new "one-way" presentation of the easel-bound subtests was incorporated.
6. Initial black and white clipart drawings were redrawn and rendered in appealing full color.
7. To expand the test's theoretical foundation, two quantitative subtests were added.
8. Two lower *g* or redundant measures from the original test (i.e., Object Memory and Mazes) were replaced with quantitative subtests.
9. To provide a measure of intelligence without short-term memory (even though all UNIT Memory subtests exhibited high

A. Friedlander Moore (✉) · B.A. Bracken
College of William and Mary, 301 Monticello Avenue, Williamsburg, VA 23185, USA
e-mail: adfriedlanderm@email.wm.edu

B.A. Bracken
e-mail: babrac@wm.edu

R.S. McCallum
Department of Educational Psychology and Counseling, University of Tennessee, 523 BEC, 1126 Volunteer Blvd, Knoxville, TN 37996-3452, USA
e-mail: mccallum@utk.edu

© Springer International Publishing AG 2017
R.S. McCallum (ed.), *Handbook of Nonverbal Assessment*,
DOI 10.1007/978-3-319-50604-3_7

*g* loadings), the option of obtaining a FSIQ with *or* without memory was configured.

10. Demonstration, sample, and checkpoint items were carefully adjusted to ensure a smooth transition between task demands on all subtests.

In addition to addressing reviewers' and consumers' concerns with the original test, the UNIT2 continues to provide its unique cognitive organization (i.e., symbolic and nonsymbolic content) and measurement of foundational cognitive abilities (i.e., memory, reasoning, and quantitative reasoning). Importantly, the UNIT2 continues to be first and foremost a strong measure of general intelligence (i.e., psychometric *g*). The UNIT2, like the original UNIT is based in part on Jensen's (1980) two-factor model of intelligence, which features memory and reasoning as the two primary sub-constructs of intelligence, Level I and Level II, respectively. Jensen's model was modified to include quantitative reasoning in the UNIT2, which added another aspect of Level II functioning to be consistent with other theories of intelligence (e.g., the Cattell, Horn, Carroll, or CHC model) and to increase the test's relevance for academic and work-force success.

Wechsler (1939) emphasized the importance of distinguishing between highly symbolic (i.e., verbal) and nonsymbolic (i.e., performance) abilities in the assessment of cognitive performance. This orientation was applied to the UNIT, with its own symbolic and nonsymbolic measures. The UNIT2 maintained this distinction. From a more current orientation, the UNIT can be conceptualized within the Gf-Gc model of fluid and crystallized abilities, as described by Cattell (1963), Horn (1968), Carroll (1993), and others (e.g., Woodcock 1990). According to McGrew and Flanagan (1998), presented in the *Intelligence Test Desk Reference*, UNIT subtests were identified as assessing a number of the Gf-Gc stratum II and III abilities. For example, Symbolic Memory was identified as a measure of visual memory (MV) from Stratum I and visual

processing (Gv) from Stratum II; Spatial Memory was identified as a measure of MV and spatial relations (SR) from Stratum I and Gv from Stratum II; Cube Design was found to assess visualization (Vz; Stratum I) and visual processing (Gv; Stratum II); Analogic Reasoning was identified as assessing induction (I; Stratum I) and Gf (Stratum II). Following the cross-battery approach that McGrew and Flanagan promote, it would make sense that Nonsymbolic Quantity and Numerical Series would be identified as measures of quantitative reasoning (Gq; Stratum II) and mathematical knowledge (KM) from Stratum I.

## Goals and Rationale for UNIT Development and Revision

Ten goals guided the development of the original UNIT, but the overarching goal was to ensure a fair and comprehensive assessment of intelligence for children and adolescents whose cognitive abilities could not be fairly assessed with language-loaded measures or with existing unidimensional, language-reduced measures. The UNIT was developed for children and adolescents who are deaf or hard of hearing, and those from different cultural backgrounds, with learning/language disabilities, with speech production impairments, and with serious emotional or intellectual limitations. For all of these individuals, the UNIT was designed to be administered in a 100% nonverbal format, and was standardized accordingly.

The UNIT authors created the test with psychometric rigor and a special sensitivity for cross-cultural assessment applications through the use of common, examinee-friendly tasks. UNIT and UNIT2 tasks also were designed to maximize existing examiner knowledge and experience to ensure the test was easily learned, administered, and interpreted by experienced examiners. The UNIT2 revision began in late 2008 and standardization started and ended in 2010 and 2015, respectively.

## Description of the UNIT2

The UNIT2 includes several test battery options that may be administered as desired or needed. These batteries include a Full-Scale Battery, a Standard Battery with Memory, a Standard Battery without Memory, and an Abbreviated Battery. Several composite and subtest scores can be calculated and interpreted for the UNIT2, including a: Full-Scale Intelligence Quotient (FSIQ), Memory Composite, Reasoning Composite, Quantitative Composite, Abbreviated Battery Quotient (ABIQ), Standard Battery with Memory Quotient (SBIQ-M), and a Standard Battery without Memory Quotient (SBIQ).

As illustrated in Table 7.1, the complete UNIT2 includes six subtests. Individual subtest scores can be derived for each of the subtests for normative and ipsative analysis of examinees' performance. Four of the subtests from the original UNIT were maintained in the UNIT2 (i.e., Symbolic Memory, Analogic Reasoning, Spatial Memory, and Cube Design). Two former UNIT subtests (i.e., Object Memory and Mazes) were replaced on the UNIT2 with two new quantitative subtests (i.e., Nonsymbolic Quantity and Numerical Series). These latter subtests were added to broaden the instrument's range of skills and abilities assessed. Table 7.1 displays the UNIT2 conceptual model, as well as its subtests, their content and function, and the cognitive abilities assessed by each subtest. Following Table 7.1 is a description of each of the UNIT2 subtests.

## UNIT2 Subtests

*Symbolic Memory*: the early items allow the youngest examinees to solve perceptual match problems; the later items require the examinees to study, recall, and recreate from memory sequences of visually-presented arrays of universal human symbols (i.e., baby, boy, girl, man, and woman) of two colors (i.e., green and black).

*Nonsymbolic Quantity*: the examinee is shown arrays of white and/or black domino-like objects that display various numerical values. Each array creates a numerical sequence, equation, analogy, or mathematical problem. The examinee must select a response option that completes the sequence, equation, analogy, or solves a mathematical problem.

*Analogic Reasoning*: the examinee selects one of four response options to complete a conceptual or geometric analogy, which is presented in a matrix format.

*Spatial Memory*: the youngest examinees must solve perceptual match problems; the older examinees are required to remember and recreate the placement of numerically increasing arrays of black and/or green chips on $1 \times 2$, $2 \times 2$, $3 \times 3$, or $4 \times 4$ cell grids.

*Numerical Series*: the examinee is presented numbers or mathematical symbols that create a perceptual match or complete a quantitative series. The examinee determines which response option best completes the series.

*Cube design*: the youngest examinees are required to solve perceptual match problems; the older examinees must complete a three-dimensional block design using between one and nine green and white blocks.

## Scores Provided

The UNIT2 subtests produce raw scores, age equivalents, scaled scores (i.e., standard scores with a mean of 10 and standard deviations set to 3), index or composite scores (standard scores with a mean of 100 and standard deviations set to 15), and percentile ranks. In addition to

**Table 7.1** Conceptual model for the UNIT-2

|  |  | Symbolic content | Nonsymbolic content |
|---|---|---|---|
|  | Memory | Symbolic memory | Spatial memory |
|  | Fluid reasoning | Analogic reasoning | Cube design |
|  | Quantitative reasoning | Numerical scales | Nonsymbolic quantity |

providing scaled scores for each subtest, the UNIT2 produces seven composite scores: three composites represent the specific cognitive ability areas assessed (i.e., Memory, Reasoning, and Quantitative Reasoning); and four include the global intelligence composites for the respective batteries (i.e., Abbreviated Battery, Standard Battery with Memory, Standard Battery without Memory, and Full-Scale Battery). Each composite produces index scores with a mean of 100 and standard deviations set to 15.

## UNIT2 Administration and Scoring

To facilitate examiners' efforts to learn to administer the UNIT2, administration guidelines and procedures were maintained from the original UNIT. Much like during the administration of the UNIT, the UNIT2 guidelines encourage examiners to consider three essential assessment-related elements: the examinee; the examiner; and the environment. The Examiner's Manual describes issues associated with these three elements in considerable detail (Bracken and McCallum 1998, 2016). Because the UNIT2 was developed to be sensitive to examinees from different cultures and with various disabilities, the UNIT2 Examiner's Manual devotes several pages to the unique needs associated with these populations.

Examiner characteristics are also very important considerations in the assessment process. A well-trained and sensitive examiner is essential for a valid assessment of diverse populations. Examiners must establish rapport, follow standardization directions carefully, be aware of the unique demands of administering the UNIT2 (e.g., administration gestures, use of pantomime, time constraints), and respond to the physical demands of the assessment process (e.g., positioning of the examiner and examinee according to the examinee's hand dominance). The UNIT2 Examiner's Manual provides visual graphics for each subtest, showing the correct placement of test materials and the position of the examinee and examiner relative to those materials.

Adept UNIT2 examiners know that they must use the language of the child to establish and maintain rapport and must use appropriate gestures to enhance examinee motivation (e.g., gesturing "thumbs up" for effort, saying "good job"). Importantly, examiners have considerable latitude to communicate the nature of the tasks to the examinees through the use of the same eight gestures created and used in the original UNIT, pantomime, and through the use of Demonstration, Sample, and Checkpoint items. Each subtest employs a simple and consistent "point-wave-shrug" sequence; that is, the examiner points to the stimulus materials, uses a sweeping hand wave to highlight the response materials, and employs the open-handed shrug to ask how the problem should be solved. UNIT2 subtests have two age-related Start Points: one for children between 5-years 0-months to 7-years 11-months of age, and a second for examinees 8 years and older. Start Points for each subtest are indicated in the Examiner's Manual and on the UNIT2 Record Booklet, as are the Discontinuation Rules.

Finally, environmental characteristics of the evaluation are important considerations for examiners. As mentioned previously, the examiner should be sensitive to the particular aspects or requirements of certain subtests, such as the use of a stopwatch and placement of blocks during the Cube Design subtest. Examiners should ensure that the testing environment is safe, quiet, and comfortable, with limited distractions. Appropriately-sized furniture and tables set to an appropriate height for the examinee should be used.

## UNIT2 Item Types

Each of the UNIT2 subtests includes four different item types. *Demonstration items* are presented by the examiner and are not scored. *Sample items* are completed by the examinee, with feedback from the examiner, and are not scored. *Checkpoint items* are completed by the examinee, with feedback from the examiner as needed, and scored. *Regular items* are completed by the examinee, and scored, with no examinee feedback allowed.

## Timing

Three UNIT2 subtests have timing elements. Symbolic Memory and Spatial Memory subtests are not timed per se, but require that stimulus materials be exposed for 5 seconds. Cube Design is the only task with a timed completion. As mentioned previously, speeded responses were de-emphasized on the UNIT2, with only Cube Design providing bonus points for speed. Bonus points on Cube Design never exceed more weight than the points accrued for a correct response. That is, maximum credit for a correct response is three points; a maximum of two additional points are credited for a speedy correct response.

## Record Booklets

Critical information on the UNIT2 administration is found in three convenient locations: The Examiner's Manual, the Administration at a Glance laminated sheet, and the UNIT2 Record Booklet. The Examiner's Manual includes the most comprehensive directions; the Administration at a Glance provides an abbreviated presentation of information in the manual and depictions of the eight gestures. The Record Booklet highlights specific administration information (e.g., Start Points, Discontinuation Rules, and Item Types) and time limits for the one timed subtest, as well as the correct responses for all items. The UNIT2 Record Booklet includes a worksheet allowing space for the examiner to transfer and convert raw scores to standard scores and a graph that can be completed to show performance visually (see Appendix A). Additionally, the back page of the UNIT2 Record Booklet contains the Interpretive Worksheet, which provides a number of tables to facilitate testing of hypotheses using different subtest normative and ipsative comparisons, levels of statistical significance, and incidence of occurrence in the population (e.g., comparisons among global scale scores, comparisons of subtest scores to the mean of all subtests, comparisons of subtest scores to means obtained from specific scales, and comparisons of pairs of subtests).

With one exception—Cube Design—subtests are scored dichotomously, with a score of 1 for correct responses and 0 for incorrect responses. With Cube Design, items 1–9 receive a score of 1 for correct responses and 0 for incorrect responses; however, for items 10–26, each item is scored 0, 1, 2, or 3 depending upon the correct placement of the blocks along three facets of the blocks. For items 17 through 26, the examinee can also earn as many as two bonus points for each design correctly completed within specified time ranges. The Cube Design subtest bonus points were based on the speed of responses of individuals during the standardization phase of the test, and were intended to add more ceiling to the subtest without overemphasizing speed of response.

## Subtest Administration

UNIT2 norms allow for administration of a two-, four-, or six-subtest battery; choice of each battery dictates which subtests may be administered, as well as influences administration time. Completion of the entire six-subtest Full-Scale Battery requires approximately 45 min; the two-subtest Abbreviated Battery requires about 15 min to administer, and the four-subtest or Standard Batteries require about 30 min. The four-subtest Standard Batteries can be used for most assessment purposes, including testing to determine eligibility and placement. The Standard Battery with Memory contains the same subtests as the original UNIT Standard Battery, so is recommended for re-evaluations where the original UNIT Standard Battery was used previously. The comprehensive Full-Scale Battery is suitable for in-depth assessment and provides the most diagnostic information because it is the most inclusive UNIT2 composite.

All items on the UNIT2 must be administered completely nonverbally, using gestures, pantomime, and modeling, as described in the UNIT2 Examiner's Manual. Only examiners who have had proper training and experience with psychological assessment and familiarity with the UNIT2 should administer the test. Individuals who have had formal graduate-level coursework in the administration and interpretation of individual standardized cognitive tests may use the UNIT2. Experienced individuals can easily acquire requisite administration skills by reading the UNIT2 Examiner's Manual and practicing its administration. There are detailed verbal directions and ample graphics in the Examiner's Manual to guide examiners. In addition, each kit includes the 8.5 × 11 inch laminated "Administration at a Glance" sheet, which contains brief subtest directions and depictions of the UNIT2 standard gestures.

The eight gestures that aid administration are common and easy for examinees to understand (e.g., nodding or "thumbs up" for yes or good effort, head shaking for no). The typical administration strategy for all subtests involves the examiner gaining eye-contact from the examinee, presenting the stimulus materials, pointing to the materials, waving a hand over the stimulus materials, and shrugging (using the open-handed shrugging gesture). The eight UNIT2 gestures are described and depicted in the UNIT2 Manual.

## Specific Administration Directions

Although UNIT2 administration is totally nonverbal, it should not create a stilted or artificial situation due to the absence of communication between the examiner and examinee. Examiners can and should talk to examinees if there is a common language, using helpful words or phrases as necessary (e.g., Bien, Bueno). It is helpful to talk with examinees to establish rapport, to obtain background information, and to provide encouragement; however, the examiner may NOT talk to the examinee about the UNIT2 administration directions, elaborate on test directions, or respond to examinees' specific queries regarding administration.

Each UNIT2 subtest requires the examiner to present stimulus material nonverbally. Administration procedures specific to each subtest on the UNIT2 follow.

*Symbolic Memory* stimulus pages are presented in Stimulus Book 1, and are exposed to the examinee for 5 s each. Symbolic Memory

items depict one or more universal human figures (i.e., baby, girl, boy, woman, and man) in varying combinations; each human figure is produced in both green and black. Examinees younger than 8 years must identify and select the matching image from options presented below the stimulus picture. For examinees older than 8 years, the stimulus page is presented for five seconds and then removed. The examinee then is instructed through modeling and gestures to replicate the sequence shown on the stimulus page. The examinee uses 1.5″ × 1.5″ response cards, each depicting one of the universal human figures, to reproduce the array shown on the stimulus page. The examinee's response has no time limits or bonus credit given for rapid performance. Materials needed include Stimulus Book 1, 10 Symbolic Memory Response Cards, and a stopwatch for timing stimulus exposure. The subtest is discontinued after the examinee obtains three consecutive scores of zero (i.e., three consecutive failed items).

On the *Nonsymbolic Quantity* subtest the examiner presents an easel-bound stimulus page in Stimulus Book 1, which includes an array of white and black domino-like objects with various numerical values. Each domino figure creates a numerical sequence, equation, analogy, or mathematical problem to be solved. The examiner points to the stimulus figure series, which ends with a red question mark. The examiner then waves a hand over the response options at the bottom of the page, points to the question mark, and shrugs to ask the examinee how the item should be completed. The examinee points to the response option presented below the stimulus that best completes the conceptual or numerical analogy, sequence, or problem. The subtest is discontinued after the examinee obtains three consecutive scores of zero (i.e., three consecutive failed items).

*Analogic Reasoning* requires the examinee to solve analogies presented in a matrix format, bound in Stimulus Book 2. The examinee must indicate which of several options best completes a two-cell or a four-cell analogy. Task solution requires the examinee to determine the relationships between concrete objects or abstract designs. For example, in the four-cell matrix the first cell might depict a fish and water in the second cell; the third cell might show a bird, and the fourth would be blank. The examinee would select the picture that best completes the matrix. In this case, a picture of the sky would be a correct response. This subtest is discontinued after the examinee obtains three consecutive scores of zero (i.e., three consecutive failed items).

On the *Spatial Memory* subtest examiners present a plate from Stimulus Book 2 showing a random pattern of green dots and black dots on a $1 \times 2$, $2 \times 2$, $3 \times 3$, or $4 \times 4$ cell grid. After viewing the stimuli for 5 s, the examinee attempts to recreate the pattern by placing green and black circular chips on a laminated response grid. To prevent a premature response, the examiner prohibits the examinee from touching the chips until the stimulus plate has been covered. Materials needed for this subtest include Stimulus Book 2, 16 Response Chips (8 green, 8 black), laminated Response Grids 1 ($1 \times 2$ on one side and $2 \times 2$ on the other) and 2 ($3 \times 3$ on one side, and $4 \times 4$ on the other), and a stopwatch to time stimulus exposure. This subtest is discontinued after the examinee obtains three consecutive scores of zero (i.e., three consecutive failed items).

*Numerical Series* requires the examiner to present a stimulus page in Stimulus Book 3 with arrays of numbers or mathematical symbols that create analogies, sequences, or problems. The examiner waves a hand over the depicted numbers and motions to a red question mark. After pointing to the question mark, the examiner shrugs, asking the examinee to select the option that best completes the series or solves the problem. The examiner discontinues the subtest after the examinee obtains three consecutive scores of zero (i.e., three consecutive failed items).

The *Cube Design* subtest requires the examinee to use between one and nine cubes to replicate two- or three-dimensional designs depicted on a stimulus plate. A laminated Response Mat provides a workspace for constructing the designs, and includes a diagonal baseline to allow the examinee to orient the blocks as shown on the stimulus plate. Each cube comprises six facets; two white sides, two green sides, and two half green, half white sides. The cubes are arranged by the examinee to reproduce the two- and three-dimensional figures depicted on the stimulus plates. Items 1 through 6 are scored 1 point if the examinee points to the correct matching option; items 7–9 are reproduced by the examinee and scored on one dimension (facet) only; items 10 through 26 earn up to 3 points, according to the correctness of the top, left, and right sides of three-dimensional figures. An additional 1 or 2 points complement the examinee's score on items 10 through 26 when the design is constructed accurately on all three scored sides within specified time limits. Cube Design items have liberal time limits to emphasize the power, rather than speeded nature of the task. Materials needed for the subtest include Stimulus Book 3, nine green and white cubes, the Response Mat, and a stopwatch. Examiners should remember that on items 7, 8, and 9 the examiner should present the response cubes so that the correct face for completing the design is *not* facing upward (i.e., avoiding an inadvertent exposure of the correct response). For items 11 and 12, one cube should be presented with a solid face up and one with a two-color side facing upward. For items 13 through 26, the cubes should be scrambled and presented so that at least one of each face (solid green, solid white, and two-color) faces upward. The examiner should also present the Cube Design Response Mat immediately before initiating Demonstration Item 10. On all items the examiner presents only the number of cubes needed to complete the design; the required number of blocks is printed in parentheses on the Record Booklet. The Cube Design subtest is discontinued after the examinee obtains three consecutive scores of zero (i.e., three consecutive failed items).

## Standardization and Psychometric Properties of the UNIT2

The UNIT2 was standardized and normed on a nationally representative sample of 1603 students from 33 states, ages 5 through 21 years. The total sample was 50.8% male and 49.2% female, and the stratification of the sample closely represented the U.S. population on all relevant variables. Stratification variables included: sex, race, ethnicity, Hispanic origin, geographic region, special education status, parent education attainment, and household income.

## Reliability

Average UNIT2 internal consistency estimates were computed for subtests and all composite scores. Average coefficient alphas range from 0.89 to 0.98 for subtests and scale across the full age range. Coefficients for Composite Scores across ages range from 0.93 (Memory Composite) to 0.98 (Standard Battery Without Memory and Full-Scale Battery). The average subtest reliability coefficients across age groups range from 0.89 (Spatial Memory) to 0.96 (Nonsymbolic Quantity, Analogic Reasoning, and Numerical Designs). Full-Scale reliability coefficients range from 0.97 (at ages 5, 6, 7, 8, and 12) to 0.99 (ages 16 and 19). Standard Battery with Memory Composite reliability coefficients range from 0.95 (ages 5 and 6) to 0.98 (age 17). Standard Battery without Memory Composite reliability coefficients range from 0.95 (age 5) to 0.99 (ages 16 and 21). Abbreviated Battery Composite reliability coefficients range from 0.94 (ages 5 and 6) to 0.98 (ages 12, 13, 14, 16, 17, 19, 20, and 21). FSIQ reliability coefficients reported by race and ethnicity are all 0.98, with the exception of American Indian/Eskimo examinees, who had a FSIQ reliability coefficient of 0.99. Full-Scale Composite reliability coefficients are all well above the recommended minimum (i.e., 0.90) for scores used in guiding selection/placement decisions (see Bracken 1987; Bracken and McCallum 1998; Wasserman and Bracken 2013).

To help ensure fairness and equity in testing, internal reliability estimates are reported in the UNIT2 Examiner's Manual for special populations (e.g., children with Learning Disabilities, Speech, and Language Impairments) and for the important decision-making points (i.e., FSIQ of

70 ± 10; 130 ± 10). In general, these coefficients are similarly impressive and comparable to those reported for the entire standardization sample.

UNIT2 stability was assessed using a sample of 199 participants divided into four age groups. Test-retest reliability over an average interval of 17.8 days was reported for the four groups and combined sample. Practice effects for the combined age sample were small and averaged 1.58 points for the Abbreviated Battery, 2.66 points for the Standard Battery with Memory, 2.15 points for the Standard Battery without Memory, and 2.45 points for the Full-Scale Battery. Obtained coefficients and those corrected for restriction and/or expansion in range are reported in the Examiner's Manual. Corrected subtest stability coefficients range from 0.75 (Spatial Memory) to 0.94 (Cube Design); corrected composite stability coefficients ranged from 0.86 (Memory) to 0.90 (Reasoning) for the overall sample. Stability coefficients for total test composites across the four batteries ranged from 0.85 (Abbreviated Battery) to 0.93 (Standard Battery without Memory and Full-Scale Battery). All of the stability coefficients for the composites exceeded 0.80, suggesting strong test–retest reliability and stability of the constructs assessed by the UNIT2. Moreover, the typical test–retest gain score was limited to less than 0.30 standard deviations.

Inter-rater scorer consistency was assessed by having two PRO-ED staff members independently score 50 protocols drawn at random from the normative sample. The resulting inter-rater coefficients ranged from 0.98 to 0.99, indicating excellent scoring consistency.

## Validity

UNIT2 validity is first and foremost based on the established body of evidence from the original test and published literature. Additional studies conducted as part of the UNIT2 norming provide further evidence of content-description validity, criterion-prediction validity, and construct-identification validity. The UNIT2 demonstrates content-description validity in the authors' rationale for choosing the UNIT2's format and content, item analysis procedures to select items during test construction, and differential item functioning analyses to investigate the presence or absence of bias in the test's items. To examine criterion-prediction validity, the UNIT2 was correlated with the seven major intelligence tests. The correlations between the UNIT2 composites and criterion tests ranged from moderate to very high levels, suggesting the UNIT2 correlates significantly and meaningfully with other tests of general intelligence.

The corrected correlation between the UNIT2 Standard Battery with Memory and the UNIT Standard Battery is 0.96, or nearly perfect. This level of agreement illustrates that the two editions are highly related in content and constructs assessed, and therefore research on and use of the first edition has considerable relevance to the findings for and use of the UNIT2. Correlations between the UNIT2 Full-Scale Battery and the Cognitive Assessment System-Second Edition (CAS2; Naglieri et al. 2014) Full-Scale are 0.66 for the CAS2 Standard Battery and 0.69 for the CAS2 Extended Battery. While these are large-magnitude correlations, they are slightly lower than when the UNIT2 was compared to other measures, as slightly different models of intelligence underpin the UNIT2 and the CAS2. The correlations between the UNIT2 Abbreviated Battery, the Standard Battery with Memory, the Standard Battery without Memory, and the Full-Scale Battery and the Wechsler Intelligence Scale for Children-Fourth Edition (WISC-IV; Wechsler 2003) are 0.70, 0.83, 0.83, and 0.84, respectively. Correlations between the four UNIT2 batteries and the Stanford-Binet Intelligence Scales–Fifth Edition (SB-5; Roid 2003) Abbreviated Battery IQ (ABIQ) are 0.59 (UNIT2 Abbreviated Battery), 0.69 (UNIT2 Standard Battery with Memory), 0.73 (UNIT2 Standard Battery without Memory, and 0.73 (UNIT2 Full-Scale Battery). Correlations between the UNIT2 Abbreviated Battery, the Standard Battery with Memory, the Standard Battery without Memory, and the Full-Scale Battery compared to the Comprehensive Test of Nonverbal Intelligence–Second Edition (CTONI-2; Hammill et al.

2009) were 0.84, 0.82, 0.85, and 0.85, respectively—all correlations of strong magnitude. The UNIT2 Abbreviated Battery, Standard Battery With Memory, Standard Battery Without Memory, and Full-Scale Battery correlated with the Woodcock–Johnson Tests of Cognitive Abilities–Third Edition (WJ III COG; Woodcock et al. 2001) in the large to very large range (0.64, 0.74, 0.82, and 0.79, respectively). These studies indicate that the UNIT2 is a sound measure of global intelligence, but may not be strongly correlated with measures of processing speed–speed was a factor downplayed in the UNIT and UNIT2 because of its inherent bias among some ethnic groups. These findings support the test creators' intention to put less emphasis on speed as a measure of intelligence within the UNIT2. The UNIT2 Abbreviated Battery, Standard Battery With Memory, Standard Battery Without Memory, and Full-Scale Battery also correlated with the Universal Multidimensional Abilities Scales (UMAS; McCallum and Bracken 2012) at moderate to very large levels (0.52, 0.63, 0.65, and 0.72, respectively).

Support for UNIT2 construct validity was provided by comparing means and standard deviations for different examinee age groups (i.e., growth curves), comparing the performance of different groups to the normative sample, correlating the UNIT2 with measures of academic achievement, and through using factor analysis to compare subtests to the constructs inherent in the UNIT2 model. The UNIT2 shows a strong relationship with age, and mean differences between various groups (i.e., low IQ, High IQ, ASD, Language Disorders, etc.) match expected performance ranges, suggesting that the UNIT2 is an effective and fair tool for assessing various populations of students. Validity studies are reported in the Examiner's Manual showing relationships between the UNIT2 and various achievement tests across several populations; most of these coefficients range from 0.54 to 0.79, with a few exceptions below or above this range.

Because the UNIT2 is based on a specific theoretical model, confirmatory factor analysis (CFA) can be used to assess the degree of fit with the model upon which it is based. According to the UNIT2 Examiner's Manual, the structural validity of the UNIT2 was empirically investigated by contrasting four CFA models across five age ranges (ages 5–7 years, 8–10 years, 11–13 years, 14–17 years, and 18–21 years) and the total sample using maximum-likelihood CFA. The four models examined included a one-factor model, a two-factor Reasoning X Memory model, a two-factor Reasoning X Quantitative model, and a three-factor Reasoning X Memory X Quantitative model. The results for these models were assessed using multiple indexes of fit: (a) Wheaton et al. (1977) relative chi square (chi square divided by degrees of freedom); (b) Tucker and Lewis's (1973) index of fit (TLI); (c) Bentler's (1990) comparative fit index (CFI); and (d) Browne and Cudeck's (1993) root mean square error of approximation (RMSEA). All four models fit the UNIT2 reasonably well, which supports interpreting the test as a measure of general ability, as well as interpreting its various Standard and Abbreviated Battery options. This factor analysis also supports an acceptable model at each age range examined, and the organization of subtests to scales on the UNIT2 (UNIT2 Manual; Bracken and McCallum 2016).

## Fairness

The UNIT was developed with an underlying model of fairness, considering five core concepts:

1. A language free intelligence test is less susceptible to bias than when a language-loaded test is the only intelligence test used;
2. An intelligence test with multiple indexes of ability is fairer that one that assesses a single dimension of ability;
3. An intelligence test that minimizes the need for previously acquired knowledge in the assessment of cognitive ability is fairer than one that does not;
4. An intelligence test that has minimal emphasis on timed tasks is fairer than one with greater emphasis on speed; and

5. An intelligence test with varied response modes is novel and therefore motivating, and less biased.

The UNIT2 maintains each of these features of fairness. The UNIT2 Examiner's Manual also devotes an entire chapter to describing the authors' efforts to reduce assessment bias (e.g., description of expert bias panels to eliminate faulty items; and presentation of reliability and internal and external validity data for several populations of interest such as African Americans, Hispanic Americans, Native Americans, Asian Americans, individuals with hearing impairments). Reliability coefficients were calculated for diverse groups for the Full-Scale Battery Composite and all coefficients were 0.97 or above across gender, 6 different ethnicities, and 12 different exceptionalities. Of interest to many users of nonverbal tests are mean score differences between minority samples and matched nonminority samples. For example, the median score differences between a sample of 224 Black/African American students and a matched sample of White examinees drawn from the standardization sample was 1.56 for the subtests and 10.40 for composite scores. The median score differences for a sample of 215 Hispanic examinees and matched controls were 0.78 for the subtests and 4.95 for the composites.

As is apparent, considerable effort was expended to establish fairness for the populations of interest to users of nonverbal tests. McCallum (1999) described the 13 criteria the authors of the UNIT used to establish fairness for the test. Readers interested in additional information about assessment fairness and equity may want to locate and read the McCallum publication.

## UNIT2 Interpretation

As described previously, the UNIT2 features four battery options: the abbreviated two–subtest battery, the standard four–subtest battery with memory, the standard four-subtest battery without memory, and the full-scale six–subtest battery. The various batteries were designed to assess memory, reasoning, and quantitative reasoning, as well as symbolic and nonsymbolic processing. Interpretation of the UNIT2 begins with the examiner's consideration of which battery should be administered. Making a choice among the four batteries depends on several issues, including the purpose for conducting the assessment (e.g., screening, diagnostic testing, placement), the estimated attention span of the student, time available to conduct the assessment, and related concerns. Once the choice of batteries has been made and the UNIT2 has been administered, actual test interpretation is conducted in multiple steps that consider data successively from the most global and reliable sources (e.g., FSIQ, Scale Scores) to increasingly more specific, yet less reliable sources (e.g., subtests, items).

UNIT2 results are interpreted from both inter- and intra-child (ipsative) perspectives. Both procedures have been employed by a variety of authors over the years and have become commonplace for the interpretation of psychoeducational tests (Bracken 1984, 1992, 1993, 1998, 2006a, b; Bracken and McCallum 1998; Kaufman 1979, Kaufman and Lichtenberger 1999; Kaufman and Kaufman 1983; McCallum 1991; Sattler 1988, 1992). The following discussion for interpreting the UNIT2 focuses on the guidelines outlined in the UNIT2 Manual (Bracken and McCallum 2016). Normative and ipsative strategies can be helpful for examining an individual's cognitive strengths and weaknesses.

## General Interpretation Guidelines

Traditional normative and ipsative interpretation should proceed from the most comprehensive and reliable scores to the most specific, least reliable scores. Test composites (e.g., FSIQs and scale scores) tend to be the most reliable scores because they include sources of variation from all of the subtests and scales that comprise the test. As such, these molar data are more reliable than the more molecular scores from individual subtests. Composite cognitive ability scores also are the best predictors of important "real-world"

outcomes, particularly academic and vocational success (Sattler 1992). Consequently, the most defensible interpretive strategy is to initially address the overall composite score and stop the interpretive process. However, whenever there is considerable variability among examinees' performance across individual subtests in a battery, the overall composite is not an ideal reflection of an examiner's true *overall* ability. When significant subtest and scale variation occurs, further interpretation of the test is warranted (Kaufman 1979; Kaufman and Lichtenberger 1999). Therefore, the UNIT2 Manual presents the following sequence for interpreting results. Three specific steps include: (1) Interpret the Global Intelligence Score, (2) Interpret the Construct-Specific Scores, and (3) Interpret Subtest Performance, including Pairwise Subtest Comparisons and Ipsative Subtest Comparisons. These three interpretation steps are described in the following sections.

### Step 1: Interpret the Global Intelligence Score

First, describe the examinee's performance at the composite level on the Abbreviated, Standard, or Full-Scale composites both quantitatively (e.g., standard scores, confidence intervals, percentile ranks) and qualitatively (e.g., descriptive classifications). Quantitative descriptions are based on interpretation of obtained scores relative to population parameters. Scores on the UNIT2 conform to the traditional normal "bell curve" and UNIT2 standard scores can be compared to global scores on other tests using the same metric (i.e., M = 100, SD = 15), such as the various Wechsler scales and the Woodcock–Johnson cognitive and academic batteries (e.g., see Shrank et al. 2014).

Score variability comes from two sources—reliable variance, shared and specific—and error variance. Because random error is normally distributed, obtained scores should be considered within a band of confidence that frames the obtained score by one or more standard error(s) of measurement (*SEm*), as determined by the level of confidence desired (e.g., 68, 95, 99%). Confidence intervals built around obtained scores define the probability that a given range of scores would include the examinee's "true" score with a given level of confidence. In addition to the *SEm*, the UNIT2 also reports bands of error associated with the "estimated true score," which takes into account regression toward the mean. As such, bands determining estimated true scores become more elliptical as scores move toward the extremes. The UNIT2 band of error (standard error of the estimate) can be found in Table 6.2 in the Examiner's Manual. Finally, qualitative descriptions can be used to describe levels of examinee functioning, using classifications provided in the UNIT2 Examiner's Manual. Qualitative classifications for the UNIT2 range from Very Superior to Very Delayed.

## Step 2: Interpret Construct-Specific Scores

The next step of UNIT2 Interpretation focuses on variability between the Memory, Reasoning, and Quantitative composites as they contribute to the estimate of overall cognitive functioning. If scores on these scales produce significant variability (i.e., significant differences between themselves), the global intelligence scale will serve as a limited estimate of the examinee's global ability, and performance on the UNIT2 construct-specific composites should be interpreted.

Memory, Reasoning, and Quantitative composites should be described both quantitatively and qualitatively. These scores should be examined for statistically significant and meaningful differences between each other. If a difference between two scales is statistically significant, that is, so large that it would not likely occur by chance, such a difference should be considered important, at least initially. As suggested by Kaufman and Lichtenberger (1999), a probability level of 0.05 is recommended to determine statistical significance; however, significant differences are not necessarily clinically meaningful or rare. If significant differences exist, their rarity within the general population should be considered (see Step 3). Tables 1 and 2 in Appendix E of the Examiner's Manual present scale deviation values considered significant.

## Step 3: Interpret Subtest Performance

Authors of the UNIT2 recommend interpretation at the most global level possible; however, significant, meaningful variability between scales should lead the examiner to consider individual subtest variability. The UNIT2 Interpretation section of the Examiner Record Form provides space to calculate normative and ipsative pairwise subtest comparisons. With the ipsative approach, a statistically significant difference necessitates further analysis. A subtest score that is significantly greater than the mean subtest score reflects a potential area of relative strength, while a subtest score that is significantly lower than the mean score reflects a potential area of relative weakness. The abilities associated with individual subtests should be used to generate hypotheses or possible explanations for individual subtest variations. Cautious interpretation of differences between subtests is recommended because their reliabilities, while robust, are lower than the composites. Item response patterns within a subtest can also be examined for clues about specific areas of ability or challenge.

The UNIT2 Manual provides hypotheses describing examinees with particular strengths or weaknesses on the global scale scores. For example, examinees who have stronger memory (than reasoning) may reproduce visual stimuli better than they can problem solved based on the recall of stimulus juxtapositions and relationships. Table 4.11 in the UNIT2 Manual shows hypotheses related to scale variations. Table 4.12 in the UNIT2 Manual also presents the primary and secondary abilities assessed by each UNIT2 subtest to assist with interpretation of strengths and weaknesses. Finally, the UNIT2 Examiner's Manual provides several examples describing results in reports, using two case studies.

Sound test interpretation can be conducted only when tests possess reasonably good psychometric properties. Several authors (e.g., Bracken 1987; Bracken and McCallum 1998; Wasserman and Bracken 2013) have recommended basic rules-of-thumb criteria for acceptable psychometric characteristics. For example, global scores used for making placement decisions should evidence reliability at a level of 0.90 or better; scores used for screening purposes should have reliability at a level of 0.80 or better. Also, subtest and scale floors, ceilings, and item gradients should be sufficiently sensitive to capture small differences in actual ability and range $\pm 2$ standard deviations. In addition, subtest specificity must meet commonly accepted criteria before subtests can be considered as measures of unique abilities or skills. That is, even though subtests within an instrument contribute to the measurement of general cognitive ability, each subtest may be a reasonably good measure of some specific cognitive skills or ability.

Finally, intelligence test scores should not be used in isolation. Critics of subtest interpretation (e.g., McDermott et al. 1990) have failed to examine the clinical value of subtest analysis when it is employed as only one aspect of data analysis that may be confirmed or refuted through other data sources (i.e., triangulation of data). Thus, UNIT2 subtest analysis should be conducted to generate hypotheses about children's unique intellectual strengths and weaknesses and *never* used without additional extra–test information that will allow the examiner to further evaluate the hypotheses that are generated.

These steps to interpret UNIT2 results can be implemented by adhering to the procedures described in the Appendix at the end of the chapter.

## Strengths and Limitations of the UNIT2

The UNIT provided a comprehensive and user-friendly assessment of intelligence, using a nonverbal administration format. The UNIT2 builds upon the original strengths of the UNIT and improves it further by addressing issues reviewers and users of the UNIT voiced about the instrument. The UNIT2 continues to be completely nonverbal, using Demonstration, Sample, and Checkpoint items, gestures and pantomime. Fives and Flanagan (2002) noted that the UNIT "is theoretically driven...

psychometrically sound...highly useful." They pointed out several specific advantages of the UNIT, including the completely nonverbal administration, its ability to measure multiple abilities, inclusion of multiple battery forms, the comprehensiveness of the normative sample, the capability to distinguish between tasks that do and do not require the use of internal verbal mediation, and an "exemplary" record form. The UNIT2 authors strove to maintain these perceived strengths, as well as address reviewers' perceived limitations. The perceived strengths and limitations of the UNIT2 are grouped into the following categories: test development, administration and scoring, standardization, reliability and validity, and interpretation.

## Test Development Strengths/Limitations

The UNIT was developed from a strong theoretical base, consistent with the models of Carroll (1993) and Jensen (1980), both of whom consider intelligence to be hierarchically structured and multifaceted. The UNIT authors consider intelligence as "the ability to problem-solve using memory and reasoning" (Bracken and McCallum 1998; p. 12). The multifaceted and hierarchical model of the UNIT is supported by a wealth of research showing the hierarchical nature of intelligence *and* the importance of memory and reasoning as basic building blocks (see Bracken and McCallum 1998, Jensen 1980). Fives and Flanagan (2002) pointed out that the UNIT is unique in that its underlying theory is both correlational and experimental. Both correlational (e.g., factor analyses) and experimental (lab manipulation) methodologies were instrumental in producing the supportive literature for the UNIT. The UNIT2 is built upon this same model, with the addition of quantitative thinking, a major element of other theories of intelligence, with special relevance for academic and work-force success. As such, the UNIT2 updated and improved upon the original UNIT.

Some perceived test development limitations of the UNIT included: (a) the age range extended from 5 years to 17 years 11 months only, leaving some high school and early college students out of the normative range; (b) the art work for Matrix Analogies and Object Memory contained black and white clipart line drawings, which may not have been maximally engaging for young children; (c) the stimulus easels were doubled-sided, which made the UNIT less user-friendly than optimal; and (d) the UNIT possessed inadequate floors or ceilings on some of its subtests.

Based on feedback and current research, The UNIT2 addressed all of these reported limitations of the UNIT. The upper age range of the UNIT2 was extended from 17 years, 11 months to 21 years, 11 months to allow for assessment of all high school seniors and many college students. The overall look of the test has been updated and enhanced (e.g., items have been redrawn and colored to make them more appealing). Administration is less confusing because of a new "one-way" presentation of the easel-based subtests.

The floors and ceilings on the original UNIT were very strong, with one exception. The floor was somewhat problematic for the youngest (5-year old) examinees with limited cognitive abilities, particularly on the Abbreviated Battery; consequently, the Abbreviated Battery was not recommended for use with cognitively limited 5-year-old examinees. Floors were much less problematic for the Standard and Extended Batteries. The UNIT2's average subtest ceilings were also evaluated across the entire age range, although emphasis was placed on the average ceiling for the oldest high-functioning examinees for whom the test is intended. The UNIT2 rectified all range issues at both ends of the distribution and currently ensures ample floors and ceilings for assessing extreme levels of cognitive functioning across the age range.

Additionally, item *difficulty gradients* are improved on the UNIT2. While the UNIT item gradients were good; care was taken to ensure that performance on each item changed the examinee's score by no more than 0.33 on the UNIT2. The UNIT2 reports consistently satisfactory item difficulty gradients across age and ability levels served by the test. Analyses reveal that the UNIT2 subtest difficulty gradients are consistently able to detect minor fluctuations in examinees' abilities across all age levels. Therefore, UNIT2 subtests have excellent floors, consistently excellent ceilings, and consistently satisfactory item difficulty gradients across the ages and ability levels served by the test.

## Administration and Scoring Strengths/Limitations

In their review Fives and Flanagan (2002) noted some of the UNIT administration/scoring innovations, including its three administration formats; a clear, yet inclusive record booklet, complete with start and stop rules, correct responses, and other useful information; a worksheet for subtest interpretation; a video tape and CD showing administration of the test; a University Training Guide (Bracken and McCallum 1999); a computer scoring/interpretation program released in 2001; use of a "81/2" × "11" laminated "Administration at a Glance" sheet with abbreviated directions and pictures of the eight administration gestures; consistently applied scoring rules; use of the same exposure times for the stimulus plates on all three memory subtests; and pictures in the Examiner's Manual showing the appropriate arrangement of test materials, examiner, and examinee for every subtest. These strengths have been maintained with the UNIT2 by keeping administration procedures identical to the UNIT and further developing optional computer scoring software.

Fives and Flanagan (2002) noted some areas of UNIT administration that they believed would have improved the instrument. As mentioned previously, administration of the UNIT could begin at either end of the stimulus easels and go in either direction, which was sometimes confusing to examiners. This concern was addressed with a new "one-way" presentation of the easel-based subtests.

Other perceived limitations of the UNIT included issues related to the scoring of the

Mazes subtest and redundancy of Object Memory. As it turned out, the subtests that were perceived as among the most difficult to administer and score were also the least psychometrically sound (i.e., Mazes and Object Memory). These subtests were eliminated and replaced with two psychometrically robust, easily administered quantitative reasoning subtests.

Other criticisms of the UNIT, which may still be perceived as problematic by some critics, include the administration directions being printed in the Examiner's Manual and on the Administration at a Glance card rather than on the easel. However, given the consistent administration format across all subtests, individual directions printed on the easel were deemed to be unnecessary and redundant.

Although the examiner can talk to the examinee during the evaluation, specific administration directions must be completely nonverbal, which may seem awkward initially. This has been another criticism of the UNIT. Similarly, the use of the eight standardized gestures may seem artificial at first. However, these procedures are a significant improvement over tests that allow ad lib use of nonstandardized gestures or verbalizations. Moreover, familiarity and practice with the tool will reduce any sense of administration awkwardness or artificiality. Additionally, the UNIT2 Examiner's Manual highlights that despite the test being administered in a completely nonverbal format, some verbal communication encouragement with the examinee is allowed if the examinee is capable; as long as communication does not relate to administration of the assessment items.

## UNIT2 Technical Properties Strengths/Limitations

Internal/external reliability and validity data are reported in the UNIT2 Manual. For example, age-related growth curves and results from exploratory and confirmatory factor analyses are shown as evidence of internal validity. Correlations with other tests of intelligence and various measures of achievement provide evidence of external validity. Other item characteristics are reported as well (e.g., strengths of item gradients and floor/ceiling).

Average internal consistency reliability indices are 0.96 and above across all four batteries (Abbreviated, Standard with and without Memory, and Full Scale), and 0.93 or above for all Composites (Memory, Reasoning, and Quantitative). As might be expected, subtest reliabilities are slightly lower, ranging from 0.89 (Spatial Memory) to 0.96 (Nonsymbolic Quantity, Analogic Reasoning, and Cube Design). The UNIT subtest with the lowest reliability (Mazes = 0.64) was removed and replaced with a quantitative subtest of higher reliability on the UNIT2. Also, the UNIT2 Examiner's Manual reports consistently high reliabilities for populations with various exceptionalities (e.g., 0.97 or above for the FSIQ for all groups). All composite scores and stability coefficients exceed 0.80, indicating acceptable reliability over a typical test-retest interval. Inter-rater reliability was also found to be exceptionally high.

Raw scores on cognitive tests such as the UNIT2 should increase with age, and they do. Additional validity is shown via factor analyses. For example, UNIT2 standard scores were intercorrelated using the entire normative sample. The resulting coefficients for the UNIT2 subtests (presented in Table 7.43 of the Examiner's Manual) are in the anticipated moderate to large range (median $r = 0.46$). The resulting coefficients for the UNIT2 composites (also presented in Table 7.43) are large in magnitude (median $r = 0.55$). These findings indicate that the UNIT2 subtest and composite measures are related but assess different aspects of general intelligence, an attribute that is most desirable for making diagnostic decisions or investigating intraindividual differences.

Much like the UNIT Examiner's Manual, the UNIT2 Manual reports results from a number of concurrent validity studies with various measures of intelligence for different populations. Coefficients between the UNIT2 and other intelligence tests range from moderate to nearly perfect, with correlations generally at 0.50 or above, showing the UNIT2 is highly related to other current, well-established tests of general intelligence. The UNIT2 Examiner's Manual also reports correlations between UNIT2 scores and those from a variety of achievement tests. The corrected correlation coefficients between the UNIT2 Standard and Full-Scale Batteries and the measures of achievement range from 0.54 to 0.79 and are all large or very large in magnitude, providing evidence of a meaningful relationship between the UNIT2 and academic achievement.

The following perceived limitation associated with the UNIT technical properties was previously noted: some subtests yielded average subtest reliabilities below 0.80 (i.e., split-half reliabilities are 0.76 and 0.64 for Object Memory and Mazes, respectively; test–retest values for five of the six subtests are below 0.80). However, the UNIT2 offers improved overall reliabilities by removing the subtests with the lowest reliabilities and adding two highly reliable subtests (i.e., Nonsymbolic Quantity and Numerical Series), each with average reliabilities of 0.96 across the age range.

## UNIT/UNIT2 Standardization Strengths/Limitations

UNIT2 standardization data were collected in 33 states and the sample included 1603 children and adolescents ranging in age from 5 years, 0 months to 21 years, 11 months and 30 days. These data were collected between 2010 and 2015 based on a stratified random selection procedure. The stratification of the sample closely represented the U.S. population and school-age population on all relevant variables (Bracken and McCallum 2016). Special needs children of various exceptionalities were included in the UNIT2 norms to the extent they were found in the general school population. Stratification variables included: sex, race, ethnicity, Hispanic origin, geographic region, special education status, parent education attainment, and household income.

Standardization data were collected by trained examiners. The UNIT2 Examiner Record Form collected for every examinee in the normative sample was subjected to a thorough and complete examination for quality control by specially trained staff members at PRO-ED. The UNIT2 improved upon some of the standardization limitations of the UNIT by including students through the age of 21 years, 11 months, to reflect the expanded age range for the test, and working to make the sample more representative of the population across several groups, particularly with bilingual and ESL samples (previously underrepresented in the sample group for the UNIT).

## UNIT2 Interpretation Strengths/Limitations

The UNIT2 Examiner's Manual provides extensive guidelines for normative and ipsative interpretation, along with an extensive number of tables showing step-by-step strategies for hypotheses generation. UNIT2 authors acknowledge the controversy surrounding the practice of ipsative interpretation, but recommend the procedure with the following caveat— ipsative test data should be interpreted cautiously, triangulated, and used carefully to generate hypotheses that are either supported or refuted with additional data. Interpretive aids include tables showing abilities assumed to underlie subtest performance, test-age equivalents, floor/ceiling and item gradient data, subtest technical properties, base-rates, and levels of statistical significance corresponding to various differences between subtest and scaled scores, test-age equivalents, prorated sums of scaled scores when a subtest is substituted, and procedures for substituting a subtest when one is spoiled. In addition, the Record Booklet offers a number of user-friendly interpretative characteristics, (e.g., an interpretative worksheet lends itself to ipsative and normative analyses;

descriptive categories are printed on the record form). To facilitate scoring and interpretation, a computer program is available (Bracken and McCallum 2016).

Despite the UNIT's interpretive strengths, there was little information in the Examiner's Manual describing base-rate interpretation procedures, as advocated by Glutting et al. (1997), although Wilhoit and McCallum (2002) described those procedures for the UNIT in a separate publication. The UNIT2 continues to use alternating symbolic and nonsymbolic subtest types; however, each Composite (Memory, Reasoning, Quantitative) consists of one symbolic subtest and one nonsymbolic subtest. There are no longer separate Symbolic and Nonsymbolic Composites.

## Fairness Strengths/Limitations

The UNIT2 Examiner's Manual includes an entire chapter devoted to describing test development efforts to ensure fairness and the results of fairness studies, as did the UNIT Manual. Some of the major characteristics used to promote fairness include: elimination of language from test administration; assessment of multidimensional constructs; elimination of achievement influences; limited influence of timed performance, use of variable response modes; use of ample teaching items; use of expert panels to select items; use of sophisticated item bias statistics to reduce content validity bias; comparison of psychometric properties across populations; use of sophisticated statistical techniques to reduce construct validity bias; comparison of mean scores across various populations; use of strategies to reduce predictive validity bias; and inclusion of children with diverse levels of ability into the standardization sample. Importantly, the mean scores of minority group individuals compared to the mean scores of the nonminority population are reported in the UNIT2 manual,

unlike with some other major intelligence tests (e.g., WISC-V) and differences between scores are generally less than differences commonly noted with other intelligence tests.

Despite the strong evidence of UNIT2 fairness the test still has some limitations. Although the UNIT and UNIT2 were developed and standardized to ensure cross-cultural fairness within the United States, neither was standardized for use in foreign countries. In addition, there are no specific methodological and statistical procedures in the UNIT2 Examiner's Manual detailing how it can be adapted for use in foreign countries when full-scale standarization is not possible (see McCallum et al. 2001 for cross-cultural adaptation guidelines).

## Summary

This chapter describes the essential characteristics of the UNIT2; its strengths and limitations, changes, and improvements. The test is multidimensional, and assesses memory, reasoning, and quantitative reasoning using both a symbolic and nonsymbolic administration format. Examinees will find the UNIT2 easy to administer, score, and interpret, following the same general format as the UNIT. The UNIT2 Examiner's Manual includes a wealth of data describing the technical properties of the test, in greater detail than other intelligence tests (e.g., tables related to the adequacy of ceilings, floors, and item gradients; and a chapter devoted to fairness and equity studies). The UNIT2 maintained all of the original strengths of the UNIT, including nonverbal assessment and computerized interpretation. In addition to retaining its strongest features, the UNIT2 also addresses several of the identified limitations of the original test by expanding the age range of the assessment, improving floors and ceilings, improving the representative sample, updating item quality both visually and color-wise, and fine-tuning the test to make it even more user-friendly.

# Appendix : UNIT Interpretive Worksheet

Step1: Interpret the Global Intelligence Score

| Scale | IQ | Confidence interval | Percentile rank | Descriptive category |
|---|---|---|---|---|
| | 90/95 Circle one | | | |
| Abbreviated battery | 90/95 | | | |
| Standard battery (with memory) | 90/95 | | | |
| Standard battery (without memory) | 90/95 | | | |
| Full scale | 90/95 | | | |

Step 2: Interpret the Construct-Specific Scores

| Scale | IQ | Confidence interval | Percentile rank | Descriptive category |
|---|---|---|---|---|
| | 90/95 Circle one | | | |
| Memory | 90/95 | | | |
| Reasoning | 90/95 | | | |
| Quantitative | 90/95 | | | |

*Note* When an examinee's scores on these three scales exhibit significant variability, the global intelligence score may not serve as a good estimate of global ability, and performance on the UNIT2 construct-specific composites should be interpreted

| Index score | Difference statistically different? | Normative frequency of the difference |
|---|---|---|
| Memory-reasoning | | |
| Memory-quantitative | | |
| Reasoning-quantitative | | |

## Step 3: Interpret Subtest Performance
### Pairwise Subtest Comparisons

| Scaled score difference | Statistically different? | Normative frequency of difference? |
| --- | --- | --- |
| Sym Mem-Spat Mem | | |
| Ana Reas-Cube Design | | |
| Nonsym Quan-Num Ser | | |

### Ipsative Subtest Comparisons:

| Subtests frequency? | Scaled score | Rounded mean difference | Statistically different? | Strength/weakness |
| --- | --- | --- | --- | --- |
| Sym Mem | | | | |
| Nonsym Quant | | | | |
| Ana Reas | | | | |
| Spat Mem | | | | |
| Num Series | | | | |
| Cube Des | | | | |

| MQ versus RQ Difference | Size needed for abnormality | Does size meet criteria? |
| --- | --- | --- |
| | 20 points (Extreme 15%) | YES | NO |
| | 23 points (Extreme 10%) | YES | NO |
| | 27 points (Extreme 5%) | YES | NO |
| | 34 points (Extreme 1%) | YES | NO |

# References

Bentler, P. M. (1990). Comparative fit index in structural models. *Psychological Bulletin, 107,* 238–246.

Bracken, B. A. (1984). *Examiner's manual: Bracken basic concept scale.* San Antonio, TX: The Psychological Corporation.

Bracken, B. A. (1987). Limitations of preschool instruments and standards for minimal levels of technical adequacy. *Journal of Psychoeducational Assessment, 4,* 313–326.

Bracken, B. A. (1992). *Examiner's manual: Multidimensional self concept scale.* Austin, TX: PRO-ED.

Bracken, B. A. (1993). *Examiner's manual: Assessment of interpersonal relations.* Austin, TX: PRO-ED.

Bracken, B. A. (1998). *Examiner's manual: Bracken basic concept scale: Revised.* San Antonio, TX: Harcourt Assessment.

Bracken, B. A. (2006a). *Examiner's manual: Clinical assessment of interpersonal relations.* Odessa, FL: Psychological Assessment Resources.

Bracken, B. A. (2006b). *Examiner's manual: Bracken basic concept scale* (3rd ed.). San Antonio, TX: Harcourt Assessment.

Bracken, B. A., & McCallum, R. S. (1998). *Universal nonverbal intelligence test.* Austin, TX: PRO-ED.

Bracken, B. A., & McCallum, R. S. (1999). *Universal nonverbal intelligence test: University training guide.* Austin, TX: PRO-ED.

Bracken, B. A., & McCallum, R. S. (2016). *Universal nonverbal intelligence test* (2nd ed.). Austin, TX: PRO-ED.

Browne, M. W., & Cudeck, R. (1993). Alternative ways of assessing model fit. In K. A. Bollen & J. S. Long (Eds.), *Testing structural equation models* (pp. 136–162). Newbury Park, CA: Sage.

Carroll, J. B. (1993). *Human cognitive abilities: A survey of factor-analytic studies.* New York: Cambridge University Press.

Cattell, R. B. (1963). Theory of fluid and crystallized intelligence. *Journal of Educational Psychology, 54,* 1–22.

Fives, C. J., & Flanagan, R. (2002). A review of the universal nonverbal intelligence test (unit) an advance for evaluating youngsters with diverse needs. *School Psychology International, 23*(4), 425–448.

Glutting, J. J., McDermott, P. A., & Konold, T. R. (1997). Ontology, structure, and diagnostic benefits of a normative subtest taxonomy from the WISC-III standardization sample. In D. P. Flanagan, J. L. Genshaft, & P. L. Harrison (Eds.), *Contemporary intellectual assessment: Theories, tests, and issues* (pp. 349–372). New York: Guilford.

Hammill, D. D., Pearson, N. A., & Wiederholt, J. L. (2009). *Comprehensive test of nonverbal intelligence* (2nd ed.). Austin, TX: PRO-ED.

Horn, J. L. (1968). Organization of abilities and the development of intelligence. *Psychological Review, 75,* 242–259.

Jensen, A. R. (1980). *Bias in mental testing.* New York: The Free Press.

Kaufman, A. S. (1979). *Intelligent testing with the WISC-R.* New York: Wiley.

Kaufman, A. S., & Kaufman, N. L. (1983). *Kaufman Assessment battery for children: Administration and scoring manual.* San Antonio, TX: Pearson.

Kaufman, A. S., & Lichtenberger, P. O. (1999). *Essentials of WAIS-III assessment.* New York: Wiley.

McCallum, R. S. (1991). The assessment of preschool children with the Stanford-Binet intelligence scale: Fourth edition. In B. A. Bracken (Ed.), *The psychoeducational assessment of preschool children* (2nd ed., pp. 107–132). Boston: Allyn & Bacon.

McCallum, R. S. (1999). A "baker's dozen" criteria for evaluating fairness in nonverbal testing. *School Psychologist, 53,* 40–60.

McCallum, R. S., & Bracken, B. A. (2012). *Universal multidimensional abilities scales.* Austin, TX: PRO-ED.

McCallum, R. S., Bracken, B. A., & Wasserman, J. (2001). *Essentials of nonverbal assessment.* New York: Wiley.

McDermott, P. A., Fantuzzo, J. W., & Glutting, J. J. (1990). Just say no to subtest analysis: A critique on Wechsler theory and practice. *Journal of Psychoeducational Assessment, 8*(3), 290–302.

McGrew, K. S., & Flanagan, D. P. (1998). *The intelligence test desk reference (ITDR): Gf-Gc cross-battery assessment.* Boston: Allyn & Bacon.

Naglieri, J. A., Das, J. P., & Goldstein, S. (2014). *Cognitive assessment system* (2nd ed.). Austin, TX: PRO-ED.

Roid, G. H. (2003). *Stanford-Binet intelligence scales* (5th ed.). Austin, TX: PRO-ED.

Sattler, J. M. (1988). *Assessment of children* (3rd ed.). San Diego, CA: Author.

Sattler, J. M. (1992). *Assessment of children* (3rd ed. rev.). San Diego, CA: Author.

Shrank, F. A., McGrew, K. S., & Mather, N. (2014). *Woodcock-Johnson IV: Test of cognitive abilities.* Rolling Meadows: Riverside.

Tucker, L. R., & Lewis, C. (1973). A reliability coefficient for maximum likelihood factor analysis. *Psychometrika, 38,* 1–8.

Wasserman, J. D., & Bracken, B. A. (2013). Fundamental psychometric considerations in assessment. In J. R. Graham & J. A. Naglieri (Eds.), *Handbook of psychology. Volume 10: Assessment psychology* (2nd ed., pp. 50–81). Hoboken, NJ: Wiley.

Wechsler, D. (1939). *Measurement of adult intelligence.* Baltimore, MD: Williams and Wilkins.

Wechsler, D. (2003). *Wechsler intelligence scale for children* (4th ed.). San Antonio, TX: Pearson.

Wheaton, B., Muthén, B., Alwin, D., & Summers, G. (1977). Assessing reliability and stability in panel models. In D. R. Heise (Ed.), *Sociological methodology* (pp. 84–136). San Francisco, CA: Jossey-Bass.

Wilhoit, B., & McCallum, R. S. (2002). Profile analysis of the Universal nonverbal intelligence test (UNIT) standardization sample. *School Psychology Review*.

Woodcock, R. W. (1990). Theoretical foundations of the WJ-R measures of cognitive ability. *Journal of Psychoeducational Assessment, 8*, 231–258.

Woodcock, R. W., McGrew, K. S., & Mather, N. (2001). *Woodcock-Johnson III test of cognitive abilities*. Rolling Meadows, IL: Riverside.

# Leiter-3: Nonverbal Cognitive and Neuropsychological Assessment

## Gale H. Roid and Christopher Koch

The need for nonverbal measures in psychology and education is more urgent than ever before. The multicultural nature of schools and society in Western countries is expanding faster in this decade than ever before due to significant immigration. And, the number of languages spoken by students in schools and universities has increased greatly causing the need for non-English measures of ability, achievement, and behavior. A recent report from the U.S. Department of Education (2016) showed 19 prominent languages spoken by students in English Language Learner (ELL) programs. Spanish was the most prominent (71% of ELL students nationally). Other prominent languages included Chinese, Arabic, Vietnamese, Haitian, Russian, Navajo, and 12 other languages ranked second or third in frequency among the 21 U.S. States with 45,000 or more ELL students. Furthermore, cognitive abilities are often listed in the clinical criteria for disorders in the DSM-5 (American Psychiatric Association 2013), frequently as "rule out" conditions. For example, for language, communication, and learning disorders (315.00, 315.1, 315.2, 315.39), the condition cannot be due to low intellectual ability to satisfy the criteria. So, using an estimate of IQ, found to be near average or above, would rule out intellectual deficiency as a reason for the disorder. Given the known probability of learning and communication disabilities in schoolchildren and adults (U.S. Department of Education 2007), combined with the frequency of non-English proficiency, the need for nonverbal cognitive assessment is well established. The recently published Leiter International Performance Scale, Third Edition (Leiter-3) provides a completely nonverbal, comprehensive measure of both cognitive and neuropsychological processes, and is the subject of this chapter.

## Goals and Rationale for Leiter-3 Development

The Leiter International Performance Scale (Leiter 1938, 1979; Roid and Miller 1997) has a long history of use in special education and psychology (Levine 1982; Roid et al. 2009). The validity and usefulness of the current edition (Roid et al. 2013) rests in part on this long history of research and development. This chapter details the development of the 3rd Edition.

Although the theoretical background and nonverbal nature of the Leiter have been highly praised, it was generally felt that the original Leiter "lacked the necessary technical characteristics to make it psychometrically adequate" (Salvia and Ysseldyke 1991, p. 208). For these reasons, the goals of the Leiter-R and Leiter-3

G.H. Roid (✉)
Testing Research, 1838 Mistwood Drive NE, Keizer, OR 97303, USA
e-mail: galeroid@gmail.com

C. Koch
George Fox University, 414 N, Meridian Street, Newberg, OR 97132, USA
e-mail: ckoch@georgefox.edu

© Springer International Publishing AG 2017
R.S. McCallum (ed.), *Handbook of Nonverbal Assessment*,
DOI 10.1007/978-3-319-50604-3_8

standardizations included a full range of psy-chometric studies and a nationally representative norm sample.

The Leiter-3 is an individually administered, nonverbal battery of 10 subtests that measure three major dimensions of cognitive ability—General Intellectual Ability (IQ), Nonverbal Memory, and Processing Speed. The Leiter-3 was designed for children, adolescents, and adults, ages 3 years, 0 months to 75+ years. Each subtest comes with pantomime or other nonvocal (un-spoken, 'nonvocal') instructions so that neither the examiner nor the examinee needs to speak aloud during the administration of each subtest. Thus, the Leiter-3 provides a fully nonverbal, nonvocal set of subtests. For hearing/speaking examinees, the examiner is encouraged to build rapport by speaking with the examinee between subtests. The Cognitive Battery subtests (4 sub-tests and one alternative) can be administered in approximately 30–40 min. These general cogni-tive subtests provide a nationally standardized estimate of nonverbal IQ. The remaining five subtests measure various memory, attention, and cognitive interference processes. This Attention Memory (A/M) Battery can be completed in another 20–30 min and provides a supplement for measuring cognitive processes associated with disorders. The A/M subtests allow examin-ers to identify strengths and weaknesses in neu-rocognitive processes suspected of affecting the IQ estimate or providing evidence for additional neuropsychological testing.

## History of the Leiter

Leiter (1938) developed the test for children and adolescents with multi-ethnic backgrounds (in Hawaii and California), using a unique "block and frame" response method, which required examinees to move wooden blocks into slots in a wooden frame to complete puzzles, figure com-pletion, numerical series, visual matching, and sequences of geometric or pictorial objects. The test did not require spoken directions from either the examiner or examinee; instead administration relied on pantomime directions and the obvious movement of blocks for responding. The test was totally revised by Roid and Miller (1997), who created a modern battery of 20 subtests with nationally standardized scale scores, for ages 2–20 (Roid et al. 2009). The test used a series of response cards or pointing responses to measure various aspects of cognitive ability (10 subtests) and 10 subtests measuring memory and attention factors. Leiter-3 is the most recent iteration.

## Theoretical Rationale

**Cognitive Model.** A unified cognitive ability model has emerged from a number of indepen-dent researchers over the last 50 years. Carroll (1993) proposed a three-stratum theory of cog-nitive abilities based on factor analysis of more than 460 data sets, including special education and multi-ethnic samples. Carroll's model included aspects of the fluid–crystallized theory of Horn and Cattell (1966) and the three-level hierarchical model documented by Gustafson (1984). Although variations in the number and names of the factors occur in different studies, one consensus shows an integrated 8-factor Cattell–Horn–Carroll model detailed by Flana-gan et al. (2013), and Schneider and McGrew (2012). At the highest level (Stratum 3) is a general intelligence or "g" factor (see Fig. 8.1). At the second level (Stratum 2) are broad factors identified as Fluid Reasoning, Crystallized Ability (or Knowledge/Verbal Comprehension), Short-Term Memory (or Working Memory), Visual-Spatial, Long-term Retrieval, Quantitative Reasoning, Processing Speed, and Auditory Processing. At the bottom level (Stratum 1) is a large number of "primary" factors, nested within the second-level factors. For example, Spatial Relations, Visualization, Perceptual Integration and Closure Flexibility are nested within Visual-Spatial Ability.

**Relationship to Theories of Autism Spec-trum Disorder (ASD).** Clearly, autism is an increasingly prevalent condition in the U.S. (CDC 2007; U.S. Department of Education 2016) and often requires nonverbal assessment (Minshew and Goldstein 1998). To meet this

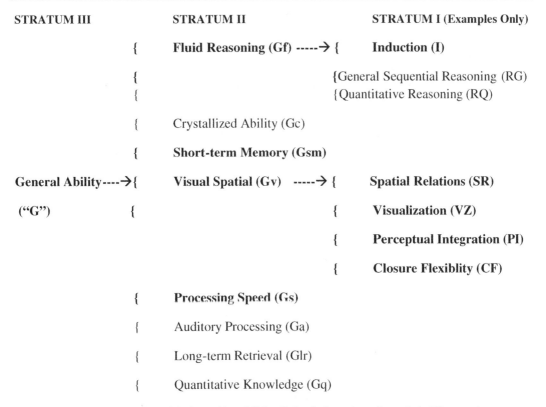

| STRATUM III | STRATUM II | STRATUM I (Examples Only) |
|---|---|---|
| | **Fluid Reasoning (Gf)** -----➔ { | **Induction (I)** |
| | { | {General Sequential Reasoning (RG) |
| | { | {Quantitative Reasoning (RQ) |
| | { Crystallized Ability (Gc) | |
| | { **Short-term Memory (Gsm)** | |
| General Ability----➔{ | **Visual Spatial (Gv)**   -----➔ { | **Spatial Relations (SR)** |
| (**"G"**)          { | { | **Visualization (VZ)** |
| | { | **Perceptual Integration (PI)** |
| | { | **Closure Flexiblity (CF)** |
| | { **Processing Speed (Gs)** | |
| | { Auditory Processing (Ga) | |
| | { Long-term Retrieval (Glr) | |
| | { Quantitative Knowledge (Gq) | |

**Fig. 8.1** Cattell–Horn–Carroll model of cognitive abilities (Leiter-3 dimensions shown in boldface type)

need, the Leiter-R (Roid and Miller 1997) was highly recommended by Klinger et al. (2012) for use with children diagnosed with ASD. Because of this and other positive reviews from clinicians, the Leiter-3 was purposely designed for use in ASD intellectual assessment. Theories of ASD were studied in detail during the development of Leiter-3 (e.g., Mayes and Calhoun 2003, 2004; Volkmar et al. 2004), including various grant proposals submitted for research funding by the senior author. For example, the theory proposed by Minshew and Williams (2007) was based on a cognitive theory of ASD called complex information processing (CIP) to explain the observed deficits in autism (Williams et al. 2006). The CIP model arose from two observations of characteristics exhibited by ASD individuals: (a) deficits on neuropsychological tests in conceptualization and complex memory and language, combined with good motor abilities, and (b) patterns of superior function in attention, simple memory and language, and visual-spatial

abilities. The Leiter-3 specifically included measures targeted for complex information processing in ASD (e.g., the subtests "Sequential Order," and "Repeated Patterns" within the nonverbal fluid reasoning portion). And, former users of Leiter who assess clients with ASD strongly recommended the "hands on" method of using the blocks to show their client responses to test items. Thus, the Leiter-3 provides clinical assessment to supplement ASD evaluations to the CIP model (Mayes and Calhoun 2003, 2004; Bishop et al. 2006). For more information on the importance of cognitive assessment for ASD, consult references such as Kuschner et al. (2007) and Mayes and Calhoun (2004).

## Description of the Leiter-3

The Leiter-3 includes two sets of subtests—a set of five cognitive ability subtests with four of them providing a nonverbal IQ and a supplementary set with two attentions, two memories, and one cognitive interference (Stroop 1935) subtests. The sets of subtests can be used separately or together. When used together, they have the advantage of being standardized on exactly the same standardization sample. Hence, the statistical significance of differences between subtest and composite scores can be calculated accurately for strength and weakness analysis.

## Leiter-3 Subtest, Administration and Scoring

Two formats of stimuli and response mode are used in these subtests: (a) colorful pictures in the stimulus book presenting the items with cards used by the examinee to respond and (b) arrays of stimuli on the easel seated above the slotted frame are used with rounded plastic blocks, with printed graphics, which can be moved into slots of the frame.

In the standard subtest order, Figure Ground is first, using the picture/card method. Form Completion is second using a combination of picture/card and block/frame, and the remaining three subtests employ the block/frame method (Classification/Analogies, Sequential Order, and the optional Visual Patterns). Subtests are described below:

1. **Figure Ground (FG).**
   FG is a basic visual interference task, but compounded by distractions. The examinee searches for a target object on the Stimulus page that is pictured on a response card. The complete target object is included in the stimulus, but since the object is embedded in increasingly complex backgrounds, the backgrounds can mask the object so that it becomes difficult to recognize. Figure ground perception is a construct which has been widely studied over decades with early studies provided by Gottschaldt (1928). Thurstone and Thurstone (1962) found that performance on this task was associated with visual closure and correlated with freedom from distractibility. Performance on this task

is related to the cognitive flexibility of the individual (i.e., the ability of perceptual shifting) since the individual must shift attention between a discrete figure and complex backgrounds, necessitating a change of perceptual set (Talland 1965). Figure Ground also requires that the individual have adequate visual scanning skills and an effective search strategy. It is a subtest which requires good inhibition from the individual, as impulsivity will result in pointing randomly to similar shapes rather than focusing on the target object embedded in the figures. This subtest lends itself to clinical qualitative observations of process such as perceptual bias to one side of the stimulus page, misidentification of objects, or perseveration (Christensen 1979).

2. **Form Completion (FC).**
   This subtest requires organization of disarranged pieces. Cognitive flexibility is tested by requiring the examinee to scan between parts and the "whole" to arrive at a solution, a process that is mostly deductive. As the examinee moves back and forth between the stimulus and response, working memory permits the individual to hold both the stimuli and possible responses in mind simultaneously as the images are constructed and deconstructed. Items are conceptually related to previous research describing Figure Ground processes (Hooper 1983) with easiest items being meaningful familiar objects. This subtest requires perceptual scanning, recognition, and the ability to perceive fragmented percepts as wholes. This task assesses a "higher level of perceptual ability" than a matching task (Dee 1970). Visual organization tasks, such as the type assessed in Form Completion, require synthesizing activities, whereas visual interference tasks, such as the type assessed in Figure Ground, require discrimination of figures from interfering elements.

3. **Classification/Analogies (CA).**
   Following extensive scaling studies using item-response theory (Lord 1980) analysis, items from the Leiter-R classification subtest

were combined with the more difficult Design Analogies' items to form the CA subtest. The classification tasks among the easier items of the subtest require pattern recognition and mental shifting of concepts. This subtest progresses into functional classification where objects which "belong together" are grouped because of usage rather than size, shape, or color (Lezak 1995; Wang 1984; Nelson 1976).

For the analogies items, in the higher difficulty level (e.g., above age 6), items are presented in the classical "matrix reasoning" format. The matrix items require solving visual analogy problems presented in tables of two columns and two rows of objects, or more of each dimension, with one "box" of the table missing. The CA items were designed to measure pattern analysis and prediction of "what goes next" in a series of objects, and classifying the most common types of abstraction and concept formation (Lezak 1995; Wang 1984; Nelson 1976). Relationships are induced from concepts (i.e., the bed "goes with" the pillow) or elements (i.e., all the pictures with a shadow "go with" the block showing a shape with a shadow). This subtest is also a measure of matrix reasoning ability which has been widely researched in previous tests (Elliot 2008; Raven et al. 1998; Roid 2003). The individual must select an appropriate response from the possible blocks based upon the perceived relationship between the figures in the matrix. Classification/Analogies measures the ability to generate rules from partial information, and inductively hypothesize what piece would complete the whole pattern. This type of task appears to be a valid measure of general ability (Carroll 1993).

4. **Sequential Order (SO)**.
The subtest requires nonverbal reasoning ability and rule generation for analyzing sequential information (Carroll 1993). The individual must understand the relationship between stimuli in order to find the missing elements at the end or in the middle of the series. The ability of the individual to perceive sequential patterns and determine the rules that govern the relationships between pictures is assessed. On this subtest, the "whole" is the final pattern which is induced from multiple stimuli.

5. **Visual Patterns (VP)**.
This subtest was created from the Leiter-R Matching subtest, combined with the Repeated Patterns subtest. At the youngest ages, this optional subtest evaluates the individual's basic ability to match visual stimuli with no memory component. This has been described as perceptual acuity, measuring visual discrimination and awareness of spatial orientation (Elliot 2008). At the youngest age levels, the task is simple, with matching by color or shape and large features being prominent. As the task progresses, attention to detail is required, as the matching dimensions become smaller and less prominent. The subtest does not include rotations or pattern reversals. It requires the ability to scan and make visual comparisons between figures while the individual is tracking several stimuli simultaneously, such as number, orientation of parts, and location of lines. This task requires basic visualization processes, but also necessitates patience and freedom from impulsivity on the part of the individual, as he or she must check different stimuli against the model as the items increase in complexity. The subtest is similar to pattern completion fluid reasoning tasks developed by Thurstone and Turnstone's (1962).

6. **Attention Sustained (AS)**.
The subtest relies on a cancellation task designed to assess prolonged visual attention, and requires good visual scanning and motoric inhibition on a rapid repetitive motor task (crossing out stimuli). This classic processing speed task was used clinically by Albert (1973), employed in research on learning disabilities by Rourke (1988), and autism by Goldstein et al. (2001). Under the name "cancellation," it was included in the Wechsler (2003, 2008) scales. Although a motor response is required, the motoric demands are quite limited. During the task,

clinicians can observe the process by which each individual accomplishes the task and if the individual does more poorly on the last item of the set of four, where the stimuli are arrayed in a random manner on the page instead of being presented in straight rows, it may be evidence of visual-spatial inattention (Lezak 1995). Poor performance on this task may reflect an underlying attention problem that is affecting performance on the other cognitive subtests. This subtest can reflect the general slowing of attention due to various brain conditions, stages of dementia, and effects of other insults to neurological function (Lezak 1995).

7. **Forward Memory (FM)**.
The FM subtest measures sequential memory span. Also, it requires an organized processing style. Sets of pictures (e.g., boat, car, and shoe) are shown and the examiner touches a sequence of pictures (beginning at one and increasing to seven pictures in the most difficult items). The examinee is taught to touch the pictures in exactly the same way as the examiner. Thus, in addition to remembering the sequence of pictures, the individual must also inhibit the memory of previous sequences of pictures. This subtest, along with Subtest 9, Reverse Memory, is similar to the Digit Span subtest of the Wechsler tests where there are both forward and reverse sequences of digits to be recalled. However, the Leiter-3 version uses visual material without vocalized examiner directions. Another advantage of the nonverbal format is that the examinee does not have to hear and comprehend the name of the picture—only its spatial position, color, and visual features. Digit Span and Forward Memory measure similar constructs—short-term memory, and in the reverse task, working memory where information is stored and manipulated in short-term memory.

8. **Attention Divided (AD)**.
The AD subtest is new in Leiter-3 and employs a game-like format. The subtest measures the ability to play a game of slapping targeted cards (marked with a red triangle) as cards with and without the target are sequentially placed in front of them. Then, examinees must learn to place soft foam disks into a container as quickly as possible. For young children, the task includes only 12 yellow disks, but older children and adults have more disks, sorting red and yellow disks into separate containers. After learning both tasks, the examinee must do both tasks at the same time (within the time it takes to present all the cards). Thus, the subtest measures concentration and executive processing of mental and motor behaviors while completing two different tasks at the same time. If the individual has difficulty with this "double or multiple tracking" (Lezak 1995, p. 551), he or she is likely to slow down or break down during the task. One young adult with diagnosed ADHD in the tryout sample vocalized his difficulty by saying "I can't do this!" The ability to attend to more than one thing at a time has been found to be very informative for teachers and parents interested in helping children pay attention in noisy classrooms. And, difficulty with dividing attention is a sensitive measure of subtle neurological deficits and, to an extent, autism (Mundy and Crowson 1997). This difficulty may be the only documentable mental change after a head injury (Lezak 1995) or other neurological condition and may be clinically important to observe, particularly, for examinees who deviate from the instructions.

9. **Reverse Memory (RM)**.
The RM subtest requires touching pictures as in the Forward Memory subtest. But, this subtest measures working memory because the examinee touches pictures in *reverse* order from that required in Forward Memory. Individuals who have less mental flexibility or become confused easily may have difficulty switching tasks from Forward Memory. For this reason, the RM subtest is administered after a diversion (e.g., another subtest, AD is administered). The RM task is complex, requiring the individual to store and juggle information using mental effort and good working memory. Reverse Memory

does not evaluate the same cognitive processes as Forward Memory and the two scales have been found to be disparate in a number of clinical groups (Banken 1985; Lezak 1995; Reynolds 1997; Sullivan et al. 1989). Raw score differences between forward and reverse memory appear to be varied and not as predictable as those with digits forward and backward (e.g., Wechsler scales typically show a 2-digit difference on average, Wechsler 1991). It appears that the gap between FM and RM on Leiter-R or Leiter-3 may increase as the span increases. For example, younger individuals may do four pictures forward, but three pictures in reverse (87%), while older individuals may do eight pictures forward, but only five pictures reversed.

10. **Nonverbal Stroop (NS).**

The subtest is a nonverbal version of a classic, cognitive interference test. The color-word Stroop test is one of the most widely used tasks for examining cognitive processing. The task is based on Stroop's (1935) original experiment in which he presented the words red, blue, green, brown, and purple twice per row in a $10 \times 10$ matrix using incongruent ink and asked participants to name the color of the ink (Experiment 2). The time to complete the task was compared to a control condition in which the same colors appeared in a $10 \times 10$ matrix but as color blocks instead of color words. It took significantly longer to name the colors of the incongruent color words than the colors of the blocks. This difference between the two conditions is commonly referred to as Stroop interference. There have been a number of variations to the task over the years including a picture–word (Rosinski et al. 1975), sorting (Tecce and Happ 1964), and emotional Stroop task (Cha et al. 2010). Of particular importance is the finding that Stroop interference can occur when the color and word are presented together but are not integrated (Dalrymple-Alford and Budayr 1966; Dyer 1973). A color block appearing alongside a color word would be an example of a nonintegrated pair. It is important to note that the color and word need to be

presented close to each other in both time (Dyer and Severance 1973) and space (Kahneman and Chajczyk 1983; Kahneman and Henik 1981) in order to be processed "together." It is generally assumed that the word is processed faster than the color from a color–word pair and must, therefore, be inhibited in order to respond correctly to the color (Dunbar and MacLeod 1984; Posner and Snyder 1975). Carroll (1993) further suggested that performance on the Stroop task is related to naming speed and reading speed. The central role of words in these explanations of the Stroop task suggests that the task itself is not possible to administer nonverbally. That assumption was challenged by presenting two color blocks, instead of a color block and a color word, and asking participants to name the color of a target block. Responses were faster when the two blocks were the same color than when the two blocks were different colors (e.g., Koch and Kubovy 1996). Thus, interference scores similar to the color–word task can be obtained without using words. Performance on this revised Stroop task parallels the performance of a variety of clinical groups with the traditional color–word task (cf., Koch and Roid 2012).

A similar task was developed for the Leiter-3 using two colored circles. To ensure that the two circles were processed together instead of as independent circles, two Gestalt grouping principles were used. First, the two circles in a pair were connected with a line creating a dumbbell (connectedness). An oval was also drawn around the pair of circles (enclosure). A nonverbal response was also needed to make the task entirely nonverbal. Consequently, a test format was selected in which a target stimulus was presented on the left with alternative stimuli presented to the right. The goal of the task is to identify, or cross out, the matching correct response among the alternatives while ignoring the distracters. Participants are given 45 s to identify as many target matches as possible. More items were identified when the circles were the same color compared to when the two circles within a pair were different colors (Koch et al. 2011; Koch and Barr 2010). The difference between the two conditions of the task is an indicator of interference.

## Scores Provided

The raw score for each of the Leiter-3 subtests is typically the sum of the correct responses marked on the Record Form. For each subtest, the distribution of raw scores, at each age, was converted into normalized scaled scores with a mean of 10 and a standard deviation of 3. To increase the sensitivity of scores in the gifted range, the scaled scores range from 1 to 20 which was used in the subtest profiles of intellectual-ability tests, instead of the standard 1–19 range. The age grouping intervals for the norms vary by age, ranging from 2-month intervals for examinees who range in age from 3 to 10, to 10-year intervals for individuals in the 30–70-year-old range.

To convert raw scores into scaled scores for each of the subtest profile scores, the examiner uses the standard norm tables for the age range that fits the examinee's chronological age. Scores are then recorded on the front of the Record Form, in a manner similar to other ability tests.

## Nonverbal Stroop Scores

Stroop (1935) required participants to name the colors of 100 color words and recorded the time to complete the task. The Color and Word Stroop Test (Golden et al. 2003) requires examinees to name as many colors as they can within 45 s. The number of correct colors is recorded. Therefore, the task has been presented measuring both time and number (accuracy). However, even if time is held constant (e.g., 45 s), it is still possible to use the total correct score as an index of speed—the more the correct items, the faster the examinee has responded accurately. Consequently, the NS task in the Leiter 3 has norms for the number of correct and number incorrect items for both the congruent and incongruent tasks. The number correct scores are primary and used in the main profile of scaled scores. The numbers

incorrect for both the congruent and incongruent have interpretative norms in the "Supplemental Attention/Memory Scores" section of the Record Form. Other indexes for examinee processing speed can be easily calculated by examiners. For instance, dividing the number of correctly identified colors by 45 s results in a colors/second time that can be used as an indicator of processing speed.

## Supplemental A/M Subtest Scores

There are five Supplemental A/M scores for an in-depth analysis of the accuracy of the individual's performance, focusing often on errors or incorrect responses. These scores were standardized on the same normative sample as the main subtest scores, but often have more restricted ranges of scores because of the predominance of individuals with zero errors. Thus, the scores are most useful as diagnostic information supplemental to the main profile scores with a profile chart that ranges from 0 to 12 rather than 0 to 20 as done with the main profile scores. Table 8.1 shows the names of the five supplemental scores and a brief explanation of their scoring and purpose.

## Nonverbal IQ and Composite Scores

To simplify scoring and facilitate the profiling, all IQ and Composite scores have been placed on the IQ scale (mean of 100 and standard deviation of 15). However, be aware that the attention and memory (A/M) Composite scores are not included in IQ calculations, for they are not measures of global intellectual ability. Rather, the A/M composites are summative indexes of factors of neuropsychological processes that are more specific than general ability.

## General Ability (Nonverbal IQ) Scores

One general ability score—the nonverbal intelligence quotient (IQ)—is available from the Leiter-3. The foundation for the IQ score is the

**Table 8.1**  The supplemental attention/memory subtest scores

| | |
|---|---|
| Attention sustained errors (ASe) | The number of incorrectly marked objects is a raw score, converted into a scaled score for exploring possible attention-deficit or impulsive responding |
| Attention divided correct (ADc) | The number of cards slapped and number of foam pieces placed correctly (added together) are converted into a scaled score. The score shows ability to split attention to two tasks simultaneously |
| Attention divided incorrect (ADi) | The number incorrect on both tasks, added together, form a score that can indicate poor motor ability, coordination issues, slowness of response, or poor executive functioning |
| Nonverbal Stroop congruent incorrect (NSci) | The number of incorrect markings for color-matched items on the first trial of NS can indicate evidence for a response pattern similar to one obtained from atypical populations (e.g., TBI, ADHD) or reflect other neurological or visual-attention difficulties |
| Nonverbal Stroop incongruent incorrect (NSii) | The number of incorrect markings for color-mismatched items on the second trial of NS can indicate even greater deficits in motor, visual, or neurological processing than the congruent incorrect score |

| Fluid Reasoning | | Visual-Spatial | | (optional Visual) |
|---|---|---|---|---|
| Classification-Analogies (CA) | Sequential Order (SO) | Figure Ground (FG) | Form Completion (FC) | Visual Patterns (VP) |

Processing Speed

| Attention Sustained (AS) | Nonverbal Stroop Incongruent—Number correct (NSic) |
|---|---|

Nonverbal Memory

| Forward Memory (FM) | Reverse Memory (RM) |
|---|---|

Additional Attention Subtest

| Attention Divided (AD) |
|---|

**Fig. 8.2**  Structure of the Leiter-3 subtests and composites nonverbal IQ

sums of the scaled scores for the subtests that compose the IQ estimate. The IQ score provides a measure of "g," or general nonverbal intelligence. Figure 8.2 shows the subtest composition of the IQ score. There are four subtest-scaled scores included in the calculation of IQ. Preference is given to using the first four cognitive subtests (FG, FC, CA, and SO) and only use Visual Patterns as a substitute if one of the other four subtests is spoiled. The reason for using Visual Patterns as a substitute is that it is slightly

lower in reliability at certain age levels compared to the other four.

To obtain the IQ score, use the scaled score information on the Record Form to organize all the subtests for summing of scaled scores for the IQ or Composite scales. Scaled scores have a mean of 10 and a standard deviation of 3. To provide more precision of measurement at low and high ends of the IQ continuum, the Leiter-3 scaled scores range from zero to 20, instead of the typical 1–19 range. Using the sum of scaled scores to estimate IQ should be familiar to many school psychologists and other assessment professionals.

The percentile equivalent of each standard score can be found in the appendix of the manual or from any standard percentile table because the IQ and Composite scores are normalized. Confidence intervals are also recommended, especially for the IQ score, because they emphasize to parents, teachers, and other professionals that all such scores have an element of measurement error. Tables for constructing the confidence intervals are provided in the appendix of the test manual. These tables provide the magnitude, based on standard errors of measurement (SEM), to create confidence intervals for the IQ and Composite scores. The user simply subtracts and then adds the confidence interval value, based on the age grouping. For example, a 99% interval is created by multiplying the SEM by 2.58 and using the rounded value to add and subtract from the IQ estimate.

## AM Battery Composite Scores

There are two Composite scores available on the Leiter-3 supplemental A/M subtests. Best practice for assessment professionals starts by considering the individual's needs and reason for referral that required the assessment. The Composite scores of Nonverbal Memory and Processing Speed provide a higher degree of test reliability than the individual subtests, and therefore should be the first line of interpretation. To simplify scoring and facilitate the profiling of composites, all scores have been placed on an IQ-type metric (mean of 100 and a standard deviation of 15). However, the metric should not imply that the Composite scores are interpreted as supplemental estimates of nonverbal IQ.

## Use of the Criterion-Referenced Growth Scale

The Leiter-3 growth scores have been developed to counteract a well-deserved criticism of standardized norm-referenced scales—that norm-referenced scaled scores do not always provide detailed information about the skills of an individual or the growth that an individual is achieving. The limitations of norm-referenced scores are particularly present for individuals who are significantly delayed for their age. For example, if a child is functioning at a very low level (scaled score of 1 or 2), he or she may never show an increase in that score due to continual comparison to the normative group for each older age category.

The metric of the growth values and the growth scale scores is similar to the W-scale used in the Woodcock series of tests (e.g., Woodcock and Dahl 1971; Woodcock et al. 2000), with scores centered on a value of 500 set at the beginning of 5th grade (10 years, 0 months). Each task on the Leiter-3 has a value from 380 to 560 along the growth scale located at the top of the Growth scale record form. The estimate of the degree of difficulty for each task is expressed by its location on the growth scale. Using the tables in the manual, it is possible to convert the raw scores for each subtest, each composite, and each IQ estimate into Growth scale scores and to identify the item growth values for each item passed or failed on the Leiter-3. These converted scores are provided to assist with program planning, determining change over time, and explain results to clients, parents, and teachers. To determine an individual's growth value on each item, first locate the item numbers for all items that the individual passes. Next, use the tables in the manual to find the actual growth values for each item. Separate tables are provided for Core Cognitive and A/M items. Those values will explain the relative item difficulty of each item passed and failed by the individual. The individual's item growth values can range from approximately 380 to 560. In addition to values for the items passed by, growth scale scores providing criterion-referenced ability estimates are available for subtests, composites, and Nonverbal IQ (Woodcock 1999). The growth scale is consistent across ages and across different collections of subtests, and provides an "anchor scale" for referencing all subtest and composite scores.

## The Leiter-3 Examiner Rating Scale

The Examiner Rating scale was originally developed for Leiter-R (Roid and Miller 1997) and is repeated in Leiter-3 with the same content. The scale has been widely used by examiners and researchers (e.g., Nordlund 1998) to provide an assessment of test-taking behavior and sensory or social–emotional factors in the examinee. The domains included in the ratings include attention, organization/impulse control, activity level, sociability, energy, feelings, regulation, anxiety, and sensory reaction. Each domain has four to eight items rated on a scale from zero to three and the sum of the ratings provide raw scores. The raw scores can be converted into scaled scores (mean 10, standard deviation 3). Two groupings of the separate domains form the Composites—Cognitive/Social and Emotional/Regulations. The Composite scores have the same metric as the Cognitive Composites—mean 100, standard deviation 15. However, in terms of national norms, most individuals have positive test behavior and typical, adaptive social-emotional behaviors. Therefore, the range of domain and Composite scores for the Examiner Rating scales are somewhat restricted above the mean scores.

## Standardization and Psychometric Properties of the Leiter-3

**Stratification**. Collection of the standardization sample began in 2010 employing the census data (U.S. Census 2009) and was updated in 2011 (U. S. Census 2011). A stratified random sample of individuals was developed, taking into account all the strata of the plan—age, gender, race/ethnicity, educational level (parent or adult individual), and geographic region. After examiners ("field researchers") were recruited for all four census regions of the United States, each was given a detailed description of the cases needed for their region.

**Examiners**. Training included a detailed description of the sampling strata, which was also printed in the demographic section of the standardization Record Form completed for all cases. The process of collecting cases for the standardization continued through 2011 and included a number of steps. For example, each field researcher developed a list of major sources for obtaining a sample in his/her vicinity for individuals within the appropriate age range. They then obtained administrative permission, selected participants based on a master list provided by the publisher, administered the Leiter-R, and conveyed the results to the publisher.

**Geographic Representation**. With 150 field researchers selected across all four U.S. Census regions, geographic randomization of the sample was enhanced. These examiners were selected to participate in the study because they were qualified professionally based on work history, education including measurement instruction, and experience with individually administered tests. Examinees were selected based on certain criteria, i.e., they had no severe physical, mental, or emotional impairment (unless included in clinical validity studies separate from norms), or other biological risk factors, and could follow basic directions.

## Description of the Sample

**Age and Gender**. Examinees were recruited at each year of age (including an oversampling of age 2.5–3 for scaling purposes). Also, identification of the sex ('gender' in this manual) was required. Some of this information was given by the parent in the cases of younger children or atypical, special cases where self-reporting was impractical. Then, categories of ages (16 categories) were used to select 1603 cases. Details of the categories are described in the Leiter-3 manual, with percentages according to each state, drawn to reflect the U.S. Census, updated as of 2011. For example, the categories for older individuals include more females, given their expected longevity in the population. The final totals, 49.8% male and 50.2% female was, as planned, as close as possible to the 50/50 target. In addition to the 13 categories of age in the sampling plan, an additional 5-age-group cate-gorization was used for many of the psychome-tric studies (e.g., factor analyses).

**Race/Ethnicity**. The Leiter-3 standardization sample includes proportions of White (Caucasian and non-Hispanic), African-American, Asian American, Hispanic, Native Americans (those with tribal affiliation or self-identification for this category), and "other/Mixed," an increasingly important category used in recent Census studies. Also, individuals of Hispanic origin were iden-tified in a special category, and were excluded from other categories (e.g., Anglo-Americans were defined as Caucasian non-Hispanic and African-American as a category excluding those of mixed Hispanic and African-American origin). Because of the primacy of language, the Hispanic category was seen as an important, mutually exclusive category of ethnicity, rather than a separate dimension paralleling racial origin. The match of the Leiter-3 sample data to U.S. Census data was extremely close for all Race/Ethnicity categories, as shown in the manual.

**Educational Level**. Based on the past expe-rience with the estimation of socioeconomic backgrounds of participants in test standardiza-tions (e.g., Roid and Miller 1997; Roid 2003), each examiner collected the educational level of examinees. For practical purposes of keeping the number of sampling strata simple and for the benefit of planning and training of examiners, only four levels of educational attainment were employed with categories similar to U.S. Census reporting categories. The four levels were (1) less than high school (11 years or less and no diploma obtained), (2) completion of 12 years and high school or General Educational Devel-opment (GED) programs, (3) completion of 1–3 years of college or post-secondary education without a bachelor degree or equivalent, and (4) any bachelor or higher degree including advanced professional degrees in law, medicine, engineering, business, etc. The proportions of examinees at each level show an extremely close match to comparable Census percentages.

**Geographic Region**. The four U.S. Census regions of the United States were used as sam-pling categories—Northeast, Midwest, South,

and West, and again show an extremely close match to U.S. Census data. After advertising widely for examiners nationwide, the publisher selected qualified and experienced examiners in each of the four geographic regions. Also, the senior author conducted training sessions for examiners in selected regions, including the West (California, Oregon, Washington, and Colorado) and South (Texas, Oklahoma, and Florida). Examiners were also recruited at regional psy-chological conferences in locations such as Philadelphia, Orlando, and Chicago. The total number of states sampled in the standardization was 36.

## Other Characteristics of the Sample

**Rural versus Urban Locations**. A demographic that now plays a reduced role in affecting cog-nitive performance averages is the size of the community in which the examinee lives (Roid 2003). However, the sample is well balanced in terms of this variable, with 24.2% of examinees coming from rural homes (small town less than 2500 population or farm and ranch locations) and 75.8% from urban homes (towns, suburban areas, medium-, and large-population cities).

**Special Groups Sampling**. Examiners were required to report any primary or secondary diagnoses of children, adolescents, or adults with DSM-IV or official special education diagnoses for any of the following conditions: Autism, Alzheimer's, delays in speech, hearing, or motor abilities, traumatic brain injury, intel-lectual deficiency or delay, ADHD, gifted-ness, learning disabilities (Reading or Other), English-as-Second Language (ESL), English Language Learner (ELL), or local designation for second-language speakers. Attempts were made to find "pure" cases with few multiple diagnoses, and this was achieved in 91% of the special cases, with the main exception being a large overlap between Reading and "Other" learning disabilities (e.g., Math, Writing, etc.). Certain examiners were assigned clinical cases for specific validity studies, but most examiners collected "typical" normative cases. For students in school, academic difficulty areas (spelling, math, reading, and handwriting) were also noted. When no diagnosis was indicated by parents or adult subjects, designation of "typical" was coded for examinees.

Because of the wide-spread implementation of U.S. policies to include individuals with special needs into the standard programs of schools and colleges, 10.7% of cases in the standardization sample had special-group status, including "gifted students" (those enrolled in official school gifted programs) and English-as-Second-Language (ESL) or Emerging Language Learner (ELL) programs.

## Reliability

The technical qualities of the Leiter-3 were researched extensively in the standardization process. In addition, the validity of the instrument was bolstered by the validity studies of the Leiter-R, from which much of Leiter-3 was derived. Except for the new subtests within Leiter-3 (AD and NS), the previous validity studies of the Leiter-R provided evidence that the new edition would have high strong validity characteristics. Studies are reviewed in the manual addressing content, construct, and criterion-related validity.

## Internal Consistency Reliability

**Cognitive Subtests**. Estimates of the internal consistency reliability of the Cognitive Battery subtests range from 0.79 to 0. 95. Importantly, because Cronbach's (1951) alpha coefficients were employed, the estimates in figure are estimates of the lower bound of internal reliability (Lord 1980). Because the reliability coefficients are the basis of standard errors of measurement, significance of subtest score differences, and other key elements of test interpretation, conservative estimates were deemed most beneficial to prevent "over interpretation" of small differences between profile scores. The optional subtest Visual Patterns (VP) had the lowest median

reliability (0.78) and the longest subtest, Sequential Order (SO) had the highest (0.95).

**A/M Subtests**. Internal consistency estimates for the A/M subtest range from 0.70 to 0.81. Because the AS number correct score and the NS Effect score have "parts" (different pages for AS and two components for Stroop Effect), alpha coefficients can be calculated for these scores.

The part scores for the Stroop Effect, the Congruent, and Incongruent trials required test–retest coefficients because they are timed tests (see section on Test–Retest Reliability). The AD subtest is a timed subtest also (completed as soon as the cards are distributed to the examinee) and has no "part scores" to calculate alpha coefficients (see section on Decision-Consistency reliability).

**IQ and Composite Scores**. In addition to the nonverbal IQ score there are two composite scores available for the Leiter-3–Nonverbal Memory and Processing Speed. For age groupings, ages 3–6, 7–11, 12–16, 17–29, and 30–75+, Table 8.2 shows the composite reliabilities for these scores. Coefficients were calculated using the formula for a composite of several tests as described by Nunnally (1978, p. 246). Average reliabilities for each age grouping were computed using Fisher's $z$-transformation of the obtained correlation reported above, then summing, averaging, and reconverting the average $z$-value into the correlation metric. As shown, the reliability of composites and IQ scores are generally higher than any of the individual subtests because of their increased length and precision.

Many psychometric experts have suggested that reliability coefficients above 0.90 are required for making life-changing decisions about individuals, such as designation as intellectually deficient (Gregory 1996; Salvia and Ysseldyke 1991). In general, the IQ and Composite scores of the Leiter-3 qualify for use in cases of major decisions about individuals.

## Test–Retest Reliability

A total of 156 individuals, ages 3–79 years (mean 21.4), were administered the Leiter-3 on

**Table 8.2** Composite score reliabilities by 5 age group

| Age group | Nonverbal IQ | | Processing speed | | Nonverbal memory | |
|---|---|---|---|---|---|---|
| | N | Rel | N | Rel | N | Rel |
| 3–6 | 337 | 0.96 | 180 | 0.94 | 176 | 0.91 |
| 7–11 | 309 | 0.98 | 230 | 0.95 | 190 | 0.93 |
| 12–16 | 352 | 0.94 | 310 | 0.95 | 298 | 0.86 |
| 17–29 | 229 | 0.94 | 209 | 0.95 | 206 | 0.82 |
| 30–75+ | 371 | 0.96 | 328 | 0.95 | 329 | 0.87 |

*Note* For processing speed, the test–retest correlations (AS = 0.93, NI = 0.91, $N$ = 120) were used for calculating composite reliabilities for all age groups

two occasions with an average delay of 7 days. The sample included 50.3% female, 10.1% African-American, and 3.4% Hispanic individuals mostly from the East and South regions of the United States. A good mixture of education levels was obtained (years of schooling completed; by parents for children and adolescents) including 10.6% less than High School, 29.8% High School or GED, 27% some college or post-secondary, and 32.6% college or advanced degree. The sample also included 34 students with conditions requiring special education services and 4 students from gifted programs. The test–retest reliabilities based on the 149 individuals in the total group who had complete data ranged from 0.74 to 0.93.

## Decision-Consistency Reliability for the Supplemental A/M Subtests Scores

The supplementary scores for the A/M set of subtests are largely diagnostic or "error" scores reflecting incorrect responses by examinees on the AS, AD, or NS subtests. The skewed distributions of error scores in psychology and education often are not described well by conventional statistics such as means, standard deviations, or correlations because of the large number of zero or low scores (Guilford and Fruchter 1978, p. 56). Because of skewness, conventional reliability indexes (e.g., test–retest correlations) do not accurately represent the

consistency of these scores. Also, due to the preponderance of zero scores, the decision-consistency methods used for criterion-referenced tests (Berk 1984) also give underestimates because of violations of "cell size" (e.g., very small numbers of examinees who have multiple errors) for statistics such as chi-square or kappa. For these reasons, the indexes of consistency (e.g., percentage of correct decisions) used in decision–classification analysis were calculated for each of the scores. The indexes estimate consistency between first and second testings based on test–retest data.

Index percentages show the consistency of test–retest data for examines who obtained "average or better scores" (such as zero errors) versus the "clinically meaningful scores" (such as multiple errors). Consistency percentages were defined by cut-off values based on the distributions of standardized scaled scores for each variable. Cut-off scores (expressed as scaled score values whereon SD below average equals 7) were determined from the full standardization sample ($N$ = 1603) and then applied to the data in the test–retest sample of 156. Consistency ranged from a percentage of 78.9% (AD, Level 2 —ages 6–10) to a high of 94% for the NS incorrect scores using a cut-off score of "less than 7." The data showed a high degree of zero-incorrect scores obtained on both test and retest administrations. Inconsistent results were often due to practice effects (more errors on the first administration of the test and fewer on retest).

## Validity

Validity is a unitary concept that includes all the sources of evidence that support the interpretations of test scores from a given test and its suggested purposes. According to the technical standards for educational and psychological tests (AERA, APA, NCME 1999), the categories of evidence for validity of a test such as Leiter-3 would include evidence based on (a) test content, (b) response processes, (c) internal structure, (d) relations to other variables, and (e) consequences of testing. This section of the chapter will review the highlights of the extensive evidence for Leiter-3 as documented more completely in the Leiter-3 test manual (Roid et al. 2013, pp. 137–168). Importantly, the validity of interpretations (e.g., identifying intellectual deficiency) with Leiter-3 stand on evidence collected for the current third edition, but also on the long history of studies for the original Leiter (Leiter 1979; Levine 1982) and the Leiter-R (Roid and Miller 1997). The historical data is relevant because all of the editions are measuring the construct of nonverbal intellectual ability and many of the features, and even a number of test items are very similar across editions. The reader desiring more complete information on all validity studies since the 1940s is referred to these previous publications and independent studies published in professional journals on the three editions.

**Evidence Based on Test Content**. Leiter-3 was constructed on a model similar to the Cattell–Horn–Carroll (CHC) theory (Flanagan et al. 2013). Content was selected from the previous edition (Leiter-R) to match two major factors of CHC theory—Fluid Reasoning (Gf) and Visual-Spatial (Gv) for the assessment of nonverbal intellectual ability. Leiter-R Full IQ had correlated 0.86 with the WISC-III Full-scale IQ, confirming that the selected subtests would measure the IQ construct. Also, the A/M composite scores for Processing Speed (attention subtests AS and NS) and Memory (FM and RM) were selected to measure the corresponding CHC factors (Gs and Gsm). Cross-battery correlation studies verified that the Leiter-3 general ability

Growth score (consisting of fluid reasoning subtests CA and SO and visual-spatial subtests FG and FC) was correlated significantly with the corresponding Woodcock-Johnson (WJ-III Cognitive Tests, (Mather & Woodcock, 2001) W-scores. Correlations ranged from 0.77 to 0.92 with median 0.85 between Leiter-3 and WJ-III CHC factors ($N = 26$, ages 5–67, median age 11 years, diverse ethnic backgrounds). Other evidence is presented in the section on "Evidence Based on Relations to Other Variables."

**Evidence Based on Response Processes**. Gregory (1996) stated that validity evidence based on content (or response processes in this case) is determined by the degree to which the tasks or items on a test are representative of the universe of behavior the test was designed to sample (p. 108). Several types of systematic sampling of item content and item writing were employed (Roid and Haladyna 1982). Also, extensive item analyses were conducted including examination of the "fit" of each item to the unidimensional construct underlying the subtest (Bond and Fox 2007), and conventional evidence of item quality (e.g., difficulty at various age levels, item versus total correlations, validity-group differentiation) was obtained during the development of Leiter-3. For example, to measure a nonverbal and nonvocal intellectual ability, the mode of response required of examinee is of vital importance. The Leiter tradition of response mode, since the early versions of the original Leiter in the 1940s, was for the examinee to move blocks (printed with test stimuli on their top side) into slots in a response frame (made of wood in early versions and in plastic in Leiter-3). With the examiner using pantomime instructions to the examinee, the block-in-frame mode of response was clearly nonverbal (except for "subvocal speech") and nonvocal—a perfect match to the construct being assessed. The block-and-frame mode of response is also valuable for children and adults that benefit from "hands on" testing materials. For the Figure Ground and Form Completion subtests, the examinee points from the response card to the target object on the stimulus booklet a highly effective and reliable response from the Leiter-R.

Also, to assure consistency with nonverbal response processes, Teaching items were employed at the starting points of each subtest. Teaching items ensure and verify that individuals would clearly understand each task prior to completing each type of item. Additionally, the use of two subtests for each CHC factor (CA and SO for Gf, FG and FC for Gv) assured that the main factors in the nonverbal IQ score were well sampled with the block-and-frame or "touch-the-picture" mode of response.

**Evidence Based on Internal Structure.** Both exploratory and confirmatory factor analyses were conducted on the standardization data for Leiter-3. Several types of extraction and rotation methods were explored for the data and the clearest factor matrices across age groups (ages 3–6 with $N = 148$; 7–11 with $N = 175$, 12–16 with $N = 291$, 17–29 with $N = 201$, and 30–75+ with $N = 309$) showed four factors. The patterns of factor loadings for each of the age groups were highly similar (Roid et al. 2013, pp. 157–158). To be concise, Table 8.3 shows the results for the age groups 7–11 and 17–29. The younger children show a tendency to have AS load with the memory subtests and for the Stroop subtest scores to split between factors. The patterns of

loadings for older teens and younger adults are quite representative of ages 17–75+ where four factors are clearly defined, although the Stroop Effect score tends to be alone as a "singleton" defining a smaller factor (Gorsuch 1983).

In addition to the exploratory analyses, a series of confirmatory factor analyses were conducted for each of the five age groupings. The singleton Stroop Effect variable was excluded for clarity and because it violated the rule of having at least two variables defining a factor in the computer program LISREL (Joreskog and Sorbom 1999). Results showed the three factor solutions provided the preferred lower values defined by Browne and Cudeck (1993). The three factors were labeled General Cognitive Ability, Nonverbal Memory, and Processing Speed. The best-fit indexes showed these 3-factor models to have the lowest values on several measures including chi-square per degrees of freedom (chi/df) and root mean-squared error of approximation (RMSEA). The range of Chi-square per degree of freedom values was 5.38–7.77 for the baseline 1-factor model and 1.07–2.73 for the 3-factor model across the five age groups. For the RMSEA index, the values ranged from 0.11 to 0.14 for the 1-factor model and 0.02–0.07 for the

**Table 8.3** Exploratory factor analysis of 11 Leiter-3 profile scores

| Name of subtest | Factor loadings for ages 3–6 | | | | Factor loadings for ages 17–29 | | | |
|---|---|---|---|---|---|---|---|---|
| Factor labels | "g" | Memory | Attn | Stroop | "g" | Memory | Attn | Stroop |
| Subtests | | | | | | | | |
| Classification/analogies | **0.43** | 0.32 | | | **0.46** | 0.23 | | |
| Form completion | **0.92** | | | | **0.48** | 0.25 | | |
| Figure ground | **0.50** | 0.26 | | | **0.74** | | | |
| Visual patterns | **0.35** | | | −0.23 | **0.62** | | | |
| Sequential order | **0.35** | 0.28 | | | **0.70** | 0.24 | | |
| Forward memory | 0.36 | **0.58** | | | 0.30 | **0.59** | | |
| Reverse memory | | **0.69** | | | 0.28 | **0.78** | 0.28 | |
| Stroop effect | | | | 0.95 | | | | **0.99** |
| NS congruent | | | 0.97 | | 0.22 | 0.22 | 0.84 | |
| NS incongruent | | | **0.77** | −0.64 | 0.27 | 0.25 | **0.88** | |
| Attention sustained | 0.25 | 0.40 | **0.28** | | | | **0.50** | |

*Note* Factor loadings with near-zero values (−0.20 to +0.20) excluded for clarity of factor patterns. Subtests intended to measure a construct (factor) are shown in boldface type

3-factor model. More detailed analyses are included in the manual (Roid et al. 2013).

Finally, in terms of internal structure, all subtests in the three composite scores (IQ, Nonverbal memory, and Processing Speed) were examined for general ability ("g") loading, and subtest general, specific, and error variance. Among the nine subtests examined, the "g" loadings ranged from 0.38 for the Stroop Incongruent score to 0.69 for Form Completion. In the tradition promoted by Kaufman (1990), these g-loadings were estimated from the first unrotated factor loading (Jensen 1980) in an exploratory factor analysis. According to the tradition described by Sattler (2001), the variance components of subtests are derived from factor analyses and data on the reliability of subtests. General variance is derived from the communality of a subtest based on the sum of squared loadings on the common factors for a particular subtest. Specific variance is obtained by subtracting the general variance from the reliability (e.g., internal consistency) index for that subtest. The remaining variance is considered error. Again, in the tradition described by Sattler (2001), the ideal pattern of variance should show general variance highest and specific variance higher than error variance. The average pattern of variance values for Leiter-3 (averaged across age groups) was 45, 37, and 18, close to the ideal pattern.

**Evidence Based on Relationships with Other Variables.** Several other well-known intellectual-ability tests were correlated with Leiter-3 in the standardization studies. First, the previous edition, Leiter-R, correlated well with the third edition, for a sample of 60 individuals, ages 3–87 (median 20) as shown in Table 8.4. All the validation samples represented in Table 8.4 had a balance of genders but wide ranges of ethnicity, race, and educational level (see Roid et al. 2013 for more details of each sample). From comparisons of Leiter-R and Leiter-3, Growth scales correlated 0.89, and IQs, 0.78. The Leiter-3 and Stanford-Binet Fifth Edition (SB5, Roid 2003) were compared for a sample of 26 individuals, ages 4–35 with a median of 8 years. Nonverbal IQ scores from the Leiter-3 and SB5 correlated 0.77 with means of 95.9 and 103.8, respectively (perhaps explained partially by the 10-year difference in standardization dates, estimated to be 0.30 IQ points higher per year, by Flynn 1987, 2012). The item-response theory scores (Change Sensitive Nonverbal score in SB5 and Growth score in Leiter-R) were correlated 0.85 with means of 493.3 and 499.3, very similar given standard deviations of 16–27.

The Woodcock-Johnson Cognitive Abilities Tests (WJ-III, Mather and Woodcock 2001) was administered to 26 individuals, ages 5–38 (median 11), along with the Leiter-3. The most relevant score measuring fluid reasoning in the WJ-III was found to correlate 0.74, as shown in Fig. 11 (Roid et al. 2013). The WJ-III W-score for the Fluid Reasoning factor-score cluster correlated 0.92 with the Leiter-3 Growth score. The two prominent Wechsler scales available at the time of the standardization (WISC-IV and WAIS-IV) also correlated 0.73 and 0.72 with the Leiter-3 IQ score, on samples of 50 and 53 individuals, respectively.

**Table 8.4** Correlations between Leiter-3 IQ scores and related intellectual-ability scales

| Intellectual-ability scales | Leiter-3 IQ score | Leiter-3 growth score |
|---|---|---|
| Leiter-R nonverbal IQ | 0.78 | – |
| Leiter-R growth score | – | 0.89 |
| SB5 nonverbal IQ | 0.77 | – |
| SB5 change-sensitive NV scale | – | 0.85 |
| WJ-III fluid reasoning cluster | 0.74 | 0.92 |
| WISC-IV perceptual reasoning index | 0.73 | – |
| WAIS-IV perceptual reasoning index | 0.72 | – |

Related Stroop measures were also correlated with the Stroop scores of the Leiter-3 (see Fig. 12, Roid et al. 2013). The traditional Stroop Color-Word Test (SCWT, Golden et al. 2003) requires the examinee to inhibit the word and respond to the color. In the NS task, the examinee must identify one color while inhibiting or ignoring the second color. Even though there is an underlying similarity between the tasks, the question of whether or not the nonverbal version is related to the color-word version is important. To address this concern, a sample of 75 college students ($M_{age}$ = 21.12) completed the Stroop Color and Word Test and the NS test from the Leiter-3. The order of the two tests was randomly varied across participants. Correlations between both tests were statistically significant providing evidence of concurrent validity, and ranged from 0.24 to 0.62.

Attention-related deficits, including inhibition, have been associated with reading disabilities (Ackerman et al. 1986; Kelly et al. 1989). Fifty-four individuals from the standardization sample had been diagnosed with a reading-related learning disability. Compared to the typically developing sample, these individuals scored significantly lower on both the congruent ($t$ (1264) = 4.82, $p < 0.001$, $d$ = 1.79) and incongruent ($t$ (1264) = 6.32, $p < 0.001$, $d$ = 1.71) NS tasks, providing evidence for the construct validity of the nonverbal task.

**Evidence Concerning Consequences of Testing with the Leiter-3**. Three lines of evidence for the effectiveness and fairness of the Leiter-3 were presented in detail in Roid et al. (2013): (a) Effective separation or fairness of differences among mean scores between typical and atypical individuals (e.g., those with disabilities), (b) Low error rates for using Leiter-3 scores for serious decisions such as identifying intellectual deficiency, and (c) fairness and lack of differential item functioning (DIF, Holland and Wainer 1993) among ethnic and racial groups.

Studies of mean scores for 11 specialized groups of individuals (e.g., those with deafness, traumatic brain injury, intellectual deficiency, ADHD, or giftedness) were reported in detail in the Leiter-3 test manual (Roid et al. 2013).

Individuals with medically diagnosed traumatic brain injury ($N$ = 28, ages 5–87 with median 21) had mean scores ranging 4.6–6.8 among the cognitive subtests and IQ mean of 77.6, as expected. The validation group for intellectual deficiency (as diagnosed with a history of special education) showed subtest score means as low as 2.5 on Form completion and an IQ mean of 71 ($N$ = 47, ages 3–35, mean 13). Similar patterns of expected mean scores were found for individuals with learning disabilities, ADHD, and autism spectrum disorder.

The classification accuracy of Leiter-3 IQ scores was examined by comparing a sample of 53 individuals with diagnosed intellectual deficiency to a random sample of 500 typical cases (with no diagnosed conditions, medical, emotional, or educational) from the normative sample. Total correct identification ("hit rate") ranged from 95.4% (using the traditional standard of IQ less than or equal to 70) to 97.1 (using 75 as the standard). False negative rates (classified typical when actually atypical) ranged from 6.6% using a standard of 65–2.4% using a standard of 75. False positive rates (classifying as atypical when truly typical) were all extremely low (0.2%). Similar results were found when using the Nonverbal Memory and Processing Speed composite scores to classify individuals with ADHD using cut-off scores of 80 to 90 (Hit rates 93.0–95.1%, false negative 3.0–3.6%, and false positive rates of 1.3% (using scores of 80–85).

In terms of fairness of measurement, several group-mean studies showed similarity of special groups to the normative sample. For example, a sample of 46 (ages 3–66) individuals with deafness or hard-of-hearing conditions showed mean scores very near 10 (the average score) for each of the cognitive subtests and near the average of 100 for IQ (97.2), indicating fairness of measurement for this group. Also, two groups of individuals with dominant spoken language other than English were administered the Leiter-3. Those with Spanish language dominance showed cognitive subtest score means ranging from 9.8 to 11.0 and an IQ mean of 101.9 ($N$ = 22, ages 5–47, median 15). A second group with a variety of non-English language dominance (although 63% Asian language) showed mean scores of 10.2–12.5 on cognitive subtests and a mean IQ of 105.8, as often found in samples of individuals with Asian educational backgrounds (e.g., Roid 2003).

Finally, extensive studies of item differential functioning (DIF, potential item bias) were conducted on contrasting samples of gender and ethnicity/race (Holland and Wainer 1993). All items within the five cognitive subtests used in the composite IQ score for Leiter-3 were calibrated using the WINSTEPS (Lincacre and Wright 2000) program for the one-parameter logistic (Rasch 1966, 1980) model, separately in normative and contrast groups. The goal was to explore the predicted item-difficulty invariance between groups (Bond and Fox 2007) by plotting the difficulties of items on graphic scatter plots (expecting a pattern of difficulties aligning together on a 45-degree line, indicating invariance). The calibrations of items were conducted on relatively large groups (as shown in Figs. 13 and 14, Roid et al. 2013) including 197 African-American, 248 Hispanic, and 1040 Caucasian non-Hispanic individuals. Out of a total of 152 items, only two items (introductory Teaching items calibrated on Anglo versus Hispanic samples) showed slight departures from the linear trend in the scatter plots. Similar analyses were conducted on items in the Nonverbal Memory subtests with similar results. Items in the Processing Speed subtests are "speeded" (timed subtests) and could not be used in this type of DIF study. Thus, evidence is compelling to conclude that the Leiter-3 is quite free from DIF, potential bias, in measurement of nonverbal intellectual ability and nonverbal memory.

## Deriving Norm-referenced Standardized Scores

**Raw Scores**. General directions for recording and scoring the individual on each subtest are provided in the manual. All Leiter-3 items are easy to administer and score; however, some subtests, such as AS and AD, require special scoring directions. For most of the subtests, rules for obtaining raw scores for items are

straightforward. Each subtest has a stop rule (e.g., stop after 5 cumulative errors). When the stop rule is reached, testing is terminated for that subtest. Each item response that is correct is counted as 1 raw score point. Incorrect item responses receive no credit. Some subtests use special procedures that differ from the general patterns for determining a subtest raw score, i.e., subtests contained in the A/M Battery. Two subtests have slightly more involved rules for obtaining subtest raw scores (Attention Sustained and or Attention Divided). The availability of very easy Teaching Trial items for each age group should assist examiners in identifying individuals who understand the nature and the expectations of a subtest. Also, the Teaching Trial items (where as many as three trials are allowed) are very useful in providing some degree of measurement or a "basal" for with cognitive delays. Since some children may have difficulty with the Teaching items it is not uncommon for an individual to initially provide two or more responses.

## Leiter-3 Interpretation

The following discussion regarding interpretation of the Leiter-3 is based upon the recommendations presented in the manual (Roid et al. 2013). The test authors recommend a hierarchical method of interpretation that begins with a thorough review of developmental, clinical, and academic history, presenting concerns, and information collected via rating scales. Next, score examination begins with the most global estimates and proceeds to more specific estimates provided by the Growth scale scores, Composites, and Subtest scores. For special interpretations and adaptations of the Leiter-3 results for individuals with deafness or hard-of-hearing conditions, please consult Appendix K of the Leiter-3 manual (Hardy-Braz 2013).

The first stage of interpretation involves examining the global estimates of nonverbal intelligence as represented by the Full-scale IQ and the Brief IQ screener of the VR Battery. Such global estimates reflect the definition of intelligence as measured on the Leiter-3 and is defined as "the general ability to perform complex nonverbal mental manipulations related to conceptualization, inductive reasoning, and visualization" (Roid and Miller 1997, p. 103). Although attention, speed of processing, and memory are regarded as pre-cursors or substrates of cognitive performance, they are also highly associated with disorders such as attention-deficit and other neuropsychological processing deficits (Hale et al. 2012). For these reasons, subtests of the AM Battery are not included in the nonverbal IQ. Instead, the AM subtests serve as "rule out" measures to assist in interpreting the effects of processing disorders on the level of global IQ scores. Performance is interpreted using standard scores, confidence intervals, percentile ranks, and descriptive classification.

The examination of Growth scores, especially for individuals who function at a low level of ability and/or are expected to be re-tested on the Leiter-3, is the next stage of interpretation. Designed using item-response theory (IRT, Lord 1980; Hambleton et al. 1991; Bond and Fox 2007), Growth scores provide an opportunity to measure small increments of growth (or decline) along the continuum of general ability as measured by the Leiter-3 (Roid and Woodcock 2000; Woodcock 1999).

The next stage of interpretation involves examination of the Composite scores of the cognitive and attention/memory batteries. The Cognitive Battery has one main composite—Nonverbal IQ. The other battery contains two composites— A/M. The Examiner Rating scales each contain two composites: Cognitive/Social and Emotional/ Regulation. Composite scores, Confidence intervals, percentile ranks, and classifications are provided in the manual to describe performance.

Leiter-3 subtests were designed to measure unitary constructs, are reliable, and unbiased based on gender, race, ethnicity, and socioeconomic factors. Thus, interpretation of performance and abilities at the subtest level is supported and is the next stage of interpretation. **Interpretation of Nonverbal Stroop Results**. Because the Stroop task is often absent from major Cognitive Batteries, it is important to explain some ideas for the interpretation of this unique new subtest. It is commonly known that attention tests, such as the Stroop, are useful for identifying processing differences but are not particularly useful for specifying a condition or disorder. Therefore, it is necessary to use Stroop scores in conjunction with other scores when making a diagnosis. Furthermore, the strong reliability of the congruent and incongruent scores and moderate reliability of the interference score suggests that it may also be beneficial to include all three scores in the clinical decision-making process. The congruent score can be viewed as an indicator of naming speed (cf., Carroll 1993) while the incongruent score may represent naming or processing speed with noise. The Stroop effect, or interference, score may represent the ability to inhibit or selectively ignore meaningful but irrelevant information.

In the case of reading-related learning disabilities, a stepwise logistic regression analysis was conducted on the Leiter-3 standardization data to determine the test scores associated with a learning disability for reading. This analysis included all three Stroop scores (i.e., congruent, incongruent, and Stroop effect). The results indicate that a model including classification/analogies, AS, NS congruent, and figure ground scores best fit the data ($X^2(4) = 35.43$, $p < 0.001$). Therefore, an attention task like the NS task may be useful for ruling in an attention-related cognitive disorder but should be combined with other construct-related measures to determine the specific disorder. Additionally, the relevant measure from the Stroop task may vary across disorders.

## Strengths and Limitations of the Leiter-3

Based on the evidence presented in this chapter, the Leiter-3 has several positive strengths and few negative weaknesses. The main strength of the Leiter-3 would be the true nonverbal character of the test, requiring no spoken directions by the examiner and no spoken responses by the examinee. In addition, the subtests have a great deal of color, are game-like, and are more engaging than some of the other nonverbal instruments that use primarily black-and-white illustrations without manipulatives such as the blocks used in the Leiter-3 cognitive subtests. Also, the Leiter-3 provides a nonverbal IQ with just four subtests, and, for differential analysis of cognitive process deficits, a companion set of memory and attention nonverbal subtests that are optional. The technical qualities are strong in terms of reliability, evidence of validity, decision-consistency accuracy, and fairness, as presented in this chapter and, more extensively in the test manual (Roid et al. 2013). One of the reviews in Buros Mental Measurements Yearbook (online at www.Buros.org by Martin Wiese, Buros Center for Testing 2014) included several positive comments about the test, stating "The Leiter-3 authors have succeeded in their goal of constructing a reliable and valid nonverbal measure of intellectual ability and Attention/Memory."

Weaknesses are few based on the reviews to date (e.g., Buros reviews by Wiese and Ward, Buros Center for Testing 2014) but include the fact that the global nonverbal IQ score is not supplemented by factor index scores for fluid reasoning and visual-spatial abilities separately. The Buros review by Susan Ward (Buros Center for Testing 2014) was largely positive but pointed to the relatively small number of subjects in criterion-group studies and lower test–retest coefficients compared to internal consistency estimates. Also, Ward's review mentioned the need for new users to study the Training DVD (available from www.stoeltingco.com) given the challenges of learning different pantomime instructions for most of the subtests. Finally, the authors are aware, and emphasize in training sessions on Leiter-3, that some individuals with disabilities (e.g., Autism) remain quite verbal and this may need additional verbal encouragement between subtests.

## Summary

The Leiter-3 is a totally nonverbal, individually administered test battery that does not require spoken directions by the examiner or vocal responses by the examinee. The wide age range (from 3 years to 75+) and combination of nonverbal general intellectual ability (IQ) and nonverbal A/M subtests makes the Leiter-3 stands out among alternative nonverbal batteries. Also, the addition of a NS effect (Stroop 1935; Golden 1976) subtest within the battery allows the assessment of more neuropsychological factors than other nonverbal batteries. Hands-on movement of blocks and cards for children with autism or other attention-impaired conditions have proven to be more engaging as a "game-like" approach to testing (M. Wiese, Buros Review online 2014).

Based on user requests, the "block and frame" response mode was restored in the third edition (where the examinee moves printed blocks into alignment with printed illustrations on the Easel attached to the frame). At the same time, the successful features and many items from the second edition (Leiter-R, Roid and Miller 1997) were retained in the new format or intact with updated stimulus materials. The scoring system for the Leiter-3 is largely unchanged from the Leiter-R and matches the style of scaled score and composite score methods (and metric) of the other instruments measuring IQ (e.g., Stanford-Binet Fifth Edition and Wechsler scales). A supplemental scoring method called "Growth Scores" is based on item-response theory (IRT) and very similar in metric to those of the Stanford-Binet 5 Change-Sensitive scores (Roid 2003) and Woodcock-Johnson W-score metrics. These IRT (Rasch Model) scores function as criterion-referenced and developmental scales helpful in tracking intellectual abilities across many years of follow-up for children and adults with continuing or chronic conditions.

The technical qualities of the Leiter-3, with extensive reliability, validity, classification accuracy, and fairness studies (summarized briefly in this chapter and more extensively in the Leiter-3 test manual), have been praised by recent reviews in the Buros Mental Measurement series (S. Ward and M. Wiese reviews online, 2014). Each area of evidence for validity (content, response processes, internal structure, relationships with other variables, and consequential validity) has been highlighted in this chapter and will surely be supplemented by more recent, independent research studies.

Finally, the Leiter-3 provides examiners with a modern, nonverbal test battery for relatively quick assessment of IQ by an individually administered instrument using a game-like format with only four subtests'. The Leiter-3 assessment of a wide range of cognitive deficits, delays, autism, learning disabilities, ADHD, or brain-injury cases as well as a fair assessment for non-English speakers and those with deafness and hard-of-hearing conditions.

# References

Ackerman, P. T., Anhault, J. M., Dykman, R. A., & Holcomb, P. J. (1986). Effortful processing deficits in children with reading or attention disorders. *Brain and Cognition, 5*, 22–40.

Albert, M. L. (1973). A simple test of visual neglect. *Neurology, 23*, 658–664.

American Educational Research Association (AERA), American Psychological Association (APA), & National Council on Measurement in Education (NCME). (1999). *Standards for educational and psychological testing*. Washington, DC: APA.

American Psychiatric Association. (2013). *Diagnostic and statistical manual of mental disorders* (DSM-V-TR) (5th ed.). Washington, DC: Author.

Banken, J. A. (1985). Clinical utility of considering digits forward and digits backward as separate components of the Wechsler Adult Intelligence Scale-Revised. *Journal of Clinical Psychology, 41*, 686–691.

Berk, R. A. (1984). *A guide to criterion-test construction*. Baltimore, MD: Johns Hopkins University Press.

Bishop, S. L., Richler, J., & Lord, C. (2006). Association between restricted and repetitive behaviors and nonverbal IQ in children with ASD. *Child Neuropsychology, 12*, 247–267.

Bond, T. G., & Fox, C. M. (2007). *Applying the Rasch model: Fundamental measurement in the human sciences* (2nd ed.). Mahwah, NJ: Routledge/Erlbaum.

Browne, M. W., & Cudeck, R. (1993). Alternative ways of assessing model fit. In K. A. Bollen & J. S. Long (Eds.), *Testing structural equation models* (pp. 136–162). Newbury Park, CA: Sage.

Buros Center for Testing. (2014). *Weise review of Leiter-3*. Lincoln, NE: Buros Institute, University of Nebraska-Lincoln. www.buros.org

Carroll, J. B. (1993). *Human cognitive abilities: A survey of factor-analytic studies*. New York: Cambridge University Press.

CDC (Centers for Disease Control). (2007). *Press release: CDC releases new data on autism spectrum disorders (ASDs) from multiple communities in the United States*. Retrieved September 6, 2007, from the Centers for Disease Control Web site: http://www.cdc.gov/od/oc/media/pressrel/2007/r070208.htm

Cha, C. B., Najmi, S., Park, J. M., Finn, C. T., & Nock, M. K. (2010). Attentional bias toward suicide-related stimuli predicts suicidal behavior. *Journal of Abnormal Psychology, 119*, 616–622.

Christensen, A. L. (1979). *Luria's neuropsychological investigation* (2nd ed.). Copenhagen: Munksgaard.

Cronbach, L. J. (1951). Coefficient alpha and the internal structure of tests. *Psychometrika, 16*, 297–334.

Dalrymple-Alford, E. C., & Budayr, B. (1966). Examination of some aspects of the Stroop color-word test. *Perceptual and Motor Skills, 23*, 1211–1214.

Dee, H. L. (1970). Visuoconstructive and visuoperceptive deficit in patients with unilateral cerebral lesions. *Neuropsychologia, 8*, 305–314.

Dunbar, K. N., & MacLeod, C. M. (1984). A horse race of a different color: Stroop interference patterns with transformed words. *Journal of Experimental Psychology: Human Perception and Performance, 10*, 622–639.

Dyer, E. N. (1973). The Stroop phenomenon and its use in the study of perceptual, cognitive, and response processes. *Memory and Cognition, 1*, 106–120.

Dyer, F. N., & Severance, L. J. (1973). Stroop interference with successive presentations of separate incongruent words and colors. *Journal of Experimental Psychology, 98*, 438–439.

Elliott, C. D. (2008). *Differential Ability Scales—Second Edition (DAS-II)*. San Antonio, TX: Pearson/Psychological Corp.

Flanagan, D. P., Ortiz, S. O., & Alfonso, V. (2013). *Essentials of cross-battery assessment* (3rd ed.). New York: Wiley.

Flynn, J. R. (1987). Massive IQ gains in 14 nations: What IQ tests really measure. *Psychological Bulletin, 101*, 171–191.

Flynn, J. R. (2012). *Are we getting smarter? Rising IQ in the 21st century*. Cambridge, UK: Cambridge University Press.

Golden, C. J. (1976). The diagnosis of brain damage by the Stroop test. *Journal of Clinical Psychology, 32*, 654–658.

Golden, C. J., Freshwater, S. M., & Golden, Z. (2003). *Stroop color and word test, children's version for ages 5–14*. Wood Dale, IL: Stoelting Co.

Goldstein, G., Johnson, C. R., & Minshew, N. J. (2001). Attentional processes in autism. *Journal of Autism and Developmental Disorders, 31*, 433–440.

Gorsuch, R. L. (1983). *Factor analysis* (2nd ed.). Hillsdale, NJ: Erlbaum.

Gottschaldt, K. (1928). Hidden figures test. In G. Talland (Ed.), *Deranged memory* (p. 1965). New York: Academic Press.

Gregory, R. J. (1996). *Psychological testing* (2nd ed.). Boston, MA: Allyn & Bacon.

Guilford, J. P., & Fruchter, B. (1978). *Fundamental statistics in psychology and education.* New York, NY: McGraw-Hill.

Gustafsson, J. E. (1984). A unifying model for the structure of intellectual abilities. *Intelligence, 8*, 179–203.

Hale, J. B., Yim, M., Schneideer, A. N., Wilcox, G., Henzel, J. N., & Dixon, S. G. (2012). Cognitive and neuropsychological assessment of ADHD. In D. Flanagan & P. Harrison, *Contemporary intellectual assessment* (pp. 687–707). New York, NY: Guilford Press.

Hambleton, R. K., Swaminathan, H., & Rogers, H. J. (1991). *Fundamentals of Item response theory.* Newbury Park, CA: Sage.

Hardy-Braz, S. (2013). General guidelines for using the Leiter-3 with deaf/hard-of-hearing (Appendix K). In G. Roid, L. Miller, M. Pomplun, & C. Koch (Eds.), *Leiter-3 manual* (pp. 277–278). Wood Dale, IL: Stoelting Co.

Holland, P., & Wainer, H. (Eds.). (1993). *Differential item functioning.* Mahwah, NJ: Routledge/Erlbaum.

Hooper, H. E. (1983). *Hooper visual organization test.* Los Angeles, CA: Western Psychological Services.

Horn, J. L., & Cattell, R. B. (1966). Refinement and test of the theory of fluid and crystallized intelligence. *Journal of Educational Psychology, 57*, 253–270.

Jensen, A. R. (1980). *Bias in mental testing.* New York: The Free Press.

Joreskog, K. G., & Sorbom, D. (1999). *LISREL 8: User's reference guide.* Chicago: Scientific Software.

Kahneman, D., & Chajczyk, D. (1983). Tests of the automaticity of reading: Dilution of Stroop effects by color-irrelevant stimuli. *Journal of Experimental Psychology: Human Perception and Performance, 9*, 497–509.

Kahneman, D., & Henik, A. (1981). Perceptual organization and attention. In M. Kubovy & J. R. Pomerantz (Eds.), *Perceptual organization* (pp. 181–211). Hillsdale, NJ: Erlbaum.

Kaufman, A. S. (1990). *Assessing adolescent and adult intelligence.* Boston, MA: Allyn & Bacon.

Kelly, M. S., Best, C. T., & Kirk, U. (1989). Cognitive processing deficits in reading disabilities: A prefrontal cortical hypothesis. *Brain and Cognition, 11*, 275–293.

Klinger, L. G., O'Kelly, S. E., Mussey, J. L., Goldstein, S., & DeVries, M. (2012). Assessment of intellectual functioning in autism spectrum disorder. In D. Flanagan & P. Harrison, Contemporary intellectual assessment, 3rd Ed. (pp. 670–686). New York, NY: Guildford Press.

Koch, C., & Barr, B. (2010). Can Task Demands Override Connectedness? *Abstracts of the Psychonomic Society, 15*, 56.

Koch, C., & Kubovy, M. (1996, June). Interference in a color-color Stroop task. Poster presented at the *Eighth Annual Convention of the American Psychological Society*, San Francisco, CA.

Koch, C., Lowen, J, & McWilliams, M. (2011, November). *Developmental differences using a nonverbal*

*Stroop task.* Poster presented at the Object Perception, Attention, & Memory 19th Annual Conference, Seattle, WA.

Koch, C., & Roid, G. (2012). *Manual for the nonverbal Stroop card sorting task.* Wood Dale, IL: Stoelting Company.

Kuschner, E. S., Bennetto, L., & Yost, K. (2007). Patterns of nonverbal cognitive functioning in young children with autism spectrum disorders. *Journal of Autism and Developmental Disorders, 37*(5), 795–807.

Leiter, R. G. (1938). *A comparative study of the general intelligence of Caucasian and Asian children as measured by the Leiter international performance scale.* Unpublished doctoral dissertation, University of Southern California, Los Angeles, CA.

Leiter, R. G. (1979). *Instruction manual for the Leiter international performance scale.* Wood Dale, IL: Stoelting Co.

Levine, M. N. (1982). *Leiter international performance scale: A handbook.* Los Angeles, CA: WPS.

Lezak, M. D. (1995). *Neuropsychological assessment* (3rd ed.). New York: Oxford University Press.

Lincacre, J. M., & Wright, B. D. (2000). *WINSTEPS v. 3.00: Rasch item analysis computer program manual.* Chicago: MESA Press.

Lord, F. M. (1980). *Applications of item response theory to practical testing problems.* Mahwah, NJ: Erlbaum.

Mather, N., & Woodcock, R. W. (2001). *Woodcock-Johnson tests of cognitive ability third edition: Technical manual.* Chicago: Riverside.

Mayes, S. D., & Calhoun, S. L. (2003). Ability profiles in children with autism. *The National Autistic Society, 6*, 65–80.

Mayes, S. D., & Calhoun, S. L. (2004). Influence of IQ and age in childhood autism: Lack of support for DSM-IV Asperger's disorder. *Journal of Developmental and Physical Disabilities, 3*, 257–272.

Minshew, N. J., & Goldstein, G. (1998). Autism and a disorder of complex information processing. *Mental Retardation and Developmental Disabilities, 4*, 129–136.

Minshew, N. J., & Williams, D. L. (2007). The new neurobiology of autism: Cortex, connectivity, and neuronal organization. *Neurological Review, 64*, 945–950.

Mundy, P., & Crowson, M. (1997). Joint attention and early social communication: Implications for research on intervention with autism. *Journal of Autism and Developmental Disorders, 27*, 653–675.

Nelson, H. E. (1976). A modified card sorting test sensitive to frontal lobe defects. *Cortex, 12*, 313–324.

Nordlund, C. B. (1998). *An examination of behavior ratings and rater differences of ADHD subjects on the Leiter-R rating scales.* Unpublished doctoral dissertation, George Fox University, Newberg, Oregon.

Nunnally, J. (1978). *Psychometric theory* (2nd ed.). New York, NY: McGraw-Hill.

Posner, M. I., & Snyder, C. R. R. (1975). Attention and cognitive control. In R. L. Solso (Ed.), *Information processing and cognition: The Loyola symposium* (pp. 55–85). Hillsdale, NJ: Erlbaum.

Rasch, G. (1966). An item analysis which takes individual differences into account. *British Journal of Mathematical and Statistical Psychology, 19*, 49–57.

Rasch, G. (1980). *Probabilistic models for some intelligence and attainment tests*. Chicago, IL: University of Chicago Press (Translated from the Danish original of 1960).

Raven, J., Raven, J. C., & Court, J. H. (1998). *Manual for Raven's progressive matrices and vocabulary scales*. Oxford, UK: Oxford Psychologists Press.

Reynolds, C. R. (1997). Forward and backward memory span should not be combined for clinical analysis. *Archives of Clinical Neuropsychology, 12*, 29–40.

Roid, G. H. (2003). *Stanford-Binet intelligence scales—Fifth edition, examiner & technical manuals*. Austin, TX: Pro-Ed.

Roid, G. H., & Haladyna, T. M. (1982). *A technology for test-item writing*. New York: Academic Press.

Roid, G. H., & Miller, L. J. (1997). *Leiter international performance scale—Revised*. Wood Dale, IL: Stoelting.

Roid, G. H., Miller, L. J., Pomplun, M., & Koch, C. (2013). *Leiter international performance scale-third edition*. Wood Dale, IL: Stoelting Company.

Roid, G. H., Pomplun, M., & Martin, J. (2009). Nonverbal cognitive assessment with the Leiter-R. In J. Naglieri & S. Goldstein (Eds.), *A practitioner's guide to assessment of intelligence and achievement*. NY: Wiley.

Roid, G. H., & Woodcock, R. W. (2000). Uses of Rasch scaling in the measurement of cognitive development and growth. *Journal of Outcome Measurement, 4*(2), 579–594.

Rosinski, R. R., Golinkoff, R. M., & Kukish, K. S. (1975). Automatic semantic processing in a picture-word interference task. *Child Development, 46*, 247–253.

Rourke, B. P. (1988). The syndrome of non-verbal learning disabilities. *Clinical Neuropsychologist, 2*, 293–330.

Salvia, J., & Ysseldyke, J. E. (1991). *Assessment*. Boston, MA: Houghton Mifflin.

Sattler, J. M. (2001). *Assessment of children: Cognitive applications* (4th ed.). La Mesa, CA: Author.

Schneider, W. J., & McGrew, K. S. (2012). The Cattell-Horn-Carroll model of intelligence. In D. Flanagan & P. Harrison, *Contemporary intellectual assessment*, 3rd Ed. (pp. 99–144). New York, NY: Guilford Press.

Stroop, J. R. (1935). Studies of interference in serial verbal reactions. *Journal of Experimental Psychology, 18*, 643–662.

Sullivan, E. V., Sagar, H. J., & Gabrieli, J. D. (1989). Different cognitive profiles on standard behavioral tests in Parkinson's disease and Alzheimer's disease. *Journal of Clinical and Experimental Neuropsychology, 11*, 799–820.

Talland, G. A. (Ed.). (1965). *Deranged memory*. New York: Academic Press.

Tecce, J. J., & Happ, S. J. (1964). Effects of shock-arousal on a card-sorting test of color-word interference. *Perceptual and Motor Skills, 19*, 905–906.

Thurstone, L. L., & Thurstone, T. G. (1962). Primary Mental Abilities (Rev.), Chicago, IL: Science Research Associates.

U.S. Bureau of Census. (2009). *Population statistics: 2008 update*. Washington, DC: Author.

U.S. Bureau of Census. (2011). *Census 2010 summary file 1 of the United States*. Washington, DC: Author.

U.S. Department of Education. (2016). National Center for Education Statistics, ED*Facts* file 141, Data Group 678, extracted May 13, 2016, from the ED*Facts* Data Warehouse (internal U.S. Department of Education source); Common Core of Data (CCD), "State Non-fiscal Survey of Public Elementary and Secondary Education," 2008–09 through 2013–14. http://nces.ed.gov/programs/digest/d15/tables/dt15_204.27.asp

U.S. Department of Education. (2007). *Data analysis system OMB #1820-0043: "Children with disabilities receiving special education under part B of the individuals with disabilities education act"*. Data updated as of July 15, 2008. Washington DC: Author, Office of Special Education Programs. Retrieved from: https://www.ideadata.org/arc_toc9.asp#partbCC

Volkmar, F. R., Lord, C., Bailey, A., Schultz, R. T., & Klin, A. (2004). Autism and pervasive developmental disorders. *Journal of Child Psychology and Psychiatry, 45*, 135–170.

Wang, P. L. (1984). *Modified Vygotsky concept formation test manual*. Chicago, IL: Stoelting Co.

Wechsler, D. (1991). *Wechsler intelligence scale for children—Third Edition (WISC-III)*. San Antonio, TX: The Psychological Corporation.

Wechsler, D. (2003). *Wechsler intelligence scale for children—Fourth edition*. (WISC-IV) San Antonio, TX: Pearson/PsychCorp.

Wechsler, D. (2008). *Wechsler adult intelligence scale—Fourth edition (WAIS-IV)*. San Antonio, TX: Pearson/PsychCorp.

Williams, D. L., Goldstein, G., & Minshew, N. J. (2006). Neurophsychologic functioning in children with autism: Further evidence for disordered complex information-processing. *Child Neuropsychology, 12*, 279–298.

Woodcock, R. W. (1999). What can Rasch-based scores convey about a person's test performance? In S. E. Embretson & S. L. Hershberger (Eds.), *The new rules of measurement: What every psychologist and educator should know* (pp. 105–128). Mahwah, NJ: Erlbaum.

Woodcock, R. W., & Dahl, M. N. (1971). *A common scale for the measurement of person ability and test item difficulty*. (AGS Paper No. 10). Circle Pines, MN: American Guidance Service.

Woodcock, R. W., McGrew, K., & Mather, N. (2000). *Woodcock-Johnson tests of cognitive ability-third edition: Examiner's manual*. Chicago: Riverside.

# Wechsler Nonverbal Scale of Ability

## Caroline M. Jaquett and Baileigh A. Kirkpatrick

The *Wechsler Nonverbal Scale of Ability* (WNV; Wechsler and Naglieri 2006) is an individual nonverbal assessment of general cognitive ability for ages 4 years and 0 months to 21 years and 11 months (4:0–21:11). The WNV was adapted from earlier versions of the Wechsler scales to minimize or eliminate nonverbal instructions and demands, while keeping the format of subtest and composite scores. Pictorial directions are unique to this assessment, and are used to communicate the directions of the subtests. Brief verbal prompts can be given if appropriate, but their use is limited and not essential. The goal of developing this nonverbal assessment was to fairly assess individuals from culturally and linguistically diverse groups (Wechsler and Naglieri 2006). This chapter discusses the development of the WNV, describes the structure and administration of the assessment, explains scoring and interpretation, discusses psychometric properties and fairness, and, finally, critiques the strengths and weaknesses of the WNV.

## Development of the WNV

The WNV provides a measure of general cognitive ability and is based on Spearman's (1904) general factor of intelligence ($g$). Wechsler's original intelligence test and the editions that have followed have measured general intelligence through subtests that differ in terms of task demands, but all together make up a Full Scale score of general cognitive ability (Wechsler 1939). There is empirical support for measuring general intelligence in this manner (see Jensen 1998). The WNV follows the Spearman and Wechsler tradition in measuring general cognitive ability as a broad composite of specific ability "slivers," and the format of the WNV is directly related to the format of previous Wechsler scales.

Although the Wechsler scales (such as the *Wechsler Intelligence Scale for Children-Fourth Edition* [WISC-IV; Wechsler 2003] and *Wechsler Adult Intelligence Scale-Third Edition* [WAIS-III; Wechsler 1997]) are reliable and valid measures of general ability, these tests may not always be the fair(est) measure of examinees who are culturally or linguistically diverse. Nonverbal tests of ability eliminate the emphasis on verbal/language skills, thus providing a more accurate assessment of the examinee's ability, rather than reflecting a deficit that is due to limited opportunity to acquire verbal skills (Naglieri and Brunnert 2009). The importance placed on assessing diverse populations using the WNV is discussed below.

C.M. Jaquett · B.A. Kirkpatrick (✉)
University of Tennessee, 535 BEC,
1122 Volunteer Blvd, Knoxville 37996, USA
e-mail: bkirkpa3@vols.utk.edu

C.M. Jaquett
e-mail: cjaquett@vols.utk.edu

© Springer International Publishing AG 2017
R.S. McCallum (ed.), *Handbook of Nonverbal Assessment*,
DOI 10.1007/978-3-319-50604-3_9

## Subtest Background

The six subtests of the WNV include Matrices, Coding, Object Assembly, Recognition, Spatial Span, and Picture Arrangement. Separate versions have been created for ages 4:0–7:11 and 8:0–21:11 as not all subtests are appropriate for all ages. The Recognition subtest was specifically developed for the WNV, and is the only subtest that is not adapted from other assessments of ability. The Matrices subtest was adapted from the *Naglieri Nonverbal Ability Test- Individual Administration* (NNAT-I; Naglieri 2003). The Coding, Object Assembly, Recognition, Spatial Span, and Picture Arrangement are similar to subtests in previous versions of the Wechsler intelligence scales (see *Wechsler Intelligence Scale for Children- Fourth Edition- Integrated Edition* [WISC-IV Integrated; Wechsler et al. 2004], WISC-IV [Wechsler 2003], *Wechsler Preschool and Primary Scale of Intelligence-Third Edition* [WPPSI-III; Wechsler 2002], WAIS-III [Wechsler 1997]). All of these subtests are described as valid and reliable, based on empirical data (Naglieri and Brunnert 2009). The tests that these subtests are based on have also been empirically validated over the years. While all of the subtests are similar in that they do not require verbal instruction or verbal responses, each of the subtests requires a different type of cognitive ability. For example, the Spatial Span subtest requires visual-spatial ability, while the Recognition subtest requires spatial recall.

## Cultural and Linguistic Diversity

Suzuki and Valencia (1997) state that ability assessments which require verbal skills do not accurately assess minority children. Children who are not assessed in their primary language are at a disadvantage, and the population of English Language Learners in U.S. schools continues to increase (National Center for Educational Statistics 2016). Furthermore, students who belong to special populations (such as those who are hearing impaired, or those who are culturally and/or linguistically disadvantaged)

are not always assessed accurately by traditional ability tests (Naglieri and Brunnert 2009). The WNV addresses the need to provide a fair (er) assessment through the use of pictorial instead of verbal directions. This emphasis is also reflected in the comparison of the performance of special populations to matched control groups during validation, and standardization groups that accurately represent the U.S. and Canadian populations. Because the overall goal of the WNV is to accurately assess ability nonverbally across a variety of examinees, a multidimensional assessment of ability is used that eliminates the examinee's use of expressive language and mathematic skills.

## Description of the WNV

The WNV, which is designed for children and adults ages 4–21, includes several test battery options based on the age of the examinee: 4:0–7:11 and 8:0–21:11. Although six subtests are included in the WNV, a practitioner never administers all six subtests. Instead, for each age band, the practitioner has the option to choose either the 4-subtest or 2-subtest option. The Full Scale Intelligence Quotient (FSIQ) can be obtained from administration of either subtest option. In addition to calculating the FSIQ, individual subtest scores can be derived for purposes of normative and ipsative analysis.

Table 9.1 displays the standard battery of tests for each age band. The tests required for the 2-subtest FSIQ (i.e., Matrices and Recognition for ages 4:0–7:11 and Matrices and Spatial Span for ages 8:0–21:11) are indicated with asterisks. Below is a description of each of the WNV subtests.

## WNV Subtests

*Matrices (MA)*: the examinee is required to identify how different shapes or geometric figures are related and select the best option that completes the relationship among the parts. The items are made up of different geometric figures (e.g., squares, circles, triangles) and colors

**Table 9.1** Standard subtest administration order, by age band, for the WNV

| 4:0–7:11 | 8:0–21:11 |
| --- | --- |
| 1. Matrices* | 1. Matrices* |
| 2. Coding | 2. Coding |
| 3. Object assembly | 3. Spatial span* |
| 4. Recognition* | 4. Picture arrangement |

*indicates subtests given in the 2-subtest battery

(i.e., black, white, yellow, blue, and/or green) in order to keep the examinee's interest. This subtest is a part of both the 2-and 4-subtest batteries.

*Coding (CD)*: the examinee is shown a key with symbols paired either with simple geometric shapes or numbers. After, the examinee is given 120 s to fill in a key with the appropriate symbol. Two forms of this task (Form A and B) are included depending on the examinee's age. Coding A is used with examinees ages 4:0–7:11 and requires the examinee to match a simple symbol (e.g., a dash or an arc) with an identifiable shape (e.g., a star or circle). Coding B is used with examinees ages 8:0–21:11 and requires the examinee to pair a number (i.e., 1–9) with a simple symbol (e.g., a slash or arc). Coding is only administered as a part of the 4-subtest battery.

*Object Assembly (OA)*: the examinee is required to assemble puzzle pieces to form a recognizable object (e.g., a ball or a tree) within a specified time limit. The number of pieces varies from 2 to 8 for each item and the items increase in number of pieces and difficulty. This subtest is administered as a part of the 4-subtest battery for ages 4:0–7:11.

*Recognition (RG)*: the examinee is required to examine a stimulus for 3 s and then choose which option is identical to the stimulus that was just seen. The stimulus figures comprised various geometric shapes (e.g., a triangle in a square) and colors (i.e., black, white, yellow, blue, and/or green). This subtest is administered as a part of both the 2- and 4-subtest batteries for ages 4:0–7:11.

*Spatial Span (SSp)*: the examinee is shown an 8-by-11-in. board with 10 blocks arranged on it. The examinee is required to touch the blocks in a specific sequential pattern either in the same, or reverse order of that performed by the examiner.

This subtest is administered in both the 2- and 4-subtest batteries for ages 8:0–21:11.

*Picture Arrangement (PA)*: The examinee is required to arrange picture cards with cartoon-like illustrations into a logical sequence (e.g., building a house) within a specified time limit. The pictures are in bright colors in order to maintain interest. This subtest is included in the 4-subtest battery for ages 8:0–21:11.

## Scores Provided

The WNV subtests produce raw scores, subtest *T* scores (i.e., standard scores with a mean of 50 and a standard deviation of 10), a composite FSIQ score (i.e., standard score with a mean of 100 and standard deviation of 15), age equivalents, and percentile ranks. Four optional scores are available to examiners who wish to more closely examine performance on the Spatial Span subtest. If close examination is desired, examiners can calculate and compare Spatial Span Forward (SSpF) versus Spatial Span Backward (SSpB), and Longest Spatial Span Forward (LSSpF) versus Longest Spatial Span Backward (LSSpB). Unlike other Wechsler assessments which provide several composite scores, the WNV only produces a single composite score: the FSIQ. This FSIQ score is obtained from the sum of all of the subtest *T* scores in the selected 2- or 4-subtest battery.

## WNV Administration and Scoring

The WNV was developed to be sensitive to examinees from various cultures and of varying ability levels; thus, the WNV Administration and Scoring Manual devotes several pages to describing the use of the instrument for examinees in these special groups. In addition, the examiner is encouraged to consider the testing environment. Specifically, the WNV is meant to be administered in a well-lit, quiet room that is free from distraction and interruptions. Only the examinee and the examiner should be in the testing room, except for in rare instances, where another adult is required for facilitation of administration. In instances in which an interpreter is used, the interpreter should be given specific instructions regarding directions to be verbally translated. Additional comments should only be translated as the examiner deems necessary. Seating arrangements are also an important aspect of the testing environment. When possible, the examiner is encouraged to sit across the table from the examinee in order to ensure a full view of the examinee's behavior. Both the examiner and the examinee must have a clear view of the stimulus book, so that the examiner can gesture to the items and pictorial directions as indicated in the Administration and Scoring Manual. In addition, the stimulus book should be positioned differently depending on the examinee's dominant hand. Examiners are encouraged to refer to the Administration and Scoring Manual for more specific regulations regarding the testing environment.

Establishing and maintaining rapport with the examinee is a crucial aspect of any testing session. Examiners must be familiar with the age, gender, and culture of the examinee they are testing, in order to determine appropriate gestures. In addition, the few verbal directions should be given in the examinee's primary language whenever possible. Verbal instructions are provided in English, French, Spanish, Chinese, German, and Dutch. However, examiners should only give verbal directions in languages in which they are proficient. Examinees should be approached differently depending on their age, the testing setting, and conditions. Examiners should approach administration in a confident manner, and establish a steady pace so that examinees do not grow bored. In order to maintain rapport, verbal (e.g., "You're working hard!") and nonverbal (e.g., smile, thumbs up)

cues should be given as appropriate. It is important, however, to not give responses that could be interpreted as indicating the correctness of the response (e.g., "Great").

The WNV is unique in that pictorial directions are given for each specific subtest. When administering pictorial directions, three gestures are used: sweep, drag, and point. When the directions state to *sweep your hand*, the examiner glides his/her hand, with palms upward, in a line just above the position(s) being indicated. *Drag your finger* indicates that the examiner should move his/her finger across the page. *Point* indicates that the examiner should briefly touch or hold his/her finger above the indicated position. Administration of the pictorial directions will require the examiner to adeptly use a combination of these three gestures. For example, administration of the Matrices subtest requires the examiner to point to each frame of the pictorial directions, point to the directions and then to the stimulus page, and then sweep his/her hand along the response options to the problem. Supplemental verbal directions are to be used as needed. If verbal directions are to be provided by a translator in a language not detailed in the manual, then these comments should be determined ahead of time.

If pictorial directions and supplemental verbal directions are ineffective for explaining the demands of the subtest, then the examiner should provide additional help as needed in order to ensure that the examinee understands subtest requirements (e.g., refer back to pictorial directions, or give additional gestures or verbal directions). The examiner should use professional judgement in order to determine the amount of additional help provided.

## WNV Item Types

Each of the WNV subtests includes demonstration and sample items in order to ensure that the examinee understands task demands before additional items are administered. Demonstration items are presented by the examiner and not scored. Sample items are completed by the examinee, with corrective feedback from the examiner, and are not scored.

**Start Points**. Specific start points for each subtest are varying according to the age of the examinee. If an examinee is suspected of a cognitive disability, then examiners should start with item 1, regardless of the examinee's age. The Spatial Span and Picture Arrangement subtests have a single start point for ages 8:0–21:11.

**Reverse Rules**. The reverse rules apply to all subtests with age-specific start points, and rules are provided in order to help determine when to administer additional items prior to the examinee's age-appropriate start point. When a reversal occurs, the examiner administers preceding items in a reverse sequence until two consecutive perfect scores are obtained or the first item is administered. Matrices, Object Assembly, and Recognition include reversal items, while Coding, Spatial Span, and Picture Arrangement do not.

**Discontinue Rules**. Discontinue rules are provided for each subtest so that the examiner can determine when to stop subtest administration. The discontinue rule typically specifies that administration should stop after an examinee receives a score of 0 on a certain number of consecutive items.

**Timing**. Three WNV subtests have strict item time limits that require precise timing: Coding, Object Assembly, and Picture Arrangement. In addition, Recognition items have a strict exposure time limit (3 s). It is imperative that the examiner have a stopwatch for these subtests in order to ensure precise timing of responses and stimulus exposures.

**Record Booklets**. Specific information detailing the WNV administration is found in the Administration and Scoring Manual and the WNV Record Booklet. The Record Booklet highlights specific administration information including start points, discontinuation rules, item types, and time limits, as well as correct responses and scoring options for all items. The front page of the Record Booklet serves as a summary page and includes areas for the examiner to calculate the examinee's chronological age, indicate the

selected test battery (4-subtest or 2-subtest), transfer and calculate subtest total raw scores, convert total raw scores to $T$ scores, and determine the Full Scale Score, Percentile Rank, and Confidence Interval (see Appendix A of the Administration and Scoring Manual). Age equivalents can be found for each specific subtest. Additional worksheets are included on the back of the front page for calculating subtest strengths and weaknesses (in the 4-subtest administration), subtest comparison (in the 2-subtest battery), and the significance of the comparison (i.e., the incidence of that difference in the population). In addition, the worksheet includes optional further analyses of the Spatial Span subtest.

## Subtest Administration and Scoring

The examiner must first determine the test battery to be administered. For each age band, as discussed above, the examiner has the option to choose either the 4- or 2-subtest battery. Choice between the two batteries depends on the goals of the assessment as well as the practical need. Although both versions have good reliability and validity, the 4-subtest battery provides a more thorough examination of general ability. However, when time is a factor, the 2-subtest option may be chosen. The 4-subtest option takes, on average, 45 min to administer, while the 2-subtest option takes 20 min to administer, on average. Refer to the Administration and Scoring Manual for more specific information on administration times.

All subtests on the WNV include pictorial directions given using specific gestures and select verbal directions, as stated above. It is imperative that examiners have proper training and experience with psychological assessment and familiarity with the WNV before administering the test. Individuals should have had formal graduate-level coursework in the administration and interpretation of individual standardized cognitive tests in order to administer the WNV. In addition to this coursework, individuals should thoroughly read the WNV Administration and

Scoring Manual and practice its administration, prior to actually administering the test. The Administration and Scoring Manual provides detailed verbal directions and ample graphics to assist with administration.

## Specific Administration Directions

Although the WNV is a nonverbal test, the absence of verbal communication can sometimes make the testing atmosphere feel uncomfortable. Thus, as much as possible, the examiner should attempt to establish rapport before, and during, test administration using common verbal phrases (e.g., Bon, Bien) and nonverbal gestures (e.g., thumbs up, nodding) as needed. If the examinee and examiner are proficient in the same language, additional verbal instructions may be given to supplement the pictorial instructions. The WNV is introduced with a set of verbal directions indicating that pictorial directions will be used for the remainder of the assessment. Each subtest requires the use of pictorial instructions in the stimulus book and supplemental verbal instructions. Examinees may also ask the examiner questions. Administration procedures specific to each subtest of the WNV are offered below. Examiners are encouraged to refer to the Administration and Scoring Manual for more specific directions.

*Matrices* stimulus pages are available in the stimulus book and are presented to the examinee. Pictorial directions in the stimulus book should be presented to the examinee using pointing and sweeping motions. The examinee is expected to point to the response option that goes in the question mark that completes each matrix. If the examinee appears confused, an additional verbal prompt is provided. The examinee uses spatial and logical reasoning to address the subtest demands and points to one of the four or five response options presented below the stimulus that best completes the figural matrix (e.g., the examinee points to a small yellow square to complete a large yellow square which has a small square missing). Three different start points are set for examinees ages 4–5, 6–15, and 16–21.

Items are scored either as a 1, indicating a correct response, or 0, indicating an incorrect response. Reverse rules indicate that examiners must reverse if either of the first two items administered is failed. This subtest is discontinued after the examinee receives 4 scores of 0 on five consecutive items. Examiners should note that this means testing is discontinued under two conditions: if the examinee misses four items in a row, or four items out of five consecutive items.

The *Coding* subtest requires the use of the Response Booklet for item completion. The Coding A form is administered to examinees ages 4:0–7:11 and the Coding B form is administered to examinees ages 8:0–21:11. Pictorial directions are indicated in the stimulus book. After the appropriate Response Booklet turned to the appropriate coding test is placed in front of the examinee, the examiner points to each frame in the pictorial directions. The examiner points to the matching shapes (Form A) or numbers (Form B) and their keyed symbols. Then the examiner demonstrates finding the matching symbol in the key and writing it in the empty box on the Response Booklet (e.g., pointing to a circle, the dash underneath it, and then writing a dash under the circle in an empty space indicated in the Response Booklet). The examinee is directed to write in the keyed symbols underneath the indicated numbers or shapes, and practices on several items, receiving corrective feedback. The examiner then uses a timer to allow the examinee 120 s to complete the rest of the items. The subtest is discontinued after 120 s or, if the subtest is completed in less time, after the examinee indicates he/she is finished. If less than 120 s are needed, the examiner indicates the exact completion time in the Response Booklet. The subtest is scored by the number of items that the examinee coded correctly, and each correctly coded item earns 1 point. On Coding A, the examinee can earn a maximum of 72 points and on Coding B, up to 144 points can be earned.

*Object Assembly* requires the examinee to fit prearranged puzzle pieces together to form a meaningful whole. The Object Assembly pieces and a stopwatch are needed for this task. Different pieces are arranged for each item. The examiner places the pictorial directions in front of the examinee as well as the puzzle pieces for the demonstration item. The examiner points to each frame in the directions while assembling the demonstration puzzle. Then the examiner disassembles the puzzle and presents the pieces to the examinee. Note that there is a standard arrangement for the puzzle piece presentation of each item. For each item, the examinee is tasked with arranging the prearranged puzzle pieces into a whole figure within a certain time limit. After demonstration and sample items, there are two start points: ages 4–5 and ages 6–7. Reverse rules indicate that items should be administered in reverse order if examinees have imperfect assembly on either of the first two items given. Item time limits are 90 s for items 1–4 and increase to 210 s for items 5–11. If the examinee does not complete the item within the time limit, the examiner stops the examinee and administers the next item. Items are scored by the number of correct junctures the examinee completes. A correct juncture indicates that the examinee correctly put two adjacent pieces together. For items 1–7, the item score is the number of junctures joined correctly within the time limit. For items 8 and 10, time bonus points (up to 3) are given on top of the number of correct junctures to reward efficient and accurate item completion. For items 9 and 11, the number of correct junctures is divided by 2, and rounded up to the higher number. Time bonus points (up to 3) are also given. The maximum raw score, including time bonus points, is 56. The subtest is discontinued after the examinee earns two consecutive scores of 0 (i.e., indicating 0 correct junctures).

*Recognition* requires the use of the stimulus book. The examiner shows the pictorial directions in the stimulus book for 3 s, and then flips the page and shows the response options. For each item, the examinee is presented with a geometric design for 3 s and then, after the examiner flips to the next page in the stimulus book, is asked to identify which of four or five response options matches the previously viewed stimulus. Items are scored either as a 1,

indicating a correct response, or 0, indicating an incorrect response. After demonstration and sample items are given, the examinee begins with one of two start points: ages 4–5 or ages 6–7. Reverse rules indicate that the examiner should reverse administer items if a score of 0 is earned on either of the first two items given. The subtest is discontinued after 4 scores of 0 are earned on five consecutive items.

*Spatial Span* requires the use of the stimulus book and the Spatial Span Board (a white board with 10 cubes arranged on top of it). The numbered side of the cubes should face the examiner. The examiner shows the Spatial Span forward pictorial directions and points to each frame. Next, the examiner taps the numbered sequence of cubes (e.g., 1–3). The examinee responds by tapping the same sequence of cubes. The trials increase in difficulty as more cubes are tapped. All examinees ages 8:0–21:11 begin with item 1. Each item includes two trials. Examinees earn one point for each trial in which they tap the correct sequence. Thus, examinees can earn scores of 0, 1, or 2 on each item, depending on if they tapped the correct sequence for 0, 1, or all trials of the item. The trials are discontinued after scores of 0 are earned on both trials of an item. To continue the subtest the next page is turned in the stimulus book showing the Spatial Span backward pictorial instructions. Similar to the directions for the Spatial Span forward component, the examiner points to the picture frames indicating the directions, and taps a sequence of number cubes. However, now the examinee responds by tapping the sequence of cubes in the opposite order of the examiner (e.g., if the examiner taps 1-3, the examinee should tap 3-1). Items are scored and discontinued in the same fashion as in the forward Spatial Span task.

*Picture Arrangement* requires the use of Picture Arrangement cards and a stopwatch. The examiner points to each frame of the pictorial directions and presents the cards for the demonstration item in the standard numerical order. The examinee is tasked with ordering each set of prearranged picture cards to tell a logical story within the time limit. A stopwatch should be used to record the time it takes the examinee to complete each item. Items 1–6 have a time limit of 45 s and items 7–13 have a time limit of 90 s. Items 1–10 and 13 are scored as either 0 or 2 points, depending on whether the examinee puts the pictures in the correct sequence. Items 11–12 can earn 1 point of credit for a specific alternative sequence as indicated in the Record Form. A maximum of 26 points can be earned. Testing is discontinued after the examinee scores 4 consecutive scores of 0.

## WNV Interpretation

As described previously, the WNV includes two battery options, the four-subtest battery or the two-subtest battery. Interpretation of the WNV begins with determining which battery was administered. As described above, both the 4- and 2-subtest batteries have adequate reliability and validity, but the four-subtest battery allows for more thorough interpretation. Consideration of the examinee, purpose of the assessment, and the time available to conduct the assessment are important concerns when making the decision between the two batteries. After the choice between the batteries has been made and the WNV has been administered, the WNV is interpreted in multiple steps that begin by examining the most reliable composite score (the FSIQ) and move to more specific, but less reliable sources of interpretation (e.g., subtests).

The WNV is interpreted from both normative (between-children) and ipsative (within-child) perspectives. These procedures have been applied in the interpretation of many intelligence tests, and are considered best practice in the field by many experts (e.g., McCallum 1991; Naglieri and Brunnert 2009; Sattler 2008). The following brief discussion of WNV interpretation focuses on the guidelines for interpretation set forth in The WNV Technical and Interpretive Manual (Wechsler and Naglieri 2006). For more information, see Naglieri and Brunnert's (2009) chapter on WNV interpretation.

## General Interpretation Guidelines

The WNV Technical and Interpretive Manual provides two different sets of interpretation guidelines depending on whether the 4-subtest or 2-subtest battery is chosen. Due to the similarity of the interpretation for these two batteries, guidelines have been combined for the purposes of this section. As stated above, interpretation begins with the global FSIQ score. This score is the most general indicator of ability ($g$) and also is the best predictor of academic achievement (Wechsler and Naglieri 2006). Although the composite score (the FSIQ) is the most reliable interpretable data point, when sizable variability exists between component scores, the FSIQ might not be the most reasonable measure of the examinee's ability (Sattler 2008). Thus, in this case, interpretation would continue to the level of the individual subtests. The WNV authors included a 5-step interpretation process in the manual. These interpretation steps are briefly described in the following sections.

### Step 1. Examine the Full Scale Score

The Full Scale score is a composite of the 2- or 4-subtest scores and is the most representative score of general ability. The score should be reported with the percentile rank, chosen confidence interval (90 or 95%), and qualitative descriptor. The Full Scale score should be interpreted after consideration of factors that could have affected testing performance such as behaviors observed during administration (e.g., inattentive behavior or restlessness) the testing session and examinee background factors. All other things being equal, the 4-subtest battery FSIQ is more robust than the 2-subtest battery.

### Step 2. Subtest-Level Analysis

The next step in WNV interpretation involves examining the $T$ scores among the various subtests. Variability between subtest scores is expected, but when significant variability occurs, interpreting the various subtests individually might be a better option. In this level of analysis, relative strengths and weaknesses can be calculated by comparing each subtest's $T$ score to the mean $T$ score of all subtests. These scores should be examined to determine if the scores are statistically significantly and meaningfully different, one from the other. This strategy allows determination of strengths and weaknesses. A subtest score that is significantly above the mean of all subtest scores is tentatively considered a relative strength, while one that is significantly below the mean of all subtest scores is assumed to be a relative weakness. Table B.1 in the Administration and Scoring Manual presents values for statistical significance. In addition to statistical significance, examiners should also be concerned with meaningful difference; that is, how often does this difference occur in the population. To assess whether the difference is rare, examiners should determine how frequently this difference occurred in the normative sample. Table B.2 in the Administration and Scoring Manual presents values for the percentage of the normative sample who obtained various discrepancies between a single subtest $T$ score and mean $T$ scores.

*Step 3. Analysis of Spatial Span (Optional)*

Examiners might be interested in the comparison of $T$ scores earned in the Spatial Span Forward and Spatial Span backward subtests. A difference equal to or greater than 13 $T$ score points between Spatial Span Forward and Spatial Span Backward is significant at $p = 0.05$ (as shown in Table C.2 of the Administration and Scoring Manual). Examiners may choose to examine and report this difference in the interpretation process as representing a difference between rote memory versus working memory.

*Step 4. Examine Intersubtest Variability (Optional)*

This step is an optional step within the 4-subtest battery interpretation process. Intersubtest variability reflects the variability of an examinee's scores across subtests. A simple examination of the difference between the highest and lowest $T$ scores will provide the examiner an indicator of this variability. Table B.5 in the Administration and Scoring Manual allows the examiner to identify the extent to which a particular level of variability occurred in the normative sample.

*Step 5. Intervention (Optional)*

The final step in interpretation occurs if there is evidence that examinee's scores are significantly different from each other or significantly below the population average. The examiner might wish to consider what effect these relative differences, i.e., strengths or weaknesses, might have on the student in academic or related contexts. Next, an examiner can use his/her knowledge of assessment theory and interventions to discuss accommodations or recommendations for next steps that the examinee might take to improve academic/social functioning.

## Standardization and Psychometric Properties

The WNV was standardized on a stratified sample of 1323 individuals (ages 4:0–21:11) from the United States and 875 individuals (ages 4:0–21:11) from Canada. In the sample from the United States, demographic variables were matched to the 2003 U.S. Bureau of the Census based on age, sex, race/ethnicity, education level, and geographic region. The Canadian stratified sample was based on demographic information from data gathered in 2001 by Statistics Canada (2002) for age, sex, ethnicity, education level, and geographic data. Higher scores were observed for individuals from the Canadian sample compared to the U.S. sample on each of the subtests when using U.S. norms. The mean 4-Subtest Battery Full Scale score was 4.10 points higher, and 2.90 points higher for the mean 2-Subtest Battery Full Scale score, for the Canadian sample (see Table 9.2).

**Table 9.2** Average performance for U.S. and Canadian samples

| Subtest/full scale score | Canada | | | U.S. | | |
|---|---|---|---|---|---|---|
| | Mean | SD | N | Mean | SD | N |
| Matrices | 51.0 | 10.2 | 875 | 50.3 | 10.1 | 1323 |
| Coding | 51.5 | 9.2 | 853 | 49.9 | 10.0 | 1305 |
| Object assembly | 54.1 | 9.8 | 250 | 50.1 | 10.1 | 391 |
| Recognition | 52.8 | 10.1 | 250 | 50.0 | 9.8 | 391 |
| Spatial span | 52.5 | 10.3 | 625 | 50.2 | 9.9 | 932 |
| Picture arraignment | 52.6 | 10.0 | 625 | 50.1 | 10.2 | 932 |
| Full scale score: 4 | 104.1 | 14.2 | 853 | 100.0 | 15.0 | 1305 |
| Full scale score: 2 | 102.9 | 15.6 | 875 | 100.0 | 15.5 | 1323 |

## Reliability

According to the WNV Manual, internal consistency estimates were obtained for the Full Scale scores as well as for all subtests for the U.S. and Canadian samples. Average reliability across ages for the U.S. sample ranged from 0.74 to 0.91 for the subtests. Average reliability across ages for the Full Scale scores (both the 4-subtest Battery and the 2-subtest Battery) was 0.91. For the Canadian sample, average reliability across ages for subtests ranged from 0.73 to 0.90. Average reliability for the Full Scale score across ages was 0.90 for the 4-subtest Battery and 0.91 for the 2-subtest Battery. Internal reliability data for special groups was also collected. Average reliability ranges for subtests can be seen in Table 9.3, and range from 0.70 to 0.98. According to Salvia et al. (2013) test scores that yield reliability coefficients of 0.90 or above can be used for making important high stakes decisions, and those ranging from 0.80 to 0.89 can be used for screening decisions.

Test–retest reliability data was gathered from a sample of 61 U.S. individuals. Test–retest intervals ranged from 10 to 31 days for those from ages 4:0 to 7:11, and 10 to 52 days for those from ages 8:0 to 21:11. For the 4:0 to 7:11 age group, test–retest corrected coefficients ranged from 0.61 to 0.84 for the subtests, 0.84 for the 4-subtest Battery Full Scale score, and 0.77 for the 2-subtest Battery Full Scale score. For the 8:0–21:11 age group, test–retest reliability corrected coefficients ranged from 0.68 to 0.78 for the subtests, 0.86 for the 4-subtest Battery Full Scale score, and 0.81 for the 2-subtest Battery Full Scale score.

## Validity

**Internal Validity.** Correlations between the subtests as well as the 4-subtest Battery Full Scale and 2-subtest Battery Full Scale scores were determined for the 4:0–7:11 and 8:0–21:11 age groups for U.S. and Canadian samples. For

**Table 9.3** Reliability coefficients for special groups

| Special group | Reliability estimate range (subtests) |
|---|---|
| ELLs | 0.70–0.96 |
| Gifted | 0.77–0.97 |
| ID-mild severity | 0.80–0.93 |
| ID-moderate severity | 0.87–0.93 |
| RWD | 0.72–0.88 |
| Language disorders | 0.74–0.97 |
| Deaf | 0.77–0.98 |
| Hard of hearing | 0.75–0.97 |

the 4:0–7:11 age group, correlation coefficients among the subtests ranged from 0.22 to 0.46 for the U.S. sample, and 0.07 to 0.34 for the Canadian sample. The correlation between the 4- and 2-subtest batteries was 0.88 for U.S. and 0.84 for Canada. For the 8:0–21:11 age group, the subtest correlations ranged from 0.20 to 0.44 for U.S. sample and 0.15–0.41 for the Canadian sample. The correlation between the 4- and 2-subtest batteries was 0.88 for both U.S. and Canada.

**Factor Analysis**. Confirmatory factor analyses were performed using a single factor model to determine the fit of the WNV to Spearman's model ($g$). This analysis was conducted for the U.S. and Canadian samples for the 4:0–7:11 and 8:0–21:11 age groups. Specificity and error variance were compared, as well as each subtest's loadings on $g$. The $g$ loadings ranged from 0.40 to 0.69 for the 4:0–7:11 age group and from 0.36 to 0.66 for the older group. In addition, each subtests' specificity exceeded the error variance, indicating that each subtest provides a systematic and unique measure of some cognitive component (Naglieri and Brunnert 2009). From confirmatory analyses, the model fit for a single factor ($g$) model revealed a good fit for both the 4:00–7:11 and 8:0–21:11 age groups. When the 8:0–21:11 age group was broken down into smaller age ranges, this model did not fit as well but was still considered adequate.

**Criterion-Related Validity**. The WNV was compared to several other measures of ability. The measures and correlations found are described below.

***Wechsler Preschool and Primary Scale of Intelligence-Third Edition (WPPSI-III)***. The WNV and WPPSI-III (Wechsler 2002) both measure ability in children ages 4:0–7:3 and have similar Matrices/Matrix Reasoning, Coding, and Object Assembly subtests. However, the WNV has pictorial directions while the WPPSI-III does not. This difference in directions is consistent across all of the following assessments described. Both the 4-subtest Full Scale Battery and 2-subtest Full Scale scores on the WNV showed moderate correlation with the WPPSI-III Full Scale IQ (0.71 and 0.67, respectively). The correlations for the equivalent subtests on the WNV

and WPPSI-III were also moderate, ranging from 0.50 to 0.70. These correlations indicate that the WNV and WPPSI-III are measuring similar constructs.

***Wechsler Intelligence Scale for Children-Fourth Edition (WISC-IV) and Wechsler Intelligence Scale for Children-Fourth Edition, Spanish (WISC-IV Sp)***. The WISC-IV (Wechsler 2003) and WISC-IV Sp (Wechsler 2005) measure cognitive ability for children ages 6:0–16:11. The Matrices/Matrix Reasoning and Coding subtests are similar in the WISC-IV, WISC-IV Sp, and WNV; however, administration of these assessments differs. Moderate correlations were obtained between the WISC-IV and WNV 4-subtest Full Scale Battery and 2-subtest Full Scale scores and WISC-IV Full Scale IQ (0.76 and 0.58, respectively). The correlations between the corresponding subtests were also moderate (0.51 and 0.78, respectively). WNV 4-subtest Full Scale Battery and 2-subtest Full Scale scores and WISC-IV Sp Full Scale IQ scores were moderate to highly correlated (0.82 and 0.67, respectively). Moderate–to-high correlations were also found between the two corresponding subtests (0.81 and 0.69, respectively). These correlations indicate that the WNV is measuring similar constructs to the WISC-IV and WISC-IV Sp.

***Wechsler Adult Intelligence Scale-Third Edition (WAIS-III)***. The WAIS-III (Wechsler 1997) measures cognitive ability for ages 16:0–21:11. The subtests that are similar between the WAIS-III and WNV are Matrices/Matrix Reasoning, Coding, and Picture Arrangement; however, the administration procedures differ between the two assessments. WNV 4-subtest Full Scale Battery and 2-subtest Full Scale scores and WAIS-III Full Scale IQs were moderately correlated (0.72 and 0.57 respectively). Correlations on the corresponding subtests were also moderate (0.67, 0.57, and 0.67 respectively). These correlations indicate that the WNV and WAIS-III are measuring similar constructs.

***Naglieri Nonverbal Ability Test-Individual (NNAT-I)***. The NNAT-I (Naglieri 2003) is a nonverbal assessment of cognitive ability for ages 5:0–17:11. The Matrices subtest on the

WNV was adapted from the NNAT-I by adding a color variation, so these subtests were hypothesized to be highly correlated. Administration differs in that the WNV includes pictorial directions and the original NNAT-1 does not. WNV 4-subtest Full Scale Battery and 2-subtest Full Scale scores and NNAT-I showed moderate correlations (0.73 and 0.71, respectively). The Matrices subtests were strongly correlated (0.67). These correlations indicate that the WNV and NNAT-I are measuring similar constructs.

*Universal Nonverbal Intelligence Test (UNIT).* The UNIT (Bracken and McCallum 1998) measures cognitive ability with no verbal directions for ages 5:0–17:11. The UNIT and WNT do not share subtests in common. WNV 4-subtest Full Scale Battery and 2-subtest Full Scale scores and UNIT Full Scale IQ showed moderate correlations (0.73 and 0.62, respectively). These correlations indicate that the WNV and UNIT are measuring similar constructs.

*Wechsler Individual Achievement Test-Second Edition (WIAT-II).* The WIAT-II (Wechsler 2001) is a measure of achievement for ages 6:0–16:11 consisting of a Reading, Mathematics, Written Language, Oral Language composite, and Total Achievement composite scores. WNV 4-subtest Full Scale Battery and 2-subtest Full Scale scores and WIAT-II Total Achievement showed moderate correlations (0.60 and 0.43, respectively). Correlations ranged from 0.28 to 0.67 for WNV Full Scale sores and the WIAT-II composite scores. These results indicate that WNV Full Scale scores are reasonably good predictive of academic achievement as measured by the WIAT-II.

# Fairness

The WNV was developed to ensure a fair and accurate assessment of all individuals, particularly those from special groups, and those who come from culturally and linguistically diverse backgrounds. As discussed, the development of the WNV placed a premium on the accurate assessment of individuals who are traditionally difficult to assess because of language constraints. This emphasis can be seen in the research and standardization that contributed to the development of the WNV. The following discussion of fairness focuses on the results described in the Technical and Interpretive Manual for the WNV (Wechsler and Naglieri 2006).

To ensure that the WNV assesses special populations fairly, data from special groups was collected. This sample consisted of students from the U.S. who fell into one of the following classifications: Gifted, Intellectual Disability (ID)-Mild Severity, ID- Moderate Severity, English Language Learners (ELLs), Reading and Written Expression Learning Disorders (RWD), Language Disorders (either Mixed Receptive-Expressive Language Disorder or Expressive Language Disorder), Deaf, or Hard of Hearing. See Table 9.4 for sample sizes and average ages of these special groups. Each of these groups was compared to a matched group of normal peers in order to determine whether the WNV provided reasonable scores when used to assess cognitive ability for individuals who belong to special groups. Each group's average Full Scale scores were as expected when compared to the control group. For example, gifted individuals were found to have significantly higher scores WNV subtest scores for the 4-subtest and 2-subtest Full Scale versions when compared to a matched control group (the gifted group's average full scale scores were 123.7 for the 4-subtest battery and 123.8 for the 2-subtest battery as compared to 104.2 and 104.0 for the control group). Also, individuals with language disorders had significantly lower Full Scale scores than their control group peers (90.5 for 4-subscale battery and 91.9 for 2-subscale compared to 98.0 and 99.1). The group differences revealed moderate effect sizes for the Full Scale scores and small effect sizes for Coding, Spatial Span, and Picture Arrangement subtests. These results are consistent with prior research that shows students with language disorders typically score 5–22 points lower on cognitive assessments than their peers and have more global deficits in cognitive functioning (Bishop 1992; Doll and Boren 1993; Johnson et al. 1999;

**Table 9.4** Sample size and age of special populations

|        | Gifted | ID-mild | ID-moderate | RWD | Language disorder | ELLs | Deaf | Hard of hearing |
|--------|--------|---------|-------------|-----|-------------------|------|------|-----------------|
| N      | 41     | 51      | 31          | 25  | 36                | 55   | 37   | 48              |
| **Age** |        |         |             |     |                   |      |      |                 |
| Mean   | 14.2   | 12.8    | 13.7        | 11.7 | 10.2             | 12.6 | 13.6 | 11.2            |
| SD     | 4.8    | 4.3     | 4.2         | 3.8 | 4.1               | 5.0  | 4.7  | 5.0             |

**Table 9.5** Performance of special groups and matched control groups

|                          | Full scale score-4 | | | | Full scale score-2 | | | |
|--------------------------|------|------|---------|---------|------|------|---------|---------|
|                          | Mean | SD   | t value | p value | Mean | SD   | t value | p value |
| **Gifted**               | 123.7 | 13.4 | −6.70  | ≤0.01   | 123.8 | 15.0 | −6.27  | ≤ 0.01  |
| Matched control group    | 104.2 | 12.3 |        |         | 104.0 | 13.2 |        |         |
| **ID-mild**              | 67.3  | 12.9 | 10.53  | ≤0.01   | 69.4  | 13.0 | 9.67   | ≤ 0.01  |
| Matched control group    | 97.4  | 15.3 |        |         | 96.8  | 15.5 |        |         |
| **ID-moderate**          | 45.9  | 8.9  | 17.54  | ≤0.01   | 49.2  | 10.1 | 16.77  | ≤ 0.01  |
| Matched control group    | 99.3  | 14.1 |        |         | 100.7 | 13.8 |        |         |
| **RWD**                  | 94.2  | 9.2  | 0.92   | 0.36    | 95.2  | 12.3 | 0.65   | 0.52    |
| Matched control group    | 97.4  | 14.7 |        |         | 97.8  | 15.8 |        |         |
| **Language disorders**   | 90.5  | 11.4 | 2.44   | 0.02    | 91.9  | 11.8 | 2.34   | 0.02    |
| Matched control group    | 98.0  | 14.2 |        |         | 99.1  | 14.2 |        |         |
| **ELLs**                 | 101.7 | 13.4 | 0.16   | 0.87    | 102.1 | 14.1 | −0.20  | 0.84    |
| Matched control group    | 102.1 | 13.4 |        |         | 101.6 | 12.7 |        |         |
| **Deaf**                 | 102.5 | 9.0  | −0.60  | 0.55    | 103.0 | 10.3 | −0.85  | 0.40    |
| Matched control group    | 100.8 | 14.3 |        |         | 100.4 | 15.5 |        |         |
| **Hard of hearing**      | 96.7  | 15.9 | 1.19   | 0.24    | 96.0  | 15.3 | 1.43   | 0.16    |
| Matched control group    | 100.5 | 14.8 |        |         | 100.4 | 14.9 |        |         |

Rose et al. 1992). These findings were in line with how individuals would be expected to perform, suggesting that the WNV can be useful as part of a comprehensive assessment of individuals who might fall into one of these categories. See Table 9.5 for specific averages for each special group's Full Scale scores compared to the matched control group. It is important to note that designation into each category was determined by different clinical professionals, thus some degree of variability in classification has to be expected. Information provided about the special populations is not meant to be totally representative, but only illustrative.

The WNV specifically places a large emphasis on individuals who are deaf or head of hearing. This population was of special interest in the development of the WNV, and the Technical and Interpretive Manual discusses group differences between this special population and a matched control group in detail. Results of comparative assessments found no differences between the deaf or hard of hearing group and the control group. These results are consistent with previous findings that found individuals who are deaf or hard of hearing perform better on nonverbal assessments than verbal assessments (Bellugi et al. 1994). This indicates that the presence of communication limitations does not impair an individual's performance on the WNV, and suggests that the WNV can be used as a fair(er) assessment of these individuals' cognitive ability.

As discussed previously, individuals from the Canadian had higher average scores than the U.S.

sample. When this was further examined using matched samples the mean differences are reduced but there is still a significant difference on the 4-subtest mean. This suggests that there are some social, economic, or educational differences between these two samples that may account for the discrepancy. Canadian children typically begin school earlier than U.S. children, Canadian parents are more likely to have obtained higher education, and the largest minority groups in Canada are French-speaking and foreign born citizens whose education levels are comparable to the majority population (Corbeil 2003). These differences are important to keep in mind to ensure fair interpretation and application of the WNV.

The WNV used a standardization sample that was matched to the U.S. and Canadian populations demographically. While this would ensure that populations are accurately represented, there is not a large amount of emphasis in the Technical and Interpretive Manual placed on differences found between different demographic groups (such as sex or race/ethnicity) or the interpretation of scores based on these demographics. This should be considered when interpreting the results on the WNV.

## Strengths and Weaknesses

The WNV is a robust and user-friendly assessment of nonverbal intelligence. It is administered in a format that "eliminates or minimizes verbal content" (technical and interpretive manual, p. 1), which makes it possible to administer to examinees from diverse cultural and linguistic backgrounds. Reviews of the WNV have applauded the instrument's easy-to-administer, attractive format, and innovative pictorial directions, and found it to be a "useful measure" (Maddux 2010; Sattler 2008, p. 697; Tindal, 2010). However, reviewers have also described some weaknesses in the instrument, such as a lack of discussion about the dated theory of intelligence that underlies the instrument and its high cost (Maddux 2010; Tindal 2010). An examination of some of the specific strengths and weaknesses of the instrument follows.

## WNV Strengths

1. *Pictorial Directions.* The pictorial directions in the WNV are unique among intelligence tests (even among other nonverbal assessments) and allow the test to be administered to a wide variety of examinees, particularly those who are not fluent in English, due to the lack of emphasis on verbal directions (Maddux 2010). An examination of the pictorial directions reveals that these directions are clear in showing the examinee the task demands for each subtest. Additional verbal and gesture instructions supplement the pictorial directions in making sure the examinee feels comfortable and knowledgeable about how to complete each subtest.

2. *Brief Battery Option.* The 2-subtest option typically takes between 15 and 20 min to administer, making it an attractive option for a quick assessment of nonverbal intelligence. This brief option could be particularly helpful in school system assessment where time is often of the essence. Even the full battery option only takes approximately 40 min on average to administer, which makes it a promising fast screening instrument (Maddux 2010).

3. *Good manuals and attractive materials.* The Administration and Scoring Manual is extensive and includes easy-to-follow step-by-step instructions for each test. Separate tabs are included with administration instructions for each age band, which makes administration relatively straightforward. The test materials are engaging, and include manipulatives and pictures, which are interesting to children. In addition, the test Manual addresses the use of the colored materials in order to account for potential concerns with color-blindness.

4. *Good standardization.* The WNV was standardized on both U.S. and Canadian samples stratified by age, sex, race/ethnicity, education level, and geographic region. Norms development and standardization is well described in the Technical and Interpretive Manual and the sampling procedures appear

to be well planned and implemented (Maddux 2010).

5. *Good overall psychometric properties*. Both the 4- and 2-subtest options have adequate reliability and validity evidence that is well-documented and presented in clearly labeled tables (Tindal 2010). The structure of the test is also supported by Factor Analysis studies.

## WNV Weaknesses

1. *Dated Theory*. In his review of the test, Maddux (2010) mentions that the theory underlying the test is somewhat dated. As previously noted, the WNV is based on Spearman's general theory of intelligence (*g*); there are more recent theoretical models (of intelligence) that could have been considered. In addition, the rationale for using Spearman's model could have been stronger.

2. *Convergent validity research*. The moderate correlations between the WNV and two other nonverbal ability measures should be noted, particularly given that the WNV is touted as a broad spectrum measure. Maddox (2010) states that the lower correlations could be a function of the different administration directions, i.e., the WNV provides pictorial directions and allows some use of verbiage. The origin of these differences might be the focus of additional research.

3. *Limited information about the construct(s) assessed by the WNV*. In his review, Tindal (2010) notes that the WNV Manual presents only limited information about the construct that the test presumes to measure, According to Tindal (2010),

   Nonverbal intelligence is a weighty construct that needs more consideration both theoretically and operationally. Yet, little to no information is presented in the manual to address this construct adequately. Theoretically, it need to be placed in a nomological net reflecting relations with other constructs... (Summary section, para. 1).

From Tindal's perspective a stronger focus on this sort of information would facilitate interpretation. However, it should be noted that the Manual provides a description of the goal of the WNV, which is to assess intelligence nonverbally and that the term nonverbal, as used in the test, refers to the content of the test and not a type of ability.

4. *Application of results to school tasks*. Although both the Administration and Scoring Manual and the Technical and Interpretive Manual address possible WNV strengths and weaknesses and offer some analysis of intervention strategies that could be employed following test interpretation and analysis, Tindal (2010) notes that these strategies are not supported by empirical or experimental evidence. Consequently, these interpretations should be considered as viable hypotheses that ought to be investigated using more classroom-specific achievement measures (Tindal 2010).

## Summary

This chapter describes the theory underlying the WNV, administration and scoring, and strengths and limitations of the test. The test assesses Nonverbal IQ in a robust, yet relatively quick and easy-to-administer format. The inclusion of pictorial directions is unique and makes the test an option if English proficiency of the examinee is a concern. The test materials are well put together, colorful and engaging. The WNV Administration and Scoring Manual and Technical and Interpretative Manual include ample information about the technical properties of the test, test development, step-by-step administration, and interpretation strategies. Although the literature contains reviews that mention both strengths and weaknesses, the test is generally characterized as psychometrically strong; it appears to offer advantages over highly verbally -laden measures for assessing students who may be disadvantaged by language - loaded instruments.

# References

Bellugi, U., O'Grady, L., Lill0-Martin, D., O'Grady Hynes, M., van Hoek, K., & Corina, D. (1994). Enhancement of spatial cognition in deaf children. In V. Volterra & C. Erting (Eds.), *From gesture to language in hearing and deaf children* (pp. 278–298). Washington, DC: Gallaudet University Press.

Bishop, D. V. (1992). The underlying nature of specific language impairment. *Journal of Child Psychology and Clinical and Experimental Neuropsychology, 24* (3), 383–405.

Bracken, B. A., & McCallum, R. S. (1998). *Universal nonverbal intelligence test.* Austin, TX: PRO-ED.

Corbeil, J. P. (2003). 30 years of education: Canada's language groups. *Canadian Social Trends, 71*(Winter), 8–12.

Doll, B., & Boren, R. (1993). Performance of severely language-impaired students on the WISC-III, language scales, and academic achievement measures. In B. A. Bracken & R. S. McCallum (Eds.), *Journal of psychoeducational assessment, WISC-III monograph, 11* (pp. 77–86). Brandon, VT: Clinical Psychology Publishing Company.

Jensen, A. R. (1998). *The "g" factor: The science of mental ability.* Westport, CT: Prager.

Johnson, C. J., Beitchman, J. H., Young, A., Escobar, M., Atkinson, L., Wilson, B., et al. (1999). Fourteen-year follow-up of children with and without speech/language impairments: Speech/language stability and outcomes. *Journal of Speech, Language, and Hearing Research, 42,* 744–760.

Maddux, C. (2010). Review of the Wechsler nonverbal scale of ability. In R. A. Spies, J. F. Carlson, & K. F. Geisinger (Eds.), *The eighteenth mental measurements yearbook.* Retrieved from the Burros Institute's Mental Measurements Yearbook online database.

McCallum, R. S. (1991). The assessment of preschool children with the Stanford-Binet intelligence scale: Fourth edition. In B. A. Bracken (Ed.), *The psychoeducational assessment of preschool children* (2nd ed., pp. 107–132). Boston: Allyn & Bacon.

Naglieri, J. A. (2003). *Naglieri nonverbal ability test-individual administration.* San Antonio, TX: Harcourt Assessment.

Naglieri, J. A., & Brunnert, K. (2009). Wechsler nonverbal scale of ability (WNV). In J. A. Naglieri, J. A., & Goldstein, S. (Eds.), *Practitioner's guide to assessing*

*intelligence and achievement* (pp. 315–338). Hoboken, NJ: Wiley.

National Center for Educational Statistics. (2016). *English language learners in public schools.* Retrieved from http://nces.ed.gov/programs/coe/pdf/coe_cgf.pdf

Rose, J. C., Lincoln, A. J., & Allen, M. H. (1992). Ability profiles of developmental language disordered and learning disabled children: A comparative analysis. *Development Neuropsychology, 8*(4), 413–426.

Salvia, J., Ysseldyke, J. E., & Bolt, S. (2013). *Assessment: In special and inclusive education* (12th ed.). Boston, MA: Houghton Mifflin.

Sattler, J. M. (2008). *Assessment of children* (5th ed.). San Diego, CA: Author.

Spearman, C. (1904). "General intelligence": Objectively determined and measured. *American Journal of Psychology, 15,* 201–293.

Statistics Canada. (2002). *2001 census of population (20% sample database) [CD-ROM].* Ottawa, Ontario, Canada: Statistics Canada.

Suzuki, L. A., & Valencia, R. R. (1997). Race-ethnicity and measured intelligence. *American Psychologist, 52,* 1103–1114.

Tindal, G. (2010). Review of the Wechsler nonverbal scale of ability. In R. A. Spies, J. F. Carlson, & K. F. Geisinger (Eds.), *The eighteenth mental measurements yearbook.* Retrieved from the Burros Institute's Mental Measurements Yearbook online database.

U. S. Bureau of the Census. (2003). *Current population survey. October 2003: School enrollment supplement file* [CR-ROM] Washington, DC: U.S. Bureau of the Census (Producer/Distributor).

Wechsler, D. (1939). *Wechsler-Bellevue intelligence scale.* New York: The Psychological Corporation.

Wechsler. D. (1997). *Wechsler adult intelligence scale,* (3rd ed.). San Antonio, TX: The Psychological Corporation.

Wechsler, D. (2001). *Wechsler individual achievement test* (2nd ed.). San Antonio, TX: The Psychological Corporation.

Wechsler, D. (2002). *Wechsler preschool and primary scale of intelligence-* (3rd ed.). San Antonio, TX: The Psychological Corporation.

Wechsler, D. (2003). *Wechsler intelligence scale for children* (4th ed.). San Antonio, TX: Harcourt Assessment.

Wechsler, D. (2005). *Wechsler intelligence scale for children- Fourth edition- Spanish.* San Antonio, TX: Harcourt Assessment.

Wechsler, D., Kaplan, E., Fein, D., Kramer, J., Morris, R., Delis, D., et al. (2004). *Wechsler intelligence scale for children- Fourth edition- Integrated edition.* San Antonio, TX: Harcourt Assessment.

Wechsler, D., & Naglieri, J. A. (2006). *Wechsler nonverbal scale of ability.* San Antonio, TX: Pearson.

# Comprehensive Test of Nonverbal Intelligence: Second Edition

# 10

## Donald D. Hammill and Nils Pearson

The *Comprehensive Test of Nonverbal Intelligence: Second Edition* (CTONI-2: Hammill et al. 2009) is the second edition of the CTONI that was published originally in 1997. Like its predecessor, the CTONI-2 was designed to give examiners an efficient means for assessing the nonverbal reasoning ability of individuals who range in age from 6–0 to 89–11. It has six subtests (i.e., Pictorial Analogies, Geometric Analogies, Pictorial Categories, Geometric Categories, Pictorial Sequences, and Geometric Sequences). Three of these subtests use pictures of familiar objects as stimuli and three use unusual geometric designs. Test-takers point to their answers; no manipulation of objects, reading, writing, or oral responses are required to take the test. This chapter describes (a) the theory underlying the CTONI-2, (b) a description of the subtests and composite scores, (c) the normative scores and their interpretation, (d) the uses of the test scores, (e) the standardization, norms, and reliability, and (f) the validity of the test.

## Goals and Rationale for CTONI-2 Development

The CTONI-2 was developed to provide a psychometrically sound measure of intelligence using a nonverbal format. Neither the CTONI nor the CTONI-2 was built to conform to any particular theory. Instead, when building the first edition of CTONI we began by reviewing the structure, content, and formats of 36 "nonverbal" measures of reasoning or problem solving that existed in 1997. We found that the authors of these tests had built 5 times more language reduced tests (i.e., tests that used simple oral instruction) than nonlanguage tests (i.e., tests that used pantomime instructions), had chosen to measure analogical, categorical, and sequential reasoning in about equal numbers, and had employed pictured objects and geometric contexts (i.e., formats) also in equal numbers. Based on this review, we decided to build a test that would provide both simple oral instructions for general use and pantomime instructions for use in those few cases where they are appropriate. Therefore, the test can be either a language reduced nonverbal test or a nonlanguage nonverbal test depending upon the type of administration opted for by the examiner. We also decided that the test would measure analogical, categorical, and sequential reasoning in both pictorial and geometric contexts (i.e., formats). Even though the underpinnings of the CTONI-2 are theoretically eclectic and pragmatic in design, its contents can readily be identified with popular

D.D. Hammill (✉) · N. Pearson
Austin, TX, USA
e-mail: dhammill@proedinc.com

© Springer International Publishing AG 2017
R.S. McCallum (ed.), *Handbook of Nonverbal Assessment*,
DOI 10.1007/978-3-319-50604-3_10

theories of intelligence Horn and Cattell (1966), Das (1972), Jensen (1980).

## Description and Administration of the CTONI-2

The subtests and composites that make up CTONI-2 and the relationship to the abilities and contacts in the test model is displayed in Table 10.1. The six subtests that make up the CTONI-2 are described briefly below followed by a description of the three composites.

### Subtest 1. Pictorial Analogies and Subtest 2. Geometric Analogies

Both the Pictorial Analogies and Geometric Analogies subtests use a 2 × 2 matrix format to measure this highly complex cognitive ability. To pass the items, the test-takers must understand that *this is to that* (the upper two boxes in the matrix) as *this is to what* (the lower two boxes in the matrix). They must demonstrate knowledge by pointing to the one of the choice items that

goes into the blank box. Example items from the Pictorial Analogies and Geometric Analogies subtests are found in Fig. 10.1.

### Subtest 3. Pictorial Categories and Subtest 4. Geometric Categories

The Pictorial Categories and Geometric Categories subtests require the test-takers to deduce the relationship between two stimulus figures and to select from the choice items the one that shares the same relationship with the stimulus figures. They have to figure out *which of these is related to those*. Example items from each subtest are found in Fig. 10.2.

### Subtest 5. Pictorial Sequences and Subtest 6. Geometric Sequences

The Pictorial Sequences and Geometric Sequences subtests use a problem-solving progression format. Test-takers are shown a series of boxes, which contain different figures that bear some sequential relationship to one another; the last

**Table 10.1** Relationship of CTONI-2 subtests to the test model

| Ability | Context | |
|---|---|---|
| | Pictorial objects | Geometric designs |
| Analogical reasoning | Pictorial Analogies | Geometric Analogies |
| Categorical reasoning | Pictorial Categories | Geometric Categories |
| Sequential reasoning | Pictorial Sequences | Geometric Sequences |

Example C

Example B

**Fig. 10.1** Pictorial analogies and geometric analogies subtests

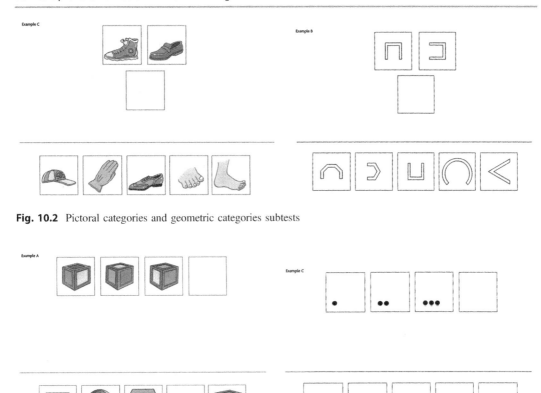

**Fig. 10.2** Pictoral categories and geometric categories subtests

**Fig. 10.3** Pictoral sequences and geometric sequences subcategories

box is blank. After viewing an array of choices, they point to the one that completes the progression in the previously displayed series of figures. They must recognize *the rule that is guiding the progression of figures.* Example items for each subtest are found in Fig. 10.3.

In addition to the subtests, the CTONI-2 also has three composites. Two composites represent the contexts used to measure the abilities (Pictorial Scale and Geometric Scale). The third composite, the Full Scale, is the overall ability score on the test). All three composites measure general intelligence. Each composite is described next.

The *Pictorial Scale* is formed by combining the scaled scores of the three subtests that use pictures of objects (i.e., Pictorial Analogies, Pictorial Categories, and Pictorial Sequences). The *Geometric Scale* is formed by combining the scaled scores of the three subtests that use images

involving points, lines, angles, surfaces, and solids (i.e., Geometric Analogies, Geometric Categories, and Geometric Sequences). The *Full Scale* composite is the best representation of general intelligence because it is the most reliable score on the CTONI-2. Because it is formed by combining the scaled scores of all six CTONI-2 subtests, the index for the Full Scale is also the best estimate of Spearman's (1923) global factor *g* in that it reflects status on a wide array of cognitive abilities.

We conclude this description of the CTONI-2 subtests and composites by calling attention to the fact that the simple act of pointing is the method of response required for all subtests. We purposely avoided complex motor responses because we did not want to bias our test against individuals who have motor impairments (e.g., people with cerebral palsy or apraxia, people recovering from stroke or other brain anomalies, or people who are simply awkward). In his description of nonverbal tests, Levin (1978) observed that the presence of complicated motor responses unnecessarily penalizes many people with disabilities. We might add that requiring complicated motor responses on a test of intelligence can be as biasing as requiring sophisticated oral (i.e., verbal) responses.

## Scores Provided

This section describes the scaled scores provided for the subtests and the index scores provided for the composites.

## Scaled Scores for the Subtests

Normative scores for the subtests are called scaled scores. They were calculated by applying a direct linear transformation to the sums of raw scores at various age levels to obtain a distribution with a mean of 10 and a standard deviation of 3. The resulting data across age levels were smoothed somewhat to allow for a consistent progression.

Subtest findings should be interpreted only in terms of the specific content and skills measured. To facilitate interpretation, we briefly describe the abilities measured by the subtests.

1. *Pictorial Analogies*: Measures the ability to recognize the relationship of two objects to each other and to find the same relationship between two different objects.
2. *Geometric Analogies*: Measures the ability to recognize the relationship of two geometric designs to each other and to find the same relationship between two different geometric designs.
3. *Pictorial Categories*: Measures the ability to select from a set of different pictures the one that is the most similar to two other related pictures.
4. *Geometric Categories*: Measures the ability to select from a set of different geometric

designs the one that is most similar to two other related geometric designs.
5. *Pictorial Sequences*: Measures the ability to select from a set of pictures the one that completes a sequence of actions shown in three pictures.
6. *Geometric Sequences*: Measures the ability to select from a set of geometric designs the one that completes a sequence of action shown in three designs.

## Indexes for the Composites

Normative scores for the composites are called indexes (another type of standard score). They were calculated by applying a direct linear transformation to the sums of scaled scores to obtain a distribution with a mean of 100 and a standard deviation of 15. The indexes for the composites are the most clinically useful scores on the CTONI-2 because they are the most reliable scores on the test. Guidelines for interpreting these important scores as discussed next. To reiterate, these composites are Pictorial Scale, Geometric Scale, and Full Scale.

**Pictorial Scale**. The index for the *Pictorial Scale* is formed by combining the subscales of the three subtests that use familiar pictured objects in their test formats. Because the pictured objects have names, examinees will likely verbalize to some extent while taking the subtests that contribute to this index. By verbalize, we mean that the examinees will talk about particular items while responding to them or silently think in words while pondering the items. In either case, most persons being tested will probably enlist their verbal skills to reach an answer for the items. Because of this, verbal ability may influence performance on the Pictorial Scale to some unknown degree. Although individuals could score high on this index without any verbal mediation at all, this is not likely in most cases.

**Geometric Scale**. The index for the *Geometric Scale* is formed by combining the subscales for the three subtests that use *unfamiliar designs* as stimuli. Because examinees have no names for the designs, any tendency to verbalize about the items is inhibited considerably. The formats of subtests that contribute to this index were specially selected to avoid verbal contamination and therefore yield results that are the purest possible estimates of intelligence when evaluated by means of nonverbal formats. Although verbalization cannot be eliminated entirely from any test (i.e., no test format can completely keep an individual examinee from using words while thinking), the selected formats do reduce the probability that incidental verbalization (oral or silent) might influence a person's answers to any appreciable extent.

In the vast majority of circumstances, these two indexes will be approximately equal (i.e., the difference between them will be inconsequential). Where large differences do occur, we suspect that the Pictorial Scale Index will be the higher index because of the mitigating influence of language ability. At this time, we cannot say for certain exactly what clinical connotations are implied by the presence of a significant difference between the two indexes.

**Full Scale**. Of all the indexes on the CTONI-2, the index for the *Full Scale* composite is the most comprehensive estimate of a person's overall, general intellectual ability because it is formed by combining the subscales of all six subtests. *Average to High* indexes (i.e., 90 and above) indicate that the person tested has attained at least a minimal level of reasoning and problem solving that is expected for his or her age. He or she can see logical and abstract relationship, reason without words, solve mental puzzles that involve progressive elements, and form meaningful associations between objects and designs. Usually, people with high scores do well in academic subjects, especially mathematics. *Low indexes* (i.e., below 90) indicate that the person tested has performed below a level that is expected for a person his or her age. He or she probably has trouble managing nonverbal

information, perceiving visual data, organizing spatially oriented material, and mastering abstract properties of visually symbols. Usually, people with low scores will also struggle academically in school.

## Standardization and Psychometric Properties of the CTONI-2

This section discusses three topics related to the CTONI-2's technical adequacy: Standardization sites, characteristics of the normative sample, and reliability of the test's subtest and composite scores.

### Standardization Sites

The standardization sample was obtained by recruiting both major and minor sites. Major sites are defined as areas of each U.S. demographic regions (Northeast, Midwest, South, and West) where at least 50 cases are collected. For the major sites, site coordinators were selected who (a) had access to individuals at the required ages (e.g., primary and secondary schools, adult recreation clubs, churches, senior activity centers, and independent living facilities) whose demographic characteristics closely matched those of the region as a whole and (b) were experienced in the administration of psychoeducational assessments. The major sites were: Birmingham, Alabama, Corpus Christi and Lubbock, Texas (*South*); Burbank, Manteca, Pleasant Grove, and Ripon, California (*West*); Rochester, New York (*Northeast*); and Bismarck and Mandan, North Dakota (*Midwest*).

Minor sites collected fewer than 50 cases. These sites were located by accessing the PRO-ED customer files and asking current users of the CTONI if they would participate in the norming effort. The examiners who responded were asked to test 20 individuals between the ages of 6-years old and 89.

## Characteristics of the Normative Sample

The CTONI-2 was normed on a sample of 2827 persons residing in 387 different zip codes in 10 states: Alabama, California, Georgia, Louisiana, Minnesota, North Dakota, New York, Texas, Virginia, and Washington. The majority of the normative sample was tested in the fall and winter of 2007 and the spring of 2008. Over ninety percent of the normative data were collected in 10 cities. At least 95% of the normative sample was tested using the English oral instructions; the remaining 5% were tested using the pantomime instructions. Because the non-English option has been recently added to the test, no individuals in the normative sample were tested using a language other than English or pantomime.

The procedures described above resulted in a normative sample that is representative of the nation as a whole. The characteristics of the sample with regard to gender, geographic region, race, Hispanic status, exceptionality status, family income, and educational level of parents are reported as percentages in Table 10.2. The percentages for these characteristics were compared with those reported in the *Statistical Abstract of the United States* (U.S. Bureau of the Census 2007) for the school-aged and adult populations. A comparison of the percentages demonstrates that the sample is representative. To further demonstrate the representativeness of the sample, selected demographic information was stratified by age. The stratified variables conform to national expectations at each age group covered by the test's norms.

## Reliability

Unreliable tests yield inaccurate results. For tests, such as the CTONI-2, reliability coefficients must approximate or exceed 0.80 in magnitude to be considered minimally reliable, coefficients of 0.90 or higher are considered most desirable (Aiken and Groth-Marnat 2006; Nunnally and Bernstien 1994; Salvia et al. 2013). Anastasi and Urbina (1997) describe three sources of error variance (content, time, and scorer). We calculated three types of correlation coefficients—coefficient alpha, test-retest, and scorer difference—to measure these three sources of error.

**Internal Consistency**. Content sampling error (i.e., internal consistency reliability) was investigated by applying Cronbach's (1951) coefficient alpha method. Coefficient alphas for the subtests and composites were calculated at 19 age intervals using data from the entire normative sample. Coefficient alphas for the composites were derived using Guilford's (1954, p. 393) formula. The average of the 19 age interval coefficients were in the 0.80 s for the subtests and in the 0.90 s for the composites. The coefficients were averaged using the Fisher z-transformation technique. The standard error of measurement (SEM) is 1 for all the subtests, 3 for the Full Scale Index, and 5 for the other two indexes.

**Test Retest**. The subjects for the test-retest analysis were 101 individuals (63 students attending regular classes in Llano, Texas, and 38 mostly adult individuals from Mandan, North Dakota). These subjects were divided into three age groups (42 aged 8 or 9; 33 aged 10–16; 26 aged 17–60). These subjects were tested twice, the time interval between testing was 2–4 weeks. The resulting coefficients were almost identical. At all age levels, the coefficients for the subtests were in the 0.80 s; those for the composites in the 0.80 or 0.90 s. The means and standard deviations between the testings were tested for significant difference at each of the three age levels and none were found to be significantly different at the 0.05 level.

**Scorer Differences**. Scorer difference reliability refers to the amount of test error due to examiner variability in scoring. Unreliable scoring is usually the result of clerical errors or improper application of standard scoring criteria on the part of an examiner. Scorer error can be reduced considerably by availability of clear administration procedures, detailed guidelines governing scoring, and opportunities to practice scoring. Nevertheless, test constructors should demonstrate statistically the amount of error in their tests due to different scorers.

**Table 10.2** Demographis characteristics of the normative sample ($n = 2827$)

| Characteristics | Percentage of school-aged sample | Percentage of school-aged population | Percentage of adult sample | Percentage of adult population |
|---|---|---|---|---|
| *Geographic Region*[a] | | | | |
| Northeast | 19 | 18 | 20 | 19 |
| South | 36 | 36 | 36 | 36 |
| Midwest | 22 | 22 | 21 | 22 |
| West | 23 | 24 | 23 | 23 |
| *Gender*[b] | | | | |
| Male | 51 | 51 | 48 | 49 |
| Female | 49 | 49 | 52 | 51 |
| *Ethnicity*[b] | | | | |
| White | 75 | 76 | 82 | 82 |
| Black/African American | 15 | 16 | 12 | 12 |
| Asian/Pacific islander | 4 | 4 | 2 | 4 |
| Two or more | 4 | 3 | 2 | 1 |
| Other | 2 | 1 | 1 | 1 |
| *Hispanic*[b] | | | | |
| Yes | 16 | 19 | 13 | 13 |
| No | 84 | 81 | 87 | 87 |
| *Parent education*[c] | | | | |
| Less than bachelor's degree | 77 | 70 | 73 | 72 |
| Bachelor's degree | 16 | 20 | 18 | 19 |
| Advanced degree | 7 | 10 | 9 | 9 |
| *Income*[d] | | | | |
| Under $10,000 | 8 | 5 | 8 | 5 |
| $10,000–$14,999 | 4 | 4 | 4 | 4 |
| $15,000–$24,999 | 10 | 11 | 10 | 11 |
| $25,000–$34,999 | 11 | 11 | 10 | 11 |
| $35,000–$49,999 | 15 | 15 | 15 | 15 |
| $50,000–$74,999 | 20 | 20 | 21 | 20 |
| $75,000 and above | 32 | 34 | 32 | 34 |
| *Exceptionality status*[e] | | | | |
| Specific learning disabilities | 2 | 5 | 1 | NA |
| Mental retardation | <1 | 1 | 1 | NA |
| Hearing impaired | 1 | <1 | 1 | NA |
| Other health impairments | <1 | 1 | 2 | NA |

(continued)

**Table 10.2** (continued)

| Characteristics | Percentage of school-aged sample | Percentage of school-aged population | Percentage of adult sample | Percentage of adult population |
|---|---|---|---|---|
| Attention deficit disorder | 3 | NA | 1 | NA |
| Other disability | 2 | 4 | 1 | NA |

[a]U.S. Census Bureau, "age and Sex for States and for Puerto Rico: April 1, 2000–July 1, 2005"; published 4 August 2006; http://www.census.gov/popest/states/asrh/SC-EST2005-02.html. My internet link http://www.census.gov/compendia/statab/tables/07s0021.xls

[b]U.S. Census Bureau, "annual estimates of the population by sex, age and race for the United States: April 1, 2000–July 1, 2005 (NC-EST2005-04)"; published 10 May 2006; http://www.census.gov/popest/national/asrh/NC-EST2005-asrh.html

[c]U.S. Census Bureau, current population survey. Data are available on the internet at http://www.census.gov/population/www/socdemo/educ-attn.html. Internet link http://www.census.gov/population/www/socdemo/educ-attn.html. My link http://www.census.gov/compendia/statab/tables/07s0216.xls

[d]U.S. Census Bureau, income, poverty, and health insurance 2004, current population report, P60-229; and internet site at http://pubdb3.census.gov/macro/032005/faminc/new07_000.htm (revised 31 January 2006)

[e]U.S. Census Bureau, current population survey. Data are available on the internet at http://www.census.gov/compendia/statab/cats/education.html

To do this, Anastasi and Urbina (1997), Rathvon (2004), and Reynolds et al. (2009), among others, recommend that two trained individuals score a set of tests independently. The correlation between scorers is a relational index of agreement. In the case of the CTONI-2, two PRO-ED staff members independently scored the same 50 protocols drawn from children in the normative sample. The scorers learned to score the test by reading the test manual and Examiner Record Booklet. The sample represented a broad range of ability and ranged in age from 6 to 60. Twenty-five were males, and 25 were females; all subjects were from the South or Midwest. The results of the scorings were correlated. The resulting coefficients all exceed 0.90 in magnitude. These coefficients provide strong evidence supporting the test's scorer reliability.

**Summary of Reliability Results**. The CTONI-2's overall reliability is summarized in Table 10.3, which shows the test's status relative to three types of reliability coefficients and three sources of test error: content, time, and scorer differences. The coefficients depicting content sampling are the average coefficients across 19 age intervals described earlier. Those relating to time sampling are the test-retest coefficients for the entire 101 sample. The coefficients relating to

scorer differences were described in the previous section.

The CTONI-2 scores satisfy the most demanding of standards for reliability, including those of Nunnally and Bernstein (1994), Reynolds et al. (2009) and Salvia et al. (2013). These authors recommend that when important decisions are to be made for individuals the minimum standard for a reliability coefficient should be 0.90. For the most part, coefficients for the CTONI-2 indexes meet this rigorous standard. These results strongly suggest that the test possesses little test error and that its users can have confidence in its results.

## Validity

In the CTONI-2 test manual, we provide numerous studies that pertain to validity including item analysis studies, correlations with age and academic ability, intercorrelations among the subtest, and a factor analysis. In this section, however, we want to discuss the three most important topics that pertain to CTONI-2's validity: the steps taken to control for test bias and the relationship between CTONI-2 and other tests of intelligence, and diagnostic accuracy analysis.

**Table 10.3** Summary of CTONI-2's reliability relative to three types of reliability (decimals omitted)

| CTONI-2 scores | Type of reliability coefficient | | |
| --- | --- | --- | --- |
| | Internal consistency | Test-retest | Scorer |
| *Subtests* | | | |
| Pictorial analogies | 83 | 85 | 98 |
| Geometric analogies | 87 | 86 | 95 |
| Pictorial categories | 82 | 81 | 99 |
| Geometric categories | 87 | 80 | 98 |
| Pictorial sequences | 84 | 85 | 99 |
| Geometric sequences | 86 | 86 | 98 |
| *Composites* | | | |
| Pictorial scale | 90 | 87 | 99 |
| Geometric scale | 91 | 86 | 98 |
| Full scale | 95 | 90 | 99 |
| Sources of test error[a] | Content sampling | Time sampling | Interscorer agreement |

[a]These sources are from Anastasi and Urbina (1997)

## Analysis of Test Bias

We were particularly interested in controlling for any test bias in CTONI-2. To this end, we conducted two studies of test bias. The first of these uses differential item functioning analysis (DIF) to detect possible bias at the item level. The second of these examines subgroup performance to detect possible bias at the subtest and composite score levels.

**Differential item functioning analysis**. The two item analysis techniques described in the previous section (i.e., the study of item difficulty and item discrimination) are traditional and popular. However, no matter how good these techniques are in showing that a test's items do in fact capture the variance involved in intelligence, they are still incomplete. Camilli and Shepard (1994) recommend that test developers should go further and perform statistical tests for item bias. Item bias, also known as differential item functioning (DIF), is said to exist when examinees from different racial or gender groups who have the same ability level perform differently on the same item (i.e., evidence indicates that one group has an advantage over another on that item). The procedures used to identify biased items are described in this section.

The logistic regression procedure developed by Swaminathan and Rogers (1990) is used for detecting DIF. This procedure compares the adequacy of two different logistic regression models to account for the ability being measured; the first model uses ability (i.e., the subtest score) alone to predict item performance (restricted model), and the second model uses ability and group membership to predict item performance (full model). This technique compares the full model with the restricted model to determine whether the full model provides a significantly better solution. If the full model does not provide a significantly better solution than the restricted model, then the differences between groups on the item are best explained by ability alone. In other words, if the full model is not significantly better than the restricted model at predicting item performance, then the item is measuring differences in ability and does not appear to be influenced by group membership (i.e., the item is not biased). Stated another way, if the full model *is* significantly better than the restricted model at predicting item performance, the item is said to exhibit uniform DIF. Uniform DIF occurs when one group consistently performs better on the item than does the other group, at all levels of ability.

To distinguish statistical significance from practical significance, we had to establish criteria for significance and magnitude. All items on the CTONI-2 were analyzed, and comparisons were made for each of the focus groups compared to the reference groups (female vs. male, African American vs. non-African American, and Hispanic vs. non-Hispanic). Because 450 comparisons were made for these analyses, a significance level of 0.001 was adopted to prevent the overidentification of potentially biased items that might occur when large numbers of comparisons are made.

Next, for those items that were flagged as statistically significant, an effect size was used to evaluate the magnitude or amount of DIF. Zumbo (1999) suggests using the $R^2$ difference ($\Delta R^2$, a weighted least-squared effect size) between the restricted model and the full model to determine the degree of an item's DIF. Using Cohen et al. (1992) conventions for small, medium, and large effects, Jodoin and Gierl (2001) suggest that an $R^2$ difference less than 0.035 indicates negligible DIF, $R^2$ greater than 0.034 but less than 0.070 indicates moderate DIF, and $R^2$ greater than 0.069 indicates large DIF. Because, we are interested only in items that may be meaningfully biased, items with moderate or large effect sizes were targeted for possible removal from the test.

Using the entire normative sample as subjects, we applied the logistic regression procedure to all items contained in each CTONI-2 subtest and made comparisons between three dichotomous groups: male versus female, African American versus non–African American, and Hispanic versus non-Hispanic. The number of comparisons found to be statistically significant at the 0.001 level is recorded in parenthesis in Table 10.4. Of all these comparisons that attained significance, none of the $R^2$ differences were greater than 0.035 indicating that while significance was found in some comparisons, the effects were negligible on the performance of the group studied.

**Demographic subgroup comparison**. In this study, we present the mean subtest and composite scores for selected demographic subgroups in the normative sample. We examined the mean subtest and composite standard scores for three mainstream subgroups (males, females, Europeans) and four minority subgroups (African–Americans, Two or more races, Hispanic, and Asian/Pacific Islander) from the normative sample. Because special attention was devoted to controlling racial and gender bias during item development, one would expect that all subgroups would score in the Average range (i.e., between 8 and 12 points on subtests and 90 and 109 points on composites) on the CTONI-2. Indeed, Table 10.5 indicates that subtest scores for all subgroups were well within the Average range, providing evidence for the fairness of the test for both mainstream and minority subgroups.

The results from logistical regression approach to test the CTONI-2 items for bias and the results from subgroup demographic means provide convincing evidence that the CTONI-2 items contain little or no bias. Finally, because timed tests depress test performance of some groups, none of the CTONI-2 subtests are timed.

## Relationship of CTONI-2 to Other Tests of Intelligence

To be valid, the CTONI-2, a test that uses non-verbal formats to measure intelligence, should be strongly related to other tests of intelligence, especially those that use nonverbal formats. To date, 11 studies have correlated the CTONI or CTONI-2 to criterion measures. For the purposes of this chapter, we will restrict our discussion to the results of 3 studies using the CTONI 2. For more information about all the studies, please refer to our manual. The demographic characteristics of the samples used in the three studies are described in Table 10.6.

The evidence relating to criterion-prediction validity has been organized into three sections: (a) a review of the correlations between CTONI-2 and the criterion measures of intellect, (b) a comparison of the means between CTONI-2 and these criterion measures, and (c) the results

**Table 10.4** Number of CTONI-2 Items with significant effect sizes (and moderate DIF results) for subgroups

| Total number of items | Male/female | African American/Non-African American | Hispanic American/Non-Hispanic American |
|---|---|---|---|
| 150 | 0 (14) | 0 (24) | 0 (14) |

*Note* Numbers in parentheses represent the number of statistically significant items for each subgroup; the other numbers represent the number of moderate effect sizes detected for each subgroup

**Table 10.5** Standard score means for normative sample and different gender and ethnic subgroups (decimals omitted, rounded values)

| CTONI-2 scores | Subgroups | | | | | | | |
|---|---|---|---|---|---|---|---|---|
| | Normative sample ($N = 2827$) | Male ($n = 1416$) | Female ($n = 1411$) | European American ($n = 2189$) | African American ($n = 385$) | Two or more races ($n = 91$) | Asian Pacific islander ($n = 102$) | Hispanic American ($n = 440$) |
| *Subtests* | | | | | | | | |
| Pictorial analogies | 10 | 10 | 10 | 10 | 9 | 10 | 10 | 10 |
| Geometric analogies | 10 | 10 | 10 | 10 | 9 | 10 | 10 | 10 |
| Pictorial categories | 10 | 10 | 10 | 10 | 9 | 10 | 10 | 10 |
| Geometric categories | 10 | 10 | 10 | 10 | 9 | 10 | 10 | 10 |
| Pictorial sequences | 10 | 10 | 10 | 10 | 9 | 10 | 10 | 10 |
| Geometric sequences | 10 | 10 | 10 | 10 | 9 | 10 | 10 | 10 |
| *Composites* | | | | | | | | |
| Pictorial scale | 100 | 100 | 101 | 102 | 94 | 103 | 102 | 99 |
| Geometirc scale | 100 | 100 | 101 | 102 | 94 | 100 | 103 | 100 |
| Full scale | 100 | 100 | 101 | 102 | 94 | 101 | 102 | 100 |

of diagnostic accuracy analyses pertaining to CTONI-2's sensitivity and specificity indexes and ROC curve statistic.

**Correlations with Criterion Measures**. In this investigation of criterion-predictive validity, we report correlation coefficients showing the relationship of CTONI-2 to 3 criterion measures of intelligence. The correlation between the CTONI-2 and the criterion measures are reported in Table 10.7. (Note: The names of the criterion tests are listed at the bottom of the table.)

In this analysis, we are asking a theoretical question: Does the CTONI-2 actually measure

general intelligence? Because the question is theoretical, it is necessary to attenuate the coefficients for any lack of reliability in the criterion test (but not in the CTONI-2) and to correct coefficients to account for any range effects that might artificially *repress* or *inflate* the size of the coefficients. Both corrected and uncorrected coefficients are reported in Table 10.7 (uncorrected coefficients appear in parentheses).

In interpreting the magnitude of these coefficients, we are guided by Hopkins (2002). He suggested that coefficients between 0.00 and 0.09 are Very Small or Trivial; coefficients between

**Table 10.6** Demographic characteristics of the samples used in the validity studies

| Sample characteristics | Sample | | |
|---|---|---|---|
| | 1 | 2 | 3 |
| Criterion tests | TONI-4 | RIAS | PTONI |
| Source of study | Hammill et al. (2009) | Firmin (2009) | Ehrler and McGhee (2008) |
| Total number of participants | 72 | 197 | 82 |
| Age range | 6–17 | 18–22 | 6–9 |
| Location | Austin, TX | Ceadarville, OH | Georgia |
| Sample Type | Normal | College | Normal |
| *Gender* | | | |
| Male | 40 | 78 | 43 |
| Female | 32 | 119 | 39 |
| *Race* | | | |
| European American | 53 | 194 | 62 |
| African American | 16 | 2 | 13 |
| American Indian/Eskimo | | | |
| Asian/Pacific Islander | | 1 | |
| Two or more | | | |
| Other | 3 | | 7 |
| *Hispanic* | | nr | |
| Yes | 42 | | 7 |
| No | 30 | | 75 |
| *Exceptionality status* | | nr | |
| No disability | 68 | | 69 |
| Disability | 4 | | 13 |

*Note* nr—not reported
PTONI—*Primary Test of Nonverbal Intelligence* (Ehrler and McGhee 2008)
RIAS—*Reynolds Intellectual Assessment Scales* (Reynolds and Kamphaus 2003)
TONI-4—*Test of Nonverbal Intelligence: Fourth Edition* (Brown et al. 2010)

0.10 and 0.29 are small; coefficients between 0.30 and 0.49 are moderate; coefficients between 0.50 and 0.69 are Large; coefficients between 0.70 and 0.89 are very large; and coefficients between 0.90 and 1.00 are Nearly Perfect. Because all these criterion tests measure intelligence, one would expect that the relationship between the CTONI-2 and the criterion tests would be large or very large.

The coefficients listed in the shaded column at the right side of the table are very important because they show the relationship between the criterion tests and the CTONI-2 Full Scale Index. The corrected coefficients in this column range from 0.76 (Very Large) to 0.86 (Very Large); the

average of these coefficients is 0.80 (Very Large).

The averaged coefficients in the shaded row at the bottom of the table are equally important because they show the relationship of the criterion measures to the Pictorial, Geometric, and Full Scale composites. These coefficients of all these composites are both Very Large in magnitude (0.78, 0.74, and 0.80, respectively).

One can conclude that the size of the coefficients in Table 10.7 provide ample evidence for the CTONI-2 predictive validity. This analysis involved different criterion tests and diverse samples of subjects. Regardless of the criterion test employed or the sample studied, the

**Table 10.7** Correlation between CTONI-2 and criterion intelligence tests (decimals deleted)

| Criterion test | Score | Sample (s) | N | Type of sample | Composites | | | Magnitude |
|---|---|---|---|---|---|---|---|---|
| | | | | | Pictorial scale | Geometric scale | Full scale | |
| TONI-4 | Total | 1 | 72 | Normal | (70) 74 | (70) 73 | (75) 79 | Very large |
| RIAS | Verbal | 2 | 197 | College | (32) 76 | (22) 62 | (31) 76 | Very large |
| RIAS | Nonverbal | 2 | 197 | College | (31) 72 | (29) 71 | (35) 78 | Very large |
| RIAS | Composite | 2 | 197 | College | (38) 84 | (32) 79 | (40) 86 | Very large |
| PTONI | Total | 3 | 82 | Normal | (86) 84 | (85) 83 | (86) 81 | Very large |
| | | | | *Average*[a] | 78 | 74 | 80 | Very large |
| | | | | Magnitude[b] | Very large | Very large | Very large | |
| | | | | | Very large | Very large | Very large | |

*Note* Values in parentheses are observed correlation coefficients; all others are corrected for attenuation due to range restriction and reliability of the criterion
PTONI—*Primary Test of Nonverbal Intelligence* (Ehrler and McGhee 2008)
RIAS—*Reynolds Intellectual Assessment Scales* (Reynolds and Kamphaus 2003)
TONI-4—*Test of Nonverbal Intelligence: Fourth Edition* (Brown et al. 2010)
[a]Fisher's average of coefficients across samples
[b]Magnitude of corrected coefficients; based on Hopkins's (2002) criteria for interpreting

coefficients that were reported are uniformly high. The results pertaining to the composites were particularly encouraging.

**Comparisons of CTONI-2 and Criterion Test Means and Standard Deviations**. When two tests are highly correlated, they are likely to be measuring the same or a similar ability. This does not necessarily mean, however, that the tests yield the same results. For example, one test may consistently score higher than another test even though they correlate well with each other. The validity of both tests is supported when the two tests produce similar means as well as correlate highly with each other.

The standard score means, standard deviations, and comparative information for the CTONI-2 and the criterion intelligence tests are presented in Table 10.8. The differences between the means of the Full Scale Index and the corresponding composite scores from the criterion tests were analyzed using the *t*-test (Guilford and Fruchter 1978) and effect size correlation methods (Hopkins 2002; Rosenthal 1994).

Conclusions based on the contents of this table are rather straightforward. In the three comparisons, the difference between the means

of the CTONI-2 and those of the criterion measures are either small or trivial. The averaged means and standard deviations in the shaded row at the bottom of the table show that the differences between means are trivial. Because all of the criterion tests represent general intelligence, one might suppose that CTONI-2 is also a valid measure of overall general intelligence.

The findings reported in Table 10.8 support the idea that for all practical purposes, regardless of the samples' characteristics or the criterion test administered, the standard scores that result from giving the CTONI-2 will be similar to those obtained from giving the criterion tests.

## Diagnostic Accuracy Analyses

The studies just reported show that the scores of the CTONI-2 are highly related to the scores of current well-established tests of cognitive ability. This provides a type of apostolic, theoretical evidence for the CTONI-2's criterion-predictive validity (i.e., if the criterion tests are indeed valid, then the CTONI-2 is valid, as well). The studies about to be discussed provide practical

**Table 10.8** Standard score means (and standard deviations) and related statistics for the CTONI-2 and criterion tests

| CTONI comparisons/ criterion tests | Sample(s) | N | Mean (SD) | Descriptive terms | t | Effect size correlations[a] | Magnitude |
|---|---|---|---|---|---|---|---|
| CTONI-2 full scale | 1 | 72 | 100 (15) | Above average | −0.40 (ns) | 0.03 | Trivial |
| TONI-4 nonverbal index | | | 101 (15) | Above average | | | |
| CTONI-2 full scale | 2 | 197 | 117 (09) | Above average | 4.92** | 0.24 | Small |
| RIAS nonverbal index | | | 113 (07) | Above average | | | |
| CTONI-2 full scale | 3 | 82 | 91 (18) | Average | −3.62** | 0.27 | Small |
| PTONI nonverbal index | | | 98 (17) | Average | | | |
| Average CTONI-2 full scale | 1,2,3 | 351 | 107 (12) | Average | 0.64 (ns) | 0.02 | Trivial |
| Average nonverbal index | | | 107 (11) | Average | | | |

[a]Values of the magnitude of the effect size between CTONI-2 nonverval intelligence composite and criterion tests according to Hopkins's (2002)
**$p < 0.01$

evidence for the CTONI-2 criterion-predictive validity using statistical procedures referred to in the literature as "diagnostic accuracy analyses." These analyses demonstrate the precision with which the CTONI-2 scores can accurately identify students whose performance on other nonverbal intelligence tests attain scores in the below average cognitive abilities category or the average and above average category and how well this can be accomplished without excessive false positives (i.e., the misclassification of typical children as below average).

Researchers such as Swets (1996), Betz et al. (2013), Dollaghan (2004), Gray et al. (1999), Pepe (2003) have long suggested that diagnostic accuracy is the preferred method of assessing the usefulness of a diagnostic measures. Dollaghan (2004) went so far as to proclaim it "the most important criterion for evaluating a diagnostic measure" (p. 395). Methods for establishing diagnostic accuracy involve the computation of a test's sensitivity and specificity indexes, and receiver operating characteristic/area under the curve (ROC/AUC).

## Sensitivity and Specificity

In the current context, the sensitivity index reflects the ability of a test to correctly identify students' who are identified as either below

average or average and above in cognitive ability. The specificity index refers to the ability of a test to correctly identify examinees who do not have a cognitive exceptionality. Sensitivity and specificity indexes are reported as proportions (i.e., percentages). The size of the proportions necessary to be considered acceptable varies depending on the purpose of the analysis (e.g., when screening for cancer, a relatively high number of false positives is tolerable in order to ensure that the number of true positives identified is high).

Educational researchers vary in their opinions about the minimum acceptable levels for sensitivity, specificity, and ROC/AUC. Wood et al. (2002) recommend that the sensitivity and specificity indexes should be at least 0.70. Janske (1978), Gredler (2000) and Kingslake (1983) prefer 0.75 for both indexes. Carran and Scott (1992) and Plante and Vance (1994) recommend a more rigorous standard of 0.80 or higher. Jenkins and others (Jenkins 2003; Jenkins et al. 2007; Johnson et al. 2009) recommend that sensitivities be high—perhaps as high as 0.90— and that specificity levels be relatively high as well.

Because the CTONI-2 is a measure of cognitive ability, an analysis of the sensitivity and specificity was conducted to examine its ability to predict scores from other measures of cognitive ability. The CTONI-2 was investigated using

**Table 10.9** Positive predictive matrix demonstrating CTONI-2's ability to predict TONI-4/PTONI

| CTONI-2 full scale | TONI-4/PTONI index score | | Total |
|---|---|---|---|
| | Below average | Average or above | |
| Below average | 41[a] | 17[b] | 58 |
| Average or above | 10[c] | 86[d] | 96 |
| Total | 51 | 103 | 154 |

*Note* N = 154
Sensitivity = 41/(41 + 10) = 0.80
Specificity = 86/(86 + 10) = 0.90
ROC/AUC = 0.83
[a]True-positives
[b]False-positives (overreferrals)
[c]False-negatives (underreferrals)
[d]True-negatives

a Full Scale cut score of 90. In this study, this cutoff score was used to predict a criterion that was dichotomized into either at-risk (i.e., standard score below 90) or not-at-risk (standard score 90 or above) based on the student's scores on the criterion measures. On both the CTONI-2 and the criterion tests, standard scores that are below 90 are considered Below Average, and scores of 90 or above are considered Average or Above Average. Using an index of 90 as the cutoff, we divided the individuals who were given the tests of intelligence into two groups— Below Average and Average or Above Average. We then created a 2 × 2 matrix for the intelligence scores attained on the TONI-4 or PTONI versus the CTONI-2 scores. The matrix for these scores is found in Table 10.9.

The data that were used for these analyses are reported in Table 10.6. Subjects in these analyses were individuals in Samples 1 and 3 described the table that had been given the CTONI-2. We could not perform this analysis on the other group that had been given the CTONI-2 (i.e., Sample 2) because it was comprised of college students, none of whom had scores below 90.

The matrix used to examine the diagnostic accuracy of the CTONI-2 when using cutoff scores of 90 is shown in Table 10.9. In this table, the number of students correctly identified by the CTONI-2 is represented by cells *a* and *d*. Cell *a* represents true positives, and cell *d* represents true negatives. The number of individuals who were not correctly identified is represented by cells *b* and *c*. Cell *b* represents false positives

(overreferrals). Cell *c* represents false negatives (underreferrals). The *sensitivity index* is calculated by dividing the number of true positives (cell *a*) by the sum of true positives and false negatives (cell *a* + cell *c*). The *specificity index* is calculated by dividing the number of true negatives (cell *d*) by the sum of true negatives and false positives (cell *d* + cell *b*). The bolded quotients in the table note correspond to the values found in Table 10.9.

Table 10.9 reports the results of the diagnostic accuracy analyses. The CTONI-2 Full Scale composite score had a classification accuracy when predicting the below average category (0.82). This score had a sensitivity of 0.80 and specificity of 0.90 exceeding the minimum standards recommended by the authorities mentioned earlier in this section and reaching the high standards.

## Receiver Operating Characteristics

The receiver operating characteristic/area under the curve (ROC/AUC) "is a measure of the overall performance of a diagnostic test and is interpreted as the average value of sensitivity for all possible values of specificity" (Park et al. 2004, p. 13). ROC/AUC is a comprehensive index of the overall accuracy of a measure and ranges from 0 (representing no predictive ability) to 1 (representing perfect predictive ability). ROC/AUC values closer to 1 are always preferred. Of the multiple measures of diagnostic accuracy, the ROC/AUC has become the preferred statistic for evaluating the overall diagnostic accuracy of a measure (Dollaghan 2004; Gray et al. 1999; Pepe 2003; Swets 1996), while specificity and sensitivity are more useful for evaluating the diagnostic accuracy of a measure at a particular cut score. Compton et al. (2006) suggest that ROC/AUCs of 0.90 and above are excellent, 0.80–0.89 are good, 0.70–0.79 are fair, and 0.69 or below are poor.

The ROC/AUC was investigated using the same data as the sensitivity and specificity study. As in the previous study, the cutoff score of 90 on CTONI-2 Full Scale was used to predict a criterion that was dichotomized into either at-risk (i.e., standard score below 90) or not-at-risk (standard score 90 or above) based on the student's scores on the criterion measures. Using these criteria, a ROC/AUC of 0.83 was attained and the magnitude of this value would be considered good by the previously noted authorities.

## CTONI-2 Interpretation

The CTONI-2 has two principle uses. The *first use* is to estimate the intelligence of people for whom traditional ability tests might be inappropriate. For such persons, the heavy language content or the complicated motor response demands of most mental ability tests can result in a serious underestimation of their intelligence. This can lead to misidentifications, faulty diagnoses, erroneous placements, low expectations, and other undesirable consequences. Use of the CTONI-2 will avoid many of the hazards that are frequently encountered when testing people who have a variety of disabilities (traumatic brain injury, post-stroke syndrome, deafness, aphasia, autism, or other language disorders) or come from cultural, linguistic, educational, or socioeconomic backgrounds that might negatively influence their performance on ability tests. The *second use* is to provide researchers with a tool that they can use to study the nature of intelligence, the interaction of verbal and nonverbal abilities, and the role of nonverbal formats in assessing thinking and reasoning. Test interpretation requires examiners to report and explain subtest, composite and the full scale score based on the test structure, and typically proceeds from presentation of composite to subtest scores.

## Strengths/Limitations of the CTONI-2

For many examiners, the CTONI-2 has become an essential complement to tests of nonverbal intelligence. The CTONI-2 provides examiners with a measure of intelligence that requires no spoken language or complex motor skills, and only a pointing response to stimulus plates presented to the examinee. No motoric manipulation of stimuli is required. Numerous studies have shown it to be reliable, valid, and unbiased with regard to gender, race, and disability. Because of this, examiners can have confidence that the CTONI-2 scores estimate the intelligence of at-risk or culturally different populations with little fear of contamination from social, ethnic, or disability bias.

## Summary

The CTONI-2 provides a psychometrically sound measure of intelligence within a nonverbal format. It is appropriate for a wide range of ages and offers subtest and composite scores. In addition to the psychometric integrity of the CTONI-2, many examiners have praised the test format because they have found most examinees seem to enjoy the challenge of solving picture puzzles with no time limit.

## References

Aiken, L. R., & Groth-Marnat, G. (2006). *Psychological testing and assessment* (12th ed.). Boston: Pearson Educational Group.

Anastasi, A., & Urbina, S. (1997). *Psychological testing* (7th ed.). Upper Saddle River, NJ: Prentice Hall.

Betz, S. K., Eickhoff, J. R., & Sullivan, S. F. (2013). Factors influencing the selection of standardized tests for the diagnosis of specific language impairment. *Language, Speech and Hearing Services in Schools, 44*, 133–146.

Brown, L., Sherbenou, R. J., & Johnson, S. K. (2010). *Test of nonverbal intelligence* (4th ed.). Austin, TX: PRO-ED.

Camilli, G., & Shepard, L. (1994). *Methods for identifying biased test items*. Thousand Oaks, CA: Sage.

Carran, D. T., & Scott, K. G. (1992). Risk assessment in preschool children: Research implications for the early detection of educational handicaps. *Topics in Early Childhood Special Education, 12*, 196–211.

Cohen, R. J., Swerdlik, M. E., & Smith, D. K. (1992). *Psychological testing and assessment*. Mountain View, CA: Mayfield.

Compton, D. L., Fuchs, D., Fuchs, L. S., & Bryant, J. D. (2006). Selecting at-risk readers in first grade for early intervention. *Journal of Educational Psychology, 98* (2), 394–409.

Cronbach, L. J. (1951). Coefficient alpha and the internal structure of tests. *Psychometrika, 16*, 297–334.

Das, J. P. (1972). Patterns of cognitive ability in nonretarded and retarded children. *American Journal of Mental Deficiency, 77*, 6–12.

Dollaghan, C. (2004). Evidence-based practice in communication disorders: What do we know, and when do we know it? *Journal of Communication Disorders, 37*, 391–400.

Ehrler, D. J., & McGhee, R. L. (2008). *Primary test of nonverbal intelligence*. Austin, TX.: PRO-ED.

Firmin, M. W. (2009). *Comparison of college students' performance on the CTONI-2, the RIAS, and three measures of school achievement*. An independent unpublished study done at Cedarville University, Cedarville, OH.

Gray, S., Plante, E., Vance, R., & Henrichsen, M. (1999). Performance of SLI and NL children on four tests of single-word vocabulary. *Language, Speech, and Hearing Services in the Schools, 30*, 196–206.

Gredler, G. R. (2000). Early childhood screening for developmental and educational problems. In B. A. Bracken (Ed.), *The psychoeducational assessment of preschool children* (pp. 399–411). Boston: Allyn & Bacon.

Guilford, J. P. (1954). *Psychometric methods* (2nd ed.). New York: McGraw-Hill.

Guilford, J. P., & Fruchter, B. (1978). *Fundamental statistics in psychology and education* (6th ed.). New York: McGraw-Hill.

Hammill, D. D., Pearson, N. A., & Wiederholt, J. L. (1997). *Comprehensive test of nonverbal intelligence*. Austin, TX: PRO-ED.

Hammill, D. D., Pearson, N. A., & Wiederholt, J. L. (2009). *Comprehensive test of nonverbal intelligence* (2nd ed.). Austin, TX: PRO-ED.

Hopkins, W. G. (2002). A scale of magnitudes for effect statistics. In *A new view of statistics*. Retrieved July 14, 2005, from http://www.sportsci.org/resource/stats/effectmag.html

Horn, J. L., & Cattell, R. B. (1966). Refinement and test of the theory of fluid and crystallized intelligence. *Journal of Educational Psychology, 57*, 253–270.

Janske, J. J. (1978). A critical review of some developmental and predictor precursors of reading disabilities. In A. L. Benton & D. Pearl (Eds.), *Dyslexia: An appraisal of current knowledge* (pp. 412–516). New York: Oxford University Press.

Jenkins, J. R. (2003, December). *Candidate measures for screening at-risk students*. Paper presented at the national research center on learning disabilities responsiveness-to-intervention symposium, Kansas City, MO. Retrieved April 3, 2006, from http://www.nrcld.org/symposium2003/jenkins/index

Jenkins, J. R., Hudson, R. G., & Johnson, E. S. (2007). Screening for service in an RTI framework: Candidate measures. *School Psychology Review, 36*, 582–599.

Jensen, A. R. (1980). *Bias in mental testing*. New York: Free Press.

Jodoin, M. G., & Gierl, M. J. (2001). Evaluating type I error and power rates using an effect size measure with the logistic regressions procedure for DIF detection. *Applied Measurement in Education, 14*(4), 329–349.

Johnson, E. S., Jenkins, J. R., Petscher, Y., & Catts, H. W. (2009). How can we improve the accuracy of screening instruments? *Learning Disabilities Research and Practice, 24*(4), 174–185.

Kingslake, B. J. (1983). The predictive (in)accuracy of on-entry to school screening procedures when used to anticipate learning difficulties. *British Journal of Special Education, 10*, 24–26.

Levin, M. D. (1978). *Developmental variation and learning disorders*. Cambridge, MA: Educators Publishing Service.

Nunnally, J. S., & Bernstein, I. H. (1994). *Psychometric theory* (3rd ed.). Baltimore: Williams & Wilkins.

Park, S. H., Goo, J. M., & Jo, C. H. (2004). Receiver operating characteristic (ROC) curve: Practical review for radiologists. *Korean Journal of Radiology, 5*(1), 11–18.

Pepe, M. S. (2003). *The statistical evaluation of medical tests for classification and prediction*. New York: Oxford.

Plante, E., & Vance, R. (1994). Diagnostic accuracy of two tests of preschool language. *American Journal of Speech-Language Pathology, 4*, 70–76.

Plante, E., & Vance, R. (1995). Diagnostic accuracy of two tests of preschool language. *American Journal of Speech-Language Pathology, 4*, 70–76.

Rathvon, N. (2004). *Early reading assessment*. New York: Guilford Press.

Reynolds, C. R., & Kamphaus, R. (2003). *Reynolds intellectual assessment scales*. Lutz, FL: Psychological Assessment Resources.

Reynolds, C. R., Livingston, R. G., & Willson, V. (2009). *Measurement and assessment in education* (2nd ed.) Boston: Allyn & Bacon.

Rosenthal, R. (1994). Parametric measures of effect size. In H. Cooper & L. V. Hedges (Eds.), *Handbook of research synthesis* (pp. 231–244). New York: Sage.

Salvia, J., Ysseldyke, J. E., & Bolt, S. (2013). *Assessment in special and inclusive education* (12th ed.). Australia: Wadsworth Cengage Learning.

Spearman, C. E. (1923). *The nature of intelligence and the principles of cognition.* New York: Macmillan.

Swaminathan, H., & Rogers, H. J. (1990). Detecting differential item functioning using logistic regression procedures. *Journal of Educational Measurement, 26,* 55–66.

Swets, J. A. (1996). *Signal detection theory and ROC analysis in psychology and diagnostics: Collected papers.* Hillsdale, NJ: Lawrence Erlbaum Associates.

U. S. Bureau of the Census. (2007). *Statistical abstract of the United States* (126th ed.). Washington, DC: Author.

Wood, F., Flowers, L., Meyer, M., & Hill, D. (2002, November). *How to evaluate and compare screening tests: Principles of science and good sense.* Paper presented at the meeting of the International Dyslexia Association, Atlanta.

Zumbo, B. D. (1999). *A handbook on the theory and methods of differential item functioning (DIF).* Ottawa, OH: Directorate of Human Resources Research, Department of national Defense.

# Test of Nonverbal Intelligence: A Language-Free Measure of Cognitive Ability

Susan K. Johnsen

The *Test of Nonverbal Intelligence* (Brown et al. 1982, 1990, 1997, 2010) was built over 30 years ago to address the increasing diversity and complexity of a society in which the evaluation of intellectual ability and aptitude was rapidly becoming common practice. The trend has continued and grown to the current day. Elementary and secondary schools, institutions of higher learning, business and industry, clinics, hospitals, and agencies in virtually every sector of society routinely assesses aptitude and ability not only in research but also in everyday decision-making (Brown 2003).

The broad use of intelligence measures demands a test that not only can be used by a variety of professionals but also can be administered to a more diverse group of people than in the past. Before nonverbal and computerized assessments, large segments of the disability community could not be tested conventionally because sensory, language, and motor impairments made it impossible for them to interact with the content of the existing tests of intelligence and aptitude. In addition, the tasks comprising most intelligence tests administered in this country employed the common language and culture of the United States, under the assumption that all "intelligent" people are able to

identify, understand, and use the English language and American cultural symbols. But in an increasingly diverse and complex society, many of the patients, clients, students, job applicants, and others who routinely take such tests may not be proficient in spoken or written English and may not be familiar with many aspects of American culture. Whether they are intelligent or not, they will score poorly on those tests of intelligence. Moreover, a large portion of people who are evaluated by schools, clinics, and hospitals fall into one of these categories: non-English speakers and individuals who are aphasic, deaf, learning disabled, or who have suffered severe neurological trauma through head injury, stroke, cerebral palsy, Alzheimer's disease, and similar conditions. Therefore, a need existed for a psychometrically sound test that could be administered reliably by professionals from many disciplines and would not equate lack of English language proficiency or limited knowledge of American culture with low intelligence or poor aptitude for learning and achievement. The *Test of Nonverbal Intelligence* (TONI) was built to fill this niche (Brown 2003, p. 191).

This chapter will (a) examine the model and philosophy underlying the TONI; (b) chronicle its development from the first edition in 1982 to the 2010 revision; (c) detail its standardization and psychometric characteristics, with particular attention to the reliability and validity of its results, the normative and standardization procedures governing its development, and empirical controls for bias; (d) describe TONI's

S.K. Johnsen (✉)
Department of Educational Psychology,
School of Education, Baylor University,
One Bear Place #97301, Waco, TX 76798, USA
e-mail: Susan_Johnsen@baylor.edu

© Springer International Publishing AG 2017
R.S. McCallum (ed.), *Handbook of Nonverbal Assessment*,
DOI 10.1007/978-3-319-50604-3_11

administration and scoring; (e) offer suggestions and guidelines for the interpretation of the test results; and (f) summarize the strengths and weaknesses of TONI.

## Goals and Rationale for TONI Development and Revision

The man who initiated the modern mental testing movement was driven more by pragmatism than by theoretical or philosophical inclinations (Brown 2003). In the early 1900s when French authorities initiated a compulsory education program, they asked Binet and his colleague Simon to design a test that would identify children who might need special assistance. In response to this request, the Binet team catalogued observable behaviors, validated their observations through scientific methods, and built an instrument with attention to simplicity, clarity, and consistency of administration (Binet and Simon 1905, 1908, 1916; Binet 1911). Despite the absence of an elaborate theoretical base, the Binet–Simon scales were straightforward and functional (Brown 2003).

The TONI follows in these practical and empirical shoes. The TONI was not built to validate a theory of intelligence, but to fill a gap. "It was intended to be free of language and complex motor requirements, to be free of significant cultural influence, and to be brief" (Brown, et al. 2010, p. 1).

After an extensive review of theories and empirical studies of intelligence, the obvious behavior to be measured by the TONI was problem solving. Problem solving is considered the essence of intelligence rather than a splinter skill or subcomponent (Kosslyn and Koenig 1992; Mayer 1992; Resnick and Glaser 1976; Snyderman and Rothman 1988; Sternberg 1981, 1984; Sternberg and Detterman 1986). The TONI therefore measures intelligence as a global construct and does not attempt to be a comprehensive measure of all intelligent behaviors. It is also a good representation of the theoretical construct of $g$ (Spearman 1923) and of fluid intelligence (Horn 1985; Horn and Cattell 1966).

Along with the characteristic of problem solving, the TONI model eliminated language and reduced cultural influences to the extent possible dictated by problems that were abstract and novel. Language was eliminated through the use of instructions, materials, and responses free of all reading, writing, speaking, and listening. It also removed the need for complex motor response by requiring a simple gesture such as nodding, blinking, or pointing.

The TONI model therefore is grounded in pragmatism as well as theory and measures overall cognitive ability. It reduces the likelihood that language and complex motor responses will mask intelligence or confound its assessment.

### History of the TONI

Most measures of intelligence and aptitude depend heavily upon language: Some require the reading of test items, others employ oral instructions or questions, many require oral responses, and a few require written responses. Even if such tests are psychometrically sound, they are inadequate for people who do not use or understand standard English such as those who are unable to read or write, who have poor or impaired linguistic skills, who are fluent in a primary language other than English, who are electively mute, or who present a language or learning disability. They also tend to have heavy cultural loading, in part because of the preeminence of written or spoken English and in part because they presume intimate knowledge of the United States (e.g., "Why are we tried by a jury of peers?") or reflect learned knowledge (e.g., usage of upper and lower case letters). On the other hand, many tests of intelligence that purport to control language also require significant manual dexterity, such as stringing beads, connecting dots, drawing a person, building with blocks, and manipulating objects (Brown 2003).

Very few tests filled this language-free and motor-reduced niche 33 years ago when TONI was first built, and those that did possess serious psychometric flaws. Most prominent among the existing measures were Raven's matrix tests

(Raven 1938, 1947, 1960, 1962, 1977), which were used widely despite dated, nonrepresentative norms and modest estimates of reliability (particularly for children), flaws that were not corrected by a 1986 book reporting North American normative studies (Raven 1986). Another widely used test at that time was *The Leiter International Performance Scales* (Leiter 1948), which was designed for children with sensory, language, or motor deficits. It was flawed by deficient normative and reliability data and reported a ratio IQ instead of standard scores, deficits that were not substantially improved by future adaptation (Arthur 1950) or revision (Levine 1982). The few tests that measured intelligence without the use of language in 1982 were not useful in practice because they did not have representative normative populations, true normative scores, or acceptable evidence of reliability and validity (Brown 2003).

Our goal, then, was to correct these problems and build a test that had acceptable norms, was reliable and valid, and estimated intellectual capacity without relying upon written or spoken language, without emphasizing American cultural familiarity, and without requiring complicated motor responses. We focused first on the test's format: stimulus material, content, administration, and response modes. (a) The stimulus material could not use words, either in written or spoken form. (b) The content had to be abstract in nature and free of linguistic representation and familiarity with the American culture. We settled on abstract/figural content. (c) Administration also had to be free of language. We elected to use pantomimed instructions. (d) Finally, the mode of response could not require speaking or writing. We settled on a multiple-choice format with a simple pointing response or any other meaningful gesture to indicate the test examinee's choice from among the options offered (Brown 2003).

With the format decided, content came next. Of all intelligent behaviors, we concluded that the one best measured in this manner is abstract reasoning and problem solving. Problem solving not only lends itself well to the language-free, culture-reduced, motor-reduced format we stipulated, but there is also substantial empirical evidence that intellectual differences among individuals are most pronounced in higher complex mental processes like abstract reasoning and problem solving, which were, therefore, likely to be powerful and stable predictors of overall, global intelligence.

We began building TONI with these qualifications in mind: (a) The test would measure a single intelligent behavior, problem solving; (b) Administration would be pantomimed, requiring only a simple responsive gesture and no reading, writing, speaking, or listening; (c) The content would be abstract/figural in nature, thereby eliminating language and also reducing cultural loading. To meet these qualifications, each item therefore posed a problem in a series of abstract figures in which one or more pieces of the figure are missing. The respondent is offered an array of four or six alternatives and asked, using oral or pantomimed directions, to select the one that solves the problem and completes the figure (see Fig. 11.1 for a practice item).

About the same time we were field testing the prototype for TONI, Jensen (1980) published his book, *Bias in Mental Testing,* in which he recommended guidelines for language-free, culturally reduced measures. He advocated (a) the use of performance tasks rather than paper-and-pencil tasks; (b) pantomimed instructions in lieu of oral or written instructions; (c) the inclusion of practice items; (d) abstract content, not pictures or reading passages; (e) content that required reasoning rather than recall of factual material; and (f) an untimed procedure. We had already incorporated these characteristics into TONI.

The following evolution of the TONI is abstracted here; full details are provided in the preface to TONI-3 and TONI-4 (Brown et al. 1997, 2010) and in its critical reviews (Johnsen et al. 2010).

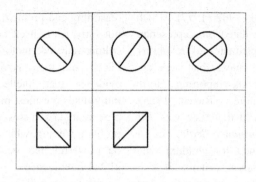

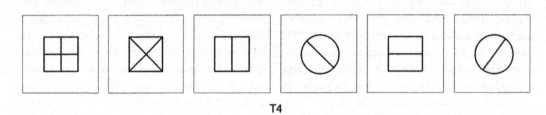

T4

**Fig. 11.1** TONI training item from the test of nonverbal intelligence, fourth edition, picture book (Brown et al. 2010)

## TONI (1982)

The first TONI (Brown et al. 1982) had two forms of 50 items each and consisted of an examiner's manual, a picture book with the stimulus drawings for the test items, and pads of Form A and Form B answer sheets to be completed by the examiner. Test items were selected empirically, assigned to Form A or Form B and arranged in easy-to-difficult order, parity between forms confirmed by coefficients of equivalence. TONI was normed on a sample of 1929 individuals, ages 5–0 years through 85–11 years, who were demographically representative of the U.S. population (U.S. Bureau of the Census 1980). Evidence for reliability and validity was provided in the manual.

## TONI-2 (1990)

TONI-2 (Brown et al. 1990) was both a revision and an upward extension of the test. Ten more difficult items were added, but scoring and administration were unchanged, as were the kit components. The normative group was 50% larger, comprising 2764 subjects, representative of the U.S. population (U.S. Bureau of the Census 1985) across age, gender, race, ethnicity, geographic region, urban/suburban/rural domicile, parental education (for minor subjects), and educational attainment (for adult subjects). The equivalence of Forms A and B was verified by coefficients of equivalence. Coefficients Alpha, immediate, and 7-day delayed alternate forms' reliability, and extraction of content sampling error from time sampling error reflected good internal consistency and stability reliability. Acceptable Coefficients Alpha, Kuder–Richardson Formula 21 coefficients, and immediate alternate forms coefficients were also reported for groups of subjects diagnosed with intellectual exceptionalities, learning disabilities, dyslexia, hearing loss, and closed head injuries; and for subjects who did not speak English or for whom English was a second language, including native Spanish speakers in Mexico and Chile, fully English-proficient bilingual speakers, limited-English proficient speakers, and non-English-proficient speakers. Validity data were extensive, incorporating our own research and independent, peer-reviewed research. Strong, positive relationships between TONI-2 and 26 other tests of intelligence, aptitude, and achievement were demonstrated, along with item analytic data, factor analyses, multiple correlation/regression, and convergent/divergent validity.

## TONI-3 (1997)

The TONI-3 (Brown et al. 1997) was shortened to enhance its quick-score characteristics. Using new measures of item bias and users' reviews, ten items from each form were removed; however, the administration and response format remained unchanged. Since all of the TONI-3 items were part of the TONI and the TONI-2, the three tests were essentially the same test for all practical purposes. All new normative data were collected, comprising 3451 individuals, representative of the U.S. population (U.S. Bureau of the Census 1990) across geographic region, gender, race, residence, ethnicity, disability status, family income, educational attainment of parents and adults, and age. The equivalence of Forms A and B was verified by coefficients of equivalence with identical means and standard deviations. Using three sources of error—content sampling, time sampling, and scorer differences—the TONI-3 evidenced consistently high reliability on both forms (e.g., 0.91–0.99). Coefficients Alphas were also reported for selective subgroups (e.g., male, female, age, African American, Hispanic, Spanish speakers in Mexico and Chile, limited-English proficient speakers, non-English proficient speakers) and individuals identified with exceptionalities (e.g., deaf, giftedness, learning disabilities) with similar results. Again, validity data were extensive, incorporating our own research and independent, peer-reviewed research. Strong, positive relationships between TONI-3 and 27 other tests of intelligence, aptitude, and achievement were demonstrated, along with item analytic data,

factor analyses, multiple correlation/regression, and convergent/divergent validity.

In addition to the evidence regarding its reliability and validity, we included an extensive discussion of how the TONI-3 conformed to prominent theories of intelligence. Some of the theories are presented below (Brown et al. 1997, p. 8):

- *Spearman's theory of intelligence* (Spearman 1923): The score generated by the TONI was hypothesized to be a good representation of Spearman's g factor.
- *Thurstones' primary mental ability theory of intelligence* (Thurstone 1938): The TONI measured the sixth primary mental ability, reasoning.
- *Guilford's Structure of Intellect model* (Guilford 1956): The TONI taps, to come extent, all of Guildford's mental operations (e.g., cognition, memory, divergent and convergent thinking, and evaluation), although memory arguable contributes the least to TONI's performance. It also seems that all of Guilford's products, particularly classes, relations, systems, and transformations, are generated in solving TONI problems. By choice, we limited the TONI to one content area, figural.
- *Cattell and Horn's two-factor theories* (Cattell 1943, 1963; Horn 1968, 1985): The TONI was built to measure fluid intelligence rather than crystallized intelligence.
- *Jensen's cognitive–associative model* (Jensen 1980): TONI requires reasoning and does not demand rote memory or previous learning, which are measures of Jensen's cognitive level.

Since the TONI does not use words, letters, or numerals, we also identified a list of specific reasoning skills that were assessed using the figural content. Adapted from Salvia and Ysseldyke's (1995) definitions and Jensen's (1980) categories, these skills were included (Brown et al. 1997, p. 23):

- *Generalization and Classification*: These items require the identification of similarities.

Given one example, the test subject must survey an array of other figures and symbols to find the one that is like it. These items may be as simple as matching a single characteristic or they may require a complex and sophisticated classification scheme.

- *Discrimination*: These items require the identification of differences, in particular the ability to review an array of stimuli and identify the figure or symbol that is different from the others presented.
- *Analogous Reasoning*: Analogies have an age-old format defined by the classic, logical formula, "A is to B as C is to _____." The problem is to determine the relationship that exists between A and B and then to find something that bears a parallel, or analogous, relationship to C. In nonverbal tests, the items usually depict figural or spatial analogies.
- *Seriation*: These items require the subject to perceive that the relationship among a series of stimuli is a sequential one and then to anticipate or complete the sequential relationship.
- *Induction*: Inductive reasoning involves the discovery of a governing principle that ties a set of figures together.
- *Deduction*: Deductive reasoning involves finding an example that illustrates a given governing principle or rule.
- *Detail Recognition*: The ability to focus on details is related to both speed and efficiency in solving problems. On measures of problem solving, detail recognition may be seen in the ability to identify parts that are missing or parts that are inferred but not actually represented. Increasing the number of details in a figure may also be used to increase the difficulty level of an item.

In summary, the TONI was built to be a measure of the common or general factor that is characteristic of intelligent behavior and assesses problem-solving skills within a nonverbal, motor-reduced format.

## TONI-4 (2010)

The TONI-4 added new items to improve the floor. These items were reordered and sorted to balance Form A and Form B in terms of difficulty and problem-solving skills measured. In addition, both verbal and nonverbal directions were provided for individuals who do not have linguistic or motor impairments. Instructions in several major foreign languages were also included for non-English-speaking examinees who did not need nonverbal directions. All new normative data were collected to ensure that the TONI-4 was representative of the U. S. population (U. S. Bureau of Census 2007). Additional evidence of the test's relationship to previous versions of the TONI and reliability and validity studies were collected. All of the TONI-4's psychometric properties will be discussed in the next section in greater detail.

## Standardization and Psychometric Properties

This section is concerned with the psychometric properties of TONI-4, beginning with empirical item selection procedures and continuing with standardization and normative procedures. Support for the reliability and validity of the test's results is detailed, concluding with a discussion of test bias.

### TONI-4 Item Selection

The TONI was developed considering Jensen's (1980) properties of culture-free tests: eliminating language through nonverbal instructions and nonverbal responses; reducing motor activity; including novel, abstract items requiring reasoning and problem solving; and eliminating any timed components. The initial TONI item pool contained 307 items, from which professionals deleted ambiguous items, items that were symbolic rather than abstract or items that involved linguistic concepts. Following this professional review, the remaining 183 items were further reduced through item analysis and assigned to Form A or Form B. The same methods were used to add ten more difficult items to create a larger ceiling with greater discriminating power for older and very bright individuals in the 1990 TONI-2 revision. The TONI-3 was reduced to 45 items per form and arranged in a new order to address bias and improve test difficulty, quality, and efficiency. Similar to the TONI-3, the TONI-4 was completely renormed with items added at the beginning and the end of the test to reduce floor and ceiling effects for a total of 60 items on each form. In addition, items were sorted according to type (e.g., matching, analogy, progression, classification, and intersection) and more evenly distributed between the two forms. Forms A and B were therefore statistically equivalent, similar to previous editions, and did not contain similar item types at similar difficulty levels.

Item selection required use of two conventional item analytic measures—item discriminating power and item difficulty. Discriminating power is observed in point-biserial correlations between individual item responses and total test scores. Item discrimination coefficients were calculated for every item in the TONI-4 pool at every age interval. Items with coefficients below 0.35 were eliminated.

Item difficulty is simply the percentage of individuals who pass an item and is used to identify items that are too easy or too difficult and to arrange items in an easy-to-difficult order. The best discriminators are items passed by about 15–85% of people at a given age interval, with a mean 50/50 pass/fail rate. Item difficulty was used to assign items to different forms of the TONI to assure that the forms were of comparable difficulty.

Items that survived these classic item analytic techniques were then subjected to differential item functioning (DIF) analysis to study possible bias with regard to gender, race, ethnicity, disability, or principal language spoken. The logistic regression procedure developed by Swaminathan and Rogers (1990) was used for detecting DIF. The procedure compares the adequacy of two different logistic regression models to account for the ability being measured; the restricted model uses ability alone to predict item performance and the full model uses both ability and group membership to predict item performance. The two models (i.e., restricted versus full) are then compared to determine which provides a significantly better solution. If the full model is better at predicting item performance than the restricted model, then the item appears to be influenced by group membership and is biased. Uniform DIF occurs when one subgroup consistently performs better on an item than the other group does at all levels of ability. For example, if both ability and male gender appear to influence test performance, then the item is biased and boys have an advantage over girls with the same ability level. All of the TONI-4 items were analyzed and comparisons made for each reference group. For those items for which the full model was a significantly better predictor than the restrictive model was, an effect size was used to evaluate the magnitude of DIF. Using Cohen et al. (1992) conventions for small, medium, and large effects, items with moderate or large effect sizes were used to target items for elimination. The logistic regression procedure was applied to all items in the TONI-4 and comparisons were made between the three dichotomous groups (i.e., female vs. male, African American vs. non-African American, and Hispanic vs. non-Hispanic). With only one item having a negligible effect, one may conclude that the test is nonbiased with regard to gender, African American, and Hispanic status.

The 120 items of TONI-4 were selected not only for their face validity as nonverbal problem-solving tasks, but also on the basis of empirical criteria: (a) strong point-biserial item-total correlations; (b) an acceptable pass/fail range; and (c) statistically insignificant indices of bias. Items were assigned to Form A and Form B and ordered from easy to difficult. Such rigorous attention to the selection and retention of items virtually ensured the reliability and validity of

TONI-4, the absence of bias in the test as a whole, and the equivalence of the two forms of the test even before norming was undertaken.

## TONI-4 Administration and Scoring

TONI-4 is a highly standardized test, with clear directions for administration and scoring. The two equivalent forms of the test accommodate situations where multiple measures are needed (e.g., evaluations of progress, effects, interventions). This section includes administration guidelines, methods of administration, and scoring procedures.

### Administration Guidelines

TONI-4 can be administered by a wide range of qualified professionals who have formal training and professional experience in assessment, including psychologists, psychological associates, educational diagnosticians, teachers, rehabilitation specialists, and speech and language therapists. They should have a basic understanding of intelligence testing and be able to (a) review and evaluate the psychometric qualities of norm-referenced tests and select a test that is appropriate for the intended purpose and for the person to be tested; (b) know the limitations and advantages of the chosen test and how they might influence test performance; (c) administer, score, and interpret the chosen test; (d) interpret the test scores to make recommendations or decisions; (e) communicate the results to the person who took the test, to parents or guardians, to other professionals, and to the lay public, as appropriate; and (f) recognize unethical, illegal, or inappropriate uses of this information. In addition, examiners should be knowledgeable about local school policies, state regulations, and the position statements of their respective professional organizations regarding test administration and interpretation and issues of confidentiality (Brown et al. 2010).

Before using the TONI-4, the examiner should study the content of the manual and be familiar with its psychometric characteristics, administration, and scoring guidelines. Examiners should practice administering the test at least three times in both oral and pantomime formats. It is critical to master the technique of the pantomime administration, which is unique to TONI-4, before giving the test.

Individuals between the ages of 6–0 through 89–11 years who understand the instructions by passing the practice items may take the test. Examiners should not administer the test to individuals who do not make meaningful gestures to the six training items. Examiners should also not administer the test to those who have serious visual problems who may not be able discriminate between response choices.

### Methods of Administration

TONI-4 is administered individually and takes about 15 minutes to administer one form. It may be administered using either oral or pantomimed directions. If the examinee speaks English proficiently, the examiner should use the oral English language instructions or alternative language instructions provided in the manual's appendix. Nonverbal directions, however, are critical for examinees who do not understand or speak Standard English or who may have a disability.

Before testing begins, the examiner should inform the examinees or parents/guardians about the purpose of the test, how the results will affect them, how the results will be recorded and scored, and who will have access to the scores. There should be a reasonable opportunity for questions. At all times, the examiner needs to protect the due process and privacy rights of the examinee, in the test situation itself and in the subsequent dissemination of test results, including the release of summary information.

Similar to any testing situation, examiners should assemble the test materials in advance and ensure that the test site is private, comfortable, well lighted, and free of distractions. The TONI-4 includes a Picture Book and an Answer and Record Form for each form. Before administering any of the items, the examiner needs to establish rapport with the person being tested.

The examiner begins by reading the oral instructions or by pantomiming the instructions for the training items, which are not scored but are used to determine if the individual understands and is able to respond meaningfully. Similar to other editions, the TONI-4 requires only a minimal motor response and the examinee has the option of pointing, gesturing or using a light beam, an eyelid switch, or other technological or mechanical option. In this special circumstance, examiners should ensure that the equipment is in working order before testing begins, and also that they understand the examinee's choices as expressed in the preferred response mode. The training items can be employed constructively for this purpose, as can a prior meeting with the person to be tested. If the examinee does not respond to the training items after two attempts to administer them, the examiner should discontinue testing.

TONI-4 is not a timed test, and although dawdling should not be encouraged, examinees should have all the time they need to make a response. The examiner should keep examinees at ease and on task and allow individuals to work at their own pace.

TONI-4 employs a basal and a ceiling. Testing begins with Item 1 if the examinee is 6–9 years of age, is suspected of having an intellectual impairment, or has experienced any difficulty with the training items. Otherwise, testing begins with Item 20. Responses are noted on the Answer and Record Form. The correct response for each item is printed inside a circle so examiners know immediately if a response is correct or incorrect. Items are arranged in an easy-to-difficult order. A basal is established with five consecutive correct responses by either testing forward or backward from Item 20. Testing is discontinued when the subject reaches the ceiling by giving three incorrect responses within five consecutive items. Older and more able subjects may proceed through all 60 items without reaching a ceiling.

## Scoring TONI-4

Since there is only one correct answer to each item, the TONI-4 is easily scored. No qualitative judgment is required. If errors occur, they tend to be related to simple addition errors or to the misapplication of basals and ceilings. These rules should be applied when scoring the TONI-4 (Brown et al. 2010, p. 11): (a) each item passed below the ceiling item is given 1 point; (b) all of the items below the basal (e.g., 5 items in a row) are given 1 point; (c) any item mistakenly administered above the ceiling is scored zero; (d) training items are not scored; and (e) the total raw score is 1 point for each item passed below the ceiling and all the items below the basal.

## Standardization and Psychometric Properties of the TONI-4

TONI-4 is both standardized and norm-referenced, meaning that it has specific administration procedures, objective scoring criteria, and an explicit frame of reference for interpreting its results, all of which reduce test error (Hammill 1987). To reduce error, each examiner needs to administer the test exactly the same. Standardization ensures that, to the extent possible, each administration of the test is the same.

One major change in the TONI-4 was the addition of oral directions. This change was made because practitioners and researchers believed that gifted or nonhandicapped students might find the nonverbal instructions "unnecessarily awkward" (Atlas 2001, p. 1259). To accommodate test users, we examined differences between oral and nonverbal instructions. Three age groups who were English speaking and not deaf or hard of hearing were tested: 6 through 8 years of age, 12 through 14 years, and 18 years or older. They were administered either Form A or Form B using nonverbal instructions and then 1 week later given the alternate form using verbal instructions. The correlations between standard scores for oral and nonverbal instructions were compared for each age group and for the full sample. Because the effect size differences observed between the first and second administrations were small and trivial, the mode of instruction did not appear to have much effect on the test's standard scores. The TONI-4 therefore now offers the examiner the option of using either oral or nonverbal (pantomime) directions. As long as the examinee speaks English proficiently, the examiner may use the oral English or alternative language instructions. However, the nonverbal instructions are essential for examinees who do not speak English proficiently. In either case, the examiner must use specific administration procedures that were used during the test's norming.

## Normative Procedures

TONI-4 was normed on a sample of 2272 people ranging in age from 6–0 through 89–11 years and matched to the U.S. population (U.S. Bureau of the Census 2007) on eight critical variables: geographic region, gender, race, Hispanic status, educational attainment, family income, exceptionality status (see Table 11.1). The norm group was also stratified by age across all of the critical variables, demonstrating not only that the normative sample is representative as a whole, but also that the stratified variables are dispersed throughout the sample's age range.

## Reliability

Test reliability is an estimate of the error associated with a test's scores and is usually reported as a reliability coefficient. Error that is external to the test itself can be controlled in part by adhering to standardized administration and scoring guidelines, but even if a test were administered perfectly, there would still be error inherent in the test itself. Studies of a test's reliability estimate the variance due to content sampling (i.e., do the test items consistently measure intelligence or the construct being assessed?), time sampling (i.e., do the test scores

vary over time?), and interscorer differences (i.e., does the test receive the same score across different scorers?). Four types of reliability are reported for the TONI-4: Coefficient Alpha, alternate forms, test–retest, and interscorer.

**Coefficient Alpha** measures the extent to which test items correlate with one another (i.e., how well do the items measure a single unidimensional construct?). Because TONI measures the single construct of intelligence, one would expect that the Coefficient Alpha would be high. Alphas are reported for Form A and Form B at each 1-year interval from 6 through 18 years and at each decade from 19 through 69 years and from 70–89. All of the 38 Coefficients Alpha for Form A and B exceed 0.93, which supports empirically the conclusion that TONI-4 is a highly reliable, internally consistent test with minimal content sampling error and can be used with confidence to test individuals at all ages (Brown et al. 2010, pp. 39–40).

Because a test is reliable at all ages, though, it does not necessarily mean that it is equally reliable for every subgroup within the population. We therefore calculated Coefficients Alpha for 13 subgroups within the normative sample: male, female, White, Black/African American, Asian/Pacific Islander, Hispanic, gifted, physical impairment, learning disability, English as a second language, attention-deficit/hyperactivity disorder, speech-language disorder, and intellectual disability. Similar to the age groups, these Alphas are all 0.92 or greater, indicating that the test is highly reliable when administered to diverse kinds of individuals (Brown et al. 2010, p. 41).

These results are similar to studies conducted with previous editions of the TONI (Johnsen et al. 2010). For TONI-1, the overall average Coefficient Alpha was 0.88 for Form A and 0.89 for Form B; for TONI-2, 0.96 for both forms; and for TONI-3, 0.92 for Form A and 0.93 for Form B. Previous editions have also shown TONI's internal consistency with different subgroups (i.e., ethnicity/gender, Spanish speaking, and exceptionality). In these 16 studies, 12 are 0.90 or higher (see Johnsen et al. 2010, pp. 8–9).

**Table 11.1** Demographic characteristics of the TONI-4 Normative Sample (N = 2272)*

| Characteristic | Percentage of school-age sample | Percentage of U.S. school-age population | Percentage of adult sample | Percentage of U. S. adult population |
|---|---|---|---|---|
| *Geographic Region* | | | | |
| Northeast | 17 | 18 | 21 | 19 |
| South | 35 | 36 | 38 | 36 |
| Midwest | 26 | 22 | 20 | 22 |
| West | 23 | 24 | 21 | 23 |
| *Gender* | | | | |
| Male | 51 | 51 | 48 | 49 |
| Female | 49 | 49 | 52 | 51 |
| *Race* | | | | |
| White | 81 | 76 | 83 | 82 |
| Black/African American | 13 | 16 | 11 | 12 |
| Asian/Pacific Islander | 2 | 4 | 3 | 4 |
| Two or more | 3 | 3 | 1 | 1 |
| Other | 1 | 1 | 1 | 1 |
| *Hispanic status* | | | | |
| Yes | 12 | 19 | 11 | 13 |
| No | 88 | 81 | 89 | 87 |
| *Educational Attainment* | | | | |
| Less than bachelor's degree | 79 | 70 | 70 | 72 |
| Bachelor's degree | 14 | 20 | 20 | 19 |
| Graduate degree | 7 | 10 | 10 | 9 |
| *Family income (in dollars)* | | | | |
| Under 15,000 | 8 | 9 | 11 | 9 |
| 15,000–24,999 | 8 | 11 | 9 | 11 |
| 25,000–34,999 | 10 | 11 | 10 | 11 |
| 35,000–49,999 | 16 | 15 | 15 | 15 |
| 50,000–74,999 | 24 | 20 | 20 | 20 |
| 75,000 and over | 35 | 34 | 34 | 34 |
| *Exceptionality status* | | | | |
| No disability | 72 | 81 | 75 | NA |
| Specific learning | 8 | 6 | 2 | NA |
| disability | 3 | 3 | 0 | NA |
| Speech-language disorder | 1 | 1 | 3 | NA |
| Other disability | 2 | 1 | 2 | NA |

Note. *NA* = not available
* Data from TONI-4 (Brown et al. 2010, pp. 30–31)

These results support TONI's internal consistency reliability, indicating its small test error due to content sampling.

**Alternate forms** Like Coefficient Alpha, immediate administration of alternate forms provides another method to estimate internal consistency. Form A and Form B of the TONI-4 were administered back-to-back to the entire normative sample and the results were correlated, correcting for any range effects that might artificially depress or inflate the size of the coefficients. The immediate alternate forms generally rounded to or exceeded 0.80, and the average corrected coefficient (0.81) is large enough to support both the equivalence of the two forms and their internal consistency (Brown et al. 2010, p. 41).

Delaying the administration of the alternate forms can estimate test error from both content sampling and time sampling. Both forms were administered to 63 people, ages 9–0 to 72–11, and then administered again 1 to 2 weeks later. The resulting average coefficients for school-age students were 0.84; for the adult sample, 0.81; and 0.84 for all subjects (Brown et al. 2010, p. 42), which supported the alternate forms' reliability and their stability.

These results are also similar to studies conducted with previous editions of the TONI (Johnsen et al. 2010). For TONI-1, the average reliability for alternate forms immediate administration was 0.85; for TONI-2, 0.86; and for TONI-3, 0.84. These results support TONI's internal consistency reliability.

**Test–retest** The test–retest method, in which a period of time elapses between two or more administrations of a test, examines the extent to which test performance is stable over time and estimates time sampling error. Three studies of the 1-week test–retest reliability of Form A and Form B are reported for school-age students, adult, and combined populations. The coefficients range from 0.82 to 0.88 for Form A and from 0.83 to 0.93 for Form B (Brown et al. 2010, pp. 42–43). Four previous studies with earlier editions of the TONI reflected similar coefficients

(e.g., 0.83 to 0.94) (Johnsen et al. 2010). All of these studies indicate that performance on TONI is relatively stable over time, with minimal time sampling error.

**Interscorer** TONI-4 has explicit instructions for identifying correct answers, tabulating raw scores, and converting raw scores to standard scores, all of which reduce the probability of scorer error. However, to evaluate this source of error, two experienced scorers rescored 50 pairs of Form A and Form B protocols, which were randomly selected from the normative sample. The ages of the sample ranged from 6 to 82 years. The quotients reported by the two scorers were correlated, yielding coefficients of nearly perfect 0.99s, indicating negligible error due to scorer differences (Brown et al. 2010, p. 44). Again, this study is similar to a previous interscorer study with the TONI-3 (Brown et al. 1997) that yielded 0.99 for each form.

**Summary of reliability results** The averaged coefficients for each of the four types of reliability using the $z$-transformation method show that TONI-4 is highly reliable, consistent with the results reported by the authors and independent researchers of previous editions. Mean reliability for Form A with regard to content sampling error is 0.93 for Form A and 0.94 for Form B; the mean with regard to time sampling error 0.88, and interscorer reliability is 0.99. For Form B, the mean reliability with regard to content sampling error was 0.96, the mean with regard to time sampling error is 0.89, and interscorer reliability is 0.99, also yielding a mean overall reliability of 0.96 (Brown et al. 2007; Johnsen et al. 2010).

## Validity

Studies of validity are concerned with whether a test measures what it says it measures. The sheer volume of studies available is important in providing a broader and deeper picture of the test. Since the TONI's initial publication in 1982, over fifty studies by the authors and independent researchers have examined its validity (Brown et al. 2010; Johnsen et al. 2010). The discussion of these data is organized here into the traditional categories of content validity, criterion-related validity, and construct validity.

**Content validity** Content validity involves the examination of the content to determine if it represents the construct being measured. As mentioned previously, the TONI items were built to measure problem solving, an overarching component of intelligence, which lends itself to a nonverbal format. To identify items for the TONI, we reviewed the theoretical research and examined earlier nonverbal tests of intelligence to create a large pool of potential test items that would conform to the desired matrix, nonverbal format and assess different types of problem-solving content. Using conventional item analytic measures (i.e., item discriminating power and item difficulty), we identified items and then distributed them to each form, making sure that the forms were equivalent and contained similar item types at similar difficulty levels. We also used differential item functioning analysis to study any influence on variables such as gender, race, ethnic group membership, or linguistic competence. This approach to the selection and retention of items ensured the content validity of the TONI-4, the absence of bias, and the equivalence of the two forms of the test.

**Criterion-related validity** Criterion-related validity procedures are used to determine the effectiveness of a test in predicting performance on assessments that measure similar constructs or performance in specific activities related to the construct. A test like the TONI-4 should therefore relate to other measures of intelligence and aptitude, especially nonverbal measures. The TONI-4 was correlated to the *Comprehensive Test of Nonverbal intelligence—Second Edition* (CTONI-2; Hammill et al. 2009) and the TONI-3 (Brown et al. 1997). Using Hopkins's (2002) criteria to evaluate coefficients, the correlation coefficients resulting from these studies were significant and large (0.73–0.79). These results

are reinforced by the overwhelming evidence of criterion–prediction validity related to previous editions of the TONI (Johnsen et al. 2010). TONI-1, TONI-2, and TONI-3 were validated against scores from 29 criterion measures: *Bilingual Verbal Ability Tests* (Muñoz-Sandoval et al. 1998), *Clinical Evaluation of Language Fundamentals—Revised* (Semel et al. 1987), *Colored Progressive Matrices* (Raven 1965), *Comprehensive Test of Nonverbal Intelligence* (Hammill et al. 1996), *Detroit Tests of Learning Ability—Adult* (Hammill and Bryant 1991), *Developmental Test of Visual-Motor Integration* (Beery 1989), *Global Assessment Scale* (Endicott et al. 1976), *Kaufman Assessment Battery for Children* (Kaufman and Kaufman 1983), *Leiter International Performance Scale* (Leiter 1948), *Leiter International Performance Scale-Revised* (Roid and Miller 1997), *Modified Gottschaldt Figures* (Thurstone 1944), *Otis-Lennon Mental Ability Test* (Otis and Lennon 1970), *Peabody Picture Vocabulary Test—Third Edition* (Dunn and Dunn 1997), *Quick Test* (Ammons and Ammons 1962), *Reynell Developmental Language Scales* (Department of Health and Education, Hong Kong, 1987), *Scholastic Abilities Test for Adults* (Bryant et al. 1991), *Scholastic Aptitude Test* (Educational Testing Service 2002), *Screening Assessment for Gifted Elementary Students* (Johnsen and Corn 1987), *Slosson Intelligence Test—Revised* (Slosson 1991), *Standard Progressive Matrices* (Raven 1938), *Test of Language Development—Intermediate, Second Edition* (Hammill and Newcomer 1988a), *Test of Language Development—Primary, Second Edition* (Hammill and Newcomer 1988b), *Universal Nonverbal Intelligence Test* (Bracken and McCallum 1996), *Wechsler Adult Intelligence Scale—Revised* (Wechsler 1981), *Wechsler Adult Intelligence Scale-Third Edition* (Wechsler 1997), *Wechsler Intelligence Scale for Children-Revised* (Wechsler 1974), *Wechsler Intelligence Scale for Children, Third Edition* (Wechsler 1991), *Wechsler Intelligence Scale for Children, Fourth Edition* (Wechsler 2003), *Woodcock-Johnson Psycho-Educational Battery* (Woodcock 1977), *Woodcock-Johnson III Tests of Cognitive Abilities* (Woodcock et al.

2001), and *Wide Range Assessment of Memory and Learning* (Sheslow and Adams 1990). The averaged coefficients across both forms and across all studies were large to very large, justifying the assumption of a strong relationship of the TONI to criterion measures: 0.63 for general measures of aptitude, 0.54 for verbal measures of aptitude, and 0.71 for nonverbal measures of aptitude. Readers are referred to the *Test of Nonverbal Intelligence Critical Reviews and Research Findings, 1982–2009* (Johnsen et al. 2010) for detailed descriptions of the subjects, research designs, and results.

**Construct validity** The following procedure was used to determine the degree to which the underlying traits could be identified and reflected the theoretical model on which the TONI is based: the constructs accounting for test performance were initially identified; then hypotheses were proposed and then verified using empirical methods. Full details are provided in the TONI-4 manual (Brown et al. 2010) and in the summary of previous research with all of the TONI editions (Johnsen et al. 2010). These hypotheses and findings are discussed in the remainder of this section:

1. *Hypothesis*: Because measured intelligence has a known developmental pattern into the late teens, plateaus through middle age, then gradually declines, raw scores TONI-4 should conform to this pattern.

*Summary of findings* TONI-4 scores follow the hypothesized pattern with a plateau beginning after 17 years of age, and a decline about age 60, correlating strongly with school-age students (i.e., 0.53 to 0.54). These results are similar to six previous studies with earlier editions (Johnsen et al. 2010). For students ages 6–0 to 17–11, the TONI correlations with age are strong and positive (A = 0.63, B = 0.60) and raw scores show hypothesized developmental patterns, increasing sharply to about age 60 years after which they decline slightly. Similar patterns are reported for

the *Comprehensive Test of Nonverbal Intelligence, Second Edition* (Hammill et al. 2009), the *Reynolds Intellectual Assessment Scales* (RIAS; Reynolds and Kamphaus 2003), and the *Wechsler Adult Intelligence Scale—Fourth Edition* (WAIS-IV; Wechsler 2008).

2. *Hypothesis*: Because it measures intelligent behavior, TONI-4 should differentiate between groups of subjects known to be average, above average, and below average intellectually.

*Summary of findings* Since the TONI-4 is most likely to be used to differentiate between individuals who vary in intelligence, the test needs to show its validity in this area and to show that it does not confer disadvantage or advantage on the basis of membership in other groups. Data show that gifted and talented individuals score 1.8 SDs above the mean, individuals with intellectual disabilities score 2 SDs below the mean, and individuals in disability groups with no intellectual impairment score in the average range. The remaining gender and ethnic subgroups all performed within the average range (ranging from 93 to 101) (Brown et al. 2010, p. 60). These findings are consistent with the data for prior editions of the TONI (Johnsen et al. 2010).

3. *Hypothesis*: Because intelligence and aptitude are strong predictors of academic success, TONI-4 should correlate strongly and positively to measures of academic achievement.

*Summary of findings* The TONI-4 was strongly correlated with three measures of reading, mathematics, and general school achievement (0.55 to 0.78) (Brown et al. 2010, p. 60). Eleven studies of this type are reported between TONI's previous editions and these tests: *Diagnostic Achievement Battery-Second Edition* (Newcomer 1990); *Diagnostic Achievement Test for*

*Adolescents, Second Edition* (Newcomer and Bryant 1993), *Kaufman Test of Educational Achievement-Second Edition* (Kaufman and Kaufman 2004), *Iowa Tests of Basic Skills* (Hieronymus and Hoover 1985), *Stanford Achievement Test* (Madden et al. 1973), *Stanford Achievement Test-Eighth Edition* adapted for deaf or hard of hearing (Holt et al. 1992), *Scholastic Abilities Test for Adults* (Bryant et al. 1991), *SRA Achievement Series* (Naslund et al. 1978), *Test of Reading Comprehension-Revised* (Brown et al. 1986), *Woodcock-Johnson Psycho-Educational Battery-Revised* (Woodcock and Johnson 1989); *Woodcock Reading Mastery Tests-Revised* (Woodcock 1998); *Wide Range Achievement Test–Revised* (Jastak and Wilkinson 1984). All of the averaged coefficients were significant and moderate to large in magnitude for each of the four categories of academic achievement (overall achievement = 0.60, language arts [writing, spelling, reading] = 0.52, math = 0.56, and other [social studies, science, reference skills] = 0.43).

4. *Hypothesis:* Because the TONI-4 was built to measure abstract reasoning and problem solving, a global component of intelligence or Spearman's *g*, the items should arrange themselves into a single large factor.

*Summary of findings*  Similar to previous studies with the TONI, all of the items were loaded on a single factor as hypothesized (Brown et al. 1997; Johnsen et al. 2010).

5. *Hypothesis*: Because they measure the same trait, TONI-4 items should correlate strongly and positively to the total test score.

*Summary of findings*  Correlating items with the total test score was used in the early stages of test construction to select good items for TONI-4. For this reason, point-biserial item-to-total coefficients are all strong and positive.

6. *Hypothesis*: Since TONI-4 was built to reduce linguistic and cultural loading in the administration and content of the test, the TONI items should evidence minimum bias.

*Summary of findings*  Measures of bias were employed at the earliest stages of test development. TONI-4 items were retained or rejected, in part, based on differential item functioning (DIF) for different subgroups (i.e., gender, race, and ethnic). In addition, test bias was minimized by including diverse groups of people from different ethnic groups in the normative sample and is representative of the most recent census (U.S. Census Bureau 2007). The statistical properties (e.g., reliability and validity) for different groups were also studied. The reliability coefficients were uniformly high for all groups (i.e., gender, race/ethnicity, intellectual ability, and English language proficiency) and mean index score differences were minimal in the normative sample supporting the assumption of minimal bias in the TONI-4. Also, the fact that TONI-4 is an untimed test and has language-reduced instructions, figural content, and motor-reduced responses increases its likelihood that its results are more fair and less biased. (Brown et al. 2010, pp. 68–69). Extensive data supporting the item discriminating power and item difficulty of the TONI are reported in *Test of Nonverbal Intelligence: Critical Reviews and research Findings, 1982–2009* (Johnsen et al. 2010).

## TONI-4 Interpretation

TONI-4 is a test of cognitive ability using nonverbal formats and pointing responses to measure general intelligence. It is particularly useful for evaluating the problem-solving ability of individuals with language and motor deficits, who are not able to perform on traditional verbal measures, and for developing educational plans and interventions. Similar to other assessments, however, it should not be used as the only source of information in making decisions and should be used in conjunction with other test scores, observations, historical data, and information from interested parties such as family members, teachers, and other professionals involved in the educational process. In all instances, where TONI-4 is used to make decisions about individuals, multiple types of data from multiple sources at multiple points in time should be collected. Test scores, grades in school, work products, job performance, self-report data, observations by the examiner and other interested parties, and other data should be accumulated over a reasonable period of time for the purpose in question (Brown 2003). No decision should be made based on a single snapshot of performance at one point in time. The American Educational Research Association, the American Psychological Association, and the National Council on Measurement in Education (2014) have collaborated in developing testing standards, which address accessibility, fairness, score interpretations, the role of testing, and other important issues. Examiners should be familiar with these standards and important developments in the field of educational testing and measurement.

Because the examiner of the TONI-4 may collaborate with others such as speech therapists, psychologists, and educational diagnosticians in interpreting the assessment data or may not even be involved in the final decision-making process, it is critical for each examiner to record all relevant information at the time the test is administered: the purposes for the test administration, any accommodations made in administration, conditions that were not standard or were limiting to the test examinee, and other information necessary for proper and accurate interpretation of the results by a person who was not present to observe them. For interpretation, it is also important to include complete information about how the test was scored, the adequacy and appropriateness of the norms, the kinds of scores reported, the standard errors of measurement, known limitations of the test, proper interpretations and misinterpretation of scores, and technical characteristics that affect the scores (Brown 2003).

## Understanding Test Scores

**Index scores** TONI-4's index scores have a distribution with a mean of 100 and a standard deviation of 15—a distribution chosen because it is widely used in other tests of intellectual abilities. They are derived or transformed from the raw score distribution and then transformed into a normalized score distribution. As interval data, these scores are intrinsically more useful because they can be subjected to arithmetic operations and statistical procedures, which make them particularly functional in research and comparisons across assessments.

An average or high index score (i.e., 90 and above) indicates that the person tested has reasoning and problem-solving skills better than his or her age-mates. They can see "logical and abstract relationships, can reason without words, can solve mental puzzles that involve complex elements, and can form meaningful associations between objects and designs" (Brown et al. 2010, p. 21). Those who perform below age expectations (i.e., below 90) may have trouble "managing nonverbal information, organizing spatially oriented materials, and mastering abstract properties of visual symbols" (Brown et al. 2010, p. 21).

**Percentile ranks** Percentile ranks, also called percentile scores or percentiles, are another normative score that are not as versatile as quotients because they cannot be manipulated arithmetically or compared across tests. They are easily understood and represent the percentage of scores in the normative sample that are higher or lower than the score in question. For example, a percentile rank of 85 means that 85% of the normative sample scored at or below that same level or that only 15% scored at a higher level. These scores are frequently shared with people who do not have a psychometric background. For more information regarding their advantages and disadvantages, examiners should read Aiken and Groth-Marnat (2006), McLoughlin and Lewis (2005), Salvia et al. (2007)

**Age equivalents.** Age equivalents are derived by calculating the average normative group's score at each 6-month interval. "Through the process of interpolation, extrapolation, and smoothing, age equivalents are generated for each raw score point on the test" (Brown et al. 2010, p. 22). Because their statistical properties are inadequate and their results are misleading, these score have been criticized extensively (Salvia et al. 2007; Reynolds et al. 2009). Because they are required by many states' education rules, we added a table to TONI-4 to generate age-equivalent scores for school-age test subjects.

## Accounting for Test Error

A test score is an estimate of performance because it may be affected by a number of variables—the test itself (its standardization and reliability), administration conditions, and characteristics of the examinee. The standard error of measurement (SEM) is a statistical means of accounting for within-test error and should always be reported when index scores are used. To help others interpret the test, examiners should calculate the upper and lower limits of the range in which the true score probably lies. In general, the SEM for the TONI-4 across all ages is about 3 points. For example, if the index score is 91, then with a 68% level of confidence, the examiner can be relatively sure that the examinee's true score is between 88 and 95 (i.e., $\pm$one SEM); with a 95% level of confidence, the true score would be between 85 and 97 (i.e., $\pm[1.96 \times 3]$); and with a 99% level of confidence, the true score would be between 83 and 99 (i.e., $\pm[2.58 \times 3]$).

## Foreign-Language, Alternate-Normed, and Cross-Validated Versions of TONI

TONI has been published in several foreign countries, sometimes with a complete renorming, and sometimes with equivalency or cross-validation research. TONI's unique language-free, culture-reduced content is appropriate for subjects without regard to their countries of residence or the languages they speak, but the test's U.S. norms may or may not be appropriate in these other settings. At this time there are three complete foreign-normed versions of TONI, one published in Spain (Brown et al. 1995), one published in the Republic of China (Wu-Tien et al, 1995), and one published in Turkey (Brown et al. 2014).

Barrett (2000) cross-validated and established the equivalency of TONI-3 in Jamaica. There have also been efforts at partial renorming and cross-validation in Chile (TONI and TONI-2) (Prado 1988; Prado et al. 1993), in Mexico (TONI) (Garcia 1988), and in India (TONI) (Parmar 1988). In addition to these renorming and cross-validation studies, additional studies with subgroups outside the United States have been conducted in countries such as Australia, Canada, Greece, Italy, South Korea, and Taiwan (Johnsen et al. 2010).

Studies have also been conducted with special populations and include children who are autism/pervasive developmental disorder (Chan et al. 2005; Edelson 2005; Kern et al. 2000); deaf, profound hearing loss or with hearing impairments (Cash 1994; Mackinson 1996; Mackinson et al. 1997); developmental disability (Auerbach 1995); dyslexia (Salas 1988); and learning disability (Lassiter and Bardos 1992). The mean scores for all of these subgroups are within the expected ranges of performance (Johnsen et al. 2010).

## Strengths and Limitations of the TONI-4

Over 30 years of research have accumulated since the TONI's first edition in 1982. Critical reviewers have noted these strengths (Aiken 1996; Althanasiou 2000; Atlas 2001; Clark 1985; De Mauro 2001; DeThorne and Schafer 2004; Handleman and Delmolino 2005; Harrington 1985; Mayo 1985; McLoughlin and Lewis 1986, 1994, 2005; Pierangelo and Giuliani 1998;

Reynolds and Fletcher-Janzen 2004; Roberts 1990; Salvia and Ysseldyke 1988; Salvia et al. 2007; Sattler 2001; Spragins 1998; Strauss et al. 2006; Watson 1992):

1. The test clearly defines the principles of nonverbal assessment and the theoretical and philosophical bases to evaluate general intelligence and aptitude. It is useful as a quick screening measure of nonverbal reasoning ability for children and adults.
2. Items consistently assess problem solving in a nonverbal, figural format and have been developed using not only classic item analytic techniques but also more advanced analyses (i.e., differential item functioning) to determine possible bias.
3. The quality and quantity of reliability and validity studies provide a rich picture of the test's usefulness. They document the test's relationship to other measures of intelligence and achievement, its efficiency in discriminating groups and potential bias, and its factor structure. The authors also are careful in providing cautions for not overgeneralizing the results.
4. The test provides two forms, allowing users opportunities to examine the effectiveness of programs and interventions.
5. New, well-constructed, and comprehensive norms have been collected for TONI-4, ensuring that they are representative of the most current U. S. census. The normative data were also stratified by age, gender, geographic region, ethnicity, and race.
6. The test is untimed allowing for individual differences, particularly for students who may need extended time. The inclusion of training items provides information to the examiner regarding the appropriateness of the test for the examinee.
7. For examinees who speak English proficiently, the examiner may administer the test using oral language instructions; for those who do not understand or speak Standard English, pantomimed instructions are available.

8. The test is particularly well suited for individuals with multiple disabilities; nearly all populations, except for the blind, may be evaluated for intelligence.
9. The manual is written clearly and is useful for psychometrically trained students and practitioners.
10. The newer computer-generated drawings in the Picture Book are substantially improved —clear and crisp. The overall test is well constructed, durable, and attractive.

Given the revisions related to the previous criticisms of the TONI, only a few weaknesses were noted in recent reviews:

1. The TONI-4 does not measure a broad array of intellectual skills and assesses only problem solving in a nonverbal, figural format.
2. While the TONI-4 has validity studies that examine the means across different groups, it does not provide separate norms.
3. More studies were suggested in examining the relationships among the test's two forms, multiple editions of the test, and exploring potential floor effects for children with autism or mental retardation.

While it is true that the TONI-4 does not measure a broad array of intellectual skills, it is a weakness only if the test is not used properly. We do encourage users to develop specialized norms for disability groups independently and continue to conduct studies with the TONI to determine the adequacy of its technical properties and its utility with different groups of examinees.

## Summary

The *Test of Nonverbal Intelligence, Fourth Edition*, is a highly standardized, norm-referenced measure of abstract reasoning and problem solving that requires no reading, writing, speaking, or listening. It is culture-reduced and largely motor-free, requiring only a point, nod, or meaningful gesture as a response. It is appropriate for use with people ranging in age from 6–0 through 89–11 years and its pantomime and oral formats makes TONI-4 particularly well suited for not only English speakers but also people who do not understand spoken or written English, either for cultural reasons or due to trauma, disease, or disability. As mentioned in the critical reviews, TONI-4 is suitable for use with almost all populations other than people who are blind or visually impaired.

TONI-4 is administered individually in about 10–15 min. It yields index scores and percentile ranks. Its two equivalent forms contain 60 items each and present a novel abstract/figural problems arranged in an easy-to-difficult order. Multiple response choices are offered to solve or complete each problem.

Finally, TONI-4 is a psychometrically sound test with over 30 years of research to support its utility. It is normed on a large, demographically representative and stratified sample of 2272 people. Empirical evidence demonstrates that the test is reliable, a valid measure of intelligence, and is relatively free of bias with regard to gender, race, ethnicity, and other relevant variables.

# References

Aiken, L. R. (1996). *Assessment of intellectual functioning* (2nd ed.). New York: Plenum Press.

Aiken, L. R., & Groth-Marnat, G. (2006). *Psychological testing and assessment* (12th ed.). Needham Heights, MA: Allyn & Bacon/Pearson.

Althanasiou, M. S. (2000). Current nonverbal assessment instruments: A comparison of psychometric integrity. *Journal of Psychoeducational Assessment, 18*, 211–229.

Atlas, J. A. (2001). Review of the test of nonverbal intelligence. In B. S. Plake & J. C. Impara (Eds.), *The fourteenth mental measurements yearbook* (3rd ed., pp. 1259–1260). Lincoln, NE: Buros Institute of Mental Measurements.

Auerbach, M. (1995). *The relationship of global intelligence, social intelligence, and nonverbal decoding ability within a developmentally disabled population.* Dissertation Abstracts International, *56*(5B), 2894.

American Educational Research Association (AERA), American Psychological Association (APA), & National Council on Measurement in Education (NCME). (2014). *Standards for educational and psychological testing.* Washington, DC: AERA

Publications. Retrieved from http://www.apa.org/science/programs/testing/standards.aspx

Ammons, R. B., & Ammons, C. H. (1962). The quick test: Provisional manual. *Psychological Reports, 11*, 11–161.

Arthur, G. (1950). *The arthur adaptation of the leiter international performance scales.* Chicago: Stoelting Company, Psychological & Educational Tests Division.

Barrett, P. (2000). *Cross-validation of the Test of Nonverbal Intelligence-Third Edition (TONI-3) for Jamaican students.* Unpublished doctoral dissertation, Auburn University, Auburn, Alabama.

Beery, K. E. (1989). *The VMI: Developmental Test of Visual-Motor Integration: Administration, scoring, and teaching manual.* Cleveland, OH: Modern Curriculum Press.

Binet, A. (1911). Nouvelles recherches sur la mésure du niveau intéllectuel chez les enfants d'éd'cole. *L'Année Psychologique, 17*, 145–210.

Binet, A., & Simon, T. (1905). Méthodes nouvelles pour le diagnostic du niveau intéllectuel des anormaux. *L'Année Psychologique, 11*, 191–244.

Binet, A., & Simon, T. (1908). Le dévelopment de l'intelligence chez les enfants. *L'Année Psychologique, 14*, 1–94.

Binet, A., & Simon, T. (1916). *The development of intelligence in children: The Binet-Simon Scale* (No. 11). Williams & Wilkins Company. (Original work published 1905)

Bracken, B. A., & McCallum, R. S. (1996). *Universal Nonverbal Intelligence Test.* Austin, TX: PRO-ED.

Brown, L. (2003). Test of nonverbal intelligence: A language-free measure of cognitive ability. In R. S. McCallum (Ed.), *Handbook of nonverbal assessment* (pp. 191–221). New York, NY: Kluwer Academic/Plenum Publishers.

Brown, L., Sherbenou, R. J., & Johnsen, S. K. (1982). *Test of nonverbal intelligence.* Austin, TX: PRO-ED.

Brown, L., Sherbenou, R. J., & Johnsen, S. K. (1990). *Test of nonverbal intelligence* (2nd ed.). Austin, TX: PRO-ED.

Brown, L., Sherbenou, R. J., & Johnsen, S. K. (1995). *Test de inteligencia no verbal: Apreciación de la habilidad cognitiva sin influencia del lenguaje.* Madrid, España: TEA Ediciones, S.A.

Brown, L., Sherbenou, R. J., & Johnsen, S. K. (1997). *Test of nonverbal intelligence* (3rd ed.). Austin, TX: PRO-ED.

Brown, L., Sherbenou, R. J., & Johnsen, S. K. (2010). *Test of nonverbal intelligence* (4th ed.). Austin, TX: PRO-ED.

Brown, L., Sherbenou, R., & Johnsen, S. (2014). *Test of Nonverbal Intelligence-4.* [ZEKA TESTİ UYGULAYICI YETİŞTİRME SERTİFİKA KURSU]. Konya, Turkey: Mevlana (Rumi) University. Turkish translation.

Brown, V. L., Hammill, D. D., & Wiederholt, J. L. (1986). *Test of reading comprehension-revised.* Austin, TX: PRO-ED.

Bryant, B. R., Patton, J., & Dunn, C. (1991). *Scholastic abilities test for adults.* Austin, TX: PRO-ED.

Cash, R. M. (1994). *An analysis of the performance of students who are hearing impaired on selected traditional measures of psychoeducational assessment.* Unpublished doctoral dissertation, Brigham Young University, Provo, UT. Retrieved from Pro-Quest Digital Dissertations database. (Publication No. AAT 9507258).

Cattell, R. B. (1943). The measurement of adult intelligence. *Psychological Bulletin, 40,* 153–193.

Cattell, R. B. (1963). Theory of fluid and crystallized intelligence: A critical experiment. *Journal of Educational Psychology, 54,* 1–22.

Chan, A. S., Cheung, J., Leung, W. W. M., Cheung, R., & Cheung, M. (2005). Verbal expression and comprehension deficits in young children with autism. *Focus on Autism and Other Developmental Disabilities, 20,* 117–124.

Clark, P. M. (1985). Review of the Test of Nonverbal Intelligence. In J. V. Mitchell Jr. (Ed.), *The ninth mental measurements yearbook* (pp. 1580–1581). Lincoln, NE: Buros Institute of Mental Measurements.

Cohen, R. J., Swerdlik, M. E., & Smith, D. K. (1992). *Psychological testing and assessment.* Mountain View, CA: Mayfield.

DeMauro, G. E. (2001). Review of the Test of Nonverbal Intelligence, Third Edition. In B. S. Plake & J. C. Impara (Eds.), *The fourteenth mental measurements year book* (pp. 1260–1262). Lincoln, NE: Buros Institute of Mental Measurements, University of Nebraska Press.

Department of Health and Education, Hong Kong. (1987). *Reynell developmental language scales (Chinese version).* Hong Kong: Author.

DeThorne, L. S., & Schaefer, B. A. (2004). A guide to child nonverbal IQ measures. *American Journal of Speech-Language Pathology, 13,* 275–290.

Dunn, L. M., & Dunn, L. M. (1997). *Peabody picture vocabulary test* (3rd ed.). Circle Pines, MN: American Guidance Service.

Edelson, M. G. (2005). A car goes in the garage like a can of peas goes in the refrigerator: Do deficits in real-world knowledge affect the assessment of intelligence in individuals with autism? *Focus on Autism and Other Developmental Disabilities, 20,* 2–9.

Educational Testing Service. (2002). *Scholastic aptitude test.* Lawrenceville, NJ: Author.

Endicott, J., Spitzer, R. L., Fleiss, J. L., & Cohen, J. (1976). The global assessment scale: A procedure for measuring overall severity of psychiatric severity. *Archives of General Psychiatry, 33,* 771–776.

Garcia, O.A. (1988). *Investigation del Test No Verbal de Inteligencia (TONI) en la Ciudad de Chihuahua.* Unpublished thesis, La Universidad Autonoma de Chihuahua, Chihuahua, Mexico.

Guilford, J. P. (1956). The structure of intellect. *Psychological Bulletin, 53,* 267–293.

Hammill, D. D. (1987). An overview of assessment practices. In D. D. Hammill (Ed.), *Assessing the abilities and instructional needs of students* (pp. 5–37). Austin, TX: PRO-ED.

Hammill, D. D., & Bryant, B. R. (1991). *Detroit tests of learning ability-adult.* Austin, TX: PRO-ED.

Hammill, D. D., Pearson, N. A., & Wiederholt, J. L. (1996). *Comprehensive test of nonverbal intelligence.* Austin, TX: PRO-ED.

Hammill, D. D., Pearson, N. A., & Wiederholt, J. L. (2009). *Comprehensive test of nonverbal intelligence* (2nd ed.). Austin, TX: PRO-ED.

Hammill, D. D., & Newcomer, P. L. (1988a). *Test of language development-intermediate* (2nd ed.). Austin, TX: PRO-ED.

Hammill, D. D., & Newcomer, P. L. (1988b). *Test of language development-primary* (2nd ed.). Austin, TX: PRO-ED.

Handleman, J. S., & Delmolino, L. M. (2005). Assessment of children with autism. In D. B. Zager (Ed.), *Autism spectrum disorders: Identification, education, and treatment* (3rd ed., pp. 269–294). London: Routledge.

Harrington, R. G. (1985). Test of Nonverbal Intelligence. In D. J. Keyser & R. C. Sweetland (Eds.), *Test critiques* (pp. 787–798). Kansas City, MO: Test Corporation of America, West Port Publishers.

Hieronymous, A. N., & Hoover, H. (1985). *Iowa tests of basic skills.* Chicago: Riverside Publishing.

Holt, J. A., Traxler, C. B., & Allen, T. E. (1992). *Interpreting the scores: A user's guide to the 8th edition Stanford achievement test for educators of deaf and hard of hearing students.* Washington, DC: Gallaudet University, Center for Demographic Studies.

Hopkins, W. G. (2002). *A scale of magnitudes for effect statistics.* Retrieved from http://www.sportsci.org/resource/stats/effectmag.html

Horn, J. L. (1968). Organization of abilities and the development of intelligence. *Psychological Review, 75,* 242–259.

Horn, J. L. (1985). Remodeling old models of intelligence. In B. Woman (Ed.), *Handbook of intelligence* (pp. 267–300). New York: Wiley.

Horn, J. L., & Cattell, R. B. (1966). Refinement and test of the theory of fluid and crystallized general intelligences. *Journal of Educational Psychology, 57,* 253–270.

Jastak, J. F., & Wilkinson, G. S. (1984). *Wide range achievement test, revised.* Wilmington, DE: Jastak Assessment Systems.

Jensen, A. (1980). *Bias in mental testing.* New York: Free Press.

Johnsen, S. K., Brown, L., & Sherbenou, R. J. (2010). *Test of nonverbal intelligence: Critical reviews and research findings, 1982–2009.* Austin, TX: PRO-ED.

Johnsen, S. K., & Corn, A. L. (1987). *Screening assessment for gifted elementary students.* Austin, TX: PRO-ED.

Kaufman, A. S., & Kaufman, N. L. (1983). *K-ABC: kaufman assessment battery for children.* Circle Pines, MN: American Guidance Service.

Kaufman, A. S., & Kaufman, N. L. (2004). *Kaufman test of educational achievement* (2nd ed.). Circle Mines, MN: American Guidance Service.

Kern, J., Cauller, L. J., & Dodd, M. (2000). Application of the Test of Nonverbal Intelligence (TONI-2) in children diagnosed with autism/PDD. *Journal of Developmental and Learning Disabilities, 4*(1), 119–131.

Kosslyn, S. M., & Koenig, O. (1992). *Wet mind: The new cognitive neuroscience.* New York: Free Press.

Lassiter, K. S., & Bardos, A. N. (1992). A comparison of learning-disabled children's performance on the test of nonverbal intelligence, K-ABC, and WISC-R. *Journal of Psychoeducational Assessment, 10*, 133–140.

Leiter, R. G. (1948). *The leiter international performance scales.* Chicago: Stoelting Company, Psychological & Educational Tests Division.

Levine, M. N. (1982). *The leiter international performance scales handbook.* Los Angeles: Western Psychological Services.

Mackinson, J. (1996). *Study of validity of the TONI-2 with deaf children.* Unpublished doctoral dissertation, Gallaudet University, Washington, DC.

Mackinson, J. A., Leigh, I. W., Blennerhassett, L., & Anthony, S. (1997). Validity of the TONI-1 with deaf and hard of hearing children. *American Annals of the Deaf, 142*, 294–299.

Madden, R., Gardner, E. R., Rudman, H. C., Karlsen, B., & Merwin, J. C. (1973). *Stanford achievement test.* New York: Harcourt Brace Jovanovich.

Mayer, R. E. (1992). *Thinking, problem solving, cognition* (2nd ed.). New York: Freeman.

Mayo, S. T. (1985). Review of the Test of Nonverbal Intelligence. In J. V. Mitchell Jr. (Ed.), *The ninth mental measurements yearbook* (pp. 1581–1583). Lincoln, NE: Buros Institute of Mental Measurements.

McLoughlin, J. A., & Lewis, R. B. (1986). *Assessing special students* (2nd ed.). Columbus, OH: Merrill.

McLoughlin, J. A., & Lewis, R. B. (1994). *Assessing special students* (4th ed.). Columbus, OH: Merrill.

McLoughlin, J. A., & Lewis, R. B. (2005). *Assessing special students* (6th ed.). Columbus, OH: Merrill.

Muñoz-Sandoval, A. F., Cummins, J., Alvarado, C. G., & Ruef, M. L. (1998). *Bilingual verbal ability tests.* Itasca, IL: Riverside.

Naslund, R. A., Thorpe, L. P., & Lefever, D. W. (1978). *SRA Achievement series.* Chicago: Science Research Associates.

Newcomer, P. L. (1990). *Diagnostic achievement battery* (2nd ed.). Austin, TX: PRO-ED.

Newcomer, P. L., & Bryant, B. R. (1993). *Diagnostic achievement test for adolescents* (2nd ed.). Austin, TX: PRO-ED.

Otis, A. S., & Lennon, R. T. (1970). *The Otis-Lennon mental ability test.* New York: Harcourt Brace Jovanovich.

Parmar, R.S. (1988). *Cross-cultural validity of the test of nonverbal intelligence.* Unpublished doctoral dissertation, North Texas State University, Denton.

Pierangelo, R., & Giuliani, G. A. (1998). *Special educator's complete guide to 109 diagnostic tests.* Upper Saddle River NJ: Prentice-Hall.

Prado, S. A. (1988). *Developing a slide projection group administration procedure for the TONI.* Unpublished manuscript, Universidad Austral del Chile, Valdivia, Chile.

Prado, S. A., Gatica, M. A., & Rojas, C. C. (1993). Instrumento de medición de actividad cognitiva libre del lenguaje: Test of Nonverbal Intelligence (T.O.N. I.). *Revista Terapia Psicológica, 19*, 23–35.

Raven, J. C. (1938). *Standard progressive matrices: A perceptual test of intelligence.* London: H. K. Lewis.

Raven, J. C. (1947). *Coloured progressive matrices.* London: H. K. Lewis.

Raven, J. C. (1960). *Guide to standard progressive matrices.* London: H. K. Lewis.

Raven, J. C. (1962). *Advanced progressive matrices.* London: H. K. Lewis.

Raven, J. C. (1965). *Guide to using the colored progressive matrices.* London: H. K. Lewis.

Raven, J. C. (1977). *The raven progressive matrices.* San Antonio: The Psychological Corporation.

Raven, J. C. (1986). *A compendium of North American normative and validity studies.* San Antonio: The Psychological Corporation.

Resnick, L. B., & Glaser, R. (1976). Problem solving and intelligence. In L. B. Resnick (Ed.), *The nature of intelligence* (pp. 205–230). Hillsdale, NJ: Erlbaum.

Reynolds, C. R., & Fletcher-Janzen, E. (Eds.). (2004). *Concise encyclopedia of special education: A reference for the education of the handicapped and other exceptional children and adults* (2nd ed.). Hoboken, NJ: Wiley.

Reynolds, C. R., & Kamphaus, R. W. (2003). *Reynolds intellectual assessment scales.* Lutz, FL: Psychological Assessment Resources.

Reynolds, C. R., Livingston, R. G., & Wilson, V. (2009). *Measurement and assessment in education* (2nd ed.). Boston: Allyn & Bacon.

Roberts, F. (1990). Review of the test of nonverbal intelligence. *Journal of Psychoeducational Assessment, 8*(2), 98–101.

Roid, G. H., & Miller, L. J. (1997). *Leiter international performance scale* (Rev ed.). Wood Dale, IL: Stoelting.

Salas, B. A. (1988). *The characteristics of dyslexic students in public schools: An operational definition.* Unpublished doctoral dissertation, University of Texas at Austin.

Salvia, J., & Ysseldyke, J. E. (1988). *Assessment* (4th ed.). Boston: Houghton Mifflin Company.

Salvia, J., & Ysseldyke, J. E. (1995). *Assessment* (6th ed.). Boston: Houghton Mifflin Company.

Salvia, J., Ysseldyke, J. E., & Bolt, S. (2007). *Assessment in special and inclusive education* (10th ed.). Boston: Houghton Mifflin.

Sattler, J. M. (2001). *Assessment of children: Cognitive applications* (4th ed.). San Diego: Author.

Semel, E., Wiig, E. H., & Secord, W. (1987). *Clinical evaluation of language functions-revised*. San Antonio: The Psychological Corporation.

Sheslow, D., & Adams, W. (1990). *Administrative manual for the wide range assessment of memory and learning*. Wilmington, DE: Jastak Assessment Systems.

Slosson, R. L. (1991). *Slosson intelligence test-revised (revised by C. L. Nicholson & T. H. Hibpsham)*. East Aurora, NY: Slosson Educational Publications.

Snyderman, M., & Rothman, S. (1988). *The IQ controversy, the media and public policy*. New Brunswick, NJ: Transaction Books.

Spearman, C. E. (1923). *The nature of intelligence and the principles of cognition*. London: Macmillan.

Spragins, A. B. (1998). *Reviews of four types of assessment instruments used with deaf and hard of hearing students, 1998 update*. Washington, DC: Gallaudet Research Institute, Gallaudet University.

Sternberg, R. J. (1981). Intelligence and nonentrenchment. *Journal of Educational Psychology, 73*, 1–16.

Sternberg, R. J. (1984). *Toward a triarchic theory of human intelligence*. Cambridge: Cambridge University Press.

Sternberg, R. J., & Detterman, D. K. (Eds.). (1986). *What is intelligence?*. Norwood, NJ: Ablex.

Strauss, E., Sherman, E. M. S., & Spreen, O. (2006). *A compendium of neuropsychological tests: Administration, norms, and commentary* (3rd ed.). Oxford: Oxford University Press.

Swaminathan, H., & Roger, H. J. (1990). Detecting differential item functioning using logistic regression procedures. *Journal of Educational Measurement, 26*, 55–66.

Thurstone, L. L. (1938). *Primary mental abilities*. Monograph No: Psychometric Monographs. 1.

Thurstone, L. L. (1944). *A factorial study of perception*. Chicago: University of Chicago Press.

U.S. Bureau of the Census. (1980). *Statistical abstract of the United States: 1980* (101st ed.). Washington, DC: U.S. Department of Commerce, Bureau of the Census.

U.S. Bureau of the Census. (1985). *Statistical abstract of the United States: 1985* (105th ed.). Washington, DC: U.S. Department of Commerce, Bureau of the Census.

U.S. Bureau of the Census. (1990). *Statistical abstract of the United States: 1990* (110th ed.). Washington, DC: U.S. Department of Commerce, Bureau of the Census.

U.S. Bureau of the Census. (2007). *Statistical abstract of the United States: 2007* (126th ed.). Washington, DC: U.S. Department of Commerce, Bureau of the Census.

Watson, T. S. (1992). Review of the Test of Nonverbal Intelligence—Second Edition. In J. Conoley & J. Kramer (Eds.), *The tenth mental measurements yearbook* (pp. 970–972). Lincoln, NE: Buros Institute of Mental Measurements.

Wechsler, D. (1974). *Wechsler intelligence scale for children-revised*. San Antonio: The Psychological Corporation.

Wechsler, D. (1981). *Wechsler adult intelligence scale-revised*. San Antonio: The Psychological Corporation.

Wechsler, D. (1991). *Wechsler intelligence scale for children* (3rd ed.). San Antonio: The Psychological Corporation.

Wechsler, D. (1997). *Wechsler adult intelligence scale* (3rd ed.). San Antonio, TX: The Psychological Corporation.

Wechsler, D. (2003). *Wechsler intelligence scale for children* (4th ed.). San Antonio, TX: The Psychological Corporation.

Wechsler, D. (2008). *Wechsler adult intelligence scale* (4th ed.). San Antonio, TX: The Psychological Corporation.

Woodcock, R. W. (1977). *Woodcock-johnson psycho-educational battery*. Allen, TX: DLM/Teaching Resources.

Woodcock, R. W. (1998). *WRMT-R: Woodcock reading mastery tests* (Rev ed.). Circle Pines, MN: American Guidance Service.

Woodcock, R. W., & Johnson, M. B. (1989). *Woodcock-johnson psycho-educational battery* (Rev ed.). Itasca, IL: Riverside.

Woodcock, R. W., McGrew, K. S., & Mather, N. (2001). *Woodcock-johnson III tests of cognitive abilities*. Itasca, IL: Riverside.

Wu-Tien, W., Chung-chien, T., Jyh-fen, H. J. W., Hsin-tai, L., & Ching-chih, K. (1995). *The chinese version of the test of nonverbal intelligence (TONI-2) and its related studies*. Taipei, Taiwan: Taiwan Normal University.

# The General Ability Measure for Adults

Amber Stieg Green, Achilles Bardos
and Maris Doropoulou

The assessment of cognitive abilities for individuals from diverse linguistic and cultural backgrounds has posed a challenge to psychologists for over a century. For example, nonverbal intelligence tests played a significant role in the psychological evaluations of recruits at the first Word War since many of them were either non-English-speaking immigrants or individuals with little or no formal schooling. They also played a significant role when evaluating the immigrants arriving at Ellis island in New York. Today, psychologists are still facing similar issues when assessing the cognitive ability of individuals in the general population who are either linguistically different from the English-speaking population and therefore are at

a disadvantage when taking tests that have verbal directions, require verbal expressive skills, or exposure to formal schooling. Given the well-documented changes of the population demographics in the United States, nonverbal intelligence tests are as important today as they were a century ago.

## Goals and Rationale for GAMA Development

The General Ability Measure for Adults (GAMA; Naglieri and Bardos 1997), is an instrument that is accessible to persons with a wide variety of backgrounds; it is a nonverbal test that is free of the confounding characteristics of expressive language skills and exposure to a formal English-speaking academic environment. Naglieri and Bardos (1997) stated that the GAMA "evaluates an individual's overall general ability with items that require the application of reasoning and logic to solve problems that exclusively use abstract designs and shapes" (p. 1). In this respect, the GAMA does not follow a particular theoretical model but rather attempts to offer an alternative to the measure of general ability after recognizing many inherent problems with tests of general ability that use subtests that have been used as measures of nonverbal ability

For a continuous update on research studies regarding the GAMA and the GAMA-2 and to obtain a training CD, the reader is encouraged to contact the author at: abardos@unco.edu.

A. Stieg Green (✉)
University of Northern Colorado, Greeley, CO, USA
e-mail: stie3366@bears.unco.edu

A. Bardos
Division of School Psychology, University of Northern Colorado, McKee Hall 289 Campus, Box 131, Greeley, CO 80639-0001, USA
e-mail: achilles.bardos@unco.edu

M. Doropoulou
Athens, Greece
e-mail: mdorop@primedu.uoa.gr

© Springer International Publishing AG 2017
R.S. McCallum (ed.), *Handbook of Nonverbal Assessment*,
DOI 10.1007/978-3-319-50604-3_12

despite the fact that their administration directions include lengthy and wordy verbal directions (see for example the Wechsler series of tests).

## History of Test Development

The primary goal for the development of the GAMA was to design a test that assesses general ability through a variety of nonverbal tasks that can be administered in various settings (individual or group) and with multiple formats using an online administration and scoring through the publisher's Q-global platform (http://www.pearsonclinical.com/psychology/products/100000200/general-ability-measure-for-adults-gama.html), various test item booklets (spiral bound, paper booklet, laminated booklet) and client response answer sheets (hand-scoring, scannable). Another goal was the development of a test that was normed on a large population so that age-specific and age-sensitive norms can be derived by including a sufficient number of individuals per age group. There were indeed a number of adult intelligence tests available at the time the GAMA was designed. However, in some cases and with very known instruments, a careful examination of their norming samples revealed serious and significant limitations in terms of both the formation of the age-norming groups as well as their sample size used to derive their norms. This is especially true for the assessment of older individuals, where one notices that the normative age groups sometimes span over 20 years (i.e., 65–85) thus including within one age group individuals who are developmentally at different life-stages and quite often include small sample sizes. An additional goal of the GAMA was the reduction of the influence of motor requirements through the elimination of manipulatives as well as the reduction of the influence of speed at the item level.

Following pilot studies of approximately 200 test items in an initial item pool, the final test was selected on the basis of a series of psychometric studies. These studies included examining mean scores by age and gender, examining biased items, computing the internal consistency coefficients for each item type as well as item difficulty and item discrimination values. Correlations with traditional individually administered tests were also obtained at the pilot stages of development. Since this is a self-administered test that can be group administered as well, the amount of time necessary for test administration was examined. A 25-minute time interval was selected.

## Description of GAMA

The GAMA is comprised of 66 items that are organized in four item types named Matching, Analogies, Sequences, and Construction.

The "Matching" subtest items require the subject to perceive the various shapes and color combinations, pay attention to details, and find the two shapes that are identical (see Fig. 12.1).

The "Analogies" subtest requires the examinee to recognize the relationship between two abstract figures in the first pair and then identify the option that completes the relationship in the second pair of designs (see Fig. 12.2).

In the "Sequence" subtest the subject is required to recognize the pattern, shape, and location of a design and complete the logical sequence of the presented pattern of designs (see Fig. 12.3).

Finally, in the "Construction" subtest, "items require the examinee to determine how several shapes can be combined to produce one of the designs" (p. 5; Naglieri and Bardos 1997) (see Fig. 12.4).

The four subtests and their scores do not represent different kinds of ability, but rather four different ways to measure general ability in nonverbal means. All items use yellow, white, black, and blue colors to enhance the presentation of the materials, making them attractive and engaging and reduce the effects of impaired color vision for some examinees.

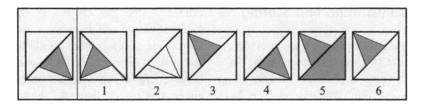

**Fig. 12.1** Matching sample item

**Fig. 12.2** Analogies
sample item

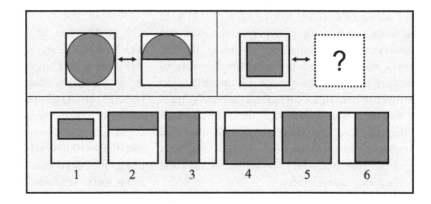

**Fig. 12.3** Sequences
sample item

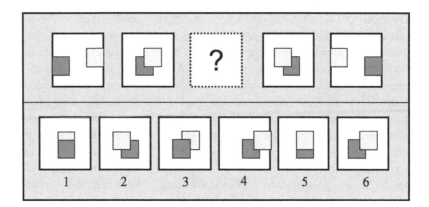

**Fig. 12.4** Construction
sample item

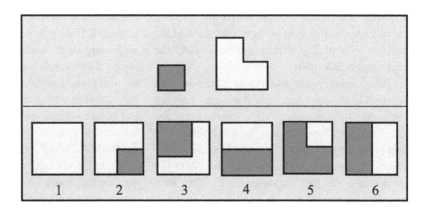

## GAMA Administration and Scoring

Administration and scoring of the GAMA is simple. The GAMA can be administered on a computer with Q-global (Pearson 2014) or using paper and pencil format. Examiners who have completed a psychological assessment course and are eligible to administer intelligence and personality tests should have no difficulty with the administration and scoring of the GAMA. In addition, with proper supervision, examiner assistants can be trained to administer the test using the guidelines provided for the various settings and with the various test materials and answer sheets. In all cases the examiner(s) must familiarize themselves with the test materials which include: the technical manual, the item booklet (spiral bound) or the group item booklet and the two types of response forms, and the self-scoring answer sheet.

Computer administration is available through Pearson's web-based application Q-global (Pearson 2014). Q-global provides on-screen test administration, scoring, and reporting. The examiner(s) should familiarize themselves with both the Q-global platform and the GAMA manual before administration. On-screen instructions and four demonstration items are presented prior to test items and accompanying stimulus. The examinee can access the instruction at any time throughout the assessment and can mark items to review at a later time. On-screen administration of the GAMA is completed entirely online; paper and pencil testing items are not required. The minimal instructions required and items are presented in English; examinees need at least a second to third grade reading level ability to read and understand the instructions and items.

When using paper and pencil administration of the GAMA, the test directions are read out loud by the examiner who encourages the examinee to follow along in the test booklet and complete the four sample items. This affords the examiner the opportunity to teach the client the proper use of the response form. The item booklets are printed in both English and Spanish. Directions for the administration of the test are printed in the last chapter of the manual to facilitate ease of use. Examinees with a second to third grade reading ability should be able to read and understand the minimal printed instructions; however, for those who are unable to read in either English or Spanish, the examiner can pantomime the test directions. Upon completion of the samples, the examinee may begin the test with the exposure of the first item.

Scoring the GAMA is also very simple. The GAMA can be scored using the Q-global web-based scoring, Q-local desktop software, or self-scoring. A Q-global account is required for the web-based scoring. If the GAMA is administered using Q-global (Pearson 2014), a score report can be generated automatically. If the GAMA is administered using paper and pencil, and the examiner wishes to score the GAMA using the Q-Global or Q-Local options, the examinee's responses for each item can be entered manually and a report can be generated. The report includes all scores, narrative, and profile graphs. For a sample please follow the link into the publisher's web site. http://images. pearsonclinical.com/images/pa/pdfs/gamaprofile. pdf. Reports can be exported and saved to a computer or network drive. When a large number of examinees are assessed, such as in assessment centers, scannable answer sheets can be used for the administration of the test which thereafter can be scanned by the user or mailed to the publisher for processing. Use of a scanner is probably the most efficient method especially in settings where numerous forms need to be processed and access to the Internet might be limited or not available for various reasons (e.g., correctional facilities). If the self-scoring record form is used, all scoring steps needed are printed on the inside cover of the record form with no need to refer to the technical manual. In the self-scoring form, the examiner will find a section to score the test and obtain subtest and total raw score, calculate the subtest scale scores (mean 10, SD = 3) and the GAMA Total IQ score (mean 100, SD = 15) using the 11 norming tables which are printed on the record form. Additional scores such as comparisons between subtest scores (an optional analysis) percentile scores, confidence intervals, and classification ranges of scores can be calculated on the form.

## Standardization and Psychometric Properties of GAMA

According to the 2014 Standards for Educational & Psychological Testing "validity refers to the degree to which evidence and theory support the interpretation of test scores for purposed uses of tests" (p. 11). Tests are used to answer specific questions. The evidence presented in the technical manual and the information generated in the professional literature about a test allows users to judge the quality of inferences that can be made by a test's score(s) or stated differently, how well the test answers those specific questions. In the next few paragraphs, evidence will be presented regarding the psychometric qualities of the GAMA in support of its claim as a measure of general cognitive ability. Tests are used to answer specific questions. The evidence presented in the technical manual and the information generated in the professional literature about a test allows users to judge the quality of inferences that can be made by a test's score(s) or stated differently, how well the test answers those specific questions. In the next few paragraphs, evidence will be presented regarding the psychometric qualities of the GAMA in support of its claim as a measure of general cognitive ability.

A normative test requires a well-designed standardization sample. The GAMA standardization sample consisted of 2360 people who ranged in age from 18–96 years and closely approximated the U.S. population according to the 1990 US census (U.S. Department of Commerce 1992, 1994) using gender, educational background, race or ethnic group, and geographic region as stratification variables. Standardization data were collected in 80 cities and 23 states across the U.S. Eleven age groups were used to collect data allowing a sufficient number of individuals to represent each age group. The sample size ranged from 219 individuals for the 70–74 age group to 310 for the 25–34 year age

group. This allowed for the calculation of sensitive age-specific norms.

The GAMA offers reliable scores. The median internal consistency across 11 age groups for the GAMA Total score was 0.90 with values ranging from 0.79 for the older group (80 plus years) to 0.94 for the 35–44 year olds. Reliability coefficients greater than 0.90 were observed in seven out of the eleven age groups of the test. Average reliabilities for the four item types were 0.65, 0.66, 0.79, and 0.81 for the Construction, Matching, Sequences, and Analogies subtests, respectively. Stability coefficients were estimated with a test-retest study that included 86 adults tested across a 2–6-week test interval. With a mean test-retest interval of 25 days, the GAMA IQ score produced a stability coefficient of 0.67. The four item types produced test–retest correlations that ranged from 0.38 (Construction) to 0.74 (Sequences). Gain scores of slightly less than one-third standard deviation was consistent across the item types and GAMA IQ Score.

Multiple sources of evidence exist regarding the instrument's validity as a measure of overall general cognitive ability. These include, the examination of developmental trends across the 11 age groups, relationships with other intelligence tests measuring similar constructs, correlations with achievement tests and performance of individuals of special populations (learning disabilities, deaf, elderly nursing home residents, individuals with traumatic brain injuries, and individuals with intellectual disabilities).

The trend of scores in the GAMA across the 11 age groups followed the expected (for adults) pattern of diminishing over time scores in visual/spatial reasoning skills. Correlations of raw scores with age ranged from −0.43 to −0.56 for the subtests and −0.59 for the GAMA IQ total score.

Mean scores and correlations with individually administered comprehensive batteries such as the Wechsler Adult Intelligence Scales (Wechsler 1981, 1997) and the Kaufman Adolescent & Adult Intelligence Scale (KAIT; Kaufman and Kaufman 1990) were also examined. The GAMA IQ scores earned were consistently similar to scores in the WAIS-R,

WAIS-III, and KAIT. In addition, high and significant correlations were obtained between the GAMA and the scale scores that measure similar constructs. This was the case for subjects selected from the regular population (Naglieri and Bardos 1997), college age populations (Lassiter et al. 2000), individuals with learning disabilities (Naglieri and Bardos 1997), individuals with intellectual disabilities (Naglieri and Bardos 1997), and individuals with traumatic brain injuries (Donders 1999; Martin et al. 2000).

In studies that utilized brief intelligence tests such as the Kaufman Brief Intelligence Test (K-BIT; Kaufman and Kaufman 1990), the Shipley Institute of Living Scale (Zachary 1991) and the Wonderlic Personnel Test (Wonderlic 1992), the GAMA performed similarly to these instruments across college age populations (Leverett et al. 2001), individuals in nursing homes (Festa et al. 1999), and individuals with sudden neurological impairment (Davis et al. 2006). These studies illustrate that the GAMA offers similar cognitive ability scores to the other instruments thus leading to similar decisions.

The relationship between the GAMA and measures of academic achievement was also examined. Significant correlations were observed with the Nelson–Denny Reading Test for a sample of college students and with the Mini-Battery of Achievement for a sample derived from the general population (Festa and Bardos 2000). Significant correlations with reading subtests on the Wide Range Achievement Test-Third Edition for a sample of adults with HIV were also observed (Ryan et al. 2008). The magnitude of the coefficients observed are similar (mid 0.50) to the ones reported between other nonverbal reasoning tests and measures of achievement. The Ryan et al. (2008) study compared the GAMA and reading among a cohort of HIV patients that consisted predominantly of ethnic/racial minorities with less than an 8th grade reading level. The GAMA demonstrated a stronger correlation with global neuropsychological functioning than reading scores on the WRAT-3. In participants with less than an 8th grade reading level, the WRAT-3 was not associated with any neuropsychological domain;

the GAMA was found to have strong significant correlations. Across all samples, the GAMA was associated less with participant's education levels than the WRAT-3. The researchers concluded that "… the GAMA appears to provide valuable information for understanding individuals who may have ineffective instruction, and it should be considered in a neuropsychological evaluation when reading scores are < 80 SS" (p. 1029).

The GAMA has been used to examine the relationship between cognitive ability and job performance. Ability scores derived from the GAMA had a correlation with and predicted job performance in a population of probation and parole staff (Ogard and Karr 1998) and in a population of public and private employees in Romania (Ispas et al. 2010). These studies suggest the GAMA may be a useful tool in employee selection.

Numerous cross culture studies have utilized the GAMA as a measure of cognitive ability. The GAMA has been normed in Romania following the same procedures applied in the United States and with a successful extension of the normative population to age 16 (Iliescu and Livinti 2008). Validity evidence has been established with a sample of Romanian university students (Brazdau and Mihai 2011), and a population of public and private employees in Romania (Ispas et al. 2010). A Dutch version of the GAMA was also used for a sample of nurses from the Netherlands that work with individuals with intellectual disabilities and severe behavior problems (Gerits et al. 2004). A study with 113 individuals (mean age 20.4 years old) in Mexico was also conducted and found the GAMA test scores to be similar to those of a matched control sample from the United States (Bardos et al. 2007). Concurrent validity studies utilizing the GAMA with other instruments, such as the Wechsler Abbreviated Scale of Intelligence (WASI; Wechsler 1999) also reported similar mean performance and significant correlations between the two tests for a sample of 59 adults (mean age 32.4 years old) in Greece (Dieti and Bardos 2012) and another sample of 63 individuals (mean age 32.7 years old) who were administered the GAMA and the Kaufman Brief

Intelligence Test (K-BIT2; Kaufman and Kaufman 2004). The GAMA was also administered to a matched sample of Greek and U.S. subjects (Petrogiannis et al. 1999), and a sample of adults from six regions in Greece (Spyridaki et al. 2014) with once again similar performance. In all of these cross-cultural studies, the differences between the samples on the GAMA Total scores were minimal, while the correlations obtained with other intelligence tests administered, were statistically significant, offering further support for the "easy transport" of a nonverbal test like the GAMA and its potential use across cultures.

In summary, the studies discussed above demonstrate that the GAMA offers reliable scores and has accumulated numerous evidence for its use and inferences that can be made by its scores as a measure of general cognitive ability.

## GAMA Interpretation

Although the administration and scoring procedures of the GAMA are simple and can be accomplished by individuals with varying degrees of training in psychological testing and assessment, interpretation of the GAMA should always be made by individuals with formal training in psychological assessment. As always, it is best to consult the local licensing boards and/or regulatory agencies regarding test administration, test interpretation, and necessary supervisory arrangements.

The GAMA was designed to offer an estimate of a person's overall cognitive ability measured in nonverbal means. The GAMA total score represents this effort; it is the most reliable score across all age groups; therefore it is the score to use when interpreting the test. Consistent with other intelligence and achievement tests, the GAMA total IQ score is organized with a mean of 100 and a standard deviation of 15. Examiners are strongly encouraged to report confidence intervals scores as well as classification ranges of a person's overall ability thus enhancing the meaning of the GAMA total IQ score. Although intra-individual subtest scores can be calculated for the four item types to determine strengths and

weakness, the four item types were not developed to represent separate cognitive abilities but rather they are different means of assessing general cognitive ability in nonverbal means.

When a strength or a weakness is found in a client's profile, the score(s) should be interpreted considering both a normative as well as an intra-individual point of view. For example, a scale score of 9 might be a weakness in a person's intra-individual profile but the score is still ranked in the average range of ability when compared to individuals the same age. This weakness will be described as a relative weakness. A score of 6 identified as a weakness in an examinee's intra-individual profile analysis is best being described as a cognitive weakness because, it is ranked below one standard deviation when compared to individuals the same chronological age.

The GAMA can also be used as a progress monitoring tool especially for those examinees whose psychological evaluation and possible subsequent therapy is associated with a traumatic brain injury. A table was developed to assist the examiner in determining if a change in scores from one administration to the other is a reliable change. The table offers the range of scores expected for such determination. Finally, in interpreting the GAMA test scores, especially when comparing the test score with other measures of cognitive ability (e.g., WAIS-IV), the examiner should consider the unique features of the test. The GAMA requires no manipulatives, has very minimal directions requiring listening comprehension skills of the English language, and performance on the test is not affected by item-specific bonus points earned for speeded performance.

Practitioners who utilize the GAMA as part of a comprehensive evaluation might wish to compare the GAMA results to scores earned in other intelligence Wechsler Adult Intelligence Scale (WAIS-IV; Wechsler 2008) or Wechsler Abbreviated Scale of Intelligence®—Second Edition (WASI-II; Wechsler 2011) or achievement tests such as the Wide Range Achievement Test—Fourth Edition (WRAT4; Wilkinson and Robertson 2004) or the Basic Achievement Skills

Inventory—Survey (BASI-Survey; Bardos 1995). Tables 12.1 and 12.2 present the values needed to consider if the performance in the GAMA is significantly different from these intelligence and achievement tests.

## Strengths and Weaknesses of GAMA

The GAMA with its administration format and excellent psychometric properties offers numerous advantages when an alternative instrument is needed to estimate a person's overall cognitive ability. Those in private practice who desire an estimate of their adult clients' cognitive ability can administer the test with minimal effort. Similarly, computer administration and group booklets can assist in the testing of small or large groups of individuals. This might be the case in correctional or personnel settings, in research studies or whenever an efficient measure of cognitive ability is desired. In addition, the GAMA can be easily adopted by researchers from other cultures who desire an adept nonverbal assessment for the testing of individuals or groups. The validity evidence from independent research studies regarding the inferences that can be made by the GAMA score as a measure of general cognitive ability is overwhelmingly supportive.

Regarding its weaknesses, the GAMA does require minimal directions requiring second grade level reading ability and/or some receptive language skills, and it only offers item booklets printed in English and Spanish. Pantomime administration of the test addresses this limitation; however, a better alternative might be translations of these brief directions in various languages. This might make the GAMA more acceptable in cultures outside the United States or for those who live in the US but do not speak English or Spanish. Computer administration is only available in English and requires a third grade reading level. Further development of on-screen administration to include pictorial instructions and instructions in various languages might increase the population of individuals who can utilize this platform.

**Table 12.1** Values needed for significance when comparing the GAMA score with the WRAT-IV or BASI-survey achievement tests

| | | $p < 0.05$ | $p < 0.10$ |
|---|---|---|---|
| WRAT-IV | Word reading | 12 | 11 |
| Blue form | Sentence comprehension | 12 | 10 |
| | Reading composite | 11 | 9 |
| | Spelling | 13 | 11 |
| | Math computation | 13 | 11 |
| WRAT-IV | Word reading | 12 | 11 |
| Green form | Sentence comprehension | 12 | 10 |
| | Spelling | 13 | 11 |
| | Math computation | 14 | 12 |
| | Reading composite | 11 | 9 |
| BASI-survey | Vocabulary | 10 | 8 |
| | Language mechanics | 10 | 8 |
| | Reading comprehension | 9 | 8 |
| | *Verbal skills total* | 11 | 10 |
| | Math computation | 10 | 8 |
| | Math application | 10 | 8 |
| | *Math skills total* | 12 | 11 |

WRAT-IV: Wide Range Achievement Test
BASI-Survey: Basic Achievement Skills Inventory—Survey

**Table 12.2** Values needed for significance when comparing the GAMA score with the WAIS-IV and WASI-II tests of intelligence

|        |          | $p < 0.05$ | $p < 0.10$ |
|--------|----------|------------|------------|
| WAIS-IV | VCI      | 9          | 11         |
|        | PSI      | 11         | 13         |
|        | WMI      | 10         | 12         |
|        | PRI      | 10         | 11         |
|        | FSIQ     | 9          | 10         |
| WASI-II | VCI      | 10         | 11         |
|        | PRI      | 10         | 12         |
|        | FSIQ (4) | 9          | 11         |
|        | FSIQ (2) | 10         | 12         |

As of the writing of this chapter, the GAMA is undergoing a national re-standardization. In addition to a more recent normative sample, the GAMA-2 will address much of the feedback we received from users in the field. For example, the GAMA-2 will:

- include a number of easier items at the beginning of the test to increase the sensitivity of the test for individuals with intellectual disabilities.
- eliminate written directions to the test in any language. These will be replaced with graphical representations that will communicate the demands of each task to be performed on the test.
- include two alternate forms of the GAMA-2 to facilitate test–retest and progress monitoring of an individual's performance.
- allow examiners to administer and generate report with the latest technologies available (e.g., tablet administration)

## Summary

The GAMA is a nonverbal test designed to evaluate an individual's overall general cognitive ability; it neither requires expressive language nor exposure to formal English-speaking academic content to complete. It offers an efficient research supported means to estimate a person's overall cognitive ability.

## References

American Educational Research Association, American Psychological Association, & National Council of Measurement in Education. (2014). *Standards for educational and psychological testing*. Washington, DC: AERA.

Bardos, A. N. (1995). *Basic achievement skills inventory—survey*. Bloomington MN: Pearson Assessments.

Bardos, A. N., Marlatt, H., Johnson, K., & Reva, K. (2007). *A cross-cultural investigation of the General Ability Measure for Adults (GAMA) in Mexico*. Paper presented at the annual meeting of the American Psychological Association, San Francisco, CA.

Brazdau, O., & Mihai, C. (2011). The consciousness quotient: A new predictor of the students academic performance. *Procedia Social and Behavioral Sciences, 11*, 245–250.

Davis, A. S., Bardos, A., & Woodward, K. (2006). Concurrent validity of the general ability measure for adults (GAMA) with sudden-onset neurological impairment. *The International Journal of Neuroscience, 116*, 1215–1221. doi:10.1080/00207450500516511

Dieti, E., & Bardos, A.N. (2012). Assessment of intelligence in Greece using the general ability measure for adults: Concurrent validity with the WAIS. In Paper presented at the 8th International Test Commission Conference, Amsterdam.

Donders, J. (1999). Psychometric intelligence in patients with traumatic brain injury: Utility of a new screening measure. *Archives of Physical Medical Rehabilitation, 80*, 346–347.

Festa, T., & Bardos, A. (2000). GAMA: Relationship to academic achievement. *Archives of Clinical Neuropsychology, 15*(8), 695–696. doi:10.1016/S0887-6177(00)800839

Festa, T., Sutton, L., Crawford, N., & Bardos, A. (1999). Measuring the cognitive ability of nursing home residents on the GAMA. *Archives of Clinical Neuropsychology, 14*(8), 664. doi:10.1016/S0887-6177(99)80086-9

Gerits, L., Derksen, J. J. L., & Verbruggen, A. B. (2004). Emotional intelligence and adaptive success of nurses caring for people with mental retardation and severe behavior problems. *Mental Retardation, 42*(2), 106–121. 10.1352/00476765(2004)42<106:EIAASO>2.0. CO;2.

Iliescu, D., & Livinți, R. (2008). *GAMA—General Ability Measure for Adults: Manual tehnicsi interpretativ*. Cluj- Napoca: Odiseea.

Ispas, D., Lliescu, D., Llie, A., & Johnson, R. (2010). Examining the criterion related validity of the general ability measure for adults: A two sample investigation. *International Journal of Selection and Assessment, 18* (2), 226–229.

Kaufman, A. S., & Kaufman, N. L. (1990). *K-BIT (Kaufman brief intelligence test) manual*. Circle Pines, MN: American Guidance Service.

Kaufman, A. S., & Kaufman, N. L. (2004). *Kaufman brief intelligence test*. John Wiley & Sons, Inc.

Lassiter, K., Maher, C. Matthews, T., Bell, N. (2000). The general ability measure for adults: A measure of Gf?. In Paper presented at the 108th annual convention of the American Psychological Association.

Leverett, P., Matthews, D., Lassiter, K., & Bell, N. (2001). Validity comparison of the general ability measure for adults with the Wonderlic personnel test. *North American Journal of Psychology, 3*(1), 173–182.

Martin, T. A., Donders, J., & Thompson, E. (2000). Potential of and problems with new measures of psychometric intelligence after traumatic brain injury. *Rehabilitation Psychology, 45*(4), 402–408. doi:10. 1037/0090-5550.45.4.402

Naglieri, J. A., & Bardos, A. N. (1997). *General ability measure for adults (GAMA)*. Minneapolis, MN: National Computer Systems.

Ogard, E., & Karr, C. (1998). *Psychological testing and concurrent validity study of probation & parole staff for the department of juvenile and adult community justice*. State of Oregon: Multnomah County.

Pearson, (2014). *Pearson clinical assessment Q-global user guide*. USA: Person Inc.

Petrogiannis, K., Bardos, A. N., & Politikos, N. (1999). A cross cultural investigation of the general ability measure for adults (GAMA) in Greece. In: Paper presented at the International Conference of Test Adaptation, Washington, DC.

Ryan, E. L., Byrd, D., Mindt, M. R., Rausch, W. J., & Morgello, S. (2008). Understanding the neuropsychological profile of hiv+participants with low literacy: Role of the general ability measure for adults (Gama). *The Clinical Neuropsychologist, 22*(6), 1018–1034. doi:10.1080/13854040701750883

Spyridaki, E. C., Simos, P., Avgoustinaki, P. D., Dermitzaki, E., Venihaki, M., Bardos, A. N., et al. (2014). The association between obesity and fluid intelligence impairment is mediated by chronic low-grade inflammation. *British Journal of Nutrition, 112*(10), 1724–1734. doi:10.1017/S0007114514002207

U.S. Department of Commerce. (1992, November). 1990 census of population, general population characteristics, United States (1 990 CP- 1 - 1). Washington, DC: Author.

U.S. Department of Commerce. (1994, January). 1990 census of population, education in the United States (1 990 CP-3-4). Washington, DC: Author.

Wechsler, D. (1981). *WAIS-R (Wechsler Adult Intelligence Scale-Revised) manual*. San Antonio, TX: The Psychological Corporation.

Wechsler, D. (1997). *WAIS-III (Wechsler Adult Intelligence Scale-Third Edition) manual*. San Antonio, TX: The Psychological Corporation.

Wechsler, D. (1999). *Wechsler Abbreviated Scale of Intelligence (WASI; Wechsler, 1999)*. Minneapolis, MN: Pearson Assessments.

Wechsler, D. (2008). *WAIS-IV (Wechsler Adult Intelligence Scale-Fourth Edition) administration and scoring manual*. San Antonio, TX: Psychological Corporation.

Wechsler, D. (2011). *Wechsler Abbreviated Scale of Intelligence (WASI-II; Wechsler, 2011)*. Minneapolis, MN: Pearson Assessments.

Wilkinson, G. S., & Robertson, G. (2004). Wide range achievement test (WRAT4). Bloomington, MN: Pearson Assessments.

Wonderlic Personnel Test and Scholastic Level Exam user's manual. (1992). Libertyville, IL: Wonderlic Personnel Test, Inc.

Zachary, R. A. (1991). *Shipley Institute of Living Scale revised manual*. Los Angeles: Western Psychological Services.

# Two Nonverbal Screeners: The Universal Multidimensional Abilities Scales and the Universal Nonverbal Intelligence Test-Group Abilities Test

## Sherry Mee Bell

The purpose of this chapter is to describe two screening instruments developed with the goal of being appropriate for the vast majority of examinees, regardless of language or cultural differences—hence the term *Universal* in their titles. Developed by R. Steve McCallum and Bruce Bracken, authors of the *Universal Nonverbal Intelligence Test* (*UNIT*; Riverside, 1998) and the *Universal Nonverbal Intelligence Test-2* (PRO-ED, 2016), these assessment tools share the goal of the *UNIT* instruments, to provide a fair assessment of examinees regardless of language abilities or language of origin. The *Universal Multidimensional Abilities Scales* (*UMAS*), designed to screen examinees in several domains related to academic success, is a six subscale rating scale completed by a teacher who knows the examinee well. The *Universal Nonverbal Intelligence Test-Group Abilities Test* (*UNIT-GAT*) is a two subtest, group administered screener of cognitive abilities. Used together or separately, these instruments efficiently provide information about examinees' levels of functioning across several domains and can be useful in the process of screening examinees for further assessment to determine eligibility for special services. These instruments share in common the philosophy that it is important to provide a fair assessment, despite cultural and language differences.

## Universal Multidimensional Abilities Scales (*UMAS*)

In the next sections I describe features of the *UMAS*, including test model and philosophy, structure (subtests), standardization characteristics, administration and scoring, and interpretation.

## Goals and Rationale for *UMAS* Development

The *UMAS* is designed as a screener of examinee (ages 5 through 17–11) behavior in six areas related to school success: (a) cognition, (b) creativity, (c) leadership, (d) literacy, (e) math, and (f) science. Unlike some other scales which focus on behaviors at one end of the intellectual continuum, the *UMAS* is designed to assess examinee performance across the range of abilities, and, thus, is designed to help identify examinees who exhibit intellectual giftedness, as well as intellectual disabilities, and specific learning disabilities. The purpose of the *UMAS* is to provide a fair assessment of all examinees, particularly those from diverse groups including individuals with speech and language disorders, who are deaf or hard of hearing, who do not speak English, and those examinees who live in poverty and/or lack exposure to mainstream

S.M. Bell (✉)
Department of Theory and Practice in Teacher Education, University of Tennessee, A204, 1122 Volunteer Boulevard, Knoxville, TN 37996-3442, USA
e-mail: sbell1@utk.edu

© Springer International Publishing AG 2017
R.S. McCallum (ed.), *Handbook of Nonverbal Assessment*,
DOI 10.1007/978-3-319-50604-3_13

cultural or language experiences. According to the authors, *UMAS* provides a fair(er) assessment in two ways: (a) by directing raters to evaluate examinees' success in each of the six domains assessed regardless of communication mode, language sophistication, etc., and (b) by requesting that raters use peer, school, and/or community standards when rating examinees.

## Description of the *UMAS*

The *UMAS* consists of six subscales (Cognition, Creativity, Leadership, Literacy, Math, and Science) that are completed by a teacher (classroom teacher, special education teacher, or other educator) who knows the examinee well. Each subscale has 15 items.

**Cognition**. Cognition items are designed to assess the rater's perceptions of examinees' cognitive abilities and focus on behaviors that can be expressed or demonstrated nonverbally or verbally, using any language system the examinee employs, (e.g., English, Spanish, American Sign Language, gestures, picture exchange system), and regardless of dialectical idiosyncrasies. The items are designed to tap problem solving, memory, use of abstract and logical thinking, quantitative reasoning, and processing speed, i.e., abilities identified as critical for academic success. According to McCallum and Bracken (2012), examinees who earn high scores on this subscale exhibit strengths in the cognitive skills necessary for mastery of academic skills in comparison to peers and those who earn low scores tend to have difficulty mastering skills needed for academic success.

**Creativity**. Creativity items are designed to assess the rater's perceptions of examinees' creativity, specifically, the ability to "produce original works or solutions that are valued by society" in "acting, dancing, drawing, music, painting, sculpting, and singing" and to exhibit originality, fluency and flexibility in their thinking (McCallum and Bracken 2012, p. 11). According to McCallum and Bracken, examinees who score high on this subscale are perceived as having "special gifts" while those who earn low

scores tend to be seen as concrete thinkers, as "more rigid, less flexible and spontaneous" than their more highly rated peers (p. 11).

**Leadership**. Leadership items assess the rater's perceptions of the extent to which examinees exhibit characteristics associated with leadership, e.g., "strong emotional sensitivity, stability, and leadership behaviors" (McCallum and Bracken, p. 11). Examinees who earn high scores on this subscale tend to be seen as leaders who can influence positively group behavior, gain others' confidence, demonstrate initiative, and influence others because of their interpersonal skills. Examinees who score low on this subscale tend to be less respected by peers, less likely to been seen as role models, and have less influence on the behavior of others.

**Literacy**. Literacy items are designed to assess the rater's perceptions of examinees' literacy skills, including reading, spelling and writing, as well as language skills, using whatever language system the examinee has available. *UMAS* items, according to McCallum and Bracken (2012), are designed to be sensitive to examinees who speak English as a second language, use American Sign Language, exhibit language disorders, and/or who are "new to the mainstream culture" (p. 11). According to McCallum and Bracken, examinees who score high on the Literacy subscale are viewed as being able to acquire knowledge easily and incidentally as well as to learn skills presented via instruction while those who score low on this subscale have difficulty acquiring academic content and mastering daily living skills, particularly those associated with functional communication.

**Math**. Math items are designed to assess the rater's perceptions of examinees' quantitative and problem solving skills. According to McCallum and Bracken (2012), examinees who score highly on this subscale are viewed as "being facile with numbers, understanding numerical relationships, solving problems quickly, and having a global ability" (p. 11) to understand mathematical relationships and patterns. Because these examinees tend to use sophisticated math strategies and are faster at calculating and estimating, they tend to be more successful in math classes then lower rated peers who grasp math relationships and patterns less quickly and who make more computation errors.

**Science**. Science items are designed to assess the rater's perceptions of examinees' appreciation of cause and effect relationships in the "natural, social, and physical environments" as well as understanding and using problem solving and appreciating classification and categorization (McCallum and Bracken 2012, p. 12). According to the authors, examinees who earn high scores on this scale tend to better understand the "causal physical and social structures within their environment" (p. 12) and they tend to gather information and analyze it in solving problems while those who earn low scores tend to use trial and error and are less systematic in their thinking.

**General Aptitude Index**. Because it is a composite determined by combining the indexes from the six subscales, the General Aptitude Index is the most comprehensive score available from the *UMAS*. In general, examinees who score in the average range or better (Index score of 90 or higher) tend to experience more school success than peers who score below 90. Examinees who score above 115 tend to be enrolled in honors, advanced placement, and/or programs for individuals who are gifted and talented. Examinees who score well below average may exhibit intellectual disabilities, autism, or other significant developmental or learning disorders.

## Scores Provided

Each subscale contains 15 items; the rater rates the examinee on each item with a score from 1 to 5 (1 = Well Below Average; 2 = Below Average; 3 = Average; 4 = Above Average; 5 = Well Above Average). For each subscale, raw scores, percentiles, and Index Scores, Standard Error of Measure, and Descriptive Terms are available. In addition, a composite or General Aptitude Index is available. Subscale Index scores and the General Aptitude Index score are standard scores with a mean set to 100 and standard deviation set to 15. Descriptive terms are based on the score's distance from the mean: Very Delayed: <70;

Moderately Delayed: 70–79; Mildly Delayed: 80–89; Average: 90–100; Mildly Advanced: 111–120; Moderately Advanced: 121–130; Very Advanced: >130.

## UMAS Administration and Scoring

Before first administering the *UMAS*, McCallum and Bracken (2012) recommend that the examiner become thoroughly familiar with the manual, conduct a practice assessment by asking a teacher to complete an *UMAS* on a non-referred child and score and interpret the practice assessment, referring to the manual to ensure accurate scoring and interpretation. The authors refer to the person who is responsible for conducting the assessment as the examiner and the person who completes the *UMAS* as the rater. The rater should be someone very familiar with the examinee in a school setting (e.g., usually the teacher most responsible for instruction of the examinee, but possibly a school counselor or administrator). The examiner must ensure the rater understands the instructions and encourage the rater to complete all items in the *UMAS* Record Booklet which includes a cover page for recording examinee information, raw scores and derived scores, a set of instructions on the inside cover page, and one page containing the 15 questions for each subscale. Completing the *UMAS* should take the rater relatively little time to complete, perhaps 10–15 minutes.

Once completed by the rater, each *UMAS* subscale is easily scored by simply adding the numbers circled in each column and writing the sum in the space provided at the bottom of each column, then adding the sum for each column to obtain a subscale raw score. The raw score for each subscale is then transferred to the front page of the Record Booklet. Percentiles, index (standard) scores, and descriptive terms for each subscale are easily located in the manual. The composite (General Aptitude Index or GAI) is determined by adding the six subscale Index scores and locating the corresponding composite Index score in the manual. Because of the inherent "local norming" feature of the *UMAS*, raw scores and corresponding derived (i.e., percentile and index) scores do not vary by age, making it easy to locate the derived scores in the manual and reducing the chance for error in looking up scores associated with most norm-referenced tests containing multiple norm tables based on age and/or grade. Scoring the *UMAS* should be quick, 10 minutes or so. The manual contains an example case study that demonstrates how to complete the Record Booklet and scoring.

## Standardization and Psychometric Properties of the UMAS

The *UMAS* has an impressive sample size; it was normed on a sample of almost 3000 (2492) school-age examinees from 22 states in the United States. The number of examinees at each age of the standardization sample ranges from 157 at age 5 to 337 at age 10. Ages 14–15 and 16–17 are treated as one age group with 204 and 122 examinees, respectively. Given that many 5 years old have not yet entered school and some 17 year olds have graduated or left school, the smaller numbers at the bottom and end of the age range of the standardization sample are reasonable. According to the authors, the "*UMAS* normative sample is representative of the United States population as a whole" (p. 16). In the *UMAS* manual, McCallum and Bracken present a table showing the percentage of examinees based on geographic region of the U.S., sex, race, and ethnicity and, indeed, the percentages are quite consistent with the U.S. Census Bureau (2011).

## Reliability

Authors present several types of evidence for the reliability of the *UMAS*. In support of internal consistency of the *UMAS* subscales, authors report coefficient alpha statistics. Average Cronbach's alpha coefficients for the six subscales range from 0.98 to 0.99 with 0.99 for the General Aptitude Scale. In support of evidence for the stability of the *UMAS*, the authors report test–

retest reliability; 80 examinees between the ages of 5 and 17 were rated twice by their teacher raters. The authors do not explicitly state the time interval between administrations but it is implied that the time interval was 2–4 weeks. Test–retest correlations for the subscales ranged from 0.84 to 0.96 and test–retest reliability was 0.96 for the General Aptitude score. Unfortunately the number of teachers who participated in the test–retest study was not reported. In addition to internal consistency and test–retest reliability, the authors provide evidence of "scorer consistency"; 31 previously scored *UMAS* protocols were rescored by trained PRO-ED staff with a resulting reliability coefficient of 0.99. However, the authors do not address inter-rater reliability, that is, similarity of scores obtained by two different teachers. It should be noted that establishing inter-rater reliability is difficult for an instrument like the *UMAS* given that most examines only have one teacher, particularly at younger ages.

## Validity

The authors present evidence for several types of validity of the *UMAS*. To support content validity, the authors present information about the value of teacher ratings, the appropriateness of the content of *UMAS* items, and results of classical item analyses. McCallum and Bracken (2012) note that "a large and growing body of research testifies to the value of teacher ratings" and cite the work of Morine-Dershimer (1978–1979a, b) and more recent work on the accuracy of teacher judgments as well as documented "agreement between teacher ratings and the results of standardized achievement tests" (p. 26). To support content validity, the authors secondly discuss the theoretical basis of the *UMAS*, noting that they conducted a broad literature review to identify behaviors appropriate for the various domains of the *UMAS*. Each subscale of the *UMAS* has 15 items, distilled from a larger item pool ranging from 21 to 26 items per subscale. In keeping with the purpose of the *UMAS*, directions are worded to ensure raters are sensitive to performance regardless of language or communication medium of the examinee. Raters are instructed to "focus on how effectively the examinee communicates, regardless of the language or medium used" (*UMAS* Record Booklet, p. 2).

Conventional item analyses were also used to establish content validity of the *UMAS*. The authors present item discrimination statistics based on a point-biserial technique in which each item is correlated with the total score, in this case, each subscale total score. The median discriminating power for the *UMAS* ranges from 0.81 to 0.93 across the age ranges across the six subscales. These data indicate high levels of discriminating power, or the degree to which an item differentiates the behavior it is designed to measure.

To provide support of the *UMAS's* ability to correlate with other similar measures, *UMAS* scores of 105 examinees were correlated with their scores from the *Gifted Rating Scales* (*GRS*; Pfeiffer and Jarosewich 2003) and the *Tennessee Comprehensive Assessment Program* (*TCAP*; Tennessee Department of Education 2011). Correlations between the three scales of the *GRS* and the *UMAS* General Aptitude Index score range from 0.65 to 0.75 (when corrected for restriction in range) and from 0.65 to 0.72 between the *TCAP* and the *UMAS* General Aptitude Index. These correlations are large to very large in magnitude (Cohen 1988; Hopkins 2002). Correlations between the *UMAS* subscale scores and the *GRS* and the *TCAP* scores are lower, as would be expected but all are significant.

McCallum and Bracken (2012) present data on the comparative means and standard deviations of the *UMAS*, *GRS*, and *TCAP*. They found no significant difference in means between the *UMAS* and the *GRS* but the *TCAP* yielded higher means. The authors concluded that the *UMAS* might underestimate end of year academic measures.

McCallum and Bracken (2012) report Receiver Operating Characteristics (Area under the Curve; ROC/AUC) as a "measure of overall performance of a diagnostic test and is interpreted as the average value of sensitivity for all possible values of specificity" (Park et al. 2004, p. 13). Citing Compton et al. (2006), they note that ROC/AUCs of 0.90 and higher are excellent, 0.80–0.89 are good, 0.70–0.79 are fair, and 0.69 or below are poor. Because the *UMAS* is designed to screen for cognitive aptitude, the authors examined the ability of the *UMAS* to discriminate between examinees with high (i.e., potentially gifted/talented examinees) versus low-to-average cognitive ability and between those with low (i.e., potential examinees with intellectual disability) versus average-to-high cognitive ability. They determined sensitivity (or percent of true positives identified), specificity (or percent of true negatives identified), and ROC/AUC for a group of 157 examinees who had IQ score data available. General Aptitude Index (GAI) cut scores of 110, 115, and 120 were used to predict membership in high cognitive ability groups and cut scores of 90, 80, and 70 were used to predict membership in low cognitive ability groups. All cut scores yielded high ROC/AUC values, ranging from 0.983 to 0.986, meeting the most stringent criteria set by Compton et al. (2006). The sensitivity and specificity values for each of the cut scores were correspondingly strong, particularly for the low cognitive ability group; only one fell below 0.90; the GAI score of 70 yielded a sensitivity index of 0.83 ("good" per Compton et al.). The specificity values for the high ability group were all above 0.90, indicating very few false positives; the sensitivity values were not as robust, 0.81 ("good") for GAI cut off of 110; 0.75 ("fair") for GAI cutoff of 15; and 0.51 ("poor") for GAI cut off of 120. So, the cut off of 120 yielded a higher than acceptable rate of false negatives. This finding, along with the fact that the *UMAS* yielded lower mean scores than the *TCAP*, suggests that using a high cut score may not identify some examinees who are potentially gifted. In fact, McCallum and Bracken recommend using a cut score of 110 for screening/identifying examinees as gifted and a cut score of 70 for screening/identifying examinees with intellectual disability because these scores yielded the fewest false positives and negatives when predicting high and low ability.

Because of the unique format of the *UMAS*, raw scores are not expected to increase by age and they do not. The correlation between age and raw scores across the ages of the *UMAS* tends to be approximately 0, supporting the idea that performance on the *UMAS* is not related to age. Given that the *UMAS* generally measures abilities important for school success, the authors assert that the subscales can be expected to correlate with one another and they do, with correlations ranging from 0.66 to 0.85.

Examinees with high IQs would be expected to earn higher scores on the *UMAS* than those with lower IQs. Examinees identified as gifted and talented and examinees identified as having an IQ measured above 120 scored significantly higher than the mean and examinees identified with IQs less than 80 scored significantly lower than the mean. Results indicate males and females score similarly. Scores of Whites, Blacks, Native Americans, and Hispanics did not differ statistically but the scores of those identified as Asian/Pacific Islander were significantly above the mean. Interestingly, examinees identified with learning disabilities scored lower, but not significantly, than the mean. The authors note that Asians tend to score higher as a group on tests of cognitive ability (e.g., Bracken and McCallum 1998) so these results support the fairness of the *UMAS* for examinees from various populations.

Both exploratory (EFA) and confirmatory (CFA) factor analyses were conducted to provide further evidence of validity. In the EFA, all items loaded significantly on their intended subscale and not on other subscales. The authors conclude that the EFA results provide strong evidence of the structure of the *UMAS*. In addition, the authors report results of a CFA and found strong evidence for both a six factor (the six subscales) and a one factor solution with the CFI, TI and MNOF exceeding 0.97 and the RMSEA = 0.08 for the six factor solution and CFI, TL< and FNI exceeding 0.96 and the RMSEA = 1.0 for the one factor solution. In general, data presented by the authors provide evidence of reliability and validity of the *UMAS*. Some additional research has been conducted to further examine psychometric properties of the *UMAS*.

## Research Supporting the Validity and Utility of the *UMAS*

In two studies, researchers have examined generally some of the psychometric properties of the *UMAS* and, specifically, the ability of the *UMAS* to accurately identify examinees who are intellectually gifted. Gray et al. (2009) administered an early eight subscale version of the *UMAS* (tentatively titled the *Universal Academic, Cognitive, Creativity, Emotions Scale or Universal ACCESS*) to 106 examinees in grades 2 through 8. Gray and colleagues reported strong internal consistency for the eight subscales, with Cronbach's alpha coefficients ranging from 0.95 to 0.98. They reported also evidence of concurrent validity, with correlation coefficients in the medium to large range ($r = 0.45$–$0.85$) between like scales on the *UMAS* and the *Gifted Rating Scales*; the *Bar-On Emotional Quotient Inventory: Youth Version* (Bar-On and Parker 2000), and the *Terra Nova Test of Basic Skills* (CTB 1996). Importantly, 53 examinees identified as intellectually gifted earned significantly higher mean scores ($p < 0.001$) on all *UMAS* subscales than 53 matched nongifted peers. Because the *UMAS* employs a "language-reduced" approach to identifying examinees' abilities, Gray et al. concluded that use of the *UMAS* will result in identification of some examinees as gifted who would be missed by traditional gifted rating scales. Further, because the *UMAS* inherently relies on local norms, use of the *UMAS*, Gray et al. concluded, will allow for examinees to be identified who would not be identified on rating scales using national norms. Gray et al. further concluded that the *UMAS* ratings were generally consistent with placement decisions based on other state-based criteria and their results provide indirect evidence supporting the use of teacher ratings in the process of identifying gifted examinees.

In a second study (Jordan et al. 2012) 47 gifted and nongifted African American and

Euro-American elementary examinees were rated by their teachers on the *UMAS*. Results of factorial multiple analyses of variance (MANOVAs) revealed no significant GAI mean differences between African American and Euro-American examinees. However, there was a significant difference in *UMAS* scores based on placement, with gifted examinees scoring higher on the GAI. A discriminant function analysis using the GAI resulted in 76.70% of participants correctly classified as gifted or nongifted, lower than the 95.3% correct classification results obtained by Gray et al. (2009). However, the Gray et al. sample consisted of gifted examinees and matched general education examinees. In contrast, of the participants in the Jordan et al. study, more than half of the nongifted examinees (13 of 23) were high achievers placed in self-contained gifted classrooms on a temporary basis. Jordan and colleagues concluded that this sample difference characteristic likely explains the reduction in discrimination between gifted examinees and high achievers in their study, as compared with the study by Gray and colleagues. They further concluded that use of the *UMAS*, multidimensional scales that minimize language and rely on local norms, has potential for identifying gifted examinees in traditionally underrepresented groups.

## UMAS Interpretation

The *UMAS* can be interpreted at the composite (GAI) level and at the subscale level. The *UMAS* yields two types of normative scores, percentiles and indexes, and corresponding terms to describe performance. Rank scores, percentiles yield information about the examinee's performance relative to peers; an examinee who scores at the 75th percentile earns a score equal to or greater than 75% of his/her peers. Equal interval scores, index scores are standard scores, with a mean set to 100 and standard deviation of 15. They allow both interindividual comparisons (comparisons between examinees) and intra-individual

comparisons, comparing performance of one examinee on various subscales within the *UMAS* (e.g., Literacy versus Math) or between the GAI or a *UMAS* subscale index score and performance on an intelligence or achievement test. These comparisons are useful for determining a pattern of performance and for identifying exceptionalities (e.g., intellectual giftedness, intellectual disabilities, and specific learning disabilities). Examinees who exhibit intellectual giftedness presumably will earn high and relatively consistent scores on intelligence tests, academic achievement tests, and on the UMAS subscales and composite. The converse presumably is true for examinees exhibiting intellectual disabilities. For examinees with specific learning disabilities, examinees presumably will show an uneven pattern across intelligence test scores, achievement test scores, and *UMAS* subscale scores. The *UMAS* manual contains a table presenting "statistically significant" ($p < 0.05$) versus "clinically useful" (per Reynolds 2003) difference scores for the *UMAS* subscales. Examiners can use the values in the table to determine if examinees' performance varies across the different domains assessed by the *UMAS*.

The *UMAS* manual contains a case example of an examinee who exhibits intellectual giftedness but with some significant variability in performance on the scales of the *UMAS*. The case provides an interesting example of interpretation at the subscale level and of considering *UMAS* data in conjunction with intelligence test data, achievement data, and background and history information.

## Strengths and Weaknesses of the UMAS

The *UMAS* is easy to administer and score. Data from the manual as well as a couple of published studies (Gray et al. 2009; Jordan et al. 2012) provide support for its reliability and validity. The authors provide evidence for accuracy of teacher ratings; however, teacher ratings are not perfect. To the extent they are not, scores will have error. There is evidence that the *UMAS* subscales predict accurately scores on other rating scales measuring similar constructs and they predict achievement test performance. However, mean scores on achievement tests reported in the manual were significantly higher than *UMAS* mean scores. Further research is needed to determine if this finding is stable, particularly given the emphasis on increased rigor and authenticity of curriculum and corresponding group achievement tests (e.g., Common Core State Standards and related achievement tests).

## Summary

The *UMAS* is a unique assessment tool that relies on teachers' ratings of examinees aged 5–17 in six domains related to academic success. Other unique features include its use of local norms and de-emphasis on use of standard English; that is, raters are instructed to rate examinees in reference to same-age peers in the local classroom or school and to rate examinees' literacy skills independent of the examinee's mode of communication. There is considerable evidence for the psychometric adequacy of the *UMAS* and it is useful for identifying examinees at both extremes of the intellectual and academic levels. The *UMAS* appears to have promise for also identifying examinees who may be twice-exceptional (with learning disabilities and intellectual giftedness) as well as examinees with autism who may exhibit splinter strengths.

## Universal Nonverbal Intelligence Test-Group Abilities Test (*UNIT-GAT*)

Like the *UMAS*, the *UNIT-GAT* is a cognitive screening tool based on the philosophy that it is important to provide a fair assessment, despite cultural and language differences. *UNIT-GAT* can be individually or group administered.

## Goals and Rationale for *UNIT-GAT* Development

The development of the *UNIT-GAT* was guided by the experience the authors gained in developing the *UNIT* and *UNIT2*, and like with those tests, several developmental goals guided its development. But the overarching goal was to ensure a fair and efficient group-based assessment of intelligence for children and adolescents whose cognitive abilities could not be fairly assessed with language-loaded measures. The *UNIT-GAT* was developed to provide a fair(er) assessment for children and adolescents who are deaf or hard of hearing, and those from different cultural backgrounds, with learning/language disabilities, with speech production impairments, and with serious emotional or intellectual limitations.

The *UNIT-GAT* authors created the test with psychometric rigor and sensitivity for cross-cultural assessment applications through the use of common, examinee-friendly tasks. *UNIT-GAT* tasks were designed to maximize existing examiner knowledge and experience to ensure that the test can be easily learned, administered, and interpreted. Currently, the *UNIT-GAT* is in its final stages of development.

## Description of the *UNIT-GAT*

The *UNIT-GAT* consists of two subtests, Analogical Reasoning and Quantitative Reasoning, for individuals aged 5 through 21–11. The Analogical Reasoning subtest is designed to measure examinees' ability to solve problems, understand relationships, and recognize perceptual similarities and differences to items presented in a matrix format. The Quantitative Reasoning subtest is designed to assess examinees' ability to solve problems using numbers and quantities and to understand quantitative patterns and relationships. *UNIT-GAT* test materials consist of the test book containing the analogic and quantitative items (the Student Test Booklet) and a Student Record booklet.

## Scores Provided

The *UNIT-GAT* yields raw scores, percentiles, and Index Scores, Standard Error of Measure, and Descriptive Terms for both the Analogical Reasoning and the Quantitative Reasoning subtests and the Composite, a full scale IQ score. Per the publisher, standard scores will be available for both Subtest Index scores and the Composite scores (e.g., mean of 10, standard deviation of 3 for the Subtest scores; mean of 100; standard deviation of 15 for the Composite score). Descriptive terms for the Composite are based on the score's distance from the mean: Very Delayed: <70; Moderately Delayed: 70–79; Mildly Delayed: 80–89; Average: 90–100; Mildly Advanced: 111–120; Moderately Advanced: 121–130; Very Advanced: >130.

## UNIT-GAT Administration and Scoring

The *UNIT-GAT* is designed for group administration but may be administered individually. Examiners should be trained in test administration and interpretation and should participate in practice testing and scoring before administering the *UNIT-GAT*. Estimated administration time for the *UNIT-GAT* is 30 minutes. Instructions indicate that the Analogical Reasoning subtest is always to be administered first. All examinees begin the Analogical Reasoning subtest by completing four sample items with modeling and prompting from the examiner and then all begin with item #1. For both subtests, examinees are instructed to choose one of four options that "best goes in the box with the question mark." Testing is timed and stopped at the end of 10 minutes. Examinees ages 5 through 8–11 record their answers directly in the Student Test Booklets and examinees aged 9 through 21–11 record their answers on a Student Answer Sheet. Once examinees complete Analogical Reasoning, examiners instruct them to turn over the Student Test Booklet and look at the first sample item. Examinees again complete four sample items with modeling and prompting by the examiner

and then begin with item #1. The examiner stops the examinees at the end of 10 min.

The *UNIT-GAT* is easily scored using a scoring key that contains the letter of the correct answer for each item. The manual contains tables from which the examiner obtains derived scores based on the examinee's raw scores and chronological age.

## Standardization and Psychometric Properties of the *UNIT-GAT*

Standardization of the *UNIT-GAT* is in final stages at this writing; additional information can be found in the examiner's manual upon publication. Preliminary data from PRO-ED are based on a sample of 1332 individuals; the average sample size for each age in the norm sample (5–21) equals 78, with the number of individuals in the 19, 20, and 21 age groups being smallest (49–55). Demographic data are not yet available.

### Reliability

Preliminary analyses indicate strong internal consistency (based on Cronbach's alpha) for both subtests and the *UNIT-GAT* Composite: for Quantitative Reasoning, coefficient alphas range from 0.89 to 0.98 across the ages 5–21 with an average of 0.95; for Analogic Reasoning, coefficient alphas range from 0.91–0.98 with an average of 0.96; and for the Composite, coefficient alphas range from 0.95 to 0.99 with an average of 0.98.

### Validity

Preliminarily, several types of evidence are available to support validity of the *UNIT-GAT*. Ability to correctly answer increasingly more items on the *UNIT-GAT* would be expected to increase with age and it does. Authors report moderate effect sizes (0.42, Quantitative Reasoning; 0.31, Analogic Reasoning) for the correlations between *UNIT-GAT* raw scores and age.

The authors also present evidence of convergent validity. As measures of cognitive ability, individual performance on the two subtests would be expected to correlate significantly and it does ($r = 0.88$) for the norm sample. In addition, correlations between the *UNIT-GAT* Composite and performance on the Test of Silent Word Reading Fluency-2 (TOSWRF-2) (Mather et al. 2014) ($r = 0.84$) and the Test of Silent Contextual Reading Fluency-2 (TOSCRF-2) (Hammill et al. 2014) ($r = 0.80$) are very large. Finally, there is preliminary evidence of construct validity. Correlations between the *UNIT-GAT* Composite and the *UNIT-2* are large to very large in magnitude: *UNIT-2* Memory, $r = 0.69$; *UNIT-2* Reasoning, $r = 0.70$; *UNIT-2* Quantitative, $r = 0.74$; and Composite, $r = 0.81$.

## Research Supporting the Validity and Utility of the *UNIT-GAT*

Browarnik (2016) explored concurrent validity of the *UNIT-GAT* Analogical Reasoning subtest and two three minute reading fluency screeners. Though test items contain no verbal content, *UNIT-GAT* Analogical Reasoning is designed to assess symbolic and nonsymbolic reasoning; symbolic reasoning has been positively correlated with reading skill (Bracken and McCallum 1998). Browarnik (2016) and colleagues administered the *UNIT-GAT*, the *TOSWRF-2*, and the *TOSCRF-2* to 140 children ages 6–15 who were enrolled in one of three Boys and Girls Clubs in the southeastern United States. Participants were rising first through seventh graders in fall, 2014, most were reading one grade level or more below their same-aged peers, and most (85.7%) were from low-income homes as determined by free/reduced price lunch. Sex demographics were 56.4% ($n = 79$) males, 44.1% ($n = 64$) females. Race demographics were 61.4% African American, 24.3% White, and 14.3% multiracial; six (4.3%) identified as Hispanic. Browarnik found that *UNIT-GAT* Analogical Reasoning scores are moderately correlated with *TOSWRF-2* Form A ($r = 0.45$, $p < 01$) and *TOSWRF-2* Form B ($r = 0.41$, $p < 0.01$). Similarly, *UNIT-GAT*

Analogical Reasoning correlates moderately with *TOSCRF-2* Form A ($r = 0.45$, $p < 0.01$) and *TOSCRF-2* Form B ($r = 0.48$, $p < 0.01$). These correlations are consistent with those between other cognitive and achievement tests (Naglieri and Bornstein 2003; Sattler 2008) and provide evidence of concurrent validity of the *UNIT-GAT*, though more research is needed to examine particularly the validity of the Quantitative Reasoning subtest.

## *UNIT-GAT* Interpretation

The *UNIT-GAT* yields an Analogical Reasoning Index, a Quantitative Reasoning Index, and a Full Scale IQ. Subscale Index scores and the Composite Index score are standard scores with a mean set to 100 and standard deviation set to 15. These scores allow both interindividual and intra-individual comparisons, similar to the *UMAS* and to other cognitive ability tests. The *UMAS* provides an estimate of overall intellectual ability as well as estimates of analogical and quantitative reasoning so it has potential to screen for intellectual giftedness, intellectual disabilities, specific learning disabilities, etc., in a language-reduced manner.

## Strengths and Weaknesses of the *UNIT-GAT*

The *UNIT-GAT* is a screener so it cannot be considered a comprehensive assessment of cognitive abilities. Given that it is in final stages of standardization, limited psychometric information is available and research is needed to support preliminary data on reliability and validity. The *UNIT-GAT* is designed as a nonverbal assessment but it does contain some verbal instructions. Verbal directions are minimized; the examiner models and prompts the examinees to complete four sample items so as to minimize effects of language differences among examinees. The *UNIT-GAT* is relatively quick to administer (two timed 10 min subtests plus instructions and modeling sample items) and is user friendly. The artwork of the stimulus items is colorful and should appeal to children.

## Summary

The *UNIT-GAT* is a group or individually administered nonverbal screening assessment of cognitive abilities containing two subtests that assess analogical (matrix) reasoning and quantitative reasoning. It also yields a Composite (Full scale) IQ. Based on preliminary psychometric data it offers promise as an efficient and fair(er) cognitive screening tool for examinees who may be unfairly assessed on traditional language-loaded measures.

## References

Bar-On, R., & Parker, J. D. A. (2000). *BarOn emotional quotient inventory: Youth version*. Multi-Health system, Incorporated.

Bracken, B. A., & McCallum, R. S. (1998). *Universal nonverbal intelligence test*. Chicago, IL: Riverside.

Browarnik., B. (2016). *Concurrent and predictive validity of the universal nonverbal intelligence test—Group ability test*. (Unpublished doctoral dissertation). University of Tennessee, Knoxville.

Cohen, J. (1988). *Statistical power analysis for the behavioral sciences* (2nd ed.). New Jersey: Lawrence Erlbaum.

Compton, D. L., Fuchs, D., Fuchs, L. S., & Bryant, J. D. (2006). Selecting at-risk readers in first grade for early intervention. *Journal of Educational Psychology, 98* (2), 394–409.

CTB. (1996). *Terra Nova comprehensive test of basic skills* (5th ed.). Monterey, CA: CTB/McGraw-Hill.

Gray, R. G., McCallum, R. S., & Bain, S. (2009). Language-reduced screening for giftedness. *Journal for the Education of the Gifted, 33*(1), 38–64.

Hammill, D. D., Wiederholt, J. L., & Allen, E. A. (2014). *TOSCRF: Test of silent contextual reading fluency—second edition examiner's manual*. Austin, TX: PRO-ED.

Hopkins, W. G. (2002). A scale of magnitudes for effect statistics. In *A new view of statistics*. Retrieved April 2, 2010, from http://www.sportsci.org/resource/stats/effectmag.html

Jordan, K. R., Bain, S. K., McCallum, R. S., & Bell, S. M. (2012). Comparing gifted and non-gifted African American and Euro-American students on cognitive and academic variables using local norms. *Journal for Education of the Gifted, 35*(3), 241–258. doi:10.1177/0162353212451701

Mather, N., Hammil, D. D., Allen, E. A., & Roberts, R. (2014). *Test of silent word reading fluency—Second edition examiner's manual*. Austin, TX: PRO-ED.

McCallum, R. S., & Bracken, B. A. (2012). *Universal multidimensional abilities scales*. Austin, TX: Pro ED, Publishing Co.

Morine-Dershimer, G. (1978–1979a). The anatomy of teacher prediction. *Educational Research Quarterly, 3* (4), 59–65.

Morine-Dershimer, G. (1978–1979b). How teachers "see" their pupils. *Educational Research Quarterly, 3*(4), 43–58.

Naglieri, J. A., & Bornstein, B. T. (2003). Intelligence and achievement: Just how correlated are they? *Journal of Psychoeducational Assessment, 21*(3), 244–260.

Park, S. H., Goo, J. M., & Jo, C.-H. (2004). Receiver operating charactering characteristic (ROC) curve: Practical review for radiologists. *Korean Journal of Radiology, 5*(1), 11–18.

Pfeiffer, S., & Jarosewich, T. (2003). *Gifted rating scales*. Upper Saddle River, NJ: Pearson.

Reynolds, C. R. (2003). Conceptual and technical problems in learning disability diagnosis. In C. R. Reynolds & R. W. Kamphaus (Eds.), *Handbook of psychological and educational assessment in children: Intelligence, aptitude, and achievement* (2nd ed., pp. 475–497). New York, NY: Guilford.

Sattler, J. M. (2008). *Assessment of children: Cognitive foundations* (5th ed.). LaMesa, CA: Jerome M. Sattler Publisher.

Tennessee Department of Education. (2011). *Tennessee comprehensive assessment program*. Retrieved from http://www.tn.gov/education/assessment/achievement.shtml

U.S. Census Bureau. (2011). *Statistical abstract of the United States: 2011* (130th ed.). Washington, DC: Author.

# Part III
# Nonverbal Assessment of Related Abilities

## John D. Wasserman

In research on personality and psychopathology assessment, the last two decades has seen a pronounced swing toward direct, face-valid, objective, and explicit assessment methods, with aggressive challenges to indirect, performance-based, projective, and implicit methods. Garb's (1999) call for a moratorium on clinical use of the Rorschach Inkblot Test was a particularly damaging brick in the battle, although his position has recently been retracted (Wood et al. 2015). More recently, Imuta and her colleagues (2013) recommended that practitioners "draw an end" (p. 7) to their use of human figure drawing tests. The restructured clinical forms of the Minnesota Multiphasic Personality Inventory (MMPI-2-RF; Ben-Porath and Tellegen 2008; and MMPI-A-RF; Archer et al. 2016) have both departed from the empirical [criterion] keying approach that characterized item selection in the original MMPI. It is almost as if one segment of assessment researchers declared to practitioners, "What matters is just what the client tells you, verbally or through endorsement of self-report items, and little else!"

Experienced clinicians, however, know that many clients cannot (or do not) accurately report their internal psychological state and that collateral informants often demonstrate limited agreement. For example, after stressing the importance of self-report assessment methodologies, Olt-

manns and Carlson (2013, p. 235) concede, "self-report measures provide a one-dimensional perspective on personality ... we are not always the best source of information regarding our own personality traits." The limitations of self-report methodologies in assessment of personality and psychopathology have been amply described (e.g., Ganellen 2007; Huprich et al. 2011), and the modest agreement between multiple informants on behavior problems has well documented in meta-analyses and cross-cultural studies across the life span (Achenbach et al. 1987; Achenbach et al. 2005; Rescorla et al. 2014, 2016). At this juncture in the history of personality assessment, the consensus recommendation for best practice in personality assessment remains to use multiple methods and multiple informants, even as the number of acceptable assessment methods is shrinking and the value of multiple informants is debated (Achenbach 2011).

Nonverbal assessment methodologies represent a possible solution to the limitations of self- and other-report assessments but suffer from a relative dearth of empirically supported tests and procedures. As part of the assessment process, the vast majority of professionals still use projective drawings for warm-up purposes (e.g., Camara et al. 2000) and implicitly observe nonverbal behaviors during interviews and test sessions (e.g., facial expressions, motor behaviors, and problem-solving approaches). At the same time, these approaches are often interpreted informally and unsystematically, relegated to a secondary status behind norm-referenced

J.D. Wasserman (✉)
9006 Crownwood Court, Suite A,
Burke, VA 22015, USA
e-mail: j.d.wasserman@cox.net
URL: http://www.johnwasserman.com

© Springer International Publishing AG 2017
R.S. McCallum (ed.), *Handbook of Nonverbal Assessment*,
DOI 10.1007/978-3-319-50604-3_14

self-report and collateral-report procedures in arriving at diagnostic and treatment-related inferences. In this chapter, some historical perspectives are recounted and a framework offered for thinking about nonverbal tests within the domain of personality and psychopathology assessment. Several approaches to nonverbal assessment of personality are reviewed, including some traditional and enduring techniques as well as some newer pioneering efforts.

In general, the use of nonverbal tools in the appraisal of personality and psychopathology is indicated for any individual who cannot or does not respond accurately to linguistically loaded measures, or when the inclusion of language in the task negatively impinges upon test score validity or reliability. Nonverbal personality assessment may be indicated with (a) individuals with neurologically based acquired language disorders (e.g., aphasia, language-based learning disabilities), (b) individuals with varied cultural, linguistic, or national backgrounds (e.g., non-English speakers), (c) individuals who are illiterate or poorly educated, (d) individuals who are deaf or hard of hearing, (e) individuals with forms of emotional disturbance that are manifested through an inability or unwillingness to produce an adequate and unconstrained sample of verbal behavior (such as may be found in cases of severe depression, some psychoses, or selective mutism), or (f) individuals who are prone to misrepresent themselves on verbal self-report measures.

As defined here, a test is operationally nonverbal if it involves a relatively brief verbal instructional set (and therefore makes limited demands on the examinee's receptive language) and requires little or no verbal response (thereby involving minimal expressive language) on the part of the examinee. These criteria exclude historically popular measures such as the Rorschach Inkblot Test (Rorschach 1921) and Thematic Apperception Test (TAT; Morgan and Murray 1935), both of which involve the presentation of nonlinguistic pictorial stimuli and the elicitation of verbal responses that can be numerous and sometimes lengthy. It is noted, however, that this operational definition is not uniform, as some researchers consider the Rorschach and TAT to be nonverbal on the basis of the pictorial nature of the test stimuli (e.g., Hong and Paunonen 2008; Paunonen and Ashton 2002).

Also excluded from the category of nonverbal assessment are tests that require reading of printed semantic material, such as the Beck Depression Inventory—II (BDI-II; Beck et al. 1996), the Minnesota Multiphasic Personality Inventory—2 Restructured Form (MMPI-2-RF; Ben-Porath and Tellegen 2008), and its adolescent version (MMPI-A-RF; Archer et al. 2016). Reading is an inherently verbal and linguistically demanding process with strong word knowledge requirements, even if little or no spoken language is involved in test administration. Reading skills are frequently impaired in individuals with language-related disorders. Additionally, most printed self-report tests are designed for use with adolescents at least 13 years of age because test content is at or above a sixth-grade reading level, leaving preschool and young school-aged children less frequently tested through written self-report methods. Even sixth-grade reading levels may be too high for many adolescents referred for psychological evaluations, since they may have language-based learning problems or disabilities that impinge upon their reading skills. Nonverbal assessment techniques using no printed verbal instructions or semantic test stimuli provide a useful alternative to the limitations of language-based self-report instruments.

## Historical Antecedents

The belief that personality and psychopathology may be most clearly understood through language probably traces its origins to Josef Breuer and Sigmund Freud's written accounts in the 1890s of the psychoanalytic "talking cure." The foundations of psychoanalysis placed a heavy emphasis on language expression and content, as per the admonition of psychoanalysts to their clients to "Say whatever comes into your mind."

The earliest psychometric attempts to measure personality were predominantly verbal self-report measures (e.g., Bernreuter 1931; Woodworth 1917) and rating scales (Scott 1919), the latter increasing in popularity when easy-to-use graphic rating scales became accepted (Freyd 1923). Isolated early efforts to use nonverbal methodologies to measure personality characteristics like honesty and trustworthiness included Hartshorne and May's (1928) nine tests, several of them nonverbal, which intentionally provided examinees with opportunities to cheat as a test of honesty.

However, the nonverbal assessment of personality can be most easily traced to Goodenough's (1926) publication of the Draw-a-Man test as a measure of intelligence, laying the groundwork for numerous derivative human figure drawing systems. In the editor's introduction to Goodenough's test, Lewis M. Terman explicitly noted its nonverbal qualities, having become sensitized to the issues of language-loaded assessments by criticisms of his Stanford–Binet intelligence scale. Goodenough speculated about the use of drawings in the assessment of personality, but it would remain for pioneers like John N. Buck (1948) and Karen Machover (1949) to more fully explore the nonintellective, characterological value of drawing tests.

With the advent of the projective testing movement, nonverbal assessment techniques showed substantial growth. Projective techniques purport to reveal the private world of the individual in a manner about which the examinee is typically unaware. Frank (1948), who coined the term *projective methods*, suggested that "The essential feature of a projective technique is that it evokes from the subject what is in various ways expressive of his private world and personality process" (p. 47). Nonverbal personality assessment techniques spawned in this era included drawing tests, finger-painting techniques, expressive movement, and other visual motor activities, as well as specialized methods such as the Szondi Test, Mosaic Test, and World Test (Bell 1948).

Challenges to psychoanalytic theory (e.g., Eysenck 1990; Holt 1992), doubts about the theoretical assumptions behind the projective

methods (Exner 1993; Wagner 1999), and poor psychometric properties for many projective tests (e.g., Dumont and Smith 1996; Smith and Dumont 1995) raised questions about the utility of projective measures. It is beyond the scope or intent of this chapter to defend the concept of projective testing, but it may not be necessary to accept the assumption of unconscious projection in order to find value in many so-called projective tests. For example, Exner (1993) reconceptualized the Rorschach as a problem-solving task in which examinee perceptions of the inkblots and the nature of articulated responses reveal both state- and trait-based aspects of psychological operations; the role of projection was relegated to a relatively minor role. A similar evolution in thinking has occurred with the projective drawings, which are thought to have potential discriminative value with clinical groups even after the psychoanalytically-oriented sign approach is abandoned in favor of a holistic or polythetic approach to interpretation (e.g., Tharinger and Stark 1990). Accordingly, it is possible to use the projectives without accepting their implicit theoretical assumptions, so long as contemporary psychometric standards are met. In the sections below, I focus on specific classes of nonverbal tests rather than theoretical considerations. We now turn our attention from theoretical limitations to specific classes of nonverbal tests.

## Approaches to Nonverbal Assessment of Personality and Psychopathology

In this section, a number of predominantly nonverbal measures of personality and psychopathology are described, including their theoretical approaches, administration and scoring, interpretation, technical adequacy, and strengths and weaknesses. The nonverbal assessments of personality and psychopathology described below are classified in three broad classes of tests adapted from those offered by Frank (1948) and Lindzey (1961), who emphasized the kind of response the technique elicits from the examinee:

- *Drawing techniques.* Drawings, depictions, or reproductions of persons, objects, and figures [e.g., Bender–Gestalt Test (Bender 1938), Draw a Person, House–Tree–Person (Buck and Warren 1992), Kinetic Family Drawings (Burns 1982)]
- *Object placement and play techniques.* Arrangement of materials and manipulatives in meaningful and interpretable ways (e.g., Erica Method, Family System Test, Mosaic Test, SandPlay, World Technique)
- *Self-rating and self-report techniques.* Rating a pictorial stimulus as it personally relates to oneself (e.g., Five-Factor Nonverbal Personality Questionnaire, Nonverbal Personality Questionnaire, Visual Analog Mood Scales).

To these could be added expressive/aesthetic techniques (e.g., finger painting, expressive movement) and pictorial preference/choice techniques (e.g., Szondi Test). While tests belonging to these classes have been developed, none are used with any frequency or approach current standards of psychometric adequacy (Bell 1948; Camara et al. 2000).

Although it remains to be proven, nonverbal methods may be sufficiently indirect so as to avoid a major limitation of verbal personality assessment methods—that they tend to be highly susceptible to deliberate efforts by examinees to misrepresent or manage their self-presentation by selectively endorsing items in a given direction. As Hutt (1985) observed, "Many of our personality tests are based on verbal responses to test stimuli. This can sometimes prove to be a serious limitation in cases in which verbal defense of façade can conceal, rather than reveal, pathology" (p. 113). Alternatively, as Frank (1939) commented with respect to projective tests, "The most important things about an individual are what he cannot or will not say" (p. 395).

## Drawing Techniques

Drawing is a commonplace and familiar activity during development, and drawing tests offer a nonthreatening start to many psychological evaluations. The study of children's drawings dates back to the 1880s, but the first popular Draw-a-Man test was offered by Goodenough (1926). Norm-referenced and standardized updates of this drawing procedure as a measure of cognitive–intellectual ability are available in the Goodenough–Harris Drawing Test (Harris 1963), Koppitz's (1968) Developmental Human Figure Drawings, the Draw a Person: A Quantitative Scoring System (Naglieri 1988), and Reynolds and Hickman's (2004) Draw-A-Person Intellectual Ability Test for Children, Adolescents, and Adults. Our focus is on personality assessment, however, and Goodenough's work spawned three main projective drawing techniques: Draw a Person (e.g., Machover 1949), House–Tree–Person (e.g., Buck 1948), and Kinetic Family Drawing (e.g., Burns and Kaufman 1970, 1972), that remain in clinical use in various forms.

Surveys of test usage show that several drawing measures still rank among the most popular with psychologists conducting assessments of personality and psychopathology: House–Tree–Person (ranked 4th), Bender–Gestalt Test (ranked 5th), Human Figures Drawings (ranked 9th), and Kinetic Family Drawings (ranked 15th) (Camara et al. 2000). Vass (1999) reports that 6530 studies on drawing tests have been published since 1950, with about 100–170 studies published per year.

In the previous edition of this book, directions for administering and scoring the leading drawing tests were briefly presented. At the current time, however, such tests are not recommended, considering the continued failure of drawing techniques for personality assessment to meet acceptable standards for evidence-based practice. A decade ago, Flanagan and Motta (2007, p. 257) conceded of drawing tasks that "evidence of their utility for diagnosis … is nonexistent." Reviews of evidence supporting the validity of human figure drawings for personality assessment have generally been negative or at best, mixed (Cummings 1986; Flanagan and Motta 2007; Kahill 1984; Klein 1986; Knoff 1993; Motta et al. 1993a; Smith and Dumont 1995; Thomas and Jolley 1998). Leading criticisms of drawing tests for personality assessment include problems with the theoretical underpinnings, interpretation that is susceptible to interpreter biases, inadequate test score reliability, inadequate normative bases, inadequate evidence of incremental validity beyond self- and other-report measures, poor prediction of future behavior and long-term outcome, and inconsistent identification of and discrimination between contrasting clinical groups. Several researchers have gone so far as to assert that the use of projective drawing techniques for personality assessment is professionally unethical (Martin 1983; Motta et al. 1993b; Smith and Dumont 1995).

The introduction of more holistic, integrative approaches to human figure drawings in the 1990s sparked some optimism that drawing tests might see a resurgence (Handler and Habenicht 1994; Swenson 1968; Tharinger and Stark 1990). At that time, polythetic scoring systems involving total scores across multiple criteria (as opposed to the use of single projective signs, which have consistently been demonstrated to lack validity) were proposed as a way to identify emotionally disturbed students (e.g., McNeish and Naglieri 1993; Naglieri and Pfeiffer 1992). The early promise of these approaches has given way to disappointment over evidence that the initial polythetic scoring systems discriminate poorly with small effect sizes between typical students and clinical groups.

An example of these unmet expectations may be found in the *Draw a Person: Screening Procedure for Emotional Disturbance* (DAP: SPED; Naglieri et al. 1991), which offered a polythetic scoring system and a nationally representative normal sample, with the objective of distinguishing between normal and emotionally disturbed samples of children. Two early investigations (McNeish and Naglieri 1993; Naglieri and Pfeiffer 1992) sampling emotionally disturbed students recommended a cut score of 55$T$ as being optimal, although this cut score would identify 31% of the normative sample as being impaired, an unacceptable false positive identification rate by any reckoning. Validity studies reported in the test manual showed that across samples of children with heterogeneous emotional disturbance, the DAP: SPED produced

mean $T$ scores from 54.8 to 57.0 (with the mean general population score being 50$T$). More recently, Matto et al. (2005) reported that a sample of emotionally disturbed students obtained a mean DAP: SPED score of 56.1$T$ (SD = 10.9$T$), more evidence of modest discrimination from typical performance.

Matto (2001, 2002) demonstrated that the DAP: SPED did not explain significant variance in externalizing behaviors but did account for 9–11% of total variance in reported internalizing behaviors, with the higher number being derived when parental report of child withdrawal was statistically controlled. Although the DAP: SPED-Internalizing behaviors relationship was statistically significant, this effect size is not sufficiently high to justify clinical use of the test. Wrightson and Saklofske (2000) reported that the DAP: SPED could statistically distinguish at modest levels between students in Canadian regular education, alternative education, and behavior disordered classes, but they reported a substantially lower level of discriminability than that found with behavior rating scales alone.

In the most recent review of validity evidence for the DAP: SPED, Bardos and Doropoulou (2014) asserted that the DAP: SPED test offers statistically significant incremental improvement beyond that which may be derived from behavior rating scales in the valid identification of emotionally disturbed students. This is certainly a reasonable contention in light of available evidence, but it does not readily translate to applied practice. When the DAP: SPED is included in a comprehensive test battery and interpreted conventionally, it is likely to contribute little to decision-making processes because of its modest effect sizes. As McGrath and Carroll (2012) concluded of the new generation of drawing tests:

> The use of individual signs from [human] figure drawings as indicators of specific personality descriptors has been largely invalidated, but the scoring systems that were subsequently developed have their own problems (p. 342).

In general, no current system of scoring and interpreting human figure drawings appears to have adequate reliability and validity for personality assessment, and it appears difficult to justify continued use of these measures for any clinical or educational decision-making purposes.

Still, judging from test usage surveys the intrinsic appeal of drawing techniques remains high, if just because practicing psychologists see human figure drawings that are occasionally meaningful and revealing. Moreover, drawings offer an easily administered, nonthreatening, warm-up to psychological testing, so drawing techniques would seem to represent a technique in search of a theory and a defensible scoring/interpretive system.

There are several new and creative, albeit unproven, approaches to the psychological use of drawings. For example, Hungarian psychologist Zoltán Vass (1998, 2012) has formulated an impressive, empirically derived taxonomy of drawing features along with a seven-step method of configuration analysis to facilitate contextual interpretation. Italian psychologist Rocco Quaglia and his colleagues articulated a developmental model of graphical expression that begins with imitative scribbles (ages 1–2 years), progressing to expressive scribbles (ages 2–3 years) in which lines begin to express emotional states, followed by dynamic, figurative scribbling, and subsequently by the development of practical esthetic figurative drawings governed by motivated logical rules (Quaglia et al. 2015). The authors describe a representative drawing task showing clear-cut developmental progressions: "Imagine that you're in a field and draw a beautiful butterfly that is flying towards you." The Levick Emotional and Cognitive Art Therapy Assessment (LECATA; Levick 2000, 2009) was only recently normed and includes six drawing tasks and covers the ages of 3–11 years. The five tasks are a drawing of anything and a story about the drawing, a self-portrait, a scribble using one color and a picture created from the scribble, a drawing of a place the examinee "would like to be" (for ages 3–5; draw an "important place" for children 6 years and up), and a drawing of a family. The LECATA was created by Myra F. Levick, a psychologist and art psychotherapist. However, the practical value of and

empirical support for these innovative approaches to the use of drawings for personality assessment, however, remains undetermined.

## Object Placement and Play Techniques

Just as paper-and-pencil drawing tasks may be used for the nonverbal appraisal of personality and psychopathology, so may object placement tasks. These types of tasks involve a meaningful arrangement or placement of a set of symbolic manipulables within structured or unstructured spatial parameters. In the Family System Test (FAST; Gehring et al. 2001; Gehring 1998), the examinee is instructed to place schematic male and female figures at varying heights and proximity on an 81-square checkerboard. Results may be interpreted as providing a representation of family relations, cohesiveness, and hierarchy. In the World Technique (e.g., Lowenfeld 1979) and its many derivative tests, examinees are typically given numerous small objects (such as people, animals, fantasy items, and items with which to build landscape or scenery) and told to do what they like with them, often constructing sandtray panoramas that are thought to symbolically represent a "miniature world" that is associated with the child's interpersonal and intrapsychic systems, as well as perceptual and thought processes. These types of procedures usually require little verbalization by examinees, although additional inquiry options are available. These object placement techniques will now be described in detail.

### Family System Test (FAST)

The FAST (Gehring et al. 2001; Gehring 1998) is a standardized figure placement technique for individuals and families with members 6 years or older. It was formulated based on structural family systems theory, and its scores yield spatial representations of family cohesion and hierarchy. Its scores are intended to describe family-oriented psychosocial issues and to facilitate the planning, execution, and evaluation of therapeutic interventions. Structural family therapy conceptualizes psychopathology as being seated in the family (and not the identified patient), with the objective of the therapist being to restructure family subsystems and transform dysfunctional transactional patterns between members (Minuchin 1974).

**Administration**. The FAST requires about 10 min to administer to individuals. Its materials include a $45 \times 45$ cm$^2$ board, divided into 81 squares. Schematic male and female figures are used, as are cylindrical blocks of three different heights that may be placed under the schematic figures to depict elevation in a hierarchy.

Verbal explanations are long in duration, although little expressive language is required of the examinee. At the outset, the examiner says, "I would now like to explain a procedure we use for representing family relations. With this board and these figures and blocks you can show how close the members of your family are to one another and how much power or influence each member has in the family. Members of the same family usually evaluate their relations differently" (Gehring and Page 2000, p. 437).

The examiner explains the concepts of emotional closeness and distance (i.e., cohesion) by placing figures side by side on adjacent squares (minimum distance), at diagonally adjacent squares (second closest distance), and at diagonally opposed corners of the board (maximum distance). The examiner also explains power or influence within the family (i.e., hierarchy) using the blocks of different sizes to elevate the figures already positioned on the board, conveying that the greater the difference in height between two figures, the more hierarchical is their relationship. Two figures at the same height have balanced or equal power within the family.

Once these concepts are understood, the FAST is administered under three conditions. First, examinees are asked to represent their current family relations (typical representation), followed by a semistructured verbal interview. Second, examinees are asked to portray their desired family structures (ideal representation), again followed by an interview. Finally, examinees are asked to depict their family in an important conflict (conflict representation), again followed by an interview.

**Scoring and Interpretation**. The three-dimensional configurations yielded on the FAST may be scored to determine the range of emotional connectedness and the degree of influence perceived to exist within and across generations for each of the three family circumstances. Cohesion and hierarchy scores can also be combined to classify family structure in each situation and can be compared across situations to determine family flexibility. Cohesion is represented by the distance between figures on the board, and hierarchy is represented by the elevation of figures with blocks. As a criterion reference, healthy families are thought to have a balanced relationship structure (cohesive and with a balanced hierarchy), clear generational borders, and a flexible organization. Pathological family organization is suggested by a number of configurations, such as when the elevation of a child figure surpasses that of a parent figure (a hierarchy reversal).

Normative FAST representations of typical family relations among nonclinical respondents are based upon a sample of nearly 600 children, adolescents, and parents from the San Francisco Bay Area, about two-thirds from intact families and one-third from single parent or blended families. Racial and ethnic composition appears to be nationally representative, with the exception of African Americans who are underrepresented (6% of the total sample). The nonclinical sample is predominantly middle class.

**Strength and Limitations**. Gehring's (1998) original objective in the development of the FAST was to create a flexible instrument that meets high clinical standards and that has an association for family-based intervention, and toward these ends, the instrument holds considerable promise.

The FAST shows early evidence of psychometric adequacy (Gehring and Marti 2001). FAST validity studies include convergent validity with common measures of family functioning (Family Cohesion and Adaptability Scale, or FACES III; and the Family Environment Scale or FES). Comparisons between the results of these instruments are suggestive that FAST indices of cohesion are relatively convergent with those offered by the FACES III and the FES, although indices of hierarchy are weakly related (Gehring and Page 2000). Discriminant validity is supported by differences between FAST representations of nonclinical respondents and members of families attending a child psychiatric outpatient clinic (Gehring and Page 2000). Based on individual representations of typical, ideal, and conflict situations by fathers, mothers, and children in the two groups, members of clinically identified families were more likely than nonclinical respondents to report their family structures as unbalanced. In eight of nine comparisons, clinical and nonclinical samples differed at statistically significant levels in their family perceptions of current family relations across situations. FAST reliability has been investigated through test–retest stability over a 1-week period with children and adolescents. Results range from $r = 0.63$ to 0.87 at the family level for cohesion and hierarchy (Gehring and Page 2000).

Some weaknesses of the FAST include its lengthy and somewhat stilted verbal instructions, as well as the lengthy verbal follow-up interviews to the three test conditions (typical, ideal, and conflict representation). Unless these interviews can be demonstrated to improve test validity incrementally, they may be unnecessary to the test (just as the lengthy inquiries following drawing tests have questionable value). The FAST offers the major assets of an efficient nonverbal depiction of family dynamics, and the excess verbiage serves only to distract from these assets and make the test less universal.

Development of the FAST began in the early 1980s in Zurich and later California, making it a relatively new international and cross-cultural endeavor. Although it clearly needs further psychometric development, the FAST is closely aligned with a well-articulated theory and family-based intervention approach. As an instrument that can both identify the nature of family pathology and direct the focus of therapeutic interventions, it offers a connection between assessment and intervention that is rare among psychological tests.

## World Techniques

Assessment procedures in which examinees are directed to arrange an array of toys and objects as they wish are sometimes referred to as *world tests*, after prototypal tests initially developed by Erik H. Erikson (Homberger 1938) and Lowenfeld (1939). Examinees usually construct panoramic constructions that are considered to reflect their perceptions of their world.

Like projective tests, the world techniques trace their origins to psychoanalytic theory and practice. Some of the earliest attempts to develop diagnostic play assessments that could be used seamlessly with play therapy were created in England by child psychoanalyst Margaret Lowenfeld, whose nonverbal techniques (the Mosaic Test, the World Technique, and Sandplay) were predicated on the belief that young, preschool children are not able to express their thoughts and feelings in constructive language although thoughts and feelings are indeed present. Preverbal (or nonverbal) thinking was considered to represent a form of pictorially based thinking preceding spoken language. In spontaneous play with pictures and toys, Lowenfeld reasoned, children symbolically express their ideas and feelings about the world. Through close observation of the play of emotionally disturbed children, it is possible to understand and gain access to the intrapsychic representations of early experiences that contribute to emotional disturbance.

Variations on the world technique include Erikson's Dramatic Productions Test (Homberger 1938), the Erica Method (Sjolund 1981, 1993; Sjolund and Schaefer 1994), and Buhler's World Test (1951a, b), Buhler and Kelly (1941). Diagnostic play assessments are reported to be more popular in Europe than in the United States (Gitlin-Weiner et al. 2000), presumably because of their association with psychoanalytic theory and their comparative lack of psychometric rigor. A scant amount of research on these measures has appeared in mainstream American psychology journals in the last 30 years. Nevertheless, object placement represents an assessment paradigm that has come to have a prominent role in the nonverbal process of play therapy.

**Administration**. Materials for Lowenfeld's (1939, 1979) World Technique include a $75 \times 50 \times 7$ cm$^3$ metal sand tray, containing sand so that the examinee can model contours and place objects as desired. Water also needs to be available. Tools to manipulate the sand, such as shovels, funnels, and molds, are placed nearby. Materials that can be shaped easily are also provided. The child has a wide array of miniature objects from various classes to use in developing the world, including people and animals, fantasy figures, scenery and landscape, items of transportation, and equipment. Other adaptations of this technique use a wooden tray instead of a sand tray. Buhler and Kelly (1941) include 150 small objects in their World Test. The Erica Method uses two metal trays (one with dry sand and one with wet sand) and 360 miniature toys including people of different ages and sizes, genders, and occupations; farm animals and wild animals; vehicles; and various objects such as fire, explosions, guns, buildings, furniture, trees, fences, and traffic signs (Sjolund 1981). A small piece of play-dough is also provided if the child wishes to create an object not available.

In Lowenfeld's World Technique, the materials are introduced with a naturalistic and simple sequence of ideas that are explained in the buildup to the task: that children think differently than adults, that many ideas and experiences that do not translate into words (Lowenfeld termed this "picture thinking" with children), that many things are easier to understand in pictures and actions than in words, that this is a natural way of thinking, and that the examiner-therapist wants to build a bridge between the worlds of children and the world of adults. The World materials are introduced, and the child is invited to make "whatever comes into your head." There are otherwise few limits placed upon the child, and Lowenfeld emphasizes the need for the construction of many successive worlds or worlds created over several therapeutic sessions.

The Erica Method is administered on three or four occasions in order to establish consistency and allow patterns to develop. Instructions are deliberately unstructured: "Here you see a lot of toys. You may use whatever you want and build

with them in the sandbox. Here is a sandbox with dry sand and here is one with wet. Which one do you want to build in?" (Sjolund 1981, p. 323). The examiner does not provide any more comments or encouragements.

**Scoring and Interpretation**. The process of scoring the World Techniques typically begins with a graphical or photographic representation of the worlds produced by the examinee. Scoring in some adaptations includes the number and choices of toys and pieces, the various forms of interaction included in the world, items used and rejected, and salient behaviors and verbalizations during and after construction. Interpretation is based upon both qualitative and objective indices. Lowenfeld (1979) described the interpretive process as beginning with attempts to understand what the objects used signify to the child: "Having drawn the 'World' we then substitute in it the qualities and concepts the child has given. When these are reassembled together the result is a picture of affect, concept, memory and experience inextricably woven together into the presentation of a total state" (p. 7). She described categories of worlds, including realistic or representational worlds, worlds in which real objects are put together in an unreal fashion, demonstrations of fantasies, and mixed types of worlds. Michael and Buhler (1945) described six objective types of abnormal worlds that may be observed in both children and adults:

- *Aggressive*: worlds in which killing, accidents, and violence occur
- *Unpopulated*: worlds in which people are omitted
- *Empty*: worlds in which few objects appear
- *Closed*: worlds in which many boundaries, fences, and enclosures are prominent
- *Chaotic or disorganized*: worlds in which the elements are poorly planned or incoherently organized
- *Rigid*: worlds in which elements are overly organized and overly symmetrical.

These types of worlds tend to be associated with emotional disturbance. Buhler and Kelly (1941) suggested that construction of two or more symptom worlds is indicative of psychopathology, with the most clinically significant world being closed and unpopulated.

The Erica Method yields information concerning the child's developmental and functional level (recognition, sorting, groupings, and relationships between toys), as well as their perception of the world (i.e., through realistic, fantasy, aggressive, chaotic, or bizarre themes). For example, the nature of relationships between the toys may be classified as conventional, meaningful, chaotic, and/or bizarre. Content analysis involves the identification of themes in one or more of the child's worlds, such as high levels of aggression (Sjolund 1981).

**Strengths and Weaknesses**. Although Lowenfeld (1979) considered her technique to be objective, recordable, and interpretable, with standardized materials and procedures, it was not originally normed-referenced, and few studies of its psychometric qualities have been conducted. Buhler (1951a) offered norms (now considered outdated), and the Erica Method includes performance norms by age (Sjolund 1981, 1993; Sjolund and Schaefer 1994). Aoki (1981) has reported adequate test–retest reliability of a World Test in adjusted and emotionally disturbed primary and middle-school students and is the only study of this type. In general, the World Technique represents a promising approach in need of further psychometric development before it can meet existing psychometric standards. As described by Sjolund and Schaefer (1994), the Erica Method currently "combines the hardiness of a formal, reality-based observation with the softness and fragility of empathic contact with the child" (p. 231).

## Self-rating and Self-report Techniques

Nonverbal assessment paradigms that do not have clear counterparts in verbal personality assessment have thus far been described, but one may ask if there are nonverbal counterparts to the so-called objective broadband and narrowband verbal self-report measures, like the MMPI-2 and MMPI-2-RF (Butcher et al. 1989) (ranked second in usage among clinical practitioners, according to Camara et al. 2000) and the Beck Depression Inventory-II (ranked tenth in usage). In this section, two relatively new nonverbal types of self-report paradigms are described that parallel verbal measures and that offer broadband and narrowband assessments of personality and psychopathology.

**Nonverbal Personality Questionnaire**. Just as verbal self-report personality inventories require examinees to respond "true" or "false" to sentence-based items according to whether the items apply to them, it is possible to respond to a series of pictorial depictions of behavior and rate their personal applicability. Pictures take more space than sentences, so fewer items may be administered so as to avoid overwhelming the examinee with an overly lengthy inventory. At the same time, psychometric properties may be maintained with fewer items when an expanded rating of response options (e.g., Likert rating scales) is offered.

The 136-item Nonverbal Personality Questionnaire (NPQ; Paunonen and Jackson 1998; Paunonen et al. 1990) and the 60-item Five-Factor Nonverbal Personality Questionnaire (FF-NPQ; Paunonen et al. 2001) represent the first instruments in a new generation of pictorial self-report inventories. These measures are distinguished by the absence of verbal content, while tapping into familiar personality constructs including Murray's (1938) need-based traits and the "big five" factor structure of personality (e.g., Goldberg 1993).

The NPQ was developed from the identification of a series of behavioral acts thought to represent exemplars of common personality traits. The behavioral acts were intended to portray the needs (traits) described in Murray's (1938) system, with many of these needs having been previously measured through verbal self-report in Jackson's (1984) Personality Research Form (PRF). Following the system of personality scale development suggested by Jackson (1971), a pool of pictorial items was first generated according to the 17 traits depicted in Murray's (1938) system of needs. For each item, a line drawing was made of a central character performing a behavior in a specific situation corresponding to the designated trait. The requirement that the examinee respond with self-ratings suggested that NPQ item contents be limited to exemplars of trait expression, with the rating describing the likelihood that the examinee would engage in the *type* of behavior pictured (rather than the specific behavior itself). Items were also created for an Infrequency validity scale, consisting of items that are likely to be endorsed by someone who completes the questionnaire randomly. NPQ items were then winnowed down through elimination of items that failed to meet minimum psychometric standards and retaining items with the best composite psychometric qualities. The NPQ has been subjected to a number of cross-cultural studies described below. Replication of a five-factor factorial structure across cultures led to the development of the abbreviated FF-NPQ scale, with most items selected from the lengthier NPQ and a few new items created.

**Administration**. For both the NPQ and the FF-NPQ, examinees are presented with a picture booklet and asked to "look at each illustration and rate the likelihood that you would engage in the type of behavior shown." Representative items are shown in Fig. 14.1. Examinee responses are given on a 7-point numerical rating scale, with 1 representing "extremely unlikely that I would perform this type of behavior" and 7 labeled "extremely likely that I would perform this type of behavior." The NPQ requires approximately 25–30 min to complete, and the FF-NPQ requires approximately 10 min to complete. Although the instruction page requires translation, the questionnaire items are inherently nonverbal and can be administered to individuals with different cultural and linguistic backgrounds.

**Scoring and Interpretation**. In the NPQ, eight items are used to score each of the Murray need-based scales, as well as the Infrequency scale that is used to detect random or dissimulated response patterns. The FF-NPQ consists of 60 items, with 12 items assigned to each of the five factors. FF-NPQ scales correspond to the "big five" personality factors: Neuroticism (N),

**Fig. 14.1** In the NPQ, examinees are asked to "Look at each illustration and rate the likelihood that you would engage in the type of behavior shown." Ratings are given on a 7-point scale. Item 112 depicts nurturance, and item 127 depicts thrill-seeking behavior. (NPQ sample items Copyright© 2004 by SIGMA assessment systems, Inc. All rights reserved. Used with permission)

Extraversion (E), Openness to Experience (O), Agreeableness (A), and Conscientiousness (C). Pending nationally representative normative studies, the NPQ and FF-NPQ should be considered research-based instruments. Based upon the psychometric characteristics and validity evidence described below, however, it is clear that these instruments hold considerable promise for expanding the breadth of cross-cultural and nonverbal personality assessment.

**Strengths and Weaknesses**. The NPQ and FF-NPQ were developed according to rigorous contemporary standards, and they appear to yield much the same information as verbal self-report measures without the attendant limitations. Moreover, their nonverbal format had made them conducive to cross-cultural studies in nearly a dozen countries (Hong and Paunonen 2008). As the NPQ pictorial paradigm undergoes evaluation by independent researchers in the coming years, it may lead to further expansion of nonverbal techniques in the assessment of personality disorders and psychopathology.

Both the NPQ and the FF-NPQ demonstrate adequate reliability. In spite of the relative brevity of NPQ scales, internal consistency tends to be adequate, with mean coefficient alpha across scales of 0.75 in a Canadian sample, 0.78 for an English sample, 0.67 across four European cultures, 0.61 for a Hong Kong sample, and 0.59 for an Israeli sample (Hong and Paunonen 2008; Paunonen et al. 1996, 2000). These reliability findings tend to compare favorably with various translations of the PRF verbal scales. The FF-NPQ scales have been reported to have a mean internal consistency of 0.80 (Paunonen et al. 2001).

Convergent validity also appears to be good. Convergence of the NPQ with PRF verbal self-report indices translated across multiple languages yields a mean $r = 0.43$, although there is variability across cultures (Paunonen et al. 1996; Paunonen et al. 2000). Hong and Paunonen (2008) argue that the correlation is somewhat suppressed because nonverbal tests are limited to depicting behaviors that are observable, while verbal tests can describe observable states as well as internal emotional states.

The FF-NPQ scales have been reported to have a mean correlation with the corresponding scales on the NEO-FFI of $r = 0.52$, with self-ratings and peer ratings of $r = 0.41$, and with 14 external behavior criteria a multiple $R = 0.25$ (Paunonen et al. 2001).

The factor structure of the NPQ has been found to be generally invariant across cultures as well as across verbal and nonverbal methods (Hong and Paunonen 2008; Paunonen et al. 1992). Exploratory principal components analyses generally yield five orthogonal factors across cultures, corresponding to the big five factors of personality. When intercorrelation matrices are compared across cultures, coefficients of congruence are consistently high (0.83), suggesting a robust and generalizable factor structure

(Paunonen et al. 1996). Metafactor-analytic methodologies are suggestive that the NPQ has robust structure across 10 or more cultures and language groups, including Canada, England, Finland, Israel, Germany, the Netherlands, Norway, Poland, Russia, and Hong Kong (Paunonen et al. 1996, 2000).

The test's psychometric properties have been reported to be the best in North American samples (Paunonen et al. 2000), presumably because some of the behaviors represented may be culture specific. For example, items portray people dreaming about graduation from the university, attending a party with dancing and drinking, playing pool, and even flying a hang glider! The degree to which these activities are predominantly Western has not been evaluated, but an international bias and review panel might recommend that some of these items be considered for deletion because they may not exemplify familiar activities to members of non-Western cultures.

As normal-range research instruments, the NPQ and FF-NPQ are in need of a nationally representative normative sample before they can be used for applied purposes. Items with strong cultural associations should be considered for deletion in favor of more universal types of items, and the item stimuli should be redrawn with more realistic figures depicted instead of stick figures. The big five model of personality has generally had limited value in the appraisal of known or suspected psychopathology although efforts to bridge research and clinical practice of personality assessment continue (e.g., Lamersa et al. 2012). The NPQ's major advantages over comparable verbal measures include better cross-cultural transferability without the need for item translations, as well as potential utility with illiterate populations or individuals with language-based disabilities (Paunonen et al. 1996).

## Visual Analog Scales

Another approach to nonverbal administration of self-report measures is to utilize graphic rating scales anchored by self-explanatory pictures.

This methodology was first described by Aitken (1969) and typically requires examinees to mark on a unipolar or bipolar graphic rating scale how they feel at a given time. The location of the mark on a standard 100 mm line relative to the polar extremes yields an interpretable score. For example, an examinee may be asked to indicate how he or she currently feels by placing a line on "X" at the appropriate segment of a scale with a happy face at one end and a sad face at the other.

Deceptive in their simplicity, visual analog scales may be used with a wide range of populations. They are readily understood by neurologically impaired individuals (Stern et al. 1991) and generally yield convergent findings with more language-loaded measures. The reliabilities of visual analog scales tapping psychiatric experiences of anxiety or depression have been shown to be robust across raters and across categorical or continuous scales (Remington et al. 1979). Visual analog scales offer a simple nonverbal alternative to narrowband self-rating measures.

A search of the *Mental Measurements Yearbook* database shows that there are few commercially available normed visual analog scales, with most containing considerable verbal test stimuli in addition to the analog scales. For example, the Derogatis Stress Profile (Derogatis 1987) includes but a single item 100-mm visual analog measure, tapping the examinee's subjective evaluation of their current level of stress (Subjective Stress Score). The Dissociative Experiences Scale (Bernstein and Putnam 1986) features a 100-mm response line for each item verbally describing a dissociative experience, requiring the respondent to mark an "X" on the spot representing the percentage of occurrence between 0 and 100. Both measures are embedded in longer verbally loaded tests.

The only norm-referenced visual analog scales are the Visual Analog Mood Scales (VAMS; Stern 1997). The VAMS includes unipolar, vertically presented scales tapping eight mood states (afraid, sad, energetic, happy, confused, angry, tired, and tense), each anchored by a neutral face at the top end and a specific mood face at the bottom end.

**Administration**. The VAMS may be administered to individuals or groups for whom conventional language-loaded measures are inappropriate, especially those with language or other cognitive deficits. It is suitable for self- or examiner administration, with examinees instructed to make one mark across the line to show how they feel, following a brief verbal explanation and demonstration. The examiner's vocal intonation and facial expression should match the valence of the mood being assessed. Administrative accommodations are provided in the manual for examinees who are unable to write. The VAMS typically requires no more than 5 min to administer.

**Scoring and Interpretation**. The VAMS is scored using a ruler that measures the distance (from 0 to 100 mm) from the neutral end of the line to the middle of the examinee's mark. For example, an examinee who makes a mark at the 34-mm receives a raw score of 34 on that scale. Raw scores for each scale may be converted to age- and gender-appropriate linear transformed $T$ scores ($M = 50$, $SD = 10$), and the $T$ scores may be graphically represented in the response booklet. The VAMS is normed for ages of 18–94 years. The VAMS was normed in its self-administered form on 579 adults between the ages of 18 and 94 years. The normative sample was representative of age, gender, and race, according to 1990 census results. Reference norms for 290 psychiatric inpatients and outpatients, including groups with major depression, mild depression, and anxiety disorders, are also available.

Six VAMS scales measure predominantly negative mood stages (fear, confusion, sadness, anger, and fatigue), and two scales measure positive mood states (vigor and happiness). Stern (1997) recommends that scores on the negative mood scales be interpreted as follows: $59T$ or lower is within normal limits, $60–69T$ is borderline, and $70T$ or greater is abnormal. For the positive mood scales, scores above $40T$ are within normal limits, scores of $31–40T$ are borderline, and scores at or below $30T$ are abnormal.

A cutoff raw score of 50 on the Sadness scale has been reported to maximize the aggregate sensitivity, positive predictive power, and negative predictive power in the differentiation of major and mild depressive disorders from demographically matched normal standardization participants. Approximately 86% of respondents who score 50 or greater on the Sadness scale would likely be diagnosed with a depressive disorder.

The VAMS may also be used to track changes in mood over time. A change of more than $30T$ may be interpreted as reflecting both a reliable and a clinically significant change in level of mood. The VAMS has been shown to be as sensitive to the therapeutic changes from electroconvulsive therapy (ECT) as verbal self-report rating scales (Arruda et al. 1996).

**Strengths and Limitations**. The VAMS shows promising psychometric evidence of validity (Stern 1997; Stern et al. 2010). Several investigations have provided convergent and discriminant validity for the VAMS, through the use of multitrait–multimethod studies (Nyenhuis et al. 1997; Stern 1997; Stern et al. 1997). In two geometrically separate samples administered both the VAMS and the Profile of Mood States (POMS; McNair et al. 1981), convergent validity was supported by statistically significant correlations between corresponding scales of the two methods relative to correlations between noncorresponding scales. Convergent validity with an adapted version of the POMS was again demonstrated with stroke patients. Correlations with the Beck Depression Inventory (BDI; Beck and Steer 1987) in two samples yielded the highest correlations with the VAMS Sad scale (ranging from $r = 0.53$ to 0.54). The VAMS has also been found to be highly correlated with the clinician's Clinical Global Improvement rating and patient self-report using a modified Center for Epidemiological Studies Depression Scale (Arruda et al. 1996). Correlations with the State-Trait Anxiety Inventory (STAI; State form; Spielberger et al. 1970) predictably yielded a high correlation with the VAMS Tense scale ($r = 0.66$).

As reported above, the VAMS shows a good capacity to discriminate between groups with mood disorders and normal comparison samples (Stern 1997). The VAMS also has been shown to be sensitive to the treatment effects of ECT

(Arruda et al. 1996). The reliability of the VAMS has been examined through two test–retest reliability studies conducted with 15-min test–retest intervals, the brief interval intended to minimize state-based fluctuations in mood state (Stern 1997). In a sample of 75 college students, reliability coefficients ranged from 0.49 (Sad) to 0.78 (Anxious, later renamed Tense). In a sample of 27 acute stroke patients, reliability coefficients ranged from 0.43 (Confused) to 0.84 (Afraid). These score reliabilities are somewhat more variable than expected.

The VAMS includes printed verbal descriptors at the poles (e.g., the word "Neutral" at one end and "Afraid" at the other), in addition to the schematic pictorial representations. The use of printed words reduces the nonverbal nature of the VAMS, insofar as word knowledge and reading ability requirements are increased. In an investigation reported by Stern et al. (1997), a group of 96 college students were administered a "no words" version of the VAMS followed in 15 min by the version with printed words. Correlations were statistically significant between each scale without words and the same scale with words, ranging from $r = 0.42$ (Tired) to $r = 0.90$ (Happy), with the exception of a low correlation for one scale that was later changed ($r = 0.26$ for the Anxious scale, later renamed Tense). The authors concluded that the VAMS has adequate content validity and can be completed accurately by patients with impaired language comprehension (Stern et al. 1997).

Finally, the VAMS is probably more vulnerable to intentional misrepresentation of an examinee's mood than any of the nonverbal instruments described in this chapter because of its obvious and transparent content. Accordingly, the VAMS should be used with caution for examinees in whom malingering or dissimulation is known or suspected.

## Summary

In this chapter, nonverbal tests and methodologies intended for the measurement of personality and psychopathology have been described. Some of the techniques date back to the beginning of personality assessment in psychology, whereas others are only a few years old. These techniques demonstrate that nonverbal measures can be constructed to tap constructs not readily assessable with traditional verbal methodologies. It is possible to use nonverbal assessment to span the full range of personality assessment, from objective to projective tests and from structured to unstructured tests. Nonverbal assessments add a potentially valuable set of tools.

In addition, nonverbal assessment methodologies are probably somewhat less transparent (or obvious) in their targeted constructs, thereby being less susceptible to the effects of examinee demand, dissimulation, and impression management. With the exception of the visual analog scales, nonverbal measures seem to be less superficially face valid than verbal self-report or behavior rating scales. Clearly, further research is necessary before nonverbal tests can be proposed as a solution to the biases associated with verbal self-report methods.

At this time, nonverbal personality assessment remains in its infancy. Some initially promising techniques have failed to meet reasonable expectations (e.g., Naglieri et al. 1991), leaving considerable room for new approaches and innovations. Adaptations of the World Technique are widely used in play therapy but generally lack psychometric rigor. The newest measures like the FAST, NPQ and FF-NPQ, and the VAMS promise to usher in a new era of instruments that can meet existing professional standards, but all need additional research. In meeting the needs of practitioners, nonverbal assessments must do more than merely match the informational yield of verbal assessments to gain acceptance. They must also expand the diversity of populations that psychologists can serve and the breadth of constructs that can be measured reliably and validly. The next major evolutionary stage in the development of nonverbal personality assessment will be the demonstration of additional incremental validity in the assessment process, relative to standard verbal personality and psychopathology assessment procedures. If nonverbal measures can be demonstrated to add

to the ability of psychologists to explain and predict behavior, then these measures can expect widespread use in the future.

# References

Achenbach, T. M. (2011). Commentary: Definitely more than measurement error: But how should we understand and deal with informant discrepancies? *Journal of Clinical Child and Adolescent Psychology, 40*(1), 80–86.

Achenbach, T. M., Krukowki, R. A., Dumenci, L., & Ivanova, M. Y. (2005). Assessment of adult psychopathology: Meta-analyses and implications of cross-informant comparisons. *Psychological Bulletin, 131,* 361–382.

Achenbach, T. M., McConaughy, S. H., & Howell, C. T. (1987). Child/adolescent behavioral and emotional problems: Implications of cross-informant correlations for situational specificity. *Psychological Bulletin, 101,* 213–232.

Aitken, R. C. B. (1969). Measurement of feelings using visual analogue scales. *Proceedings of the Royal Society of Medicine, 62,* 989–993.

Aoki, S. (1981). The retest reliability of the sand play technique: II. *British Journal of Projective Psychology & Personality Study, 26,* 25–33.

Archer, R. P., Handel, R. W., Ben-Porath, Y. S., & Tellegen, A. (2016). *Minnesota multiphasic personality inventory-adolescent restructured form (MMPI-A-RF).* Minneapolis, MN: University of Minnesota Press.

Arruda, J. E., Stern, R. A., & Legendre, S. A. (1996). Assessment of mood state in patients undergoing electroconvulsive therapy: The utility of visual analog mood scales developed for cognitively impaired patients. *Convulsive Therapy, 12,* 207–212.

Bardos, A. N., & Doropoulou, M. (2014). Draw-a-person screening procedure for emotional disturbance validity evidence. In L. Handler & A. D. Thomas (Eds.), *Drawings in assessment and psychotherapy: Research and application* (pp. 42–57). New York: Routledge.

Beck, A. T., & Steer, R. A. (1987). *Beck depression inventory manual.* San Antonio, TX: The Psychological Corporation.

Beck, A. T., Steer, R. A., & Brown, G. K. (1996). *Beck depression inventory manual* (2nd ed.). San Antonio, TX: The Psychological Corporation.

Bell, J. E. (1948). *Projective techniques: A dynamic approach to the study of the personality.* New York: Longmans, Green.

Bender, L. (1938). *A visual motor gestalt test and its clinical use. Research monograph No. 3.* New York: American Orthopsychiatric Association.

Ben-Porath, Y. S., & Tellegen, A. (2008). *MMPI-2-RF (Minnesota multiphasic personality inventory-2 restructured form): Manual for administration, scoring, and interpretation.* Minneapolis, MN: University of Minnesota Press.

Bernreuter, R. G. (1931). *Bernreuter personality inventory.* Stanford, CA: Stanford University Press.

Bernstein, E. M., & Putnam, F. W. (1986). Development, reliability, and validity of a dissociation scale. *Journal of Nervous and Mental Disease, 174,* 727–735.

Buck, J. N. (1948). The H-T–P technique: A qualitative and quantitative scoring manual. *Journal of Clinical Psychology, 4,* 317–396.

Buck, J. N., & Warren, W. L. (1992). *House–tree–person projective drawing technique (H–T–P): Manual and interpretive guide.* Los Angeles: Western Psychological Services.

Buhler, C. (1951a). The World test: A projective technique. *Journal of Child Psychiatry, 2,* 4–23.

Buhler, C. (1951b). The World test: Manual of directions. *Journal of Child Psychiatry, 2,* 69–81.

Buhler, C., & Kelly, G. (1941). *The World test. A measurement of emotional disturbance.* San Antonio, TX: The Psychological Corporation.

Burns, R. C. (1982). *Self-growth in families: Kinetic family drawings (K–F–D): Research and application.* New York: Brunner/Mazel.

Burns, R. C., & Kaufman, S. H. (1970). *Kinetic family drawings (K–F–D): An introduction to understanding children through kinetic drawings.* New York: Brunner/Mazel.

Burns, R. C., & Kaufman, S. H. (1972). *Actions, styles, and symbols in Kinetic family drawings (K–F–D): An interpretive manual.* New York: Brunner/Mazel.

Butcher, J. N., Dahlstrom, W. G., Graham, J. R., Tellegen, A., & Kaemmer, B. (1989). *Minnesota multiphasic personality inventory—2 (MMPI-2): Manual for administration and scoring.* Minneapolis: University of Minnesota Press.

Camara, W. J., Nathan, J. S., & Puente, A. E. (2000). Psychological test usage: Implications in professional psychology. *Professional psychology: Research & practice, 31,* 141–154.

Cummings, J. A. (1986). Projective drawings. In H. M. Knoff (Ed.), *The assessment of child and adolescent personality* (pp. 199–244). New York: Guilford.

Derogatis, L. R. (1987). The Derogatis stress profile (DSP): Quantification of psychological stress. *Advances in Psychosomatic Medicine, 17,* 30–54.

Dumont, F., & Smith, D. (1996). Projectives and their infirm research base. *Professional psychology: Research and practice, 27,* 419–421.

Exner, J. E. (1993). *The Rorschach: A comprehensive system. Volume 1: Basic foundations* (3rd ed.). New York: Wiley.

Eysenck, H. J. (1990). *The decline and fall of the Freudian empire.* Washington, DC: Scott-Townsend.

Flanagan, R., & Motta, R. W. (2007). Figure drawings: A popular method. *Psychology in the Schools, 44*(3), 257–270.

Frank, L. K. (1939). Projective methods for the study of personality. *Journal of Psychology, 8,* 389–413.

Frank, L. K. (1948). *Projective methods.* Springfield, IL: Charles C. Thomas.

Freyd, M. (1923). The graphic rating scale. *Journal of Educational Psychology, 14,* 83–102.

Ganellen, R. J. (2007). Assessing normal and abnormal personality functioning: Strengths and weaknesses of self-report, observer, and performance-based methods. *Journal of Personality Assessment, 89,* 30–40.

Garb, H. N. (1999). Call for a moratorium on the use of the Rorschach Inkblot in clinical and forensic settings. *Assessment, 6,* 313–317.

Gehring, T. M. (1998). *The Family system test (FAST).* Seattle WA: Hogrefe & Huber.

Gehring, T. M., Debry, M., & Smith, P. K. (Eds.). (2001). *The Family system test: Theory and application.* Philadelphia, PA: Brunner-Routledge.

Gehring, T. M., & Marti, D. (2001). Concept and psychometric properties of the FAST. In T. M. Gehring, M. Debry, & P. K. Smith (Eds.), *The Family system test (FAST): Theory and application* (pp. 3–27). Philadelphia, PA: Brunner-Routledge.

Gehring, T. M., & Page, J. (2000). Family system test (FAST): A systemic approach for family evaluation in clinical practice and research. In K. Gitlin-Weiner, A. Sandgrund, & C. Schaefer (Eds.), *Play diagnosis and assessment* (2nd ed., pp. 419–445). New York: Wiley.

Gitlin-Weiner, K., Sandgrund, A., & Schaefer, C. (Eds.). (2000). *Play diagnosis and assessment* (2nd ed.). New York: Wiley.

Goldberg, L. R. (1993). The structure of phenotypic personality traits. *American Psychologist, 48*(1), 26.

Goodenough, F. L. (1926). *Measurement of intelligence by drawings.* New York: World Book AQ: Company.

Handler, L., & Habenicht, D. (1994). The Kinetic family drawing technique: A review of the literature. *Journal of Personality Assessment, 62,* 440–464.

Harris, D. B. (1963). *Children's drawings as measures of intellectual maturity.* New York: Harcourt, Brace & World.

Hartshorne, H., & May, M. (1928). *Tests of honesty and trustworthiness.* New York: Association Press.

Holt, R. R. (1992). The contemporary crises of psychoanalysis. *Psychoanalysis & Contemporary Thought, 15,* 375–403.

Hong, R., & Paunonen, S. V. (2008). Nonverbal personality assessment. In G. J. Boyle, G. Matthews, & D. H. Saklofske (Eds.), *Handbook of personality theory and testing* (pp. 485–507). London: Sage.

Homberger, E. [Erikson, E. H.] (1938). Dramatic productions test. In H. A. Murray (Ed.), *Explorations in personality: A clinical and experimental study of fifty men of college age* (pp. 552–582). New York: Oxford University Press.

Huprich, S. K., Bornstein, R. F., & Schmitt, T. A. (2011). Self-report methodology is insufficient for improving the assessment and classification of Axis II personality disorders. *Journal of Personality Disorders, 25*(5), 557–570.

Hutt, M. L. (1985). *The Hutt adaptation of the Bender-Gestalt test* (4th ed.). New York: Grune & Stratton.

Imuta, K., Scarf, D., Pharo, H., & Hayne, H. (2013). Drawing a close to the use of human figure drawings as a projective measure of intelligence. *PLoS ONE, 8* (3), e58991.

Jackson, D. N. (1971). A sequential system for personality scale development. In C. D. Spielberger (Ed.), *Current topics in clinical and community psychology* (Vol. 2, pp. 61–92). New York: Academic Press.

Jackson, D. N. (1984). *Personality research form manual.* Port Huron, MI: Research Psychologists.

Kahill, S. (1984). Human figure drawing in adults: An update of the empirical evidence, 1967–1982. *Canadian Psychology, 25,* 269–292.

Klein, R. G. (1986). Questioning the clinical usefulness of projective psychological tests for children. *Journal of Developmental and Behavioral Pediatrics, 7,* 378–382.

Knoff, H. M. (1993). The utility of human figure drawings in personality and intellectual assessment: Why ask why? *School Psychology Quarterly, 8,* 191–196.

Koppitz, E. M. (1968). *Psychological evaluation of children's human figure drawings.* New York: Grune & Stratton.

Lamersa, S., Westerhofa, G. J., Kovácsb, V., & Bohlmeijera, E. T. (2012). Differential relationships in the association of the Big Five personality traits with positive mental health and psychopathology. *Journal of Research in Personality, 46*(5), 517–524.

Levick, M. F. (2000). *The Levick emotional and cognitive art therapy assessment (LECATA* rev ed.). Boca Raton, FL: South Florida Art Psychotherapy Institute.

Levick, M. F. (2009). *Levick emotional and cognitive art therapy assessment: A normative study.* Bloomington, IN: AuthorHouse.

Lindzey, G. (1961). *Projective techniques and cross-cultural research.* New York: Appleton-Century-Crofts.

Lowenfeld, M. (1939). The world pictures of children; A method of recording and studying them (Paper read on March 23rd, 1938 to the medical section of the British Psychological Society). *British Journal of Medical Psychology, 18,* 65–101.

Lowenfeld, M. (1979). *The World Technique.* London: Allen & Unwin.

Machover, K. (1949). *Personality projection in the drawing of the human figure (A method of personality investigation).* Springfield, IL: Charles C. Thomas.

Martin, R. P. (1983). The ethical issues in the use and interpretation of the Draw-a-person test and other similar projective procedures. *School Psychologist, 38* (6), 8.

Matto, H. C. (2001). Investigating the clinical utility of the Draw-a-person: Screening procedure for emotional disturbance (DAP:SPED) projective test in assessment of high-risk youth. A measurement validation study. *Dissertation Abstracts International, 61*(2), 2920.

Matto, H. C. (2002). Investigating the validity of the Draw-a-person: Screening procedure for emotional disturbance: A measurement validation study with high-risk youth. *Psychological Assessment, 14*(2), 221–225.

Matto, H. C., Naglieri, J. A., & Clausen, C. (2005). Validity of the Draw-a-person: Screening procedure for emotional disturbance (DAP: SPED) in strengths-based assessment. *Research on Social Work Practice, 15*(1), 41–46.

McGrath, R. E., & Carroll, E. J. (2012). *The current status of "projective" "tests"* American Psychological Association, Washington, DC. doi:http://dx.doi.org/10.1037/13619-018

McNair, D. M., Lorr, M., & Droppleman, L. F. (1981). *Profile of mood states.* San Diego, CA: Educational and Industrial Testing Service.

McNeish, T. J., & Naglieri, J. A. (1993). Identification of individuals with serious emotional disturbance using the Draw a person: Screening procedure for emotional disturbance. *Journal of Special Education, 27,* 115–121.

Michael, J. C., & Buhler, C. (1945). Experiences with personality testing in the neuropsychiatric department of a general hospital. *Diseases of the Nervous System, 6,* 205–211.

Minuchin, S. (1974). *Families & family therapy.* Cambridge, MA: Harvard University Press.

Morgan, C. D., & Murray, H. A. (1935). A method for investigating phantasies: The thematic apperception test. *Archives of Neurology and Psychiatry, 34,* 289–306.

Motta, R. W., Little, S. G., & Tobin, M. I. (1993a). A picture is worth less than a thousand words: Response to reviewers. *School Psychology Quarterly, 8,* 197–199.

Motta, R. W., Little, S. G., & Tobin, M. I. (1993b). The use and abuse of human figure drawings. *School Psychology Quarterly, 8,* 162–169.

Murray, H. A. (1938). *Explorations in personality.* New York: Oxford University Press.

Naglieri, J. A. (1988). *Draw a person: A quantitative scoring system.* San Antonio, TX: The Psychological Corporation.

Naglieri, J. A., McNeish, T. J., & Bardos, A. N. (1991). *Draw a person: Screening procedure for emotional disturbance (DAP: SPED).* Austin, TX: PRO-ED.

Naglieri, J. A., & Pfeiffer, S. I. (1992). Performance of disruptive behavior disordered and normal samples on the Draw a person: Screening procedure for emotional disturbance. *Psychological Assessment, 4,* 156–159.

Nyenhuis, D. L., Stern, R. A., Yamamoto, C., Luchetta, T., & Arruda, J. E. (1997). Standardization and validation of the Visual analog mood scales. *The Clinical Neuropsychologist, 11,* 407–415.

Oltmanns, T. F., & Carlson, E. (2013). Informant reports and the assessment of personality disorders using the five-factor model. In T. A. Widiger & P. T. Costa (Eds.), *Personality disorders and the five-factor model of personality* (3rd ed., pp. 233–248). Washington, DC: American Psychological Association.

Paunonen, S. V., & Ashton, M. C. (2002). The nonverbal assessment of personality: The NPQ and the FF-NPQ. In B. de Raad & M. Perugini (Eds.), *Big five assessment*. Hogrefe & Huber: Göttingen, Germany.

Paunonen, S. V., Ashton, M. C., & Jackson, D. N. (2001). Nonverbal assessment of the big five personality factors. *European Journal of Personality, 15*, 3–18.

Paunonen, S. V., & Jackson, D. N. (1998). *Nonverbal personality questionnaire (NPQ)*. Port Huron, MI: Sigma Assessment Systems.

Paunonen, S. V., Jackson, D. N., & Keinonen, M. (1990). The structured nonverbal assessment of personality. *Journal of Personality, 58*, 481–502.

Paunonen, S. V., Jackson, D. N., Trzebinski, J., & Forsterling, F. (1992). Personality structure across cultures: A multimethod evaluation. *Journal of Personality and Social Psychology, 62*, 447–456.

Paunonen, S. V., Keinonen, M., Trzebinski, J., Forsterling, F., Grishenko-Roze, N., Kouznetsova, L., et al. (1996). The structure of personality in six cultures. *Journal of Cross-Cultural Psychology, 27*, 339–353.

Paunonen, S. V., Zeidner, M., Engvik, H. A., Oosterveld, P., & Maliphant, R. (2000). The nonverbal assessment of personality in five cultures. *Journal of Cross-Cultural Psychology, 31*, 220–239.

Quaglia, R., Longobardi, C., Iotti, N. O., & Prino, L. E. (2015). A new theory on children's drawings: Analyzing the role of emotion and movement in graphical development. *Infant Behavior & Development, 39*, 81–91.

Remington, M., Tyrer, P. J., Newson-Smith, J., & Cicchetti, D. V. (1979). Comparative reliability of categorical and analog rating scales in the assessment of psychiatric symptomatology. *Psychological Medicine, 9*, 765–770.

Rescorla, L. A., Achenbach, T. M., Ivanova, M. Y., et al. (2016). Collateral reports and cross-informant agreement about adult psychopathology in 14 societies. *Journal of Psychopathology and Behavioral Assessment, 38*, 381–397.

Rescorla, L. A., Bochicchio, L., Achenbach, T. M., et al. (2014). Parent–teacher agreement on children's problems in 21 societies. *Journal of Clinical Child and Adolescent Psychology, 43*(4), 627–642.

Reynolds, C. R., & Hickman, J. A. (2004). *Draw-a-person intellectual ability test for children, adolescents, and adults: Examiner's manual*. Pro-Ed.

Rorschach, H. (1921). *Psychodiagnostik*. Bern: Ernst Bircher.

Scott, W. D. (1919). *Personnel system of the U.S. army* (Vol. 2). Washington, DC: U.S. Government Printing Office.

Sjolund, M. (1981). Play-diagnosis and therapy in Sweden: The Erica-method. *Journal of Clinical Psychology, 37*, 322–325.

Sjolund, M. (1993). *The Erica method: A technique for play therapy and diagnosis: A training guide*. Greeley, CO: Carron.

Sjolund, M., & Schaefer, C. E. (1994). The Erica method of sand play diagnosis and assessment. In K. J. O'Connor & C. E. Schaefer (Eds.), *Handbook of play therapy* (Vol. 2, pp. 231–252)., Advances and innovations New York: Wiley.

Smith, D., & Dumont, F. (1995). A cautionary study: Unwarranted interpretations of the draw-a-person test. *Professional psychology: Research & practice, 26*, 298–303.

Spielberger, C. D., Gorsuch, R. L., & Lushene, R. E. (1970). *The State-trait anxiety inventory*. Palo Alto, CA: Consulting Psychologists Press.

Stern, R. A. (1997). *Visual analog mood scales professional manual*. Odessa, FL: Psychological Assessment Resources.

Stern, R. A., Arruda, J. E., Hooper, C. R., Wolfner, G. D., & Morey, C. E. (1997). Visual analogue mood scales to measure internal mood state in neurologically impaired patients: Description and initial validity evidence. *Aphasiology, 11*, 59–71.

Stern, R. A., Daneshvar, D., & Poon, S. (2010). The Visual Analog Mood Scales. In S. Brumfitt (Ed.), *Psychological well being and acquired communication impairments* (pp. 116–136). West Sussex, United Kingdom: Wiley-Blackwell.

Stern, R. A., Rosenbaum, J., White, R. F., & Morey, C. E. (1991). Clinical validation of a visual analogue dysphoria scale for neurologic patients (Abstract). *Journal of Clinical and Experimental Neuropsychology, 13*, 106.

Swenson, C. H. (1968). Empirical evaluations of human figure drawings: 1957–1966. *Psychological Bulletin, 70*, 20–44.

Tharinger, D. J., & Stark, K. D. (1990). A qualitative versus quantitative approach to evaluating the draw-a-person and kinetic family drawing: A study of mood-and anxiety-disorder children. *Psychological Assessment, 2*, 365–375.

Thomas, G. V., & Jolley, R. P. (1998). Drawing conclusions: A re-examination of empirical and conceptual bases for psychological evaluation of children from their drawings. *British Journal of Clinical Psychology, 37*, 127–139.

Vass, Z. (1998). The inner formal structure of the H-T-P drawings: An exploratory study. *Journal of Clinical Psychology, 54*, 611–619.

Vass, Z. (1999). *Projektív rajzvizsgálat algoritmusokkal (A számítógépes formai elemzés módszerének bemutatása a szkizofrénia képi kifejezodésének tükrében)* (Analysis of projective drawings with algorithms. The method of computer assisted formal analysis, validated in visual expression of schizophrenia). Unpublished doctoral dissertation, Budapest: Eötvös Loránd University of Sciences.

Vass, Z. (2012). *A psychological interpretation of drawings and paintings. The SSCA method: A systems analysis approach*. Pécs, Hungary: Alexandra

Publishing/Pècsi Direkt Ltd. (Available from http://kre.academia.edu/VassZoltán)

Wagner, E. E. (1999). Defining projective techniques: The irrelevancy of "projection". *North American Journal of Psychology, 1*, 35–40.

Wood, J. M., Garb, H. N., Nezworski, M. T., Lilienfeld, S. O., & Duke, M. C. (2015). A second look at the validity of widely used Rorschach indices: Comment on Mihura, Meyer, Dumitrascu, and Bombel (2013). *Psychological Bulletin, 141*, 236–249.

Woodworth, R. S. (1917). *Personal data sheet*. Chicago: C. H. Stoelting Company.

Wrightson, L., & Saklofske, D. H. (2000). Validity and reliability of the Draw a person: Screening procedure for emotional disturbance with adolescent students. *Canadian Journal of School Psychology, 16*, 95–102.

# The Nonverbal Assessment of Academic Skills

# 15

## Craig L. Frisby

In the previous version of this chapter which appeared in McCallum (2003), the discussion of nonverbal assessment of academic skills began with an overview of academic skill areas commonly assessed in educational settings (see Frisby 2003, Table 12.1, p. 242). This was followed by a discussion of the three conditions in which the nonverbal assessment of academic skills is most likely to occur with high frequency.

In the first condition, instead of an examiner orally giving directions that require a verbal or behavioral response from the examinee, the respondent (parent, teacher, or other caregiver) observes and records the presence of naturally occurring academic skill behaviors (which may or may not be displayed verbally) by an examinee. Adaptive behavior consists of skills learned throughout human development and performed in response to expectations from communities within which the examinee lives. Adaptive behaviors consist of conceptual, social, and practical skills that are learned which enable persons to function in their everyday lives (Tasse 2013). *Adaptive Behavior Scales* are a form of nonverbal assessment that fits this category, as the respondent simply can read and write responses on the scale protocol.

Some examples among many can be gleaned from an older adaptive behavior scale (Lambert et al. 1993). Here, respondents can rate a school-aged child on the following items that involve the demonstration of academic skills by students up to age 21: Select and mark the highest level of writing (cannot write/print any words; writes/prints name; writes/prints at least ten words; writes/prints whole sentences; writes/prints short notes or memos; writes understandable and complete letters or stories); Select and mark the highest level of mathematical calculation (has no understanding of numbers; discriminates between "one" and "many" or "a lot"; counts two objects by saying "one … two"; mechanically counts to ten; counts ten or more objects; does simple addition and subtraction; performs division and multiplication).

In the second condition, examinees with disabling conditions that involve severe speech and physical impairments (such as cerebral palsy) are unable to speak or write intelligibly due to a variety of neurological, physical, emotional, and/or cognitive limitations. In order to demonstrate academic skills, these individuals need various forms of assistive technology (AT) to demonstrate what they know and can do that can provide alternative ways of demonstrating expressive language communication. The information in Table 15.1 describes internet-based links and resources for AT updates since Frisby (2003), with an emphasis on AT resources for the deaf and/or hard-of-hearing.

In the third condition, individuals with some degree of hearing loss may require test instructions to be read directly from print, which are administered by means of a nonverbal sign

C.L. Frisby (✉)
University of Missouri, 5A Hill Hall,
Columbia, MO 65211, USA
e-mail: FrisbyCL@missouri.edu

© Springer International Publishing AG 2017
R.S. McCallum (ed.), *Handbook of Nonverbal Assessment*,
DOI 10.1007/978-3-319-50604-3_15

**Table 15.1** Internet links to assistive technology (AT) information/resources emphasizing the needs of the deaf and hard of hearing

| Links providing definitions/explanations of key concepts for nonspecialists | http://www.pbs.org/parents/education/learning-disabilities/strategies-for-learning-disabilities/communication-strategies/aac/ http://www.pbs.org/parents/education/learning-disabilities/strategies-for-learning-disabilities/communication-strategies/ http://www.californiaearinstitute.com/hearing-device-center-listening-device-classroom-bay-area.php http://www.asha.org/uploadedFiles/AIS-Hearing-Assistive-Technology.pdf |
|---|---|
| Links providing pictures, descriptions, and/or videos of AT devices | http://www.greatschools.org/gk/articles/assistive-technology-for-kids-with-learning-disabilities-an-overview/ http://www.closingthegap.com/ http://www.closingthegap.com/category/new-and-updated-products/ https://www.microsoft.com/enable/at/types.aspx http://www.nidcd.nih.gov/health/hearing/pages/assistive-devices.aspx http://www.dhs.state.mn.us/main/idcplg?IdcService=GET_DYNAMIC_CONVERSION&RevisionSelectionMethod=LatestReleased&dDocName=id_003399 http://www.harriscomm.com/equipment.html http://www.harriscomm.com/equipment.html |
| Links for AT training programs | http://www.csun.edu/cod/training-programs |
| Links of advocacy organizations for deaf and/or hard-of-hearing | http://www.nidcd.nih.gov/directory/Bykeyword.aspx?key1=8 |

language. In turn, examinee responses are given either in writing of by nonverbal sign language.

Compared to the previous version of this chapter, the remainder of this chapter will go into greater depth on this third condition—i.e., the application of nonverbal assessment issues and practices involving individuals who are deaf or hard of hearing (HOH).

## Prevalence of Deafness and Hearing Loss

Hearing impairment can be attributed to either congenital (present at, or acquired soon after birth) or acquired (occurring at any age due to infectious diseases, chronic ear infections, otitis media, use of particular drugs, regular exposure to excessive noise, or head injury) causes (World Health Organization 2015). In 2012, the World Health Organization estimated that 5.3% of the world's population (approximately 360 million persons) have a disabling hearing loss (World Health Organization 2012). According to more

recent National Center for Disease Control (CDC) Early Hearing Detection and Intervention (EHDI) summary data for 2013, out of nearly 4 million births that occurred in 49 states, 5 territories, and the District of Columbia who received a hearing screen, 1.5 out of 1000 infants were diagnosed as having some hearing loss (Centers for Disease Control and Prevention 2013). According to National Institute on Deafness and Other Communication Disorders (NIDCD) estimates, more than 90% of deaf children are born to hearing parents (National Institute on Deafness and Other Communication Disorders 2015).

## Types and Categories of Hearing Loss

Sounds are measured in decibels (abbreviated dB). A rocket at takeoff is roughly equivalent to 180 dB. Normal city traffic is roughly equivalent to 90 dB. A soft whisper is roughly equivalent to 30 dB (http://www.hear-it.org/what-db-and-frequency). A hearing healthcare professional can administer assessments by testing each ear individually using either headphones or earplugs. A tone is administered, and the examiner asks the examinee to either press a button or raise their hand. The examiner adjusts the frequency of sounds in order to assess the softest sounds the examinee is able to hear at different pitches.

The results of a hearing test are displayed in the form of an audiogram, which illustrates the examinee's hearing threshold at various sound frequencies (for an example see: http://www. hear-it.org/Audiogram). A "hearing threshold" is defined as the softest sound that can be heard before it is inaudible to the examinee. A hearing threshold of between 0 and 25 decibels is considered normal.

Newborn babies are tested for hearing before they leave the hospital. Persons who may acquire a hearing loss after this time can be initially identified, assessed, and diagnosed by ear, nose, and throat physicians (called otolaryngologists), audiologists (working in universities, hospitals, clinics, or schools) or hearing aid specialists.

The most common categories of hearing loss classifications are mild, moderate, severe, and profound hearing loss (see http://www.hear-it. org/Defining-hearing-loss). Persons may experience different degrees of hearing loss at different pitches of sound (http://www.medel.com/blog/ degree-of-hearing-loss/). For example, a person may experience a mild hearing loss in low frequencies (e.g., the barking of a dog) yet experience profound hearing loss in high sound frequencies (e.g., the ringing of a doorbell).

People with *mild hearing loss* can hear sounds between 25 and 40 decibels with their better ear. They may not be able to hear sounds like a ticking clock or a dripping faucet (http://www. medel.com/blog/degree-of-hearing-loss/). Persons who suffer from mild hearing loss have some difficulties keeping up with conversations in the context of noisy surroundings.

People with *moderate hearing loss* can hear sounds between 40 and 70 decibels with their better ear. Persons with moderate hearing loss have difficulty keeping up with conversations or hearing the ringing of a telephone when they do not use a hearing aid.

Persons with *severe hearing loss* can hear sounds between 70 and 95 decibels. In everyday life, persons in this category may not be able to hear loud conversations or traffic noise without assistive devices such as middle ear or cochlear implants (see next section). Persons in this category require a hearing aid for daily living and often rely on lipreading while using hearing aids. Many also use sign language.

Finally, persons who suffer from *profound hearing loss* cannot hear sounds softer than 90–120 dB. Persons suffering from profound hearing loss may be unable to hear very loud sounds such as airplane engines, moving trucks, or loud fire alarms. Only cochlear implants are effective for this group. Persons within this category rely mostly on lipreading and/or sign language for communication.

## Assistive Devices for Hearing Loss

Assistive hearing devices differ according to the degree of invasiveness in their physical application to the human body, and the degree of hearing loss for which it serves as a solution. An *outer ear hearing aid* can only make sounds that enter the ear canal louder. A *conductive hearing loss* is caused by problems in the middle ear (as opposed to outer or inner ear) which houses the ear drum. For persons who suffer from conductive hearing loss, sound cannot take the natural path through the outer and middle ear to the inner ear, and a middle ear implant may be needed. A *middle ear implant* consists of an externally worn audio processor that sits atop (through the use of strong magnets) a surgical implant that is inserted under the skin above and slightly behind the ear. Sounds are picked up by the microphone in the audio processor, which converts sound into electrical signals. These signals in turn are transmitted through the skin to the implant. The implant, in turn, transmits the signals via a wire to a floating mass transducer (or FMT) which is physically adjacent to the inner ear. The FMT converts the signal into mechanical vibrations that directly stimulate the middle ear structure, causing it to vibrate. These vibrations then conduct sound to the inner ear where they are passed on to the brain and are perceived as sound (see video at http://www. medel.com/int/vibrant-soundbridge).

Like middle ear implants, a *bone conduction implant* consists of an externally worn audio processor that sits atop (through the use of strong magnets) a surgical implant that is inserted under the skin and attached to the temporal bone (above and slightly behind the ear). Here, the microphone in the external processor picks up sound waves, which are converted to electrical signals that are transmitted to the bone-attached implant under the skin. Mechanical vibrations are transmitted to the skull, and the skull bone conducts the vibrations to the inner ear (bypassing the outer and the middle ear). The inner ear processes the mechanical vibrations and transmits the acoustic information to the brain, similar to natural hearing (see video at http://www.medel. com/int/bonebridge/).

*Sensorineural hearing loss* occurs when there are problems with the cochlea (the sensory hearing organ in the inner ear) or with the auditory nerve attached to the cochlea. For this type of hearing loss, outer ear external hearing aids provide little to no benefit. *Cochlear implants* are generally considered to be the only medical intervention that seeks to restore the sense of hearing for persons with severe to profound sensorineural hearing loss. A small audioprocessor externally sits atop (through the use of strong magnets) a surgically implanted device inserted under the skin (above and slightly behind the ear). Sound signals are picked up by the external audioprocessor and transmitted via an electrode surgically implanted into the cochlea and passed on to cochlea nerve fibers. The impulses are then passed on to the auditory cortex of the brain where they are perceived as sound (see http://www.medel.com/chchlear-implants/). Cochlear implants work by bypassing nonfunctioning parts of the inner ear and providing electrical stimulation directly to the nerve fibers in the cochlea.

## Deafness, Hearing Impairments, and Special Education

According to the Institute on Disability (2014), 1.1% of all disabled students aged 6–12 nationwide were served under the IDEA Part B Hearing Impaired category in 2012. The distribution of deaf and hard-of-hearing students receiving special education services in schools may not necessarily be similar to the total numbers of deaf and hard-of-hearing students attending schools (Mitchell and Karchmer 2011). Unlike blindness, there is no legal standard that provides a clear-cut definition of who is or is not deaf (Mitchell and Karchmer 2011). Hearing loss and impairments exist in degrees, and there is no legal threshold beyond which a student is considered to be "legally deaf". The federal government has two categories for serving students with hearing impairments (only) in special education: (1) "Deafness" is defined as a hearing impairment that is so severe, that a child is impaired in processing linguistic information through hearing, with or without amplification, that adversely affects a child's educational performance, and (2) "Hearing Impairment" is defined as an impairment in hearing, whether permanent or fluctuating that adversely affects a child's performance but is not included under the definition of deafness (Center for Parent Information and Resources 2015).

## Difficulties Experienced by Deaf or Hard of Hearing Students for Language/Literacy Development

Mayer and Trezek (2015) describe four developmentally sequenced phases of language/literacy development for children without sensory impairments: acquiring a language (phase 1), thinking with language (phase 2), linking language to print (phase 3), and developing literacy for learning and educational purposes (phase 4). Deaf and HOH children experience this same developmental sequence (Williams 2004), however they graduate secondary school many grade levels behind their hearing peers in reading levels (Traxler 2000), with many leaving school functionally illiterate (Marschark et al. 2002). However, these dire statistics cannot be assumed to be unaffected by the emergence of technologies such as cochlear implants (Archbold 2010; Archbold and Mayer 2012).

## Phase 1: Acquiring a Language

Learning to read and write is built on a foundation of how well a child has developed skills in spoken, signed, or a combination spoken/signed language (Mayer and Trezek 2015). Nearly all hearing children acquire a complex and rule-governed grasp of core grammar even in the absence of formal instruction (Gee 2001). Regardless of individual differences in SES and other sociocultural variables, all children possess the biological capacity to acquire vocabulary and rule-governed grammar in their native language. Research indicates that a typical six-year old child will accrue at least 2600 words in his/her expressive vocabulary and between 20,000 and 40,000 words in their receptive vocabulary (Owens 2012). However, these numbers can vary significantly as a function of individual differences in intellectual ability, SES-related differences in the home environment, and the presence of language disabilities (Kaiser et al. 2011; Neuman 2011; Vasilyeva and Waterfall 2011).

The following four environmental conditions are necessary in order for formal language/literacy instruction to have maximum effect: (1) adequate exposure to both quality and quantity of language, (2) fully functioning language input channels, (3) meaningful language/literacy interactions with caregivers, and (4) caregivers who themselves are capable users of language (Mayer 2007). With respect to the first condition (adequate exposure to both quality and quantity of language), adequate language opportunities must be present in the child's environment from birth, the purpose of which is to "mediate activities in which [children] are interested and that matter to them (e.g.,

bath time, playing games, going for a walk)" (p. 31). Unfortunately, deaf and HOH children are most vulnerable in being disadvantaged in the second condition. Here, it simply cannot be assumed that deaf and HOH children have fully acquired face-to-face exposure to spoken English in the same way as hearing children. In addition, most deaf children are born to hearing parents who had no expectation that their children would be deaf (Mitchell and Karchmer 2004). Many deaf children of hearing parents have different early environments than those of hearing children of hearing parents. These include, but are not limited to, barriers to full access of the language of their families, and/or hearing parents not being fully equipped to handle the special needs of a deaf child (Marschark et al. 2002). A deaf child born to parents who are deaf—and who also are skilled in the use of sign language—will begin to acquire sign language at home as comfortably and naturally as a hearing child acquires spoken language from hearing parents. However, deaf children growing up in homes with hearing parents can only be exposed to the learning of sign language if the parents learn it as well either before the child is born or learn it with their child's learning of it. Deaf children who are exposed to a school learning environment in which sign language is taught can often learn sign language more quickly than their hearing parents (National Institute on Deafness and Other Communication Disorders 2015).

Thus, the combination of an incomplete exposure to spoken language, and the fact that reading and writing learning is based on such a system, results in low literacy levels among students with severe to profound hearing impairments (Geers 2006). However, those deaf children born into homes in which at least one parent is proficient in a signing communication can display age-appropriate development in the signed language (Baker and Woll 2008). Advanced hearing technological interventions (e.g., cochlear implants, bone conducting hearing implants) also show promise for bring hearing impaired children up to age-appropriate language skills (Archbold 2010).

## Phase 2: Thinking with Language

Approximately at three years of age, children are able to differentiate between social language (use of language for communicating with others) and self-language (use of an inner mental language to communicate with oneself). Theorists essentially argue that the quality of self-language is tied directly to the quality of acquiring a first language (Phase 1), and that the quality of self-language in turn influences the quality of reading and writing learning in the first language (Watson 2001). According to Mayer and Trezek (2015), "… deaf children … have not developed competence in any face-to-face language, [and] … they will not have developed inner speech and thus not have a full language to think with. This will have significant repercussions for all aspects of learning, including the development of reading and writing" (p. 35). The bottom line here is that children must be able to think in the same language as the materials from which they will be learning to read and write.

## Phase 3: Linking Language to Print

When acquiring a spoken language (in the case of hearing children) or a signed language (in the case of many deaf or HOH children), the words or signs are a direct, symbolic representation of the events and objects being referred to. Said differently, a spoken word or a sign provides a "straight-line" representation of the object (called a "first-order representation", see Mayer and Trezek 2015). In contrast, writing is a "second-order" symbol system that reflects a visual representation of a spoken work or sign (and not a direct "straight-line" representation of it). To make sense of written words, the word must first be mapped onto the spoken (or signed) representation of the word. Here, hearing children must make connections at the phoneme-grapheme level to decode or encode the word, and then access the word in the mental lexicon.

Unfortunately, many deaf children lack full control of the primary spoken or signed language that needs to be read or written. If deaf children have difficulty expressing themselves in the face-to-face form of the language, and have not as yet developed a complete internal representation of that language, then they will not be able to make sense of written text (as they lack the requisite linguistic foundation).

## Phase 4: Developing Literacy for Learning and Educational Purposes

As children enter Phase 4, it is assumed that the connection between face-to-face language (Phase 1) and print (Phase 3) has been established, basic decoding and encoding skills have been mastered, and that comprehension and generation of text are now possible (Mayer and Trezek 2015). In this phase, children must gain mastery of two complementary modes of language: basic interpersonal communication skills and cognitive-academic language proficiency (see Cummins 2000). The former language mode refers to mastery of the ways in which persons speak and write in everyday, informal communication (e.g., "Bob always eats macaroni at every meal"), versus using language in more formalized academic settings that are far removed from everyday informal language contexts (e.g., "Bob's passion for macaroni was not clearly understood by his older siblings"). This latter mode involves reading and writing with more abstract topics, employing lower frequency grammar, as well as more complex sentence structures (Mayer and Trezek 2015).

The challenges of mastering Phase 4 language are more pronounced with deaf children. Here, they must develop mastery of academically oriented school-based texts without complete control of the language within which they are expected to read and write.

## Modes of Language Used for Communicating with Deaf and HOH Individuals

In the context of spoken language, words are produced by using the mouth and voice to make sounds. For persons who are profoundly deaf, speech sounds cannot be heard, and only a small fraction of speech sounds can be discerned from lipreading. A "sign language" is based on the idea that deaf persons must rely to a significant degree on their visual skills to properly communicate and receive information (National Institute on Deafness and Other Communication Disorders 2015).

American Sign Language (hereafter abbreviated as ASL) uses hand shapes, hand positions, hand movements, facial expressions, and body movements to convey meaning. As one among many examples, asking a question in regular speech involves a slight raising of the voice pitch at the end of a question. In contrast, communication in ASL asks a question by raising the eyebrow, widening the eyes, and tilting the body forward (National Institute on Deafness and Other Communication Disorders 2015). ASL makes use of finger spelling to convey letters of the alphabet, signs representing ideas, and manual gestures that represent common words. ASL is not simply a manual version of English (as are Signed Exact English and Pidgin Signed English), but it is an independent language that has its own grammar and syntax. No one form of sign language is universal, as different sign languages (as well as regional variations within the same sign language) are used within and across different countries.

*Manually Coded English (MCE)* is an umbrella term that describes communication systems for deaf people that represent exactly the grammar and vocabulary of the English language. For example, MCE systems include word suffixes and prefixes that are not provided in ASL. Some examples of names for MCE systems are Signed Exact English (SEE), Manual English, fingerspelling, and Signed English.

*Signed Exact English* (abbreviated SEE) is a system of manual communication that strives to be an exact representation of English vocabulary and grammar. It does not represent "its own unique language", as does ASL, but quite simply is a means for signing the English language. This is used by persons who adhere to the educational philosophy that the learning of SEE would make it easier for deaf persons to learn how to speak "regular" English (Gustason and Zawolkow 2006).

*Pidgin Signed English* (PSE) is the term associated with a hybrid system of ASL and English. Many deaf persons (who may have become deaf later in life) learn and use spoken English first in life, then learn to sign much later in life. As a result, they use a mixture of ASL and English by signing most of the English words in a sentence but approximate an English syntax (Valli and Lucas 2000).

The choice of whether or not children and youth learn and use ASL or MCE has sociopolitical overtones (e.g., see https://www.quora.com/What-are-some-of-the-controversies-cultural-or-political-disputes-within-deaf-culture). Since ASL tends to be the preferred method of communication for Deaf communities, and MCE tends to be taught and used in instructional contexts seeking integration with hearing communities, the choice of method has implications for self-identification, the need for acceptance in particular communities, and civil rights issues.

*Cued speech* is the name given to a visual mode of communication for deaf persons that uses handshapes and hand placements (in order to distinguish consonant and vowel sounds) in combination with the mouth movements of speech (National Cued Speech Association 2015). Handshapes, hand placements, and mouth/lip movements are used in tandem to form syllables and words. Cued speech enables deaf persons to visually distinguish among phonemes (smallest units of speech sounds) in spoken language (see https://www.youtube.com/watch?v=6B18_G_8JHs).

The mode used to communicate with deaf children in the classroom will also vary by setting. For example, some schools for the deaf use sign language almost exclusively, whereas a fully mainstreamed student may have no one who signs in their learning environment (Luetke-Stahlman and Nielsen 2003). Some deaf and hard-of-hearing students can speech-read to some degree, but this is difficult because approximately half of language sounds are distinguishable from other sounds (Williams 1994).

## Large-Scale Academic Achievement Testing with Deaf Students

Accountability for schools that serve students with disabilities, which include deaf and hard-of-hearing students, is a standard feature of federal legislation requiring the inclusion of all students in state and district-wide assessment programs (for a review, see Qi and Mitchell 2012). Such standards require testing accommodations for students with disabilities for enabling their participation in large-scale assessment programs.

Many students who are deaf or hard of hearing have concomitant disabilities (e.g., learning disabilities, cerebral palsy, mental retardation, emotional disturbance, and attention deficit disorders; see Gallaudet Research Institute 2005). Even when students have only hearing problems, this causes significant impediments to their participation in statewide standardized assessments.

Unfortunately, psychometric challenges arise when assessing deaf and HOH students with standardized tests originally designed for hearing students. First, significant portions of deaf and HOH students are not on grade level, nor do they receive comparable levels of instruction in the general curriculum compared to hearing students —despite Individuals with Disabilities Education Act Amendments of 1997 mandates (Qi and Mitchell 2012). Second, many deaf and HOH students receive classroom instruction through American Sign Language (ASL) or through another visual communication mode, which in turn limits their English proficiency. Translation of statewide standardized achievement tests into ASL is limited to only a few states (e.g., see Foster 2008).

The Guidelines for Accessible Assessments Project (GAAP) is a federally funded effort led by the Maryland State Department of Education and the Measured Progress Innovation Lab, working in conjunction with 17 partner states, the National Center for Educational Outcomes (NCEO), the National Center for Accessible Media (NCAM), and national accessibility experts and educators to develop research-based

guidelines for the representation of test items in audio and American Sign Language. GAAP has published guidelines intended to aid state departments of education, assessment consortia, and test vendors in creating standardized ASL versions of test items. The aim of the guidelines is to ensure that ASL versions of test items provide quality access to students who use ASL to communicate and/or learn content in the classroom, while still measuring the same construct as is measured in the English text version of the assessment. The GAAP ASL guidelines are accompanied by sample items (available at http://gaap.measuredprogress.org/gaap/) created by the GAAP ASL Working Group, a team with collective expertise in assessment, accessibility, instruction, content and academic standards, and ASL (Measured Progress Innovation Lab 2015).

The Stanford Achievement Test (SAT) has been the only national large-scale assessment regularly used to monitor the academic achievement of deaf and HOH students since the 1970s, and yearly norming study data can be accessed from the Gallaudet Research Institute (https://research.gallaudet.edu/Demographics/annsrvy.php). When a new edition of the SAT is created, the Gallaudet University's Office of Research Support and international Affairs (RSIA) constructs a representative sample of deaf and hard of hearing students (using Annual Survey of Deaf and hard of Hearing Youth data) and includes norming tables using this information in the new edition of the test. When schools elect to give the SAT to deaf and/or HOH students, they can contact RSIA, who in turn provides them with test documents and special forms that schools fill out and send back to RSIA with student test responses. Pearson Assessments will score the test using normal procedures (i.e., by providing raw scores, scaled scores, and grade equivalents) but will not provide normative data (since their norms coincidence only with the general population). Pearson then sends the scored school data to RSIA directly, where reports are generated that will include age-based deaf and HOH norms (see http://www.gallaudet.edu/rsia/research-support/research-services/stanford-test-scoring.html).

## The Use of Accommodations When Testing Deaf Students

Assessment *accommodations* are meant to increase access to the test content while allowing for the score to be interpreted in the same manner as that for a test taken without an accommodation. However, there are additional accommodations that are more specific to language characteristics of students who are deaf or hard of hearing, including (a) having an interpreter translate test directions, reading passages, or test items by either using sign language, a signed system, or a read-aloud approach; and (b) allowing the students to respond using sign language and having their responses recorded by a scribe who back-translates those responses into English (Cawthon and Leppo 2013). When an interpreter or other sign language based accommodations are used, there are potentially significant implications for the role the resultant scores play in high-stakes decisions. According to Cawthon et al. (2011):

> Language translations are rarely exact, and the translation from English to ASL involves different grammatical structures and ways of representing information. As a result, and ASL-translated item may be harder, easier, or simply measure a different construct than the original item (p. 198).

When attempting to administer a test under standardized conditions, a computer-based strategy can be used that integrates recordings of test content administered in a signed format, using either avatars (computerized representations of human figures) or actual humans (Russell et al. 2009). Cawthon et al. (2011) describe a study designed to ascertain the effects of an ASL administration on Iowa Test of Basic Skills (ITBS) reading and math proficiency scores. In the ASL condition of the study, test directions and test items were provided both in ASL on a DVD (shown on a computer screen) and in a written version in a test booklet. For reading and math items, an item was first presented in print on a screen, then it was visually demonstrated in ASL, and then the print version was presented again on the screen. After the second print exposure on the screen, participating students were given time to respond to the items in their test booklets. Using psychometrically equivalent versions of test items across ASL and non-ASL administration conditions, the authors found no significant differences between the two conditions in the average percent of items that were correctly answered.

## Individually Administered Assessments

Individually administered tests of academic achievement give teachers and diagnosticians opportunities to assess a larger pool of academic skills in both receptive and expressive modes. Numerous state departments of education provide internet-based information documents listing a wide variety of instruments and methods that can be used in assessing students who are deaf or HOH, in response to local, state, or federal mandates developed since the passage of No Child Left Behind (No Child Left Behind 2002) and the Individuals with Disabilities Education Improvement Act of 2004 (Individuals with Disabilities Education Act 2004; see for example Outreach Services for Deaf and Hard-of-Hearing Children 2013). Such documents describe how both informal (e.g., teacher interviews, student interviews and observations, curriculum-based assessments, portfolios) and formal assessments (e.g., intelligence tests, behavior rating scales, reading/math achievement tests) may be useful for these populations. Many of the state department materials include assertions that various tests can be used to assess deaf and/or HOH students, yet they provide no information on norming studies or specific information as to how they can be administered nonverbally to these populations. This does not necessarily mean that there is no norming or alternative administration information on deaf and HOH students for a particular test, only that the state department information document may not include this information (however another state department document may do so).

For the purposes of this chapter, nonverbal individually administered academic skill assessments for deaf and HOH groups are subdivided into two broad categories: (1) instruments requiring examinees to indicate correct answers to test items by choosing (typically via a pointing response) among an array of visually presented options (thereby demonstrating receptive understanding); and (2) instruments requiring examinees to express nonverbally answers to test items (typically via using a sign language), which demonstrates expressive language skills. Some instruments include both categories of item types.

Instruments within both categories do not require examiners to administer test items verbally. This review does not include those instruments that were not developed for deaf children, but on which research may have been conducted and published using participants with cochlear implants. Individually administered nonverbal tests of academic skills requiring receptive understanding are listed in Table 15.2, along with the references.

The American Sign Language Receptive Skills Test (2013) uses a video presentation format (see sample pictures at http://www.signlang-assessment.info/index.php/american-sign-language-receptive-skills-test.html). The child watches a video of a deaf adult who introduces the test and then presents the test sentences. The test consists of three practice sentences and 42 test sentences that assess children's understanding of ASL grammar (e.g., number/distribution, negation, noun/verb distinction, location/action spatial verbs, size and shape specifiers, handling classifiers, role shift, conditionals). After the video presentation of the ASL sentence, the child responds by pointing to the most appropriate picture from a choice of four that appears on the screen. The child's score on the test is converted to a standard score using the standardization table.

The *Carolina Picture Vocabulary Test* (CPVT; Layton and Holmes 1985a, PRO-ED) is a norm- referenced, validated, individually administered, receptive sign vocabulary test for children between the ages of 4–0 and 11–6 who are deaf or hearing impaired (see http://www.proedinc.com/customer/productView.aspx?ID=557). The population ($N = 767$) used in the standardization research was based on a nationwide sample of children who use manual signs as their primary means of communication.

The Tests of Early Reading Ability Deaf and Hard of Hearing (TERA-D/HH; 1991) was reviewed in the last edition of this handbook (Frisby 2003). According to the Administration Manual (Reid et al. 1991):

**Table 15.2** Receptive language scales requiring a nonverbal pointing response to orally spoken or signed stimuli

| Scale | Age range | Sample receptive language skills assessed | Citations |
|---|---|---|---|
| American Sign Language Receptive skills test (ASL RST) | 3–13 | ASL grammar: Number/distribution; Negation; Noun/Verb distinction; Spatial verbs; Size/shape specifiers; Handling classifiers; Role shift; Conditionals | Allen and Enns (2013) Enns et al. (2013) |
| Carolina picture vocabulary test (CPVT) for deaf and hearing impaired | 4–0 to 11–6 | Receptive sign vocabulary | Kline and Sapp (1989) Layton and Holmes (1985b) White and Tischler (1999) |
| Test of Early Reading Ability Deaf or Hard of Hearing (TERA-D/HH) | 3–13 | Ability to construct meaning; knowledge of alphabet and its functions; awareness or print conventions | Reid et al. (1991) |

The examiner must be proficient in the use of communication methods that are most comfortable and appropriate for the students being tested. These include ASL, manual English, total communication and fingerspelling. Qualified persons would include teachers skilled in test administration who are certified to teach deaf and hard of hearing students and diagnosticians with manual communication competence or with access to a certified interpreter (p. 9).

According to the TERA-D/HH manual, there are no precise statements as to what method was used to administer the TERA-D/HH to the normative population. However, the description of the TERA-D/HH sample shows that the primary method of teaching the students in the sample included Auditory/Oral only (16%), Sign and Speech (83%), and Cued Speech (1%; T. Cooter, personal communication, December 30, 2015).

Individually administered nonverbal tests of academic skills requiring expressive ASL skills are listed in Table 15.3, along with the references.

The American Sign Language Proficiency Assessment (ASL-PA; Haug 2005) is a screening measure designed to assess the level and monitor the acquisition process of ASL skills in deaf children between the ages of 6–12. ASL-PA items are based on ASL language acquisition studies. Eight morphological and syntax structures of ASL are identified and assessed, the order of which reflects their sequence of acquisition (Haug 2005): (1) one-sign/two-sign utterances, (2) non-manual markers (yes/no questions, wh-questions, topic, conditional), (3) deictic (denoting a word or expression whose meaning is dependent on the context in which it is used) pointing, (4) referential shifting (role shift and multiple role position), (5) verbs of motion (simple path movement, central object handshape classifier, and secondary object handshape classifiers), (6) aspects and number (aspect, duality, and distribution), (7) verb agreement (verb agreement inflection reveals two features: real world location marked and abstract location marked), and (8) noun–verb pairs (noun–verb pair production and multiple noun–verb production).

According to Maller et al. (1999), the ASL-PA is a criterion-referenced test useful for assessing a child's individual expressive ASL skills against a predetermined level based on language mastery objectives or the child's own past performance on the ASL-PA scale (p. 264). The test takes about one half hour to administer and about 1–2 h to code and score data for one child. The assessor needs to have linguistic knowledge of ASL in order to administer the test. Due to the tests early stages of development, no large or nationally representative sample norms are currently available. For more detailed information on how to obtain this test, readers are encouraged to contact the Gloss Institute (at http://glossinstitute.org/).

The ASL Development Observation Record (available at http://successforkidswithhearingloss.com/wp-content/uploads/2011/12/ASL-Stages-of-Development-Assmt.pdf) was developed by the Early Childhood Education program at the California School for the Deaf in Fremont, in order to document the ASL language development of deaf children from the time they enter early intervention/early childhood to kindergarten. The observation record also serves as a criterion-referenced hierarchy to guide teacher in assessing their own role as language models and how they use language with children. This instrument is available through the ASL Resource Teacher, Early Childhood Education Program, California School for the Deaf, Fremont (CSDF), 39350 Gallaudet Drive, Fremont, CA 94538.

The MacArthur Communication Development Inventory for American Sign Language (ASL-CDI) is a parent report checklist measure that assesses early signing production in children between the ages of 8–36 months. The ASL-CDI uses a recognition format, where parents check off signs observed from their child's communications at home.

The ASL-CDI includes a receptive language component (called "Early Understanding") that requires parents to indicate whether or not the child to demonstrate understanding of signed phrases such as "Come here", "Open your mouth", and "Are you tired/sleepy?" The vocabulary portion of the scale assesses expressive language, where parents indicate whether or

**Table 15.3** Expressive language scales requiring knowledge of American Sign Language

| Scale | Age range | Sample receptive language skills assessed | Citations |
|---|---|---|---|
| American Sign Language proficiency assessment | 6–12 | Broad range of linguistic structures of ASL | Maller et al. (1999) |
| ASL development observation record | 3 months–6 years | Handshapes, headshakes, using body shifts, eye gazes, and facial expressions for role-playing | ASL Resource Teacher, Early Childhood Education Program, California School for the Deaf, 39350 Gallaudet Drive, Fremont, CA 94538 |
| MacArthur communication development inventory for American Sign Language | 8–36 months | Vocabulary relating to things in the home, people, action words, description words, pronouns, prepositions, question words, sentences, and grammar | Anderson and Reilly (2002) |
| Systematic analysis of language transcripts (SALT) | 3–16 | A 30-min play session is videotaped every 6 months, and every spoken and/or signed language utterance is transcribed | Miller et al. (2011) |
| Test of American Sign Language (TASL) | Deaf students 8–15 years | Classifier Production, Sign Narrative production, Story Comprehension, Classifier Comprehension, Time Marker Test, Map Marker Test | Strong and Prinz (2000) |
| Visual communication and sign language (VCSL) Checklist | Birth–5 years | Developmentally appropriate markers of ASL acquisition | Simms et al. (2013) |

not the child has demonstrated evidence of using signs for words within the broad categories of animals, clothing, games/routines, action signs, furniture/rooms, toys, people, food/drinks, connecting signs (e.g., "and", "because", "but"), prepositions/locations, outside things (e.g., "backyard", "ladder", "shovel"), pronouns, places to go, quantifiers, question signs, small household items, vehicles, signs about time, helping verbs, and descriptive signs.

The Systematic Analysis of Language Transcripts (SALT) software helps users to manage the process of eliciting, transcribing, and analyzing language samples (Miller et al. 2015). According to promotional materials for SALT software, these materials can analyze any language sample that can be represented orthographically, which include written samples, samples that are produced using communication devices or sign language, and language samples

other than English (Miller and Nockerts 2011). However, in order to allow users to make direct comparisons to a database of pre-collected language samples, the program provides elicitation protocols that, if followed, allow for the comparison of the language samples to those provided by typical speakers. A computerized SALT editor allows users to transcribe the sample using SALT transcription conventions. By using simple drop-down menus, the SALT software compares the transcribed language sample to a database of similar transcripts (according to the age of the child and a particular elicitation protocol) on the following indicators (this list is not exhaustive): entire transcript word length, number of different words provided, elapsed time for entire language sample, syntax/morphology indices, omissions, and errors. SALT generates a profile of the speakers' targeted strengths and weaknesses. The SALT program also allows users to generate their own measures when there is no appropriate comparison database. For language sample protocols consisting primarily of ASL language, users can analyze samples themselves, or they can request samples to be translated by a SALT consultant by special request (Karen Andriacchi, personal communication, January 4, 2016). Caution is advised, however, since the SALT transcription database does not include samples elicited in ASL.

Test of American Sign Language (TASL) was developed within the context of a larger research project between San Francisco State University and the University of California, Santa Cruz. The purpose of the research project was to investigate the relationship between ASL and English literacy skill (Prinz et al. 1994; Strong and Prinz 1997, 2000). The TASL, developed for deaf students between the ages of 8–15, consists of two production and four comprehension measures (see description in Haug 2005). Beginning with the production tests, the *Classifier Production Test* consists of a 5 min cartoon shown to students. The cartoon is then presented again in ten separate segments. Students are then videotaped using ASL to describe each segment, which are then scored for the presence of different size, shape, and movement markers in the classifiers. The *Sign Narrative Test* consists of pictures from a children's book (without text) that is given to the students, who in turn are required to sign the story in ASL. The students are videotaped and their responses are scored using a checklist for the presence of ASL grammar and narrative structures.

The comprehension measures include the *Story Comprehension Test*, where a video is shown of an ASL narrative presented by a native signer. While watching the video, students are asked questions about the content and are videotaped providing their responses. For the *Classifier Comprehension Test*, pictures of multifaceted objects are shown to students, and they view a deaf individual describing each object in five different ways. On an answer sheet with video freeze frames of each description, the students mark the one option that provides the best description. For the *Time Marker Test*, six representations of specific periods of time are shown on a video. On a calendar-like answer sheet, the students indicate the corresponding dates for the time periods. For the *Map Marker Test*, a video shows ways objects are located in given environments (e.g., vehicles at a crossroads or furniture in bedroom). For each description, the students select the correct representation from a selection of photographs within an answer booklet. After scores from these tests are tallied, TASL scores are divided into thirds representing low, medium, and high levels of ASL ability.

The Visual Communication and Sign Language (VCSL) Checklist was designed to document the developmental milestones of children from birth to age 5 who are visual learners and are acquiring sign language. During the earliest stages of scale development, teachers at the Laurent Clerc Center's Kendall Demonstration Elementary School (KDES) on the campus of Gallaudet University piloted the VCSL Checklist for two years with children who were deaf or hard of hearing, were exposed to ASL beginning at birth, and who were without additional known disabilities (Simms et al. 2013). These children had typical ASL development and no language delays. Each milestone was listed in age-based groups with developmentally appropriate use of ASL grammatical structures for each age. Each child's sign language acquisition was marked as "not yet emerging," "emerging," "inconsistent use," or "mastered."

Examples of VCSL items (see Simms et al. 2013) include "Copies physical movements involving the arms, hands, head, and face", "Follows the eye gaze of the signer" (Birth to 1 year of age); "Uses beginning ASL handshapes for letters and numbers", "Answers where and what questions" (1–2 years); "Names objects/animals/people in pictures when asked", "Counts from 1 to 5" (2–3 years of age); "Uses plain verbs to connect subjects and objects (e.g., he like ice cream), "Understands quantity (e.g., full, empty, some)" (3–4 years); "Counts from 5 to 10", "Uses expanded sentences involving two traits (e.g., mother bear is big and mean)" (4–5 years).

## Future Directions

### Growth of Cochlear Implants

As discussed earlier, a cochlear implant is a device that can be surgically implanted under the skin that can help provide a sense of sound to profoundly deaf or hard-of-hearing persons. While cochlear implants cannot restore "normal hearing", they bypass damaged portions of the ear and directly stimulate the auditory nerve in the brain. Cochlear implants give deaf persons a functional representation of sounds in the environment. Most importantly, they enable deaf persons to understand speech (for important details, see Cooper and Craddock 2006).

According to the National Institute on Deafness and Other Communication Disorders (NIDCD), since 2000 cochlear implants have been FDA-approved for use in eligible children beginning at 12 months of age. For young children who are deaf or severely hard-of-hearing, implantation while young exposes them to sounds during an optimal period to develop speech and language skills. When these children receive a cochlear implant followed by intensive therapy before 18 months of age, they are better able to hear, comprehend sound and music, and speak than their peers who receive implants at older ages. Studies have also shown that eligible children who receive a cochlear implant at a young age develop language skills at a rate comparable to children with normal hearing, and many succeed in mainstream classrooms (for more information, see NIDCD 2014; see also May-Mederake 2012).

Due to the increased presence of cochlear implants, tests standardized on hearing populations can be administered to test takers with cochlear implants. It comes as no surprise that many research studies empirically compare the academic skill test performance of children and youth with cochlear implants at different stages of development (e.g., López-Higes et al. 2015), or compare deaf students with cochlear implants to those with only "traditional" hearing aids (e.g., Geers and Hayes 2011).

## Psychometric Issues for Assessment of the Deaf

State departments of education often publish information sheets on assessing academic skills in deaf and hard-of-hearing populations (e.g., see Rose et al. 2008; West Virginia Department of Education, n.d.), however the recommended assessments are often instruments normed for hearing populations that have no substantial norms for deaf populations (which by definition would include standardized procedures for nonverbal administration). These instruments can be used under the unspoken assumption that the populations for whom the assessments are intended have cochlear implants (or other hearing assistive devices), or that they will be administered (and responses recorded) using a nonverbal sign language or some other form of nonverbal communication. The nonverbal administration of tests normed on hearing populations is not to be recommended, as the psychometric properties of the altered administration have not been established.

Individually administered academic skill assessments that are developed, normed, and scored for nonverbal ASL administration are indeed a step in the right direction. However these instruments require a highly developed level of ASL knowledge and skill in the test administrator, or access to prerecorded videos needed for item administration. The increase in the usage and effectiveness of cochlear implants with each passing decade calls into question the need for spending the time and financial resources necessary for developing a nationally representative set of individually administered academic achievement measures standardized on persons with no hearing capabilities at all. Even if progress could be made on this front, test developers may need to consider a wider variety of academic skills that can be assessed (beyond receptive/expressive language skills) to give a fuller picture of academic functioning.

## Summary

As noted at the beginning of this chapter, the first version (of the chapter) appeared in McCallum (2003) and began with a discussion of nonverbal assessment of academic skills, with an overview of academic skill areas commonly assessed in educational settings (see Frisby 2003, Table 12.1, p. 242). This was followed by a discussion of the three conditions in which the nonverbal assessment of academic skills is most likely to occur with high frequency. In the first condition, instead of an examiner orally giving directions that require a verbal or behavioral response from the examinee, a respondent (parent, teacher, or other caregiver) observes and records the presence of naturally occurring academic skill behaviors (which may or may not be displayed verbally) by an examinee. Adaptive behavior instruments provide an example of this sort of format. For example respondents can rate the highest level of mathematical calculation (has no understanding of numbers; discriminates between "one" and "many" or "a lot"; counts two objects by saying "one ... two"; mechanically counts to ten; counts ten or more objects; does simple addition and subtraction; performs division and multiplication). In the second condition, examinees with disabling conditions that involve severe speech and physical impairments (such as cerebral palsy) are unable to speak or write intelligibly due to a variety of neurological, physical, emotional, and/or cognitive limitations. In order to demonstrate academic skills, these individuals need various forms of assistive technology (AT) to demonstrate what they know and can do, that can provide alternative ways of demonstrating expressive language communication. In the third condition, individuals with some degree of hearing loss may require test instructions to be read directly from print, which are administered by means of a nonverbal sign language. In turn, examinee responses are given either in writing of by nonverbal sign language. Compared to the previous version of this chapter, this chapter focused with greater detail on this third condition—i.e., the application of nonverbal assessment issues and practices involving individuals who are deaf or hard of hearing (HOH).

## References

Allen, T. E., & Enns, C. E. (2013). A Psychometric study of the ASL Receptive Skills Test when administered to deaf 3-, 4-, and 5-year old children. *Sign Language Studies, 14*(1), 58–79.

Anderson, D., & Reilly, J. (2002). The MacArthur communicative development inventory: Normative data for American Sign Language. *Journal of Deaf Studies and Deaf Education, 7*(2), 83–119.

Archbold, S. (2010). *Deaf education: Changed by cochlear implantation?* Nijmegen, Netherlands: Thesis Radboud University Nijmegen Medical Centre.

Archbold, S., & Mayer, C. (2012). Deaf education: The impact of cochlear implantation? *Deafness Education International, 14*(1), 2–15.

Baker, A. E., & Woll, B. (2008). *Sign language acquisition.* Amsterdam, Netherlands: John Benjamin.

Cawthon, S. W., & Leppo, R. (2013). Assessment accommodations on tests of academic achievement for students who are deaf or hard of hearing: A qualitative meta-analysis of the research literature. *American Annals of the Deaf, 158*(3), 363–376.

Cawthon, S. W., Winton, S. M., Garberoglio, C. L., & Gobble, M. E. (2011). The effects of American Sign Language as an assessment accommodation for students who are deaf or hard of hearing. *Journal of Deaf Studies and Deaf Education, 16*(2), 198–211.

Center for Parent Information and Resources. (2015). *Categories of Disability under IDEA.* Accessed November 2015 from http://www.parentcenterhub.org/repository/categories/#deafness

Centers for Disease Control and Prevention. (2013). Summary of 2013 national CDC EHDI data. Accessed November 2015 from http://www.cdc.gov/ncbddd/hearingloss/2013-data/2013_ehdi_hsfs_summary_a.pdf

Cooper, H., & Craddock, L. (Eds.). (2006). *Cochlear implants: A practical guide* (2nd ed.). New York: John Wiley.

Cummins, J. (2000). *Language, power and pedagogy: Bilingual children in the crossfire.* Clevedon, United Kingdom: Multilingual Matters.

Enns, C. E., Zimmer, K., Boudreault, P., Rabu, S., & Broszeit, C. (2013). *American Sign Language Receptive Skills Test.* Winnipeg, MB: Northern Signs Research.

Foster, C. (2008). One state's perspective on the appropriate inclusion of deaf students in large-scale assessment. In R. C. Johnson & R. E. Mitchell (Eds.), *Testing deaf students in an age of accountability* (pp. 115–135). Washington, DC: Gallaudet University Press.

Frisby, C. L. (2003). Nonverbal assessment of academic achievement with special populations. In R. S. McCallum (Ed.), *Handbook of nonverbal assessment* (pp. 241–258). New York, NY: Kluwer.

Gallaudet Research Institute. (2005). *Regional and national summary report of data from the 2003–2004 Annual Survey of Deaf and Hard of Hearing Children and Youth.* Washington, DC: Gallaudet University.

Gee, J. P. (2001). A sociocultural perspective on early literacy development. In S. Neuman & D. Dickinson (Eds.), *Handbook of early literacy research* (Vol. 1, pp. 30–42). New York, NY: Guilford Press.

Geers, A. (2006). Spoken language in children with cochlear implants. In P. Spencer & M. Marschark (Eds.), *Advances in spoken language development of deaf and hard of hearing children* (pp. 244–270). New York, NY: Oxford University Press.

Geers, A., & Hayes, H. (2011). Reading, writing, and phonological processing skills of adolescents with 10 or more years of cochlear implant experience. *Ear and Hearing, 32*(1), 49–59.

Gustason, G., & Zawolkow, E. (2006). *Signing exact English.* Los Alamitos, CA: Modern Signs Press.

Haug, T. (2005). Review of sign language assessment instruments. In A. Baker & B. Woll (Eds.), *Sign language acquisition* (pp. 51–85). John Benjamins Publishing Company.

Individuals with Disabilities Education Act, 20 U.S.C. § 1400 (2004).

Institute on Disability. (2014). *Annual disability statistics compendium.* Retrieved September 2015 from http://disabilitycompendium.org/compendium-statistics/special-education/11-3b-special-education-students-ages-6-21-served-under-idea-part-b-by-select-diagnostic-categories

Kaiser, A. P., Roberts, M. Y., & McLeod, R. H. (2011). Young children with language impairments: Challenges in transition to reading. In S. B. Neuman & D. K. Dickinson (Eds.), *Handbook of early literacy research* (Vol. 3, pp. 228–241). New York, NY: Guilford Press.

Kline, M., & Sapp, G. L. (1989). Carolina picture vocabulary test: Validation with hearing-impaired students. *Perceptual and Motor Skills, 69,* 64–66.

Lambert, N., Nihira, K., & Leland, H. (1993). *AAMR adaptive behavior scale—School* (2 ed.), Austin, TX: PRO-ED.

Layton, T. L., & Holmes, D. W. (1985a). *Carolina picture vocabulary picture test.* Austin, TX: PRO-ED.

Layton, T. L., & Holmes, D. W. (1985b). *Carolina picture vocabulary test (for deaf and hearing impaired).* Modern Education Corporation.

López-Higes, R., Gallego, C., Martín-Aragoness, M., & Melle, N. (2015). Morpho-syntactic reading comprehension in children with early and late cochlear implants. *Journal of Deaf Studies and Dear Education, 20*(2), 136–146.

Luetke-Stahlman, B., & Nielsen, B. (2003). The contribution of phonological awareness and receptive and expressive English to the reading ability of Deaf students with varying degrees of exposure to accurate English. *Journal of Deaf Studies and Deaf Education, 8,* 464–484.

Maller, S. J., Singleton, J. L., Supalla, S. J., & Wix, T. (1999). The development and psychometric properties of the American Sign Language Proficiency Assessment (ASL-PA). *Journal of Deaf Studies and Deaf Education, 4*(4), 249–269.

Marschark, M., Lang, H. G., & Albertini, J. A. (2002). *Educating deaf students: From research to practice.* New York: Oxford University Press.

Mayer, C. (2007). What matters in the early literacy development of deaf children. *Journal of Deaf Studies and Deaf Education, 12,* 411–431.

Mayer, C., & Trezek, B. J. (2015). *Early literacy development in deaf children.* New York, NY: Oxford University Press.

May-Mederake, B. (2012). Early intervention and assessment of speech and language development in young children with cochlear implants. *International Journal of Pediatric Otorhinolaryngology, 76*(7), 939–946.

McCallum, R. S. (Ed.). (2003). *Handbook of nonverbal assessment.* New York, NY: Kluwer.

Measured Progress Innovation Lab. (2015). *Guidelines for the development of American Sign Language versions of academic test content for K-12 students.* Accessed January 2016 from http://gaap.measuredprogress.org/gaap/docs/GAAP_ASL_Guidelines.pdf

Miller, J., Andriacchi, K., & Nockerts, A. (2011). *Assessing language production using SALT software: A clinician's guide to language sample analysis.* SALT Software, LLC.

Miller, J., Andriacchi, K., & Nockerts, A. (2015). *Assessing language production using SALT software: A clinician's guide to language sample analysis* (2 ed.). SALT Software, LLC.

Miller, J.F., & Nockerts, A. (2011). *Using SALT software to assess the language production of school-aged children.* American Speech-Language Hearing Association, Powerpoint presentation.

Mitchell, R. E., & Karchmer, M. A. (2004). Chasing the mythical ten percent: Parental hearing status of deaf and hard of hearing students in the United States. *Sign Language Studies, 4*(2), 138–163.

Mitchell, R.E. & Karchmer, M.A. (2011). Demographic and achievement characteristics of deaf and hard-of-hearing students. In M. Marschark & P.E. Spencer (Eds.), *The Oxford handbook of deaf studies, language, and education* (pp. XXXX). New York: Oxford University Press.

National Cued Speech Association. (2015). *About cued speech.* Accessed December 2015 from http://www.cuedspeech.org/cued-speech/about-cued-speech.php

National Institute on Deafness and Other Communication Disorders. (2014). *Cochlear implants.* Accessed January 2016 from http://www.nidcd.nih.gov/health/hearing/pages/coch.aspx

National Institute on Deafness and Other Communication Disorders. (2015). *American Sign Language.*

Accessed December 2015 from http://www.nidcd.nih.gov/health/statistics/pages/quick.aspx

Neuman, S. (2011). The challenge of teaching vocabulary in early education. In S. Neuman & D. Dickinson (Eds.), *Handbook of early literacy research* (Vol. 3, pp. 358–372). New York, NY: Guilford Press.

No Child Left Behind Act of 2001, Pub.L. No. 107–110, § 115, Stat. 1425. (2002).

Outreach Services for Deaf and Hard-of-Hearing Children. (2013). *Guidelines for the assessment and educational evaluation of deaf and hard-of-hearing children in Indiana*. Accessed December 2015 from http://www.in.gov/isdh/files/Assessment_Guideline_updated_Nov_2013.pdf

Owens, R. E. (2012). *Language development: An introduction*. Upper Saddle River, NJ: Pearson Education.

Prinz, P., Strong, M., & Kuntze, M. (1994). *The Test of ASL*. Unpublished test. San Francisco: San Francisco State University, California Research Institute.

Qi, S., & Mitchell, R. E. (2012). Large-scale academic achievement testing of deaf and hard-of-hearing students: Past, present, and future. *Journal of Deaf Studies and Deaf Education, 17*(1), 1–18.

Reid, D. K., Hresko, W. P., Hammill, D. D., & Wiltshire, S. (1991). *Test of early reading ability—deaf or hard of hearing*. Austin, TX: Pro-Ed.

Rose, S., Barkmeier, L., Landrud, S., Klansek, V., McAnally, P., Larson, K., et al. (2008). *Assessment of students who are deaf and hard of hearing*. Minnesota Department of Education, Minnesota Resource Center: Deaf/Hard of Hearing.

Russell, M., Kavanaugh, M., Masters, J., Higgins, J., & Hoffmann, T. (2009). Computer-based signing accommodations: Comparing a recorded human with an avatar. *Journal of Applied Testing Technology, 10*(3). Retrieved from http://www.testpublishers.org/assets/documents/computer_based.pdf

Simms, L., Baker, S., & Clark, M. D. (2013). The standardized visual communication and sign language checklist for signing children. *Sign Language Studies, 14*(1), 101–124.

Strong, M., & Prinz, P. (1997). A study of the relationship between American Sign Language and English Literacy. *Journal of Deaf Studies and Deaf Education, 2*(1), 37–46.

Strong, M., & Prinz, P. (2000). Is American Sign Language skill related to English Literacy? In C. Chamberlain, J. P. Morford, & R. Mayberry (Eds.), *Language acquisition by Eye* (pp. 131–142). Mahwah, NJ: Lawrence Erlbaum Publishers.

Tasse, M. J. (2013). Adaptive behavior. In M. L. Wehmeyer (Ed.), *The Oxford handbook of positive psychology and disability* (pp. 105–115). New York, NY: Oxford University Press.

Traxler, C. (2000). The Stanford Achievement Test, 9th edition: National norming and performance standards for deaf and hard or hearing students. *Journal of Deaf Studies and Deaf Education, 5*, 337–348.

Valli, C., & Lucas, C. (2000). *Linguistics of American Sign Language: An introduction* (3rd ed.). Washington, DC: Gallaudet University Press.

Vasilyeva, M., & Waterfall, H. (2011). Variability in language development: Relation to socioeconomic status and environmental input. In S. Neuman & D. Dickinson (Eds.), *Handbook of early literacy research* (Vol. 3, pp. 36–48). New York, NY: Guilford Press.

Watson, R. (2001). Literacy and oral language: Implications for early literacy acquisition. In S. Neuman & D. Dickinson (Eds.), *Handbook of early literacy research* (Vol. 1, pp. 43–53). New York, NY: Guilford Press.

West Virginia Department of Education. (n.d.). *Assessment tools for students who are deaf or hard of hearing*. Accessed January 2016 from https://wvde.state.wv.us/osp/AssessmentTools.pdf

White, A., & Tischler, S. (1999). Receptive sign vocabulary tests: Tests of single-word vocabulary or iconicity? *American Annals of the Deaf, 144*(4).

Williams, C. (1994). The language and literacy worlds of three profoundly deaf preschool children. *Reading Research Quarterly, 29*(2), 125–135.

Williams, C. (2004). Emergent literacy development of deaf children. *Journal of Deaf Studies and Deaf Education, 9*, 352–365.

World Health Organization. (2012). WHO global estimates on prevalence of hearing loss. Accessed November 2015 from http://www.who.int/pbd/deafness/WHO_GE_HL.pdf?ua=1

World Health Organization. (2015). Deafness and hearing loss (fact sheet). Accessed November 2015 from http://www.who.int/mediacentre/factsheets/fs300/en/

# Functional Behavioral Assessment of Nonverbal Behavior

Merilee McCurdy, Christopher H. Skinner
and Ruth A. Ervin

Interest in functional behavioral assessment (FBA) procedures may be traced to several factors. First, a long established and evolving research base has demonstrated that FBA procedures can play an important role in preventing and remedying problem behaviors, particularly in people with disabilities (Anderson et al. 2015; Ervin et al. 2001). Second, psychologists and educators often have sought to enhance service delivery by linking assessment procedures to interventions, thereby unifying these primary service activities (Batsche and Knoff 1995; Gresham and Lambros 1998). Additionally, recent statutory changes in how students with disabilities are served have enhanced interest in FBA across psycho-educational professionals (Nelson et al. 1999; Telzrow 1999; Yell and Shriner 1997).

Researchers and practitioners have demonstrated how FBA procedures can be used to identify the function of various behaviors, thus leading to interventions that have successfully reduced inappropriate behaviors (Mueller et al. 2011). The goal of a functional behavior analysis is to identify and define the referral problem by gathering and reviewing information from a variety of sources, determine the function of the behavior, develop a behavior intervention plan based on the identified function, and evaluate the effectiveness of this plan. In doing so, practitioners may rely on descriptive functional assessment methods, such as informant reports (interviews, rating scales) and direct observations (narrative, empirical). In addition, they may conduct experimental functional analyses, which involve a manipulation of environmental variables to identify causal relationships between these variables and behavior. However, the use of a functional analysis is not common outside research settings (Oliver et al. 2015; Steege and Scheib 2014).

Because many FBA procedures do not require clients or students to provide verbal or written reports of their behavior or conditions surrounding those behaviors, FBA procedures are particularly well suited for determining the function of behaviors of students with communication skills deficits (e.g., students with severe and profound disabilities who are nonverbal, students with autism who have poor receptive and expressive language skills) (Gann et al. 2015). Although some FBA procedures do require examiner–eaminee verbal or written communication, throughout this chapter we will describe and provide examples of how FBA procedures can be used to identify the function of various behaviors in nonverbal students.

M. McCurdy (✉) · C.H. Skinner
Department of Educational Psychology &
Counseling, University of Tennessee, 520 BEC,
1126 Volunteer Blvd, Knoxville
TN 37996-3452, USA
e-mail: mccurdy2@utk.edu

C.H. Skinner
e-mail: cskinne1@utk.edu

R.A. Ervin
University of British Columbia, 2125 Main Mall,
Vancouver, BC V6T 1Z4, Canada
e-mail: Ruth.ervin@ubc.ca

© Springer International Publishing AG 2017
R.S. McCallum (ed.), *Handbook of Nonverbal Assessment*,
DOI 10.1007/978-3-319-50604-3_16

## Foundations of FBA

Psychoeducational professionals employ FBA procedures and traditional standardized assessment procedures for similar reasons (e.g., to identify or confirm problems and to collect data that enhances their ability to develop more effective procedures to prevent and remedy problems). Furthermore, FBA and traditional assessment models depend on similar assessment techniques such as parent or teacher interviews, rating scales, and direct observation (Shapiro and Kratochwill 2000).

Although FBA and traditional models of assessment have similar broad goals and employ similar data gathering techniques, FBA is based on a different set of assumptions. Many traditional psycho-educational theories view problem behaviors as symptoms of deeper, underlying, within-student problems. For example, disruptive behaviors may be caused by intra-individual traits, conditions, or disorders (e.g., attachment disorders, attention-deficit/hyperactivity disorder). Generally, these causal variables are thought to be stable and somewhat resistant to change (Hartmann et al. 1979; Nelson and Hayes 1979). In many instances it is not possible to directly observe these within-subject causal variables, conditions, or traits. Thus, traditional assessment procedures often rely on student communications to collect data related to these within-student variables. For example, a teenager may keep a diary, a young child may be asked to verbally respond to vague stimuli (e.g., ink blots, pictures, sentence fragments), or a clinical child or adolescent interview may be used as part of the assessment or diagnostic process. Because students' verbal (e.g., clinical interview) or written (e.g., sentence completion) responses are often used to assess these internal (within-subject) causal variables, determining if a student has these underlying problems can prove challenging when student–assessor communication is hindered. However, as the current text indicates, researchers have made and continue to make important advances in this area.

Under a behavioral model, specific problems are not viewed as mere symptoms of underlying, within-student traits or disorders. Rather, the behaviors themselves are of interest and altering these behaviors is considered a valid psycho-educational goal (Nelson and Hayes 1979). Furthermore, under an operant behavioral model, behaviors are assumed to be caused by or maintained by an interaction between current environmental conditions and an organism's past learning history (McComas et al. 2000; Sprague et al. 1998). Therefore, the focus of a *functional* behavioral model of assessment is to identify the current environmental conditions that are maintaining or reinforcing behaviors of interest (i.e., target behaviors).

Identifying environmental conditions that maintain specific behaviors may allow one to make inferences with respect to a student's past learning history. These inferences may be useful in that they may allow the researcher to determine what events in the subject's past may contribute to current problems, which in turn may allow researchers to develop prevention programs. Although preventing problems is an important goal, in many cases it is often difficult to determine when and why a specific behavior first presented. For example, it may not be possible to determine why a person first began to engage in echolalic speech (i.e., repeating words and phrases) or hand flapping (e.g., repetitive waving of hands in front of one's eyes). Regardless of etiology, it is often possible to determine what current environmental conditions are *maintaining* these behaviors (Townsend 2000). When attempting to remedy problems, FBA procedures tend to focus on current environmental conditions that are maintaining current aberrant behaviors (Hartmann et al. 1979).

Although there are many behavioral theories (Malone 1990; Staddon 1993), FBA procedures are most closely associated with B.F. Skinner's operant psychology (Ervin et al. 2001). Operant psychology is concerned with how behaviors operate on the environment. Environmental conditions that maintain behaviors are positive and negative reinforcement. Positive reinforcement occurs when under specific antecedent stimulus conditions, consequent stimuli (e.g., reinforcing stimuli) are delivered contingent upon behavior *and* this process increases the probability of that behavior reoccurring when those antecedent conditions reoccur. Negative reinforcement occurs when stimuli are removed contingent upon behavior *and* this process increases the probability of that behavior reoccurring when those antecedent stimulus conditions reoccur. FBA procedures are designed to specify reinforcement contingencies that are currently maintaining target behaviors. Specification includes delineating antecedent conditions, target behaviors, and consequent events that are contingent upon target behaviors.

Specifying maintaining contingencies may allow psycho-educational professionals to develop more effective treatments (Bergan and Kratochwill 1990; Sprague et al. 1998). For example, suppose that FBA data suggest that a student's hand flapping behavior is being maintained or reinforced by teacher attention. Treatment may then be constructed whereby teachers remove attention contingent upon hand flapping, but maintain or deliver attention contingent upon more desirable behavior (e.g., differential reinforcement of other behaviors—DRO, differential reinforcement of incompatible behaviors—DRI). Now suppose that hand flapping is being maintained by the removal of teacher attention (i.e., negative reinforcement). In this situation, the DRO and DRI interventions are likely to strengthen, rather than reduce the handflapping behavior (Townsend 2000).

## Nonverbal Behavioral Assessment Procedures

FBA procedures differ from traditional assessment procedures and general behavioral assessment procedures because the focus is on identifying and specifying the contingencies that are reinforcing target behaviors within the natural environment (Carr 1993). Interviewing target students and other self-report techniques (e.g., checklist and rating scales) may allow one to gather data designed to specify these contingencies. These self-report measures can provide rich and detailed information. However, in the current chapter we exclude these assessment procedures for several reasons. First, when communication is problematic (e.g., the subject does not speak) collecting this type of data can be extremely difficult. One of the primary advantages of FBA procedures is that they do not rely on subject reports. Thus, FBA is particularly useful for assessing nonverbal behavior and the contingencies that may be maintaining these behaviors.

In addition, many students simply do not have the verbal and/or cognitive skills to provide FBA data via self-report. Given FBA's roots in operant conditioning research and the study of lower level organisms' behavior (e.g., laboratory pigeons), it is not surprising that FBA procedures have been developed and successfully applied across human behavior where students or clients have limited verbal skills or severe communication disorders. FBA procedure have been used to identify the function of specific behaviors in students with severe disabilities and communication deficits including students with severe mental retardation, students with autism, and students with severe mental illness (e.g., Durand and Crimmins 1987; McComas et al. 2000; Townsend 2000; Worcester et al. 2015). Although FBA procedures can be used across behaviors and students, one strength of these procedures for assessing behavior when verbal communication is hindered (e.g., students with speech or hearing deficits, students with autism, students who do not speak) is that many FBA procedures do not require verbal communication between the examiner and the examinee.

For these reasons, FBA procedures have been developed that rely less on self-reports for identifying the function of student behaviors. Rather, procedures used to identify variables (e.g., positive and negative reinforcement contingencies) that may be maintaining target behaviors in the natural environment typically include informant reports (e.g., interviews, rating scales), direct observation in natural environments (e.g., A-B-C recording, scatter-plot recording), and observation in modified or analog environments (e.g., experimental functional analysis). Next, these types of functional assessment techniques will be described and analyzed.

## Informant Reports: Interviews and Rating Scales

**FBA interviews**. Perhaps the most common and most researched procedures for collecting functional assessment data via informant interviews are based on the structured interview format develop by Bergan (1977) and expanded on by others (e.g., Bergan and Kratochwill 1990; Sheridan et al. 1996). There are three structured interviews that are essential to Bergan and Kratochwill's behavioral consultation model of service delivery—Problem Identification Interview (PII), Problem Analysis Interview (PAI), Treatment Evaluation Interview (TEI).

Initially the series of interviews focuses on the target behaviors and related goals. These goals include defining target behaviors, estimating target behavior levels, and developing data collection systems designed to measure target behaviors. However, in this first interview, the focus is also on soliciting information from informants that may indicate contingencies of reinforcement that are maintaining target behaviors within natural environments. Thus, structured interviews are designed to collect data that (a) indicates when and where target behaviors are more likely to occur, (b) specifies sequential events that precede and follow target behaviors, and (c) identifies procedures that have been attempted to remedy problems.

In the final two interviews, obtained data can allow one to identify other variables that may impact treatment selection, implementation, and evaluation. These variables include (a) teacher or parent skills, (b) acceptability or perceptions regarding specific interventions, (c) resources (time, other responsibilities) available to apply to the problem, (d) goals with respect to immediacy, levels, and stability of desired behavior, (e) priorities when multiple behaviors are problematic, and (f) maintenance issues and generalization procedures. Using the interviews above, a plan is developed and evaluated for effectiveness.

**Strengths and limitations of FBA interviews**. Initial referrals often fail to provide information that specifies target behaviors. The flexible verbal exchange that occurs during structured interviews with referring agents (e.g., teachers or parents) may be the most efficient procedure for obtaining clear, operational definitions of target behaviors, especially when these behaviors are atypical or unusual. Through verbal exchange, these interviews also can be used to develop data collection procedures that can be used to (a) confirm problems, (b) evaluate and precisely measure characteristics of target behaviors (e.g., rate, variability, duration, intensity), (c) establish treatment objectives and goals, and (d) provide baseline data that allow one to evaluate the effects of interventions (Bergan 1977).

Interviews also allow psycho-educational professionals to determine when and where the behavior is most likely to occur. Data on variability across settings, activities, and time allow one to schedule direct observation sessions. Additionally, this type of data may assist in identifying the function of target behaviors. Suppose a target behavior is most likely to occur only during a specific activity (e.g., communication training). These data suggest that the conditions during communication training differ from other conditions and somehow reinforce this target behavior. For example, the target behavior may be reinforced in this setting because it allows the student to escape or avoid this activity or some specific stimuli associated with this activity (e.g., the instructor who conducts communications training). Perhaps the communication instructor is more likely to attend to or reinforce target behaviors during these instructional activities.

Interview data can be used to collect reports on sequential events that immediately precede target behaviors, antecedents, and those that immediately follow target behaviors, consequences. Because reinforcement is stronger when it immediately follows target behaviors, establishing this sequence of events may help identify consequent events (i.e., positive and negative reinforcing events) that are maintaining target behaviors (Neef et al. 1993, 1994). Obtaining sequential data is critical because many reinforcing events are conditioned. Therefore, an event that serves as a reinforcer for some behaviors, under some conditions, for some children, may serve as a neutral stimulus or punishing event across other conditions, behaviors, or children (Kazdin 2001). The flexibility of verbal exchanges provided via informant interviews allows one to specify atypical idiosyncratic contingent relationships.

However, not all events that immediately follow behaviors are functionally related to those behaviors. One of the primary advantages of interview data is that it allows psycho-educational professionals to collect data on events that do not immediately follow target behavior, but may be reinforcing target behaviors. For example, during an outdoor activity a child may engage in aggressive behavior (e.g., throwing a ball at a peer), which is followed by the teacher removing the child from the activity. However, escape or avoidance may not be functionally related to the target behavior. Instead, the responses from the child's peers after returning to the classroom may reinforce the behavior. Thus, the reinforcing event that is maintaining the behavior (e.g., peer responses, thus the function of the behavior is peer attention) may be more temporally distant from the target behavior than another event (e.g., removal from the activity) that frequently tends to occur immediately after the target behavior, but is not functionally related to the target behavior.

Temporally distant antecedent events also can impact functional relationships. For example, Ray and Watson (2001) found that inappropriate classroom behaviors served different functions dependent upon whether the student woke on time or late. When the student woke late, aggressive behaviors were maintained by escape and when the student woke on time aggressive behaviors were maintained by access to tangible reinforcers. Interviews provide a means to collect data on delayed reinforcers and antecedent events or establishing operations (see Michael 1993 for a discussion of establishing operations) that are functionally related to target behaviors.

Interview data also may allow one to determine what interventions have been previously implemented and the impact of these interventions. The significance of determining what has been tried in the past is clear. For example, a parent may report

use of time out at home but the child's negative behaviors only increased. Such a report may suggest that the target behavior is being reinforced by escape-avoidance as opposed to attention.

Reports of previous interventions and their success should be interpreted with caution. Some interventions require high levels of integrity for them to be effective. However, research on treatment integrity suggests that many interventions are not carried out accurately or consistently (Noell et al. 1997; Reynolds and Kamphaus 2015; Sterling-Turner et al. 2001; Watson and Robinson 1996). Additionally, some interventions may have a gradual effect that is difficult to detect without precise measurement. Therefore, sometimes when informants report that an intervention failed, the intervention may have actually been working but the effect was gradual and subtle. Consequently, when an informant reports that an intervention was not effective, this lack of effectiveness may have little implication for determining the function of the behavior unless the treatment was implemented with integrity and evaluation of intervention effectiveness was precise. Again, the flexibility inherent in the interview process may allow one to discern whether previous interventions were implemented with integrity and evaluated appropriately.

**FBA rating scales**. Checklists and rating scales have long played a role in diagnosing students. These instruments include general or broad-band assessment instruments (e.g., Behavior Assessment System for Children— Reynolds and Kamphaus 2015) and narrow-band instruments designed to measure specific behaviors (e.g., Social Skills Improvement System— Gresham and Elliott 2008) or disorders (e.g., ADHD Rating Scale-IV: DuPaul et al. 1998). Psychometric properties associated with these instruments and the ability to compare response patterns to a normative sample have allowed practitioners to use these instruments for screening, diagnostic, and treatment evaluation purposes. However, little data have been collected to show how they lead to function-based interventions (Merrell 2000).

Researchers have begun to develop informant report measures designed to indicate the function of target behaviors. The Motivational Assessment Scale (MAS; Durand and Crimmins 1988b) is a teacher report instrument that can be used after target behaviors have been identified. Teachers respond to a series of questions across a seven-item Likert scale (never to always) designed to indicate conditions when target behaviors are more likely to occur. Scores are summed across four possible functions of the target behavior including sensory, negative reinforcement or escape-avoidance, positive reinforcement—social attention, and positive reinforcement—access to tangibles. For example, a score of always on the item that asks if the target behavior occurs following a request to perform a difficult task suggests that the behavior may be serving an escape-avoidance function. However, a response of always to an item that asks if the behavior occurs whenever the teacher ceases attending to the child would suggest that the behavior is being reinforced with attention.

The Problem Behavior Questionnaire (PBQ: Lewis et al. 1994) is similar in that the target behavior is already defined and responses are based on how often this behavior occurs under specific conditions. However, this measure focuses on five conditions. Four conditions are concerned with the consequence of the behavior including escaping peers, obtaining peer attention, escaping adults, and obtaining adult attention. The last category focuses solely on antecedent or settings events that may consistently precede target behaviors (e.g., is the behavior more likely to occur following disruptions of schedules). Again, scores are summed and results are designed to indicate the function of specific behaviors.

**Strengths and limitations of FBA rating scales.** Once a target behavior is specified or defined, perhaps the most obvious advantage of checklists and rating scales is that they provide a time and resource efficient procedure for identifying the function of that behavior. Although these instruments may provide a general indication of behavioral function (e.g., escape-avoidance), typically these instruments do not indicate specific antecedent and consequent events, conditions, or stimuli that are functionally related to that behavior within the specific environment of concern

(e.g., escaping feedback from a teacher versus avoiding doing a task). Therefore, other data collection procedures (e.g., interview) may be needed to more precisely identify these variables.

In one of the earliest investigations of the validity of checklist and rating scales, Durand and Crimmins (1988a) collected MAS, direct observation data, and experimental functional analysis data in an attempt to determine the function of self-injurious behavior in eight participants. Results showed that the three assessment procedures tended to correlate. These results suggest that the MAS is a valid procedure for determining the function of a student's self-injurious behavior.

Crawford et al. (1992) conducted a study that required eight staff members (four residential and four vocational trainers) to complete the MAS for four subjects who engaged in high rates of stereotypic behavior. MAS results showed agreement (i.e., results indicated the same function) among all four vocational staff. However, MAS results from the residential staff were inconsistent as identification of function varied across staff completing the instrument. Furthermore, direct observation data (A-B-C) did not always suggest the same function as MAS data. Similarly, Townsend (2000) found that MAS results identified different functions of echolalic behaviors than experimental functional analysis results. Barton-Arwood et al. (2003) examined item-by-item intrarater reliability over 1 and 4 weeks for the MAS and the PBQ. Reliability was variable for both scales but more so for the MAS with very few reliability coefficients above 0.80. Additionally, behavioral function was not stable across assessments. While there are explanations for this instability of function (e.g., function changes over time, multi-function behaviors), stability is a concern for both measures.

Research and development of FBA checklists and rating scales has just begun. While some studies have found evidence supporting the reliability and validity of these measures, results from other studies suggest psychometric weaknesses with these instruments (Akande 1994; Crawford et al. 1992; Sigafoos et al. 1994; Thompson and Emerson 1995; Townsend 2000). Clearly more research is needed to establish the validity and reliability of these instruments (Sturmey 1994). The limitations of informant report rating scales are well-known. Merrell (2000) summarizes these limitations including response bias (i.e., halo effects, leniency/severity effects, and central tendency). However, these effects have been primarily investigated with respect to measures of target behaviors or within-student constructs (e.g., diagnostic measures). Researchers should conduct similar studies of FBA checklists and rating scales to determine if these limitations impact informant reports designed to indicate the function of the behavior, as opposed to the presence, level, or severity of behaviors, symptoms, or disorders.

Merrell (2000) discusses error variance that can be attributed to source (who provides the ratings), settings (ratings vary across settings where the child is observed), and temporal variance (ratings change over time). When constructs of interest are assumed to be relatively stable, variance across source, settings, and time is assumed to be an index of error. However, variance across source, settings, and time is not always viewed as error under behavioral models. In fact, variability across conditions is often necessary for determining the function of a behavior. Thus, many procedures used to evaluate traditional measures may have to be adjusted. Regardless, as Shriver et al. (2001) indicate, FBA procedures are used to assess a construct (i.e., a functional relationship) and if these procedures are to have applied value they must accurately indicate variables that are maintaining target behaviors within natural settings. Because FBA checklist and rating scales are relatively more structured than other FBA procedures (e.g., interviews), these instruments may prove invaluable in developing procedures for evaluating the quality (e.g., reliability and validity) of FBA data.

## Direct Observation in Natural Environments

One of the advantages of an operant model of psychology is that both target behaviors and variables that are functionally related to target behaviors can often be directly observed. Thus,

behavioral psychology has long employed direct observation procedures as an integral part of assessment. There are many procedures that can be used to record direct observation data (see Skinner et al. 2003 for a comprehensive review). Below, we will discuss and provide examples of narrative and empirical procedures for recording FBA data.

**Narrative recordings**. Narrative recordings merely require an observer to write a description of student behaviors and events surrounding those behaviors. Narrative recordings can provide a flexible and rich description of a child's behavior. These recordings that describe target behaviors can be used to help specify or operationally define target behaviors. Furthermore, narrative descriptions of target behaviors can provide general information about the behavior (e.g., rate, intensity, and topography) that may be necessary for developing empirical data collection systems that allow one to more precisely measure target behavior levels and evaluate the effects of intervention procedures.

One example of a narrative recording is a communications log that may be used by parents and teachers to communicate with each other (Skinner et al. 2003). Thus, a parent may send daily narrative reports that describe a student's behavior and events surrounding that behavior to a teacher. For example, a narrative report from a parent may indicate that a student wet his bed last night, had difficulty falling asleep, or was noncompliant during preschool morning routines. These data may provide information on setting events that may influence the student's behavior in school (Ray and Watson 2001).

When serious behaviors occur, educators are often required to write an incident report or a narrative description of the behavior that includes events that preceded the behavior and how they reacted to or dealt with the behavior. This form of narrative recording is similar to narrative antecedent-behavior-consequent (A-B-C) recording. During A-B-C recording an observer may use the occurrence of a previously defined target behavior or class of target behaviors (often based on interview data or previous observations) as a stimulus or cue to write a description of the target behavior (e.g., Tommy began to throw instructional materials), general conditions that preceded the target behavior (e.g., Mrs. Smith was conducting instruction is shape identification with Ralph while Mrs. Jones was providing food preparation training to the other four students), specific events that immediately preceded the target behavior (e.g., Mrs. Smith took a plastic triangle away from Tommy that he was chewing), and events that immediately followed the target behavior (e.g., Mrs. Smith ceased shape instruction and held Tommy's hands next to his side).

**Strengths and limitations of narrative recordings**. Narrative recordings of events surrounding target behaviors may allow one to identify antecedent and consequent events that are functionally related to target behaviors. Thus, in our above example, narrative recording data suggests that the aggressive behavior may be positively reinforced by the teacher holding Tommy's hands to his side or negatively reinforced by the cessation of instruction. Additionally, these data suggest that taking the shape away from Tommy is an antecedent event that often precedes aggressive behavior. In addition, narrative recording can be used as a first step in a functional behavior assessment. During the narrative recording, operational definitions of the target behavior can be developed, the setting can be explored, and hypothesis can begin to be developed.

It is often impossible to translate narrative recordings to empirical data. Therefore, it may be difficult to use narrative data to measure behaviors with enough precision so that these data can be used to evaluate gradual changes or trends in target behaviors. Thus, the utility of narrative recordings for evaluating intervention effects is limited. Additionally, without empirical data it may be difficult to determine if target behaviors are more likely to occur under some conditions than others (Skinner et al. 2000a). Conditional probability data are often useful, if not critical for determining the function of a behavior.

**Empirical recording procedures**. Empirical recording procedures typically require an observer to record the presence of a previously defined behavior or event with a tally. Thus, the first step in constructing empirical recording procedures is to operationally define the behaviors or events to be recorded. Next, a data recording system must be established. For low-rate, discrete behaviors frequency counts are often used which can be translated into rate data (e.g., two disruptive outbursts in 30 min). However, for high rate or continuous behaviors interval recording systems are often used to estimate durations of behavior. With whole interval recording, a behavior or event must occur for an entire interval for it to be recorded as present. With partial-interval recording, the behavior or event must be present only for an instant during the interval for it to be recorded as present. With momentary time sampling, the behavior or event must be observed at the moment an interval begins for it to be recorded as present (Powell et al. 1977; Shapiro 2011).

**Strengths and limitations of direct observation in empirical recording procedures**. Empirical recording procedures yield precise data that allow for more immediate evaluation of treatment effects and conditional probabilities. Additionally, empirical recordings allow target behaviors to be verified with a level of precision that may be necessary when important decisions are being made. Finally, with empirical recording systems, observers typically record the presence of a behavior or event by tallying (i.e., writing a slash in a specified place) as opposed to providing written descriptions of behavior. These characteristics of empirical recording allow observers to collect more precise data on multiple behaviors and events in a more continuous manner than narrative recording (Skinner et al. 2000b). Collecting data on multiple behaviors and events (e.g., teacher directions, teacher feedback) in a continuous manner allows observers to obtain a record of the temporal sequence of these events that may assist with identify antecedent and consequent conditions that surround target behaviors.

Researchers have developed various direct observation systems (e.g., State-Event Classroom Observation System; Saudargus 1992). However, their utility for establishing functional relationships has not been empirically validated across cases. Furthermore, because settings, target behaviors, and consequent conditions may vary across cases, researchers often develop their own direct observation system. In order to do this, interview data and narrative recordings may be used to establish observation targets (e.g., target behaviors and antecedent and consequent events) and characteristics of these targets (rates, levels, intensity, continuity) that should be considered when developing interval recording systems (Skinner et al. 2000b).

Empirical recording observations in natural environments may be ideal when target behaviors are being reinforced immediately. However, these systems may be less useful for collecting data on delayed reinforcement. For example, a child may misbehave and immediately receive a teacher reprimand contingent upon the misbehavior. However, the reprimand may have no functional relationship to the behavior. Instead, the child may be misbehaving in order to receive delayed peer attention at recess (Skinner et al. 2000b).

Data collected in natural settings is often considered more valid than data collected in analog settings because one does not have to assume that behaviors would be constant across artificial and natural conditions. However, the process of observing behaviors can cause reactivity, which may impact the validity of assessment data. For example, when an independent observer enters the classroom to record behaviors, the classroom environment has been altered and the presence of this observer may impact target student behavior, teacher behavior, and peer behavior.

Researchers have identified a variety of variables that impact subject or target student reactivity including (a) what the child is told about the observer's presence, (b) perceived power of the observer, and (c) obtrusiveness of the observer and their behaviors (Johnston and Bolstad 1973). There are several procedures that can be used to reduce reactivity. Independent observers should not orient themselves directly and continuously toward target students, respond to any activities that occur during observation periods, or communicate with students (Skinner et al. 2000a). They should enter the room as unobtrusively as possible (e.g., before class begins) and station themselves where they are less likely to command student attention (e.g., the back of the room). Finally, reactivity tends to fade over time. Thus, initial assessments may produce behaviors and events less typical (i.e., more reactivity) than subsequent assessments.

In order to reduce reactivity, teachers should not inform target students or peers why the observer is in the room. However, it is difficult to reduce teacher reactivity, as they typically know why you are present, which student is the focus of your observations, and what behaviors and events may be of particular interest. While direct observation data in natural environments may yield precise and verifiable data, caution is required when interpreting these data because it is not possible to determine the precise impact of reactivity. For example, a teacher who typically reprimands a student who fails to follow directions may be more likely to redirect the student or ignore the student when an independent observer is present. This reactivity may mislead observers in their attempts to identify the function of a particular behavior under typical (e.g., nonreactive) environmental conditions.

## Experimental Functional Analyses in Analog or Natural Contexts

As described above, data gathered through interviews, rating scales, and/or observations are analyzed and interpreted to formulate hypotheses regarding functional relations between environmental variables and target behaviors. In some cases, when data are clear and consistent, it may be sufficient to develop hypotheses and intervention strategies directly from these data sources. In other cases, particularly when data gathered from various descriptive sources (interviews, observations, rating scales) are ambiguous and difficult to interpret, it may be necessary to actually *test* hypotheses through an "experimental functional analysis." According to Cone (1997), the process of verifying causal hypotheses can be accomplished through formal systematic manipulations (e.g., withdrawal designs, alternating treatments designs) or through less formal means (e.g., structuring observations to compare naturally occurring situations associated with low and high rates of the target behavior). A review of the research literature on school-based applications of functional assessment (Ervin et al. 2001b) suggests that this verification phase is almost always (i.e., 90% of cases) included in research studies, making it a critical feature of FBA.

## Analog Experimental Functional Analyses

One purpose of an experimental functional analysis is to use experimental methods to infer a causal relationship (always an approximation) between the environmental events (context) and a specified response (target behavior) to further understanding these relationships. In 1977, Carr reviewed the research on self-injurious behavior and hypothesized there was a functional relationship between self-injury and its consequences in certain settings. This hypothesis sparked subsequent studies wherein experimental methods were used to evaluate this premise (e.g., Carr and Newsom 1985; Iwata et al. 1982/1994). For example, Iwata et al. (1982/1994) conducted systematic manipulations of environmental variables to examine four proposed functions of self-injurious behavior (i.e., escape from demands, gaining adult attention, access to tangible items, and access to sensory stimulation) across nine individuals with developmental disabilities. In order to establish tight experimental control (i.e., precisely control independent variables or reinforcement procedures and precisely measure the dependent variable, student behavior levels), manipulations were conducted in modified or analog environments. Conditions were randomly scheduled in a multi-element design and session length was also held constant and kept brief (i.e., 15-min) for each of the conditions. Results indicated that self-injurious behavior was functionally related to different

environmental consequences across different individuals. Data indicated clearly distinguishable outcomes for seven of the nine participants and inconclusive outcomes for two participants.

Other studies have continued this line of analog experimental functional analysis research, extending applications across behaviors, populations, and settings (Beavers et al. 2013; Carr et al. 1980; Derby et al. 1994; Northup et al. 1991). A variety of procedures for conducting analog experimental functional analyses are available in the literature. For example, procedures developed by Iwata et al. (1982/1994) have been modified to include the use of protective equipment (i.e., helmets, padding) and consultation from medical professionals when conducting experimental manipulations of variables that covary with self-endangering behavior. Other researchers have included the manipulation of antecedent events (events that precede the occurrence of problem behaviors) such as instructional demands (e.g., Durand and Crimmins 1987) and task preference (e.g., Cooper et al. 1992) in addition to the traditional emphasis on the manipulation of consequences. Across studies, analog experimental manipulations can vary on several dimensions, including: (a) what variables should be manipulated (antecedents, consequences), (b) how they should be manipulated (e.g., schedules of reinforcement, length of sessions, sequence of sessions, number of sessions), and (c) how to record and interpret data. These factors need to be considered when preparing to collect experimental functional assessment data.

**Experimental Functional Analyses in Natural Contexts.** When the primary purpose of a functional assessment is to develop an intervention strategy, it may not be necessary to confirm the hypothesized behavior function through an analog functional analysis, unless descriptive data regarding function (interviews, ratings scales, observations) are ambiguous. If sufficient evidence (interviews, observations) indicates a clear functional relationship between problem behavior and environmental events, then it may be appropriate to consider the selection of an assessment-based, functionally relevant intervention strategy (Dunlap and Kern 1996).

Functionally relevant interventions will directly address the behavioral function (e.g., escape from task) in a number of ways. First, an intervention strategy may consider accommodations to reduce motivation for the problem behavior by addressing the antecedent context/situations (e.g., changing task demands). Second, the intervention strategy might focus on teaching an acceptable alternative behavior that serves the same purpose as the problem behavior (e.g., using a picture card to request a break when behavior is maintained by escape from task). Third, the intervention strategy might focus on weakening the functional relation between the problem behaviors and maintaining consequences (e.g., disconnecting the link between aggression and escape from task demands). Alternatively, the intervention might focus on strengthening the connection between an appropriate behavior that is incompatible with the problem behavior and access to the identified reinforcer.

Working from a functional assessment model, a number of specific, functionally relevant interventions might be useful. When selecting specific interventions, careful consideration should be given to how the intervention addresses functional relations, as well as to practical constraints (time, resources), and individual teacher and/or student preferences. In cases when the functional assessment does not identify a clear function of the behavior, an experimental analysis of the effects of hypothesized intervention strategies can be conducted to determine which intervention strategy should be selected. This can be accomplished through comparisons across various interventions (alternating treatments design) or through comparisons between a hypothesized intervention strategy and baseline conditions (no intervention).

Several studies have employed this intervention hypothesis testing approach to functional assessment. For example, Dunlap et al. (1995) examined the effects of systematically manipulating functionally relevant curricular variables that were identified by teachers of three elementary students with various disabilities (i.e., autism, mental retardation, emotional and behavior disordered). Results supported hypotheses that the modified classroom activities would lead to reductions in problem behaviors and increases in on-task behavior. In another study, Lalli et al. (1993) successfully evaluated the effects of functionally relevant intervention strategies during ongoing classroom activities across three children with severe to profound mental retardation. In this study, Lalli et al. also trained teachers to conduct experimental analysis to confirm hypothesized functions of behavior (teacher attention) in the classroom.

**Strengths and Weaknesses of Analog and Natural Experimental Functional Analyses**. Experimental functional analysis data can be used to empirically confirm behavior function and/or the utility of functionally relevant intervention strategies. When experimental analyses indicate clear and consistent functional relations between environmental variables (e.g., task demands, attention, hypothesized intervention strategies) and target behaviors (e.g., off-task, aggression, compliance), then these analyses contribute to our understanding of behavior environment relations and our ability to influence these relations to promote desired change. Whether these analyses are conducted in analog or natural settings may be of issue depending on the purpose of the assessment.

Analog functional analyses allow for more control of extraneous variables than might be possible in more natural contexts. Thus, it may be helpful to conduct manipulations in modified environments, particularly when preliminary information (e.g., unstructured interviews, rating scales, direct observation data) is ambiguous or unclear. Further, because analog analyses allow for careful control of the context (environmental conditions) under study, it is sometimes possible to conduct these analyses over relatively brief time periods. The potential utility of brief, analog analyses is illustrated in the findings of assessments conducted across 79 outpatients with mild to severe mental retardation who exhibited various behaviors (self-injury, aggression, destruction, and stereotypy). Across these cases, manipulations of environmental contingencies demonstrated behavioral control during 84% of cases, supporting generalizability and utility of brief experimental functional analyses for high frequency behaviors exhibited by individuals with developmental disabilities (Derby et al. 1992).

This tight experimental control and brevity of assessment may, however, come at the cost of what Cone (1997) refers to as "representational validity," the extent to which a measure faithfully portrays the target of assessment. According to findings of a study conducted by Derby et al. (1994), brief functional analyses are useful in generating hypotheses about distinct functions of high rate behaviors, but extended functional analyses are preferable when screening for multiple functions of behavior and in determining functional response classes. Practical applications of functional experimental analyses should be conducted with consideration of potential limitations of this methodology. Although these experimental analyses can contribute to the "believability" of functional assessments, they may be especially difficult to conduct in practical settings for several reasons. First, many practitioners (educators, clinicians) are not trained in such techniques. Second, such techniques require time and resources (space, extra personnel) that may not be readily available in applied settings (e.g., residential treatment centers, outpatient clinics, schools). Third, such techniques, which are often used several times each day, may deprive students of access to appropriate learning, employment, and/or social environments. Finally, research has yet to directly compare the cost-benefit ratios of experimental functional analysis procedures to that of other methods of assessment and intervention selection.

Trial-based functional analyses may provide solutions to some of these limitations (Austin et al. 2015; Sigafoos and Saggers 1995). In comparison to traditional session-based functional analyses, trial-based functional analyses are brief and can be interspersed into typical classroom activities using 2 min repeated trials instead of 10 min sessions. In a comparison of the two methods, Bloom et al. (2011) found that the results of the two functional analyses matched 60% of the time. The trial-based functional

analysis may be a valid option for use in schools. Given that the trials can take place throughout the school day, it is important for teachers to implement the trials as they have a constant presence. Past research has shown that teachers and other school personnel can implement functional analyses (Kunnavatana et al. 2013).

## Case Example

Donny is an 8-year-old boy who was diagnosed with Autism by school personnel and Oppositional Defiant Disorder by a local psychologist using criteria outlined in the Diagnostic Statistical Manual—Fifth Edition (American Psychiatric Association 2013). While Donny could communicate using gestures and a few signs, his verbal communication skills were extremely limited. Donny attended a self-contained special education classroom in a public school setting and lived at home with his mother and father. He often would respond aggressively (e.g., hit, throw items, yell) or run from an adult when given a direct instruction. These behaviors were reported primarily in the school environment. While Donny's mother also reported these behaviors at home, she often did not give direct instructions for fear of an aggressive outburst.

According to teachers, Donny's negative behaviors occurred during in-seat assignments and small group activities (e.g., circle time, morning welcome). During assignments, Donny would run from his seat area and disrupt the class. While running, he would knock items off of shelves and throw items at his classmates. These behaviors were considered unsafe, in part due to the medical needs of his classmates. For example, one student had a diagnosed heart condition while another had braces on his legs and was unsteady when standing. If required to remain in his seat, Donny would rip up his assignment, squirm to leave his seat, hit his teacher, or throw his pencil (Fig. 16.1).

In order to directly assess the possible functions of Donny's behaviors, an experimental functional analysis was designed which included four conditions: (a) free play, (b) attention,

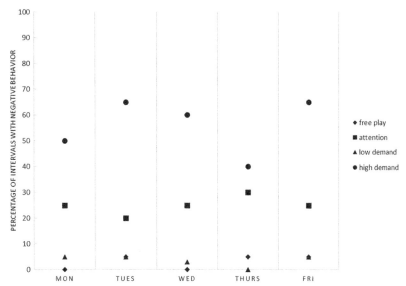

**Fig. 16.1** Experimental FBA data for Donny's negative behavior across conditions. Data reflect the percentage of intervals that negative behaviors occurred

(c) low demand, and (d) high demand (see Iwata et al. 1982/1994). During the free play condition, Donny was allowed to play with preferred items and was provided noncontingent praise on a 30-second fixed interval schedule. Attention was not provided contingent upon negative or positive behaviors. When in the attention condition, Donny sat with his teacher while she graded papers and he had access to the same preferred activities he was given during the free play condition. Donny was provided attention contingent upon his negative behavior. For example, when Donny threw his pencil, the teacher would respond by saying, "Donny, you should not throw pencils. Please do not do that again." If Donny attempted to leave the work area, attention was provided through redirection and verbal attention such as, "Donny, you must finish your worksheet. I know you can do it. Please sit down." The teacher responded to each occurrence of negative behaviors in the same manner to assess the effects of positive reinforcement (in the form of social attention).

Two demand conditions were examined and a three-prompt command strategy was used in each. First, the command was presented verbally. If the command was not followed, the command was repeated with a visual prompt. If the command plus visual prompt did not result in

compliance, the command was repeated with a physical prompt. This physical prompt would result in compliance to the command. In the low demand condition, Donny was given a preferred task to complete (e.g., identifying letters on the Letter Cards), while in the high demand condition, Donny was given a nonpreferred task to complete (e.g., completing the Morning Worksheet). In each demand condition, the task was removed contingent upon negative behaviors. These two conditions were designed to assess the degree to which Donny's negative behaviors were sensitive to escape from task demands and the impact of the task preference.

Each condition was presented for 10 min each day for a period of five days. The school psychologist conducted observations of the occurrence of Donny's negative behaviors (i.e., running, aggressive behavior) during these conditions through the use of a 5-second partial-interval recording procedure. The results of the functional analysis indicated that Donny's negative behaviors did not occur during the free play condition or during the low task demand condition. However, running behavior escalated slightly during the attention condition and was most prevalent during the high task demand condition. For aggressive behaviors, throwing items was elevated in the attention condition while hitting was elevated in the high task demand condition.

The school psychologist met with Donny's parents and teacher to discuss the assessment results and implications for intervention. Everyone agreed the data gathered through teacher interviews and observations clearly and consistently indicated that Donny's negative behaviors (i.e., aggression and running) occurred at higher rates during demand situations with low preference tasks. In addition, teacher attention did impact negative behaviors. Because the data were fairly clear and consistent, it was decided that the next step would be to develop an intervention based on the assessment results.

Since the primary function of Donny's aggressive and running behavior was identified in the functional analyses as negative reinforcement (i.e., escape from nonpreferred tasks), escape extinction procedures were implemented. Using these procedures, Donny was not allowed to escape tasks or commands by engaging in negative behavior; however, he could briefly escape the task by engaging in positive behaviors. Additionally, Donny received teacher attention (e.g., praise, pat on the back) for positive behaviors. The intervention was comprised of three main steps. First, Donny was presented with a verbal command and given five seconds to comply. If Donny complied, verbal and physical reinforcement was provided and a small break with access to preferred toys was allowed. If Donny did not comply, the command was repeated with a visual prompt (e.g., pointing). Again, Donny was given five seconds to comply and reinforcement was provided following compliance. However, if Donny did not comply, the command was repeated and he was provided a physical prompt (e.g., hand-over-hand technique). Praise and a brief break were provided following assisted compliance.

Using escape extinction combined with teacher praise and attention reduced Donny's negative behaviors. After a month using this treatment, Donny was often compliant with the initial verbal instruction and the teacher would use the visual prompt for clarification and to gain compliance. Teacher praise and access to preferred tasks continued to improve compliance.

Donny's case demonstrates how FBA data can be used to form hypotheses with respect to the function of target behaviors within natural environments. By identifying the function of the behavior, the school team has a better chance of developing a successful intervention. In this manner, FBA data may help prevent professionals (e.g., teachers) and others (e.g., parents) from developing and implementing interventions that are unlikely to be successful. Such failures can cause professionals (e.g., teachers) and parents to become frustrated and have a debilitating effect on a future problem solving behavior. If the team is successful, then specific psycho-educational programming may become more effective and efficient.

## Summary

Although covert behaviors such as thoughts and feelings (self-efficacy, optimism) are considered important to behaviorists (see Skinner 1974), FBA is based on an operant model of psychology where overt behaviors are maintained by their effects on the environment. Because covert behaviors cannot impact the environment (some researchers investigating extrasensory perception such as telekinesis may disagree), behavioral assessment procedures have traditionally measured observable behaviors and how they operate in their environments (e.g., observable reinforcement delivered contingent upon target behaviors). Thus, behavioral assessment and FBA have traditionally been less dependent upon self-reporting to assess variables of interest. This has led to numerous demonstrations of the effectiveness of FBA indicating the function of behaviors in individuals who are nonverbal or who have other communication skill deficits.

In the current chapter we indicated how FBA procedures can be used to identify natural environmental contingencies that are maintaining the behavior of individuals who lack the verbal skills to communicate information about the function of their behavior (e.g., nonverbal students).

These data can then be used to develop interventions based on this within-subject data. Although FBA procedures are based on sound theory, the development and evaluation of such procedures is in its infancy and future research is needed to improve the quality of these procedures so that educators can efficiently determine the function of target behaviors. Additionally, combining FBA and treatment effectiveness research may allow researchers to develop function-by-treatment models of linking assessment to intervention, which may allow educational professionals to develop more effective prevention and remediation procedures across subjects, based on the assessed function of target behaviors.

# References

Akande, A. (1994). The motivation assessment profiles of low-functioning children. *Early Child Development and Care, 101*, 101–107.

American Psychiatric Association. (2013). *Diagnostic and statistical manual of mental disorders* (5th ed.). Arlington, VA: American Psychiatric Publishing.

Anderson, C. M., Rodriquez, B. J., & Campbell, A. (2015). Functional behavior assessment in schools: Current status and future directions. *Journal of Behavioral Education, 24*, 338–371.

Austin, J. L., Groves, E. A., Reynish, L. C., & Francis, L. L. (2015). Validating trial-based functional analyses in mainstream primary school classrooms. *Journal of Applied Behavior Analysis, 48*, 274–288.

Barton-Arwood, S. M., Wehby, J. H., Gunter, P. L., & Lane, K. L. (2003). Functional behavior assessment rating scales: Intrarater reliability with students with emotional or behavioral disorders. *Behavioral Disorders, 28*, 386–400.

Batsche, G. M., & Knoff, H. M. (1995). Linking assessment to intervention. In A. Thomas & J. Grimes (Eds.), *Best practices in school psychology-III* (pp. 569–586). Washington, DC: National Association of School Psychologists.

Bergan, J. R. (1977). *Behavioral consultation*. Columbus, OH: Merrill.

Bergan, J. R., & Kratochwill, T. R. (1990). *Behavioral consultation in applied settings*. New York: Plenum Press.

Beavers, G. A., Iwata, B. A., & Lerman, D. C. (2013). Thirty years of research on the functional analysis of problem behavior. *Journal of Applied Behavior Analysis, 46*, 1–21.

Bloom, S. E., Iwata, B. A., Fritz, J. N., Roscoe, E. M., & Carreau, A. B. (2011). Classroom application of a trial-based functional analysis. *Journal of Applied Behavior Analysis, 44*, 19–31.

Carr, E. G. (1977). The motivation of self-injurious behavior: A review of some hypotheses. *Psychological Bulletin, 84*, 800–816.

Carr, E. G. (1993). Behavior analysis is not ultimately about behavior. *The Behavior Analyst, 16*, 47–49.

Carr, E. G., & Newsom, C. (1985). Demand-related tantrums. *Behavior Modification, 9*, 403–426.

Carr, E. G., Newsom, C. D., & Binkoff, J. A. (1980). Escape as a factor in the aggressive behavior of two retarded children. *Journal of Applied Behavior Analysis, 13*, 101–117.

Cone, J. D. (1997). Invited essay: Issues in functional analysis in behavioral assessment. *Behaviour Research and Therapy, 35*, 259–275.

Cooper, L. J., Wacker, D. P., Thursby, D., Plagmann, L. A., Harding, J., Millard, T., et al. (1992). Analysis of the effects of task preferences, task demands, and adult attention on child behavior in outpatient and classroom settings. *Journal of Applied Behavior Analysis, 25*, 823–840.

Crawford, J., Brockel, B., Schauss, S., & Miltenberger, R. G. (1992). A comparison of methods for the functional assessment of stereotypic behavior. *Journal of the Association for Persons with Severe Handicaps, 17*, 77–86.

Derby, K. M., Wacker, D. P., Peck, S., Sasso, G., DeRaad, A., Berg, W., et al. (1994). Functional analysis of separate topographies of aberrant behavior. *Journal of Applied Behavior Analysis, 27*, 267–278.

Derby, M., Wacker, D., Sasso, G., Steege, M., Northup, J., Cigrand, K., et al. (1992). Brief functional assessment techniques to evaluate aberrant behavior in an outpatient setting: A summary of 79 cases. *Journal of Applied Behavior Analysis, 25*, 713–721.

Dunlap, G., Foster-Johnson, L., Clarke, S., Kern, L., & Childs, K. E. (1995). Modifying activities to produce functional outcomes: Effects on the problem behaviors of students with disabilities. *Journal of the Association for Persons with Severe Handicaps, 20*, 248–258.

Dunlap, G., & Kern, L. (1996). Modifying instructional activities to promote desirable behavior: A conceptual and practical framework. *School Psychology Quarterly, 11*, 297–312.

DuPaul, G. J., Power, T. J., Anastopoulos, A. D., & Reid, R. (1998). *ADHD rating scale-IV: Checklists, norms, and clinical interpretation*. New York: Guilford Press.

Durand, V. M., & Crimmins, D. B. (1987). Assessment and treatment of psychotic speech in an autistic child. *Journal of Autism and Developmental Disorders, 17*, 17–28.

Durand, V. M., & Crimmins, D. B. (1988a). Identifying variables maintaining self-injurious behavior. *Journal of Autism and Developmental Disorders, 18*, 99–117.

Durand, V. M., & Crimmins, D. B. (1988b). Motivational assessment scale. In M. Hersen & A. Bellack (Eds.),

*Dictionary of behavioral assessment techniques* (pp. 309–310). Elmsford, NY: Pergamon.

Ervin, R. A., Ehrhardt, K. E., & Poling, A. (2001a). Functional assessment: Old wine in new bottles. *School Psychology Review, 30*, 173–179.

Ervin, R. A., Radford, P. M., Bertsch, K., Piper, A. L., Ehrhardt, K. E., & Poling, A. (2001b). A descriptive analysis and critique of the empirical literature on school-based functional assessment. *School Psychology Review, 30*, 193–210.

Gann, C. J., Gaines, S. E., Antia, S. D., Umbreit, J., & Liaupsin, C. J. (2015). Evaluating the effects of function-based interventions with deaf or hard-of-hearing students. *Journal of Deaf Studies and Deaf Education, 20*(3), 252–265.

Gresham, F. M., & Elliott, S. N. (2008). *Social skills improvement system rating scales manual.* Minneapolis, MN: NCS Pearson.

Gresham, F. M., & Lambros, K. M. (1998). Behavioral and functional assessment. In T. S. Watson & F. M. Gresham (Eds.), *Handbook of child behavior therapy* (pp. 3–22). New York: Plenum Press.

Hartmann, D. P., Roper, B. L., & Bradford, C. C. (1979). Some relationships between behavioral and traditional assessment. *Journal of Behavioral Assessment, 1*, 3–21.

Iwata, B., Dorsey, M., Slifer, K., Bauman, K., & Richman, G. (1982/1994). Toward a functional analysis of self-injury. *Journal of Applied Behavior Analysis, 27*, 197–209. (Reprinted from *Analysis and Intervention in Developmental Disabilities, 2*, 3–20, 1982).

Johnston, S. M., & Bolstad, O. D. (1973). Methodological issues in naturalistic observation: Some problems and solutions. In L. A. Hamerlynch, L. E. Handy, & E. J. Marsh (Eds.), *Behavior change: Methodology, concepts, and practices* (pp. 7–68). Champaign, IL: Research Press.

Kazdin, A. E. (2001). *Behavior modification in applied settings*, 6th ed. Belmont, CA: Wadsworth.

Kunnavatana, S. S., Bloom, S. E., Samaha, A. L., & Dayton, E. (2013). Training teachers to conduct trial-based functional analyses. *Behavior Modification, 37*, 707–722.

Lalli, J. S., Browder, D. M., Mace, F. C., & Brown, K. (1993). Teacher use of descriptive analysis data to implement interventions to decrease students' maladaptive behavior. *Journal of Applied Behavior Analysis, 10*, 141–150.

Lewis, T. J., Scott, T. M., & Sugai, G. (1994). The problem behavior questionnaire: A teacher based instrument to develop functional hypotheses of problem behavior in general education settings. *Diagnostique, 19*, 103–115.

Malone, J. C. (1990). *Theories of learning: A historical approach.* Belmont, CA: Wadsworth.

McComas, J. J., Hoch, H., & Mace, F. C. (2000). Functional analysis. In E. S. Shapiro & T. R. Kratochwill (Eds.), *Conducting school-based assessment of child and adolescent behavior* (pp. 78–101). New York: Guilford Press.

Merrell, K. W. (2000). Informant reports: Theory and research in using child behavior rating scales in school settings. In E. S. Shapiro & T. R. Kratochwill (Eds.), *Behavioral assessment in schools: Theory research and practice* (2nd ed., pp. 233–256). New York: Guilford Press.

Michael, J. (1993). Establishing operations. *The Behavior Analyst, 16*, 191–206.

Mueller, M. M., Nkosi, A., & Hine, J. F. (2011). Functional analysis in public schools: A summary of 90 functional analyses. *Journal of Applied Behavior Analysis, 44*, 807–818.

Neef, N. A., Mace, F. C., & Shade, D. (1993). Impulsivity in students with serious emotional disturbance: The interactive effects of reinforcer rate, delay, and quality. *Journal of Applied Behavior Analysis, 23*, 37–52.

Neef, N. A., Shade, D., & Miller, M. S. (1994). Assessing the influential dimensions of reinforcers on choice in students with serious emotional disturbance. *Journal of Applied Behavior Analysis, 24*, 389–408.

Nelson, R. O., & Hayes, S. C. (1979). Some current dimensions of behavioral assessment. *Behavioral Assessment, 1*, 1–16.

Nelson, J. R., Roberts, M. L., Rutherford, R. B., Mathur, S. R., & Aaroe, L. A. (1999). A statewide survey of special education administrators and school psychologists regarding functional behavioral assessment. *Education and Treatment of Children, 22*, 267–279.

Noell, G. H., Witt, J. C., Gilbertson, D. N., Ranier, D. D., & Freeland, J. T. (1997). Increasing teacher intervention implementation in general education settings through consultation and performance feedback. *School Psychology Quarterly, 12*, 77–88.

Northup, J., Wacker, D., Sasso, G., Steege, M., Cigrand, K., Cook, J., et al. (1991). A brief functional analysis of aggressive and alternative behavior in an outclinic setting. *Journal of Applied Behavior Analysis, 24*, 509–522.

Oliver, A. C., Pratt, L. A., & Normand, M. P. (2015). A survey of functional behavior assessment methods used by behavior analysts in practice. *Journal of Applied Behavior Analysis, 48*, 1–13.

Powell, J., Martindale, B., Kulp, S., Martindale, A., & Bauman, R. (1977). Taking a closer look: Time sampling and measurement error. *Journal of Applied Behavior Analysts, 10*, 325–332.

Ray, K. P., & Watson, T. S. (2001). Analysis of temporally distant events on school behavior. *School Psychology Quarterly, 16*(3), 324–342.

Reynolds, C. R., & Kamphaus, R. W. (2015). *Behavior assessment system for children* (3 ed.). Upper Saddle River, NJ: Pearson Education, Inc. Sanetti, Collier-Meek, Long, Byron, & Kratochwill.

Saudargus, R. A. (1992). *State-event classroom observation system (SECOS).* Knoxville: University of Tennessee, Department of Psychology.

Shapiro, E. S. (2011). *Academic skills problems: Direct assessment and intervention* (4th ed.). New York: Guilford Press.

Shapiro, E. S., & Kratochwill, T. R. (2000). Introduction: Conducting a multidimensional behavioral assessment. In E. S. Shapiro & T. R. Kratochwill (Eds.), *Conducting school-based assessments of child and adolescent behavior* (pp. 1–20). New York: Guilford Press.

Sheridan, S. M., Kratochwill, T. R., & Bergan, J. R. (1996). *Conjoint behavioral consultation: A procedural manual.* New York: Plenum Press.

Shriver, M. D., Anderson, C. M., & Proctor, B. (2001). Evaluating the validity of functional behavioral assessment. *School Psychology Review, 30*, 180–192.

Sigafoos, J., & Saggers, E. (1995). A discrete-trial approach to the functional analysis of aggressive behaviour in two boys with autism. *Journal of Intellectual and Developmental Disability, 20*, 287–297.

Sigafoos, J., Kerr, M., & Roberts, D. (1994). Inter-rater reliability analysis of the MAS: Failure to replicate with aggressive behavior. *Research in Developmental Disabilities, 15*, 333–342.

Skinner, B. F. (1974). *About behaviorism.* New York: Knopf.

Skinner, C. H., Dittmer, K. I., & Howell, L. A. (2000a). Direct observation in school settings: Theoretical issues. In E. S. Shapiro & T. R. Kratochwill (Eds.), *Behavioral assessment in schools: Theory research and practice* (2nd ed., pp. 19–45). New York: Guilford Press.

Skinner, C. H., Freeland, J., & Shapiro, E. S. (2003). Applying behavioral assessment procedures to the problem solving process. In C. R. Reynolds & R. Kamphaus (Eds.), *Handbook of educational and psychological assessment of children: Personality, behavior, and context* (2nd ed.). New York: Guilford.

Skinner, C. H., Rhymer, K. N., & Mcdaniel, E. C. (2000b). Naturalistic direct observation in educational settings. In E. S. Shapiro & T. R. Kratochwill (Eds.), *Conducting school-based assessments of child and adolescent behavior* (pp. 21–54). New York: Guilford Press.

Sprague, J., Sugai, B., & Walker, H. (1998). Antisocial behavior in schools. In T. S. Watson & F. M. Gresham (Eds.), *Handbook of child behavior therapy* (pp. 451–474). New York: Plenum Press.

Staddon, J. E. R. (1993). *Behaviorism: Mind, mechanism and society.* London: Duckworth.

Steege, M. W., & Scheib, M. A. (2014). Best practices in conducting functional behavioral assessment. In P. L. Harrison & A. Thomas (Eds.), *Best practices in school psychology* (pp. 273–286). Bethesda, MD: National Association of School Psychologists.

Sterling-Turner, H. E., Watson, T. S., Wildmon, M., Watkins, C., & Little, E. (2001). Investigating the relationship between training type and treatment integrity. *School Psychology Quarterly, 16*, 56–67.

Sturmey, P. (1994). Assessing the functions of aberrant behaviors: A review of psychometric instruments. *Journal of Autism and Developmental Disorders, 24*, 293–304.

Telzrow, C. F. (1999). IDEA amendments of 1997: Promise or pitfall for special education reform? *Journal of School Psychology, 37*, 7–28.

Thompson, S., & Emerson, E. (1995). Inter-informant agreement on the motivation assessment scale: Another failure to replicate. *Mental Handicap Research, 8*, 203–208.

Townsend, B. J. K. (2000). *A functional analysis of the echolalic behavior of three children with autism in a residential school setting.* (Unpublished doctoral dissertation). Mississippi State University, Starkville.

Watson, T. S., & Robinson, S. L. (1996). Direct behavioral consultation: An alternative approach to didactic consultation. *School Psychology Quarterly, 11*, 267–278.

Worcester, L., McLaughlin, T. F., Barretto, A., & Blecher, J. (2015). Use of a functional behavior assessment to address tantrum behavior with a preschooler with developmental delays. *International Journal of English and Education, 4*, 522–538.

Yell, M. L., & Shriner, J. G. (1997). The IDEA amendments of 1997: Implications for special and general education teachers, administrators, and teacher trainers. *Focus on Exceptional Children, 30*, 1–19.

# Nonverbal Neuropsychological Assessment

17

## John D. Wasserman

At the outset, it is important to acknowledge that the term *nonverbal* cannot begin to approximate the multitude of mental operations executed by people during complex behaviors, even when no spoken or written communications are involved. Recent advances in cognitive neuroscience show that human behaviors, when measured with neuroimaging technologies, correspond to the activation of highly connected neural networks with integrated processes and dynamic interactions across multiple network distributions (van den Heuvel and Sporns 2013; Sporns and Betzel 2016). Many of these networks span functionally heterogeneous brain regions and are not modality-specific, activating in response to more than one sensory input or even nonsensory-based ideation. The 1990s-era discovery of *mirror neurons*, multimodal association neurons that increase activity during execution of certain actions or while seeing/hearing corresponding actions performed by others (see, e.g., Rizzolatti and Craighero 2004), has stimulated a dawning awareness now supported by research that a wide range of cognitive activities involve neural simulations or reenactments (Barsalou 2008). For example, perceiving the handle of a coffee cup activates a grasping simulation (Tucker and Ellis 1998); judging the weight of an object lifted by someone else activates motor and somatosensory

systems (Bosbach et al. 2005); mental rotation of objects is accompanied by motor simulations of turning (Richter et al. 2000); and retrieval of a word stimulates the sensory modality operations performed when the word was encoded (Buckner and Wheeler 2001). Stating that a test is *nonverbal* says very little about the many verbal areas of the brain that may be activated by its performance. At best, *nonverbal* describes the overt requirements of a test, not the internal mental processes that may be required for performance.

When contrasted with *verbal* assessment, however, the practice of *nonverbal* assessment is practical and easy to understand, accounting for its century-long duration. *Nonverbal assessment* simply describes measurement in which an effort has been made to minimize the use of language (in instructions, materials, and responses) because language functioning per se may be irrelevant to the cognitive construct being measured. For example, there is value in identifying relatively spared mental functions in an individual with a known language disorder, so administration of tasks with minimal receptive and expressive language requirements may be helpful and instructive. If tests have lengthy spoken instructions, the examinee with a language disorder may potentially perform at lower levels, even if the measure is intended to tap abilities unrelated to language. Likewise, it is usually ill-advised to administer a measure in the English language to a person proficient in another language (and not in English), since results will invariably underestimate true ability. We would also be exceedingly cautious about administering

17

J.D. Wasserman (✉)
Burke, VA, USA
e-mail: j.d.wasserman@pobox.com
URL: http://www.johndwasserman.com

© Springer International Publishing AG 2017
R.S. McCallum (ed.), *Handbook of Nonverbal Assessment*,
DOI 10.1007/978-3-319-50604-3_17

a measure in spoken English to an individual who is Deaf, unless an American Sign Language (ASL) translator or appropriate augmentative device is available. Accordingly, use of nonverbal assessment tools in neuropsychology is indicated for individuals whose English language functioning is likely compromised by their cultural–linguistic, educational, or medical background, including the following special populations: (a) individuals with acquired or developmental speech and language disorder; (b) individuals with limited English proficiency, for whom translated or adapted tests are not available; (c) individuals who are Deaf or hard of hearing; and (d) individuals who, by virtue of their education or cultural experience, cannot be assessed validly with language-based tasks. Nonverbal assessment of language-impaired individuals may provide a truer representation of neurocognitive functioning than can be expected with language-loaded measures, because the role of language as an intervening factor in explaining deficient test performance is minimized. At the same time, it should be considered best practice to first document an examinee's existing language proficiency and competencies with conventional language measures, including the nature and severity of language impairment. For example, it is reasonable to administer an aphasia battery or an English proficiency measure before proceeding to the nonverbal neuropsychological assessment.

Within the scope of clinical practice, neuropsychological assessment involves measurement of higher order dimensions of cognition, principally in the domains of attention and executive functions, memory and new learning ability, language and communication, and visual–spatial cognition. There are few investigations pertaining to the structure of wide-ranging neuropsychological batteries, but in an investigation of Spanish speaking adults administered a neuropsychological battery with "minimal linguistic components" (p. 127), Ardila and Pineda (2000) extracted five relatively independent nonverbal cognitive factors: "attention, executive function, memory, visuoperceptual and visuoconstructive abilities" (p. 135). This chapter addresses nonverbal

assessment in these neuropsychological domains, noting that related areas of testing commonly included in neuropsychological batteries (e.g., appraisal of intelligence, personality, and psychopathology) are described elsewhere in this volume and that testing of lower sensory and motor functions already tend to be somewhat independent of language.

## A Working Definition of "Nonverbal" Tests

The verbal–nonverbal dichotomy cannot be equated with the auditory–visual sensory modality distinction, as there are nonverbal aspects to auditory processing (e.g., processing of environmental and musical sounds) and verbal aspects to visual processing (e.g., identification of meaningful, semantically processed visual details). Efforts to simplify the verbal–nonverbal dichotomy by defining functions in terms of underlying cerebral lateralization (left hemisphere vs. right hemisphere) also represent an oversimplification of reality, since some aspects of language are seated in the right cerebral hemisphere, and some spatial processing is seated in the left cerebral hemisphere. De Renzi (1982) criticized the association of verbal–nonverbal functioning with lateralized left- and right hemisphere cortical functions: "There is no need to spend time to demonstrate that labeling the right hemisphere specialization as 'non verbal' is heuristically unsatisfactory" (p. 186). Benton (1988/2000) concluded that the verbal–nonverbal dichotomy remains a practical, albeit flawed, way to think about cortical functions. As implied in the brief discussion of neural networks in the introduction to this chapter, behavior always has a multitude of cortical and subcortical underpinnings. Most human behaviors involve a *microgenesis*, or unfolding, of multiple simultaneous complex processes that change over a span of seconds—activating circuits and pathways throughout the entire brain, never just one cerebral hemisphere.

Traditional clinical wisdom holds that the inability to communicate *meaning* is the defining characteristic of disorders of language. Beginning in 1863, Jackson (1915) studied language disorders and speculated that at the heart of language disorders was a central deficit in the ability to convey meaning or the formulation of propositions. Finkelnburg (1870/1979) described language disorders as an inability to manipulate any symbols for communication (*asymbolia*), making it difficult for affected individuals to use even nonverbal gestures or pantomime for communication. Head (1926) built upon the Jacksonian tradition to argue that impaired symbol formation and expression in any context—language and nonlanguage tasks—is the central processing disorder in aphasia. Contemporary theorists continue to emphasize the integral role of *meaning* in language and communication, irrespective of whether communication is spoken, written, or gestural (e.g., Caplan 1994). This tradition, however, might lead us toward the untenable position that meaningful content is inherently *verbal* (language-based), while content that is not meaningful is *nonverbal*. Fortunately, Barsalou (1999) has theorized that symbolic operations transcend language, for they are part of perceptual processes that record and conceptually interpret experience, as well as driving internal mental simulations.

With these considerations in mind, we offer a working operational definition of *nonverbal tests* that relies upon their objective, observable, and overt performance requirements. The most obvious definition is that nonverbal neuropsychological tests involve no expressive or receptive language requirements from the examinee, but there are so few tests that meet this requirement that it is unduly restrictive. Accordingly, we must arbitrarily define *nonverbal neuropsychological tests* as instruments (a) requiring minimal receptive language of the examinee (usually not more than several sentences to be comprehended as part of the spoken instructions), (b) utilizing stimuli that are not semantic or numerical symbols (e.g., logographs, letters, words, or numbers), (c) requiring minimal expressive language (i.e., only very brief written or spoken verbal responses) on the part of the examinee, and (d) having a theoretical or

empirical relationship with the integrity of functioning in the brain.

Our rationale for permitting brief spoken instructions (requiring a little receptive language/comprehension) in a nonverbal test while minimizing expressive language/production is threefold: (a) expressive language deficits, particularly in naming and word finding ability, are almost universal in language disorders, whereas receptive language deficits are comparatively rarer; (b) receptive language is developmentally acquired before expressive language and tends to be less impaired in developmental disorders than expressive language (e.g., Ballantyne and Sattler 1991; Clark and Hecht 1983; Fraser et al. 1963); and (c) the sparing of language comprehension relative to language expression after acquired brain injury parallels the better-known sparing of recognition memory relative to free recall memory (e.g., Channell and Peck 1989). All things being equal, the ability to comprehend ideas is more resilient to brain injury than the expression of ideas.

Our rationale for excluding printed stimuli that involve semantic or numerical symbols (e.g., letters, words, logographic characters, and numbers) is that most of these graphic forms tend to be semantically represented and therefore heavily dependent upon linguistic processes. For example, most forms of numerical processing are mediated by some form of semantic representation (McCloskey and Macaruso 1995). The now ubiquitous rapid automatized naming tests (see Wolf and Denckla 2005 for the most recent update of the RAN/RAS tests) are based on the finding that (in)efficiency at accessing and mentally retrieving semantically stored material is associated with a host of language-based learning disabilities, including dyslexia, dysgraphia, and dyscalculia. The exclusion of test stimuli using letters, numbers, or words from our definition of nonverbal tests leads us to abandon some of the best known neuropsychological measures including the Trail Making Test (Army Individual Test Battery 1944) and the Halstead Category Test (Halstead 1947) from the Halstead–Reitan Neuropsychological Battery (Reitan and Wolfson 1985). The evidence from tests like the

RAN/RAS convincingly shows that processing of even isolated letters and numbers can be compromised in language-related disorders (e.g., Wolf and Denckla 2005).

It is theoretically possible to conduct an assessment of language-related functions with nonverbal measures, although there is little reason to do so. For example, language functions such as auditory processing and symbolic communication may be measured with nonverbal tools of sound processing (Seashore et al. 1960; Spreen and Benton 1969) and pantomime/gesture recognition (Benton et al. 1994). Several measures of receptive language and comprehension meet our defining criteria for nonverbal neuropsychological tests (e.g., DiSimoni 1978; Dunn and Dunn 2007; Spreen and Benton 1969), because they involve brief verbal directives to point or manipulate objects with no expressive language.

## Representative Nonverbal Tests by Neurocognitive Domain

In this section, we describe applied and theoretical dimensions of assessment within the major neurocognitive domains of attention and executive functions, memory and new learning ability, and visual–spatial cognition. Representative nonverbal measures that tap central neuropsychological functions are described, including information about the constructs they measure, their administration, scoring, and interpretation, and their limitations. These instruments rank among the most widely utilized by practitioners (see Butler et al. 1991; Camara et al. 2000; Rabin et al. 2005). In many instances, there may be as many as half a dozen or more adaptations for a given procedure, so only a limited number of representative adaptations can be described in text. For example, there are at least 10 scoring systems for the Rey–Osterrieth Complex Figure (ROCF; Troyer and Wishart 1997).

In this volume, the psychometric properties of nonverbal tests typically are described in detail. In this chapter, however, the psychometric properties of nonverbal neuropsychological

measures are not directly addressed, in part because existing psychometric standards have not been traditionally or rigorously applied to neuropsychological tests. It has only been in more recent years that neuropsychological tests have undergone standardizations with nationally representative normative samples (e.g., Delis et al. 2001; Korkman et al. 2007; White and Stern 2001, 2003). Moreover, many neuropsychological tests yield multiple interpretive indices, with variable psychometric qualities, that are evaluated with reference to a large number of independently published norms varying widely in quality. Accordingly, it is difficult to make brief summary statements about psychometric adequacy for almost any neuropsychological test. Thoughtful discussions concerning the psychometric properties of neuropsychological tests are available in Mitrushina et al. (2005) and Strauss et al. (2006).

## Attention and Executive Functions

Attention and executive functions are interrelated constructs. At the simplest level of analysis, attention involves the allocation of cognitive resources in a given direction, whereas executive functions control the implementation of behaviors with some intended outcome. Theoretical models of attention include elements from the executive functions (Mirsky 1996), whereas most models of the executive functions include elements (e.g., inhibition) that are central to attention (Eslinger 1996). In some test batteries, attention and executive functions are separated (e.g., Naglieri et al. 2014; White and Stern 2001, 2003), whereas in others, they are combined (Korkman et al. 2007). Some new conceptualizations of disorders of attention emphasize underlying deficits in executive functions (Barkley 2015; Tannock and Schachar 1996). I have always found the approach of Stuss and Benson (1986) to be helpful, that is, that attention and executive functions are hierarchically organized mental processes with executive functions at an upper, superordinate level and attention at a lower level, although the picture is undoubtedly more complex. In this section, we distinguish between attention and executive functions with the recognition that measures of each construct may be readily applied to the other.

In neuropsychology, *attention* is used to describe a wide range of behaviors and processes beginning as soon as environmental events are detected by the senses and involving the subsequent and ongoing allocation of cognitive resources. Attention has the net effect of facilitating cognitive and behavioral performance by filtering and managing incoming stimulation, permitting selection and control of behavioral responses, and maintaining performance over time (Cohen 1993). Although a number of kinds of attention have been described (e.g., Parasuraman 1998), most cognitive and neuropsychological models tend to include just a few core types (Cohen 1993; Koelega 1996; Stankov 1988; van Zomeren and Brouwer 1994):

- *Selective attention*: Ability to preferentially attend to a particular signal while inhibiting attention to competing signals; related to the concept of *focus*.
- *Sustained attention*: Ability over time to maintain a response set or readiness to respond to unpredictable events; related to the concept of *vigilance*.
- *Divided attention*: Ability to simultaneously attend to multiple events or perform multiple tasks; related to the concept of *multitasking*.

In comparison with attention, the *executive functions* refer to a cluster of activating and inhibitory psychological processes that control the formulation, implementation, coordination, and monitoring of sequences of behavioral responses according to short- and long-term goals (Eslinger 1996). The executive functions tend to be most strongly associated with activity in the prefrontal cortex, as the active force behind voluntary and deliberate behavior (Pribram 1973; Tranel et al. 1995). In his most recent theoretical formulation, Barkley (2012) considers *executive functioning* to be a meta-construct operationally defined as behavioral self-regulation across time for the attainment of one's goals, typically using social and cultural means. In his view, executive functions are self-directed activities that change subsequent behaviors in the service of some objective. There is some variation in the classes of self-regulatory behaviors identified as *executive functions*, but they generally include (a) response inhibition; (b) working memory; (c) organization, strategizing, and planning; (d) cognitive flexibility and shifting; (e) emotional self-regulation and self-motivation; and (f) self-awareness and self-monitoring (e.g., Barkley 2012).

In the following sections, representative nonverbal measures tapping various aspects of attention and executive functions are reported. Some of the theoretical dimensions cited above have few formal measures and are not included.

**Tests of selective and sustained attention.** Although there are many measures of selective and sustained attention, the best-known tests with nonverbal forms of administration are the continuous performance tests (CPTs). Developed nearly five decades ago (Rosvold et al. 1956), the CPTs represent a family of measures intended to assess diverse aspects of attention, along with elements of impulsivity. Ranging from about 10 to 25 min in length, the CPTs involve continuous presentation at either regular or variable intervals of low interest stimuli and require the examinee to respond (or *not respond*) to selected stimuli under specific conditions, usually by pressing a button or switch.

Four major continuous performance tests—Conners' continuous performance tests (Conners CPT 3 and Conners CATA), the *Integrated Visual and Auditory Continuous Performance Test* (IVA2), the *Gordon Diagnostic System* (GDS), and the *Test of Variables of Attention* (TOVA and TOVA-A)—currently dominate CPT assessment (Riccio et al. 2001). Of these, only the *Test of Variables of Attention* (TOVA) and its auditory version (TOVA-A) utilize nonlanguage stimuli (i.e., neither letters nor numbers) (Leark et al. 2007). After a 3-min practice test, the TOVA tests for 21.6 min (11 min for 4–5 year olds). Stimuli in the TOVA are two geometric figures, one of which is the target; the auditory version TOVA-A uses two tones, the higher tone being the target. Both measures are nonsequential with a fixed interstimulus interval. The test developers recommend administering the visual and auditory TOVAs about 90 min apart or on different days. The instructions for each version of TOVA are provided verbally and include the brief practice test for both the visual and auditory versions to ensure that the examinee understands the testing conditions and instructions. The tests are computer scored and normed for ages 4 years through 80+ years, generating a score and narrative printout (Leark et al. 2007). Results are reported as raw scores, percentages, standard scores, and standard deviations. Scoring indices on the TOVA, like most CPTs, include indices of response variability, errors of omission (traditionally associated with inattention), errors of commission (impulsivity or disinhibition), correct response time (decision time to respond correctly) and postcommission response time (inhibitory responding after making an error), anticipatory responses (number of guesses), and response sensitivity (the ratio of hit rate to false alarm rate).

In the most comprehensive treatment to date, Riccio et al. (2001) have summarized the strengths and weaknesses of the CPTs:

- Most CPT paradigms are sensitive to most types of central nervous system dysfunction;
- CPT performance is adversely affected by metabolic disorders with cognitive sequelae, by schizophrenic disorders, by pervasive developmental disorders, by most externalizing disorders in children, and by some internalizing disorders;
- CPTs tend not to be sensitive to disorders of mood or affect;
- CPTs have high levels of sensitivity and specificity for all forms of Attention-Deficit Hyperactivity Disorder (ADHD), but only when ADHD or a typical presentation with no impairment are the only two diagnostic possibilities (and differential diagnosis is not involved);
- Reliance on CPTs as a primary diagnostic tool in determining the presence of ADHD will result in an unacceptably high number of false-positive errors (i.e., overdiagnosis of ADHD).

Although the CPTs provide norm-referenced information about multiple aspects of attention, the examiner must also consider the testing time investment and examinee motivation relative to the interpretive yield for these unengaging tasks. I sometimes introduce CPT tasks as measures of a person's capacity to remain attentive during very boring classroom or work experiences.

Visual search and cancellation tests constitute a second major class of measures thought to tap selective and sustained attention. These tasks typically involve the presentation of a printed stimulus array with instructions to mark (or *cancel*) specified targets with a pencil. Computerized versions with touchscreen input are rapidly emerging (Dalmaijer et al. 2014). For example, an examinee may be asked to make a mark on all of the cats appearing in a semirandomly organized array of printed line drawings of animals. A more figural nonverbal stimulus may be found in the Landolt C cancellation tasks, which employ circles with or without a gap for targets and distractors (Parton et al. 2006). Performance on cancellation tasks is typically measured according to speed, although errors of commission or omission may be respectively interpreted as indicating difficulty with impulsiveness or inattention, especially if they are concentrated in one hemispatial field. With neglect syndromes, automated computation facilitates identification of visual field inattention severity. For example, the center of cancellation (CoC) is the average horizontal position of cancelled targets, standardized so that a value of −1 corresponds with the leftmost targets and +1 with the rightmost targets (e.g., Rorden and Karnath 2010). Depending upon specific parameters of the test stimuli, cancellation tasks require selective and sustained visual attention, visual scanning, visual discrimination, access to a full visual field, psychomotor coordination, lower order (for simple detection) and higher order (for decision-making) processing speed, and selection and implementation of visual search strategies. Task demands may be varied according to the randomness or structure of the stimulus array, the density and discriminability of the target stimuli relative to distractors, the nature of the decision to be made (e.g., mere detection of a target vs. comparison of multiple targets), the size of the visual field to be searched, and the use of target stimuli from different domains (e.g., letters, digits, pictures, or abstract figures; Cohen 1993). For example, the tests of directed attention of Mesulam (1985) sometimes show dissociated patterns of performance between detection of the letter "A" (poor performance) and abstract geometric figure detection (adequate performance) in patients with left hemisphere lesions (Kaplan 1988), presumably because of the enhanced role of the left cerebral hemisphere in the processing of letter stimuli. A hemiattentional neglect syndrome is suggested when errors of omission are substantially greater for the examinee's left visual field than right. Profound neglect for the left hemiattentional visual field has been demonstrated in adults with right cerebral hemisphere impairment (Heilman et al. 1993). A generalized slowing of performance may be evident, however, in examinees with a variety of diffuse and focal neurological conditions.

Cancellation tasks differ from the CPTs through use of paper-and-pencil materials (compared to computerized presentation of stimuli), a single frame simultaneous presentation (compared to a multiframe, sequential presentation), self-paced performance (versus computer pacing), heightened demands on visual–spatial scanning (versus stimuli presented within a more limited visual field), and heightened demands for visual search strategies (different strategies are required for CPTs). They are similar to the CPTs insofar as they measure sustained and selective attention, usually under conditions of limited interest.

When the stimuli are randomly or semirandomly organized in the array, there are at least two ways of noting the spatial progress of the search over time. The color coding method, recommended by Mesulam (1985), requires that the task be performed with colored pencils, a different color being handed to the examinee after the identification of a specified number of

targets or after a specified period of time. An alternative method is simply to have the examiner draw a diagram indicating the sequence of targets circled by the examinee. Normal adults and adolescents typically conduct a systematic, planful search beginning on the left and proceeding to the right in horizontal or vertical rows even in the random arrays (Kaplan 1988; Mesulam 1985). Children younger than 8 or 9 years usually scan and mark shapes in a random, unsystematic sequence. Some assessment procedures require the examinee to draw their plan of search for an object lost in an open field (e.g., Wilson et al. 1996), permitting easy determination of the efficiency and systematicity of visual searches.

The paper-and-pencil visual search and cancellation tasks offer several important strengths, namely that they are child and adult friendly, simple to administer without computer equipment, and useful for screening visual field deficits. Their chief limitations are short administration duration, thereby limiting their use as measures of sustained attention, and limited prediction of clinical attention-deficit disorders. Normative performance on most of visual search and cancellation tests is dependent on speed, with few errors of omission or commission expected. As a result, children with visual–motor impairments may produce depressed performance, even if there is no attention deficit. Moreover, children, adolescents, and adults with known attention deficits have been shown in general to be prone to fast, inaccurate, impulsive task performance rather than slow, accurate, and reflective performance (Campbell et al. 1977; Cohen et al. 1972; Hopkins et al. 1979), so tests such as the visual cancellation tasks that can be completed easily without errors may suffer from diminished clinical sensitivity.

**Tests of response inhibition**. Assessment of the executive functions may also include tests that require an examinee to suppress a competing response voluntarily, whether it is a highly automatized response or simply an easier, faster, or shorter pathway to task execution. Tests that involve the suppression of an automatic, easier, or preferred response are considered to tap neural processes of response inhibition. Sergeant et al. (1999) have described 12 assessment paradigms operationalizing response inhibition, a few of which are described below.

A classic and largely nonverbal measure of response inhibition is the Matching Familiar Figures Test (MFFT; Kagan et al. 1964), in which the examinee is asked to identify which of six choices is perfectly identical to a target picture. The test consists of an elementary set of 12 items and an adolescent/adult set of 12 items. All but one of the six choices (or up to eight choices for the adolescent/adult set) differ in some small, detailed respect from the target, and a careful and deliberate comparison of the choices to the target is required for accurate responding. The MFFT involves spoken directions, only two sentences of which are essential, and requires only a pointing response from the examinee. The examiner records time to the first response, total number of errors for each item, and the order in which errors are made. Responses continue to be coded for each item until the examinee makes a maximum of six errors or gets the item correct. In general, the MFFT is intended to detect children and adolescents who do not take sufficient time to examine the response options carefully, thereby demonstrating an impulsive response style (Kagan 1965). The MFFT generally yields more errors in individuals with impulsivity-attentional problems compared with normal controls (Douglas et al. 1988; Milich et al. 1994), but performance on it may be depressed for reasons other than defective response inhibition including low intelligence, poor search strategies, and inadequate awareness of the need to inhibit responses until all options have been examined (Schachar and Logan 1990).

Measures of the ability to inhibit motor responding include the motor impersistence tests, the go/no-go tests and their variants, motor programming, and graphic pattern generation tests (e.g., Cohen 1993; Denckla 1985; Goldberg et al. 2001). For the most part, these tests are mastered with perfect performance expected at adolescent or preadolescent ages and have very low ceilings. *Motor impersistence* refers to the inability to sustain a directed act or intention and can be demonstrated using a variety of body parts including the limbs, eyes, eyelids, jaw, and tongue (Denckla 1985; Heilman et al. 1993). In the Benton–Iowa neuropsychological battery, motor impersistence is assessed with eight tests requiring the maintenance of a movement or posture (e.g., keeping eyes closed, protruding tongue) (Benton et al. 1994). Norms are provided for ages 5–11, as most adolescents and adults perform these tests without error.

The go/no-go paradigm described by Drewe (1975) and other forms of reciprocal responding (see Luria 1966) involve presentation of a series of stimuli (either verbal or nonverbal) to which the examinee must respond according to specified rules, usually inhibiting the inclination to reciprocate with a response identical to the stimulus or to perseverate to previously given responses. A simple nonverbal version of this task involves instructing the examinee to raise a finger ("go") when the examiner taps once on the table but to refrain from any movement ("no-go") when the examiner taps twice (Trommer et al. 1991). The children's game of *Simon Says* may be considered a go/no-go task of behavioral inhibition in which the directed action is to be performed if "Simon says" ("go"), but the action should not be performed if the prefatory phrase "Simon says" is omitted from the directive ("no-go"). The simplest nonverbal form of the reciprocal programming task appears in the NEPSY Knock and Tap subtest, in which the examiner tells the examinee, "When I do this (knock lightly on the table with your knuckles), you do this (tap lightly on the table with your palm). But if I do this (tap lightly), you do this (knock lightly)" (Korkman et al. 1998, p. 171). The task, which is normed for ages 5–12, requires the examinee to respond to a series of knocks and taps with responses that require suppression of the natural inclination to be stimulus bound and echopraxic. This task was not included in the NEPSY-II (Korkman et al. 2007). There are innumerable variations on these clinical paradigms, but relatively few of them are norm referenced.

Measures of motor alternation, sequencing, and programming can be utilized to examine diverse aspects of executive functions, including motor inhibition. Assessment of the formulation, execution, coordination, and maintenance of intentional motor action programs can include varied motor sequences, such as from repetitive sequences touching each of the four fingers to the thumb (a fingers–thumb sequence); sequentially shifting the position of one hand from closed fist to open palm down to open palm held vertically (a fist–palm–side sequence); or alternating simultaneous bilateral hand movements from left palm—right fist to left fist—right palm to left palm—right fist and so on, each program maintained for a specified period of time. The regulation and maintenance of motor tone during execution of these programs with smooth, fluid, and coordinated movements constitutes what Luria (1973) termed a "kinetic melody" that heavily involves activity in the premotor cortex as well as other cortical and subcortical regions. The phenomenon of motor overflow, in which another part of the body moves involuntarily in conjunction with the intentional execution of motor sequences, is considered to be a neurological soft sign that reflects selective motor disinhibition (Denckla 1985, 1994). Various test batteries including most adaptations of Luria's neuropsychological examination measure motor programming at graded levels of complexity for children and/or adults (e.g., Denckla 1985; Goldberg et al. 2001; Korkman et al. 2007).

Graphic pattern generation tests typically involve the motor reproduction and continuation of recurring alternating figures, with the expectation that examinees with executive dysfunction may experience difficulty alternating between figures. Examinees are typically asked to reproduce and continue a pattern with either semantic stimuli (e.g., alternating m's and n's: mnmnmnmn) or figural stimuli (e.g., alternating peaks and plateaus). Luria (1966) described the reproduction of a series of alternating patterns from a written model, and Goldberg et al. (2001) included a Graphical Sequences Test in their Executive Control Battery for adults.

Leading measures of behavioral inhibition such as the Stroop task (Stroop 1935), in which an examinee must selectively attend to and name the color of ink a word is printed in while suppressing the more automatic, prepotent response of reading the word, have reading requirements that make them less than optimal for nonverbal assessment. Stroop alternatives without reading requirements include the Day–Night task which requires that children say the opposite of what the stimulus card represents (i.e., saying "day" when shown a black card with a moon and stars, or saying "night" when shown a white card with a sun) (Gerstadt et al. 1994). The NEPSY-II Inhibition subtest uses a similar methodology to achieve the Stroop effect (Korkman et al. 2007), but both the Day–Night and Inhibition procedures have expressive language requirements that exclude them from our nonverbal compilation. Similar effects may be achieved, however, through computerized testing with no verbal response required. On the Bivalent Shape Task (Esposito et al. 2013), for example, colored shape stimuli appear in the center of the computer screen with the instruction to *match the shape* to either of two choices—a red circle or a blue square. Instructions for this task, albeit with possibly unnecessary verbiage, state:

> The next computer game is the Shape Game. You are going to match the circles to the circle picture at the bottom and the squares to the square picture at the bottom. We are going to practice first. The first few we do will make a 'ding' if you do it correctly and an 'eh' if you do it incorrectly. That we can make sure you know how to play! The sound will go away after the first few, but that does not mean you are playing it wrong; just keep playing. Let's play the Shape Game! (Esposito et al. 2013, p. 359).

Some stimuli match according to shape and color, while others match ignore the color and respond according to shape. The same approach to responding may be applied to other computerized Stroop-like measures.

**Tests of organization, strategizing, and planning**. Executive functions also include the capacity to formulate and execute an organized sequence of actions with the objective of accomplishing a goal, or *planning*. For complex tasks, planning tends to be hierarchical, so that a task is broken into smaller subtasks, each with its own intermediate goal that can be accomplished in the service of the higher order objective. Because planning involves the generation of divergent response options, sorting through the options, and selecting one for implementation, it necessarily involves behavioral inhibition, sequential processing, working memory, strategy formation, and ongoing monitoring to appraise progress toward the goal. Lezak (1982) argues that planning is essential for independent, creative, and socially constructive behavior.

Disk transfer problems, such as the Tower of London (TOL; Shallice 1982) and Tower of Hanoi (TOH; Simon 1975), utilize variations of a look-ahead problem-solving assessment paradigm dating back some seven decades (Ewert and Lambert 1932). These tasks differ in their cognitive demands, with the TOL solution matching some specified final position and the TOH solution involving placement of all disks on one specified peg. At the same time, they share the qualities of being sensitive to sequential planning abilities, with the quality of performance being measured by the number of moves (or trials) required to arrive at the goal state. Problem-solving strategies used to solve the tower tasks include rote approaches, goal recursion strategies, perceptual strategies, and move-pattern strategies, all dependent upon tradeoffs between perceptual and memory functions (Simon 1975). The TOL and TOH have both been shown to yield impaired performance in individuals with frontal lobe lesions (Levin et al. 1996; Pennington and Ozonoff 1996). Commercial adaptations of these paradigms with contemporary norms are available for the *Tower of Hanoi* (D-KEFS Tower; Delis et al. 2001) and the *Tower of London* (TOL—Drexel University, Second Edition; Culbertson and Zillmer 2001). The tower tasks are largely nonverbal, with the examinee response being evident through the sequence of moves. At least one experimental investigation has shown tower tasks to have a substantially lower language load than other executive function measures (Remine et al. 2008).

Planning and strategizing is also thought to be associated with paper-and-pencil drawing and reproduction of graphic figures, such as the Bender–Gestalt Test and the ROCF. The sequence of placements of the nine Bender–Gestalt figures on a blank sheet of paper has been hypothesized to reveal organization and planning attitudes and skills (Hutt 1985), and likewise spatial management of elements of other drawings (e.g., person, house, tree, family) within the constraints of an 8.5 × 11 in. (21.59 × 27.9 cm) sheet of paper may also reveal planning deficits. The person with poor planning abilities may leave insufficient space on the page to complete a drawing. Reproduction by direct copy or memory of complex graphic figures such as the ROCF may also be rated according to the planning based on the order in which elements are drawn, the overall placement of the figure on the page, the placement of elements within the figure, and the overall integrity of the structure of the figure (Stern et al. 1999; Waber and Holmes 1986).

**Tests of cognitive flexibility and shifting**. Cognitive flexibility refers to the ability to establish an attentional focus, mental set, or problem-solving approach, and then to appropriately switch to another set according to environmental demands or task requirements. In its pathological form, impaired cognitive flexibility results in a concrete and perseverative style that can be manifested by repeated execution of the same actions or sequence of actions in unsuccessful attempts to accomplish a goal. The individual with adequate cognitive flexibility can shift fluidly and comfortably from one idea to another.

The test most widely used to measure the ability to shift mental set is the Wisconsin Card Sorting Test (WCST; Grant and Berg 1948; Heaton et al. 1993). This test meets our criteria as *nonverbal*, since it has relatively brief instructions and one-word examiner feedback for each response. The WCST requires the examinee to sort up to 128 response cards next to one of four stimulus (or *key*) cards according to a categorical principle, which must be deduced from feedback ("correct" or "incorrect") provided by the examiner after each response. Instructions are fairly nonspecific, requiring examinees to impose organization upon an ambiguous task ("I cannot tell you how to match the cards, but I will tell you each time whether you are right or wrong"; Heaton et al. 1993, p. 5). Sorting principles include matching key card stimuli on several dimensions of the stimuli depicted on each response card. Unknown to the examinee, the examiner will switch the correct sorting principle after the examinee provides 10 consecutive correct responses as a way of eliciting set-shifting abilities. The test continues until six categories have been correctly deduced, all 128 cards have been sorted, or 64 cards have been sorted if not even one category has been deduced.

Scoring on the WCST is challenging even for experienced examiners and should be facilitated with a computer-scoring program. During the test, the examiner indicates on a record form the basis for each card sorted, that is, the identity of the dimensions on which the response card matches the key card. The WCST yields 16 scoring indices, each of which is norm referenced for ages 6 years, 6 months through 89 years, 11 months. Norms are also stratified by education for adults. Percentile ranks, $T$ scores, and standard scores are available.

The degree to which the examinee can respond to the new feedback, deduce that the sorting principle has changed, and alter their actions accordingly are the most important performance dimensions tapped by the WCST. Perseverative responses are defined as persistent responses based upon a stimulus characteristic that is incorrect. Once a perseverated-to principle is established, responses that match that principle are scored as *perseverative*, whereas responses that do not match the perseverated-to principle are *nonperseverative*. We will not address additional scoring indices here, except to note that the WCST provides indices describing the ease with which an individual can formulate a conceptual set, maintain that set when responding, and shift away from that set according to changing task requirements. In general, the WCST is considered to provide a valid measure of executive functions that is sensitive (but not specific) to frontal lobe dysfunction (Heaton et al. 1993).

The strength of the WCST is its largely non-threatening (and low difficulty) format, as well as its minimally verbal instructions and nonverbal stimuli. The examinee is not required to speak during administration (although it is common for the examiner to ask about the examinee's approach after completion of the test). The fractionation of scores including the index of perseverative responding is useful in understanding and identifying the specific processes that may be impaired. At the same time, the WCST has the significant weakness of sometimes putting the examiner in the position of providing negative verbal feedback over a prolonged period of time. Several indices on the WCST (e.g., number of correct sorts) have truncated ranges and low ceilings, rendering them most useful only when significant impairment is present.

In the tradition of the Goldstein-Scheerer Object Sorting Test (Goldstein and Scheerer 1941), the NEPSY-II Animal Sorting subtest taps concept formation, cognitive flexibility, and self-monitoring (Korkman et al. 2007). The examinee is given eight cards and is asked to sort them into two groups of four cards, each with something in common that the examinee must name; then the examinee must sort the cards into two *different* groups of four, again naming the basis for the sorting. In essence, this task measures how many different ways a person can (re)conceptualize a single situation or a set of stimuli. Unlike the D-KEFS Sorting Test (Delis et al. 2001), the NEPSY-II Animal Sorting requires no reading, but unfortunately for nonverbal assessment purposes it does require limited verbal expression to convey the concept by which the cards have been sorted.

Another means by which cognitive flexibility may be tapped is through fluency tasks, which require productive output under timed, controlled conditions. Deficits in flexibility may manifest in markedly perseverative output (e.g., Jones-Gotman and Milner 1977). Verbal fluency tasks, for example, ask an examinee to generate the names of as many different animals as possible, or as many different words starting with a particular letter, within a 60 s time limit. When the initial production strategy runs dry, can the examinee shift to another, and later still another, strategy? On design fluency tasks, which involve asking an examinee to make as many different graphical designs as possible according to specified rules within a given time limit, the same challenges to performance may be found, especially as initial strategies become unproductive. Design fluency tasks may be found in the NEPSY-II (Korkman et al. 2007) and the D-KEFS batteries (Delis et al. 2001) and involve very little verbalization after initial instructions are provided.

## Memory and New Learning Ability

The study of nonverbal memory and learning processes may be traced to some of the earliest studies of amnesia and formal memory assessment. Ribot (1882), who formulated the *law of regression* (stating that memory for recent events is more susceptible to disruption than older memories), described modality-specific amnesias and the loss of memory for symbols. Binet and Simon (1905/1916), in their first intelligence scales at the beginning of the 20th century, included separate procedures to assess retention of visual and verbal material. Their nonverbal memory tests included memory for pictures and figures, both memory assessment procedures that survive to the present day. Early memory assessment resources included Whipple's (1915) compendium that classified tests according to sensory modality involved (visual, auditory, or visual–auditory) and form of visual presentation (simultaneous or successive), as well as multidimensional memory batteries that included nonverbal/performance measures, picture recognition measures, and design reproduction tasks (e.g., Babcock 1930; Wells and Martin 1923). By the time that David Wechsler published his first memory scale in 1945, there were there were over 80 available measures of learning, memory, and association, including eight tests or batteries with emphases on memory for figural, pictorial, or visual stimuli (Hildreth 1939). Since mid-twentieth century, the most widely utilized memory battery has been the Wechsler Memory Scale (e.g., Wechsler 1945, 2009), which always included at least one nonverbal task as a core

subtest. Certainly, nonverbal memory testing is not new.

The clinical distinction between verbal and nonverbal assessment in contemporary clinical memory assessment is usually credited to Milner (1971, 1975), who demonstrated its utility in understanding the sequelae of unilateral temporal lobe damage. Although the significance of lateralized brain injuries to the cerebral hemispheres is not as differentiated with children as with adults, there has been substantial evidence of modality- and material-specific sequelae in memory functioning (e.g. Bauer et al. 1993; Warrington 1984). The link between functioning in the left temporal lobe and verbal memory has proven fairly consistent (e.g., Jones-Gotman et al. 2000), but evidence for linkage between functioning in the right temporal lobe and visual–spatial nonverbal memory is considerably weaker (e.g., Barr 2003; Willment and Golby 2013), perhaps due to unresolved questions about the verbalization of visual–spatial memory performances across a variety of measures. Difficulty extracting nonverbal memory factors from neuropsychological batteries have also led some researchers to wonder if nonverbal memory is a distinct neurocognitive construct, independent from visual–spatial processing in general and conducive to contrasts with verbal memory (e.g., Barr 2003; Heilbronner 1992). Still, most omnibus clinical memory batteries and reviews of best practice include nonverbal memory tasks, typically involving stimuli that are visual–figural, visual–pictorial, visual–spatial, perceptual, novel and unfamiliar, difficult to verbalize, and difficult to encode verbally (Moye 1997).

**Tests of Short-Term/ Working Memory**. The distinction between short-term and long-term memory may be traced back as far as James (1890), who coined the expression "primary memory" to describe awareness of the "specious present" (a span of time extending for several seconds), as distinct from the storehouse of "secondary memory … [which] is the knowledge of a former state of mind after it has already once dropped from consciousness; or rather it is the knowledge of an event, or fact, of which meantime we have not been thinking" (pp. 643–648). James's distinction between primary and secondary memory set the stage for more contemporary distinctions between immediate/short-term memory and long-term memory. Because of the imprecise manner in which short-term and long-term memory are differentiated, practitioners have adopted more functional descriptions of memory tests, that is, those that involve immediate recall (more short-term memory) versus those that involve delayed recall (more long-term memory), and those that involve presentation within normal short-term memory capacity (memory span tasks) and those that are intended to exceed normal short-term memory capacity (supraspan tasks). Working memory is a newer concept, just a few decades old, for which the first generation of clinical measures has just been developed.

At present, short-term memory usually refers to "a limited capacity store" involving uninterrupted sequential recall of material immediately after it is presented (Cowan 2001; Miller 1956; Watkins 1974). Short-term memory is usually considered to last from a few seconds to a few minutes. Usually tapped by digit span or block span tasks, short-term auditory sequential memory tends normatively to be slightly greater than that of immediate visual sequential memory (Orsini et al. 1987). For simultaneously presented information, however, short-term span of visual apprehension is comparatively unlimited. Short-term memory typically involves passive, temporary, static, and superficial processing of material that is mentally activated and stimulated by sensory input (e.g., seeing and immediately reproducing a simple sequence of visual–motor actions).

There are two main classes of nonverbal short-term span tasks, both analogs to auditory digit span tasks: the Knox Cubes paradigm (Arthur 1943; Knox 1914; Stone and Wright 1980) and the Corsi Block Tapping paradigm (Corsi 1972; Milner 1971). The Knox Cubes approach involves tapping a sequence of four 1-in. (2.5 cm.) cubes, placed along a straight line 4 in. (10.1 cm.) apart. The examinee is to reproduce the sequence, span, and location of the taps. Stone and Wright (1980) introduced an updated and Rasch-scaled version of this test that extends from age 2 years through the full range of adulthood. A second approach based upon Corsi's (1972) dissertation increases the spatial demands of block span. Corsi attached nine wooden cubes to a small board, with the cubes numbered on the side facing the examiner for ease of presentation and scoring. Sequences from two to eight cubes are tapped by the examiner at the rate of one block per second, at the completion of which the examinee reproduces the spatial sequence of taps. The Corsi blocks are available near to their original three-dimensional form in the WISC-V Integrated Spatial Span subtest (Wechsler and Kaplan 2015), with two-dimensional adaptations available in several other measures (e.g., Adams and Sheslow 2003; Williams 1991). These measures are all adequately normed, but they likely involve different neural systems of memory than digit span because of their high visual–spatial demands.

Working memory has been defined as the capacity to hold information in mind and perform some active manipulation, operation, or transformation; working memory tends to be more active, flexible, dynamic, and predictive of real-life outcome than short-term memory (e.g., Goldman-Rakic 1995; Richardson et al. 1996). Working memory has been implicated as an essential aspect of the higher order intellectual functions of language, perception, and logical reasoning (Baddeley 1986; Baddeley and Hitch 1974). The emergent role of working memory as a necessary prerequisite for human thinking abilities has been elegantly described by Goldman-Rakic and Friedman (1991): "… the brain's working memory function, i.e., the ability to bring to mind information and hold it 'on line' in the absence of direct stimulation, may be its inherently most flexible mechanism and its evolutionarily most significant achievement. It confers the ability to guide behavior by representations of the outside world rather than by immediate stimulation and thus to base behavior on ideas and thoughts" (p. 73).

Working memory operates "across a range of tasks involving different processing codes and different input modalities" (Baddeley 1986,

p. 35), and distinctive auditory–verbal and visual–spatial subsystems have been hypothesized. The visual–spatial subsystem, which we discuss now because of its association with nonverbal abilities, has been termed the *visuospatial sketchpad* but is now simply described as *visuospatial working memory* (Baddeley 2000). It probably consists of a system that passively stores visual images along with a companion system that maintains, refreshes, or transforms the images. The mental manipulation or transformation of images associated with working memory is thought to be mediated by prefrontal, executive processes. Visuospatial working memory may be disrupted by irrelevant movement or distracting visual stimuli (e.g., patches of color) and can be dissociated into separate visual and spatial components (Baddeley 2000). Baddeley (1986, p. 109) emphasized spatial over visual processing by defining the visuospatial working memory as "a system especially well adapted to the storage of spatial information, much as a pad of paper might be used by someone trying for example to work out a geometric puzzle."

The newest edition of the Wechsler Memory Scale (WMS-IV; Wechsler 2009) introduced two new visual working memory procedures. In Spatial Addition, the examinee is sequentially shown two grids with blue and red circles (5 s of exposure) and is then asked to add or subtract the location of the circles based on a simple set of rules. In Symbol Span, the examinee is briefly shown a series of abstract symbols on a page and is then asked to select the symbols from an array of symbols in the same order they were presented. The diagnostic quality of these measures remains to be determined, but joint factor analyses of the WAIS-IV and the WMS-IV suggested that they collectively form a plausible visual working memory factor, with good model fit to the standardization data in confirmatory factor analyses (Holdnack et al. 2011). When scores are combined, the two subtests yield a Visual Working Memory Index in the WMS-IV (Wechsler 2009).

Another approach to tapping working memory with minimal language may be found in adaptations of the *n*-back procedure, originally developed by Kirchner (1958). In brief, *n*-back procedures involve presentation of a sequence of stimuli, with the examinee indicating when the current stimulus matches the stimulus presented *n* steps previously. The task requires constant updating of items presented and is made considerably more difficult by requiring active comparisons with more steps back. A promising computer-administered nonverbal n-back test may be found in the *Tasks of Executive Control* (TEC: Isquith et al. 2010), which permits the levels of working memory (i.e., the number of steps back), as well as comparison of performance under conditions *with* and *without inhibitory control* requirements.

**Tests of long-term memory**. Long-term memory refers to effective consolidation, storage, and retrieval of newly learned material over time. In clinical practice, it is usually assessed through recall or recognition following a 20- or 30-min intervening time interval after initial presentation, although the interval may span minutes, hours, days, or longer. It may be distinguished from short-term memory and working memory through its capacity, which exceeds short-term memory span, and its duration, which exceeds the seconds or minutes during which short-term memory processes can remain active. Long-term memory is considered to constitute a relatively permanent memory store from which elements can be retrieved into active mental working space. As conceptualized by Anderson and Bower (1973), "working memory is not structurally separate from long-term memory, but it is the currently active partition of long-term memory" (p. 216).

Measures of recognition memory for meaningful pictorial content constitute a leading way to use nonverbal methods to assess memory in ecologically relevant ways. These measures typically involve the exposure of one or more pictured objects (e.g., flowers) for several seconds in sequence or simultaneously, followed by a recognition trial in which the examinee must point to the matching object from several choices, including foils that are members of the same semantic class (e.g., different types of flowers) in order to minimize the benefits of verbal mediational strategies. One of the most ecologically relevant tests of this type is the *Wide Range Assessment of Memory and Learning* (WRAML2) Picture Memory subtest (Adams and Sheslow 2003). In Picture Memory, the child is shown a pictorial scene for 10 s and is instructed to look at all parts and to "Take a picture of it in your mind." The initial scene is then removed, and a second, similar scene is presented. The child is asked to mark with an "X" all parts of the picture that have been changed, moved, or added. Errors on the first scene are corrected. Four pictorial scenes are presented altogether. Scoring consists of one point for each correctly identified element in the four scenes. There is no penalty for guessing, although subjects are encouraged to "Just mark the things you are sure of." The admonition to "take a picture in your mind" encourages visual processing. However, this instruction also interrupts spontaneous learning processes and imposes a suggested mnemonic strategy upon the child.

Memory for faces is considered to constitute another ecologically relevant form of nonverbal memory, although its clinical utility as part of memory assessment has yet to be fully and convincingly demonstrated. The first generation of contemporary tests utilizing memory for faces included the Denman Neuropsychology Memory Scale (Denman 1987) and the Recognition Memory Test—Faces test (Warrington 1984). The newest face memory procedures involve simultaneous or sequential presentation of multiple faces and subsequent recognition, using either multiple choice or signal detection paradigms. For example, the NEPSY Memory for Faces subtest (Korkman et al. 2007) involves the serial presentation of faces during which the examinee is directed to verbally identify the gender of each picture (in order to facilitate attention and encoding processes); immediately afterwards, the child is asked to recognize the target pictures from arrays of three faces. Faces have been modified on this task to minimize peripheral details that might facilitate identification, theoretically reducing the benefits from verbal mediation. A 15–25 min delayed recognition is also utilized.

A more abstract nonverbal memory procedure involves the use of paper-and-pencil constructional tasks with immediate and/or delayed recall of figural material (Larrabee and Crook 1995). Figural reproduction tasks date at least to Binet and Simon (1905/1916; see also Binet and Henri 1894), in which two designs were each exposed for 10 s followed by immediate reproduction. Among the most widely utilized design reproduction tests are the Benton Visual Retention Test, the Rey–Osterrieth Complex Figure reproduction from memory, and the Wechsler Memory Scale Visual Reproduction subtest (Butler et al. 1991; Rey 1941; Sivan 1992; Wechsler 2009). The Benton Visual Retention Test—Fifth Edition (Sivan 1992) requires that the examinee view each design for 10 s and immediately reproduce the designs from memory (administration A). Reproductions are scored by an objective system, including the number of errors and types of errors (omissions, distortions, perseverations, misplacements, and size errors). In order to parse out the effects of visuoconstructional ability without memory demands, the examinee may also reproduce each design while the design remains in view (administration C). The inclusion of a direct copy supplemental procedure to a figure reproduction memory test permits separation of memory impairment from constructional impairment. This has been a historic criticism of visual memory testing procedures, i.e., that they are confounded by visuospatial processing ability (Larrabee and Crook 1995). Measures of figure reproduction from memory as a rule should optimally include separate norms for direct copy reproduction and reproductions from memory. Moye (1997) has reviewed the construct validity and clinical utility for a number of measures of figural memory.

Recognition memory tasks for abstract figural stimuli are another leading methodology used clinically to assess nonverbal learning and memory (Larrabee and Crook 1995). Stimuli usually involve abstract designs or geometric shapes that are either exposed a single time or recurrently in series. The examinee must then choose the identical stimuli from multiple choices on an immediate and delayed basis. An example of such tasks is the Continuous Visual Memory Test (CVMT; Trahan and Larrabee 1988), which uses complex ambiguous designs that are not conducive to verbal mediation in a signal detection paradigm. The test has small expressive language requirements, as examinees must indicate whether they have seen the stimuli before. Recognition paradigms are especially useful for fine motor-impaired clinical populations.

## Visual–Spatial Cognition

Spatial cognition has generally been defined to include perception, analyses, and manipulation of stimuli in personal or extrapersonal space. Lohman (1996) emphasizes imagery when he suggests, "Spatial ability may be defined as the ability to generate, retain, retrieve, and transform well-structured visual images" (p. 98). Carroll (1993) includes both perceptual processes and internal operations when he states "Spatial and other visual perceptual abilities have to do with individuals' abilities in searching the visual field, apprehending the forms, shapes, and positions of objects as visually perceived, forming mental representations of those forms, shapes, and positions, and manipulating such representations 'mentally'" (p. 304). In their compendium of measures of spatial cognition over 80 years, Eliot and Smith (1983) note that "measures of psychological space typically entail visual problems or 'tasks' which require individuals to estimate, predict, or judge the relationships among figures or objects in different contexts" (p. iv).

The neural underpinnings of spatial cognition tend to vary according to the quality of the processing and nature of the information being processed, with the abilities to orient in space, reproduce constructions, and recognize objects through visual or tactile cues most strongly associated with the adequacy of right hemisphere processing of spatial information (De Renzi 1982). Two separate cortical visual systems have been identified by Mishkin et al. (1983), one a ventral system specialized for object vision (*what* was seen) and the other a dorsal system specialized for spatial vision (*where* it was seen). Consequently, a visual–spatial assessment should tap not only visual content but also visual location.

Performance on specialized tasks such as recognition and learning of unfamiliar faces appears to be mediated by different strategic approaches, with an analytical–sequential approach tending to involve more left hemisphere activity and a global synthetic approach involving more activity by the right hemisphere (De Renzi 1982). The global–local visual processing distinction proposed by Navon (1977) originally reported evidence supporting the hypothesis that perception proceeds from the global, configural aspect of visual objects to the analysis of more local details. More recent investigations have suggested that individuals with focal left hemisphere damage are more likely to have difficulty reproducing local, meaningful details, whereas individuals with focal right hemisphere damage appear to experience particular difficulty reproducing global, configural forms (Delis et al. 1988). While we consider many aspects of spatial cognition to have neural underpinnings in the right cerebral cortex, it is clear that analysis of meaningful detail in pictorial material may be seated in the left hemisphere.

Disorders of spatial cognition may take a variety of forms, including various *agnosias* (disorders of recognition), *apraxias* (disorders of intentional movement), and inattention syndromes (De Renzi 1982). Benton and Tranel (1993) have provided a more behaviorally defined system of classifying disorders including visuoperceptual disorders, visuospatial disorders, and visuoconstructional disorders. Visuoperceptual disorders include visual object agnosias, defective visual analysis and synthesis, impairment of facial recognition (including the *prosopagnosias*, or loss of ability to identify familiar faces), and impairment in color recognition. Visuospatial disorders include defective localization of points in space, defective judgment of direction and distance, defective topographical orientation, unilateral visual neglect, and Balint's syndrome. Visuoconstructional disorders include defective assembling performance and defective graphomotor performance.

**Tests of visuospatial perception**. The integrity of visuospatial processes may be assessed with tests that exclude motor responses or with tests that require perceptual–motor integration. In this section, we describe several measures of nonmotor visuospatial perception. Constructs tapped in this domain of functioning include facial discrimination, figure–ground perception, form constancy, perception of position and direction, spatial relations, visual closure, visuospatial discrimination, and visuospatial working memory, among others. The degree to which these constructs may be differentiated remains an important research question.

Several test batteries assessing diverse aspects of visual perception and processing have been published. For example, the developmental test battery of visual perception originally created by Marianne Frostig in 1964 has been recently revised for children (DTVP-3; Hammill et al. 2014) and adolescents/adults (DTVP-A; Reynolds et al. 2002). These batteries include measures of figure–ground perception, visual closure, and form constancy that are administered with brief verbal instructions and multiple choice pointing responses. Visual–perceptual test batteries with similar content may be found for children and adolescents (TVPS-3; Martin 2006) and across the full-age range from childhood to older adulthood (MVPT-4; Colarusso and Hammill 2015).

Three well-researched visual–perceptual measures from the Benton–Iowa neuropsychological battery readily lend themselves to nonverbal assessment: Facial Recognition, Judgment of Line Orientation (JLO), and Visual Form Discrimination (Benton et al. 1994). All three of these tests involve simultaneous presentation of the target stimulus and a multiple choice array of responses (so as to avoid significant memory demands), succinct verbal instructions, and pointing as an acceptable nonverbal response. Screening for adequate visual acuity is recommended prior to administration of most measures of visuospatial cognition.

The Facial Recognition test (Benton et al. 1994) assesses the capacity to identify and discriminate photographs of unfamiliar human faces and is available in two forms, a 27-item short form and a 54-item long form. Administered in a spiral bound booklet, the test involves matching of front-view photographs with identical photographs, with three-quarter-view photographs, and with varied front-view photographs under different lighting conditions. Instructions are brief (e.g., "You see this young woman? Show me where she is on this picture."), and the test is normed for ages 6 through adult. Age- and education-corrected norms are provided for adults (Benton et al. 1994).

The JLO test taps spatial perception and orientation and is available in two 30-item forms. Administered from a spiral bound booklet, it involves matching a pair of stimulus lines (appearing at full length for easier items and partial length for more difficult items) to a multiple choice array of lines (including full-length representations of the correct responses) drawn from a common origin. Instructions are brief ("See these two lines? Which two lines down here are in exactly the same position and point in the same direction as the two lines up here?"). Examinees can respond by either saying the numbers of the line corresponding to the choices or pointing to the correct responses. Successful performance is suggestive of adequate visuospatial perception of direction, orientation, and position. The JLO is normed for ages 7 through adult (Benton et al. 1994).

The Visual Form Discrimination test involves discrimination between complex geometric configurations differing in minor characteristics. Administered from a spiral bound booklet, it consists of 16 items in which the examinee is asked to match a multiple element stimulus design with the identical design from four multiple choice options ("See this design? Find it among these four designs"). The multiple choices are designed in such a way that one features a rotation of a major part of the stimulus design, one features a major distortion of the stimulus design, and one features a rotation in a small figure peripheral to the central design elements. Scores on Visual Form Discrimination are reported to be particularly sensitive to right cerebral hemisphere posterior lesions, although performance may be compromised by lesions elsewhere in the brain and a variety of functional deficits (e.g., sustained attention). The Visual Form Discrimination test is normed for ages 19–74, but the majority of adults have near-perfect performance due to low test ceilings (Benton et al. 1994).

**Tests of perceptual–motor integration**. The assessment of visual–motor integration is most commonly accomplished through paper-and-pencil direct reproduction of figural stimuli, with the leading tests including the Bender–Gestalt Test (Bender 1938; Brannigan and Decker 2003), Beery-Buktenica Developmental Test of Visual–Motor Integration (VMI; Beery and Beery 2010), and the Rey–Osterrieth Complex Figure (Osterrieth 1944; Rey 1941) according to published surveys of neuropsychological test usage (e.g., Butler et al. 1991). Measures of visual–motor integration typically require multiple subprocesses: visual–perceptual patterning, visual–perceptual analysis, fine motor abilities, and the transformation and organization of visual–perceptual analyses into coordinated motor programs. Neuropsychological underpinnings of perceptual motor tasks are relatively nonspecific, involving activity in the motor cortex contralateral to the preferred hand, a variety of right hemisphere functions (and, to some extent, the left as well as interhemispheric connections), and activity in cerebellar and subcortical nuclei, all thought to be operating in a dynamic, parallel fashion (e.g., Grafton et al. 1992). As the organizational demands in figural reproduction increase (e.g., progressing from reproduction of simple to complex geometric figures), the role of the executive/prefrontal functions becomes more prominent in visual–motor integration.

Perhaps the simplest geometric form copying measure of visual–motor integration is the VMI (Beery and Beery 2010), now in its sixth edition and normed from ages 2 through 99 years.

The VMI consists of 27 geometric figures to be copied with a pencil or a pen, with no erasures permitted. It is supplemented by two tests, one of visual perception and one of motor coordination, intended to parse out the degree to which these narrower abilities contribute to deficient performance. Instructions for the main visual–motor integration test are minimally verbal ("Make one like that. Make yours right here."), and testing ends after three consecutive no-credit reproductions. Each item may be scored as correct or incorrect, according to one or more criteria. The VMI is most useful for young children or impaired older children, but its score ceiling is low and near-perfect performance is usually evident in early adolescence.

Visual–motor reproduction of complex figures offers an assessment methodology with higher test score ceilings, as well as the opportunity to more closely examine elements of visuospatial analysis and motor reproduction of basic figures that are spatially integrated. The best known of the complex figures was published by Andre Rey in 1941, although alternative complex figures are available (e.g., Strauss et al. 2006). Assessment with the ROCF usually involves three phases (direct copy, immediate recall, and 20- to 30-min delayed recall). The direct copy phase administration requires placement of the ROCF stimulus in front of the examinee along with pencil and blank paper, with the essential instructions to "Copy this figure as carefully and as accurately as you can." There is some variation in these instructions, depending upon the specific normative and scoring system utilized. There is no time limit. Some ROCF administrative methods involve switching the examinee's writing tools during the production with colored markers to track the sequential development of the drawing, although a graphical flow chart may also be utilized. When the colored markers are utilized, several sentences are typically added to instructions to explain how the examinee will be handed different colored markers during task performance. Once completed, the overall quality of the reproduction may be scored according to Osterrieth's (1944) criteria using norms and scoring elaborations described by Lezak (1995) or norms collected by Meyers and Meyers (1995). Alternatively, the reproduction may be scored on a number of normed qualitative dimensions (e.g., Stern et al. 1999; Troyer and Wishart 1997; Waber and Holmes 1985) such as accuracy, organization, rotation, perseveration, confabulation, and asymmetry.

A third class of perceptual motor tests involves performance in three dimensions, unlike the paper-and-pencil reproductions we have already described in this section. Manipulation of objects in three-dimensional space may be sensitive to neural impairment that is not evident in paper and pencil constructions and reproductions (e.g., Critchley 1953; De Renzi 1982). Block-building tasks to reproduce a model appear in several test batteries of early childhood (e.g., Elliott 2007; Korkman et al. 2007), but some more complex tasks of three-dimensional block construction involving blocks of varying sizes and shapes are also available (e.g., Benton et al. 1994).

## Summary

In this chapter, I have described nonverbal measures of specific abilities within the neuropsychological domains of attention and executive functions, memory and new learning ability, and visual–spatial cognition. The clinical approaches, applications, and limitations of representative tests within each domain have been described. Clinical indications for nonverbal neuropsychological assessment have been described, as well as the history of selected nonverbal assessment procedures.

The vast array of options available to the practitioner wanting to utilize nonverbal tests suggests that the current state of nonverbal neuropsychological assessment is healthy and vibrant. Computer-administered assessment options are proliferating, lending themselves to nonverbal forms of response via the click of a mouse or use of a touchscreen. Nearly every important domain of neuropsychological assessment (with the exception of expressive language) now includes tests with reduced language requirements, suggesting that in the future, it may be possible to conduct a reasonably comprehensive neuropsychological assessment without requiring that the examinee speak. This prospect has particular benefits for examinees who may otherwise not be served because there are no psychologists who speak their native language or because they have lost expressive language functions.

At the same time, it is important to thoroughly research some of the underlying assumptions behind nonverbal assessment, i.e., that it enhances test fairness and reduces construct irrelevant test performance variance with specific populations of examinees. For example, Alfredo Ardila and Monica Rosselli have persuasively made the case that impoverished and illiterate samples demonstrate depressed nonverbal task performances in areas of attention and executive functions, memory, and visual–spatial constructional ability (Ardila and Rosselli 1989; Rosselli and Ardila 2003; Rosselli et al. 1990). We are still surprised to see psychological tests described as "virtually culture-free" (Beery and Beery 2010, p. 1), long after such claims should have been discredited.

It may also be argued that enhancing the nonverbal administration of most neuropsychological tests may improve test validity and reduce the construct irrelevant variance introduced by the high language loads of most neuropsychological measures. Excessive instructional verbiage may tax examinee language comprehension and memory, thus unintentionally tapping extraneous neuropsychological constructs. We recommend that test developers routinely abbreviate instructional sets and provide alternative gestural instructions in test manuals. Assessment paradigms need ultimately to target their intended neuropsychological constructs in the truest and most focused manner possible, and sometimes language may constitute an impediment to assessment. Nonverbal testing provides a good solution when, to borrow a phrase, words get in the way.

# References

Adams, W., & Sheslow, D. (2003). *Wide range assessment of memory and learning* (2nd ed.). Wilmington, DE: Wide Range.

Anderson, J. R., & Bower, G. H. (1973). *Human associative memory*. Washington, DC: Winston.

Ardila, A., & Pineda, D. A. (2000). Factor structure of nonverbal cognition. *International Journal of Neuroscience, 104*, 125–144.

Ardila, A., & Rosselli, M. (1989). Neuropsychological assessment in illiterates: Visuospatial and memory abilities. *Brain and Cognition, 11*(2), 147–166.

Army Individual Test Battery. (1944). *Manual of directions and scoring*. Washington, DC: War Department, Adjutant General's Office.

Arthur, G. (1943). *A point scale of performance tests. Clinical manual* (2 ed., Vol. 1, Rev.). New York: The Commonwealth Fund.

Babcock, H. (1930). An experiment in the measurement of mental deterioration. *Archives of Psychology, 117*, 1–105.

Baddeley, A. (2000). Short-term and working memory. In E. Tulving & F. I. M. Craik (Eds.), *The Oxford handbook of memory* (pp. 77–92). New York: Oxford University Press.

Baddeley, A. D. (1986). *Working memory*. New York: Oxford University Press.

Baddeley, A. D., & Hitch, G. J. (1974). Working memory. In G. A. Bower (Ed.), *The psychology of learning and motivation* (pp. 47–89). New York: Academic Press.

Ballantyne, A. O., & Sattler, J. M. (1991). Validity and reliability of the Reporter's Test with normally achieving and learning disabled children. *Psychological Assessment, 3*(1), 60–67.

Barkley, R. A. (2012). *Executive functions: What they are, how they work, and why they evolved*. New York: Guilford.

Barkley, R. A. (Ed.). (2015). *Attention-deficit hyperactivity disorder: A handbook for diagnosis and treatment* (4th ed.). New York: Guilford.

Barr, W. B. (2003). Delineating the functions of the nondominant hemisphere. *Epilepsy & Behavior, 4*(6), 797–798.

Barsalou, L. W. (1999). Perceptual symbol systems. *Behavioral and Brain Sciences, 22*(4), 577–660.

Barsalou, L. W. (2008). Grounded cognition. *Annual Review of Psychology, 59*, 617–645.

Bauer, R. M., Tobias, B., & Valenstein, E. (1993). Amnesic disorders. In K. M. Heilman & E. Valenstein (Eds.), *Clinical neuropsychology* (3rd ed., pp. 523–602). New York: Oxford University Press.

Beery, K. E., & Beery, N. A. (2010). *The Beery-Buktenica developmental test of visual motor integration with supplemental developmental tests of visual perception and motor coordination* (6th ed.). Bloomington, MN, NJ: NCS Pearson.

Bender, L. A. (1938). *A visual motor gestalt test and its clinical use. Research monograph number 3*. New York: American Orthopsychiatric Association.

Benton, A., & Tranel, D. (1993). Visuoperceptual, visuospatial, and visuoconstructive disorders. In K. M. Heilman & E. Valenstein (Eds.), *Clinical neuropsychology* (3rd ed., pp. 165–213). New York: Oxford University Press.

Benton, A. L. (1988/2000). Neuropsychology: Past, present, and future. In F. Boller & J. Grafman (Eds.), *Handbook of neuropsychology* (Vol. 1, pp. 3–27). New York: Elsevier Science. Reprinted in Benton, A. L. (2000). Neuropsychology: Past, present, and future. In A. Benton (Ed.), *Exploring the history of neuropsychology: Selected papers* (pp. 3–40). New York: Oxford University Press.

Benton, A. L., Sivan, A. B., Hamsher, K. D., Varney, N. R., & Spreen, O. (1994). *Contributions to neuropsychological assessment: A clinical manual* (2nd ed.). New York: Oxford University Press.

Binet, A., & Henri, V. (1894). Recherches sur le développement de la mémoire visuelle des enfants [Investigations on the development of visual memory in children]. *Revue philosophique, 37*, 348–350. Translated in R. H. Pollack & M. J. Brenner (Eds.). (1969), *The experimental psychology of Alfred Binet: Selected papers* (pp. 127–129). New York: Springer.

Binet, A., & Simon, T. (1905/1916). *The development of intelligence in children* (E. Kite, Trans.). Baltimore: Williams & Wilkins (Original work published 1905).

Bosbach, S., Cole, J., Prinz, W., & Knoblich, G. (2005). Inferring another's expectation from action: The role of peripheral sensation. *Nature Neuroscience, 8*(10), 1295–1297.

Brannigan, G. G., & Decker, S. L. (2003). *Bender visual-motor Gestalt test* (2nd ed.). Itasca, IL: Riverside Publishing.

Buckner, R. L., & Wheeler, M. E. (2001). The cognitive neuroscience of remembering. *Nature Reviews Neuroscience, 2*(9), 624–634.

Butler, M., Retzlaff, P. D., & Vanderploeg, R. (1991). Neuropsychological test usage. *Professional Psychology: Research & Practice, 22*(6), 510–512.

Camara, W. J., Nathan, J. S., & Puente, A. E. (2000). Psychological test usage: Implications in professional psychology. *Professional Psychology: Research & Practice, 31*(2), 141–154.

Campbell, S. B., Endman, M. W., & Bernfeld, G. (1977). A three-year follow-up of hyperactive preschoolers into elementary school. *Journal of Child Psychology and Psychiatry, 18*(3), 239–250.

Caplan, D. (1994). Language and the brain. In M. A. Gernsbacher (Ed.), *Handbook of psycholinguistics* (pp. 1023–1053). San Diego, CA: Academic Press.

Carroll, J. B. (1993). *Human cognitive abilities: a survey of factor-analytic studies*. New York: Cambridge University Press.

Channell, R. W., & Peek, M. S. (1989). Four measures of vocabulary ability compared in older preschool children. *Language, Speech, and Hearing Services in Schools, 20*(4), 407–419.

Clark, E. V., & Hecht, B. F. (1983). Comprehension, production, and language acquisition. *Annual Review of Psychology, 34*(1), 325–349.

Cohen, N. J., Weiss, G., & Minde, K. (1972). Cognitive styles in adolescents previously diagnosed as hyperactives. *Journal of Child Psychology and Psychiatry, 13*(3), 203–209.

Cohen, R. A. (1993). Attentional control: Subcortical and frontal lobe influences. In R. A. Cohen (Ed.), *The neuropsychology of attention* (pp. 459–482). New York: Plenum Press.

Colarusso, R. P., & Hammill, D. D. (2015). *Motor-free visual perception test* (4th ed.). Novato, CA: ATP Assessments.

Corsi, P. (1972). *Human memory and the medial temporal region of the brain.* Unpublished doctoral dissertation, McGill University, Montreal, Quebec, Canada.

Cowan, N. (2001). The magical number 4 in short-term memory: A reconsideration of mental storage capacity. *Behavioral and Brain Sciences, 24*(1), 87–185.

Critchley, M. M. (1953). *The parietal lobes.* London: Arnold.

Culbertson, W. C., & Zillmer, E. A. (2001). *Tower of London—Drexel University, Second Edition (TOL$^{DX}$): Technical manual.* N. Tonawanda, NY: MHS.

Dalmaijer, E. S., Van der Stigchel, S., Nijboer, T. C. W., Cornelissen, T. H. W., & Husain, M. (2014). Cancellation tools: All-in-one software for administration and analysis of cancellation tasks. *Behavior Research Methods, 47*(4), 1065–1075.

De Renzi, E. (1982). *Disorders of space exploration and cognition.* New York: Wiley.

Delis, D. C., Kaplan, E., & Kramer, J. H. (2001). *Delis-Kaplan executive function system.* San Antonio, TX: The Psychological Corporation.

Delis, D. C., Kiefner, M., & Fridlund, A. J. (1988). Visuospatial dysfunction following unilateral brain damage: Dissociations in hierarchical and hemispatial analysis. *Journal of Clinical and Experimental Neuropsychology, 10*(4), 421–431.

Denckla, M. B. (1985). Revised neurological examination for subtle signs. *Psychopharmacology Bulletin, 21*(4), 733–800.

Denckla, M. B. (1994). Measurement of executive function. In G. R. Lyon (Ed.), *Frames of reference for the assessment of learning disabilities: New views on measurement issues* (pp. 117–142). Baltimore, MD: Paul H. Brookes.

Denman, S. B. (1987). *Denman neuropsychology memory scale.* Charleston, SC: Denman.

DiSimoni, F. (1978). *The token test for children.* Hingham, MA: Teaching Resources Corporation.

Douglas, V. I., Barr, R. G., Amin, K., O'Neill, M. E., & Britton, B. G. (1988). Dosage effects and individual responsivity to methylphenidate in attention deficit disorder. *Journal of Child Psychology and Psychiatry, 29*(4), 453–475.

Drewe, E. A. (1975). Go–no go learning after frontal lobe lesions in humans. *Cortex, 11*(1), 8–16.

Dunn, L. M., & Dunn, D. M. (2007). *Peabody picture vocabulary test* (4th ed.). Minneapolis, MN: Pearson.

Eliot, J., & Smith, I. M. (1983). *An international directory of spatial tests.* Windsor, UK: NFER-Nelson.

Elliott, C. D. (2007). *Differential ability scales-second edition (DAS-II).* San Antonio, TX: Pearson.

Eslinger, P. J. (1996). Conceptualizing, describing, and measuring components of executive function. In G. R. Lyon & N. A. Krasnegor (Eds.), *Attention, memory, and executive function* (pp. 367–395). Baltimore: Brookes.

Esposito, A. G., Baker-Ward, L., & Mueller, S. T. (2013). Interference suppression vs. response inhibition: An explanation for the absence of a bilingual advantage in preschoolers' Stroop task performance. *Cognitive Development, 28*(4), 354–363.

Ewert, P. H., & Lambert, J. F. (1932). Part II: The effect of verbal instructions upon the formation of a concept. *Journal of General Psychology, 6*(2), 400–413.

Finkelnburg, D. C. (1870/1979). Vortrag in der niederrheinische Gessellschaft der Aerzte. *Berliner klinische wochenschrift, 7,* 449. In Duffy, R., & Liles, B. Z. (1979). Finkelnburg's 1870 lecture on aphasia with commentary. *Journal of Speech and Hearing Disorders, 44.*

Fraser, C., Bellugi, U., & Brown, R. (1963). Control of grammar in imitation, comprehension, and production. *Journal of Verbal Learning and Verbal Behavior, 2*(2), 121–135.

Gerstadt, C., Hong, Y., & Diamond, A. (1994). The relationship between cognitive and action: Performance of 3½—7 year children on a Stroop Day-Night test. *Cognition, 53*(2), 129–153.

Goldberg, E., Podell, K., Bilder, R., & Jaeger, J. (2001). *Executive control battery (ECB).* Melbourne: PsychPress.

Goldman-Rakic, P. S. (1995). Architecture of the prefrontal cortex and the central executive. In J. Grafman, K. J. Holyoak, & F. Boller (Eds.), *Annals of the New York academy of sciences. Structure and functions of the human prefrontal cortex* (Vol. 769, pp. 71–83). New York: New York Academy of Sciences.

Goldman-Rakic, P. S., & Friedman, H. (1991). The circuitry of working memory revealed by anatomy and metabolic imaging. In H. Levin, H. Eisenberg, & A. Benton (Eds.), *Frontal lobe function and dysfunction* (pp. 72–91). New York: Oxford University Press.

Goldstein, K., & Scheerer, M. (1941). Abstract and concrete behavior: An experimental study with special tests. *Psychological Monographs, 53*(2) (Whole no. 239).

Grafton, S. T., Mazziotta, J. C., Woods, R. P., & Phelps, M. E. (1992). Human functional anatomy of visually guided finger movements. *Brain, 115*(2), 565–587.

Grant, D. A., & Berg, E. A. (1948). A behavioral analysis of degree of reinforcement and ease of shifting to new responses in a Weigl-type card sorting problem. *Journal of Experimental Psychology, 38*(4), 404–411.

Halstead, W. C. (1947). *Brain and intelligence*. Chicago: University of Chicago Press.

Hammill, D. D., Pearson, N. A., & Voress, J. K. (2014). *Developmental test of visual perception, Third edition* (DTVP-3). Examiner's manual. Austin, TX: Pro-Ed.

Head, H. (1926). *Aphasia and kindred disorders of speech*. New York: Macmillan.

Heaton, R. K., Chelune, G. J., Talley, J. L., Kay, G. G., & Curtiss, G. (1993). *Wisconsin card sorting test manual* (Rev ed.). Odessa, FL: Psychological Assessment Resources.

Heilbronner, R. L. (1992). The search for a "pure" visual memory test: Pursuit of perfection? *The Clinical Neuropsychologist, 6*(1), 105–112.

Heilman, K. M., Watson, R. T., & Valenstein, E. (1993). Neglect and related disorders. In K. M. Heilman & E. Valenstein (Eds.), *Clinical neuropsychology* (3rd ed., pp. 279–336). New York: Oxford University Press.

Hildreth, G. H. (1939). *A bibliography of mental tests and rating scales* (2nd ed.). New York: The Psychological Corporation.

Holdnack, J. A., Zhou, X., Larrabee, G. J., Millis, S. R., & Salthouse, T. A. (2011). Confirmatory factor analysis of the WAIS-IV/WMS-IV. *Assessment, 18*(2), 178–191.

Hopkins, J., Perlman, T., Hechtman, L., & Weiss, G. (1979). Cognitive style in adults originally diagnosed as hyperactives. *Journal of Child Psychology and Psychiatry, 20*(3), 209–216.

Hutt, M. L. (1985). *The Hutt adaptation of the Bender-Gestalt Test* (4th ed.). New York: Grune & Stratton.

Isquith, P. K., Roth, R. M., & Gioia, G. A. (2010). *Tasks of executive control (TEC)*. Professional manual. Lutz, FL: Psychological Assessment Resources.

Jackson, J. H. (1915). Reprints of some of Hughlings Jackson's papers on affections of speech. *Brain, 38*, 28–190.

James, W. (1890). *The principles of psychology*. New York: Henry Holt.

Jones-Gotman, M., Harnadek, M. C., & Kubu, C. S. (2000). Neuropsychological assessment for temporal lobe epilepsy surgery. *Canadian Journal of Neurological Sciences, 27*(Suppl. 1), S39–S43, Discussion S50-32.

Jones-Gotman, M., & Milner, B. (1977). Design fluency: The invention of nonsense drawings after focal cortical lesions. *Neuropsychologia, 15*(4), 653–674.

Kagan, J. (1965). Reflection-impulsivity and reading ability in primary grade children. *Child Development, 36*, 609–628.

Kagan, J., Rosman, B. L., Day, L., Albert, J., & Phillips, W. (1964). Information processing in the child: Significance of analytic and reflective attitudes. *Psychological Monographs, 78*(1), 1–37.

Kaplan, E. (1988). A process approach to neuropsychological assessment. In T. Boll & B. K. Bryant (Eds.), *Clinical neuropsychology and brain function: Research, measurement, and practice* (pp. 129–167).

Washington, DC: American Psychological Association.

Kirchner, W. K. (1958). Age differences in short-term retention of rapidly changing information. *Journal of Experimental Psychology, 55*(4), 352–358.

Knox, H. A. (1914). A scale, based on the work at Ellis Island, for estimating mental defect. *Journal of the American Medical Association, 62*(10), 741–747.

Koelega, H. S. (1996). Sustained attention. In O. Neumann & A. F. Sanders (Eds.), *Handbook of perception and action* (Vol. 3, pp. 277–331). San Diego, CA: Academic Press.

Korkman, M., Kirk, U., & Kemp, S. (1998). *NEPSY: A developmental neuropsychological assessment*. San Antonio, TX: The Psychological Corporation.

Korkman, M., Kirk, U., & Kemp, S. (2007). *NEPSY II* (2nd ed.). San Antonio, TX: Harcourt.

Larrabee, G. J., & Crook, T. H. (1995). Assessment of learning and memory. In R. L. Mapou & J. Spector (Eds.), *Clinical neuropsychological assessment: A cognitive approach* (pp. 185–213). New York: Plenum.

Leark, R. A., Greenberg, L. K., Kindschi, C. L., Dupuy, T. R., & Hughes, S. J. (2007). *Test of variables of attention: Professional manual*. Los Alamitos, CA: The TOVA Company.

Levin, H. S., Fletcher, J. M., Kufera, J. A., Harward, H., Lilly, M. A., Mendelsohn, D., et al. (1996). Dimensions of cognition measured by the Tower of London and other cognitive tasks in head-injured children and adolescents. *Developmental Neuropsychology, 12*(1), 17–34.

Lezak, M. D. (1982). The problem of assessing executive functions. *International Journal of Psychology, 17*(1–4), 281–297.

Lezak, M. D. (1995). *Neuropsychological assessment* (3rd ed.). New York: Oxford University Press.

Lohman, D. (1996). Spatial ability and *g*. In I. Dennis & P. Tapsfield (Eds.), *Human abilities: Their nature and measurement* (pp. 97–116). Hillsdale, NJ: Lawrence Erlbaum.

Luria, A. R. (1966). *Higher cortical functions in man*. New York: Basic Books.

Luria, A. R. (1973). *The working brain: An introduction to neuropsychology*. New York: Basic Books.

Martin, N. A. (2006). *Test of visual perceptual skills* (3rd ed.). Novato, CA: ATP Assessments.

McCloskey, M., & Macaruso, P. (1995). Representing and using numerical information. *American Psychologist, 50*, 351–363.

Mesulam, M. M. (1985). *Principles of behavioral neurology*. Philadelphia: Davis.

Meyers, J. E., & Meyers, K. R. (1995). *Rey complex figure and recognition trial*. Odessa, FL: Psychological Assessment Resources.

Milich, R., Hartung, C. M., Martin, C. M., & Haigler, E. D. (1994). Behavioral disinhibition and underlying processes in adolescents with disruptive behavior disorders. In D. K. Routh (Ed.), *Disruptive behavior disorders in childhood: Essays honoring Herbert C. Quay* (pp. 109–138). New York: Plenum.

Miller, G. A. (1956). The magic number seven, plus or minus two: Some limits on our capacity for processing information. *Psychological Review, 63*(2), 81–93.

Milner, B. (1971). Interhemispheric differences in the localization of psychological processes in man. *British Medical Bulletin, 27*, 272–277.

Milner, B. (1975). Psychological aspects of focal epilepsy and its neurological management. In D. P. Purpura, J. K. Penry, & R. D. Walter (Eds.), *Advances in neurology* (Vol. 8, pp. 299–321). New York: Raven Press.

Mirsky, A. F. (1996). Disorders of attention: A neuropsychological perspective. In G. R. Lyon & N. A. Krasnegor (Eds.), *Attention, memory, and executive function* (pp. 71–95). Baltimore, MD: Brookes.

Mishkin, M., Ungerleider, L. G., & Macko, K. A. (1983). Object vision and spatial vision: Two cortical pathways. *Trends in Neurosciences, 6*, 414–417.

Mitrushina, M., Boone, K. B., Razani, J., & D'Elia, L. F. (2005). *Handbook of normative data for neuropsychological assessment* (2nd ed.). New York: Oxford University Press.

Moye, J. (1997). Nonverbal memory assessment with designs: Construct validity and clinical utility. *Neuropsychology Review, 7*(4), 157–170.

Naglieri, J. A., Das, J. P., & Goldstein, S. (2014). *Cognitive assessment system* (2nd ed.). Austin, TX: Pro-Ed.

Navon, D. (1977). Forest before the tree: The precedence of global feature in visual perception. *Cognitive Psychology, 9*(3), 353–383.

Orsini, A., Grossi, D., Capitani, E., Laiacona, M., Papagno, C., & Vallar, G. (1987). Verbal and spatial immediate memory span: Normative data from 1355 adults and 1112 children. *The Italian Journal of Neurological Sciences, 8*(6), 539–548.

Osterrieth, P. A. (1944). Le test de copie d'une figure complex: Contribution a l'étude de la perception et de la mémoire. *Archives de Psychologie, 30*, 286–356.

Parasuraman, R. (Ed.). (1998). *The attentive brain.* Cambridge, MA: MIT Press.

Parton, A., Malhotra, P., Nachev, P., Ames, D., Ball, J., Chataway, J., et al. (2006). Space re-exploration in hemispatial neglect. *NeuroReport, 17*(8), 833–836.

Pennington, B. F., & Ozonoff, S. (1996). Executive functions and developmental psychopathology. *Journal of Child Psychology and Psychiatry and Allied Disciplines, 37*, 51–87.

Pribram, K. H. (1973). The primate frontal cortex—executive of the brain. In K. H. Pribram & A. R. Luria (Eds.), *Psychophysiology of the frontal lobes* (pp. 293–314). New York: Academic Press.

Rabin, L. A., Barr, W. B., & Burton, L. A. (2005). Assessment practices of clinical neuropsychologists in the United States and Canada: A survey of INS, NAN, and APA Division 40 members. *Archives of Clinical Neuropsychology, 20*(1), 33–65.

Reitan, R. M., & Wolfson, D. (1985). *The Halstead-Reitan neuropsychological test battery.* Tucson, AZ: Neuropsychology Press.

Remine, M. D., Care, E., & Brown, P. M. (2008). Language ability and verbal and nonverbal executive functioning in Deaf students communicating in spoken English. *Journal of Deaf Studies and Deaf Education, 13*(4), 531–545.

Rey, A. (1941). L'examen psychologique dans les cas d'encephalopathie traumatique. *Archives de Psychologie, 28*, 286–340.

Reynolds, C. R., Pearson, N. A., & Voress, J. K. (2002). *Developmental test of visual perception, Adolescent and adult (DTVP-A). Examiner's manual.* Austin, TX: Pro-Ed.

Ribot, T. (1882). *Diseases of memory.* New York: Appleton.

Riccio, C. A., Reynolds, C. R., & Lowe, P. A. (2001). *Clinical applications of continuous performance tests: Measuring attention and impulsive responding in children and adults.* New York: Wiley.

Richardson, J. T. E., Engle, R. W., Hasher, L., Logie, R. H., Stoltzfus, E. R., & Zacks, R. T. (1996). *Working memory and human cognition.* New York: Oxford University Press.

Richter, W., Somorjai, R., Summers, R., Jarmasz, M., Menon, R. S., et al. (2000). Motor area activity during mental rotation studied by time-resolved single-trial fMRI. *Journal of Cognitive Neuroscience, 12*(2), 310–320.

Rizzolatti, G., & Craighero, L. (2004). The mirror-neuron system. *Annual Review of Neuroscience, 27*(1), 169–192.

Rorden, C., & Karnath, H.-O. (2010). A simple measure of neglect severity. *Neuropsychologia, 48*(9), 2758–2763.

Rosselli, M., & Ardila, A. (2003). The impact of culture and education on non-verbal neuropsychological measurements: A critical review. *Brain and Cognition, 52*(3), 326–333.

Rosselli, M., Ardila, A., & Rosas, P. (1990). Neuropsychological assessment in illiterates: II. Language and praxic abilities. *Brain and Cognition, 12*(2), 281–296.

Rosvold, H. E., Mirsky, A. F., Sarason, I., Bransome, E. D., & Beck, L. H. (1956). A continuous performance test of brain damage. *Journal of Consulting Psychology, 20*(5), 343–350.

Schachar, R., & Logan, G. (1990). Impulsivity and inhibitory control in normal development and childhood psychopathology. *Developmental Psychology, 26*(5), 710–720.

Seashore, C. E., Lewis, D., & Saetveit, J. G. (1960). *Seashore measures of musical talents.* New York: The Psychological Corporation.

Sergeant, J. A., Oosterlaan, J., & van der Meere, J. (1999). Information processing and energetic factors in attention-deficit/hyperactivity disorder. In H. C. Quay & A. E. Hogan (Eds.), *Handbook of disruptive behavior disorders* (pp. 75–104). New York: Kluwer Academic/Plenum.

Shallice, T. (1982). Specific impairments of planning. *Philosophical Transactions of the Royal Society of London, Series B: Biological Sciences (London), 298* (1089), 199–209.

Simon, H. A. (1975). The functional equivalence of problem solving skills. *Cognitive Psychology, 7*(2), 268–288.

Sivan, A. B. (1992). *Benton visual retention test* (5th ed.). San Antonio, TX: The Psychological Corporation.

Sporns, O., & Betzel, R. F. (2016). Modular brain networks. *Annual Review of Psychology, 67,* 613–640.

Spreen, O., & Benton, A. L. (1969). *Neurosensory center comprehensive examination for aphasia.* Victoria, British Columbia: University of Victoria Department of Psychology.

Stankov, L. (1988). Aging, attention, and intelligence. *Psychology and Aging, 3*(1), 59–74.

Stern, R. A., Javorsky, D. J., Singer, E. A., Harris, N. G. S., Somerville, J. A., Duke, L. M., et al. (1999). *Boston qualitative scoring system for the Rey— Osterrieth complex figure.* Odessa, FL: Psychological Assessment Resources.

Stone, M. H., & Wright, B. D. (1980). *Knox's cube test.* Chicago: Stoelting.

Strauss, E., Sherman, E. M. S., & Spreen, O. (2006). *A compendium of neuropsychological tests: Administration, norms, and commentary* (3rd ed.). New York: Oxford University Press.

Stroop, J. R. (1935). Studies of interference in serial verbal reactions. *Journal of Experimental Psychology, 18*(6), 643–662.

Stuss, D. T., & Benson, D. F. (1986). *The frontal lobes.* New York: Raven Press.

Tannock, R., & Schachar, R. (1996). Executive dysfunction as an underlying mechanism in behavior and language problems in ADHD. In J. H. Beitchman, et al. (Eds.), *Language, learning and behavior disorders* (pp. 128–155). Cambridge: Cambridge University Press.

Trahan, D. E., & Larrabee, G. J. (1988). *Continuous visual memory test.* Odessa, FL: Psychological Assessment Resources.

Tranel, D., Anderson, S. W., & Benton, A. L. (1995). Development of the concept of executive function and its relationship to the frontal lobes. In F. Boller & J. Grafman (Eds.), *Handbook of neuropsychology* (Vol. 9, pp. 125–148). Amsterdam: Elsevier.

Trommer, B. L., Hoeppner, J. B., & Zecker, S. G. (1991). The Go—No-Go Test in attention deficit hyperactivity disorder is sensitive to methylphenidate. *Journal of Child Neurology, 6*(1 suppl), S128–S131.

Troyer, A. K., & Wishart, H. A. (1997). A comparison of qualitative scoring systems for the Rey-Osterrieth Complex Figure Test. *The Clinical Neuropsychologist, 11*(4), 381–390.

Tucker, M., & Ellis, R. (1998). On the relations between seen objects and components of potential actions. *Journal of Experimental Psychology: Human Perception and Performance, 24,* 830–846.

van den Heuvel, M. P., & Sporns, O. (2013). Network hubs in the human brain. *Trends in Cognitive Sciences, 17*(12), 683–696.

van Zomeren, A. H., & Brouwer, W. H. (1994). *Clinical neuropsychology of attention.* New York: Oxford University Press.

Waber, D. P., & Holmes, J. M. (1985). Assessing children's copy productions of the Rey-Osterrieth Complex Figure. *Journal of Clinical and Experimental Neuropsychology, 7*(3), 264–280.

Waber, D. P., & Holmes, J. M. (1986). Assessing children's memory productions of the Rey-Osterrieth Complex Figure. *Journal of Clinical and Experimental Neuropsychology, 8*(5), 563–580.

Warrington, E. K. (1984). *Recognition memory test.* Windsor, UK: NFER-Nelson.

Watkins, M. J. (1974). Concept and measurement of primary memory. *Psychological Bulletin, 81*(10), 695–711.

Wechsler, D. (1945). A standardized memory scale for clinical use. *Journal of Psychology, 19*(1), 87–95.

Wechsler, D. (2009). *Wechsler memory scale—Fourth edition: Administration and scoring manual.* San Antonio, TX: Pearson.

Wechsler, D., & Kaplan, E. (2015). *Wechsler intelligence scale for children, Fifth edition, Integrated (WISC-V Integrated).* San Antonio, TX: Pearson.

Wells, F. L., & Martin, H. A. (1923). A method of memory examination suitable for psychotic cases. *American Journal of Psychiatry, 80*(2), 243–257.

Whipple, G. M. (1915/1973). *Manual of mental and physical tests* (Part II, 2nd ed.). New York: Arno Press.

White, T., & Stern, R. A. (2001, 2003). *Neuropsychological assessment battery (NAB). Psychometric and technical manual.* Lutz, FL: Psychological Assessment Resources.

Williams, J. M. (1991). *Memory assessment scales professional manual.* Odessa, FL: Psychological Assessment Resources.

Willment, K. C., & Golby, A. (2013). Hemispheric lateralization interrupted: Material-specific memory deficits in Temporal Lobe Epilepsy. *Frontiers in Human Neuroscience, 7*(Article 546), 1–8.

Wilson, B. A., Alderman, N., Burgess, P. W., Emslie, H., & Evans, J. J. (1996). *Behavioral assessment of the dysexecutive syndrome* (BADS). Bury St. Edmunds, UK: Thames Valley Test Company.

Wolf, M., & Denckla, M. B. (2005). *Rapid automatic naming and rapid alternating stimulus tests (RAN/RAS). Examiner's manual.* Austin, TX: Pro-Ed.

# Index

*Note*: Page numbers followed by *f* and *t* indicate figures and tables, respectively

© Springer International Publishing AG 2017
R.S. McCallum (ed.), *Handbook of Nonverbal Assessment*,
DOI 10.1007/978-3-319-50604-3

Made in the USA
Las Vegas, NV
21 February 2024

86056790R00184